BIOGRAPHICAL DIRECTORY
OF
ANTHROPOLOGISTS BORN BEFORE 1920

GARLAND REFERENCE LIBRARY
OF THE HUMANITIES
(Vol. 439)

ABOUT THE EDITORS

Michele Calhoun is Reference and Public Services Librarian, Field Museum of Natural History.

Dale Christoffersen is Computer Consultant, Loyola University of Chicago.

Yvonne M. Damien is Reference Librarian and Subject Bibliographer for Anthropology, Fine Arts, Nursing, and Theatre, Loyola University of Chicago, E. M. Cudahy Library.

David L. Easterbrook is Principal Bibliographer, University of Illinois at Chicago.

Gregory A. Finnegan is Humanities and Social Sciences Reference-Bibliographer, Dartmouth College, Baker Library.

Fr. Francis X. Grollig, S.J., is Professor of Anthropology and Director of Latin American Studies Program, Loyola University of Chicago.

Thomas L. Mann is Bibliographer for Slavic Literature and the Social Sciences, Northwestern University.

Hans E. Panofsky is Curator of Africana, Northwestern University.

Robert B. Marks Ridinger is Subject Librarian for Anthropology, Geography, Sociology and Foreign Languages, Northern Illinois University.

Margo L. Smith, Ph.D., is Professor of Anthropology and Chairperson of that department, Northeastern Illinois University.

Sol Tax is Professor Emeritus of Anthropology at the University of Chicago.

Christopher Winters is Bibliographer for Geography, Anthropology and Maps, University of Chicago Library.

Kathleen Zar is the Head of Reference and Subject Services for the John Crerar Library, the University of Chicago.

BIOGRAPHICAL DIRECTORY OF ANTHROPOLOGISTS BORN BEFORE 1920

Compiled by
Library-Anthropology Resource Group
(LARG)

General Editor
Thomas L. Mann

Editorial Board
Michele Calhoun
Dale Christoffersen
Yvonne M. Damien
David L. Easterbrook
Gregory A. Finnegan
Fr. Francis X. Grollig
Hans E. Panofsky
Robert B. Marks Ridinger
Margo L. Smith
Sol Tax
Christopher Winters
Kathleen Zar

GARLAND PUBLISHING, INC. • NEW YORK & LONDON
1988

© 1988 Library-Anthropology Resource Group (LARG)
All rights reserved

Library of Congress Cataloging-in-Publication Data

Biographical Directory of Anthropologists Born Before 1920.

(Garland Reference Library of the Humanities; vol. 439)
Includes index.
1. Anthropologists—Biography—Bibliography.
I. Mann, Thomas L.   II. Library-Anthropology Resource Group (Chicago, Ill.)   III. Series: Garland Reference Library of the Humanities; v. 439.

Z5111.B56 1988 [GN20] 016.306′092′2 [B] 87-29219
ISBN 0-8240-5833-X (alk. paper)

Printed on acid-free, 250-year-life paper
Manufactured in the United States of America

The Editorial Board of Library-Anthropology Resource Group (LARG) has unanimously agreed to dedicate this, our fourth publication, to Sol Tax. Sol Tax is not only the founder of LARG, but is also the only member of LARG's Editorial Board to appear in this directory.

In the early 1970's, when Sol was organizing the IX International Congress of Anthropological and Ethnological Sciences, he envisioned the preparation of a resource volume which would list all of the anthropological serials held by the major university and research libraries in the Chicago area in order to facilitate local research. Sol contacted some local anthropologists and librarians to recruit their collaboration in this project. Thus LARG was born. Although only Sol, from the University of Chicago; Fr. Francis X. Grollig, S.J., from Loyola University; and Hans Panofsky, from the Melville Herskovits Library of Northwestern University remain from the original group, LARG has met monthly since 1971, has broadened its membership, and has produced three publications prior to this one: two editions of the original serials project, expanded into an international list and issued as *SERIAL PUBLICATIONS IN ANTHROPOLOGY* (1973), revised edition (1982), and *ANTHROPOLOGICAL BIBLIOGRAPHIES: A SELECTED GUIDE* (1981). Sol's initial concept of producing anthropological reference materials from the collaboration of anthropologists and librarians clearly has met a need.

During all of this time, we have benefitted greatly from Sol's wisdom and guidance.

CONTENTS

Preface ix
Acknowledgments xi
Introduction xiii
Statistical Summaries xv
Biographical Directory 1
Index 219

PREFACE

This is a biographical directory of persons born before 1920 who have contributed to the discipline of anthropology. For each person the entries include dates of birth and death, birthplace, profession, major contributions and published sources of biographical information. The information has been compiled by members of the Library-Anthropology Resource Group (LARG), which is a cooperative group of anthropologists and librarians who have been meeting monthly since January 1971 at research libraries in the Chicago area to discuss bibliographic needs in the field of anthropology and to explore the development of useful reference publications.

The *Biographical Directory* provides a ready reference source for biographies of people who have contributed to anthropology in a broadly defined sense as the study of humankind. The historical development of anthropology is in large measure an outgrowth of the lifelong contributions of people from various professions and geographic areas, so no restrictions beyond a birthdate earlier than 1920 were placed on inclusion of a name, so long as the person made a contribution to the field.

The growth of any discipline is a result of the contributions of all those who contributed to it. Therefore, this directory has been made as broadly inclusive as possible in terms of the profession, period, and contribution of those persons listed. We were, however, dependent on the location of a biographic source before a name could be added, with the result that some worthy persons have unintentionally been omitted. It is planned that this first compilation will be followed by a revised edition which will add newly located biographies. Indeed, in addition to guiding the scholar to already existing biographies, the lack of a name in this directory might stimulate knowledgeable people to write new biographies of contributors to the field of anthropology and thus serve to expand our record of the history of our discipline.

This directory adds significantly to the scope and efficiency of research into the biographies of specific individuals and through them into the history of the field of anthropology itself.

ACKNOWLEDGMENTS

The Editorial Board thanks the following people for their contributions to this project:

    Mike Dooley, Loyola University of Chicago.
    Sandy Dooley, Loyola University of Chicago.
    Paul Hockings, University of Illinois in Chicago.
    Dolores Lopez, Loyola University of Chicago.
    Georgeanna North, Loyola University of Chicago.
    Pamela E. Sandstrom, Harvard University.
    Elizabeth Tate, Northwestern University.

We also thank Loyola University of Chicago for its generous contribution of computer time for storing, sorting, and printing the manuscript.

INTRODUCTION

The primary function of this volume is to bring together in one reference source as many citations to biographical information as the group could provide. It does not present new information, but cumulates in a single, readily used volume, basic biographical information about the person and references to published sources of biographical information, thus eliminating the time-consuming hunt through myriad sources. This greatly increases the efficiency of locating biographical information on a particular person. Biographies were found by searching relevant biographical reference works, directories, anthropological journals, histories of anthropology, library subject catalogs, National Union Catalog (NUC), Online Computer Library Center (OCLC), and Research Libraries Information Network (RLIN). This not only saves the user time, but also insures a more complete listing of sources than an individual researcher could hope to discover on his own.

When the editors found a name in *Biography Index,* the reader is referred to that standard reference source to obtain the specific citations. All sources were included as located, so that the length and depth of information referred to varies from brief data in some directories to full-length monographs. Citation style also varies according to the information available to the compiler, but all follow this basic pattern: (for books) author, title (date), page; (for journals) title, volume: page, date.

This directory is international in scope, but coverage of any particular country depended on the existence of written biographies or other sources of information. It is therefore inevitable that names are lacking in this directory, because LARG could list only those which could be discovered in the sources consulted. Similarly, some information will in some cases be lacking in the Statement of Contributions, because of the sources and our decision to keep it brief.

Many sources were examined and are referred to with complete bibliographic information in the Directory; however, those that are referred to most often are cited with the following abbreviations:

Am Anth	*American Anthropologist*
Am Antiq	*American Antiquity*
Am J Arch	*American Journal of Archaeology*
Anth News	*Anthropology Newsletter*
Biog Index	*Biography Index*
Columbia	*Columbia Encyclopedia*
Int Dir Anth	*International Directory of Anthropologists,* 1st, 2nd, 3rd, 4th, 4th rev., 5th editions

Int Enc Soc Sci	*International Encyclopedia of the Social Sciences*
Jes Rel	*Jesuit Relations and Allied Documents*
Nat Cyc Am Biog	*National Cyclopedia of American Biography*
Nat Dir Lat Am	*National Directory of Latin Americanists*
Nat Un Cat	*National Union Catalog*
New Int Enc	*New International Encyclopedia*
NY Times	*New York Times*
Rev Arch	*Revue Archeologique*

We have used some standard bibliographic abbreviations, which require no explanation.

In addition to giving citations to the original sources of biographical information for each name included, when available we provide the following categories of information for each entry: dates of birth and death, place of birth, profession, and contributions to anthropology. However, since we were dependent on those original sources for additional information, full data could not be obtained for some entries. The content of each brief statement of contribution to anthropology was particularly dependent on the biographical source and the style of the person who compiled the particular entry and should not be considered definitive and complete.

It should be noted that the biographies referred to often include a listing of the scholar's publications in addition to biographical information, and can thus lead to the author's corpus of writings in books and journals.

The index terms were drawn as keywords directly from the computer record of the text, specifically from the "Statement of Contributions." There is no standardization of terms; rather, each "Statement of Contributions" was written by the various contributors and based on information contained in the various biographical sources and entered into the computer record as presented. Also, the brief statement gives a summary, not a full accounting of each person's contributions. Nonetheless, the Index to this work does provide a basic means for locating many persons who were actively involved in research on a particular topic or geographic region.

Statistics

A natural and interesting byproduct of the computer data are the following tables and graphs which indicate the number of persons included in this directory, categorized by country of birth, birth and death year groupings, and specific careers and professions.

COUNTRY	TOTAL	COUNTRY	TOTAL	COUNTRY	TOTAL
Algeria	2	Greece	9	Northern Ireland	1
Angola	2	Greenland	2	Norway	21
Argentina	17	Guatemala	15	Oman	1
Australia	26	Honduras	1	Panama	2
Austria	17	Hungary	18	Paraguay	10
Bechuanaland	1	Iceland	1	Peru	14
Belgium	20	India	12	Philippines	1
Bermuda	1	Indonesia	4	Poland	28
Bolivia	10	Iran	2	Portugal	8
Brazil	15	Iraq	1	Rhodesia	2
British India	1	Ireland	11	Romania	9
Bulgaria	4	Italy	50	Samoa	1
Canada	30	Japan	32	Scotland	34
Caroline Islands	1	Kenya	3	Senegal	1
Ceylon	2	Kingdom of Sardinia	1	Sierra Leone	1
Chile	8	Korea	4	South Africa	18
China	15	Latvia	2	Spain	59
Colombia	13	Lebanon	2	Sweden	22
Cuba	3	Lesotho	6	Switzerland	20
Czechoslovakia	16	Leyden	1	Tunisia	1
Dahomey	3	Liberia	5	Turkey	4
Denmark	19	Lithuania	2	U S S R	75
Ecuador	19	Mailand	1	United Kingdom	1
Egypt	13	Mexico	24	United States	652
El Salvador	5	Mongolia	1	Uzbekistan	1
England	258	Moravia	2	Venezuela	9
Estonia	5	Morocco	1	Virgin Islands	1
Finland	10	Mozambique	1	Wales	4
France	276	Netherlands	22	West Indies	1
Gabon	2	New Zealand	16	Yugoslavia	6
Germany	151	Nigeria	4	Zaire	1
Ghana	3	North China	1		

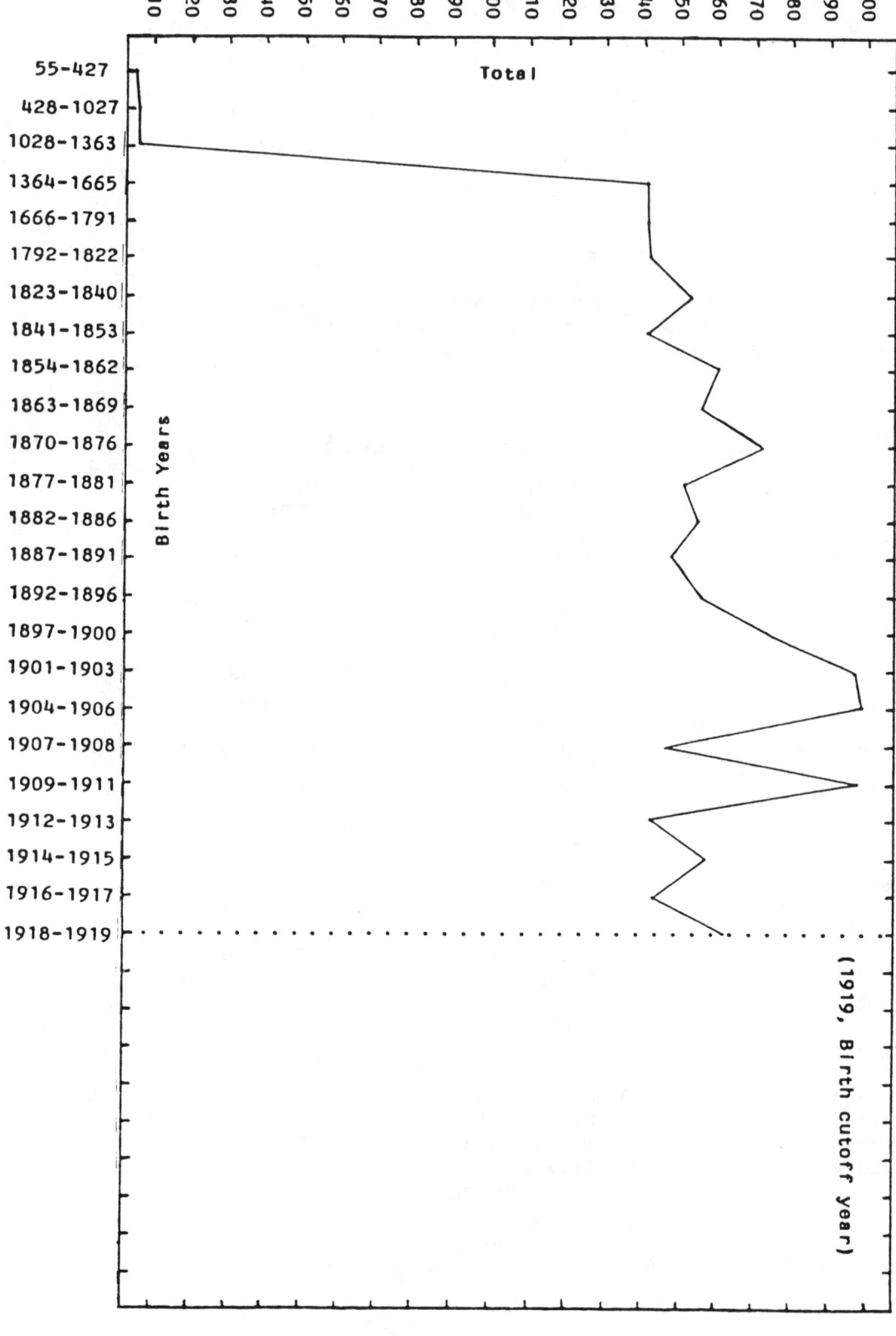

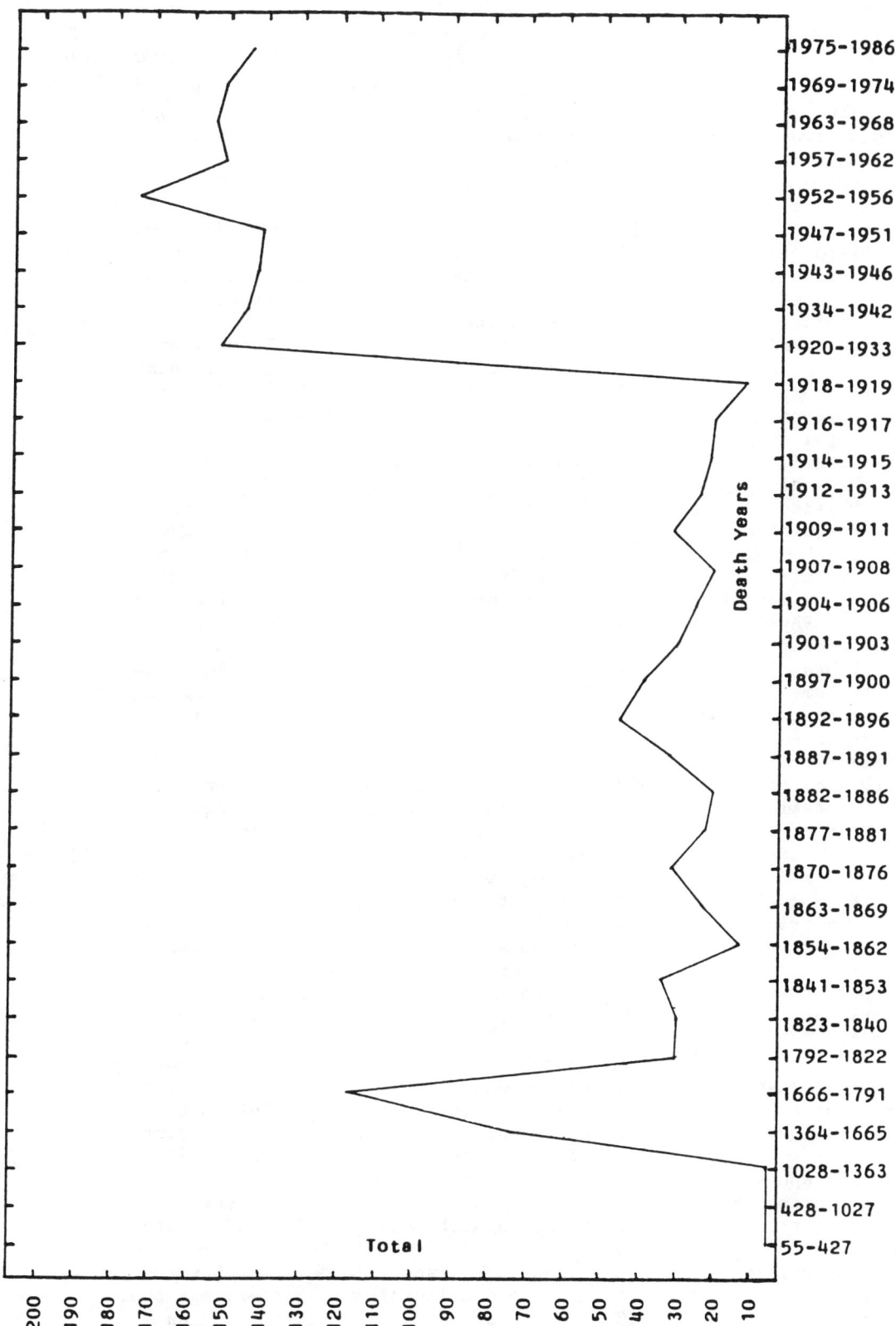

CAREER	TOTAL	CAREER	TOTAL	CAREER	TOTAL
Acculturationist	2	Cartographer	2	Ethnologist (cont.)	
Administrator	10	Ceramicist	2	Ecological	1
Colonial	6	Chemist	1	Japanese	1
Museum	1	Chieftain	1	Paleo-	1
Africanist	4	Kwakiutl	1	Prehistoric	1
Anatomist	32	Seneca	1	Religious	1
Anthropologist	555	Chiropractor	1	Socio-Cultural	1
Agricultural	1	Choreographer	1	Ethnomusicologist	6
Applied	9	Chronicler	1	Ethnopharmacologist	1
Biological	9	Classicist	6	Ethnopsychologist	1
Cultural	28	Clergyman	17	Ethologist	1
Applied	1	Collector	1	Evolutionist	3
Economic	1	Ethnological	1	Cultural	1
Forensic	1	Composer	4	Explorer	87
Legal	2	Communication Theorist	1	Arctic	2
Linguistic	1	Conservationist, Soil	1	Farmer	2
Medical	11	Conservator, Museum	1	Folklorist	202
Physical	88	Criminologist	1	Ethnological	1
Applied	1	Critic	2	Genealogist	3
Psychological	8	Art	5	Geneticist	8
Social	49	Culturist, Folk	1	Behavioral	1
Cultural	3	Culturologist	1	Population	1
Physical	1	Curator	3	Geographer	30
Theoretical	2	Art	1	Cultural	2
Urban	1	Museum	29	Economic	1
Anthropometrist	2	Dancer	1	Ethnological	1
Anthropotaxonomist	1	Demographer	2	Geologist	24
Antiquarian	9	Dentist	3	Grammarian	2
Arabist	1	Diplomat	16	Guide	1
Archeologist	889	Director, Field	1	Hellenist	1
Avocational	1	Motion Picture	3	Hieroglyphologist	1
Biblical	2	Museum	11	Histologist	1
Classical	2	Diver	1	Historian	188
Cross-Cultural	1	Ecologist	5	Architectural	3
Ethnological	1	Cultural	3	Art	19
Historic	1	Physical	1	Economic	1
Mayan	1	Economist	8	Social	1
Archer	1	Educator	21	Humanist	1
Architect	8	Egyptologist	83	Hunter	1
Archivist	9	Engineer	9	Iconographer	1
Artist	14	Civil	2	Illustrator	1
Folk	1	Engraver	1	Scientific	1
Assyriologist	12	Entomologist	4	Indianist	1
Astronomer,		Environmentalist	2	Informant	1
Archeological	1	Epigrapher	3	Interpreter	3
Banker	2	Ethnobotanist	5	Journalist	12
Bibliographer	10	Ethnographer	36	Judge	3
Anthropological	1	Ethnohistorian	19	Lawyer	21
Biochemist	3	Ethnolinguist	2	Leader, Creek Nation	1
Biologist	6	Ethnologist	464	Iroquois	1
Biostatistician	1	Comparative	1	Lesotho	1
Bishop	4	Cross-Cultural	3	Lexicographer	1
Botanist	13	Urban	1	Librarian	6
Bureaucrat	1	Cultural	3	Linguist	140
Businessman	12	Economic	1	Anthropological	4

Statistical Summaries

CAREER	TOTAL	CAREER	TOTAL	CAREER	TOTAL
Linguist (cont.)		Paleoarcheologist	1	Researcher, Medical	1
Classical	1	Paleobotanist	1	Scholar	4
Ethnological	1	Paleodemographer	1	Biblical	5
Sociological	1	Paleontologist	49	Buddhist	1
Mathematician	2	Human	3	Scientist	5
Matriculturist	1	Vertebrate	1	Social	2
Merchant	13	Paleopathologist	4	Sculptor	2
Missiologist	1	Petroglyphologist	5	Servant, Civil	50
Missionary	105	Philanthropist	4	Colonial Civil	1
Portugese	1	Philologist	27	Public	2
Monk, Buddhist	1	Comparative	1	Singer	1
Museologist	21	Philosopher	20	Folk	1
Bio-	1	Photographer	7	Sinologist	31
Musician	5	Physician	49	Social Worker	1
Folk	3	Physicist	1	Sociologist	74
Musicologist	15	Physiologist	4	Ethno-	3
Ethno-	4	Poet	9	Rural	1
Mythologist	6	Politician	16	Soldier	10
Naturalist	19	Potter	1	Statistician	2
Navigator	3	Prehistorian	16	Surgeon	6
Numismatist	5	Priest	138	Military	1
Nun, Catholic	1	Primatologist	9	Surveyor	3
Nutritionist	2	Printer	2	Taxonomist	1
Officer, Army	6	Producer, Theatrical	1	Theologian	5
British Colonial	1	Psychiatrist	6	Topographer	1
Military	4	Social	1	Trader	4
Naval	9	Psychoanalyst	2	Indian	1
Opthalmologist	1	Psychoanthropologist	2	Traveler	11
Orientalist	157	Psychologist	12	Turcologist	1
Ornithologist	3	Animal	1	Trade unionist	1
Osteologist	2	Cultural	1	Veterinarian	1
Primate	1	Social	2	Writer	57
Osteometrist	1	Publisher	3	Song	3
Osteopath	1	Rabbi	1	Zooarcheologist	1
Otologist	1	Radiologist	2	Zoologist	13
Paleoanthropologist	4	Reformer, Social	3	Ethnological	1

Biographical Directory
of
Anthropologists Born Before 1920

0001 ABADIE, MAURICE (1885-), France. Ethnologist. Wrote on Turkey, Africa, China. Source: Nat Un Cat.

0002 ABBEVILLE, CLAUDE D' (1632-). Priest. Wrote about missions to Brazil. Source: Nat Un Cat.

0003 ABBOTT, CHARLES C (1843-1919), Delaware Valley, New Jersey, United States. Archeologist. Archeology of the Delaware Valley (New Jersey and Pennsylvania). Source: Am Anth 22:70-1 Ja '20.

0004 ABDALLAH, YOHANNA, Mozambique. Historian, priest. Wrote one of the first histories of his people, the Yao, of Malawi, published in 1919. Source: Crosby, Cynthia A., Historical Dictionary of Malawi (1976), p 1.

0005 ABEL, LELAND J (1914-). Archeologist. Pueblo ceramic taxonomy horizons & salvage archeology. English colonial archeology. Source: Int Dir Anth 5.

0006 ABERLE, DAVID FRIEND (1918-), United States. Ethnologist. Kinship systems. Indians of Western U.S., Northwest Coast & Alaska. Sources: Int Dir Anth 3, 5.

0007 ABRAHAM, DONALD P. Historian. Collected a large body of Shona oral tradition and wrote basic articles on Shona (Rhodesia) using Portuguese archives. Source: Rasmussen, R. Kent, Historical Dictionary of Rhodesia/Zimbabwe (1979), p 9.

0008 ABSOLON, KAREL (1877-1960), Czechoslovakia. Archeologist. Fieldwork at the Hallstatt period site of Byci Skala (Czechoslovakia). Sources: Biog Index: 5/Illustrated London News 237:717 O 22 '60.

0009 ACKERKNECHT, ERWIN HEINZ (1906-), Germany. Ethnologist, physical anthropologist. Medical- and psycho-pathology of S. American Indians. Sources: Nat Un Cat/Int Dir Anth 3.

0010 ACOSTA, JOAQUÍN (1800-1852), Colombia. Historian. Wrote an account of the discovery and colonization of Colombia. Source: Davis, Robert H., Historical Dictionary of Colombia (1977), p 44.

0011 ACOSTA, JOSEPH DE (1539-1600), Spain. Priest. Wrote history of Spanish colonial period in Peru to 1590. Sources: Columbia/Heath, Dwight B., Historical Dictionary of Bolivia (1972), p 8.

0012 ADACHI, BUNTARO (1865-). Wrote on ethnology of Japan. Source: Nat Un Cat.

0013 ADAM, LEONHARD (1891-), Germany. Anthropologist. Primitive art of Indians of N. America. Sources: Nat Un Cat/Int Dir Anth 3.

0014 ADAMS, FRED T (1918-). Cultural anthropologist. Social structures & organizations. Demography. Source: Int Dir Anth 5.

0015 ADAMS, G BRENDAN (1917-). Linguist. Phonology, relationship of words to things. Celtic languages. Source: Int Dir Anth 5.

0016 ADAMS, HENRY (1838-1918), Boston, Massachusetts, United States. Historian, writer. Helped Ari'i Ta'ima'i to write her memoirs of Tahitian life. Source: Columbia.

0017 ADANDE, ALEXANDRE SENOU (1913-), Porto Novo, Dahomey. Ethnologist, archivist, political figure. Wrote on art and material culture of Benin. Source: DeCalo, Samuel, Historical Dictionary of Dahomey (1976), p 2-3.

0018 AFANAS'EV, ALEKSANDR NIKOLAEVICH (1826-1871), Russia. Folklorist. Published collections of Russian folk tales. Source: Columbia.

0019 AFZELIUS, ADAM (1730-1837). Botanist. Wrote the first systematic botanical work on West African flora. Source: Foray, Cyril P., Historical Dictionary of Sierra Leone (1977), p 2.

0020 AGASSIZ, LOUIS (1807-1873), Moutiers-en-Vuly, Switzerland. Geologist, zoologist. Gave impetus to study of science directly from nature; opposed Darwinism, extended theory of recapitulation. Led expedition to the Amazon Basin in 1865-1866. Sources: Columbia/Levine, Robert M., Historical

Dictionary of Brazil (1979), p 5.

0021 AGBO, CASIMIR (1889-), Ouidah, Dahomey. Historian. Wrote an extensive work, *Histoire de Ouidah du XVIe au XXe siecle* (1959), contributing to regional history of this city and area. Source: DeCalo, Samuel, Historical Dictionary of Dahomey (1976), p 6-7.

0022 AGUADO, PEDRO (1513-), Colombia. Priest. Wrote an account of Colombia as it was in the 16th century. Source: Davis, Robert H., Historical Dictionary of Columbia (1977), p 45.

0023 AGUILAR, CARLOS H (1917-). Archeologist. Ceramics, metallurgy & shamanism in Meso-America. Worked at Guayabo de Turrialba (Costa Rica). Source: Int Dir Anth 5.

0024 AGUIRRE, JUAN FRANCISCO (1758-1811), Spain. Surveyor. Left a diary describing the Buenos Aires region (Argentina) in the late colonial period. Source: Wright & Nelsham, Historical Dictionary of Argentina (1978), p 10-1.

0025 AHARONI, YOHANAN (1919-1976). Biblical archeologist. Worked at Masada (Israel); founded the Institute of Archeology in Tel Aviv. Sources: Biog Index: 10 & 11/N Y Times p 34 F 12 '76/ Biblical Archaeologist 39:53 My '76.

0026 AIYAPPAN, AIYAPPAN (1905-), India. Social anthropologist. Tribal ethnography & welfare administration in India. Sources: Int Dir Anth 3, 5.

0027 AKHMANOVA, OLGA (1908-), U.S.S.R. Linguist. General phonetics, lexicography, terminology, syntax & style. Source: Int Dir Anth 5.

0028 ALARCÓN, HERNANDO de (fl early 16th century-1541), Spain. Explorer. Explored Southwest U.S. in 1540s. Source: Columbia.

0029 ALBANEL, S J, Fr. CHARLES (1616-1696), Auvergne, France. Priest. Missionary to New France; wrote on N. American Indians. Source: Jes Rel.

0030 ALBENINO, NICOLAO de (1514-ca. 1570), Florence, Italy. Historian. Wrote a history of the early colonial period in Quito (Ecuador) and the revolt of Gonzalo Pizzaro. Source: Bork & Maier, Historical Dictionary of Ecuador (1973), p 14.

0031 ALBENQUE, ALEXANDRE (1909-1951), France. Archeologist. Sources: Biog Index: 2/Rev Arch series 6 37:190-1 Ap '51.

0032 ALBERTIS, LUIGI MARIA D' (1841-1901), Voltri, Italy. Explorer. Conducted several expeditions to the Fly River and other areas of Papua New Guinea; collected botanical and ethnographic specimens. Source: Craig & King, Historical Dictionary of Oceania (1981), p 67.

0033 ALBIZZATI, CARLO (1888-1950). Archeologist. Specialist in Etruscan, Greek, and Roman archeology and art. Reconstructed the Dionysius statue of Praxiteles in 1922. Sources: Biog Index: 2/N Y Times p 27 O 16 '50.

0034 ALBRIGHT, WILLIAM FOXWELL (1891-1971), Coquimbo, Chile. Orientalist, archeologist. Biblical archeology of Palestine. Sources: Biog Index: 1 4 5 6 9 10 11 12 & 13/Int Dir Anth 2, 3/ Biblical Archaeologist 42:37-47 Win '79.

0035 ALCEDO Y HERRERA, ANTONIO LEANDRO de (1735-1812), Quito, Ecuador. Soldier, historian. Wrote a historico-geographical dictionary of Spanish America, including ethnographic data on Argentina. Sources: Bork & Maier, Historical Dictionary of Ecuador (1973), p 14/ Wright & Nelsham, Historical Dictionary of Argentina (1978), p 17.

0036 ALCEDO Y HERRERA, DIONISIO de (1690-1777), Madrid, Spain. Historian, civil servant. Wrote a detailed description of equatorial America and a separate volume on the province of Guayaquil (Ecuador). Source: Bork & Maier, Historical Dictionary of Ecuador (1973), p 15.

0037 ALDERSON, EDWIN ALFRED HARVEY (1859-1927). Soldier. Wrote an account of the 1897 Shona Revolt (Rhodesia). Source: Rasmussen, R. Kent, Historical Dictionary of Rhodesia/Zimbabwe (1979), p 17.

0038 ALEGRÍA, RICARDO E (1918-). Anthropologist. Specialist in Puerto Rican culture. Sources: Nat Dir Lat Am/Biog Index: 10.

0039 ALEXANDER, HARTLEY BURR (1873-1939), United States. Philosopher, anthropologist. Mythology & rituals of Indians in Southeast U.S. Sources: Biog Index: 4 & 6/Int Dir Anth 1, 2/Nat Cyc Am Biog 46:538-9 '63.

0040 ALFARO, ANASTASIO (1865-1951), Costa Rica. Archeologist. Wrote several monographs on Costa Rican archeology and ethnology. Source: Creedman, Theodore, Historical Dictionary of Costa Rica (1977).

0041 ALFÖLDI, ANDREAS (1895-). Historian, archeologist. Wrote about the festival of Isis in Rome under the Christian emperors of the IVth century. Sources: Biog Index: 10/Antike Kunst 18 no 2:45-6 '75.

0042 ALLARD, ELISABETH M A A J (1904-), Netherlands. Sociologist. Biculturalism & social organization of Eurasian minorities. Sources: Int Dir Anth 3, 5.

0043 ALLDRIDGE, THOMAS JOSHUA (1847-). Author, civil servant. Wrote two books describing Sierra Leone in the early 20th century; witnessed much of the 1898 Hut Tax War. Source: Foray, Cyril P., Historical Dictionary of Sierra Leone (1977), p 4.

0044 ALLEN, GRANT (1848-1899), Kingston, Ontario, Canada. Author. Known for books discussing scientific knowledge in biology & anthropology. Source: Encyclopedia Britannica, 11th ed.

0045 ALLIOT, HECTOR (1862-), Gironde, France. Archeologist. Associated with Farah Pasha in explorations at Tyre (Asia Minor, Lebanon). Also worked among the Ute, Hopi & Pueblo Indians. Source: New Int Enc.

0046 ALLIOT, MAURICE (1903-1960), France. Archeologist, Egyptologist. Excavated and wrote extensively about Edfu (Egypt). Sources: Biog Index: 6/Rev Arch 1:50-2 Ja '61.

0047 ALLOUEZ, S J, Fr. CLAUDE JEAN (1613-1689), St.-Didier-en-Foret, France. Priest. Missionary to New France; wrote on N. American Indians. Source: Jes Rel.

0048 ALLYN, HARRIET MAY (1883-1957), United States. Anthropologist. Indians of West U.S. Sources: Biog Index: 4/Int Dir Anth 1, 2, 3/N Y Times p 27 Jl 9 '57.

0049 ALMAGRO BASCH, MARTIN (1911-). Archeologist. European & African prehistory. Source: Int Dir Anth 5.

0050 ALMEIDA, ANTONIO de (1900-1984), Portugal. Bio-anthropologist. Anthropometrics, ethnology & prehistory of S. Angola and Portugese Timor. Studied the Bijugo. One of first to publish on medical anthropology. Sources: Int Dir Anth 5/Am Anth 1/86:3.

0051 ALMGREN, OSCAR (1869-1945), Sweden. Archeologist. Archeology of Sweden. Sources: Biog Index: 2/Rev Arch series 6, 37:206-7 Ap '51.

0052 ALPERT, HARRY (1912-). Sociologist. Ethnological & sociological theory & policy in France & U.S. Source: Int Dir Anth 5.

0053 ALSVIK, HENING (1911-). Ethnologist, museologist. Painting & applied arts of Norway. Source: Int Dir Anth 5.

0054 ALVARADO, LISANDRO (1858-1929), El Tocuxo, Venezuela. Ethnologist, historian. Wrote widely on Venezuelan linguistics, ethnography and folklore. Sources: Biog Index: 4/Hispania 40:425-9 D '57/ Rudolph & Rudolph, Historical Dictionary of Venezuela (1971), p 12.

0055 ALVARES, S J, Fr. MANUEL (1580-1619). Missionary. Worked 1607-1617 among peoples of Sierra Leone peninsula; wrote account of history and customs of the region at this time. Source: Foray, Cyril P., Historical Dictionary of Sierra Leone (1977), p 5.

0056 ALVAREZ-OSSORIO, FRANCISCO (1868-1953). Archeologist. Sources: Biog Index: 3/ Archivo Espanol de Arte y Arqueologia 26 no 88:459-60 '53.

0057 ALVEAR Y PONCE DE LEÓN, DIEGO de (1749-1830), Spain. Civil servant. Wrote a 5-volume history of his travels in Paraguay and La Plata (Argentina), useful for description of the region. Source: Kolinski, Charles J., Historical Dictionary of Paraguay (1973), p 8.

0058 AMBROSETTI, JUAN BAUTISTA (1865-1917), Gualeguay, Argentina. Archeologist, ethnographer, folklorist. Founded archeology as a discipline in Argentina; first to study Argentine folklore on a scientific basis. Archeology of the Calchaqui region of Argentina. Sources: Am Anth 19:533-35 O '17/Wright & Nelsham, Historical Dictionary of Argentina (1978), p 35.

0059 AMEGHINO, FLORENTINO (1854-1911), Lujan, Argentina. Geologist, paleontologist, anthropologist. Studied the human occupation of the Argentine Pampas and wrote extensively on the prehistory and environment of the area. Theories of fossil man in South America met with opposition during his lifetime; was responsible for one of the largest South American fossil mammal collections ever gathered. Sources: Biog Index: 3/Wright & Nelsham, Historical Dictionary of Argentina (1978), p 35/ Carnegie Magazine 28:240-3 S '54.

0060 AMIN, AHMAD (1886-1954), Egypt. Author. Compiled a dictionary of Egyptian folklore. Source: King, Joan W., Historical Dictionary of Egypt (1984), p 135.

0061 AMIOT, JOSEPH MARIA (1718-1794). Priest. Jesuit missionary to China. Wrote 15 vols. on history, sciences, & customs of Chinese. Authority on Manchu language. Source: Columbia.

0062 AMMAR, ABBAS MOUSTAIA (1907- 1974), Egypt. Anthropologist. Sources: Biog Index: 10/N Y Times p 36 D 16 '74.

0063 AMMIANUS, MARCELLINUS (ca. 330-ca. 400), Antioch, Antakya, Turkey. Historian. History of the Roman Empire, AD 96-378. Source: Columbia.

0064 AMMON, OTTO (1842-1916), Karlsruhe, Germany. Anthropologist. Known for anthropological literature and discovery of "Ammon's Law". Source: New Int Enc.

0065 AMSBURY, CLIFTON (1910-). Socio- psycho-anthropologist. Social & psychological aspects of peasant-based cultures of preindustrial societies. Source: Int Dir Anth 5.

0066 AMUNÁTEGUI ALDUNATE, MIGUEL LUIS (1828-1888), Chile. Historian. Wrote several historical works valuable for understanding the events of the 19th century in Chile. Source: Bizzarro, Salvatore, Historical Dictionary of Chile (1972), p 27-8.

0067 ANASTASIO, ANGELO (1914-). Ethnologist. Intergroup relations, community studies in N. America. Anthropology & history of wind instruments in music. Source: Int Dir Anth 5.

0068 ANASTASIUS MARIA, FATHER (1866-1947). Orientalist. Specialist in Arab philology and history; compiled a thirty-volume dictionary of Arabic. Sources: Biog Index: 1/N Y Times p 21 Ja 10 '47/Isis 38 no 3-4:246 '48.

0069 ANDAGOYA, PASCUAL de (1495-1548), Spain. Explorer. Wrote an account of early explorations in Colombia; first to sail down Colombia's Pacific Coast. Source: Davis, Robert H., Historical Dictionary of Colombia (1977), p 48-9.

0070 ANDERSON, A HAMILTON (1901-1967), Melbourne, Australia. Archeologist. First archeological commissioner of British Honduras; worked at sites of Awe Cave,

Santana, Caracol and Xuantunica. **Sources**: Biog Index: 8/Am Antiq 33:90-2 Ja '68.

0071 **ANDERSON, ARTHUR JAMES OUTRAM** (1907-), United States. Anthropologist. Ethnohistory of pre-Hispanic Mexico. **Sources**: Nat Dir Lat Am/Int Dir Anth 3.

0072 **ANDERSON, CLIFFORD C** (1870-1951). Archeologist. Authority on Mound Builders and the mounds at Fort Ancient near Lebanon, Ohio (U.S.). **Sources**: Biog Index: 2/Museum News 29:4 S 1 '51.

0073 **ANDERSON, ROBERT** (1914-), United States. Ethnologist. History of American ethnology. Fieldwork among the Cheyenne Indians. **Sources**: Int Dir Anth 3, 5.

0074 **ANDRADE, MARIO RAUL de MORAIS** (1893-1945), Sao Paulo, Brazil. Musicologist, folklorist. Leader of the Modernist movement in Brazil, a movement which sought to renovate Brazilian literature; wrote criticism on literature, folklore, music; wrote about philology and linguistics. **Sources**: Biog Index: 1 & 7/Americas 17:27-9 Ja '65.

0075 **ANDRÉ, S J, Fr. LOUIS** (1623-1715), Saint Remy, Bouches du Rhone, France. Priest. Missionary to New France; wrote on N. American Indians. **Source**: Jes Rel.

0076 **ANDREWS, EDWARD WYLLYS, IV** (1916-1971), Chicago, Illinois, United States. Archeologist. Investigated the Northern Lowland Maya. Excavated & restored Dzibilchaltun in Yucatan (Mexico), which evidenced longest, continuous occupation by Maya. **Sources**: Nat Dir Lat Am/Am Anth 75:295-8 F '73/Am Antiq 37:394-403 Jl '72/ N Y Times p 22 Jl 5 '71.

0077 **ANDREWS, EUGENE PLUMB** (1866-1957). Archeologist. Known as an historian of archeology; some fieldwork in classical archeology. **Sources**: Biog Index: 4 & 7/Nat Cyc Am Biog 47:177-8 '65/ N Y Times p 86 S 22 '57.

0078 **ANDREWS, JOSEPH,** England. Sailor. Visited interior provinces of Argentina en route to Potosi in 1825 and wrote an account of the trip useful for its detailed description of life and customs. **Source**: Wright & Nelsham, Historical Dictionary of Argentina (1978), p 39.

0079 **ANDRIESESCU, IOAN G** (1888-1944), Romania. Archeologist. Initiator of prehistoric studies in Romania; published much on Romanian archeology. **Sources**: Biog Index: 2/Rev Arch series 6 34:73 Jl '49.

0080 **ANGEL, JOHN LAWRENCE** (ca. 1915-1986), England. Physical anthropologist. Specialized in anatomy, forensic anthropology, paleodemography. ecology, and classical archeology. Researched demography & social biology in Greece & Turkey; paleopathology & microevolution in Eastern Mediterranean; stature, growth & health in U.S. populations. **Sources**: Biog Index: 12 & 13/Anth News 28:1:4/Int Dir Anth 3, 5/ American Journal of Physical Anthropology 51:508-16 N '79/ People Weekly 19:59-60 My 16 '83.

0081 **ANGELINO, HARRY R** (1910-). Psychologist. Poverty, intelligence & enculturation of the young. Culture & personality studies. **Source**: Int Dir Anth 5.

0082 **ANKERMANN, BERNHARD** (1859-). Studied African musical instruments. **Source**: Nat Un Cat.

0083 **ANNING, MARY** (1799-1847). Paleontologist. **Source**: Biog Index: 11.

0084 **ANSEROV, NIKOLAI IVANOVICH** (1893-1944), Russia. Anthropologist, anatomist. Physical anthropology in Azerbaijan. **Sources**: Great Soviet Encyclopedia, New York, Macmillan (1973), v. 2, p 120 /Ocherki zhizni i deiatel'- nosti gistologov i anatomov Moskvy (1967).

0085 **ANTHONY, BARBARA W** (1916-). Archeologist. Old World Archeology. Stillbay industry & Middle Stone Age in Africa. African proto-historic cultures. **Source**: Int Dir Anth 5.

0086 **ANTI, CARLO** (1889-1961),

Villafranca Veronese, Italy. Archeologist. Wrote about ancient theatres and the cultural context in which they were built. <u>Sources</u>: Biog Index: 7/Rev Arch 2:204-5 O '63.

0087 ANTONIEWICZ, WŁODZIMIERZ (1893-), Poland. Archeologist. Pre- & proto-history of Poland. Pastoral life & archeology of Slavs. <u>Sources</u>: Int Dir Anth 3, 5.

0088 ANUCHIN, DIMITRII NIKOLAEVICH (1843-1923), St. Petersburg, Russia. Anthropologist, ethnologist, archeologist, geographer. Wrote extensively on Central Asian peoples, Ainu of Japan; founded a school of anthropologists & ethnographers at Moscow University and a museum. Continued the work of A. P. Bogdanov and was one of the founders of the scientific study of anthropology in Russia. <u>Sources</u>: Great Soviet Encyclopedia, New York, Macmillan (1973), v. 2, p 186 /Karpov, G.V. Put' uchenogo Moscow (1958)/Who Was Who In the USSR (1972), p 25.

0089 APARICIO, FRANCISCO de (1892-), Province of Buenos Aires, Argentina. Anthropologist. Archeology & applied anthropology of S. America. <u>Sources</u>: Nat Un Cat/Int Dir Anth 2, 3.

0090 ARAI, SHOJI (1899-), Japan. Anatomist. Anthropometric studies of the Yuzurihara (Japan) & Micronesians. <u>Source</u>: Int Dir Anth 5.

0091 ARAMBOURG, CAMILLE (1885-), Paris, France. Paleontologist. Human paleontology of Europe, Africa, Near & Middle East. <u>Sources</u>: Int Dir Anth 3/Nat Un Cat.

0092 ARBERRY, ARTHUR JOHN (1905-), England. Orientalist. <u>Source</u>: Biog Index: 5.

0093 ARBOLEDA, JOSÉ RAFAEL (1916-), Colombia. Ethnohistorian. Ethnohistory of the negro of Columbia. History of religion in S. America. <u>Sources</u>: Int Dir Anth 3, 5.

0094 ARBOUSSET, JEAN THOMAS (1810-1877), France. Missionary. The customs of the Basotho in Lesotho. Explored the Lesotho region, identifying the source of the Orange River. Left detailed accounts of his travels and of then-contemporary Basotho society under Moshoeshoe I. <u>Source</u>: Haliburton, Gordon, Historical Dictionary of Lesotho (1977), p 9.

0095 ARCELIN, FABIEN (1876-1942), Chalon-sur-Saone, France. Archeologist, radiologist. Archeology of Solutre (France). <u>Sources</u>: Biog Index: 1/Rev Arch 26:88 Jl '46.

0096 ARENDS, TULIO (1918-), Venezuela. Bio-anthropologist. Genetics of Indians of Venezuela. <u>Source</u>: Int Dir Anth 5.

0097 ARENSBERG, CONRAD MAYNADIER (1910-), New York, New York, United States. Anthropologist. Ethnology, linguistics, folklore & applied anthropology of Europe, Middle East, India, China, Korea, Japan; urban anthropology. <u>Sources</u>: Int Dir Anth 1, 3, 5.

0098 ARIAS RENGELL HIDALGO, JOSÉ ANTONIO (1744-1787), Lerma, Argentina. Historian. Wrote the first history of the conquest of the northern areas of Argentina. <u>Source</u>: Wright & Nelsham, Historical Dictionary of Argentina (1978), p 52.

0099 ARIENS KAPPERS, CORNELIUS UBBO (1877-1946). Anthropologist. Wrote on Asia, Armenia & Near East. <u>Source</u>: Nat Un Cat.

0100 ARI'I TA'IMA'I, Princess (1821-1897), Tahiti. Chieftain. Created (with the aid of American historian Henry Adams) a memoir of her life reflecting the structure of Tahitian society in the 19th century. <u>Source</u>: Craig & King, Historical Dictionary of Oceania (1981), p 13.

0101 ARISS, ROBERT McLEOD (1908-), United States. Ethnologist. Curing practices & cults of the American Indians of the Southwest. <u>Sources</u>: Int Dir Anth 3 5/Nat Dir Lat Am.

0102 ARKELL, ANTHONY JOHN (1898-), England. Ethnohistorian. Area studies of the Sudan, Egypt & Libya. <u>Sources</u>: Int Dir Anth 3,

5.
0103 ARMILLAS, PEDRO (1914-), Spain. Cultural anthropologist. Evolution of civilization in Mexico & Central America;pre-Columbian land use. Sources: Nat Dir Lat Am/Int Dir Anth 5.
0104 ARMSTRONG, ROBERT GELSTON (1917-). Ethnologist. African studies, languages & oral literature. Source: Int Dir Anth 5.
0105 ARMSTRONG, ROBERT PLANT (1919-1984). Anthropologist. Ethnoesthetics in Africa. Source: Anth News (Oct. 1984) p 3.
0106 ARNASON, JON (1819-1888). Folklorist. Folklore of Iceland. Sources: Biog Index: 1 & 7.
0107 ARNAUD, EXPEDITE COELHE (1916-), Brazil. Anthropologist. Brazilian cultural anthropology. Source: Int Dir Anth 5.
0108 ARNE, TURE ALGOT JOHNSSON (1879-), Stockholm, Sweden. Anthropologist. European & Asian prehistory, Islamic art and archeology, Chinese prehistory. Studies in archeology of Siberia & Iran. Antiquities of Sweden & Russia. Sources: Int Dir Anth 3/Nat Un Cat.
0109 ARNOT, FREDERICK STANLEY (1858-1914). Missionary, explorer. Missions to South Africa. Traveled extensively over much of Zambia, parts of Zaire & Angola. Sources: Grotpeter, John J., Historical Dictionary of Zambia (1979), p 14/ Nat Un Cat.
0110 ARRIOLA, MANUEL (1873-1927), Guatemala. Historian. Published *Etimologias nacionales*, on Guatemalan languages. Source: Moore, Richard E., Historical Dictionary of Guatemala (1973), p 25.
0111 ARSANZ DE ORSULA Y VELA, BARTAMOLAML (1676-1736). Historian. Wrote a history of colonial Potosi (Bolivia) up to 1735. Source: Heath, Dwight B., Historical Dictionary of Bolivia (1972), p 26.
0112 ARTAMONOV, MIKHAIL ILLARIONOVICH (1898-), Vygoleva, Russia. Anthropologist, historian. Bronze and Iron Ages of the Ukraine and Northern Caucasus, and archeology of the early Slavs, Scythians and Khazars. Sources: Great Soviet Encyclopedia, New York, Macmillan (1973), v. 2, p 371 /Klein, L.S., "K semidesiatiletiiu M. I. Artamonova." Sovetskaia arkheologiia, 1968, no. 4.
0113 ARTSIKHOVSKII, ARTEMII VLADIMIROVICH (1902-), Russia. Archeologist. Antiquities of Novgorod and Moscow (Russia). Source: Great Soviet Encyclopedia, New York, Macmillan (1973), v. 2, p 384.
0114 ARVIEUX, JAMES HENRY (1635-1702). Orientalist. Source: Biog Index: 6.
0115 ASBJORNSEN, PETER CHRISTEN (1812-1885), Norway. Author, folklorist. Sources: Biog Index: 1 2 7 8 12 & 13/ Commire, Anne. Something about the Author, v 15. Gale '79.
0116 ASCH, MOSES (ca. 1905-1986), Warsaw, Poland. Folklorist, businessman. Developed library of 2,000 albums of traditional music from around the world. Sources: Biog Index: 3 & 7/Anth News 27:9:3/ Senior Scholastic 89:22 N 11 '66.
0117 ASHMUN, JEHUDI (1794-1828), Champlain, New York, United States. Missionary. Wrote a history of the first two years of the Liberian settlement. Source: Dunn & Holsoe, Historical Dictionary of Liberia (1985), p 20.
0118 ASÍN PALACIOS, MIGUEL (1871-1944), Spain. Orientalist. Sources: Biog Index: 1 & 3.
0119 ASMUS, GISELA (1905-), Germany. Anthropologist. Prehistoric anthropology of North & Central Europe. Source: Int Dir Anth 5.
0120 ATKINS, JOHN (1685-1757). Traveler. Wrote on travels to Guinea, Brazil, West Indies. Source: Nat Un Cat.
0121 ATKINSON, MARY JOURDAN (1898-). Cultural anthropologist. Ethnohistory & acculturation studies of Indians in Southwest U.S. and Blacks in Texas. Source: Int

Dir Anth 5.

0122 AUBERY, S J, Fr. JOSEPH (1674-1756), Gisors, Normandy, France. Priest. Missionary to New France; wrote on N. American Indians. Source: Jes Rel.

0123 AUBREY, JOHN (1626-1697). Archeologist. Sources: Biog Index: 1/ Powell, Anthony. John Aubrey & His Friends. Scribner '48/Time 53:110+ My 9 '49.

0124 AUDOLLENT, AUGUSTE MARIE HENRI (1864-1943), Paris, France. Archeologist. Excavated Roman ruins in North Africa as well as at Clermont-Ferrand (France). Sources: Biog Index: 1/Rev Arch series 6 25:62-3 Ja '46.

0125 AUFENANGER, HENRY (1905-). Ethnologist. Spiritual & material culture of New Guinea & S Pacific. Source: Int Dir Anth 5.

0126 AUL, JUHAN MIHKELEVICH (1897-), Estonia. Anthropologist, zoologist. Anthropology of modern Estonians, Latvians, Swedes, Ingrians, and Udmurts. Source: Great Soviet Encyclopedia, New York, Macmillan (1973), v. 2, p 510.

0127 AULNEAU, S J, Fr. JEAN PIERRE (1705-1736), Moutiers sur Hay, France. Priest. Missionary to New France; wrote on N. American Indians. Source: Jes Rel.

0128 AUPIAIS, FRANCIS (1877-1945), Saint Nazaire, France. Missionary, ethnologist. Founded the review *La Reconnaissance Africaine*. Wrote extensively on ethnology of Africa, viz *Les proverbes* (1926). Source: DeCalo, Samuel, Historical Dictionary of Dahomey (1976), p 23.

0129 AURIGEMMA, SALVATORE (1885-1964). Archeologist. Sources: Biog Index: 7/Bollettino d'Arte 49:191-2 Ap '64.

0130 AUVRAY, HENRY (1878-1947), Tours, France. Archeologist. Archeology of Tours region. Source: Rev Arch series 6 39:101-2 Ja '52.

0131 AVAUGOUR, S J, Fr. LOUIS d' (1669-1732), France. Priest. Missionary to New France; wrote on N. American Indians. Source: Jes Rel.

0132 AYONE, JEAN-REMY (1914-). Civil servant. Prepared a paper for the 1944 Brazzaville conference on the respective roles of African and Western cultures in an evolving Africa. Source: Gardiner, David E., Historical Dictionary of Gabon (1981), p 34-5.

0133 AYROUT, HENRI-HABIB (1907-1969). Wrote on Egyptian social life & culture. Source: Nat Un Cat.

0134 AYZAC, FÉLICIE d' (1801-). Anthropologist. Source: Biog Index: 8.

0135 AZADOVSKII, MARK KONSTANTINOVICH (1883-1954), Siberia. Ethnologist. Source: Nat Un Cat.

0136 AZARA, FÉLIX de (1746-1821), Spain. Civil servant. Wrote memoirs and several books on the geography and history of Paraguay. Source: Kolinski, Charles J., Historical Dictionary of Paraguay (1973), p 18.

0137 AZEVEDO, THALES de (1904-). Anthropologist. Acculturation of Italian immigrants & race relations between blacks & whites in Brazil. Source: Int Dir Anth 5.

0138 AZIKIWE, NNAMDI (1904-), Onitsha, Nigeria. Civil servant. Igbo mythology; Governor-general of Nigeria, 1961-63, President, 1963-66. Source: West Africa 15, Aug. 1983, p 1889.

0139 BA, AMADOU HAMPATE. Historian. Wrote historical and ethnographic studies on the Futani people of the Inland Niger Delta in Mali. Source: Imperato, Pascal J., Historical Dictionary of Mali (1977), p 19.

0140 BACH, ADOLF (1890-). Linguistic geography, especially German. Source: Nat Un Cat.

0141 BACHHOFER, LUDWIG (1894-1976). Art historian. Wrote: on Far Eastern art, e.g., *Chinesische Kunst*, 1923; *Die Kunst der japanischen Holzschnittmeister*, 1922. Sources: Biog Index: 11/Archives of Asian Art 31:110-12

'77.

0142 BACHOFEN, JOHANN JAKOB (1815- 1887). Anthropologist. Source: Biog Index: 7.

0143 BACKHOUSE, EDMUND TRELAWNY (1873-1944), England. Historian. Sources: Biog Index: 5 & 11/ Trevor-Roper, Hugh. Hermit of Peking: the Hidden Life of Sir Edmund Backhouse. Knopf, 1977.

0144 BACON, FRANCIS H (1856-). Archeologist. Wrote a 5-volume account of the excavation of the site of Assos in Turkey, 1881-1885. Sources: Biog Index: 10/Archaeology 27:83-95 Ap '74.

0145 BACOT, JACQUES (1877-1965). Wrote on Tibet. Source: Nat Un Cat.

0146 BADE, WILLIAM FREDERIC (1871-1936). Biblical scholar, archeologist. Sources: Biog Index: 4/Dictionary of Australian Biography sup 2:16-17 '58.

0147 BADEN-POWELL, DONALD FORLYS WILSON (1897-), England. Human paleontology, prehistory. Europe. Source: Int Dir Anth 2.

0148 BADEN-POWELL, ROBERT STEPHEN SMYTH (1857-1941). Soldier. Wrote an account of the 1897 revolt of the Shona in Rhodesia. Source: Rasmussen, R. Kent, Historical Dictionary of Rhodesia/ Zimbabwe (1979), p 25.

0149 BADER, OTTO NIKOLAEVICH (1903-), Aleksandrovnoc, Russia. Anthropologist. Paleolithic and Bronze Age in Russia. Source: Great Soviet Encyclopedia, New York, Macmillan (1973), v. 2, p 536.

0150 BAEGERT, JAKOB (1717-1772), Germany. Studies on Indians of Mexico. Source: Nat Un Cat.

0151 BAELZ, ERWIN O. E. von (1849-1913), Germany. Wrote on travels to Japan and China. Source: Nat Un Cat.

0152 BAERREIS, DAVID ALBERT (1916-), New York, United States. Anthropologist, archeologist. Ethnohistory & paleoecology of U.S. Sources: Nat Dir Lat Am/Int Dir Anth 3, 5.

0153 BÁEZ, CECILIO (1862-1941), Paraguay. Sociologist, historian. Author of several works on Paraguay's cultural revolution. Source: Kolinski, Charles J., Historical Dictionary of Paraguay (1973).

0154 BAGBY, PHILIP HAXALL (1918-1958), Richmond, Virginia, United States. Anthropologist. Focused on the study of comparative civilizations & culture and its causes. Sources: Biog Index: 5/Am Anth 61:1075 D '59.

0155 BAGEHOT, WALTER (1826-1877). Social scientist. Pioneer analysis of the inter-relationship between the natural social sciences. Source: Columbia.

0156 BAHRAMI, MEHDI (1905-1951), Persia, Iran. Orientalist. Source: Biog Index: 3 5.

0157 BAILEY, HAROLD WALTER (1899-), Australia. Orientalist. Source: Biog Index: 12.

0158 BAILEY, JOHN HAYNES (1909-1948), Dansville, New York, United States. Archeologist. Site survey in areas of Iowa, Illinois and Champlain Valley, Vermont, New York. Sources: Biog Index: 2/Int Dir Anth 2/Am Antiq 14:214-15 Ja '49.

0159 BAILEY, WILFRED C (1918-), United States. Cultural anthropologist. Anthropology of education. Community organization & culture change. Sources: Int Dir Anth 3, 5.

0160 BAILLOQUET, S J, Fr. PIERRE (1612-1692), Saints, France. Priest. Missionary to New France; wrote on N. American Indians. Source: Jes Rel.

0161 BAINES, JERVOISE ATHELSTANE (1847-). Ethnologist. Ethnology of India. Source: Nat Un Cat.

0162 BAIRD, GEORGE HUSBAND (1761-1840), Scotland. Orientalist. Source: Biog Index: 4.

0163 BAKE, ARNOLD ADRIAAN (1899-). Folklore, folk music, comparative musicology, India. Source: Int Dir Anth 2.

0164 BAKER, FRANK (1841-1918), Pulaski, New York, United States. Biologist, physician. Edited

American Anthropologist in 1890s; anatomy specialist. Source: Am Anth 19:186-188 Je '19.

0165 BAKER, SAMUEL WHITE (1821-1893), England. Explorer. Explored the headwaters of the Nile in the Lake Victoria region and left an excellent account of the culture and customs of the people of the Nile region of the Sudan. Source: Voll, John Obert, Historical Dictionary of the Sudan (1978), p 39.

0166 BAKER, SHIRLEY WALDEMAR (1836-1903), London, England. Missionary. Promulgated a comprehensive set of laws for Tonga. Source: Craig & King, Historical Dictionary of Oceania (1981), p 22.

0167 BAKO, FERENC (1917-), Hungary. Ethnologist. Folk architecture, culture & community, ethnic groups in Hungary. Source: Int Dir Anth 5.

0168 AL-BAKRĪ, ABŪ ʿUBAYD (1028-1094), Spain. Geographer. *Al-Masalik wa al-mamalik*, key description of world as known to Muslim Spaniard in 11th century, particularly important for African studies. Sources: Imperato, Pascal J., Hisotrical Dictionary of Mali (1977), p 45/ Encyclopaedia of Islam, New ed., v. 1, p 155-157.

0169 BALASSA, IVAN (1917-), Hungary. Anthropologist. The history of farming and plows in Europe. Source: Int Dir Anth 5.

0170 BALDUS, HERBERT (1899-1970), Germany. Anthropologist. First to systematize the studies of South American ethnology. Compiled bibliographies of all publications about groups of Indians living in or who lived in Brazil. Source: Am Anth 74:1307-12 O '72.

0171 BALDWIN, ARTHUR. Missionary. Left a journal describing politics in the Lozi area of Zambia, 1891-1893. Source: Grotpeter, John J., Historical Dictionary of Zambia (1979), p 17.

0172 BALDWIN, CHARLES CANDEE (1834-1895), Middletown, Connecticut, United States. Lawyer. Ohio archeology. Source: Am Anth 8(old series):180 Ap 1895.

0173 BALDWIN, GORDON C (1908-), United States. Archeologist. Pueblo Indians of Arizona. Sources: Biog Index: 11/Int Dir Anth 1 2 3/ Commire, Anne. Something about the Author, v 12. Gale.

0174 BALFOUR, HENRY (1863-1939), Croydon, England. Anthropologist. Curator of Pitt-Rivers Museum, Oxford, 1891-1939. Specialist in technology of prehistory & prehistoric archeology. Sources: Biog Index: 2/Dictionary of National Biography 1931-40:35-7 '49.

0175 BALLESTER TORMO, ISIDRO (1876-1950). Archeologist. Sources: Biog Index: 3/ Archivo Espanol de Arte y Arqueologia 25 no 86:413 '52.

0176 BALODIS, FRANCIS ALEKSANDRA (1882-1947), Valmiera, Latvia. Archeologist. Specialist on archeology of Latvia; published a survey of excavations at Sanai, 1919-1922; focused on history of Latvia in regional context. Sources: Biog Index: 1/Journal of Central European Affairs 8:91 Ap '48.

0177 BALOUT, LIONEL FERDINAND FELIX (1907-), France. Paleontologist. Prehistory of Mediterranean & North & East Africa. Source: Int Dir Anth 5.

0178 BALSAN, FRANÇOIS (1902-). Traveler to Arabia, South Africa, Baluchistan, Afghanistan, Ethiopia. Source: Nat Un Cat.

0179 BAÑADOS ESPINOSA, JULIO (1858-1894), Chile. Journalist. Created several objective accounts of Chilean history. Source: Bizzarro, Salvatore, Historical Dictionary of Chile (1972), p 35-6.

0180 BANCROFT, HUBERT HOWE (1832- 1918), Granville, Ohio, United States. Publisher, historian. Collection of primary source material on history of the U.S. West. Source: Columbia.

0181 BANDELIER, ADOLPH FRANCIS ALPHONSE (1840-1914). Archeologist, ethnologist. Ethnology of Western U.S. Indians. Sources:

Biog Index: 2 3 7 & 9/ Pioneers in American Anthropology: the Bandelier-Morgan Letters. Univ. of New Mexico Press, 1940/ The Southwestern Journals of Adolph F. Bandelier. Univ. of New Mexico Press, 1966.

0182 BANKS, JOSEPH (1743-1820), London, England. Naturalist, botanist. Accompanied Cook's expedition around the world and brought back first marsupial fauna of Australia; explored Hebrides & Iceland where he discovered the great geysers. Sources: Columbia/New Int Enc.

0183 BAPTISTA, PEDRO J. Wrote a diary describing a nine year trek from Luanda, Angola to Tete, Mozambique, 1802-1811. Source: Grotpeter, John J., Historical Dictionary of Zambia (1979), p 19.

0184 BARAMKI, DIMITRI CONSTANTINE (1909-), Lebanon. Archeologist. Numismatics, ceramics, art & architecture of the Near East. Source: Int Dir Anth 5.

0185 BARBEAU, MARIUS (1883-1969), Canada. Anthropologist, folklorist. Anthropology of Canadian Indians. Sources: Biog Index: 2 5 8 & 11/Int Dir Anth 2, 3/ Journal of American Folklore 82:264-6 Jl '69/N Y Times p 43 Mr '69.

0186 BARBER, EDWIN ATLEE (1851-1916). Archeologist. Sources: Biog Index: 13/Stillinger, Elizabeth. Antiques. Knopf '80.

0187 BARDON, LOUIS (1877-1944), France. Priest, archeologist. Archeology of Correze (France). Sources: Biog Index: 1/Rev Arch 27:80 Ja '47.

0188 BARJAKTAROVIĆ, MIRKO (1912-), Yugoslavia. Ethnologist. Ethnic differentiation and interrelations in Yugoslavia. Source: Int Dir Anth 5.

0189 BARKER, GEORGE CARPENTER (1912-1958), Omaha, Nebraska, United States. Anthropologist. Specialized in the language of Mexican-American youth and the social functions of language. Sources: Biog Index: 5/Int Dir Anth 3/Am Anth 60:932-3 O '58.

0190 BARLOW, FRANK OSWELL (1880-1951), England. Anthropologist. Restoration and casts of fossil remains, especially human. Chief preparator in the Geological Department of the British Museum (Natural History); was associated with Sir Arthur Smith Woodward and the reconstruction of the Piltdown specimens. Sources: Biog Index: 2/Nature 168:1103-4 D 29 '51/ Museum Journal 51:234-5 D '5.

0191 BARLOW, ROBERT HAYWARD (1918- 1951), United States. Poet, archeologist. Anthropology of Central America & Mexico. Sources: Biog Index: 2/Int Dir Anth 3/Poetry 78:115-18 My '51/ Am Antiq 16:347 Ap '51, 53:543 O '51.

0192 BARNES, JOHN ARUNDEL (1918-), England. Social anthropologist. Social networks. Kinship theories. Mathematical models. Sources: Int Dir Anth 3, 5.

0193 BARNETT, HOMER GARNER (1906- 1985), Bisbee, Arizona, United States. General ethnology, applied anthropology & culture change, ethnology of N. America & Micronesia. Studies on Indians of North America; research focused on cultural social change; fieldwork in British Columbia (Salish) and Micronesia (Palau). Sources: Nat Un Cat/Int Dir Anth 1, 2, 3/Anth News 9/85.

0194 BARNETT, LIONEL DAVID (1871-1960), England. Orientalist. Keeper of the Department of Oriental Printed Books and Manuscripts in the British Museum, 1908-1936. Sources: Biog Index: 5/Illustrated London News 236:221 F 6 '60.

0195 BARNICOT, NIGEL ASHWORTH (1914-1975), England. Physical anthropologist. Genetics of human & non-human primates. Sources: Biog Index: 11/Int Dir Anth 3, 5/ American Journal of Physical Anthropology 45:173 S '76.

0196 BARNOUW, VICTOR (1915-), Netherlands. Ethnologist. Culture & personality studies of the Chippewa of N. America & Sindhi of India. Sources: Int Dir Anth 3, 5.

0197 BARNS, JOHN WINTOUR BALDWIN (1912-1974), England. Egyptologist. Specialist on papyrology. Sources: Biog Index: 10/Journal of Egyptian Archaeology 60:3 '74.

0198 BAROCELLI, PIETRO (1887-), Modena, Italy. Archeologist. Prehistoric archeology of Italy. Sources: Nat Un Cat/Int Dir Anth 3.

0199 BARÓN CASTRO, RODOLPO (1909-), El Salvador. Wrote extensively on colonial period of El Salvador. Source: Flemion, Philip F., Historical Dictionary of El Salvador (1972), p 23.

0200 BARRETT, MURRAY JAMES (1916-). Dentist. Dental anthropology of central Australia. Source: Int Dir Anth 5.

0201 BARRINGTON, THEOPHILUS (1657- 1679), Little Baddow, Essex, England. Archeologist, historian. Sources: Biog Index: 11/Antiquity 51:49-51 Mr '77.

0202 BARROS ARAÑA, DIEGO (1830-1906), Chile. Historian. Wrote a 10 volume account of the war for Chile's independence and general works, including a large number of individual biographies. Source: Bizzarro, Salvatore, Historical Dictionary of Chile (1972), p 38-9.

0203 BARROSO, GUSTAVO (1888-1959), Brazil. Folklorist. Directed restoration of the colonial mining center of Ouro Prieto (Brazil). Sources: Biog Index: 1 & 5/N Y Times p 32 D 4 '59.

0204 BARRY, HERBERT (1898-). Wrote on Russian social life & customs. Source: Nat Un Cat.

0205 BARTELS, MAXIMILIAN CARL AUGUST (1843-1904). Ethnologist. Source: Nat Un Cat.

0206 BARTH, HEINRICH (1821-1865), Hamburg, Germany. Explorer, historian. Worked in British service in Africa. Studied Fulani & Hausa in Africa. Explored West Africa between 1845 and 1855, leaving detailed accounts of Mali, Northern Nigeria & Cameroon. His works are still considered as basic ethnographic sources for these regions. Sources: Columbia/Imperato, Pascal J., Historical Dictionary of Mali (1977), p 23.

0207 BARTHOUX, JULES (1881-1965), France. Archeologist. Archeology of Afghanistan. Sources: Biog Index: 7/Rev Arch 1:103-4 Ja '65.

0208 BARTOCCINI, RENATO (1893-1963). Archeologist. Specialist in Etruscan archeology; located the cities of Vulci and Feronia in Italy; worked at the site of Leptis Magna (Libya) in 1924. Sources: Biog Index: 6/N Y Times p 37 O 11 '63/Time 82:114 O 18 '63.

0209 BARTÓK, BÉLA (1881-1945), Hungary. Composer, folk musician. Wrote: *The Hungarian Folk Song* (tr. 1931). Collector of folk music, especially of Eastern Europe (Hungary & Yugoslavia). Transcribed Yugoslav folk melodies. Source: Columbia.

0210 BARTOLD, VASILII VLADIMIROVICH (1869-1930). Orientalist. Source: Biog Index: 12.

0211 BARTON, GEORGE AARON (1859-1942). Orientalist, clergyman. Source: Biog Index: 3.

0212 BARTON, ROY FRANKLIN (1883-1947), Illinois, United States. Ethnographer, dentist. Specialist in Philippine peoples & cultures, particularly Ifugao & Kalinga. Sources: Biog Index: 2/Am Anth 51:91-5 Ja '49.

0213 BASADRE, JORGE (1903-), Tacna, Peru. Historian. Wrote studies of Peruvian history useful for background ethnographic data. Source: Alisky, Historical Dictionary of Peru (1979), p 16-7.

0214 BASCOM, WILLIAM RUSSEL (1912-1981), Princeton, Illinois, United States. Africanist, ethnologist, folklorist, anthropologist. Ethnology of African peoples. Folklore. Afro-Cuban religion. Kiowa culture, Zomba religion and kinship, African themes in Gullah culture and Cuba, and Ponape cultures; specialist in Zomba religion and folklore, African art, and the nature and function of folklore. Sources: Am Anth 88:154 '86/Int Dir Anth 1, 2, 3, 5/Nat Dir Lat Am.

0215 BASEDOW, HERBERT (1881-1933), Kent Town, Adelaide, South Australia, Australia. Geologist, politician, anthropologist. Chief protector of Aborigines for the Commonwealth in the Northern Territories. Lived for years among the Aborigines. Authority on the Aboriginal Question and anthropology of Australian tribes. Sources: Biog Index: 2/Dictionary of Australian Biography 1:57, '49/ Who Was Who, 1929-1940.

0216 BASEHART, HARRY W (1910-). Socio-cultural anthropologist. Ethnographic fieldwork among the Matengo of Tanzania & the N. American Apache & Oneida. Source: Int Dir Anth 5.

0217 BASTIAN, ADOLF (1825-1905). Ethnologist. Source: Biog Index: 9.

0218 BASTIDE, ROGER (1898-), France. Ethno-sociologist. Race relations between whites & blacks in Brazil. African & Afro-American religions. Sources: Int Dir Anth 3, 5.

0219 BATAILLON, PIERRE-MARIE (1810-1877), Saint-Cyr-Des-Vignes, France. Missionary. Pioneered conversion of peoples of Wallis Island. Source: Craig & King, Historical Dictionary of Oceania (1981), p 23.

0220 BATES, DAISY (1861-1951). Ethnologist. Sources: Biog Index: 2 3 7 8 9 & 10.

0221 BATESON, GREGORY (1904-1980), England. Anthropologist, philosopher, photographer. Fieldwork in New Guinea, Melanesia. Psychological anthropology, as related to evolution & adaptation. Analysis of human thought & behavior. Sources: Biog Index: 11 12 & 13/ International Encyclopedia of the Social Sciences, v. 18/ Lipset, David. Gregory Bateson: the Legacy of a Scientist. Prentice-Hall '80/ Am Anth 84:379-394 Jn '82/Afterimage 8:4 O '80/N Y Times p D-13 Jl 7 '80/ N Y Times Biog Service 11:939 Jl '80/Newsweek 96:61 Jl 21 '80/ Publishers Weekly 218:83 Jl 25 '80/Time 116:49 Jl 21 '80.

0222 BATESON, WILLIAM (1861-1926). Studies on sociology and evolution. Source: Nat Un Cat.

0223 BATRAWI, AHMED A (1902-), Egypt. Physical anthropologist. Physical anthropology of Nubia. Sources: Nat Un Cat/Int Dir Anth 3.

0224 BATTEL, ANDREW (fl. 1589-). Traveler to Angola, Kongo, Brazil. Source: Nat Un Cat.

0225 BAUMANN, HERMANN (1902-), Germany. Ethnologist. Sources: Nat Un Cat/Int Dir Anth 3.

0226 BAUMANN, JEAN-A (1910-). Anatomist. Medical anthropology. Anthropometric methodology. Source: Int Dir Anth 5.

0227 BAUMGARTEL, ELISE JENNY (1892-1977), Germany. Archeologist. Archeology of Egypt. Sources: Biog Index: 11/Int Dir Anth 3.

0228 BAUR, ERWIN (1875-1933). Studied ethnology & human heredity. Source: Nat Un Cat.

0229 BAUR, PAUL VICTOR CHRISTOPHER (1872-1951), Cincinnati, Ohio, United States. Archeologist. Curator of Classical Archeology at Yale Univ. Sources: Biog Index: 2/Am J Arch 55:67 Ja 52/Archaeology 4:187 Autumn 51/ Museum News 29:4 S 1 '51/N Y Times p 31 Je 6 '51/ School & Society 73:382-3 Je 16 '51.

0230 BAUXAR, J JOSEPH (1910-). Archivist, ethno-archeologist. Ethnoarcheology of Illinois & Tennessee. Source: Int Dir Anth 5.

0231 BAYBARS, AL-MANSURI (-1325), Egypt. Historian. Wrote a detailed study of the development of Islam and the rise of Egypt. Source: King, Joan W., Historical Dictionary of Egypt (1984), p 205.

0232 BEAGLEHOLE, ERNEST (1906-1965), New Zealand. Psychologist. Combined anthropology with psychology to shape the field of ethno-psychology. Was instrumental in establishing anthropology in New

Zealand. <u>Sources</u>: Int Dir Anth 3/Am Anth 69:68-70 F '67.

0233 **BEAGLEHOLE, JOHN CAUTE** (1901- 1971), Wellington, New Zealand. Historian. Edited the journals of Captain James Cook and wrote a definitive study of the exploration of the Pacific Ocean. <u>Source</u>: Craig & King, Historical Dictionary of Oceania (1981), p 25.

0234 **BEAGLEHOLE, PEARL** (1910-), United States. Ethnology of Pukapuka (Tuamotu Islands). Wrote on Hopi Indians. <u>Sources</u>: Nat Un Cat/Int Dir Anth 1.

0235 **BEALS, RALPH LEON** (1901-), United States. Ethnologist, anthropologist. Peasant communities, marketing systems in Latin America. <u>Sources</u>: Int Dir Anth 1, 2, 3, 5/Nat Dir Lat Am.

0236 **BEAN, ROBERT BENNETT** (1874-1944), United States. Anatomist, physical anthropologist. Anthropology of Virginia & the Philippine Islands. <u>Sources</u>: Biog Index: 1/Int Dir Anth 1, 2/Am Anth 48:70-4 Ja '46.

0237 **BEARDSLEY, RICHARD KING** (1918-1978), Colorado, United States. Anthropologist. Japanese community studies. <u>Sources</u>: Biog Index: 11 12 & 13/Int Dir Anth 3/Am Anth 81:636-9 S '79/ Anth News S '78.

0238 **BEATTLE, JOHN HUGH MARSHALL** (1915-). Ethnologist. Theoretical studies in ritual & small scale political organizations in Africa. <u>Source</u>: Int Dir Anth 5.

0239 **BEAUBIEN, PAUL L** (1903-1962), Ford, Kansas, United States. Archeologist. Regional archeologist for the Midwest Region, U.S. National Park Service; excavated the Convento area at Tumacacori National Monument. <u>Sources</u>: Biog Index: 7/Am Antiq 29:486 Ap '64.

0240 **BEAUBOIS, S J, Fr. NICOLAS IGNACE de** (1689-ca. 1763), Orleans, France. Priest. Missionary to New France; wrote on N. American Indians. <u>Source</u>: Jes Rel.

0241 **BEAZLEY, JOHN DAVIDSON** (1885- 1970), Glasgow, Scotland. Archeologist. Wrote extensively on Greek vases. <u>Sources</u>: Biog Index: 2 & 9/Burlington Magazine 112:541-2 Ag '70/ Gazette des Beaux Arts 76:sup 32 D '70/Rev Arch 297-9 '70.

0242 **BECHER, HANS** (1918-). Ethnologist. Material culture. Social organization of kinship relations of the Amazon Basin. <u>Source</u>: Int Dir Anth 5.

0243 **BECK, EARL CLIFTON** (1891-). Folklorist. Tracked down lumberjack ballads and their origins in the American northwoods. <u>Sources</u>: Biog Index: 1/American Forests 52:216+ My '46.

0244 **BECK, WALTER GEORGE** (1909-), Germany. Ethnologist. Ethnology of Australia, Indonesia, and Africa. <u>Sources</u>: Nat Un Cat/Int Dir Anth 3.

0245 **BECKER, CARL JOHAN** (1915-), Denmark. Archeologist. Neolithic culture in Early Iron Age Scandinavian settlements. <u>Sources</u>: Int Dir Anth 3, 5.

0246 **BECKWITH, MARTHA WARREN** (1871-1959), United States. Folklorist. Folklore of Polynesia & Hawaiian Islands. <u>Sources</u>: Biog Index: 6/Int Dir Anth 1, 2, 3/ Journal of American Folklore 75:341-53 0 '62.

0247 **BEDDOE, JOHN** (1826-1911). Anthropologist. Anthropology of India; ethnology of Europe, Scotland. <u>Source</u>: Nat Un Cat.

0248 **BÉGOUEN, HENRI** (1863-1956), Chateauroux, France. Archeologist. Prehistory of Europe. <u>Sources</u>: Biog Index: 4/Rev Arch 50:76-9 Jl '57.

0249 **BÉHAGLE, FERDINAND de** (-1899). Explorer. Identified sources of Tomi & Gribingui rivers (Central African Republic). <u>Source</u>: Kalck, Pierre, Historical Dictionary of the Central African Republic (1980), p 13.

0250 **BEHRENDT, KARL HERMANN** (1817- 1878). Ethnologist. <u>Sources</u>: Biog Index: 2/Zucker, Adolf Eduard, ed. Forty-eighters. Columbia Univ. Press '50 p 277.

0251 BEHRENS, HERMANN (1915-). Archeologist. Studies of the New Stone Age in Europe. Source: Int Dir Anth 5.

0252 BELAIEFF, JUAN (1874-1957), Russia. Army officer. Conducted the first surveys of the Chaco region (Argentina) and studied the indigenous peoples of the area. Source: Kolinski, Charles J., Historical Dictionary of Paraguay (1973), p 23.

0253 BELIN-MILLERON, JEAN ETIENNE FERNAND (1909-). Linguist. Rural semiotics & history of ethnology in France. Comparative methodology of the human sciences. Source: Int Dir Anth 5.

0254 BELL, BETTY BONITA (1918-), United States. Anthropologist. Mesoamerican archeology. Present-day social planning in Latin America. Source: Nat Dir Lat Am.

0255 BELL, EARL HOYT (1903-1963), United States. Sociologist, anthropologist. Plains Indians of the United States. Sources: Biog Index: 6 & 7/Int Dir Anth 1, 2, 3/Am Anth 66:614-⌐ Je '64.

0256 BELL, GERTRUDE MARGARET LOWTHIAN (1868-1926). Archeologist. Sources: Biog Index: 2 3 4 5 6 8 11 12 & 13/ Geography Journal 145:302-4 Jl '79/Tidrick, Kathryn, Heart-beguiling Araby. Cambridge Univ. Press '81 p 187-92/Antiquity 50:190-3 S '76/ Contemporary Review, F '52.

0257 BELL, HAROLD IDRIS (1879-1967), Epworth, Lincolnshire, England. Egyptologist. Papyrologist who was the Keeper of the British Museum. Sources: Biog Index: 3 7 & 8/Illustrated London News 250:12 Ja 28 '67/ Journal of Egyptian Archaeology 53:131-9 D '67, 40:3-6 '54.

0258 BELL, ROBERT E (1914-), United States. Archeologist. Dendrochronology in the prehistoric Mississippi Valley & Eastern U.S. Archeology in Ecuador. Sources: Int Dir Anth 3, 5/Nat Dir Lat Am.

0259 BELTRAMI, LUCA (1854-1933), Milano, Italy. Art historian, archeologist. Sources: Biog Index: 2/Isis 40 no 4:354 '49.

0260 BELZONI, GIOVANNI BATTISTA (1778-1823), Padua, Italy. Archeologist. Compiled a huge collection of Egyptian artifacts for the British Museum; left documentation of the tomb of Seti I. Sources: Biog Index: 4 5 6 & 10/Archaeology 26:48-51 Ja '73.

0261 BENEDICT, PAUL KING (1912-), United States. Anthropologist. Anthropology of India & SE Asia. Sources: Nat Un Cat/Int Dir Anth 3.

0262 BENEDICT, RUTH FULTON (1887-1948), New York, New York, United States. Cultural anthropologist, ethnologist. Studied American Indians & contemporary European and Asian cultures. Cultural configuration. National character. Role of culture in individual's personality formation. Popularized notion of culture. Attacked racism & ethnocentrism. Sources: Biog Index: 1 2 4 5 6 10 12 & 13/Int Dir Anth 1, 2/Columbia/ Mead, Margaret, Ruth Benedict, New York, Columbia Univ. Press (1975)/ Am Anth 51:457-68 Jl '49/American Scholar 49:504-9 Aut '80/ Journal of American Folklore 92:445-76 O '79.

0263 BENET, SULA (1906-), Poland. Socio-anthropologist, folklorist. Ethnology & folklore of Europe & the Caucasus. Sources: Biog Index: 8/Int Dir Anth 3, 5.

0264 BENFEY, THEODOR (1809-1881), Norton, Hanover, Germany. Orientalist. Researched Sanskrit language & literature; studied influence of ancient Indian material on the folklore of Asia & Europe. Source: New Int Enc.

0265 BENNETT, JOHN WILLIAM (1915-), United States. Cultural ecologist. Human & cultural ecology. Human geography. Natural resources in Asia & N. America. Sources: Int Dir Anth 3, 5.

0266 BENNETT, LOUISE (1919-), Jamaica. Folklorist. Folklore and dance in Jamaica. Sources: Biog Index: 9/Int Dir Anth 3.

0267 BENNETT, WENDELL CLARK

(1905- 1954), United States. Anthropologist. Archeology, ethnology, linguistics of South America. Conducted excavations at Tiahuanaco and elsewhere in Bolivia. Sources: Biog Index: 3/Int Dir Anth 1, 2, 3/Heath, Dwight B., Historical Dictionary of Bolivia (1972), p 36/Int Dir Anth 1 2 3/ Am Anth 56:269-73 Ap '54/Archaeology 6:244 D '53/Museum News 31:301 '53/ N Y Times p 7 S 7, p 56 S 8 '53/Nature 172:936-7 N 21 '53/ School & Society 78:94 S 19 '53/Science 119:674 My 14 '54/ Am Antiq 19:265-70 Ja '54.

0268 BENOIT, FRANÇOIS (1870-1947), France. Art historian, architectural historian. History of art and architecture including that of the Classical World. Source: Rev Arch series 6 39:100-1 Ja '52.

0269 BENT, JAMES THEODORE (1853-1897), England. Antiquarian, archeologist, explorer. Research on coast of Asia Minor, Bahrein Islands. Wrote on the Hadhramaut (Yemen), Mashonaland (Rhodesia) and Ethiopia. Directed first survey and excavation of the ruins at Great Zimbabwe in 1891. Sources: Columbia/Rasmussen, R. Kent, Historical Dictionary of Rhodesia/ Zimbabwe (1979), p 32.

0270 BENVENISTE, ÉMILE (1902-1976). Linguist. Sources: Biog Index: 12/Nat Un Cat.

0271 BENZONI, GIROLAMO (1519-1572), Italy. Historian. Wrote one of the earliest accounts of the exploration of Central America. Source: Creedman, Theodore, Historical Dictionary of Costa Rica (1977), p 18.

0272 BERCHMANS, JULES ETIENNE (1883-1951), Liege, Belgium. Sculptor, archeologist. Wrote on classical Greek art. Sources: Biog Index: 3 & 4/Rev Arch series 6 48:68-70 Jl '56.

0273 BERESFORD, GEORGE READ EDWARD (1815-1857), United Kingdom. Banker. Archeology & photography of Delhi (India); author of *The Handbook of Delhi*. Source: Dictionary of International Biography.

0274 BERG, GOSTA (1903-), Sweden. Ethnologist. History of agricultural techniques. Food & food preparation in European & Scandinavian countries. Sources: Int Dir Anth 3, 5.

0275 BERGMANN, JOSEPH G L (1911-). Archeologist. Studies of the Middle Paleolithic of Central Europe. Prehistory & early history of Germany. Source: Int Dir Anth 5.

0276 BERNAL, IGNACIO (1910-), France. Archeologist. Archeology & bibliography of Mexico & Mesoamerica. Sources: Int Dir Anth 3, 5.

0277 BERNARDI, BERNARDO (1916-). Ethnologist. Social systems & religions in East Africa. Source: Int Dir Anth 5.

0278 BERNART, LUELEN (1866-1946), Ponape, Caroline Islands. First Micronesian to compile the legends, mythologies & chants basic to Ponapean culture and traditional values. Source: Craig & King, Historical Dictionary of Oceania (1981), p 26.

0279 BERNATZIK, EMMY (1904-). Ethnologist. Problems of applied ethnology in W. Africa. Impact & damage of contact with civilization. Culture change. Source: Int Dir Anth 5.

0280 BERNATZIK, HUGO ADOLF (1897-), Austria. Anthropologist. Ethnology, primarily Egyptian, Sudan, Siam, Indochina. Sources: Nat Un Cat/Int Dir Anth 3.

0281 BERNDT, CATHERINE HELEN (1918-), New Zealand. Ethnologist. Aboriginal culture in Australia. European mass culture in Australia. Sources: Int Dir Anth 3, 5.

0282 BERNDT, RONALD MURRAY (1916-), Australia. Ethnologist. Social control & sociocultural change. Aborigines of Australia. Sources: Int Dir Anth 3, 5.

0283 BERNET KEMPERS, AUGUST JOHAN (1906-), Netherlands. Ethnologist. Indo-Javanese archeology & prehistory. Source: Int Dir Anth 5.

0284 BERNIER, FRANÇOIS (1620-

1688), Angers, France. Visited Syria, Egypt, Arabia & India; wrote classic account of his travels to India. Source: New Int Enc.

0285 BERNSTAM, ALEKSANDR NATANOVICH (1909-1956), Kerch, Russia. Archeologist, historian, Orientalist. Archeology of the Semirech'e, T'ien-shan, Pamiro-Alai, and Fergana peoples of Middle Asia. Study of Central Asia and its nomadic people took him to Kazakhstan, Kirghiz, Tian-Chou, Altai, Pamirs and Fergana. Sources: Biog Index: 5/ Great Soviet Encyclopedia, New York, Macmillan (1973), v. 3, p 214/ Tolstov, S.P. "A.N. Bernshtam" Sovetskaia etnografiia, 1957, no. 1/ Artibus Asiae 20 no 2-3:187 '57.

0286 BERRY, JACK (1918-), England. Linguist. Comparative study of African languages & Jamaican Creole. Sources: Int Dir Anth 3, 5.

0287 BERSU, GERHARD (1889-1964), Jauer, Germany. Archeologist. Archeology of Germany, particularly during Roman period. Sources: Biog Index: 7/Rev Arch 2:191-4 O '64.

0288 BERT'E-DELAGARD, ALEKSANDR L'VOVICH (1842-1920), Sevastopol', Russia. Archeologist, numismatist. Early coin minting in the area north of the Black Sea. Source: Great Soviet Encyclopedia, New York, Macmillan (1973), v. 3, p 218.

0289 BERTHO, JACQUES. Ethnologist, missionary. Wrote many articles on the ethnology of southern Dahomey and Togo. Source: DeCalo, Samuel, Historical Dictionary of Dahomey (1976), p 26.

0290 BERTILLON, ALPHONSE (1853-1914), France. Environmentalist, criminologist, anthropologist. Devised the "Bertillon System," a classification of skeletal & body types. Sources: Biog Index: 2 4 7 8 & 9/Columbia.

0291 BERTLING, CORNELIS TJENKO (1894-), Netherlands. Ethnology of Indonesia. Sources: Nat Un Cat/ Int Dir Anth 3.

0292 BERTONI, GUILLERMO T (1889-), Paraguay. Linguist. Specialized in the study of the Guarani languages of Paraguay. Source: Kolinski, Charles J., Historical Dictionary of Paraguay (1973), p 26.

0293 BESCHEFER, S J, Fr. THIERRY (Theodoric) (1630-1711), Chalons, France. Priest. Missionary to New France; wrote on N. American Indians. Source: Jes Rel.

0294 BESSAIGNET, PIERRE OCTAVE HENRI (1914-), France. Anthropologist. Socio-economic anthropology. Research in primitive money. Sources: Int Dir Anth 3, 5.

0295 BESSIEUX, JEAN-REMY (1803-1876), Villieux, Montpellier, France. Missionary. Published a grammar of the Mpongwe language (1847) of Gabon. Source: Gardiner, David E., Historical Dictionary of Gabon (1981), p 41-2.

0296 BESSON, MARIUS (1876-1943), Turin, Italy. Bishop, historian, archeologist. Historian of the origins of Christianity in Switzerland and archeologist of the period of the Great Invasion. Sources: Biog Index: 1/Rev Arch 26:92 Jl '46.

0297 BEST, ELSDON (ca. 1856-1931), New Zealand. Ethnologist, museum curator. Specialist in culture of Maori (New Zealand) and Tuhoe tribe. One of the founders of the Polynesian Society. Source: Am Anth 34:134 Mr '32.

0298 BETANZOS, PEDRO de, La Coruna Province, Spain. Missionary. Wrote a dictionary of Guatemalan Indian languages. Source: Creedman, Theodore, Historical Dictionary of Costa Rica (1977), p 18.

0299 BETILLON, ALPHONSE (1853-1914). Environmentalist, anthropologist. Source: Biog Index: 7.

0300 BETT, HENRY (1876-1953). Clergyman, folklorist. Studied nursery rhymes and children's stories, linking them to original cultural contexts and meanings. Sources: Biog Index: 3/N Y Times p 29 Ap 8 '53.

0301 BEUCHAT, HENRI (1878-1916), France. Ethnologist, archeologist. Did fieldwork throughout the Americas. Source: Am Anth 18:104-10 Ja '16.

0302 BEULE, CHARLES ERNEST (1826-1874), Saumur, France. Archeologist. Discovered the propylaea of the Acropolis (Greece); made excavations at the site of Carthage. Source: New Int Enc.

0303 BEVAN, ANTHONY ASHLEY (1859- 1933), London, England. Orientalist. Specialist in Arabic & Semitic languages and literatures. Sources: Biog Index: 2/Dictionary of National Biography 1931-1940:75-5 '49.

0304 BEYER, HENRY OTLEY (1883-1966), Iowa, United States. Anthropologist. Spent many years doing research & teaching in the Philippines. First to chair the Anthropology Department at the Univ. of the Philippines. Sources: Biog Index: 7 & 10/Int Dir Anth 3/Am Anth 76:361-2 Je '74.

0305 BEYSOLOW, THOMAS E (1857-1948), Bendu, Liberia. Jurist. Wrote several books discussing the development of Liberia. Source: Dunn & Holsoe, Historical Dictionary of Liberia (1985), p 26.

0306 BHANDARKAR, RAMKRISHNA GOPAL (1837-1925), India. Social reformer, Orientalist. Source: Biog Index: 9.

0307 BIANCHI BANDINELLI, RANUCCIO (1900-1975), Italy. Archeologist. Specialist in Classical art, history and archeology; worked in Italy and Libya. Sources: Biog Index: 2 10 & 12/Gazette des Beaux Arts 93:supp 32 Ja '79/ Archaeology 28:125 Ap '75/Connaissance Arts no 277:23 Mr '75/ N Y Times p 32 Ja 18 '75.

0308 BIARD, S J, Fr. PIERRE (1567-1622), Grenoble, France. Priest. Missionary in New France; wrote on N. American Indians. Source: Jes Rel.

0309 BIASUTTI, RENATO (1878-), Italy. Ethnology and anthropogeography. Sources: Nat Un Cat/Int Dir Anth 3.

0310 BIBIKOV, SERGEI NIKOLAEVICH (1908-), Sevastopol', Ukraine. Archeologist. Paleolithic, Neolithic, and early metal periods in the Crimea, Urals, and Dnestr River valley. Source: Great Soviet Encyclopedia, New York, Macmillan (1973), v. 3, p 248.

0311 BIDAGA, see: Son of Many Beads.

0312 BIDNEY, DAVID (1908-1987), Ukraine, Russia. Socio-cultural ethnologist, anthropological theoretician. Philosophy of the social sciences & history; theoretical anthropology & philosophy. Sources: Anth News 28:4(1987):4/Int Dir Anth 3, 5.

0313 BIEBER, MARGARETE (1879-1978), Schonau, Germany. Archeologist. Specialist in Greek and Roman art. Sources: Biog Index: 10 11 & 12/Nat Cyc Am Biog 60:277-8 '81/ Am J Arch 82:273-5 Fall '78/Archaeology 28:74-5 Ap '75/ N Y Times Biog Service 9:155 F '78, p 36 F 28 '78.

0314 BIESANZ, JOHN BERRY (1913-), United States. Anthropologist. Analysis of culture in Central America, Caribbean and Paraguay. Sources: Int Dir Anth 3/Nat Dir Lat Am.

0315 BIESANZ, MAVIS HILTUNEN (1919-). Social anthropologist. Ethnographic research in Panama & Costa Rica. Source: Int Dir Anth 5.

0316 BIGELOW, ROBERT SIDNEY (1918-). Geneticist. Genetics & studies on aggression. Source: Int Dir Anth 5.

0317 BIGOT, S J, Fr. JACQUES (1651-1711), Bourges, France. Priest. Missionary in New France; wrote on N. American Indians. Source: Jes Rel.

0318 BINDER, TEODORO (1919-). Anthropologist. Ethno-medicine & mythology in the Americas. Source: Int Dir Anth 5.

0319 BINETEAU, S J, Fr. JULIEN (1660-1699), La Fleche, Sarthe, France. Priest. Missionary in New France; wrote on N. American

Indians. Source: Jes Rel.

0320 BINGER, LOUIS-GUSTAVE (1856-1936), Strasbourg, France. Explorer, civil servant. First European to explore Kongo; visited Baromo, Ouagadougou & Grand Bassam. Explored Southern Mali, Baurbena, Ivory Coast & Ghana in 1887-1889. Wrote a detailed account of this journey useful as an ethnographic source. Contributed to linguistic publications by Faidherbe. Sources: New Int Enc/Imperato, Pascal J., Historical Dictionary of Mali (1977), p 24/ World Who's Who in Science, 1968, p 178.

0321 BINGHAM, HIRAM, Jr (1831-1908), Honolulu, Hawaii, United States. Missionary. Compiled a dictionary of the language of the Gilbert Islands. Source: Craig & King, Historical Dictionary of Oceania (1981), p 28.

0322 BINGHAM, HIRAM (1789-1869), Bennington, Vermont, United States. Missionary. Developed a written language for Hawaiian. Source: Craig & King, Historical Dictionary of Oceania (1981), p 27.

0323 BINGHAM, HIRAM (1875-1956), Honolulu, Hawaii, United States. Explorer, historian, politician, missionary. Discovered & described the site of Machu Picchu in Peru. Sources: Columbia/Craig & King, Historical Dictionary of Oceania (1981), p 27-8/ World Who's Who in Science, 1968, p 178.

0324 BIRCH, SAMUEL (1813-1885), England. Egyptologist. Composed a dictionary of hieroglyphics. Translated *The Book of the Dead*. Source: Columbia.

0325 BIRD, JAMES (1797-1864). Bombay Medical Establishment, secretary to Bombay Asiatic Society, 1844-47; wrote on various subjects (historical and archeological) connected with India, including Buddhism and Jainism. Source: Dictionary of International Biography.

0326 BIRD, JUNIUS BOUTON (1907-), United States. Anthropologist. Anthropology of N. & S. America. Sources: Nat Dir Lat Am/Int Dir Anth 2, 3.

0327 BIRDSELL, JOSEPH BENJAMIN (1908-), South Bend, Indiana, United States. Physical anthropologist. Human genetics and evolution; origins of Australian man. Source: American Men and Women of Science, ed. by J.C. Press, 12th ed., New York, Bowker, 1973.

0328 BIRDWHISTELL, RAY L (1918-). Communications theorist. Kinesics, paralanguage & communication theory. Source: Int Dir Anth 5.

0329 BIRKET-SMITH, KAJ (1893-), Denmark. Ethnologist. Anthropometry of Inuit. Ethnology of Greenland. Sources: Nat Un Cat/Int Dir Anth 3.

0330 BISHOP, CARL WHITING (1881-1942), Japan. Prehistoric archeology of China. Sources: Nat Un Cat/Int Dir Anth 1, 2.

0331 BISSCHOP, ERIC de (1891-). Traveler to Kaimiloa. Source: Nat Un Cat.

0332 BITTREMIEUX, LEO (1880-1946). Ethnologist. Studied the Congo, Belgium. Source: Nat Un Cat.

0333 BLACK, DAVIDSON (1884-1934). Anatomist, paleontologist. Research on Peking man. Sources: Biog Index: 7/Am Anth 36:319 Je '34.

0334 BLACK, GLENN ALBERT (1900-1964), United States. Archeologist. Indians of Indiana. Sources: Biog Index: 7/Int Dir Anth 1, 2, 3/Am Antiq 31:402-5 Ja '66.

0335 BLACKMAN, AYLWARD MANLEY (1883-1956), England. Egyptologist. Directed field excavations at the site of Sesebi, Sudan. Sources: Biog Index: 4/Journal of Egyptian Archaeology 42:102-4 '56/ N Y Times p 17 Mr 10 '56/Nature 177:731-2 Ap 21 '56.

0336 BLACKMAN, WINIFRED SUSAN (-1950). Anthropologist, Egyptologist. Study of the daily life, beliefs and customs of modern Egyptian peasantry. Sources: Biog Index: 2/Nature 167:135 Ja 27 '51.

0337 BLACKWOOD, BEATRICE MARY (1889-1975), London, England.

Anthropologist, ethnologist. Work in New Guinea, Melanesia. Her extensive photographs of the Kukukuku of New Guinea are a pictorial record of a modern Stone Age culture. Sources: Biog Index: 11/Am Anth 78:321-2 Je '76/Oceania 46:235-7 Mr '76.

0338 BLAGDEN, CHARLES OTTO (1864- 1949), England. Orientalist. Student of Eastern Asia; wrote *Pagan Races in the Malaya Peninsula*. Sources: Biog Index: 2/Isis 42 no 1:49 '51.

0339 BLANC, ALBERTO CARLO (1906-1960), Italy. Paleontologist. Archeology of Europe. Sources: Biog Index: 5 & 6/Int Dir Anth 3.

0340 BLAVATSKII, VLADIMIR DMITRIEVICH (1899-), St. Petersburg, Russia. Archeologist. Archeology of classical cities of Charaxes, Phanagoria, Panticapaeum, and the north shore of the Black Sea. Source: Great Soviet Encyclopedia, New York, Macmillan (1973), v. 3, p 362.

0341 BLEEK, WILHELM HEINRICH IMMANUEL (1827-1875), Berlin, Germany. Philologist. Expedition to Natal; studied philological peculiarities of the South African languages. Source: Encyclopedia Britannica, 9th ed.

0342 BLEGEN, CARL W (1887-1971), Minneapolis, Minnesota, United States. Archeologist. Specialist in archeology of Mycenaean Greece and Troy; excavated at Pylos in 1939 and located an archive of Linear B tablets. Sources: Biog Index: 9 & 10/Britannica Book of the Year 1972:519 '72/ N Y Times p 40 Ag 26 '71.

0343 BLEICHSTEINER, R (1891-1954). Wrote on Himalayan Lamaism. Source: Nat Un Cat.

0344 BLINKENBERG, CHRISTIAN SORENSEN (1863-1948), Denmark. Archeologist. Member of the staff of the Danish National Museum, 1888-1916; taught archeology at the Univ. of Copenhagen, 1911-1926; conducted excavations of Lindos at Rhodes, 1902-1905. Sources: Biog Index: 2/Antiquaries Journal 28:224 Jl '48.

0345 BLISS, FREDERICK JONES (1859-1937). Archeologist. Researched in Syria. Excavated at Tel-el-Hesy & Jerusalem. Sources: Biog Index: 4/New Int Enc/ Dictionary of Australian Biography sup 2:44-5 '58.

0346 BLOCH, HAYIM (1881-). Folklorist. Sources: Biog Index: 5/Commentary 29:65-6 Ja '60.

0347 BLOCH, RAYMOND (1914-). Wrote about antiquity in Etruria; also wrote on history of Rome. Source: Nat Un Cat.

0348 BLOCK, GWENDOLINE HARRIS (1906-1956), Johannesburg, South Africa. Editor. Editor of numerous university anthropological publications. Source: Am Anth 59:126 F '57.

0349 BLOM, FRANS FERDINAND (1893-1963), Copenhagen, Denmark. Archeologist, explorer. Mexico, Central America, especially Mayan culture. Excavated at Pueblo Bonito, and extensively in Central America. Sources: Biog Index: 5 6 7 & 11/Int Dir Anth 1, 2, 3/ Who's Who in Latin America 3rd ed., Ronald Hilton ed., Stanford Univ. Press (Blaine Ethridge Edition, 1971) vol. I, p 13.

0350 BLOM, GERTRUDE DUBY (1901-). Ethnologist, photographer, writer. Lacandon Maya. Reforestation & agricultural changes in Mexico. Champion of the Maya from her base in San Cristobal de las Casas, Chiapas, Mexico. Source: Int Dir Anth 5.

0351 BLONDEL, CHARLES AIMÉ ALFRED (1876-1939). Wrote on social & ethno-psychology. Source: Nat Un Cat.

0352 BLOOMFIELD, LEONARD (1887-1949), Chicago, Illinois, United States. Linguist. Comparative aspects of Germanic languages. Sources: Columbia/Int Dir Anth 1, 2.

0353 BLOOMFIELD, MAURICE (1855-1928), Bielitz, Austria. Philologist. Wrote extensively on ancient Indian epics, particularly the Rig-Veda; also studied history and culture of ancient India. Sources: Biog Index: 3/Nat Cyc Am Biog 37:509-510 '51.

0354 BLUNT, EDWARD ARTHUR HENRY (1877-). Wrote on society, economy of India. Source: Nat Un Cat.

0355 BLYDEN, EDWARD W (1832-1912), St. Thomas, Virgin Islands. Writer, educator. Created several works reawakening intellectual movement in Africa. Source: Dunn & Holsoe, Historical Dictionary of Liberia (1985), p 27.

0356 BOAS, FRANZ (1858-1942), Minden, Westphalia, Germany. Anthropologist. Insisted on rigorous methodology in establishing the science of anthropology. Worked with Inuit & Indians of British Columbia. Applied statistical methods to biometric study. Worked in Mexican stratigraphic archeology. Did linguistic analysis from language structures. Sources: Biog Index: 1 2 3 4 5 6 7 & 13/Columbia/ Am Anth 62:1-17 '60, 45(no. 3, pt. 2) Jl '43/ International Encyclopedia of the Social Sciences, v. 2/Nat Cyc Am Biog/ Social Education 44:5 Mr '80/Zusne, L., Biographical Dictionary of Psychology, Westport, Conn., Greenwood, 1984/Boelscher, Marianne. "Boas, Franz" (In Makers of Modern Culture. Facts on File '81, p 54-55).

0357 BOATRIGHT, MODY COGGIN (1896- 1970), Mitchell County, Texas, United States. Folklorist. Collected folklore of West Texas, including some dealing with the oil industry. Sources: Biog Index: 9 & 10.

0358 BOCCARD, EUGÈNE de (1879-1957), Fribourg, Switzerland. Archeologist, editor. Edited numerous French-language archeology publications. Sources: Biog Index: 5/Rev Arch 1:220-1 Ap '58.

0359 BOCK, BERNHARD (1902-). Linguist. Education & social anthropology. Source: Int Dir Anth 5.

0360 BODKER, LAURITS LAURSEN (1915-). Folklorist. Folk culture & folk festivals in Denmark. Source: Int Dir Anth 5.

0361 BOECKH, AUGUST (1785-1867), Karlsruhe, Germany. Philologist. Specialist on Greek arts; scholar of philology. Source: Encyclopedia Britannica, 9th ed.

0362 BOELAERT, EDMOND (1899-), Belgium. Ethnologist. Ethnology of West Africa. Sources: Nat Un Cat/Int Dir Anth 3.

0363 BOEMUS, JOHANN (late 15th cent.-), Aub, Franconia, Germany. Ethnologist. Published detailed descriptions of the cultures of Europe, Asia & Africa based on the writings of others; focused on Ethiopia, but described 40 cultures in all. Sources: Biog Index: 3/Am Anth 55:284-94 Ap '53.

0364 BOESCH, ERNEST EDUARD (1916-). Socio-psychologist. Socio-psychological research in central & northeastern Thailand. Source: Int Dir Anth 5.

0365 BOETHIUS, AXEL (1889-1969). Archeologist. Sources: Biog Index: 9/Britannica Book of the Year 1970:579 '70.

0366 BOGDANOV, ANATOLII PETROVICH (1834-1896), Nizhnedevitsk, Russia. Anthropologist, zoologist. Inaugurated Russian anthropology. Founder of the anthropology department at Moscow Univ. and the anthropology division of the Society of Amateur Naturalists. Sources: Great Soviet Encyclopedia, New York, Macmillan (1973), v. 3, p 389 /Levin, M.G. "A.P. Bogdanov i russkaia antropologiia" Sovetskaia etnografiia (1946), no. 1/ Bol'shaia Sovetskaia Entsyklopediia, 2nd ed.

0367 BOGDANOV, LEONIDAS STANISLAS (1881-1945), Russia. Orientalist. Source: Biog Index: 1.

0368 BOGGIANI, GUIDO (1861- ca. 1902), Italy. Artist, ethnologist, ethnographer. Ethnology of South America. Expert on the Indian tribes of the Paraguayan Chaco; wrote several basic ethnographies. Lived with Guaycurue Indians in the Chaco, 1887-93 and 1896; wrote a dictionary of their language and collected legends. Studied indigenous peoples of Paraguay; published ethnography of the Cadiueios. <u>Sources</u>: Am Anth 4:568/Nat Un Cat/Kolinski, Charles J., Historical Dictionary of Paraguay (1973), p 28/Wright & Nelsham, Historical Dictionary of Argentina (1978), p 103.

0369 BOGGS, RALPH STEELE (1901-), United States. Linguist, folklorist. U.S. & Mexican folklore. <u>Sources</u>: Biog Index: 8 & 10/Int Dir Anth 3.

0370 BOGGS, STANLEY HARDING (1914-), United States. Archeologist. Pre-Columbian Central America. Development of archeological sites & museums. <u>Sources</u>: Int Dir Anth 2, 3, 5/Nat Dir Lat Am.

0371 BOGOIAVLENSKII, SERGEI KONSTANTINOVICH (1871-1947), Moscow, Russia. Historian, archeologist. Migration and burial mounds in the Baltic and in the region of Moscow (Russia). <u>Sources</u>: Great Soviet Encyclopedia, New York, Macmillan (1973), v. 3, p 394 /Bakhrushin, S.V. "S.K. Bogoiavlenskii kak istorik" Voprosy istorii, 1948, no. 8.

0372 BOGORAZ, VLADIMIR GERMANOVICH (1865-1936). Ethnographer, merchant. Ethnology of eastern & northern Siberia & North Pacific coast of North America; published on Chukchee and other tribes of Siberia. <u>Source</u>: Am Anth 39:314-5 Ap '37.

0373 BOHM, JAROSLAV (1901-1962), Holasov, Moravia. Archeologist. Wrote about Scythians and about prehistory of Czechoslovakia. <u>Sources</u>: Biog Index: 7/Rev Arch 2:205-6 O '63.

0374 BOHNDORFF, FREDERICK. Interpreter. First European to travel across region between Kordofan and the Mbomou River (Central African Republic). <u>Source</u>: Kalck, Pierre, Historical Dictionary of the Central African Republic (1980), p 17.

0375 BOHTLINGK, OTTO von (1815-1904), Germany. Orientalist. <u>Source</u>: Biog Index: 7.

0376 BOISSARD, JEAN-JACQUES (1528- 1602), Besancon, France. Poet. Formed collection of holy monuments and artifacts of Rome & vicinity. <u>Source</u>: Encyclopedia Britannica, 9th ed.

0377 BOISSELIER, GEORGES (1876-1943), France. Archeologist. Director of several archeological excavations in region of La Torche (France). <u>Sources</u>: Biog Index: 1/Rev Arch 26:89 Jl '46.

0378 BOISSEVAIN LESSER, ETHEL (1913-), United States. Anthropologist. Indians of Eastern U.S.; prehistoric art of Eastern Europe and Near East. <u>Sources</u>: Int Dir Anth 2, 3, 5.

0379 BOLAÑOS, LUIS de (1550-1629), Marchena, Spain. Missionary. Wrote a book of prayers and a catechism in Guarani. <u>Source</u>: Wright & Nelsham, Historical Dictionary of Argentina (1978), p 104.

0380 BOLINGER, DWIGHT LeMERTON (1907-), Topeka, Kansas, United States. Linguist. Wrote on many aspects of language. <u>Source</u>: Nat Dir Lat Am.

0381 BOLNAT, GEORGES (1885-1943), France. Veterinarian, archeologist. Archeology of Northern France. <u>Sources</u>: Biog Index: 1/Rev Arch series 6 25:205-6 Ap '46.

0382 BOLTON, HENRY CARRINGTON (ca. 1842-1903). Folklorist. Published on folklore of many cultures. <u>Source</u>: Am Anth 5:739-740.

0383 BOMAN, ERIC (1867-1924), Falun, Sweden. Archeologist, musicologist. Fieldwork in Northern Argentina, Bolivia & the Atacama Desert (Chile); wrote first systematic description of Northern Argentina from an archeological viewpoint. <u>Sources</u>: Wright & Nelsham, Historical Dictionary of Argentina (1978), p 106 /Am Anth 28:325-326 Ja '26.

0384 BOMILCAR, ALVARO (1874-1957), Brazil. Journalist. Wrote a pamphlet attacking prevalent attitudes of race prejudice in Brazil in the early 20th century. Source: Levine, Robert M., Historical Dictionary of Brazil (1979), p 33.

0385 BONCH-OSMOLOVSKII, GLEB ANATOL'EVICH (1890-1943), Blon, Belorussia. Anthropologist, archeologist. Early Paleolithic and first discovery of Neanderthal man in what is now the U.S.S.R. Source: Great Soviet Encyclopedia, New York, Macmillan (1973), v. 3, p 450.

0386 BONE, EDOUARD L (1919-). Physical anthropologist. Ecology & primate evolution. Source: Int Dir Anth 5.

0387 BONIFACE, S J, Fr. FRANÇOIS (1635-1715), Arras, France. Priest. Missionary in New France; wrote on N. American Indians. Source: Jes Rel.

0388 BONIFACY, AUGUSTE (1856-1931). Ethnologist. Indo-China. Source: Nat Un Cat.

0389 BONNECAMPS, S J, Fr. JOSEPH PIERRE de (1707-1790), Vannes, France. Priest. Missionary in New France; wrote on N. American Indians. Source: Jes Rel.

0390 BOODBERG, PETER ALEXIS (1903- 1972). Philologist. Sources: Biog Index: 10/American Oriental Society Journal 94:1-13 Ja '74.

0391 BOOY, THEODOUR de (1882-1919), Hellevoetsluis, Netherlands. Archeologist. Did extensive archeological fieldwork in the West Indies: Bahamas, Jamaica, Santo Domingo, Cuba, Trinidad, Puerto Rico, Martinique & Danish West Indies. Also, conducted ethnological studies of the Motilone (Venezuela). Source: Am Anth 21:182-185.

0392 BORDEN, CHARLES EDWARD (1904- 1978), United States. Philologist, archeologist. British Columbian prehistory. Sources: Biog Index: 13/Anth News Jn '79/Am Antiq 45:472-6 Jl '80.

0393 BORDES, FRANÇOIS (1919-1981), France. Archeologist. Authority on manufacture and use of stone tools, and on Neanderthal period of Paleolithic Europe. Sources: Biog Index: 13/N Y Times p A-31 My 7 '81/ N Y Times Biog Service 12:600 My '81/Newsweek 97:100 My 18 '81.

0394 BORELLI, JULES (1853-1941). Traveler to Ethiopia, East Africa. Source: Nat Un Cat.

0395 BOREUX, CHARLES (1874-1944), France. Egyptologist. Sources: Biog Index: 2/Rev Arch series 6 37:197-8 Ap '51.

0396 BORISKOVSKII, PAVEL IOSIFOVICH (1911-), Russia. Archeologist, historian. Paleolithic research, especially monuments, in western U.S.S.R. & S.E. Asia. Sources: Int Dir Anth 5/ Great Soviet Encyclopedia, New York, Macmillan (1973), v. 3, p 467.

0397 BOSANQUET, ROBERT CARR (1871- 1935), London, England. Archeologist. Specialist in archeology of Greece; directed excavations at Melos, on Crete, and at Sparta. Director, British School of Archaeology, Athens, 1899-1905; also worked on Roman sites in Wales. Sources: Biog Index: 2/Dictionary of National Biography 1931-40:90-1 '49.

0398 BOSCH, FREDERIK DAVID KAN (1887-), South Africa. Archeologist. Interest in Indian archeology. Source: Int Dir Anth 3.

0399 BOSCH-GIMPERA, PEDRO (1891-1974), Spain. Anthropologist, archeologist, historian. World prehistoric studies. Emphasis on formation of the Mexican peoples. Old & New World archeology, history & ethnology. Sources: Int Dir Anth 3, 5/Anth News Ja '75.

0400 BOTKIN, BENJAMIN ALBERT (1901-), Boston, Massachusetts, United States. Folklorist. Collected and published American folklore; headed the folklore division of the Federal Writers Project; many volumes. Sources: Biog Index: 4 & 10/Nat Un Cat/ Kunitz, Stanley Jasspon ed., Twentieth Century Authors; 1st sup. Wilson '55 p 101-2/N Y Times p 30 Jl '75.

0401 **BOTTA, PAUL EMILE** (1802-1870), France. Archeologist. Source: Biog Index: 3.

0402 **BOTTIGER, KARL AUGUST** (1760-1835), Reichenbach, Germany. Archeologist. Source: New Int Enc.

0403 **BOUCHER, S J, Fr. JEAN-BAPTISTE** (1641-1686), Soissons, France. Priest. Missionary in New France; wrote on N. American Indians. Source: Jes Rel.

0404 **BOUCHER de CRÈVECOEUR de PERTHES, JACQUES** (1788-1868), France. Archeologist. Discovered early stone tools in France. First to establish man in the Pleistocene epoch. Source: Columbia.

0405 **BOUGAINVILLE, LOUIS ANTOINE de** (1729-1811), Paris, France. Navigator. His writings helped to popularize Rousseau's theory of the morality of man in nature. Inspired Diderot to write a defense of sexual freedom. Wrote: *Description d'un voyage autour du monde* (2 vols, 1771-1772). Directed exploration of Tuamotu archipelago and Tahiti; wrote a journal of this voyage containing valuable ethnographic data. Sources: Columbia/Craig & King, Historical Dictionary of Oceania (1981), p 33.

0406 **BOUIS, EDMOND de** (1818-1870), France. Naval officer. Wrote extensively on the life and culture of pre-contact Tahiti. Source: Craig & King, Historical Dictionary of Oceania (1981).

0407 **BOUISSINGAULT, JEAN BAPTISTE** (1802-1887), France. Naturalist. Wrote a description of his travels and scientific investigations in Colombia. Source: Davis, Robert H., Historical Dictionary of Colombia (1977), p 65.

0408 **BOULANGER, ANDRE** (1886-1958). Classicist, archeologist. Wrote on ancient Greek religion as well as Greek culture in the Middle East. Sources: Biog Index: 5/Rev Arch 1:204-6 Ap '59.

0409 **BOURDARIE, PAUL**. Founded the Academy of Colonial Sciences; started the *Revue Indigene* in 1906. Source: Kalck, Pierre, Historical Dictionary of the Central African Republic (1980), p 21.

0410 **BOURDIER, FRANCK PAUL LEONARD** (1910-). Geologist. Geology and prehistory of France. Source: Int Dir Anth 5.

0411 **BOURKE, JOHN GREGORY** (1846-1896). Army officer, ethnologist. Source: Biog Index: 12.

0412 **BOURLIÈRE, FRANÇOIS** (1913-). Physiologist. Ecology. Human development & the aging process. Source: Int Dir Anth 5.

0413 **BOUTEILLER, MARCELLE** (1904-), France. Ethnologist. Shamanism. Sources: Nat Un Cat/Int Dir Anth 3.

0414 **BOUVART, S J, Fr. MARTIN** (1635-1705), Chartres, France. Priest. Missionary in New France; wrote on N. American Indians. Source: Jes Rel.

0415 **BOVALLIUS, CARL** (1849-1907), Sweden. Archeologist. Wrote a rare pamphlet on Nicaraguan archeology and crafts on basis of visit to Central America, 1881-83. Source: Meyer, Harvey K., Historical Dictionary of Nicaragua (1972), p 43.

0416 **BOWDEN, ABERDEEN ORLANDO** (1881-1946), United States. Sociologist, archeologist, anthropologist. American Indian culture from Midwest to West Coast. Sources: Biog Index: 1/Int Dir Anth 1, 2/School & Society 63:134 F 23 '46.

0417 **BOWDITCH, CHARLES PICKERING** (1842-1921), Boston, Massachusetts, United States. Philanthropist, archeologist. Supported numerous archeological expeditions in Mexico and Central America. Sources: Biog Index: 3/Russel, Foster William. Mount Auburn biographies. Mount Auburn Cemetary '53 p 22/Am Anth 23:353-9 D '21.

0418 **BOYD, ELIZABETH** (1903-1974), United States. Museum curator. Spanish art & architecture of Mexico. Source: Anth News F '75.

0419 **BOYD, LYLE GIFFORD** (1907-), United States. Biochemist, archeologist. Blood-group properties of Egyptian mummies. Sources: Biog Index: 1/Int Dir Anth 2, 3.

0420 BOYD, WILLIAM CLOUSER (1903-), Cambridge, Massachusetts, United States. Physical anthropologist. Physical anthropology. Genetics. Sources: Int Dir Anth 2, 3.

0421 BOYER, PAUL JEAN MARIE (1864- 1950), Cormery, Touraine, France. Orientalist. Director of the School of Oriental Languages in Paris whose main interest was linguistic studies, particularly Russian philology; textbook on Russian grammar considered of fundamental importance to students. Sources: Biog Index: 2/Am J Arch 54:134-5 Ap '50.

0422 BOYER, RUTH McDONALD (1918-), United States. Anthropologist, ethnologist. Indians of Southwest U.S., Peru & Alaska. Sources: Int Dir Anth 5/Nat Dir Lat Am.

0423 BOYLE, DAVID (1842-1911), Greenock, Scotland. Archeologist. Archeology of Canada, especially Ontario. Sources: Biog Index: 1/ Royal Canadian Institute, Toronto. Centennial volume, 1849-1949/ Am Anth 13:159-64 Mr '11.

0424 BOYLE, JOHN ANDREW (1916-1978), France. Orientalist. Source: Biog Index: 12.

0425 BRADFORD, JOHN SPENCER PURVIS (1918-1975), England. Archeologist. Sources: Biog Index: 11/Int Dir Anth 3/Antiquity 49:246-7 D '75.

0426 BRAIDWOOD, ROBERT J (1907-), United States. Archeologist. On the staff of the Oriental Institute, Chicago, Illinois. Ancient Near Eastern & Egyptian prehistoric civilizations. Sources: Biog Index: 9/Int Dir Anth 2, 5/Archaeology 25:84 Ap '72.

0427 BRAILOIU, CONSTANTIN (1893-). Folklorist. Source: Nat Un Cat.

0428 BRAINERD, GEORGE WALTON (1909-1956), United States. Anthropologist. Specialist on the culture of prehistoric Maya; also excavated in Arizona and American Southwest. Sources: Biog Index: 4 & 6/Int Dir Anth 2, 3/Nat Cyc Am Biog 46:86-7 '63/ Am Anth 58:908-12 O '56/Am Antiq 22:165-8 O '56/ Publishers Weekly 169:1345 Mr 10 '56.

0429 BRAM, JOSEPH (1904-1974), Russia. Anthropologist, sociologist. Cultural nationalism & bilingualism. Social change & development. Sources: Int Dir Anth 3, 5/Nat Dir Lat Am/Anth News My '74.

0430 BRAND, DONALD DILWORTH (1905-), Peru. Geographer. Ethnobiology of Mesoamerica & Andean countries. History of explorations. Sources: Int Dir Anth 1, 2, 3, 5.

0431 BRANT, CHARLES S (1919-). Ethnologist. Studied Inuit & Apache; sociocultural change in India. Source: Int Dir Anth 5.

0432 BRASSEUR de BOURBOURG, CHARLES ÉTIENNE (1814-1874), Bourbourg, France. Missionary, archeologist. Served as archeologist to the French expedition to Mexico. Source: New Int Enc.

0433 BRATANIC, BRANIMIR (1910-1986), Yugoslavia. Ethnologist. Ethnological cartography. Comparative study of European plowing implements. Sources: Anth News 27:7:4/Int Dir Anth 3, 5.

0434 BRAUNHOLTZ, HERMANN JUSTUS (1888-), England. Ethnologist. Ethnology of Africa. Sources: Biog Index: 3/Nature 172:939 N 21 '53.

0435 BRAVO CARBONEL, JUAN, Spain. Civil servant. Wrote extensively on the land and culture of what was then known as Spanish Guinea. Source: Liniger-Gounaz, Max, Historical Dictionary of Equatorial Guinea (1979), p 21.

0436 BRAZZA, PIERRE SAVARGNAN de (1852-1905). Politician. Expanded French influence over large portions of future Central Africa. Source: Kalck, Pierre, Historical Dictionary of the Central African Republic (1980), p 21-2.

0437 BREASTED, JAMES HENRY (1865-1935), United States. Orientalist, historian, archeologist. Sources: Biog Index: 2 6 & 11/Int Dir Anth 1/ Pioneer to the Past: The Story of James Henry Breasted, Archeologist; told by his son. Univ. of Chicago Press '77.

0438 BRÉBEUF, S J, JEAN de, Saint (1593-1649), Normandy, France. Priest, Jesuit. Missionary in New France. Martyr. Worked with Huron & Iroquois Indians (New York & Canada). Sources: Columbia/Jes Rel.

0439 BRECCIA, ANNIBALE EVARISTO (1876-1967), Offagna, Italy. Archeologist, Egyptologist. Director of Greek-Roman Museum in Alexandria; extensive fieldwork in Egypt, 1928-1967. Sources: Biog Index: 8/N Y Times p 25 Jl 29 '67.

0440 BREEKS, JAMES WILKINSON (1830-1872). Civil servant. Administrator in the Indian Civil Service, 1867-72; commissioner of Nilgiris; wrote an important monograph on, and collected for museums, artifacts of the Nilgiri peoples (which include the Kota and Toda). Source: Dictionary of International Biography.

0441 BRELSFORD, WILLIAM VERNON. Author, civil servant. Founder of the Rhodes-Livingstone Institute in Lusaka. Authored extensive works on ethnic groups of Zambia, in particular the Bemba. Source: Grotpeter, John J., Historical Dictionary of Zambia (1979), p 29.

0442 BREREWOOD, EDWARD (1565-1613). Wrote on numismatics, logic, language, religion. Source: Nat Un Cat.

0443 BREUIL, HENRI (1877-1961), Mortain, France. Archeologist, priest. Founder of theory that cave art was produced by Paleolithic man; drew and described many cave sites in Europe, Ethiopia and South Africa; discoverer of the "White Lady" of the Brandberg, Cape Province, South Africa. Sources: Biog Index: 3 4 6 & 8/Int Dir Anth 3/Antiquity 35:257-8 D '61/ Illustrated London News 239:341 Ag 26 '61/N Y Times p 29 Ag 22 '61/ Nature 191:1246 S 23 '61/Newsweek 58:46 S 4 '61/Time 78:57 S 1 '61.

0444 BREW, JOHN OTIS (1906-), United States. Archeologist. Primitive technology & prehistory of Southwestern U.S. Sources: Biog Index: 8/Int Dir Anth 2, 3, 5.

0445 BREWER, JOHN MASON (1896-). Folklorist. Sources: Biog Index: 2 8 & 10.

0446 BREYSIG, KURT (1866-1940). Wrote on anthropology, sociology. Source: Nat Un Cat.

0447 BRIAN, LUIGI (1915-). Physical anthropologist. Anthropometry. Biological aspects of senescence. Source: Int Dir Anth 5.

0448 BRIDGES, ESTEBAN LUCAS (1874- 1949). Traveler to Tierra del Fuego (Chile and Argentina); wrote on Ona Indians. Source: Nat Un Cat.

0449 BRIDGES, THOMAS (1841-1898). Wrote on the Yahgan (of Tierra del Fuego) and on their language. Source: Nat Un Cat.

0450 BRIFFAULT, ROBERT (1876-1948). Anthropologist. Sources: Biog Index: 4 & 7.

0451 BRIGGS, JEROME ROBERT (1915-). Archeologist, ethnologist. Intertribal trade relations between N. American Indians. Source: Int Dir Anth 5.

0452 BRIGGS, KATHERINE MARY (1898- 1980), London, England. Folklorist. Collected and analyzed folktales of Great Britain and wrote several major studies of the field; compiled a definitive dictionary of the subject. Sources: Biog Index: 13/Journal of American Folklore 94:228 Ap/Jn '81/ Publishers Weekly 218:22 N 7 '80.

0453 BRIGGS, LLOYD CABOT (1909-1975), United States. Applied anthropologist. Ethnology, archeology & physical anthropology of North Africa. North African, Middle Eastern & Western European ethnographic fieldwork. Honored by France for his work in Africa. Sources: Biog Index: 10/Int Dir Anth 3, 5/Anth News S '75/ N Y Times p 32 My 19'75.

0454 BRIGHAM, WILLIAM TUFTS (1841-1926). Ethnologist. Sources: Biog Index: 3/Russel, Foster William. Mount Auburn biographies. Mount Auburn Cemetary '53 p 26.

0455 BRITTEN, JAMES (1846-1924), Chelsea, England. Botanist, folklorist. Member of the staff of the Botany Department of the British Museum; one of the founding members of the Folklore Society; founding member of the English Dialect Society for which he published, *Old Country and Farming Words*, 1880. Sources: Biog Index: 12/Folklore 89:71-4 Spr '78.

0456 BRITTON, ROSWELL SESSOMS (1897-1951), Shanghai, China. Sinologist, mathematician. Authority on the oracle bone writings of the Shang Dynasty (China). Sources: Biog Index: 2/N Y Times p 77 F 4 '51/ School & Society 73:92-3 F 10 '51.

0457 BRIUSOV, A IA (1885-1966), Russia. Archeologist. Neolithic and Bronze Ages of European Russia. Sources: Great Soviet Encyclopedia, New York, Macmillan (1973), v. 4, p 87/ Raushenbakh, V.M. "K 80-letiiu A. Ia. Briusova" Sovetskaia arkheologiia, 1965, no. 3.

0458 BROCA, PIERRE PAUL (1824-1880), France. Surgeon, anthropologist. Sources: Biog Index: 1 9 12 & 13/Science Digest 89:84-7+ S '81/ New Scientist 81:776-7 Mr 8 '79.

0459 BROGGER, ANTON WILHELM (1884- 1951), Stockholm, Sweden. Archeologist. Director of the University Oldsaksamling and the Viking Ship Museum; main interest was the Viking age. Sources: Biog Index: 3/Antiquaries Journal 32:268 Jl '52.

0460 BROHOLM, HANS CHRISTIAN (1893-), Copenhagen, Denmark. Archeology of Europe; field research in Italy & Greece. Interest in Neolithic, Bronze Age, & early Iron Age of Middle, Northern and Western Europe. Source: Int Dir Anth 2.

0461 BROMILOW, WILLIAM EDWARD (1857-1929), Australia. Missionary. Created a dictionary and grammar of the language of Dobu (British New Guinea). Source: Craig & King, Historical Dictionary of Oceania (1981), p 39-40.

0462 BRONDSTED, PETER OLOF (1780-1842), Jutond, Denmark. Archeologist. Archeology in Greece. Source: New Int Enc.

0463 BRONEER, OSCAR THEODORE (1894-), Sweden. Archeologist. Directed excavations at Corinth; located and excavated the Sanctuary of Poseidon at Isthmia (Greece). Sources: Biog Index: 8 & 9/Archaeology 23:84 Ap '70.

0464 BROOM, LEONARD (1911-). Ethnologist, sociologist. Social stratification & mobility. Source: Int Dir Anth 5.

0465 BROOM, ROBERT F (1866-1951), Scotland. Anthropologist. S. African fossil hominoid discoveries at Sterkfontein and Kromdraai. Physical anthropology & paleontology in E. & S. Africa. Major contributor to knowledge on Australopithecus. Sources: Biog Index: 1 2 3 & 10/Int Dir Anth 3/N Y Times, Ap 7 '51.

0466 BROWER, JACOB VRANDENBERG (1844-1905), York, Michigan, United States. Archeologist. Specialized in archeology of Minnesota & Kansas, United States. Source: Am Anth 7:362-3 Ap '05.

0467 BROWN, BARNUM (1873-1963), Carbondale, Kansas, United States. Paleontologist. Chief interest was pre-hominid vertebrates but discovered what were at the time among the earliest Indian remains. Sources: Biog Index: 1 2 3 7 8 & 12/ Brown, Lillian (MacLaughun) I Married a Dinosaur. Dodd '50/ Nature 44:467-70 N '51/American Association of Petroleum Geologists, Bulletin 48:1595-7 S '64/Nat Cyc Am Biog 51:483 '69/ Journal of Geological Education 28:193-8 S '80.

0468 BROWN, FRANK EDWARD (1908-). Archeologist. Director for Rome Academy. Sources: Biog Index: 7/Archaeology 19:52 Ja '66.

0469 BROWN, GEORGE GORDON (1896-

1955), New Brunswick, Canada. Anthropologist, colonial administrator. Pioneer in "racial impact"; ethnology of the Hehe (Tanzania); pioneer in applied anthropology; educational anthropology in Samoa; studied administrators as well as those administered; focused on problems of human interaction and adjustment (war relocation in the U.S., and Cree community health). Sources: Biog Index: 4 & 5/Int Dir Anth 2, 3/Am Anth 60:571-3 Je '58.

0470 BROWN, INA CORINNE (1896-), United States. Anthropologist. Social anthropology of W. Africa & the Congo. Sources: Biog Index: 3/Int Dir Anth 3/Murrow, Edward Roscoe. This I believe. Simon & Schuster '52 p 17-8.

0471 BROWN, RALPH DUNCAN (1907-1952), Minneapolis, Minnesota, United States. Archeologist. Worked at several sites in Minnesota, especially the Harvey Rockshelter; also at Kincaid Mounds in Illinois. Sources: Biog Index: 3/Am Antiq 18:387 Ap '53.

0472 BROWN, SUSAN ELLEN (1895-). Ethnologist. Household studies in the Caribbean. Fieldwork among the Cibao of the Dominican Republic. Source: Int Dir Anth 5.

0473 BROWN, WILLIAM NORMAN (1892-1975), Baltimore, Maryland, United States. Orientalist. Authority on Sanskrit, as well as the philosophy and art of India and South Asia. Sources: Biog Index: 10 & 11/N Y Times p 30 Ap 26 '75.

0474 BROWNBACK, JOHN HAROLD (1897- 1952). Biologist, folklorist. Expert on Pennsylvania German folklore. Sources: Biog Index: 3/N Y Times p 25 Jl 16 '52/School & Society 76:62 Jl 26 '52.

0475 BROWNE, EDWARD GRANVILLE (1862-1926), England. Orientalist. Sources: Biog Index: 4 5 9 & 11/Historical Journal 21:399-408 Je '78.

0476 BROŽEK, JOSEF MARIA (1913-). Physical anthropologist. Studies of human body growth & composition. Nutritional anthropometry. Source: Int Dir Anth 5.

0477 BRUCE, JAMES (1730-1794). Explorer. Traveled widely in northern Ethiopia and Sudan, 1769-1771, and wrote major account of this area in this period. Source: Prouty & Rosenfeld, Historical Dictionary of Ethiopia (1981), p 29-30.

0478 BRUCE, RICHARD ISAAC (1840-1924), Ireland. Colonial administrator. Wrote on the history and language of the Marri Baluchis of Pakistan. Sources: Dictionary of International Biography/Who Was Who, 1916-1928.

0479 BRUES, ALICE M (1913-). Physical anthropologist. Studies on human genetics. Source: Int Dir Anth 5.

0480 BRUGSCH, HEINRICH KARL (1827- 1894), Berlin, Germany. Egyptologist. Source: New Int Enc.

0481 BRUHL, GUSTAV (1826-1903). Archeologist. Founder of American Anthropological Association; published on pre-Hispanic Mexico. Source: Am Anth 5:176 Ja '03.

0482 BRUNNER, HELLMUT (1913-). Egyptologist. Language & literature of ancient Egypt. Source: Int Dir Anth 5.

0483 BRUNTON, ALEXANDER (1772-1854), Scotland. Orientalist. Source: Biog Index: 4.

0484 BRUNTON, GUY (1878-), England. Field director, british school of archaeology. British Museum expedition to Egypt, interest in Egyptian archeology. Source: Int Dir Anth 2.

0485 BRUTSCH, ALBERT, Rev (1916-), Geneva, Switzerland. Archeologist, historian. Wrote extensively on all aspects of Lesotho life & Basotho culture; maintained the manuscript archives at Morija. Source: Haliburton, Gordon, Historical Dictionary of Lesotho (1977), p 28.

0486 BRUYAS, S J, Fr. JACQUES (1635-1712), Lyons, France. Priest. Missionary in New France; wrote on N. American Indians. Source: Jes Rel.

0487 BRY, THEODOR de (1528-1598), Liege, Belgium. Engraver, publisher. Wrote on voyages & travels. Source: Columbia.

0488 BRYANT, ALFRED T., Rev. Missionary. Authority on the Swazi & Zulu of Southern Africa, with emphasis on their political history. Source: Historical Dictionary of Swaziland (1975), p 15.

0489 BUCH, CHRISTIAN LEOPOLD VON (1774-1853), Stolphe, Pomerania, Germany. Paleontologist, geologist, geographer. His geologic studies demonstrated that enormous changes in the earth's surface had occurred. Sources: Biog Index: 2/Encyclopedia Britannica, 9th & 11th ed/EI.

0490 BUCHANAN, THOMAS (1808-1841), Fort Covington, New York, United States. Civil servant. Served as first governor of Liberia, 1839-1841, and wrote a series of articles on its history. Source: Dunn & Holsoe, Historical Dictionary of Liberia (1985), p 33.

0491 BUCHI, ERNST CARL (1914-). Physical anthropologist. Blood groups & dermatoglyphics. Source: Int Dir Anth 5.

0492 BUCK, PETER HENRY (1880-1951), Urenui, New Zealand. Anthropologist. Ethnology of New Zealand and the Pacific. Studied the Maori of New Zealand and pre-contact Polynesian migration. Sources: Biog Index: 1 2 3 & 9/Int Dir Anth 1, 2, 3/Craig & King, Historical Dictionary of Oceania (1981), p 41.

0493 BUCKLER, WILLIAM HEPBURN (1867-1952), Paris, France. Archeologist. Practiced law from 1893-1904 and as a result published works such as *The Origin and History of Contract in Roman Law*, 1894. Was a distinguished diplomat and was Special Agent in the Embassy in London, 1914-1918. From 1910-1914 he was the Assistant Director at Sardis (Turkey) and helped finance excavations there. Was a learned linguist and became involved with the untranslated Lydian language. Sources: Biog Index: 3/Am J Arch 56:179 Jl '52/ Antiquaries Journal 32:263 Jl '52.

0494 BUDGE, WALLIS (1857-1934), England. Assyriologist, Egyptologist. Published extensively in Egyptology; principal work was as translator of hieroglyphic texts and excavation at various sites in Egypt & Sudan; created standard edition of *The Book of the Dead*. Sources: Biog Index: 2 & 4/ Dictionary of National Biography 1931-1940:121-3 '49.

0495 BUHLER, CHARLOTTE (1893-). Psychiatrist. Ethnological use of life histories. Source: Int Dir Anth 5.

0496 BUHLER, JOHANN GEORG (1837-1898). Professor of Indian philology and archeology; authority on Sanskrit and ancient inscriptions. Source: Dictionary of International Biography.

0497 BUHOCIU, OCTAVIAN (1919-). Ethno-folklorist. Folklore of southeastern Europe. Source: Int Dir Anth 5.

0498 BULARD, MARCEL (1877-1952), Cirey-sur-Blaise, France. Archeologist. Wrote extensively on ruins at Delos (Greece). Sources: Biog Index: 3/Rev Arch series 6 43:210-13 '54.

0499 BULCK, GASTON van (1903-). Wrote on ethnology, African languages and society, and Missions to the Congo. Source: Nat Un Cat.

0500 BULIĆ, FRANE (1846-1934), Yugoslavia. Archeologist. Began the first archeological research in Dalmatia (Yugoslavia). Source: Great Soviet Encyclopedia, New York, Macmillan (1974), v. 4, p 172.

0501 BULL, LUDLOW (1886-1954), New York, New York, United States. Egyptologist. Sources: Biog Index: 3 5 & 12/N Y Times p 19 Jl 2 '54/ Nat Cyc Am Biog 42:690 '58.

0502 BULLE, HEINRICH (1867-1945), Bremen, Germany. Archeologist. Director of the University Museum (the Martin Wagner Museum),

Wurzberg, Germany. Main field of interest was Greek art. Interest in Greek theatre produced publications on Greek vases. Sources: Biog Index: 1/Am J Arch 50:406 Jl '46.

0503 BULLEID, ARTHUR (1862-1951), England. Physician, archeologist. Discoverer of the Iron Age 'B' site, known as the Glastonbury Lake Village in Somerset, England. Sources: Biog Index: 2 3 & 7/Antiquaries Journal 32:264 Jl '52/ Isis 43 no 2:117 '52/Nature 169:221-2 F 9 '52.

0504 BULLEN, ADELAIDE KENDALL (1908-), United States. Physical anthropologist. Wide range of studies from mental fatigue to cross cultural language behavior to skeletal materials. Sources: Nat Dir Lat Am/Int Dir Anth 3, 5.

0505 BULLEN, RIPLEY PIERCE (1902-1976), United States. Anthropologist, archeologist, engineer. Studies in West Indies, Antilles & Southeastern U.S. Sources: Biog Index: 12/Int Dir Anth 3, 5/Nat Dir Lat Am/ Nat Cyc Am Biog 60:185-6 '81/Am Antiq 43:622-5 O '78.

0506 BULLOCK, CHARLES (1880-1952). Ethnographer, civil servant. Wrote several books on the Ndebele & Shona of Rhodesia. Source: Rasmussen, R. Kent, Historical Dictionary of Rhodesia/Zimbabwe (1979), p 42.

0507 BUNAK, VICTOR VALERIANOVICH (1891-), Russia. Physical anthropologist, archeologist. Anthropometry of the peoples from Central Europe to the Caucasus. General development of human characteristics. Human morphology, race, and development, and applied anthropology in the mass economy of the U.S.S.R. Sources: Int Dir Anth 5/ Great Soviet Encyclopedia, New York, Macmillan (1973), v. 4, p 176/ Nesturkh, M.F. "V. V. Bunak" Sovremennaia antropologiia. Moscow, 1964.

0508 BUNZEL, RUTH LEAH (1898-). Archeological work on North American Pueblo and Zuni Indians. Source: Nat Un Cat.

0509 BURCHENAL, ELIZABETH (1877-1959). Folklorist. Specialist on folk dance and folk art. Sources: Biog Index: 5 8 & 13/ Notable American Women, the Modern Period. vol. IV, Belknap Press '80, p 121-2/ Journal of Health, Physical Education, Recreation 31:43 My '60/ N Y Times p 86 N 22 '59/Wilson Library Bulletin 34:328 Ja '60.

0510 BURCKHARDT, JAKOB CHRISTOPH (1818-1897), Switzerland. Historian. One of the originators of the cultural interpretation of history. Believed that a pattern of culture is peculiar to each age. Focused on Renaissance in Italy. Source: Columbia.

0511 BURCKHARDT, JOHN LEWIS (1784- 1817). Orientalist. Sources: Biog Index: 9 & 11/New Int Enc.

0512 BURGESS, EDWARD SANFORD (1855-1928), Little Valley, New York, United States. Botanist. Introduced anthropology for the first time in a women's college; focused on interracial & ethnic relationships; wrote about Paleolithic man; studied the Romansch-speaking people (Switzerland). Source: Am Anth 30:481-482.

0513 BURGESS, JAMES (1832-1916), Kirkmaui, Dumfriesshire, Scotland. Director general of the archeological surveys of India, 1886-1889. Sources: Dictionary of International Biography/Who Was Who, 1916-1928.

0514 BURGH, ROBERT FREDERICK (1907-1962), Denver, Colorado, United States. Archeologist. Specialist in archeology of Southwest U.S.; created first site plan of Awatovi; contributed to work on Anasazi basketry. Sources: Biog Index: 6/Int Dir Anth 2, 3/Am Antiq 28:83-6 Jl '62.

0515 BURGMANN, ARNOLD (1909-), Dinslaken, Niederrhein, Germany. Linguist, ethnologist. Missionary of the Societas Verbi Divini; wrote on Polynesian linguistics. Sources: Biog Index: 13/Anthropos

74 no 3-4:321-5 '79.

0516 BURKE, JOHN GREGORY (1787-1848). Ethnologist, genealogist. Source: New Int Enc.

0517 BURKITT, ROBERT JAMES (1869-1945), Ireland. Archeologist, ethnologist. Specialized in Guatemala: ethnology, languages & folklore. Source: Am Anth 47:609-610 O '45.

0518 BURLAND, COTTIE ARTHUR (1905-), England. Ethnologist. Pre-Columbian religion in Mexico. Folklore of Britain. Sources: Int Dir Anth 3, 5.

0519 BURLIN, NATALIE (Curtis) (1875-1921). Folk musician, folklorist. Sources: Biog Index: 1/Howard, John Tasker. Our American Music. 3rd ed. rev Crowell '46 p 617.

0520 BURNE, CHARLOTTE SOPHIA (1850-1923), Staffordshire, England. Folklorist. Assembled the folklore of Shropshire in her best known work, *Shropshire Folklore*; president of the Folklore Society in 1910. Sources: Biog Index: 10/Folklore 86:167-74 Aut '75.

0521 BURNELL, ARTHUR COKE (1840-1882). Civil servant. Linguistics and ethnography of India. Source: Dictionary of International Biography.

0522 BURNETT, SWAN MOSES (1847-1906), New Market, Tennessee, United States. Opthalmologist, otologist. Published on the Melungeons & the development of social science. Source: Am Anth 8:200-201 Ja '06.

0523 BURNOUF, EUGÈNE (1801-1852), Paris, France. Orientalist. Study of Indian & Persian languages. Attempted the deciphering of the cuneiform inscriptions of Persepolis. Source: New Int Enc.

0524 BURRAGE, CHAMPLIN (1874-1951). Archeologist. Specialized in scripts of Crete, Hittites and Indus Valley. Sources: Biog Index: 2 & 3/Nat Cyc Am Biog 38:533-4 '53/ N Y Times p 27 Ja 10 '51.

0525 BURROWS, EDWIN GRANT (1891-1958), United States. Anthropologist. Ethnology of Polynesia and Hawaii. Sources: Biog Index: 4 5 & 7/Nat Cyc Am Biog 47:254 '65/ Int Dir Anth 1, 2, 3/Am Anth 61:97-8 F '59.

0526 BURROWS, ERIC (1882-1938), England. Assyriologist. Source: Biog Index: 3.

0527 BURROWS, MILLAR (1889-1980), Wyoming, Ohio, United States. Orientalist. Directed restoration, excavation and publication of *The Dead Sea Scrolls*; wrote widely on Biblical relationships of the Scrolls. Sources: Biog Index: 4 & 12/Current Biography 17:17-9 Jl '56/ Current Biography Yr Bk 1956:88-90 '57, 1980:451 '80/N Y Times p 28 My 3 '80/ N Y Times Biog Service 11:652 My '80.

0528 BURROWS, RONALD MONTAGU (1867-1920). Antiquarian. Studied finds in Crete. Source: Nat Un Cat.

0529 BURSZTA, JÓZEF (1914-), Poland. Ethnologist. History of folk culture of Polish peasantry. Source: Int Dir Anth 5.

0530 BURTON, FREDERICK RUSSELL (1861-1909). Composer, folklorist. Sources: Biog Index: 1/Howard, John Tasker. Our American Music. 3rd ed. rev Crowell '46 p 617.

0531 BURTON, RICHARD FRANCIS (1821-1890), England. Orientalist, explorer. Traveled over much of Central & East Africa; wrote descriptive accounts of Arabia, India, Dahomey & N. America. Sources: Biog Index: 3 4 5 6 7 8 9 10 11 & 12/ Dictionary of International Biography/Time 83:110 F 28 '64/Kurtz, Laura S., Historical Dictionary of Tanzania (1978), p 26-7.

0532 BURTON-BRADLEY, BURTON GYRTH (1914-). Psychiatrist. Mixed-race society in Papua, New Guinea. Cross-cultural psychiatry. Source: Int Dir Anth 5.

0533 BUSCHAN, GEORG HERMAN THEODOR (1863-1942). Ethnologist. Medical ethnology and prehistory. Sources: Biog Index: 2/Isis 42 no 2:145 '51.

0534 BUSHE-FOX, JOCELYN PLUNKET (1880-1954), Cordara, Co. Longford, England. Archeologist. Main interest was in Roman pottery in England; made excavations at Wroxeter, 1912-13; Hengistbury Head, 1911-12; Swarling, 1921; and Richborough, 1922-39; was Chief Inspector of Ancient Monuments from 1933 until 1945. Sources: Biog Index: 3 & 4/Antiquaries Journal 35:283 Jl '55.

0535 BUSHNELL, ALBERT (1818-1879), Rome, New York, United States. Missionary. Expert on the Mpongwe language of Gabon into which he translated portions of scripture. Source: Gardiner, David E., Historical Dictionary of Gabon (1981), p 50.

0536 BUSHNELL, DAVID IVES, Jr (1875-1941), Missouri, United States. Archeologist. Studies of the American Indians of the eastern United States. Source: Am Anth 44:104-7 Ja '42.

0537 BUSHNELL, GEOFFREY HEXT SUTHERLAND (1903-1978), England. Archeologist. Ecuador & Peru. Sources: Biog Index: 1/Int Dir Anth 3, 5/Nature 162:445 S 18 '48/ Anth News My '79.

0538 BUSK, GEORGE (1807-1886). President of Anthropological Institute, 1873-74. Source: New Int Enc.

0539 BUTEUX, S J, Fr. JACQUES (1600-1652), Abbeville, France. Priest. Missionary in New France; wrote on N. American Indians. Source: Jes Rel.

0540 BUTLER, HOWARD CROSBY (1872-1922). Archeologist. Sources: Biog Index: 1 & 11.

0541 BUTLER, PERCY MILTON (1912-). Zoologist. Comparative & functional anatomy of teeth in mammals, including primates. Source: Int Dir Anth 5.

0542 BUTRUS GHĀLĪ, MIRIT. Civil servant. Researched extensively on Coptic archeology and anthropology. Source: King, Joan W., Historical Dictionary of Egypt (1984), p 218-9.

0543 BUXTON, LEONARD HALFORD DUDLEY (1889-1939). Anthropology, ethnology of Asia. Source: Nat Un Cat.

0544 BYERS, DOUGLAS SWAIN (1903-1978), United States. Anthropologist, archeologist. Paleo-Indians of northeastern N. America, Mexico, and Guatemala. Sources: Nat Dir Lat Am/Biog Index: 13/Int Dir Anth 1, 2, 3, 5/ Am Antiq 44:708-10 O '79.

0545 BYRES, JAMES (1734-). Architect, archeologist. Sources: Biog Index: 10/Apollo 99:446-61 Je '74.

0546 BYRON, JOHN (1723-1786), Newstead, England. Naval officer. Explored the Gilbert & Tuamotu Islands, 1764-1766, and left a journal with ethnographic data on these areas. Source: Craig & King, Historical Dictionary of Oceania (1981), p 42.

0547 CABALLERO DE BEDOYA, RAMÓN (1881-), Paraguay. Philologist. Specialist on the Guarani language of Paraguay. Source: Kolinski, Charles J., Historical Dictionary of Paraguay (1973), p 36.

0548 CABRÉ AGUILÓ, JUAN (1882-1947), Spain. Archeologist. Sources: Biog Index: 2/Rev Arch series 6 38:56-8 Jl '51.

0549 CÁCERES, MARIANO (1856-), El Salvador. Author. Composed several poems and stories which reflect Salvadoran customs of the 19th century. Source: Flemion, Philip F., Historical Dictionary of El Salvador (1972), p 28.

0550 CÁCERES FREYRE, JULIÁN (1916-), Buenos Aires, Argentina. Artist, anthropologist. History of Argentine anthropology. Cave art & petrography. Sources: Int Dir Anth 3, 5.

0551 CADILLA de MARTÍNEZ, MARIA (1886-1951), Puerto Rico. Folklorist. Collected folktales of Puerto Rico, as well as songs and traditions of the island; first to do major work in the area. Sources: Biog Index: 3 & 13/Journal of American Folklore 65:216 Jl '52/ Notable American Women, the Modern Period. vol. IV,

Belknap Press '80, p 129-30.

0552 CADOGAN, LEON (1899-), Paraguay. Ethnographer. Specialist on the culture of the Guarani Indians of Paraguay. Source: Kolinski, Charles J., Historical Dictionary of Paraguay (1973), p 38.

0553 CAESAR, JULIUS (100-44 BC), Rome, Italy. Descriptions of Celtic & Germanic peoples. Source: Columbia.

0554 CAHEN, ÉMILE (-1942). Archeologist. Archeology of France & Greece. Sources: Biog Index: 2/Rev Arch series 6 35:92 Ja '50.

0555 CAILLIE, RENÉ (1799-1838), France. Explorer. Traveled extensively in West Africa in late 1820s; first European to visit Timbuctoo (Mali) for centuries, published account of this trip. Sources: Columbia/O'Toole, Thomas E., Historical Dictionary of Guinea (1978), p 14.

0556 CALANCHA, ANTONIO de la (1584-1654). Traveled through Peru where he examined ancient ruins. Source: New Int Enc.

0557 CALDWELL, ROBERT (1814-1891). Compared Christianity and Hinduism, went on missions to India. Source: Nat Un Cat.

0558 CALKIN, CARLETON IVERS (1914-). Anthropologist. Source: Nat Dir Lat Am.

0559 CALLAHUAZO, JAUNTO (ca. 18th Cent-), Ibarra, Ecuador. Historian. Wrote an account from a native viewpoint of the civil war between the last two Incas, Atahualpa & Huascar. Source: Bork & Maier, Historical Dictionary of Ecuador (1973), p 32-3.

0560 CALLAWAY, HENRY (1817-1890). Bishop. Went on missions to South Africa, particularly among the Zulu. Source: Nat Un Cat.

0561 CALVERLEY, AMICE MARY (1896-1959), London, England. Egyptologist. Expert on the Temple of Seti I at Abydos (Egypt); recorded inscriptions there photographically; 5 volumes published. Sources: Biog Index: 5 & 12/N Y Times p 87 Ap 12 '59.

0562 CALVERT, JOHN (1813-1892), Pickering, New York, United States. Missionary. Translated and printed many texts in Fijian. Source: Craig & King, Historical Dictionary of Oceania (1981), p 43.

0563 CALVETE DE ESTRELLA, JUAN CRISTÓBAL (1525-1593), Savinena, Spain. Historian. Wrote a history of Ecuador during the period of Gonzalo Pizarro's activity. Source: Bork & Maier, Historical Dictionary of Ecuador (1973), p 33.

0564 CALZA, GUIDO (1888-1946), Milan, Italy. Archeologist. Conducted extensive excavations at the site of Ostia, former port of Imperial Rome. Sources: Biog Index: 1/Am J Arch 50:407-8 Jl '46/N Y Times p 25 Ap 24 '46.

0565 CAMANO y BAZAN, JOAQUIN (1737-1820), La Rioja, Argentina. Missionary. Wrote linguistic and cartographic studies on Argentina. Source: Wright & Nelsham, Historical Dictionary of Argentina (1978), p 137.

0566 CÁMARA-BARBACHANO, FERNANDO (1919-). Ethnologist. Salvage archeology of Indian groups of Mexico. Sociocultural change. Source: Int Dir Anth 5.

0567 CÂMARA CASCUDO, LUÍS (1898-), Brazil. Folklorist. Published several studies of Brazilian regional life including a study of the fishing vessels of the northeast coast. Source: Levine, Robert M., Historical Dictionary of Brazil (1979), p 41.

0568 CAMBIER, ERNEST FRANÇOIS (1844-1909). Explorer. Accompanied first expedition of the African International Association. Source: New Int Enc.

0569 CAMDEN, WILLIAM (1551-1623), England. Antiquarian, historian. Collected materials of antiquarian interest. Revived study of Anglo-Saxons. Source: Columbia.

0570 CAMERON, GEORGE GLENN (1905- 1979). Archeologist, linguist, Orientalist. Middle Eastern languages. History of Iran before Alexander the Great. Near Eastern archeology. Sources: Biog Index: 12/Int Dir Anth 5.

0571 CAMIEN, LAITEN LESTER (1906-). Archeologist. Historical archeology of Mexican-American homes. Source: Int Dir Anth 5.

0572 CAMP, CHARLES LEWIS (1893-1975), Jamestown, North Dakota, United States. Paleontologist. Led an expedition to Sterkfontein (1947-48) which located Australopithecine skeletal fragments; specialist in folk history of American West. Sources: Biog Index: 10/N Y Times p 22 Ag 16 '75.

0573 CAMPA, ARTHUR LEON (1895-), Guaynas, Mexico. Historian. Spanish folklore. History of Hispanic cultures. Sources: Int Dir Anth 3, 5.

0574 CAMPBELL, ARCHIBALD (1787-). Wrote an account of his Pacific travels giving detailed data on Hawaii under King Kamehameha I. Source: Craig & King, Historical Dictionary of Oceania (1981), p 43.

0575 CAMPBELL, GEORGE (1824-1892). Civil servant, ethnologist. Author of *The Ethnology of India* and other ethnographic writings. Source: Dictionary of International Biography.

0576 CAMPBELL, JOHN LORNE (1906-). Folklorist. Sources: Biog Index: 3/Schafer, Bruno, Comp. They Heard His Voice. McMullen '52 p 123-35.

0577 CAMPBELL, JOSEPH (1904-), New York, New York, United States. Folklorist. Specialist in myth and symbol; analyzed religions showing different expressions of common experiences. Sources: Biog Index: 4 11 & 12/N Y Times p 14 Ap 15 '79.

0578 CAMPER, PIETER (1722-1789), Leyden. Known for contributions to human and comparative anatomy, obstetrics. Source: New Int Enc.

0579 CAMPS CAZORLA, EMILIO (1903-1952). Archeologist. Sources: Biog Index: 3/ Archivo Espanol de Arte y Arqueologia 25 no 1:209 '52.

0580 CANBY, JOEL SHACKELFORD (1919-), Denver, Colorado, United States. Anthropologist, archeologist. Archeology of Middle America. Sources: Int Dir Anth 3/Nat Dir Lat Am.

0581 CANDLIN, ALFRED HUGH STANTON (1911-1977). Orientalist. Source: Biog Index: 11.

0582 CANELAS, MANUEL (1718-1773), Cordoba, Argentina. Missionary. Wrote account of his work and the customs of the Mocabi Indians in Santa Fe province (Argentina). Source: Wright & Nelsham, Historical Dictionary of Argentina (1978), p 142.

0583 CANINA, LUIGI (1795-1856), Casale, Italy. Archeologist. Superintended excavations at Tusculum. Wrote on Etruscan & Roman archeology. Source: New Int Enc.

0584 CANNON, ROBERT (1909-1964). Anthropologist, film maker. Expert on the use of the camera in fieldwork. Sources: Biog Index: 7/Am Anth 67:453-4 Ap '65.

0585 CANNON, WALTER BRADFORD (1871-1924), United States. Physiologist. Introduced the concept of homeostasis. Source: Columbia.

0586 CANTACUZINO, GEORGES (1900-). Archeologist, archivist. Neolithic cultures & ethnography of Balkan regions. Source: Int Dir Anth 5.

0587 CAPART, JEAN (1877-1947), Brussels, Belgium. Egyptologist. Chief conservator of the Musees Royaux d'Art et d'Histoire of Brussels, 1925-1942. Sources: Biog Index: 1 & 4/ Brussels, Musees Royaux d'Art et d'Histoire Bulletin 28:2-5 '56.

0588 CAPELL, ARTHUR (1902-), Sydney, Australia. Comparative linguistics of Oceania & Australia. Sources: Int Dir Anth 2, 3, 5.

0589 CAPPANNARI, STEPHEN C (1917-1974), Massachusetts, United States. Anthropologist, psychiatrist. Psychological anthropology of southern Italy & southern California. Italian rural studies. Ethnographic work on Pomo & Kawaiisu of California and on South

Italian peasants. Sources: Int Dir Anth 3, 5/Am Anth 81:335-7 Je '79/Anth News O '74.

0590 CAPPIERI, MARIO (1854-), Trieste, Italy. Physical anthropologist. Peoples of the Mediterranean, Central Asia & India. Sources: Int Dir Anth 3, 5.

0591 CAPPS, EDWARD (1902-1969). Archeologist. Specialist in Greek sculpture. Sources: Biog Index: 9/Archaeology 23:251 Je '70.

0592 CARAMELEA, VASILE V (1915-). Ethnologist. History of social & cultural anthropology. Source: Int Dir Anth 5.

0593 CARBALLO GARCIA, JESÚS (1874-1961). Priest, archeologist. Sources: Biog Index: 6/ Archivo Espanol de Arte y Arqueologia 34 no 103:224-5 '61.

0594 CARDIEL, JOSÉ (1704-1782), La Guardia, Spain. Explorer, missionary. Made many trips of exploration from northern Paraguay to southern Argentina and wrote accounts. Source: Wright & Nelsham, Historical Dictionary of Argentina (1978), p 148.

0595 CARDINAL, ALLAN WOLSEY (1887-1956), Tendring, Essex, England. Anthropologist. Worked for the British Colonial Government in northern Gold Coast (Ghana) and wrote baseline ethnography of "Northern Territories" peoples. Source: Who Was Who, 1951-1960, p 183.

0596 CAREY, HENRY AMES (1895-1965), Pennsylvania, United States. Anthropologist, archeologist. Studied anthropology and archeology of American Indians and Near East. Sources: Biog Index: 9/Int Dir Anth 1, 2, 3/Nat Cyc Am Biog 52:399-400 '70.

0597 CAREY, WILLIAM (1761-1834), England. Orientalist, missionary. Traveled to India as a Baptist missionary; translated the Bible into Bengali and other Indian languages; the mission at Serampore printed this Bible as well as the third edition of Roxburgh's Flora Indica of which Carey was editor in 1832. Sources: Biog Index: 1 2 3 4 5 6 7 8 10 11 12 13-4/Taxon 31:60 Mr '82.

0598 CARHEIL, S J, Fr. ÉTIENNE de (1634-1726), Chateau de la Guichardaye, Carentoir, France. Priest. Missionary in New France; wrote on N. American Indians. Source: Jes Rel.

0599 CARLSON, GUSTAV G (1909-), Gwinn, Michigan, United States. Ethnologist. Studies of peasantry in Europe & China. Primitive art of the Comanche Indians of U.S. Sources: Int Dir Anth 2, 3, 5.

0600 CARNARVON, 5TH Earl of, see: MOLYNEUX, GEORGE.

0601 CARNEGIE, DAVID (1855-1910). Missionary. Wrote an account of the life and customs of the Matabele. Source: Rasmussen, R. Kent, Historical Dictionary of Rhodesia/Zimbabwe (1979), p 46.

0602 CARNOCHAN, FREDERIC GROSVENOR (1890-1952). Ethnologist. Did fieldwork in Tanzania while collecting zoological specimens; wrote book on the Nyamwezi people. Sources: Biog Index: 3/N Y Times p 15 Ag 4 '52.

0603 CARO, RODRIGO (1573-1647). Archeologist. Sources: Biog Index: 3/ Archivo Espanol de Arte y Arqueologia 24 no 1-2:5-22 '51.

0604 CARO-ALVAREZ, JOSÉ (1910-1978), Dominican Republic. Pre-Columbian Caribbean Arawakan art. Source: Anth News My '78.

0605 CARPENTER, CLARENCE RAY (1905-1975), United States. Psychologist, anthropologist, primate behaviorist. Established Macaque population at Santiago Island research station in Puerto Rico. Sources: Biog Index: 8 10 & 11/ American Journal of Physical Anthropology 45:175 S '76/Anth News My '75.

0606 CARPENTER, RHYS (1889-1980). Archeologist. Founded school of classical archeology in the U.S.; specialist in cultural geography of Mediterranean, Greek archeology; worked on Greek colonies in Spain. Sources: Biog Index: 9 12 & 13/Art in America 68:160 Mr '80/ N Y Times p A-15 Ja 4 '80/N Y

Times Biog Service 11:15 Ja '80/ Am J Arch 84:260 Ap '80.

0607 **CARRINGTON, JOHN FREDERICK** (1914-), Rushden, England. Botanist. Music & ethno-biology of Africa. Comparative study of African languages, especially those of West Africa & Zaire. Sources: Int Dir Anth 3, 5.

0608 **CARRIÓN CACHOT de GIRARD, REBECA**, Peru. Archeologist. Director of the National Museum of Anthropology and Archeology, Lima, Peru; studied the pre-Inca civilization of the Paracas Peninsula in Peru; also the Chavin civilization of the Central Andes. Sources: Biog Index: 2/Americas 2:6-9+ Ja '50.

0609 **CARTER, EDWARD CLARK** (1878-1954). Orientalist. Sources: Biog Index: 3 & 6.

0610 **CARTER, GEORGE F** (1912-), San Diego, California, United States. Geographer. Early man and origins of agriculture in N. America. Sources: Int Dir Anth 1, 2, 3, 5.

0611 **CARTER, HOWARD** (1874-1939), England. Painter, archeologist, Egyptologist. Excavated (1906-1922) in Valley of the Kings, near Luxor, Egypt. Discovered tomb of King Tutankhamen. Sources: Biog Index: 2 4 6 8 9 12 & 13/Columbia/ Burton, Harry. Discovery of Tutankhamen's tomb, Grosset & Dunlap '77/ Vandenberg, Philipp. Golden Pharoah. MacMillan '80/ Dictionary of National Biography, '49.

0612 **CARVALHO, GERARDO A de** (1914-). Ethnographer. Afro-Brazilians. Source: Int Dir Anth 5.

0613 **CASAGRANDE, JOSEPH BARTHOLOMEW** (1915-1982), Cincinnati, Ohio, United States. Anthropologist, ethnologist. Linguistic studies of the Navajo & Comanche Indians of the U.S. Inter-ethnic relations in Ecuador & the Andes. The Indians of Ecuador; ethnolinguistics, psycholinguistics. History of anthropology. Sources: Am Anth 87:883-888 '85/Int Dir Anth 5/Nat Dir Lat Am/ American Men and Women of Science, ed. by J.C. Press, 12th ed., New York, Bowker, 1973.

0614 **CASALIS, JEAN EUGÈNE ARNAUD** (1812-1891), Orthez, France. Missionary. Served as political adviser to Moshoeshoe I; wrote extensive diaries and other accounts invaluable to Basotho history of the 19th century. Source: Haliburton, Gordon, Historical Dictionary of Lesotho (1977), p 30.

0615 **CASAS, BARTOLOMÉ de LAS** (1474-1566), Seville, Spain. Missionary, historian, priest. Worked for the improvement of Indian conditions, especially for abolition both of Indian slavery and of the forced labor of the encomienda; championed Amerindian rights; wrote *Historia de las Indias*, a classic history of early Indian-Spanish relationship. Sources: Biog Index: 13/Columbia/Briggs & Alisky, Historical Dictionary of Mexico (1981), p 64/ Historical Dictionary of Guatemala (1973), p 119-20/Heath, Dwight B., Historical Dictionary of Bolivia (1972), p 54/Rudolph & Rudolph, Historical Dictionary of Venezuela (1971), p 32-3/Moore, Richard E., Helps, Sir Arthur, Life of Las Casas. Gordon Press '80/ Parish, Helen Rand, Las Casas as a Bishop. U.S. Govt print office '80.

0616 **CASEY, DERMOT ARMSTRONG** (1897-1977), Australia. Archeologist. Archeology and ethnology of Australia & Western Pacific. Sources: Biog Index: 11/Int Dir Anth 2, 3/Antiquity 52:92 Jl '78.

0617 **CASO y ANDRADE, ALFONSO** (1896-1970), Mexico City, Mexico. Anthropologist, archeologist, lawyer. Director, Museo Nacional. Made important contributions to knowledge of Mixtec & Zapotec cultures through excavation of Monte Alban, 1931-43, Oaxaca, Mexico. Sources: Biog Index: 9 10/Int Dir Anth 1, 3/ Who's Who in Latin America 3rd ed., Ronald Hilton ed., Stanford Univ. Press (Blaine Ethridge edition, 1971) vol. I, p 21/Am Anth 75:877-85 Je '73/ Am

Antiq 36:449-50 O '71.

0618 CASOT, S J, Fr. JEAN JOSEPH (1728-1800), Switzerland. Priest. Missionary in New France; wrote on N. American Indians. Source: Jes Rel.

0619 CASSADY, RALPH (1901-1978), United States. Economist. Traditional marketing in Oaxaca, Mexico. Source: Anth News Jn '78.

0620 CASSANI, JOSÉ (1673-1750), Spain. Missionary. Wrote a history of Jesuit mission efforts in the Orinoco region and llanos' of Colombia. Source: Davis, Robert H., Historical Dictionary of Colombia (1977), p 76.

0621 CASSELL, CHRISTIAN ABAYOMI (1906-), Monrovia, Liberia. Lawyer. Author of *Liberia: History of the First African Republic* (1970). Source: Dunn & Holsoe, Historical Dictionary of Liberia (1985), p 36.

0622 CASSON, STANLEY (1889-1944), England. Archeologist. Prehistory & classical Greek archeology. Sources: Biog Index: 2/Int Dir Anth 2/Rev Arch series 6 36:114-7 Jl '50.

0623 CASTAÑEDA PAGANINI, RICARDO (1908-), Guatemala. Historian. Authored two books on the Mayan cities of Tikal (Guatemala) and Palenque (Mexico). Source: Moore, Richard E., Historical Dictionary of Guatemala (1973), p 49.

0624 CASTELLVÍ, MARCELINO de (ca. 1911-1953), Spain. Priest. Published on the languages of the Amazon region. Sources: Biog Index: 3/Am Anth 55:239 Ap '53.

0625 CASTILLERO REYES, ERNESTO de JESÚS, Ocu, Panama. Historian. Wrote several histories of the Panamanian region. Source: Hedrick & Hedrick, Historical Dictionary of Panama (1970), p 25.

0626 CASTILLO, JESÚS (1877-1946), Guatemala. Composer. The leading authority on Guatemala's Indian music and musical instruments. Source: Moore, Richard E., Historical Dictionary of Guatemala (1973), p 49.

0627 CASTRÉN, MATTHIAS ALEXANDER (1813-1852), Finland. Philologist. One of the first to study Finno-Ugaritic languages. Source: Columbia.

0628 CASTRO, JOÃO de (1500-1548), Lisbon, Portugal. Explorer. Went on expedition to the Red Sea. Source: New Int Enc.

0629 CATHERWOOD, FREDERICK (1799- 1854), Hoxton Parish, London, England. Artist, archeologist, architect. Drew the ruins of Copan and other Maya sites. Spent ten years, 1824-1834, traveling in the Near East making detailed drawings of ancient ruins; his drawings of Egyptian remains were some of the first ever done by a trained architect; in 1839 he accompanied John Lloyd Stephens to Central America to draw for the first time the Mayan ruins of Quirigua, Palenque, Chichen Itza, Uxmal, and Tulum in Mexico. Sources: Biog Index: 1 2 5 6 7 8 & 10/Meyer, Harvey K., Historical Dictionary of Honduras (1976), p 62-3/Natural History 56:104 Mr '47.

0630 CATLIN, GEORGE (1796-1872), Wilkes-Barre, Pennsylvania, United States. Artist, lawyer, traveler. Portraits, tribal scenes, manners, customs, & conditions of the N. American Indians. Source: Columbia.

0631 CATON-THOMPSON, GERTRUDE (1888-1985), England. Archeologist, anthropologist. Conducted archeological excavations at Great Zimbabwe; formulated theories of origin of culture in Zimbabwe region. Attempted to settle issue of origin and dating of stone ruins of Zimbabwe, Dhlo Dhlo, etc. Supported thesis of African origin; argued for dating to 8-9th century. Most extensive work done on Maund Ruin, Great Zimbabwe. Excavated at Fayum Lake & Kharga (Egypt), Zimbabwe, and Hadhramaut (Yemen). Sources: Int Dir Anth 1, 2, 3/Anth News 3/86/Rasmussen, R. Kent, Historical Dictionary of Rhodesia/Zimbabwe (1979), p 47.

0632 CAYTON, HORACE ROSCOE

(1903- 1970), Seattle, Washington, United States. Sociologist. Afro-American community studies. Sources: Encyclopedia of Black America 1981. p 221-2/ Who's Who in Colored America (1950, 7th ed.) p 95.

0633 CEBALLOS NOVELO, ROQUE JACINTO (1885-), Hunucma, Yucatan, Mexico. Published on Teotihuacan, the Acolhua period, Tepoztlan and Teopanzolco, and Tenayuca. Source: Who's Who in Latin America 3rd ed., Ronald Hilton ed., Stanford Univ. Press (Blaine Ethridge edition, 1971) vol. I, p 24.

0634 CECCHI, ANTONIO (1849-1896), Pesaro, Italy. Joined Italian geographical expedition to Abyssinia, also went to Massawa. Source: New Int Enc.

0635 CENTURIÓN, CARLOS R. (1902-1969), Paraguay. Historian. Published a history of the evolution of a distinctive Paraguayan culture. Source: Kolinski, Charles J., Historical Dictionary of Paraguay (1973), p 48-9.

0636 Ceram, C W, see: MAREK, KURT W.

0637 ČERNÝ, JAROSLAV (1898-1970), Pilsen, Czechoslovakia. Egyptologist. Specialist in Late Egyptian language; focused work on the site of Deir el Medina. Sources: Biog Index: 8 & 9.

0638 CERULLI, ENRICO (1898-), Naples, Italy. Ethnologist. Ethiopic studies in history & ethnology. Sources: Int Dir Anth 2, 3, 5.

0639 CERVALLOS, PEDRO FERMIN (1812-1893), Ambato, Ecuador. Historian. Created a 6 volume *Historia del Ecuador*. Source: Bork & Maier, Historical Dictionary of Ecuador (1973), p 40.

0640 CESNOLA, LUIGI PALMA di (1832-1904). Archeologist. Sources: Biog Index; 7 & 9.

0641 CEVALLOS, JOSÉ ANTONIO (1860-), El Salvador. Writer. Published *Recuerdos Salvadorenos*, a compilation of documentary sources of Salvadoran history. Source: Flemion, Philip F., Historical Dictionary of El Salvador (1972), p 35.

0642 CHABOT, JEAN-BAPTISTE (1860-1948), Vouvray, France. Orientalist, historian. Wrote much on Eastern Christianity and started the major series *Corpus scriptorum Christianorum orientalium*. Source: Rev Arch series 6 40:40-66 Jl '52.

0643 CHACÓN TREJOS, GONZALO (1890- 1969), Costa Rica. Author. Wrote a volume on traditions of Costa Rica. Source: Creedman, Theodore, Historical Dictionary of Costa Rica (1977), p 40.

0644 CHAFFANJON, JEAN (ca. 1854-1913). Studied the archeology and ethnology of the Orinoco (Venezuela); assembled anthropological collections from northern & Central Asia. Source: Am Anth 16:373.

0645 CHALLAYE, FÉLICIEN (1875-). Wrote account of the inspection mission of 1905 done by Commissioner Brazza to investigate colonial crime in the Congo and Upper Chari. Source: Kalck, Pierre, Historical Dictionary of the Central African Republic (1980), p 25.

0646 CHAMBERLAIN, ALEXANDER FRANCIS (1865-1914). Anthropologist. Sources: Biog Index: 1/ Royal Canadian Institute, Toronto. Centennial volume, 1849-1949. The Institute '49, p 180/Am Anth 16:377-48 Ap '14.

0647 CHAMPE, JOHN LELAND (1895-1978), Nebraska, United States. Anthropologist. Fieldwork among Plains Indians. Expert witness in several Indian land claims cases. Sources: Biog Index: 13/Int Dir Anth 2/Am Antiq 45:268-71 Ap '80/ Am Anth 81:338-41 Je '79/Anth News My '78.

0648 CHAMPION, SELWYN GURNEY (1874-1949). Folklorist, physician. Sources: Biog Index: 2/British Medical Journal no 4647:255 Ja 28 '50/ Lancet 257:1245-6 D 31 '49.

0649 CHAMPOLLION, JEAN FRANÇOIS (1790-1832), France. Egyptologist, hieroglyphologist. Deciphered hieroglyphic writing of the Rosetta Stone, making possible the reading of all inscriptions of pharaonic Egypt. Wrote first modern study of ancient Egypt by a European. Sources: Biog Index: 3 4 6 & 10/King, Joan W., Historical Dictionary of Egypt (1984), p 229.

0650 CHAMPOLLION-FIGEAC, JACQUES JOSEPH (1778-1867). Archeologist, Egyptologist. Sources: Biog Index: 7 & 10/Wilson Library Bulletin 49:232 N '74.

0651 CHAO, PAUL K Y (1919-), China. Ethnologist. Kinship & village organization of North & Central China. Source: Int Dir Anth 5.

0652 CHAO, YUEN REN (1882-). Linguist. Dialectology & symbolic systems of China. Source: Int Dir Anth 5.

0653 CHAPMAN, CARL HALEY (1915-). Archeologist, archivist. Worked especially with the Osage Indians, Missouri & eastern U.S. Source: Int Dir Anth 5.

0654 CHAPMAN, JAMES (1831-1872). Explorer. Source: Stevens, Richard P., Historical Dictionary of the Republic of Botswana (1975), p 31.

0655 CHAPOUTHIER, FERNAND (1899-1953). Archeologist. Sources: Biog Index: 3 & 4/Rev Arch series 6 47:204-11 Ap '56.

0656 CHAPPLE, ELIOT DINSMORE (1909-), United States. Psychological anthropologist. Studied adolescent sociopaths & psychopaths in U.S. Sources: Int Dir Anth 1, 2, 3, 5.

0657 CHARBONNEAUX, JEAN (1895-1969), Genlis, France. Archeologist. As Chief of Dept. of Greek and Roman Antiquities at Louvre, he improved the collections enormously. Sources: Biog Index: 8/Rev Arch 1:119-20 '69.

0658 Chardin, Pierre Teillard de, see: TEILLARD de CHARDIN.

0659 CHARLEVOIX, PIERRE FRANÇOIS XAVIER de (1682-1761), France. Jesuit, historian. Missionary to New France. Only full description of the interior of America in the first third of the 18th century. Source: Columbia.

0660 CHARLIN, JORGE IRIBARREN (1908-1977), Chile. Archeologist. Expert in Chilean archeology. Source: Anth News Mr '77.

0661 CHARNAY, DÉSIRÉ (1828-1915), France. Photographer. Led an expedition to the Maya areas of Central America to excavate, clear and photograph the ruins; published a book covering this work. Source: Meyer, Harvey K., Historical Dictionary of Honduras (1976), p 71-2.

0662 CHASE, RICHARD (1904-). Folklorist. Sources: Biog Index: 4 5 & 6/Elementary English 40:677-86 N '63/ Fuller, Muriel, ed. More Junior Authors. Wilson '63 p 43-5.

0663 CHATTERJEE, BAJRA KUMAR (1904-), Calcutta, India. Anthropologist. Study of ancient human remains of India & the Middle East. Sources: Int Dir Anth 3, 5.

0664 CHAUCHETIÈRE, S J, Fr. CLAUDE (1645-1709), Saint-Porchaire-de-Potiers, France. Priest. Missionary in New France; wrote on N. American Indians. Source: Jes Rel.

0665 CHAUMONOT, S J, Fr. PIERRE JOSEPH MARIE (1611-1693), Chatillon, France. Priest. Missionary in New France; wrote on N. American Indians. Source: Jes Rel.

0666 CHAVERO, ALFREDO (1841-1906), Mexico City, Mexico. Founder of the American Anthropological Association; comparative study of Mexican calendar systems (especially Aztec & Palenque). Source: Am Anth 8:701-3 O '06.

0667 CHAVEZ FRANCO, MODESTO (1872-1952), Santa Rosa, Ecuador. Historian, folklorist. Collected and published historical material on the Guayaquil region (Ecuador). Source: Bork & Maier, Historical Dictionary of Ecuador (1973), p 41.

0668 CHEBOKSAROV, NIKOLAI NIKOLAEVICH (1907-1980), Russia. Ethnologist, anthropologist. Did work in East Asia and also wrote about general problems of anthropology. Sources: Great Soviet Encyclopedia, New York, Macmillan (1982), v. 29, p 76 /Alekseev, V.P. and G.G. Stratanovich. "N.N. Cheboksarov" Sovetskaia etnografiia, 1967, no. 3.

0669 CHENET, GEORGES (1881-1951), France. Archeologist. Archeology of ancient Near East, Syria. Sources: Biog Index: 3/Int Dir Anth 1, 2/Rev Arch series 6 41:193 Ap '53.

0670 CHENU, PAUL (1868-1956), France. Archeologist. Wrote extensively on archeology of the Cher (France). Sources: Biog Index: 5/Rev Arch 1:89 Ja '59.

0671 CHEPURKOVSKII, EFIM MIKHAILOVICH (1871-1950), Ukraine. Anthropologist. Applied statistical methods to anthropological research of the Russian people. Source: Great Soviet Encyclopedia, New York, Macmillan (1982), v. 29, p 103.

0672 CHEVALIER, AUGUSTE. Explorer, botanist. Wrote *French Central Africa* (1908), in which he describes the destruction of villages and dislocation of populations by large companies. Source: Kalck, Pierre, Historical Dictionary of the Central African Republic (1980), p 26.

0673 CHEWINGS, CHARLES (1859-1937), Near Mount Bryan, Australia. Geologist, anthropologist. Wrote on aborigines. Sources: Biog Index: 2/Dictionary of Australian Biography 1:161 '49.

0674 CHI, LI (1896-). Archeologist. Study of prehistoric stone artifacts & early decorative arts of China. Source: Int Dir Anth 5.

0675 CHIA, LAN PO (1908-), China. Paleontologist. The study of early man in China. Sources: Int Dir Anth 2, 5.

0676 CHIANG, YEE (1903-1977), Kiu Kiang Province, China. Sinologist. Specialist in East Asian languages, cultures, sculpture and calligraphy. Sources: Biog Index: 1 2 3 4 5 & 11/N Y Times p 8-13 O 21 '77/ N Y Times Biog Service 8:1477-8 O '77.

0677 CHIL y NARANJO, GREGORIO (-1901). Physician, museum director. Expert on archeology of the Canary Islands. Source: Am Anth 4:358 Ap '02.

0678 CHILD, FRANCIS JAMES (1825-1896). Educator, folklorist. Sources: Biog Index: 3 8 9 & 11/American Renaissance in New England.

0679 CHILDE, VERE GORDON (1892-1957), Sydney, Australia. Archeologist. Sociological and economic interpretation of archeological discoveries. Sources: Biog Index: 1 4 5 & 13/Int Dir Anth 2, 3/ Gathercole, Peter. Childe, Vere Gordon (In Makers of Modern Culture. Facts on File '81 p 104 5)/ Trigger, Bruce G. Gordon Childe, Revolutions in Archaeology. Columbia Univ. Press '80/Am Anth 60:733-6 Ag '58.

0680 CHINNERY, ERNEST WILLIAM PEARSON (1887-), Canberra, Australia. Archeologist. Worked in Tanganyika. Ruanda-Urundi, Papua & New Guinea. Sources: Biog Index: 1/Int Dir Anth 1, 2, 3/ United Nations Bulletin 5:604 Ag 1 '48.

0681 CHIRI, MASHIO (1909-1961), Japan. Anthropological linguist. Ainu scholar of Ainu culture. Studied the Ainu language in order to make his people known to the world from "an insider's point of view". Sources: Biog Index: 10/Am Anth 75:868-76 Je '73.

0682 CHODZIDLO, TEOFIL (1909-), Poland. Ethnologist. Ethnology & comparative religions of Siberian peoples. Source: Int Dir Anth 5.

0683 CHOLENEC, S J, Fr. PIERRE (1641-1723), St.-Pol-de-Leon, Finistere, France. Priest. Missionary in New France; wrote on N. American Indians. Source: Jes Rel.

0684 CHOLLOT-VARAGNAC, MARTHE (1918-). Archeologist. Paleolithic symbolism & prehistory in France, the Pyrenees & Dordogne. Source: Int Dir Anth 5.

0685 CHOMBART de LAUWE, PAUL-HENRI (1912-). Sociologist.

French society, especially the family. Source: Nat Un Cat.

0686 CHRISTALLER, THEODOR (1840-1896). Teacher. Created first German-Douala dictionary and wrote a grammar of the language of the Douala of Cameroon. Source: Levine & Nye, Historical Dictionary of Cameroon (1974), p 27.

0687 CHRISTENSEN, BODIL (1896-). Ethnologist. Photographic records of customs, superstitions & Indian textiles of Mexico. Source: Int Dir Anth 5.

0688 CHRISTY, HENRY (1810-1865). Archeology of S. France. Source: Nat Un Cat.

0689 CH'U, WAN-LI (1907-), China. Historian, bibliographer. Chinese history of the Yin & Chou Dynasties. Chinese bibliographies. Source: Int Dir Anth 5.

0690 CHURCHILL, EDMUND (1912-). Statistician. Statistical applications in anthropometry. Source: Int Dir Anth 5.

0691 CHURCHILL, WILLIAM (1859-1920), New York, New York, United States. Diplomat. Specialized in Polynesian linguistics & ethnology. Source: Am Anth 22:201 Je '20.

0692 CIEZA de LÉON, PEDRO de (1518-1560), Seville, Spain. Explorer, soldier, historian. Wrote *Chronicle of Peru*, useful source of data on the Pacific regions of South America and the early Spanish explorations. Sources: Columbia/Bork & Maier, Historical Dictionary of Ecuador (1973), p 43/Davis, Robert H., Historical Dictionary of Colombia (1977), p 80.

0693 CLAPPERTON, HUGH (1788-1827), Annan, Dumfriesshire, Scotland. Explorer. Wrote a journal about his West African exploration in the 1820s in which he described areas of Nigeria, including the Hausa states, as well as parts of Cameroon. One of the first Europeans to see Lake Chad. Sources: New Int Enc/Nat Un Cat/Levine & Nye, Historical Dictionary of Cameroon (1974), p 27.

0694 CLARK, IAN MELVILLE (1914-1967), England. Engineer, Orientalist. Expert on Japanese gardens. Sources: Biog Index: 8/Oriental Art 13:325 Winter '67.

0695 CLARK, JOHN DESMOND (1916-), England. Prehistorian, ethnologist, archeologist. African peoples. Primate behavior relative to hominid evolution. Founder of archeology in Zambia; author of extensive works on the prehistory of South Central Africa. Sources: Int Dir Anth 2, 3, 5/Grotpeter, John J., Historical Dictionary of Zambia (1979), p 60.

0696 CLARK, JOHN GRAHAME DOUGLAS (1907-), Kent, England. Archeologist. Prehistoric archeology & Northwestern European "food gathering" cultures. Sources: Biog Index: 3 & 10/Int Dir Anth 1, 3/ Current Anthropology 14:262 O '73/Who's Who, 1985.

0697 CLARK, WALTER EUGENE (1895-1960), Digby, Nova Scotia, Canada. Orientalist. Specialist on India and its culture, chief area of research was Sanskrit. Sources: Biog Index: 5 & 12/N Y Times p 84 O 2 '60/Int Dir Anth 3.

0698 CLARKE, CHARLES BARRON (1832- 1906), Andover, Massachusettes, United States. Educator. Numerous papers on anthropology. Sources: Dictionary of International Biography/Who Was Who, 1897-1916.

0699 CLARKE, LOUIS COLVILLE GRAY (1881-1960), England. Archeologist. American archeology & ethnology. Director, Fitzwilliam Museum, Cambridge Univ. Sources: Biog Index: 5 & 6/Int Dir Anth 2/Apollo 76:377-83 Jl '62.

0700 CLARKE, ROBERT. Physician. Wrote two histories of Sierra Leone in 19th Century. Source: Foray, Cyril P., Historical Dictionary of Sierra Leone (1977), p 39.

0701 CLARKE, ROY RAINBIRD (1914-1963), England. Archeologist. Prehistoric & Roman archeology of England. Sources: Biog Index: 6/Int Dir Anth 2/ Illustrated

London News 242:777 My 18 '63.

0702 CLAUSON, GERARD (1891-). Philologist. Comparative Turkish philology. Source: Int Dir Anth 5.

0703 CLAUSS, LUDWIG FERDINAND (1892-). Ethnopsychology. Source: Nat Un Cat.

0704 CLAVIJERO, FRANCISCO JAVIER (1731-1787). Historian. Wrote a history of Mexico. Source: Briggs & Alisky, Historical Dictionary of Mexico (1981), p 48.

0705 CLEMENTS, FORREST EDWARD (1900-), Missouri, United States. Ethnologist. American ethnology & N. American archeology. Southern plains & lower Mississippi "Mound" buildings. Sources: Int Dir Anth 1, 2.

0706 CLERMONT-GANNEAU, CHARLES SIMON (1846-1923), Paris, France. Orientalist. Helped discover the "Moabite Stone"; explored Palestine, Syria, Tripolitania, Cyrenaica. Source: New Int Enc.

0707 CLIFFORD, ELSIE (1885-1976). Archeologist. Amateur archeologist who concentrated her digging in Gloucester (England); among her excavations were Roman villas and chambered long barrows, notably Bagendon. Sources: Biog Index: 11/Antiquity 51:3 Mr '77.

0708 CLINE, HOWARD FRANCIS (1915-). Anthropologist. Source: Nat Dir Lat Am.

0709 CLOSS, ALOIS (1893-), Neumarkt, Austria. Paleo-ethnologist. Paleoethnology involving reflections concerning Germany & Indo European peoples. Sources: Int Dir Anth 3, 5.

0710 CLOZEL, FRANÇOIS. Explorer. Led expedition to upper Sangha district of Central African Republic, 1894-1895. Source: Kalck, Pierre, Historical Dictionary of the Central African Republic (1980).

0711 CLUTESI, GEORGE CHARLES (1905-). Painter, folklorist. Sources: Biog Index: 10/Bibliog Profiles (Canadian Lib Assn) '75 p 34-36.

0712 COBA ROBALINO, JOSÉ MARÍA (1880-1935), Pillaro, Ecuador. Folklorist. Wrote extensively on the customs and folklore of Ecuador. Source: Bork & Maier, Historical Dictionary of Ecuador (1973), p 43.

0713 COBO, BERNABÉ (1582-1657). Missionary. Wrote description of classic Inca culture. Source: Heath, Dwight B., Historical Dictionary of Bolivia (1972), p 68-9.

0714 COCCHIARA, GIUSEPPE (1904-1965). Folklorist. Source: Nat Un Cat.

0715 CODERE, HELEN (1917-), Winnipeg, Manitoba, Canada. Anthropologist. Economic & political anthropology & social change among the Kwakiutl Indians; Rwanda. Sources: Int Dir Anth 3, 5.

0716 CODRINGTON, ROBERT HENRY (1830-1922), Wroughton, England. Anthropologist. Linguistics of Melanesian languages. Studied culture and languages of the Solomon Islands and northern New Hebrides. Fieldwork in Melanesia. Sources: Nat Un Cat/Craig & King, Historical Dictionary of Oceania (1981), p 55/Am Anth 25:130 Ja '23.

0717 CODY, BERTHA PARKER THURSTON (1907-1978), Charlotte, New York, United States. Archeologist, ethnologist. Anthropology & museum activities of New York State. Sources: Int Dir Anth 1, 2, 3/Anth News Jn '79.

0718 COE, JOFFRE LANNING (1916-), Greensboro, North Carolina, United States. Archeologist. Archeology of the Eastern U.S., especially North Carolina. Sources: Int Dir Anth 2, 3, 5.

0719 COEDÈS, GEORGES (1886-1969), Paris, France. Orientalist. Archeology & linguistics of India, S.E. Asia, and Indonesia. Sources: Biog Index: 9/Int Dir Anth 3.

0720 COELHO, GEORGE V (1918-). Ethnologist. Prejudices in cross-cultural education in U.S. Source: Int Dir Anth 5.

0721 COHEN, MARCEL (1884-), Paris, France. Socio-linguist.

Socio-linguistics. Sources: Int Dir Anth 3, 5.

0722 COILLARD, FRANÇOIS (1834-1904). Missionary. Wrote account of the Shona people of Rhodesia during the 1870s. Source: Rasmussen, R. Kent, Historical Dictionary of Rhodesia/Zimbabwe (1979), p 67.

0723 COKER, DANIEL (1785-), Baltimore, Maryland, United States. Civil servant. Left a diary describing the experiences of the first group of immigrants to Liberia. Source: Dunn & Holsoe, Historical Dictionary of Liberia (1985), p 42.

0724 COLANI, MADELEINE (1866-), Germany. Paleontology & paleobotany of Indo-China. Sources: Nat Un Cat/Int Dir Anth 1, 2.

0725 COLBACCHINI, ANTONIO (1881-). Priest. Wrote about culture of Bororo Indians of the Mato Grosso in Brazil. Source: Nat Un Cat.

0726 COLBERT, EDWIN HARRIS (1905-). Paleontologist. Sources: Biog Index: 2 3 & 7.

0727 COLE, FAY-COOPER (1881-1961), Plainwell, Michigan, United States. Anthropologist, archeologist, ethnologist. Physical anthropology & archeology of Mississippi Valley. Authority on peoples and cultures of Malaysia; published on Tinguian culture and folklore of Mindanao, Philippines. Sources: Biog Index: 6/Int Dir Anth 1, 2, 3/Am Anth 65:641-8 Je '63/ Am Antiq 27:573-5 Ap '62/Britannica Book of the Year 1962:505 '62/ N Y Times p 35 S 5 '61/Science 135:412-3 F '62.

0728 COLE, JOHN AUGUSTUS ABAYAMI, Rev, Ilorin, Nigeria. Missionary. Wrote ethnography on the "Poro" society of Sierra Leone; compiled a reader at basic level in the Mende language; studied herbal medicines. Source: Foray, Cyril P., Historical Dictionary of Sierra Leone (1977), p 42-3.

0729 COLLIE, GEORGE LUCIUS (1857-1954). Geologist, anthropologist. Sources: Biog Index: 5/Wisconsin. State Historical Society. Dictionary of Wisconsin Biography. The Society '60 p 83.

0730 COLLIER, DONALD (1911-), Sparkill, New York, United States. Archeologist, ethnologist, anthropologist. Plains Indians. Middle & S. America ethnology. Andean archeology. Sources: Int Dir Anth 3, 5/Nat Dir Lat Am.

0731 COLLIER, JOHN (1884-1968). Sociologist, anthropologist. Sources: Biog Index: 3 6 8 10 & 11/Philp, Kenneth R. John Collier's Crusade for Indian Reform, 1920-1954.

0732 COLLINGWOOD, ROBIN GEORGE (1889-1943), England. Historian, philosopher. Reconstructed Roman Britain from study of coins & inscriptions. Prehistoric archeology of Celtic countries. Sources: Columbia/Int Dir Anth 2.

0733 COLLINS, HENRY B (1899-), Geneva, Alabama, United States. Archeologist. Art & archeology of N. American Inuit. Sources: Int Dir Anth 1, 2, 3, 5.

0734 COLLIS, MAURICE (1889-), England. Orientalist. Sources: Biog Index: 3 4 & 9.

0735 COLLIVER, FREDERICK STANLEY (1908-). Geologist, prehistorian. Prehistoric & ethnographic bibliography of Queensland, Australia. Source: Int Dir Anth 5.

0736 COLQUHOUN, ARCHIBALD ROSS (1848-1914). Civil servant. First resident commissioner of Mashonaland, Rhodesia, 1890-1891; wrote period autobiography. Source: Rasmussen, R. Kent, Historical Dictionary of Rhodesia/Zimbabwe (1979), p 68.

0737 COLSON, ELIZABETH F (1917-), Hewitt, Minnesota, United States. Social anthropologist. Long term study of social & economic change in Southern Zambia. Sources: Int Dir Anth 3, 5.

0738 COLT, HARRIS DUNSCOMBE (1901- 1973). Philanthropist, archeologist. Sources: Biog Index: 10/Am Antiq Soc Proc 84 pt 1:21-4 '74.

0739 COLTON, HAROLD SELLERS

(1881- 1970), Philadelphia, Pennsylvania, United States. Archeologist, zoologist. Ancient populations of Northern Arizona. Sources: Biog Index: 9/Int Dir Anth 1, 2, 3/ Biological Bulletin 143:13-14 Ag '72.

0740 COMAS CAMPS, JUAN (1900-1979), Alayor, Minorca, Spain. Physical anthropologist, paleoanthropologist. Directed Monte Alban excavations in Mexico. Study of native American inhabitants & race. History of anthropology & prehistory of Mexico. Published on physical anthropology of Mexico & Central America. Sources: Biog Index: 13/Int Dir Anth 1, 2, 3, 5/ Who's Who in Latin America 3rd ed., Ronald Hilton ed., Stanford Univ. Press (Blaine Ethridge edition, 1971) vol. I, p 28-9/ Instituto de Investigaciones Antropologicas. In Memoriam: Juan Comas Camps. U N A M '80 (includes complete bibliog)/Anth News My '79/ Hispanic American Historical Review 60:95-6 F '80/ Human Organization 38:325-6 Fall '79.

0741 COMBS, JOSIAH HENRY (1886-1960), Kentucky, United States. Philologist, folklorist. Scholar of southern Appalachian dialect and folklore, specialized in music and stories. Sources: Biog Index: 6/Journal of American Folklore 75:354-5 O '62.

0742 COMHAIRE, JEAN LOUIS LEOPOLD (1913-), Belgium. Sociologist. Urbanization with special regard to social stratification in Africa & Haiti. Sources: Int Dir Anth 2, 3, 5.

0743 COMISEL, EMILIA (1913-). Folklorist. Ethnology & folkmusic of Romania. Source: Int Dir Anth 5.

0744 COMPTON, CARL BENTON (1905-). Anthropologist, archeologist. Precolumbian culture of Tzeltal Mayan area of Guatemala & Mexico. Sources: Int Dir Anth 5/Nat Dir Lat Am.

0745 COMTE, AUGUSTE (1798-1857), France. Philosopher. Social reformer. Founder of positivism. Analyzed human social evolution. Classified human intellectual development into three stages. Source: Columbia.

0746 CONNOLLY, CORNELIUS JOSEPH (1883-1954), Stellarton, Nova Scotia, Canada. Priest, anthropologist. Physical anthropology; brain morphology. Sources: Biog Index: 3 & 5/Int Dir Anth 1, 2, 3/ Kerr, J. Ernest. Imprint of the Maritimes. Christopher '59.

0747 CONTENAU, GEORGES (1877-1964), Laon, France. Archeologist. Wrote on Babylon and Assyria. Sources: Biog Index: 7/Rev Arch 2:69-71 Jl '64.

0748 CONTI-ROSSINI, CARLO (1872-1949), Italy. Ethnologist, linguist. Archeology of the Middle East & Ethiopia. Source: Nat Un Cat.

0749 CONTOLEON, ALEXANDRE-EMMANUEL (1859-1943), Smyrna, Greece. Archeologist. Conservator of antiquities at Delphi for many years. Sources: Biog Index: 1/Rev Arch series 6 25:207-8 Ap '46.

0750 CONVERSE, HARRIET ARNOT MAXWELL (1836-1903), Elmira, New York, United States. Anthropologist, folklorist. Myths and legends of the Iroquois in New York State; assembled significant collections of artifacts from the Iroquois and other members of the Six Nations. Sources: Siegel, P.A. & K.T. Finley, Women in the Scientific Search, Metuchen, N.J., Scarecrow, 1985/Notable American Women, 1607-1950, vol. I, Belknap Press '71, p 375-7.

0751 COOK, JAMES (1728-1779), England. Explorer, navigator, naval officer. Most known for discoveries in the S. Pacific. Conducted three voyages of exploration, 1768-1779, compiling geographic and ethnographic knowledge of Hawaii, Fiji, the Tuamotus and other S. Pacific Island groups. Sources: Columbia/Craig & King, Historical Dictionary of Oceania (1981), p 63.

0752 COOK, SHERBURNE FRIEND (1900- 1974), United States.

Anthropologist. Dated prehistoric bone by chemical analysis. Population studies. Sources: Nat Dir Lat Am/Anth News Ja '75.

0753 COOKE, CHARLES WYTHE (1887-), Baltimore, Maryland, United States. Geologist, paleontologist. Proposed geomorphological explanation for Mayan collapse: the silting up of the lakes near Mayan cities. Sources: Biog Index: 8/Nat Cyc Am Biog vol. K, p 45-48 '67.

0754 COOKE, CRANMER KENRICK (1906-), England. Bibliographer, archeologist. Stone Age Africa, especially south of the Congo River. Sources: Int Dir Anth 3, 5.

0755 COOKE, HERBERT BASIL SUTTON (1915-), Johannesburg, South Africa. Paleontologist. Fossil mammals & Pleistocene chronology of Africa. Sources: Int Dir Anth 2, 3, 5.

0756 COON, CARLTON STEVENS (1904- 1981), Wakefield, Massachusetts, United States. Archeologist, physical anthropologist. Prehistoric archeology. Ethnology & the study of races. Worked in Arabia, Balkans, N. Africa. Discovered (1939) Neanderthal man. Sources: Biog Index: 4 5 10 & 13/Int Dir Anth 1, 2, 3, 5/Columbia/ Coon, Carleton Stevens. Adventures & Discoveries the autobiography of Carleton S. Coon. Prentice-Hall '81/ Current Biography 42:42 Jl '81/Current Biography Yr Bk 1981:460 '82/ Expedition II 23:3 Summer '81/N Y Times p 19 Je 6 '81/ N Y Times Biog Service 11:15 Ja '80/Newsweek 97:107 Je 15 '81/ Time 117:84 Je 22 '81.

0757 COOPER, JOHN MONTGOMERY (1881-1949), Maryland, United States. Priest, anthropologist. Ethnology of Canadian Native Americans. Sources: Biog Index: 1 & 2/Int Dir Anth 1, 2/ Washington Academy of Science Journal 40:64 F '50/Am Anth 52:64-74 Ja '50/ Science 109:578 Je 3 '49/Catholic Education Review 47:435-41 S '49.

0758 COOPER, PAUL LEMEN (1909-1961), Cuba City, Wisconsin, United States. Archeologist. Midwest American archeology. Sources: Biog Index: 6/Int Dir Anth 1, 2, 3/Am Antiq 27:571-2 Ap '62.

0759 CORAL RÉMUSAT, GILBERTE de (1904-1943), France. Archeologist, Orientalist. Archeology of Southeast Asia, particularly Khmer art. Sources: Biog Index: 1 & 3/Isis 43 no 1:55 '52/ Rev Arch series 6 25:206-207 Ap '46.

0760 CORBETT, JOHN MAXWELL (1913-), New York, New York, United States. Anthropologist, archeologist. Archeology of the Americas. Sources: Int Dir Anth 3/Nat Dir Lat Am.

0761 CORBIN, HENRY (1903-1978), France. Orientalist. Source: Biog Index: 12.

0762 CORDEIRO da MATTA, JOAQUIN DIAS (1857-1894), Cabiri, Angola. Linguist, historian. Compiled a Kimbundu-Portugese dictionary (1893), a Kimbundu grammar (1892) and collected proverbs and riddles (1891); sought to revive traditional values of Angolan culture via his writings. Source: Martin, Phyllis M., Historical Dictionary of Angola (1980), p 40.

0763 CORDERO CRESPO, LUÍS (1883-1912), Surampalti, Ecuador. Lawyer. Compiled a dictionary of the Quechua language and worked on other dialects of Ecuador. Source: Bork & Maier, Historical Dictionary of Ecuador (1973), p 48.

0764 CORDIER, HENRI (1849-1925), New Orleans, Louisiana, United States. Historian. History of France & E. Asia. Sources: New Int Enc/Nat Un Cat.

0765 CORDUN FASTICOVSKY, VAL (1919-), Romania. Folklorist. Folktales, folk medicine & gypsies in Romania. Source: Int Dir Anth 5.

0766 CORNEVIN, ROBERT (1919-), Malesherbes, France. Historian, evolutionist. History of political, economic & cultural evolution in Africa; foremost scholar on the history of Togo. Sources: Int Dir Anth 5/DeCalo, Samuel,

Historical Dictionary of Togo (1976).

0767 CORRÊA, ANTONIO AUGUSTO MENDES (1888-). Anthropology of Portugal. Source: Nat Un Cat.

0768 CORRENTI, VENERANDO (1908-). Physical anthropologist. Skeletal architecture of the human pelvis. Anthropology applied to sports. Source: Int Dir Anth 5.

0769 CORSO, RAFFAELE (1883-), Nicotera, Italy. Anthropologist, ethnographer. Ethnology & folklore of Europe and E. & S. Africa. Sources: Int Dir Anth 1, 2, 3.

0770 CORTAZAR, AUGUSTO RAÚL (1910-), Salta, Argentina. Librarian, folklorist. Theory, method, technique & history of folklore in Argentina. Sources: Biog Index: 1/Int Dir Anth 3, 5/Library Journal 72:834 My 15 '47.

0771 CORTE, MATTEO DELLA (1875-1962). Archeologist. Directed excavations at Pompeii (Italy), 1928-1942; published extensively on results of work there. Sources: Biog Index: 7/Archeology 18:230 Autumn '65.

0772 CORTES, MANUEL JOSÉ (1811-1865). Historian. Wrote the first history of Bolivia. Source: Heath, Dwight B., Historical Dictionary of Bolivia (1972), p 84.

0773 CORY, GEORGE EDWARD (1862-1935). Historian. Wrote a multivolume history of the British settlement in Southern Africa to 1820. Source: Saunders, Christopher, Historical Dictionary of South Africa (1983), p 50.

0774 COTTER, JOHN LAMBERT (1911-), Denver, Colorado, United States. Bibliographer, archeologist. Historical sites archeology. Sources: Int Dir Anth 2, 3, 5.

0775 COTTRELL, LEONARD (1913-). Archeologist. Source: Biog Index: 8.

0776 COUNT, EARL WENDEL (1899-), Irvington, New York, United States. Anthropologist. Evolution of function; biosocial evolution of Homo sapiens; scientific concept of race. Sources: Int Dir Anth 1, 2, 3, 5.

0777 COUPERUS, MOLLEURUS (1906-). Paleoanthropologist. Dating techniques & cranial studies of fossils. Research into skin diseases in Tanganyika. Source: Int Dir Anth 5.

0778 COUTIL, LÉON (1856-1943), Andelys, France. Painter, archeologist. Archeology of Normandy. Sources: Biog Index: 1/Int Dir Anth 1, 2/Rev Arch series 6 25:63 Ja '46.

0779 COUVERT, S J, Fr. MICHEL GERMAIN de (1653-1715), Bayeux, France. Priest. Missionary in New France; wrote on N. American Indians. Source: Jes Rel.

0780 COUVREUR, SÉRAPHIN (1835-1919). Linguist. Chinese and French languages. Source: Nat Un Cat.

0781 COVARRUBIAS, MIGUEL (1904-1957), Mexico. Painter, archeologist, anthropologist. Indian art of Mexico and Central America. Sources: Biog Index: 1 2 3 4 5 & 9/Texas Quarterly il 12:279-80 Autumn '69.

0782 COVES, ELLIOT (1842-1899). Ornithologist. Elucidated the ethnology of the "Great West" region of the United States from the journals of the early explorers of this area. Source: Am Anth 2:187.

0783 COWAN, HENDRIK KAREL JAN (1907-), Batavia, Indonesia. Linguist. Statistical research dealing with linguistic relationships & quantitative classification of West German dialects. Comparative linguistics. Sources: Int Dir Anth 3, 5.

0784 COWELL, EDWARD BYLES (1826-1903), England. Orientalist. Source: Biog Index: 2.

0785 COWLEY, ARTHUR ERNEST (1861- 1931), England. Orientalist. *Jewish documents at the time of Ezra Aramaic papyri of the 5th Century BC*. Sources: Biog Index: 2/Dictionary of National Biography 1931-1940:194-5 '49 /Who Was Who 1929-1940.

0786 COX, JOHN HARRINGTON (1863-

1945), Illinois, United States. Folklorist. Focused on American regional folklore; created one of first major regional collections for the southern U.S. Sources: Biog Index: 1/Southern Folklore Quarterly 10:111 Mr '46/ Journal of American Folklore 59:315-6 Jl '46.

0787 CRAMPEL, PAUL (1864-1891), Nancy, France. Civil servant. Led expeditions in various areas of Central Africa: Gabon and Cameroon (1888), Central African Republic (1890/91). Source: Kalck, Pierre, Historical Dictionary of the Central African Republic (1980), p 34-5.

0788 CRAWFORD, JOHN (1783-1868). Physician. Wrote on languages and ethnology of Malaya and Indonesia. Source: Dictionary of International Biography.

0789 CRAWFORD, OSBERT GUY STANHOPE (1886-1957), Bombay, India. Archeologist. Archeology officer of British Ordinance Survey on field trips to Sudan, Near & Middle East. Sources: Biog Index: 4 5 & 11/Int Dir Anth 1, 2, 3/ Antiquity 50:18 J 6 S '76.

0790 CRAWLEY, ALFRED ERNEST (1869- 1924). Ethnologist. Marriage customs. Sports customs. Source: Nat Un Cat.

0791 CREMER, JEAN HENRI (1880-1920), Brive, France. Anthropologist, physician. Compiled a large body of folklore and linguistic data on western Upper Volta; compiled a grammar of the Kasena language (1924), a French-Fulani dictionary (1923) and ethnographic material on the Bobo (all posthumously issued). Source: McFarland, Daniel Miles, Historical Dictionary of Upper Volta (1978), p 71.

0792 CREPIEUL (Crespieul), S J, Fr. FRANCOIS de (1638-1702), Arras, France. Priest. Missionary in New France; wrote on N. American Indians. Source: Jes Rel.

0793 CRÉQUI-MONTFORT, GEORGES de. Linguist. Fieldwork in early 18th century Bolivia. Source: Heath, Dwight B., Historical Dictionary of Bolivia (1972), p 85.

0794 Crespieul, see: CREPIEUL.

0795 CREVAUX, JULES NICOLAS (1847- 1882). Explorer. Visited and explored the Chaco region of Bolivia. Source: Heath, Dwight B., Historical Dictionary of Bolivia (1972), p 86.

0796 CROFT, KENNETH (1917-), Ripley, Texas, United States. Linguist, anthropologist. Source: Nat Dir Lat Am.

0797 CROOKE, WILLIAM (1848-1923). Civil servant. Administrator in the Indian Civil Service; wrote extensively on ethnography of India. Sources: Columbia/Dictionary of International Biography/ Who Was Who, 1916-1928.

0798 CROW, JOE MEDICINE (1911-). Anthropologist. Source: Biog Index: 9.

0799 CROWLEY, CORNELIUS JOSEPH (1911-), New York, New York, United States. Source: Nat Dir Lat Am.

0800 CROWTHER, SAMUEL ADJAI (1806- 1892), Oshogun, Nigeria. Missionary. Compiled a vocabulary of Yoruba and translated New Testament into language of Nigeria. Source: Foray, Cyril P., Historical Dictionary of Sierra Leone (1977), p 49-51.

0801 CRUM, WALTER EWING (1865-1944), Capelrig, Renfrewshire, Scotland. Egyptologist. Specialist in Coptic studies; numerous publications and contributions to Egyptian publications dealing with the Copts; compiled a comprehensive dictionary of Coptic. Sources: Biog Index: 5 & 12/ Dictionary of National Biography 1941-1950:189-90, '59.

0802 CRUXENT, JOSÉ M (1911-), Barcelona, Spain. Anthropologist, archeologist, museologist. Aesthetic & visual components of art & technology in pre-Hispanic art forms in Meso-America & Venezuela. Sources: Int Dir Anth 3, 5.

0803 CUADRADO RUIZ, JUAN (1886-1952). Archeologist. Sources: Biog Index: 3/ Archivo Espanol de

Arte y Arqueologia 25 no 86:414 '52.

0804 CUBILLOS CHAPARRO, JULIO CAESAR (1919-), Colombia. Archeologist. Archeology of Andes, especially Colombia. Source: Int Dir Anth 5.

0805 CUERVO, RUFINO JOSÉ (1844-1911), Colombia. Linguist. Colloquial usage of Spanish in Colombia. Source: Davis, Robert H., Historical Dictionary of Colombia (1977), p 100.

0806 CUISINIER, JEANNE (1890-). Folklore & dance customs, especially in Asia. Source: Nat Un Cat.

0807 CULIN, STEWART (1858-1929), Philadelphia, Pennsylvania, United States. Ethnologist. Customs and games among Chinese & N. American Indians. Sources: New Int Enc/ Nat Un Cat.

0808 CULWICK, ARTHUR THEODORE (1905-), Ireland. Anthropologist. Extensive work in Africa especially Tanzania. Sources: Int Dir Anth 2/Nat Un Cat.

0809 CULWICK, GERALDINE MARY (1905-), England. Nutritionist, social anthropologist. Studied the food economy & nutrition of East and Central Africa, especially the Sudan & Tanzania. Sources: Int Dir Anth 2, 3.

0810 CUMMINGS, BYRON (1860-1954), Westville, New York, United States. Archeologist. Human culture in prehistoric Southwest U.S. Sources: Biog Index: 3 & 6/Int Dir Anth 1, 2, 3/ Nat Cyc Am Biog 44:568-9 '62/Am Anth 56:871-2 O '54.

0811 CUMMINS, HAROLD (1893-), Markleville, Indiana, United States. Anatomist. Studied the variation of dermatoglyphics between racial groups. Sources: Int Dir Anth 1, 2, 3.

0812 CUNHA, J GERSON DA (1842-1900), Arpora, Goa, India. Antiquarian, physician. Many papers on archeology before Royal Asiatic Society. Source: Dictionary of International Biography.

0813 CUNNINGHAM, ALEXANDER (1814- 1893). Archeologist, engineer. Pioneer of Indian archeology. Archeological Surveyor to governor of India, 1861-65; Director of the Archeological Survey, 1870-85. Sources: Biog Index: 8/Dictionary of International Biography.

0814 CUNNINGTON, EDWARD BENJAMIN HOWARD (ca. 1861-1950), England. Archeologist. Source: Museum Journal 50:299-300 Mr '51.

0815 CUNNINGTON, WILLIAM (1754-1810). Antiquarian, archeologist. Source: Biog Index: 10.

0816 CUNOW, HEINRICH (1862-1936). Anthropologist, historian, economist. Wrote especially about the Incas. Source: Nat Un Cat.

0817 CUOQ, Fr. JEAN ANDRÉ (1821-1898). Priest. Customs & languages of the Algonkians and Iroquois. Source: Nat Un Cat.

0818 CURLE, ALEXANDER ORMISTON (1866-1955). Archeologist. Director of the Royal Scottish Museum, 1919-1931; supervised many excavations for the Society of Antiquarians of Scotland. Sources: Biog Index: 3 & 4/Antiquaries Journal 35:284 Jl '55.

0819 CURR, EDWARD MICKLETHWAITE (1820-1889), Hobart, Tasmania, Australia. Ethnologist, antiquarian. Published a four-volume work, *The Australian Race*, 1886-1887, on Aboriginal languages and tribes. Sources: Biog Index: 2 & 10/Oceania 46:12-15 S '75.

0820 CURRELLY, CHARLES TRICK (1876-1957). Archeologist. Sources: Biog Index: 4 & 6/Art News 61:32-4+ F '63.

0821 CURTIN, JEREMIAH (1838-1906), near Milwaukee, Wisconsin, United States. Folklorist. Studied the languages & mythology of the Iroquois, Modoc, Yuchi, Potawatomi, Sauk, Shawnee & peoples of Northern California & Oregon for Bureau of American Ethnology. Published on the mythology & folklore of Ireland, Russia, the Slavs, the Magyars & the Mongols and on the ethnology of Western Mongols. Sources: Biog Index: 7/Slavic

Review 24:189-214 Je '65/ Am Anth 9:237-238 Ja '07.

0822 **CURTIS, NATALIE** (1875-1921), New York, New York, United States. Ethnomusicologist. Recorded American Indian and Black American music. Source: Notable American Women, 1607-1950, vol. I, Belknap Press '71, p 420-1.

0823 **CUSHING, FRANK HAMILTON** (1857-1900), Medina, New York, United States. Archeologist, ethnologist. Published on the Zuni and other Pueblo peoples. First professional anthropologist to live extensively with American Indians; famous for studies of Zuni Pueblo. Sources: Biog Index: 8 & 12/Smithsonian 10:96-8+ Ag '79/ Am Anth 2:354-80 Ap '00, 2:768-71 O '00.

0824 **ĆWIRKO-GODYCKI, MICHEL** (1901-), Poland. Physical anthropologist. Postnatal development of man. Sources: Int Dir Anth 1, 2, 5.

0825 **CZAPLICKA, MARIE ANTOINETTE** (-1921), Poland. Anthropologist. Anthropology of Siberian peoples & the Turks of Central Asia. Sources: Nat Un Cat/Am Anth 23:252-3 Ap '21.

0826 **CZEKANOWSKI, JAN** (1882-), Poland. Anthropologist. Ethnology, physical anthropology, & linguistics of Slavic peoples and also of West Africa, Congo, East & Southern Africa. Sources: Int Dir Anth 3/ Great Soviet Encyclopedia, New York, Macmillan (1982), v. 29, p 271/ Alekseev, V.P. "Pamiati Iana Chekanovskogo" Voprosy antropologii, 1966, no. 23/ "Pr. J. Czekanowski" Przeglad antropologiczny, 1965, v. 31, no. 2.

0827 **CZERMAK, WILHELM** (1889-1953), Austria. Archeologist, Egyptologist. Semitic languages. Sources: Biog Index: 3/Int Dir Anth 1, 2, 3/N Y Times p 15 Mr 14 '53.

0828 **DABBS, JACK AUTREY** (1914-), Murcury, Texas, United States. Linguist. Language in Mexico. Onomastics. Source: Nat Dir Lat Am.

0829 **DABLON, S J, Fr. CLAUDE** (1618-1697), Dieppe, France. Priest. Missionary in New France; wrote on N. American Indians. Source: Jes Rel.

0830 **DAHLGREN-JORDAN, BARBRO** (1912-), Mexico. Ethnologist. Ethnography of prehispanic to 19th century Mixtecs of Oaxaca, Mexico. Socio-economic importance of myths for belief & religion. Wrote *La Mixteca, Su Cultura e Historia Prehispanicas* (2nd ed.). Source: Int Dir Anth 5.

0831 **DAIGRE, JOSEPH Rev.** Missionary. Wrote a volume on his experiences in Ubangui-Shari which depicts excessive behavior of the colonial government. Source: Kalck, Pierre, Historical Dictionary of the Central African Republic (1980), p 36.

0832 **DAL', VLADIMIR IVANOVIC** (1801-1872). Folklorist, lexicographer. Source: Biog Index: 10.

0833 **DALMAS, S J, Fr. ANTOINE** (1636-1693), Tours, France. Priest. Missionary in New France; wrote on N. American Indians. Source: Jes Rel.

0834 **DALTON, EDWARD TUITE** (1815-1880). Military officer. Wrote: "The Descriptive Ethnology of Bengal" (1872). Source: Dictionary of International Biography.

0835 **DALTON, ORMONDE MADDOCK** (1866-1945), Cardiff, Wales. Archeologist. Served on British Museum staff; wrote numerous books and articles on Near Eastern and European prehistoric collections; translator of several classical works as well. Sources: Biog Index: 5/ Dictionary of National Biography 1941-1950 p 195-6 '59.

0836 **DAMANE, MOSEBI** (1919-), Masitise, Lesotho. Historian. Foremost Basotho historian: wrote extensively on Basotho praise poems, Moorosi's Rebellion, and a general history of Lesotho. Source: Haliburton, Gordon, Historical Dictionary of Lesotho (1977), p 40-1.

0837 **DAMPIER, WILLIAM** (1652-1715), East Coker, Somersetshire, England. Explorer. Wrote an account of several years privateering in the Pacific which describes the Marianas Islands. Sources: Columbia/Craig & King, Historical Dictionary of Oceania (1981), p 68-9.

0838 DANBY, HERBERT (1889-1953), England. Orientalist. Sources: Biog Index: 3/Illustrated London News 222:579 Ap 11 '53.

0839 DANIEL, GLYN EDMUND (1914-1986). Archeologist. Specialized in the megalithic chamber tombs of Britain & France. The first systematic historian of archeology. Brought archeology to the general public. Source: Anth News 28:3:3.

0840 DANIEL, JOHN FRANKLIN (1910-1948), Ann Arbor, Michigan, United States. Archeologist. Directed excavations in Turkey & Cyprus. Sources: Biog Index: 1 & 2/Am J Arch 52:front O '48/ N Y Times p 76 D 19 '48.

0841 DANIELLI, JACOPO (-1901). Industrialist. Published on the anatomy of the peoples of Nias & Engano; specialist in morphology of human dentition. Source: Am Anth 5:176 '03.

0842 DANKAH, JOSEPH KWANE KYORETINI BOAKYE (1895-1965), Bepong, Kwawu, Gold Coast, Ghana. Lawyer, author, philosopher, naturalist, politician. Politician in the Gold Coast Colony. Wrote in support of idea that Akan people were descended from the inhabitants of the medieval empire of Ghana. Source: Dictionary of African Biography: vol. 1, Ethiopia-Ghana. New York: Reference Publications Inc., 1977, p 230-3.

0843 DANZEL, THEODORE WILHELM (1886-1954), Germany. Anthropologist. Cultural psychology, general ethnology & psychology of religion in Mexico, Africa & China. Sources: Dictionary of Universal Biography/Int Dir Anth 1, 2, 3.

0844 DAPPER, OLFERT (1639-1689). Geographer, traveler. Wrote descriptions of much of Asia and Africa. Of particular note for ethnographers are his descriptions of West African coastal states, Kingdom of Kongo and land of the Hottentots in Southern Africa. Source: Foray, Cyril P., Historical Dictionary of Sierra Leone (1977), p 53-4.

0845 DARK, PHILIP JOHN CROSSKEY (1918-). Anthropologist. Aesthetic & visual anthropology. Art & technology in Africa, Oceania, Northwest Coast of North America & among Mixtecs of Mexico. Sources: Int Dir Anth 5/Nat Dir Lat Am.

0846 DART, RAYMOND ARTHUR (1893-), Brisbane, Australia. Paleontologist, physical anthropologist. Extracted "Taung Baby" & named the discovery Australopithecus africanus. Worked on protoculture of Negro, Hottentot & Bushmen. Demonstrated that man had originated in Africa; showed that in transformation from ape to man brain enlargement came late: evolution was "mosaic" in character. Sources: Int Dir Anth 1, 2, 5/ International Encyclopedia of the Social Sciences, v. 18.

0847 DARWIN, CHARLES ROBERT (1809-1882), Shrewsbury, England. Naturalist. Theory of organic evolution through natural selection. Sources: Columbia/Dictionary of National Biography/ Charles, Darwin, Thomas uxley, ed. by Gavin de Beer, London, Oxford Univ. Press, 1974/ Bettany, George Thomas, Life of Charles Darwin, London, W. Scott, 1887.

0848 DARWIN, FRANCIS (1848-1925), England. Botanist. Assistant to and biographer of his father, Charles Darwin. Source: Columbia.

0849 DAS, SUDHIR RANJAN (1910-), India. Physical anthropologist. Human genetics research. Source: Int Dir Anth 5.

0850 DASTUGUE, JEAN (1910-). Paleopathologist. Pathology of Cro-Magnon. Source: Int Dir Anth 5.

0851 DAUMAS, FRANÇOIS (1812-1871), France. Missionary. Traveled into the Blue Mountains (Lesotho) with Thomas Arbousset in 1836, left account of journey. Source: Haliburton, Gordon, Historical

Dictionary of Lesotho (1977), p 41-2.

0852 **DAVENPORT, CHARLES BENEDICT** (1866-1944), Stamford, Colorado, United States. Zoologist, demographer. Development of human child. Sources: International Encyclopedia of the Social Sciences, v. 6/ Int Dir Anth 1, 2.

0853 **DAVID, JOSÉ HENRIQUE SANTOS** (1919-). Physical anthropologist. Genetic polymorphism in growth & development. Source: Int Dir Anth 5.

0854 **DAVID-NEEL, ALEXANDRA** (1868-1969), France. Orientalist, explorer. Sources: Biog Index: 8 9 & 11.

0855 **DAVIDSON, BASIL** (1914-), Bristol, England. Africanist, historian. History and culture of Africa. Source: International Who's Who 82-83.

0856 **DAVIDSON, DANIEL SUTHERLAND** (1900-1952), Cohoes, New York, United States. Anthropologist. Australian and American ethnology. Sources: Biog Index: 3/Int Dir Anth 1, 2, 3/N Y Times p 48 D 28 '52/ Am Anth 56:873-6 O '54.

0857 **DAVIDSON, JAMES WIGHTMAN** (1915-1975), Wellington, New Zealand. Historian. Wrote a four-volume geographical handbook of the Pacific Islands, and many articles and books on Pacific history. Source: Craig & King, Historical Dictionary of Oceania (1981), p 69.

0858 **DAVIDSON, LEVETTE JAY** (1894-1957), Eureka, Illinois, United States. Folklorist. Folk culture of the American West. Sources: Biog Index: 5/Journal of American Folklore 71:150-1 Ap '58.

0859 **DAVIES, ANNA MacPHERSON** (1881-1965), Salonika, Greece. Egyptologist. Specialized in copying Egyptian hieroglyphics and tomb paintings, especially those of Thebes. Sources: Biog Index: 7/Journal of Egyptian Archaeology 51:196-9 D '65.

0860 **DAVIES, OLIVER** (1905-). Archeologist. South African prehistory, especially in the Iron Age. Sources: Int Dir Anth 1, 5.

0861 **DAVIS, ARTHUR KYLE** (1897-1972). Folklorist. Sources: Biog Index: 10/Southern Folklore Quarterly 37:127-9 Je '73.

0862 **DAVIS, EDWARD MOTT** (1918-), United States. Archeologist. U.S. prehistoric Caddoan & Paleolithic Indian archeology. Radiocarbon dating. Balkan prehistory. Neolithic to Iron Age in Yugoslavia. Source: Int Dir Anth 5.

0863 **DAVIS, EMMA LOU** (1905-), United States. Archeologist. Graphic & plastic arts. Psychotherapy, aging, status of women, population pressures in the U.S. Source: Int Dir Anth 5.

0864 **DAVIS, MARY GOULD** (1882-1956). Folklorist, librarian. Sources: Biog Index: 2 4 & 8.

0865 **DAVIS, THOMAS** (1918-). Physician, anthropologist. Sources: Biog Index: 3/Davis, Thomas & Davis, Lydia (Henderson) Doctor to the Islands. Little '54/Time 60:61-2 N 17 '52, 60:59-60 S 15 '52.

0866 **DAVIS, WILBUR ARTHUR** (1915-). Archeologist. North American prehistoric archeology; Pacific marine environment; theory of technological systems. Source: Int Dir Anth 5.

0867 **DAWKINS, WILLIAM BOYD** (1838-1929). Archeologist. Early man in Britain. Source: Columbia.

0868 **DAWSON, CARL ADDINGTON** (1887-1964), Prince Edward Island, Canada. Sociologist, anthropologist. Set up sociology as a discipline in Canada; focused his field research on western Canadian frontier. Sources: Biog Index: 7/American Sociological Review 29:752-3 O '64.

0869 **DAWSON, GEORGE MERCER** (1849-1901), Pictou, Nova Scotia, Canada. Geologist, ethnologist. Ethnographer of Canadian Rockies, British Columbia & Yukon Valley; wrote on the Haida, Kwakiutl and Shuswap peoples; headed 1896 Ethnological Survey of Canada. Source: Am Anth 3:159-163 Ja '01.

0870 DAWSON, JOHN WILLIAM (1820-1899), Pictou, Nova Scotia, Canada. Botanist, geologist. Pioneer in paleobotany. Published on the Hebrew scriptures & human evolution. Sources: Columbia/Am Anth 2:187 Ja '00.

0871 DAWSON, WARREN ROYAL (1888-1968), Ealing, England. Egyptologist. Compiled *Who Was Who In Egyptology*, (1951); specialized in medicine and documents of Ancient Egypt. Sources: Biog Index: 9/Journal of Egyptian Archaeology 55:211 Ag '69.

0872 DAY, DONALD (1899-). Folklorist. Sources: Biog Index: 3/Murrow, Edward Roscoe. This I Believe: 2. Simon & Schuster '54 p 46-7.

0873 DAY, GORDON MALCOLM (1911-). Ethnohistorian. Evaluation of oral traditions. American Society Ethnohistory. Source: Int Dir Anth 5.

0874 DEBETS, GEORGII FRANTSEVICH (1905-1969), Russia. Anthropologist. Studied the racial and ethnic backgrounds of the peoples of the U.S.S.R. Sources: Great Soviet Encyclopedia, New York, Macmillan (1975), v. 7, p 132 /"Debets, G.F." Sovetskaia etnografiia, 1969, no. 1.

0875 DEBO, ANGIE ELBERTHA (1890-), Kansas, United States. Librarian. Ethnohistorian of Choctaw Indians, historian of Indians in United States. Source: Glenna Matthews and Gloria Valencia-Weber, "Against Great Odds: The Life of Angie Debo," Organization of American Historians, OAH Newsletter, May 1985, p 8-11.

0876 DÉCHELETTE, JOSEPH (1862-1914), Roanne, France. Archeologist. Archeology of France. Sources: Biog Index: 6/Antiquity 36:245-7 D '62/Rev Arch 2:219-20 O '62/ Rev Arch II:323-25 1914/Livre d'or de Joseph Dechelette, Centenaire, 1862-1962.

0877 DECORSE, LIEUTENANT. Wrote account of state of the Sara region of the Central African Republic in early 20th century which depicted effect of slave raids on local population. Source: Kalck, Pierre, Historical Dictionary of the Central African Republic (1980), p 38.

0878 DEEVEY, EDWARD S (1914-). Ecologist. Research in ecology, paleolimnology in Meso-America. Source: Int Dir Anth 5.

0879 DEFFONTAINES, PIERRE (1894-). Geographer, ethnologist. Source: Biog Index: 8.

0880 DEFRISE-GUSSENHOVEN, ÉLISABETH (1912-), Antwerp, Belgium. Physical anthropologist. Statistical analysis in human biometry. Sources: Int Dir Anth 3, 5.

0881 DEGERBØL, MAGNUS (1895-), Denmark. Zoologist, archeologist. Domestication of recent prehistoric & protohistoric vertebrates. Inuit & Norse archeology. Sources: Int Dir Anth 1, 2, 3, 5.

0882 Degonnor, see: GONNOR.

0883 DEHN, WOLFGANG (1909-). Archeologist. Celtic & Megalithic archeology in Central & Western Europe. Source: Int Dir Anth 5.

0884 De JARNETTE, DAVID LLOYD (1907-), Bessemer, Alabama, United States. Archeologist. Historic & prehistoric archeology of the Weiss Reservoir, Alabama. Sources: Int Dir Anth 1, 2, 3, 5.

0885 De KIEWET, CORNELIS (1903-). Historian. Wrote several books describing British policy under the Empire toward South Africa. Source: Saunders, Christopher, Historical Dictionary of South Africa (1983), p 52.

0886 De LAET, SIGFRIED JAN LEO (1914-). Archeologist. Historic & prehistoric archeology of Bronze & Iron Age in Benelux, Belgium. Source: Int Dir Anth 5.

0887 DELAFOSSE, MAURICE (1870-1926), France. Africanist, administrator, ethnologist, linguist. Wrote extensively on language, culture & history of many ethnic groups in West Africa. Source: Imperato, Pascal J., Historical Dictionary of Mali (1977), p 37-8.

0888 DELAGE, FRANCK (1873-1950), France. Archeologist. Prehistoric

& Gallo-Roman archeology. **Sources**: Biog Index: 3/Int Dir Anth 1, 2/Rev Arch series 6 41:196-7 Ap '53.

0889 De LAGUNA, FREDERICA ANNIS (1906-). Anthropologist. Ethnography of Inuit of Alaska and Northwest Greenland. **Sources**: Biog Index: 10/Int Dir Anth 5/Biography News 2:512 My '75.

0890 DELANY, MARTIN ROBINSON (1812-1885). Ethnologist, army officer. **Sources**: Biog Index: 6 8 & 9.

0891 DELARUE, PAUL ALFRED (1889-1956), Saint-Dider, France. Folklorist. Specialist in folktales of France. **Sources**: Biog Index: 4/Journal of American Folklore 70:262-3 Jl '57.

0892 DELBRUCK, RICHARD (1875-), Germany. Biologist, archeologist. Nobel prize for physiology or medicine. **Sources**: Biog Index: 6 & 8/Int Dir Anth 1, 2/Science 166:479-81 O 24 '69.

0893 De LEEUWE, JULES (1913-). Sociologist. Social organization & stratification in Australia. Replication in cross-cultural research of the marriage system. **Source**: Int Dir Anth 5.

0894 DELORIA, ELLA CARA (1888-1971), South Dakota, United States. Anthropologist, linguist. Linguistics & ethnology of Sioux especially Oglala & Dakota. **Sources**: Biog Index: 9 11 & 13/ Notable American Women, the Modern Period. vol. IV, Belknap Press '80, p 183-5.

0895 DELOUGAZ, PINHAS PIERRE (1901-1975). Archeologist, Orientalist. Specialist in Iranian archeology; directed excavations at Chogha for the Oriental Institute of Chicago; also specialized in archeology of Mesopotamia, in particular the Diyala region. **Sources**: Biog Index: 10/N Y Times p 42 Ap 2 '75.

0896 de LUMLEY, HENRY, Marseilles, France. Archeologist, human paleontologist. Human paleontology. **Sources**: Biog Index: 10/ Mary, Leakey, Disclosing the Past, an Autobiography, Leakey, Mary D., McGraw-Hill, 1986, p 174.

0897 DEMBINSKA, MARIE (1916-). Historian. European medieval technology & social change. **Source**: Int Dir Anth 5.

0898 DEMIEVILLE, PAUL (1894-1979), Lausanne, Switzerland. Sinologist. Professor Emeritus of the College de France; co-editor of *T'oung Pao*; wrote extensively on Sinological and Buddhist themes. **Sources**: Biog Index: 12/American Oriental Society Journal 99:553 Jl S '79.

0899 DENHAM, DIXON (1786-1828), London, England. Explorer. Visited Chari River area and Lake Chad region (in present-day Nigeria, Niger, Cameroon and Chad), 1822; visited Borneo including its capital, Kuka, 1823-24; left a journal account of the trip. **Sources**: Levine & Nye, Historical Dictionary of Cameroon (1974), p 271/ Dictionary of National Biography, v. 5, p 792.

0900 DENIKER, JOSEPH (1852-1918), France. Naturalist, anthropologist. **Sources**: Dictionary of Universal Biography/ Encyclopedia Britannica, 11th ed.

0901 DENNIS, GEORGE (1814-1898). Archeologist. Wrote: *Cities and Cemeteries of Etruria*, 1848; fieldwork and antiquarian excavations for the British Museum in Benghazi (Libya), Smyrna (Turkey) and Palermo (Italy). **Sources**: Biog Index: 10/Antiquity 48:190-95 S '74.

0902 DENON, DOMINIQUE VIVANT (1747-1825). Archeologist. Brought artifacts to Louvre. **Source**: Columbia.

0903 DENSMORE, FRANCES THERESA (1867-1957), Red Wing, Minnesota, United States. Musician, ethnomusicologist. Major recording and study of American Indians. **Sources**: Biog Index: 1 4 11 & 13/Int Dir Anth 1, 2, 3/ Notable American Women, the Modern Period. vol. IV, Belknap Press '80, p 185-6/ Who Was Who In America, vol 3, 1960 p 222.

0904 DEONNA, WALDEMAR (1880-1959), Cannes, France. Archeologist. Wrote on ancient civilization and art, particularly that of Greece; also on Swiss art, especially that of the Geneva region. Sources: Biog Index: 5/Rev Arch 2:103-6 Jl '59.

0905 DEPELCHIN, HENRI (1822-1900). Missionary. Traveled widely on the Limpopo Basins of Southern Africa and Zambezi, 1879-1882; left account of these travels. Source: Rasmussen, R. Kent, Historical Dictionary of Rhodesia/Zimbabwe (1979), p 76.

0906 DERANIYAGALA, PAUL EDWARD PIERIS (1900-), Ceylon. Archeologist. Paleolithic & Neolithic archeology; human paleontology in Ceylon. Sources: Int Dir Anth 3, 5.

0907 DERRY, DOUGLAS ERITH (1874-1961), Middlesex, England. Egyptologist, physical anthropologist. Physical anthropology of Egypt, Nubia, Syria. Sources: Biog Index: 5 & 12/Int Dir Anth 2, 3.

0908 DESKAHEH, CHIEF (ca. 1872-1925). Iroquois leader. Prominent in Canadian Indian affairs. Source: Am Anth 28:328 Ja '26.

0909 DESMOND, GERALD RAYMOND (1904-), Ellensburg, Washington, United States. Ethnologist. The Yakima Band of Sahaptin-speaking N. American Indians. Sources: Int Dir Anth 3, 5.

0910 DESPLAGNES, LOUIS. Archeologist, ethnographer. Directed an archeological expedition in Central Mali, 1907-1908, in Inland Niger Delta; published first detailed study of region in 1907 monograph. Source: Imperato, Pascal J., Historical Dictionary of Mali (1977), p 37.

0911 Dessalines d' Orbigny, see: ORBIGNY, ALCIDE DESSALINES d'.

0912 De TERRA, HELMUT (1900-), Marburg, Germany. Anthropologist, paleontologist, archeologist. Discovered the remains of "Tepexpan Man" near Mexico City in 1947. Sources: Biog Index: 1/New Yorker 23:21-2 My 10 '47.

0913 DETWEILER, ALBERT HENRY (1906-1970), Perkassie, Pennsylvania, United States. Archeologist, architectural historian. Participated in and wrote about numerous excavations throughout Middle East; expert on ancient architecture. Sources: Biog Index: 8 9 & 10/Nat Cyc Am Biog 55:152-3 '74.

0914 DEUEL, THORNE (1890-1984), Millbrook, New York, United States. Ethnologist, archeologist, anthropologist. Cultural typology of primitive cultures. Analyzed & compared whole (e.g., Hopi, Cheyenne, etc.) cultures. Indian history of the Middle West. Sources: Int Dir Anth 1, 2, 3, 5/Anth News (May 1984) p 3.

0915 DEVEREUX, GEORGE (1908-1985). Anthropologist, psychologist. Did fieldwork on the Mohave and Hopi (U.S.), also in Melanesia and in Vietnam; studied sex and childrearing practices. Source: Anth News 4/86:3.

0916 De WAAL MALEFIJT, ANNEMARIE (1914-), Amsterdam, Netherlands. Researcher on Caribbean anthropology, culture change, Javanese in Surinam, history of anthropology. Source: American Men and Women of Science, ed. by J.C. Press, 12th ed., New York, Bowker, 1973, p 540 (Soc. & Behav. Sci.).

0917 DIAMOND JENNESS, C C (1886-1969), New Zealand. Anthropologist. Inuit & Indian peoples of Canada. First to call attention to the Dorset Inuit culture. Source: Am Anth F '71.

0918 DIAS, MARGOT (1908-), Nuremberg, Germany. Ethnologist. Traditional art & musical instruments in Mozambique & Angola. Sources: Int Dir Anth 3, 5.

0919 DIAS de DEUS, ANTONIO (1901-1955). Archeologist. Sources: Biog Index: 4/ Archivo Espanol de Arte y Arqueologia 28 no 1:193 '55.

0920 DÍAZ de GUZMÁN, RUY (1560-1629), Asuncion, Paraguay. Explorer, historian. First native historian of Paraguay. Published the first history of the Rio de la

Plata, Argentina, from its discovery and conquest up to 1573. Sources: Wright & Nelsham, Historical Dictionary of Argentina (1978), p 246 /Kolinski, Charles J., Historical Dictionary of Paraguay (1973), p 84.

0921 DÍAZ DEL CASTILLO, BERNAL (1495-1581), Spain. Soldier. Wrote the best account of Cortes' conquest of Mexico. Source: Briggs & Alisky, Historical Dictionary of Mexico (1981), p 67-8.

0922 DÍAZ MACHICADO, PARFERIO (1909-), Bolivia. Historian. Wrote multi-volume history of Bolivia. Source: Heath, Dwight B., Historical Dictionary of Bolivia (1972), p 90.

0923 DÍAZ UNGRÍA, ADELAIDA G de (1913-). Physical anthropologist. Microevolutionist. Worked among the Yupa of Venezuela. Source: Int Dir Anth 5.

0924 DÍAZ VASCONCELOS, LUÍS ANTONIO (1906-), El Salvador. Historian. Wrote on law and legal institutions among the Maya. Source: Moore, Richard E., Historical Dictionary of Guatemala (1973), p 75.

0925 DICKESON, MONTROVILLE W (fl-1837). Archeologist. Sources: Biog Index: 11/Design Quarterly 101:32-4 N '76.

0926 DIEHL, CHARLES (1859-1944), Strasbourg, France. Archeologist. Major figure in Byzantine studies; had great influence on study of classical world in general. Sources: Biog Index: 2/Rev Arch series 6 35:93-7 Ja '50.

0927 DIETERLEN, GERMAINE (1903-), France. Ethnologist. African religion, myths, rituals, art & pharmacopias. Worked particularly on Dogon people of Mali. Sources: Int Dir Anth 3, 5.

0928 DIETERLEN, HERMAN (1850-1933), France. Missionary. Wrote extensively on Basotho history and culture in both French and Sesotho. Source: Haliburton, Gordon, Historical Dictionary of Lesotho (1977), p 42-3.

0929 DIETSCHY, HANS (1912-), Switzerland. Ethnologist. Social organization & kinship system of Karaja Indians of Brazil. Sources: Int Dir Anth 2, 3, 5.

0930 DIGGS, IRENE (1906-), Monmouth, Illinois, United States. Anthropologist, ethnologist. Ethnohistory of descendants of Africans in the U.S. & Latin America. Sources: Int Dir Anth 3, 5/Nat Dir Lat Am.

0931 DILLON, PETER (1788-1847), Martinique, West Indies. Explorer, trader. Wrote an account of the customs, religion and cannibalism of the people of Vanuatu (New Hebrides). Source: Craig & King, Historical Dictionary of Oceania (1981), p 72.

0932 DIXON, ROLAND BURRAGE (1875- 1934), Worcester, Massachusetts, United States. Anthropologist, ethnologist. Specialist in the ethnology of California; fieldwork in New Zealand, Tasmania, Australia & Fiji; first to use a combination of physical traits to describe a race; published on human migration, Oceanic mythology. Wrote on mixed ancestry of American Indians and on similarities in objects used by early man; created major collection of Oceanic artifacts at Peabody Museum. Sources: Biog Index: 3 & 4/Nat Cyc Am Biog 39:237-8 '54/ Am Anth 38:291-300 Ap '36.

0933 DOBIE, JAMES FRANK (1888-1964). Folklorist. Sources: Biog Index: 3 4 5 7 8 9 10 & 11.

0934 DOBRIZHOFFER, MARTIN (1717-1791), Graz, Styria, Austria. Naturalist. Catholic missionary in Paraguay. Source: Dictionary of Universal Biography.

0935 DOBZHANSKII, THEODOSIUS GRIGORIEVICH (1900-1975), Nemirov, Russia. Zoologist, geneticist. Published 43 papers on the "genetics of natural populations". Genetic basis of human evolution. Genetic diversity. Sources: Biog Index: 11/Int Dir Anth 5/ International Encyclopedia of the Social Sciences, v. 18/ Current Biography

Yr Bk 1976:466 '77/Zygon 10:449-50 D '75.

0936 DOCKSTADER, FREDERICK J (1919-). Anthropologist, ethnologist, museologist. Museum director. Arts & aesthetics of N. American Indians. Sources: Biog Index: 7/Int Dir Anth 5/Nat Dir Lat Am/ Nat Cyc Am Biog J:518-9 '64.

0937 DODGE, ERNEST STANLEY (1913-1980), Trenton, Maine, United States. Museum director, anthropologist, ethnohistorian. Material culture of the Polynesian Islands. Ethnohistory & art of N. American Indians. Sources: Int Dir Anth 2, 3, 5/Biog Index: 12/N Y Times p D-13 F 11 '80/ N Y Times Biog Service 11:191 F '80/Publishers Weekly 217:16 Mr 14 '80/ American Antiquarian Society Proceedings 90:299-302 O 15 '80.

0938 Doerpfeld, Wilhelm, see: DORPFELD, WILHELM.

0939 DOI, TAKUJI (1912-), Japan. Ethnologist, folklorist. Burial customs, cemeteries & tombstones. Buddhist rites for the dead in Japan. Source: Int Dir Anth 5.

0940 DOKE, CLEMENT MARTYN (1893-1980), Bristol, England. Anthropologist, linguist. Comparative history of Bantu languages, grammar and linguistics. Sources: Int Dir Anth 1, 3/African Studies 39:1 (1980), p 99-102.

0941 DOLE, GERTRUDE EVELYN (1915-). Anthropologist, ethnologist. Kuikuru & Amahuaca cultures of Brazil and Peru respectively. Comparative kinship nomenclature & organization. Foundations of contemporary evolutionism. Sources: Int Dir Anth 5/Nat Dir Lat Am.

0942 DOLLARD, JOHN (1900-), Wisconsin, United States. Anthropologist. Interdisciplinary anthropological integration of race relations. Tested theories with cross-cultural data. Source: International Encyclopedia of the Social Sciences, v. 18.

0943 DOLORES, JUAN (1880-1948), Mexico. Construction teamster. Alfred Kroeber's, and J. Alden Mason's Papago informant; wrote on Papago kinship and folklore. Source: Am Anth 51:96-7 Ja '49.

0944 DOMOTOR, TEKLA (1914-). Folklorist. Hungarian customs, folk customs, drama, theatre & poetry. Source: Int Dir Anth 5.

0945 DONNADIEU, ALPHONSE-ALEXANDRE (1877-1959), Caylus, France. Physician, archeologist. Archeology of the Frejus Region, France. Sources: Biog Index: 5/Rev Arch 2:98-9 Jl '59.

0946 DOR, LEOPOLD (1881-1960), Marseille, France. Lawyer, archeologist. Wrote about ancient Greeks. Sources: Biog Index: 6/Rev Arch 1:213-4 Ap '61.

0947 DORPFELD, WILHELM (1853-1940), Germany. Archeologist. Director, German Archaeological Institute in Athens. Greek archeology and architecture. Sources: Biog Index: 2/Int Dir Anth 1/Isis 41 no 1:56 '50.

0948 DORSEY, GEORGE AMOS (1868-1931). Anthropologist, museum curator. Raised large sums to support anthropological research and assemble ethnographic collections for museums; popularized science; published on Arapaho dance. Sources: Biog Index: 3/Am Anth 54:162-3 Ap '52.

0949 DORSINFANG-SMETS, ANNIE (1911-). Archeologist, ethnologist. Social anthropology. Joking relationships. Mexican archeology. Source: Int Dir Anth 5.

0950 DORSON, RICHARD MERCER (1916- 1981), New York, New York, United States. Anthropologist, folklorist. Folklore of North America; directed Indiana University Folklore Institute. Sources: Int Dir Anth 3/Folklore 93:112 '82.

0951 DOUDIET, ELLENORE W (1912-). Archeologist. Building methods, history & food habits in U.S. Source: Int Dir Anth 5.

0952 DOUGLAS, FREDERICK HUNTINGTON (1897-1956), Evergreen, Colorado, United States. Anthropologist, museum curator. Native American ethnography. Collected

U.S. Indian & Oceanic art; used museum exhibits to show viewer the aesthetic merit of cultures popularly considered "inferior" or "primitive". Sources: Biog Index: 4 & 5/Int Dir Anth 1, 2, 3/Am Anth 60:737 Ag '58.

0953 DOUGLASS, ANDREW ELLICOTT (1819-1901), United States. Archeologist. Florida Indians. Source: Am Anth 3:586-7 Jl '01.

0954 DOVER, CEDRIC (-1961), Calcutta, India. Ethnologist, entomologist. Studied contemporary attempts to develop a scientific study of minority problems. Sources: Biog Index: 6/Nature 193:625-6 F 17 '62.

0955 DOZIER, EDWARD PASQUAL (1916- 1971), New Mexico, United States. Anthropologist. Native American. Scholar & interpreter of Pueblo Indian life. Advanced the theory of "compartmentalization" to explain the durability of native life. Sources: Biog Index: 2 9 & 11/Newsweek, Mr 24 '52/Am Anth 74:740 Jn '72.

0956 DRAGHI LUCERO, JUAN (1897-), Lujan de Cuyo, Argentina. Folklorist. Recorded regional folklore of various Argentinean provinces. Source: Wright & Nelsham, Historical Dictionary of Argentina (1978), p 254.

0957 DRAGO, CIRO (1895-1960). Archeologist. Sources: Biog Index: 6/Bollettino d'Arte 46:379-80 O '61.

0958 DRAKE, FRANCIS (1540-1596), Devonshire, England. Navigator. Explored much of New World. Source: Columbia.

0959 DRAKE, ST. CLAIR (1911-). Anthropologist. Sources: Biog Index: 1/Current Biography 7:8-11 Ja '46/ Current Biography Yr Bk revised 1946:103-6 '47.

0960 DREUILLETE, S J, Fr. GABRIEL (1613-1681), Gurat, France. Priest. Missionary in New France; wrote on N. American Indians. Source: Jes Rel.

0961 DRIBERG, JACK HERBERT (1888-1946), India. Anthropologist. Social anthropology of Africa. Sources: Biog Index: 1/Int Dir Anth 2/ New Statesman & Nation 31:117 F 16 '46/Nature 157:257-8 Mr 2 '46.

0962 DRIOTON, ÉTIENNE (1889-1961), France. Priest, Egyptologist. Wrote extensively about ancient Egypt. Sources: Biog Index: 5 6/Rev Arch 2:83-5 Jl '61.

0963 DRIOUX, GEORGES (1888-1949), Langres, France. Historian, archeologist. Archeology of Haute-Marne (France). Sources: Biog Index: 3/Rev Arch series 6 40:67 Jl '52.

0964 DRIVER, HAROLD EDSON (1907-), Berkeley, California, United States. Anthropologist. Native American ethnology, particularly of Sierra Nevada area & Northwest California. Sources: Int Dir Anth 1, 2, 3/Nat Dir Lat Am.

0965 Du BRUHL, E LLOYD (1909-). Anatomist, physical anthropologist. Phylogenetic mechanisms in hominid head & neck. Oral anatomy of mammals. Genetic control in evolution of behavior. Source: Int Dir Anth 5.

0966 Du PERON, S J, Fr. FRANÇOIS (1610-1665), Lyons, France. Priest. Missionary in New France; wrote on N. American Indians. Source: Jes Rel.

0967 Du POISSON, S J, Fr. PAUL (1692-1729), Epinay, France. Priest. Missionary in New France; wrote on N. American Indians. Source: Jes Rel.

0968 Du SOMERARD, ALEXANDRE (1779- 1842). Archeologist, taxonomist. Art collector. Sources: Biog Index: 11/History & Theory 17 no 3:251-66 '78.

0969 Du TOIT, S J (1847-1911). Clergyman. Worked to establish Afrikaans as a separate language; wrote a grammar of Afrikaans (1876). Source: Saunders, Christopher, Historical Dictionary of South Africa (1983), p 8.

0970 DUBOIS, CHARLES (1874-1955), Bondange, Belgium. Priest, archeologist. Sources: Biog Index: 4/ Brussels, Musees Royaux d'Art et d'Histoire Bulletin S 4 27:111 '85.

0971 DUBOIS, MARIE EUGÈNE FRANÇOIS THOMAS (1858-1940), Netherlands. Paleontologist, physical anthropologist. Quantitative evolution, relationship of brains & phylogenetic evolution of brain in vertebrates. Sources: Biog Index: 5 & 12.

0972 DuCHAILLU, PAUL BELLONI (1831-1903). Explorer. First European to visit many parts of Gabon: two expeditions for Boston and Philadelphia museums resulted in accounts of life and customs of coastal and interior peoples at this period, 1855-1865. Source: Gardiner. David E., Historical Dictionary of Gabon (1981), p 69.

0973 DUCKWORTH, WYNFRID LAURENCE HENRY (1870-1956). Anatomist, anthropologist. Interests in anatomy, archeology, teratology, primatology, anthropology and general natural history. Wrote: *Morphology and Anthropology*, 1904. Sources: Biog Index: 4/British Medical Journal no 4964:462-3 F 25 '56/ Lancet 270:306 F 25 '56/Nature 177:505-6 Mr 17 '56.

0974 DUELL, PRENTICE (1894-1960), New Albany, Indiana, United States. Archeologist. Egyptian and Etruscan archeology; ancient Mediterranean painting. Sources: Biog Index: 5 & 6/Int Dir Anth 1, 2, 3/ Nat Cyc Am Biog 44:226-7 '62.

0975 DUFF, ROGER SHEPHERD (1912-), New Zealand. Prehistorian, ethnologist. Typology of Neolithic adzes. Polynesian prehistory. Moa hunter, Maori phase. Sources: Int Dir Anth 2, 5.

0976 DUGDALE, WILLIAM (1605-1686). Antiquarian. Wrote on antiquities of England. Source: Columbia.

0977 DUMEZIL, GEORGES (1898-1986), Paris, France. Mythologist. Focused on comparative mythology & Indo-European studies. Developed the "tripartite ideology" (functions performed by kings & priests, warriors, and workers from the foundation of all Indo-European mythologies). Used Durkheim's sociology. Elected to the Academie Francaise. Sources: Anth News 28:3:3/ International Encyclopedia of the Social Sciences, v. 18.

0978 DUMITRESCU, HORIA (1902-), Romania. Anthropologist. Microscopic morphology in laboratory animals. Regional, ecological &, demographic social anthropology. Sources: Int Dir Anth 1, 5.

0979 DUMONT, LOUIS CHARLES JEAN (1911-), Thessalonika, Greece. Social anthropologist. Hierarchies. Comparison of ideologies & institutions. Kinship theory in India & Australia. Sources: Int Dir Anth 3, 5.

0980 DUMONT D'URVILLE, JULES-SÉBASTION-CÉSAR (1790-1842), Corde-sur-Noireau, France. Explorer. Led two voyages of discovery between 1826 and 1840 and published two massive compilations of geographic and ethnographic data on many Pacific island groups. Source: Craig & King, Historical Dictionary of Oceania (1981), p 74.

0981 DUNĂRE, NICOLAE (1916-). Ethnologist. Classification of popular ornaments, costumes & human habitats in mountainous regions of Eastern Europe. Source: Int Dir Anth 5.

0982 DUNBABIN, THOMAS JAMES (1911- 1955), Australia. Archeologist. Assistant Director of the British School at Athens, 1936-1945. Participated in the excavation of the Perachora site in 1936 and prepared the resultant material for publication. His notion of combining historical background and archeological data were most evident in his publication, *The Western Greeks*, 1948. Sources: Biog Index: 3 & 4/Am J Arch 59:323 O '55/ Antiquaries Journal 35:284 Jl '55/Archaeology 8:205 S '55.

0983 DUNBAR, JOHN BROWN (1841-1914), Nebraska, United States. Educational administrator.

Authority on Pawnee Indians; prepared material on Potawatomi linguistics. Source: Am Anth 16:142-3 Ja '14.

0984 DUNCAN, GEORGE STEWART (1860- 1946). Archeologist. Sources: Biog Index: 2/Nat Cyc Am Biog, '49.

0985 DUNGLAS, EDOUARD (1891-1952), Paris, France. Geographer, historian. Wrote a history of the state of Ketou (in present-day Benin); also a study of Fon traditions. Source: DeCalo, Samuel, Historical Dictionary of Dahomey (1976), p 57.

0986 DUNHAM, DOWS (1890-). Egyptologist. Directed fieldwork in Saqqara, Dahshur and Giza (Egypt); first to establish chronology of Meroe (Sudan) and to excavate there. Sources: Biog Index: 4 & 12/Am J Arch 84:190 Ap '80.

0987 DUNHAM, KATHERINE (1910-). Anthropologist, dancer, choreographer. Sources: Biog Index: 8 9 10 11 & 12/ Beckford, Ruth. Katherine Dunham, a biography M Decker '79/ Dunham, Katherine. Touch of Innocence. Books for Libraries '80.

0988 DUNLOP, ROBERT GLASCOW (1815- 1847), Scotland. Merchant. Wrote an account of his travels to the Central America in the 1840s. Source: Creedman, Theodore, Historical Dictionary of Costa Rica (1977), p 58.

0989 DUNNING, ROBERT WILLIAM (1918-), Canada. Social anthropologist. Inuit social organization & change. Source: Int Dir Anth 5.

0990 DUPONT, PIERRE (1908-1955), Paris, France. Archeologist. Archeology of India & Southeast Asia. Sources: Biog Index: 4/Int Dir Anth 3/Artibus Asiae 18 no 2:178-82 '55.

0991 DUPOUY, WALTER (1906-), Puerto Cabello, Venezuela. Archeologist, ethnologist, folklorist. Worked on Venezuelan folklore. Sources: Int Dir Anth 3, 5.

0992 DUQUESNE de LA MADRID, JOSÉ DOMINGO (1748-1822), Colombia. Priest. Wrote a dissertation on the calendrical system of the Chibcha Indians of Colombia. Source: Davis, Robert H., Historical Dictionary of Colombia (1977), p 105.

0993 DURAN y DIAZ, JOAQUIN, Spain. Soldier. Wrote the first descriptive and statistical almanac of Colombia. Source: Davis, Robert H., Historical Dictionary of Colombia (1977), p 105.

0994 DURKHEIM, EMIL (1858-1917). Sociologist. Major social theorist. Wrote at length on the differences between primitive and modern societies. Source: Columbia.

0995 DUSENBERRY, VERNE (1906-1966), Iowa, United States. Ethnologist. Compiled data on Cree & Chippewa people. Did extensive fieldwork on Northern Cheyenne Indian Reservation. Source: Am Anth Ap '68.

0996 DUTTON, BERTHA PAULINE (1903-), Algona, Iowa, United States. Anthropologist. Ethnography of Mexico & Central America. Sources: Nat Dir Lat Am/Int Dir Anth 2, 3.

0997 DUYVENDAK, JAN JULIUS LODEWIJK (1889-1954), Harlingen, Netherlands. Sinologist. Chinese history. Sources: Biog Index: 3/Int Dir Anth 1, 3.

0998 DYEN, ISIDORE (1913-). Genetic linguistics, lexicostatistics & grammar. Source: Int Dir Anth 5.

0999 DYGGVE, EJNAR (1887-1961), Liban, Denmark. Archeologist. Archeology of Europe, North Africa, Near & Middle East. Sources: Biog Index: 6/Int Dir Anth 3/Rev Arch 1:99-100 Ja '62.

1000 DYK, WALTER (1899-1972), Germany. Anthropologist, linguist. Pioneered in the use of naturalistic language in his ethnographic studies of the Navajo. Also worked on Wishram grammar. Sources: Biog Index: 10/Int Dir Anth 1, 2/Am Anth 76:86-7 Mr '74.

1001 DZIERŹYKRAY-ROGALSKI, TADEUSZ (1918-), Poland. Anthropologist, paleopathologist. Research in Egypt. Medical anthropology. Source: Int Dir Anth 5.

1002 EASBY, DUDLEY T (1905-). Anthropologist. Source: Nat Dir Lat Am.

1003 EASTMAN, MARY (Henderson) (1818-). Folklorist. Sources: Biog Index: 10/Southern Folklore Quarterly 39:271-89 S '75.

1004 EBERHARD, WOLFRAM (1909-). Sociologist, folklorist. Modern & historical folklore. Classical astronomy & society in China. Source: Int Dir Anth 5.

1005 EBERS, GEORG MORITZ (1837-1898), Germany. Egyptologist. Source: Biog Index: 7.

1006 ECKE, GUSTAV (1896-1971), Bremen, Germany. Orientalist. History of Chinese art. Sources: Biog Index: 10/Int Dir Anth 1, 2.

1007 ECKSTROM, FANNIE PEARSON HARDY (1865-1946), Brewer, Maine, United States. Folklorist, historian. Authority on Penobscot Indians. Source: Notable American Women, 1607-1950, vol. I, Belknap Press '71, p 549-51.

1008 EDEL, MAY (Mandelbaum) (1909-1964), Brooklyn, New York, United States. Anthropologist. Physical anthropology, linguistics of Africa, Uganda especially. Sources: Biog Index: 6 & 7/Int Dir Anth 1, 2, 3/Am Anth 68:986-9 Ag '66.

1009 EDWARDS, AMELIA ANN BLANFORD (1831-1892), London, England. Egyptologist. Largely responsible for the founding of the Egypt Exploration Fund, 1882, which sought to preserve Egyptian antiquities. Wrote: *A Thousand Miles up the Nile*, 1877. Sources: Biog Index: 1 6 13-4/ Journal of Egyptian Archaeology 33:66-89 D '47/Antiquity 56:81-3 Jl '82/ Dictionary of National Biography Supp. II:601-603.

1010 EELLS, MYRON (1843-1907), Walker's Prarie, Washington, United States. Minister, missionary. Expert on the linguistics and ethnology of the peoples of Oregon (Twana, Chinook). Source: Am Anth 10:500-1 Jl '08.

1011 EFIMENKO, PETR PETROVICH (1884-1969), Russia. Archeologist. Created a periodization of the Paleolithic sites of European Russia. Source: Great Soviet Encyclopedia, New York, Macmillan (1975), v. 9, p 76.

1012 EGGAN, DOROTHY WAY (1901-1965), Indiana, United States. Anthropologist. Viewed dreams in their cultural perspective, studied Hopi personality. Published a series of papers on the importance & significance of dreams for anthropology. Sources: Biog Index: 8/Am Anth 69:731-2 D '67.

1013 EGGAN, FRED (1906-), Seattle, Washington, United States. Ethnologist. Numerous studies of N. American Indians, also of Philippines. Social organization & structure. Sources: Int Dir Anth 1, 2, 3, 5/ International Encyclopedia of the Social Sciences, v. 18.

1014 EGGEN, DERICK RUSSEL (1906-), Seattle, Washington, United States. Ethnologist. Worked with Choctaw, Cheyenne, Arapaho, & Hopi Indians. Source: International Encyclopedia of the Social Sciences, v. 18.

1015 EHRENFELS, UMAR R von (1901-), Prague, Czechoslovakia. Ethnologist. Work in India. Sources: Int Dir Anth 3, 5.

1016 EHRHARDT, SOPHIE (1902-), Tubingen, Germany. Physical anthropologist. Sources: Int Dir Anth 1, 2, 3, 5.

1017 EHRICH, ROBERT W (1908-), New York, New York, United States. Anthropologist. Ethnological & archeological theory as related to Old World archeological interpretation. Sources: Int Dir Anth 1, 2, 3, 5.

1018 EISELEY, LOREN COREY (1907-1977), Lincoln, Nebraska, United States. Anthropologist, author, paleontologist. Advanced public understanding of social science. Paleolithic Indian horizons; indexed fauna & evolutionary concepts. Neanderthal man. Sources: Biog Index: 5 6 7 9 10 & 11/Int Dir Anth 1, 2, 3, 5/ Georgia

Review 31:854-71 Wint '77/Anth News S '77/Current Biography 38:43 S '77/ Current Biography Yr Bk 1977:462 '78/N Y Times p 28 Jl 11 '77/ N Y Times Biog Service 8: 931 Jl '77/Science News 112:63 Jl 9 '77/ Time 110:61 Jl 25 '77.

1019 EISNER, JAN (1885-1967), Czechoslovakia. Archeologist, historian. Archeology of Slovakia and the origins of the Slavs. Source: Great Soviet Encyclopedia, New York, Macmillan (1982), v. 29, p 340.

1020 EKHOLM, GORDON FREDERICK (1909-), St. Paul, Minnesota, United States. Archeologist, anthropologist. Studied archeological & ethnographic relations between the early civilizations of Asia & those of the New World. Sources: Columbia/Int Dir Anth 1, 2, 3/Nat Dir Lat Am.

1021 ELDERKIN, GEORGE WICKER (1879-1965), Chicago, Illinois, United States. Archeologist. Directed the first excavations at Antioch (Turkey) in 1932; specialized in history of cults & religions of classical world. Sources: Biog Index: 7/N Y Times p 35 D 20 '65/ Publishers Weekly 189:279 Ja 24 '66.

1022 ELIOT, CHARLES NORTON EDGECUMBE (1862-1931), Sibford Gower, Oxfordshire, England. Diplomat, Orientalist, linguist. Familiar with many rarely used languages; contributed first grammar in English of the Finnish language; studied Hindu, Buddhist religions. Sources: Biog Index: 2/ Dictionary of National Biography 1931-1940:254-5 '49.

1023 ELISEEV, ALEKSANDR VASIL'EVICH (1859-1895), Sveaborg, Finland. Traveler. Explorer of Asia Minor & Africa. Wrote extensive monographs and collected ethnological, anthropological data on Asia Minor, Africa, Europe. Source: Great Soviet Encyclopedia, New York, Macmillan (1975) v. 9, p 116.

1024 ELISSÉEFF, SERGE (1889-). Orientalist. Wrote on Japanese culture. Sources: Biog Index: 4 & 11.

1025 ELKIN, ADOLPHUS PETER (1891-1979), West Maitland, New South Wales, Australia. Archeologist, physical anthropologist. Oceanic & Australian aboriginal research. Social organization, culture mythology of the Australian Aborigines. Sources: Biog Index: 13/Int Dir Anth 1, 3, 5/Am Anth 83:368-71 Je '81/ Anth News O '79/Oceania 14:161-7 O '79/Mankind 12:162-3 D '79/ Wise, Tigger. Self-Made Anthropologist: the Life of A.P. Elkin. Allen & Urwin, 1985.

1026 ELLENBERGER, DANIEL FREDERIC (1835-1920), Switzerland. Missionary. Wrote a comprehensive historical work on the Basotho using Sesotho. Source: Haliburton, Gordon, Historical Dictionary of Lesotho (1977), p 47.

1027 ELLENBERGER, VICTOR (1879-1974), Masitise, Lesotho. Missionary. Wrote account of the P.E.M.S. mission work in Lesotho; also account of extermination of the Bushmen in Lesotho. Source: Haliburton, Gordon, Historical Dictionary of Lesotho (1977), p 47-8.

1028 ELLENBOGEN, BERT L (1917-). Anthropologist. Source: Nat Dir Lat Am.

1029 ELLIOT, HENRY MIERS (1808-1853). Civil servant. Wrote on peoples of India's Northwest Frontier. Source: Dictionary of International Biography.

1030 ELLIOT, WILLIAM ALLEN (1851-). Civil servant. Published first Sindebele and Chisona dictionaries; wrote an account of the Ndebele of Rhodesia in 1910. Source: Rasmussen, R. Kent, Historical Dictionary of Rhodesia/Zimbabwe (1979), p 84.

1031 ELLIS, WILLIAM (1794-1872), London, England. Printer, missionary. Developed a form of writing for the Hawaiian language. Included in his work antiquarian materials on Polynesia. Sources: Columbia/ Craig & King, Historical

Dictionary of Oceania (1981), p 79.

1032 ELMENDORF, MARY LINDSAY (1917-). Ethnologist. Latin American peasant women & community development. Source: Int Dir Anth 5.

1033 ELMENDORF, WILLIAM W (1912-), Victoria, British Columbia, Canada. Ethnologist. U.S. coastal Salish status ranking & intergroup ties. Sources: Int Dir Anth 3, 5.

1034 ELSASSER, ALBERT B (1918-). Anthropologist. Domestication of plants & animals. Fossil man. Old World physical anthropology. Source: Int Dir Anth 5.

1035 ELWIN, VERRIER (1902-1964), Dover, England. Anthropologist, author. Pioneer Indian anthropologist. Sources: Biog Index: 6 7 & 10/Am Anth 67:448-52 Ap '65.

1036 EMBREE, JOHN FEE (1908-1950), New Haven, Connecticut, United States. Social anthropologist, ethnologist, diplomat. Social anthropology of Japanese in Hawaii. Specialist in Japanese culture which he used in applied anthropology during World War II. Published on Thai social organization. Sources: Biog Index: 2/Int Dir Anth 1, 2, 3/ American Sociological Review 15:116-17 F '51/ Far Eastern Quarterly 11:219-25 F '52/ Human Organization 9:4 Winter '50, 10:33-4 Spring '51/Am Anth 53:376-82 Jl '51/ Isis 42 no 1:49 '51/N Y Times p 16 D 23 '50/School & Society 72:447 D 30 '50.

1037 EMERSON, J NORMAN (1917-1978), Toronto, Ontario, Canada. Archeologist. Ontario prehistory. Sources: Int Dir Anth 3/Anth News Ap '79.

1038 EMERSON, NATHANIEL BRIGHT (1839-1915). Physician, folklorist. Sources: Biog Index: 3/Halford, Francis John. Nine Doctors & God. Univ. of Hawaii '54 p 304-5.

1039 EMERY, WALTER BRYAN (1903-1971), England. Egyptologist. Desert exploration, history & ancient architecture of Egypt. Sources: Biog Index: 2 9 & 10/Int Dir Anth 2.

1040 EMLEN, JOHN T (1908-). Zoologist, primatologist. Social behavior of free ranging gorillas. Source: Int Dir Anth 5.

1041 EMRICH, DUNCAN (1908-), Turkey. Folklorist. Collected folksongs of the United States. Sources: Biog Index: 3 4 & 11/Current Biography 16:14-15 Mr '55/ Current Biography Yr Bk 1955:180-2 '56/Time 66:44+ Jl 18 '55/ Commire, Anne. Something about the Author, Gale.

1042 ENGEL, FREDERIC ANDRE (1908-), Peru. Archeologist. Agricultural ecologies & regions. Holocene settlements. Prehistoric demography, artifacts & fabrics of Peru. Source: Int Dir Anth 5.

1043 ENGELBACH, REGINALD (1888-1946), Devonshire, England. Archeologist, Egyptologist. Studies of ancient Egypt, including *The Aswan Obelisk*. Sources: Biog Index: 1 & 2/Chronique d'Egypte 21:206-7 Jl '46/ Isis 41 no 1:56 '50/Journal of Egyptian Archaeology 32:97-99 S '46.

1044 ENGELMANN, GEORGE JULIUS (1847-1903), Missouri, United States. Surgeon. Assembled important collection of Missouri artifacts (lithics & ceramics); published on "primitive" peoples and contemporary female health. Source: Am Anth 5:739 O '03.

1045 ENGELMANN, HUGO OTTO (1917-). Sociologist. Social theory referring to social anthropology & psychology. Changes & differences in structure of experience. Source: Int Dir Anth 5.

1046 ENGERRAND, GEORGE CHARLES MARIUS (1877-1961), Libourne, France. Anthropologist, geologist. Published on European prehistory, human races, colonists in Texas & Australia, human growth, Maya dental nutrition, Aztec artifacts & Mexican folk medicine. Sources: Biog Index: 6/Int Dir Anth 2/Am Anth 64:1052-6 O '62.

1047 ENGLERT, SEBASTIAN (1888-1969), Augsberg, Bavaria, Germany.

Missionary. Wrote a detailed account of the ethnology, linguistics, & archeology of Easter Island; collected island folklore and legends. Sources: Craig & King, Historical Dictionary of Oceania (1981), p 80-1/ Am Anth 71:1109-11 D '69.

1048 ENJALRAN, S J, Fr. JEAN (1639-1708), Rodez, France. Priest. Missionary in New France; wrote on N. American Indians. Source: Jes Rel.

1049 ENTHOVEN, REGINALD EDWARD (1869-1952). Anthropologist, civil servant. Student of Hindu anthropology and folklore; did service in Bombay where, as Census Superintendent for Bombay Presidency, produced report which led to appointment as honorary Superintendent of Ethnography in Bombay; also in charge of ethnographical survey of the Presidency. Sources: Biog Index: 3/Isis 43 no 4:367 '52/Nature 169:1080-1 Je 28 '52.

1050 ERICHSEN, WOLJA (1890-1966), Denmark. Egyptologist. Demotic scholar devoted to Egyptian philology whose works include *Demotische Lesestucke*, 1937. Sources: Biog Index: 8/Journal of Egyptian Archaeology 52:1 D '66.

1051 ERIO, PAUL. Wrote report on conscription of local populations as porters by Europeans (1912). Source: Kalck, Pierre, Historical Dictionary of the Central African Republic (1980), p 46.

1052 ERKES, EDUARD (1891-1958), Genua, Germany. Sinologist. Specialist in Chinese culture. Wrote: *Chinesische Literatur*, 1922; *Die Chinesische Religion*, 1927; *Das Alteste Dokument zur Chinesischen Kunstgeschichte, T'-ien-wen*, 1931. Sources: Biog Index: 5 & 12/Artibus Asiae 21 no 2:167-70 '58.

1053 ERSKINE, JOHN ELPHINSTONE (1805-1887), Cardross, Scotland. Naval officer. Wrote a journal of a visit to Samoa, Tonga, Fiji, the New Hebrides and New Caledonia in the period 1848-1853 useful for information on Samoan warfare. Source: Craig & King, Historical Dictionary of Oceania (1981), p 82.

1054 ESPEJO-NÚÑEZ, JULIO (1911-), Peru. Archeologist, bibliographer. History of ceramics of ancient Peru. Source: Int Dir Anth 5.

1055 ESTEVA-FABREGAT, CLAUDIO (1918-). Ethnologist. Pyrenean and Fang culture & acculturation; theory & methodology. Source: Int Dir Anth 5.

1056 ESTRADA, EMILIO (1916-1961), Guayaquil, Ecuador. Archeologist. Created chronology and surface survey for cultural sequence on the coast of Ecuador. Sources: Biog Index: 6/Am Antiq 28:78-81 Jl '62.

1057 ETHERIDGE, ROBERT, Jr (1847-1920), Cheltenham, England. Diplomat, paleontologist, ethnologist. Wrote on Aborigines. Sources: Biog Index: 2/Dictionary of Australian Biography 1:273 '49.

1058 ETTINGHAUSEN, RICHARD (1906-1979), Frankfurt, Germany. Art historian, museum curator. One of the world authorities on the arts of Islam; many publications, especially *Islamic Art* (1962). Sources: Biog Index: 11/N Y Times p 6-18 Ap 3 '79/ N Y Times Biog Service 10:459 Ap '79.

1059 ETTLINGER, ELLEN (1902-). Folklorist. Amulets, devotional pictures & superstitions of Celtic countries. Source: Int Dir Anth 5.

1060 EVANS, ARTHUR JOHN (1851-1914), England. Archeologist. Fieldwork at Knossos (Greece); discovered Minoan civilization and Linear B. Sources: Biog Index: 2 4 5 6 7 8 & 13/Int Dir Anth 2/ Archaeology, 3:134-9 S '50/Horwitz, Sylvia L. Find of a Lifetime: Sir Arthur Evans & the discovery of Knossos. Viking Press '81/ Expedition 23:4-12 Spr '81.

1061 EVANS, JOHN (1823-1908), England. Published on ancient British coins, bronze and stone artifacts. Source: Am Anth 10:355-6 Ap '08.

1062 EVANS-PRITCHARD, EDWARD EVAN (1902-1973), Crowborough, Sussex, England. Social anthropologist, ethnohistorian. Ethnohistory of Southern Sudan, especially Azande, Nuer and Anuak. Sources: Biog Index: 1 10 & 13/Int Dir Anth 1, 2, 3/ International Encyclopedia of the Social Sciences, v. 18/ Douglas, Mary Tew. Edward Evans-Pritchard. Viking Press '80/ Makers of Modern Culture. Facts on File '81, p 160-1/ Times Higher Education Supplement p 12 Jl 4 '80.

1063 EWERS, JOHN CANFIELD (1909-), Cleveland, Ohio, United States. Ethnologist. Blackfoot Indian studies. Arts, crafts, collections of U.S. Plains. Sources: Int Dir Anth 2, 3, 5.

1064 EWING, S J, Fr. J FRANKLIN (1905-1968), New York, New York, United States. Anthropologist, archeologist. Excavated at Ksar Akil, Lebanon (1948), the Beirut area (1938-40) and Byblos; made a study of the Maronites of Lebanon; also did work in Philippines on the hill tribes of Mindanao. Sources: Biog Index: 8/Int Dir Anth 3/N Y Times p 47 My 21 '68/ Time 91:62 My 31 '68.

1065 EZELL, PAUL HOWARD (1913-), Wyoming, United States. Anthropologist. Prehistory of West Texas. Sources: Int Dir Anth 2/Nat Dir Lat Am.

1066 FA-HSIEN, (fl. 399-414), China. Writer. Pilgrim. Traveler. Source: Dictionary of Universal Biography.

1067 FABILA, ALFONSO (1897-), Amanalco, Mexico. Bureaucrat, ethnologist. Published on the Mexican "Indian problem"; worked in several government agencies dealing with cultures & Indian affairs. Source: Who's Who in Latin America 3rd ed., Ronald Hilton ed., Stanford Univ. Press (Blaine Ethridge edition, 1971) vol. I, p 39.

1068 FABRÉ, GABRIELLE (1907-1960). Archeologist. Sources: Biog Index: 5/Rev Arch 2:84-5 Jl '60.

1069 FAGG, BERNARD E B (1915-), London, England. Archeologist. African prehistory, particularly West African prehistory. Source: Int Dir Anth 3.

1070 FAGG, WILLIAM BULLER (1914-), London, England. Anthropologist, art historian. Nigerian art, archeology, and general ethnology of Africa;social history of art. Source: Int Dir Anth 3.

1071 FAHNBULLEH, VARNEY JAKEMA (1892-1975), Gbesse, Liberia. Civil servant. Pioneered in the study of the ethnic groups of Liberia. Source: Dunn & Holsoe, Historical Dictionary of Liberia (1985), p 70.

1072 FAIDHERBE, LOUIS LÉON (1818-1889), Lille, France. Civil servant, administrator. Sent exploratory missions into Mali and spread French power in West Africa; wrote several major works on the region. Source: Imperato, Pascal J., Historical Dictionary of Mali (1977), p 47.

1073 FAIRBANKS, CHARLES H (1913-), Bainbridge, New York, United States. Archeologist. Studies of the prehispanic & colonial U.S., Creek & Seminole Indians. Sources: Int Dir Anth 3, 5.

1074 FAIRMAN, HERBERT WALTER (1907-), England. Egyptologist. Egyptian archeology, especially, hieroglyphic inscriptions of the Ptolemaic period. Sources: Biog Index: 1/Int Dir Anth 2.

1075 FALCK, KJELL (1919-), Honefoss, Norway. Ethnologist. Economy & social organization in Madagascar. Sources: Int Dir Anth 3, 5.

1076 FALCONBRIDGE, ANNA MARIA. Author. First Englishwoman to publish an account of her experiences in the Sierra Leone colony. Source: Foray, Cyril P., Historical Dictionary of Sierra Leone (1977), p 66-7.

1077 FALKENBERG, JOHANNES (1911-), Oslo, Norway. Ethnologist. Australian kinship systems. Sources: Int Dir Anth 3, 5.

1078 FALKNER, THOMAS (1702-1784), Manchester, England. Missionary. Wrote the first description of the interior of Patagonia (Argentina) including much useful ethnographic data. Source: Wright & Nelsham, Historical Dictionary of Argentina (1978), p 288-99.

1079 FARIÑA NÚÑEZ, ELOY (1885-1929), Paraguay. Journalist. Wrote a study of Guarani Indians of Paraguay. Source: Kolinski, Charles J., Historical Dictionary of Paraguay (1973), p 95.

1080 FARMAKOVSKII, BORIS VLADIMIROVICH (1870-1928), Russia. Archeologist. Specialized in Greece, Rome, and the Black Sea region. Source: Great Soviet Encyclopedia, New York, Macmillan (1981), v. 27, p 104.

1081 FARMER, MALCOLM F (1915-), Los Angelos, California, United States. Archeologist. Anthropology of the U.S. Southwest. Sources: Int Dir Anth 3, 5.

1082 FARRAND, LIVINGSTON (1867-1939), Newark, New Jersey, United States. Anthropologist. Conducted a study with James Cattell, begun in 1894, of Columbia University students through physical and mental measurement, the goal of which was to analyze personality and ability development in the light of the nature vs nurture theory espoused by Francis Galton. Sources: Science 90:583-4 '39/American Journal of Psychology 53:302 '40/ Dictionary of Australian Biography, 22/Nat Cyc Am Biog, 40/ N Y Times 23:1 N 9 '39/Who Was Who in America, 1/ Zusne, L., Biographical Dictionary of Psychology, Westport, Conn., Greenwood, 1984.

1083 FATHAUER, GEORGE H (1918-). Ethnologist. Matrilineal kinship of the U.S. Mojave. Source: Int Dir Anth 5.

1084 FAUBLÉE, JACQUES (1912-), Saint Quentin, France. Linguist. Malagasy language components. Ethno-sociology. Ethnology of the Eurasians. Rock engravings & paintings. Sources: Int Dir Anth 3, 5.

1085 FAULKNER, RAYMOND O (1894-), England. Egyptologist. Wrote a dictionary of Middle Egyptian; translated many Egyptian texts. Sources: Biog Index: 10/Journal of Egyptian Archaeology 60:5-7 '74.

1086 FAURÉ, GABRIEL (1877-1962). Archeologist. Sources: Biog Index: 6/Rev Arch 2:222-3 O '62.

1087 FAURIEL, CLAUDE CHARLES (1772-1844), France. Philosopher, critic, historian. Source: Dictionary of Universal Biography.

1088 FAVRET, PIERRE MARCEL (1875-1950), Vauchamps, Marne, France. Priest, archeologist. Prehistoric & protohistoric archeology of France. Sources: Biog Index: 3/Int Dir Anth 1, 2/Rev Arch series 6 42:96-9 Jl '53.

1089 FAZY, ROBERT (1872-1956), Switzerland. A non-professional with a great interest in the civilizations of Asia and Africa; one of the founders of the Societe suisse des Amis de l'Extreme-Orient in 1939 and a contributor to its Bulletin. Sources: Biog Index: 4/Artibus Asiae 19 no 1:72 '56.

1090 FEDER, ERNEST (1913-). Ethnologist. Agrarian policy, employment, reforms, colonization, social & labor relations in Latin America. Source: Int Dir Anth 5.

1091 FEDERMANN, NICHOLAS (1502-1546), Germany. Explorer. Led a joint expedition to Colombia, 1535-1538, and wrote an account of its discoveries. Source: Davis, Robert H., Historical Dictionary of Colombia (1977), p 111.

1092 FEJOS, PÁL (1897-1963), Budapest, Hungary. Motion picture director, anthropologist. Published on the ethnography of the Yaqui of Mexico; one of the first to recognize the significance of Carbon-14 to archeology; supported anthropological research & publications for 20 years as director of the Wenner-Gren Foundation. Sources: Biog Index: 6 7 11 12 & 13/Int Dir Anth 3/ Film Quarterly 32:28-37 Wint '78-79/Cinema, v. 1. Viking Press '80 p 339-40/ Am Anth 66:110-15 F '64, 65:667-8 Je '63/N

Y Times p 35 Ap 24 '63/ Neewsweek 61:63 My 6 '63/Nat Cyc Am Biog 49:143-4 '66/Am Antiq 30:81-2 Jl '64/ Koszarski, Richard. Hollywood directors, 1914-1940. Oxford '76 p 222-6/ Whitemore, Don (and others). Passport to Hollywood. McGraw '76 p 424-40.

1093 FELL, BARRY (1917-1971). Archeologist. Proposed many trans-Atlantic voyages by various groups (Welsh & Basques); claimed to have verified these from inscriptions. Sources: Biog Index: 10/Newsweek 85:81-2 My 26 '75.

1094 FENOLLOSA, ERNEST FRANCISCO (1853-1908). Poet, Orientalist. Source: Biog Index: 6.

1095 FENTON, RICHARD (1746-1821), Rhosson, Wales. Archeologist, lawyer, topographer, poet. Made early survey of historical sites in Pembrokshire, Wales. Sources: Biog Index: 10/Country Life 158:700-1 S 18 '75.

1096 FENTON, WILLIAM NELSON (1908-), New Rochelle, New York, United States. Archeologist. Ethnohistory of the Iroquois of New York State. Source: American Men and Women of Science, ed. by J.C. Press, 12th ed., New York, Bowker, 1973.

1097 FERDON, EDWIN NELSON (1913-), St. Paul, Minnesota, United States. Anthropologist. Sources: Int Dir Anth 3/Nat Dir Lat Am.

1098 FERGUSON, FRANCES NORTHEND (1915-). Anthropologist. Ancient and modern trade values & attitudes in India & U.S.; body symbolism and social experience. Source: Int Dir Anth 5.

1099 FERGUSON, GEORGE EKEM (1864-1897), Anomabu, Ghana. Surveyor, political officer, geographer. British colonial surveyor, political officer & geographer of Fanti ethnicity. Explored, mapped and annexed the Northern Territories of the Gold Coast. Known for his linguistic and ethnographic knowledge of the Voltaic peoples; killed before he could write a planned geography. Source: Dictionary of African Biography: vol. 1, Ethiopia-Ghana. New York: Reference Publications Inc., 1977, p 241-7.

1100 FERGUSON, THOMAS STUART (1915-). Anthropologist. Source: Nat Dir Lat Am.

1101 FERNÁNDEZ, LEÓN (1840-1887), Costa Rica. Historian. Compiled early documentary sources on Costa Rican history and founded the National Archives. Source: Creedman, Theodore, Historical Dictionary of Costa Rica (1977).

1102 FERNÁNDEZ de ENCISCO, MARTÍN (1470-1528), Spain. Cartographer. Wrote an account of geography of Colombia's coastline. Source: Davis, Robert H., Historical Dictionary of Colombia (1977), p 112.

1103 FERNÁNDEZ de OVIEDO y VALDÉZ, GONZALO see: OVIEDO y VALDEZ, GONZALO F d

1104 FERNÁNDEZ de PIEDRAHITA, LUCAS (1624-1688), Bogota, Colombia. Priest. Wrote a history of the Spanish conquest of Colombia. Source: Davis, Robert H., Historical Dictionary of Colombia (1977), p 112.

1105 FERNÁNDEZ GUARDIA, RICARDO (1867-1950), Costa Rica. Historian. History of Costa Rica. Source: Creedman, Theodore, Historical Dictionary of Costa Rica (1977), p 71-2.

1106 FERRAGNE, MARCEL (1914-), Canada. Missionary. Edited & wrote some sixty books on Basotho culture, history, anthropology and literature. Source: Haliburton, Gordon, Historical Dictionary of Lesotho (1977), p 48.

1107 FETT, PER HARRY (1909-), Oslo, Norway. Historian. Norway. History of settling. Rock carvings. Migration period weapons. Sources: Int Dir Anth 3, 5.

1108 FEWKES, JESSE WALTER (1850-1930), United States. Ethnologist, archeologist. Pueblo Indians, especially the Zuni; archeology of the West Indies. Sources: Dictionary of Universal Biography/Am Anth 33:92-7 Ja '31.

1109 **FEWKES, VLADIMIR JAROSLAV** (1901-1941), Nimburk, Czechoslovakia. Archeologist. Excavated in Europe, and at the Irene Mound (Georgia, United States); published on the Neolithic in Europe, especially Bohemia, on conservation for museum technicians, and on ceramics. <u>Source</u>: Am Anth 44:476-477 Jl '42.

1110 **FIELD, HENRY** (1902-1986), Chicago, Illinois, United States. Physical anthropologist, archeologist, explorer, musicologist. Anthropometry & prehistory in S. W. Asia. Excavated at Kish (Mesopotamia); science advisor to two United States Presidents. <u>Sources</u>: Biog Index: 3 4 8 & 10/Int Dir Anth 1, 2, 3, 5/ Biography News 2:1219-21 N '75/Tribune, January 12, 1986/Anth News 3/86.

1111 **FIGEAC, JOSE** (1899-). Educator. Authored several books on Salvadoran history. <u>Source</u>: Flemion, Philip F., Historical Dictionary of El Salvador (1972), p 55.

1112 **FIGGINS, JESSE D** (1867-1944), Frederick Co., Maryland, United States. Naturalist, museum executive. Recognized the significance of the association of man made tools with the bones of extinct animals; focused the attention of archeologists on the association of fluted points and mammoth remains; published on Folsom & Yuma artifacts. <u>Source</u>: Am Anth 48:75-77 Ja '46.

1113 **FIGUEIRA, LUIZ** (1573-1643), Portugal. Portugese missionary & philosopher. <u>Source</u>: Dictionary of Universal Biography.

1114 **FIGUERAS PACHECO, FRANCISCO** (1880-1960). Archeologist. <u>Sources</u>: Biog Index: 6/ Archivo Espanol de Arte y Arqueologia 34 no 103:222-3 '61.

1115 **FILIP, JAN** (1900-), Czechoslovakia. Archeologist. Archeology of Central Europe and the Celts. <u>Source</u>: Great Soviet Encyclopedia, New York, Macmillan (1981), v. 27, p 202.

1116 **FILIPOVIĆ, MILENKO S** (1902-1969), Yugoslavia. Ethnologist, ethnographer. Balkan ethnologies, emphasized population movements, material culture & folkloristic customs. <u>Sources</u>: Biog Index: 8 & 9/Int Dir Anth 2, 3/Am Anth 72:558-60 Je '70.

1117 **FILLMORE, JOHN COMFORT** (1843- 1898). Musicologist, folklorist. <u>Sources</u>: Biog Index: 5/Wisconsin. State Historical Society. Dictionary of Wisconsin Biography. The Society '60 p 129-30.

1118 **FINCK, FRANZ NIKOLAUS** (1867-1910), Germany. Linguist. Recorded variations on the minority languages of Europe, especially of the Caucasus Mountains. <u>Source</u>: Am Anth 12:724-7 O '10.

1119 **FINE, REUBEN** (1914-). Psychoanthropologist. Personality structure, culture & mental health. Psychotherapy & analysis. <u>Source</u>: Int Dir Anth 5.

1120 **FINLAY, HAROLD JOHN** (1901-1951), Cronilla, India. Paleontologist. Micropaleontology of New Zealand; expert in molluscan systems. <u>Sources</u>: Biog Index: 2/Nature 167:796-7 My 19 '51.

1121 **FINN, DANIEL** (1886-1936). Priest, archeologist. <u>Sources</u>: Biog Index: 4/Nash, Robert, ed. Jesuits. Newman '56 p 149-58.

1122 **FIRTH, RAYMOND WILLIAM** (1901-), near Auckland, New Zealand. Economic anthropologist, social anthropologist. Published materials on the Tikopia of the Solomon Islands. Social structure & religion of Solomons. Anthropological treatment of symbols. <u>Sources</u>: Biog Index: 5/Int Dir Anth 2, 5/ International Encyclopedia of the Social Sciences, v. 18/Am Anth 61:896 O '59.

1123 **FISCHER, ANN** (1919-1971), Kansas, United States. Anthropologist. Advanced the role of anthropology in public health & social work. Maintained active interest in roles & rights of women in anthropology. <u>Sources</u>: Biog Index: 8 & 9/Am Anth 75:292-4 F '73.

1124 FISHBERG, MAURICE (ca. 1873-1934/35). Physician. Published on the physical anthropology of Eastern European Jews. Source: Am Anth 37:168.

1125 FISHER, CLARENCE STANLEY (1876-1941), Philadelphia, Pennsylvania, United States. Archeologist. Led and wrote about several excavations to the Near East, particularly Egypt. Sources: Biog Index: 4/Nat Cyc Am Biog 40:286-7 '55.

1126 FISON, LORIMER (1832-1907). Clergyman, anthropologist. Aboriginal Studies. Sources: Biog Index: 2 & 10/Oceania 46:6-7 S '75/Am Anth 10:176 Ja '08/ Dictionary of Australian Biography, '49.

1127 FLEISCH, HENRI (1904-), Jonvelle, France. Philologist. Arabic philology, dialects, semiotics & phonetics. Sources: Int Dir Anth 3, 5.

1128 FLEISCHMANN, JAROSLAV (1916-). Anatomist. Somatotyping. Source: Int Dir Anth 5.

1129 FLETCHER, ALICE CUNNINGHAM (1838-1923), Cuba. Ethnologist, anthropologist, archeologist. Authority on culture of Omaha and other Plains Indian groups. A founder of the School of American Archeology and of the American Anthropological Association. Did fieldwork among the Sioux, Omaha, Winnebago & Pawnee; assembled ethnological collections for museums; secured funding for the preservation of Serpent Mound (Ohio); secured land for the Omaha & Winnebago; expert on Plains Indian music; published principally on the Omaha & Sioux. Sources: Biog Index: 7 & 10/American West 12:12-15 Jl '75/ Am Anth 25:254-257 Ap '23.

1130 FLETCHER, ROBERT (1823-1912), Bristol, England. Physician. Published on anthropometry of Civil War recruits, drafted and enlisted men & substitutes, tattooing, myths, criminal anthropology, ethnomedicine. Source: Am Anth 114:687-90 O '12.

1131 FLETCHER VALLS, DOMINGO (1912-). Archeologist. Neolithic, Bronze Age & Second Iron Age periods in Spain. Source: Int Dir Anth 5.

1132 FLINT, EARL, United States. Discovered the site of Acahualinca (Nicaragua) in 1978, which was later worked on by S.R. Lathrop. Source: Meyer, Harvey K., Historical Dictionary of Nicaragua (1972), p 164.

1133 FLÓREZ de OCÁRIZ, JUAN (1612-1692), Spain. Chronicler. Wrote a history of the leading Spanish families of Colombia. Source: Davis, Robert H., Historical Dictionary of Colombia (1977), p 113.

1134 FLORIA, STEN ARVID (1905-). Geologist. Postglacial dating, phosphate investigations. Littoral deposits with culture layer stratigraphy. Source: Int Dir Anth 5.

1135 FLOWER, WILLIAM HENRY (1831-1899). Director of natural history museum. Source: Dictionary of Universal Biography.

1136 FLOYD, LOIS GRAY (1910-1978), United States. Ethnopsychologist, anthropologist. Spanish Gypsy culture. Sources: Biog Index: 11/Anth News F '79/N Y Times p 16 D 25 '78.

1137 FOCK, GERHARD J (1907-). Paleoarcheologist. African rock engravings. Archeological distribution of animals. Source: Int Dir Anth 5.

1138 FOGEL, EDWIN MILLER (1874-1949). Folklorist. Specialist on the folklore of Germany and the settlers of the Pennsylvania Dutch country. Sources: Biog Index: 2/N Y Times p 17 D 17 '49.

1139 FOLKMAR, DANIEL (-1932), Roxbury, Wisconsin, United States. Civil servant. Worked in the Philippines. Source: Am Anth 34:741 O '32.

1140 FORCE, MANNING FERGUSON (1824-1899), Washington, D.C., United States. Attorney, judge. Wrote on prehistoric inhabitants of Western Europe and on the mound builders of Ohio. Source: Am

Anth 1:590-592 Jl 1899.

1141 FORD, CLELLAN STEARNS (1909-1972), Worchester, Massachusetts, United States. Anthropologist. Worked to develop & expand Human Relations Area Files into a strong supporting unit for cross-cultural research. Sources: Biog Index: 10/Int Dir Anth 2, 3/Am Anth 76:83-5 Mr '74.

1142 FORD, JAMES ALFRED (1911-1968), Water Valley, Mississippi, United States. Archeologist. Laid groundwork for archeological chronologies in Southeast, especially lower Mississippi valley. Excavated Marksville, Menard & Hopewell. Sources: Biog Index: 8/Int Dir Anth 1, 2, 3/Am Anth 70:1161-7 D '68/ Am Antiq 34:62-71 Ja '69/N Y Times p 37 F 26 '69.

1143 FORD, VIRGINIA (1914-). Medical anthropologist. Medical care on the U.S. Dakota Indian Teton Reservation. Source: Int Dir Anth 5.

1144 FORDE, CYRIL DARYLL (1902-1973), England. Archeologist, ethnologist. Director of the African Institute (1944-1970). Fieldwork in New Mexico, Arizona, Nigeria. Sources: International Encyclopedia of the Social Sciences, v. 18/ Int Dir Anth 1, 2, 3.

1145 FORKE, ALFRED (1867-1944), Bad Schoningen near Braunschweig, Germany. Sinologist. Wrote: *World Conception of the Chinese*, 1925. Sources: Biog Index: 2/Isis 42 no 2:146 '51/Artibus Asiae no 9:148-9 '46.

1146 FORRER, ROBERT (1886-1947), Switzerland. Archeologist. Prehistory of Europe. Sources: Biog Index: 3/Int Dir Anth 2/Rev Arch series 6 39:95-8 Ja '52.

1147 FORSTEMANN, ERNST WILHELM (1822-1906), Germany. Linguist. Specialist on the hieroglyphic writing of Middle America, especially the Dresden Codex of the Maya. Source: Am Anth 9:153-9 Ja '07.

1148 FORSTER, JOHANN GEORGE ADAM (1754-1794), near Danzig, Poland. Naturalist. Wrote a narrative of Captain Cook's voyage, 1772-1775, which was influential for both its views on "primitive" society and for the information it contained on the ethnography of Pacific island groups. Source: Craig & King, Historical Dictionary of Oceania (1981), p 93.

1149 FORSTER, JOHANN REINHOLD (1729-1798), Dirschau, Germany. Naturalist. Specialist in N. American zoology. Wrote a scientific account of the second voyage of Captain Cook, 1772-1775, containing much ethnographic material. Sources: Columbia/Craig & King, Historical Dictionary of Oceania (1981), p 93.

1150 FORTES, MEYER (1906-1983), South Africa. Anthropologist. Political anthropology. Kinship systems & social organization in Africa. Sources: Biog Index: 2/Int Dir Anth 2, 5/Nature 165:176 F 4 '50.

1151 FORTIER, ALCÉE (1856-1914). Folklorist, linguist. Published on Louisiana folklore. Sources: Biog Index: 3/Herrin, M H. Creole Aristocracy, Exposition '52 p 107-9/ Rand, Clayton, Stars in Their Eyes. Dixie Press '53 p 204-5/ Am Anth 16:373 Ap '14.

1152 FORTUNE, GEORGE (1915-). Linguist. Grammar, dialects, tradition & modern literature in the Shona language of Zimbabwe. Source: Int Dir Anth 5.

1153 FORTUNE, REO FRANKLIN (1903-). Specialist on Melanesia, especially New Guinea. Source: New Zealander. 2nd. His. of M. Mead.

1154 FOSTER, GEORGE McCLELLAND (1913-), Sioux Falls, South Dakota, United States. Social anthropologist. Peasant societies. Latin American & Hispanic American societies. Sources: Int Dir Anth 3, 5/Nat Dir Lat Am.

1155 FOSTER, LAURENCE (1903-1969), Florida, United States. Anthropologist. Cultural anthropology. Sources: Biog Index: 8/Int Dir Anth 1, 2/N Y Times p 35 Ag 18

'69.

1156 FOSTER, MARY LE CRON (1914-). Linguist. Semantic analysis of Tarascan & the Mixezoque languages of Mexico. Comparative American Indian linguistics. Source: Int Dir Anth 5.

1157 FOUCART, GEORGE (1865-1944), Versailles, France. Egyptologist. History of religion in general, particularly ancient Egyptian religion. Sources: Biog Index: 1 & 2/Rev Arch series 6 36:103-106 Jl '50.

1158 FOUCHER, ALFRED CHARLES AUGUSTE (1865-1952), France. Orientalist. Traveled to India, Indochina, Cambodia, Java, Persia; was interested in the religious art of these countries and its archeological and philological association. Sources: Biog Index: 3/Artibus Asiae 15 no 4:348-51 '52.

1159 FOUILLÉE, ALFRED JULES ÉMILE (1838-1912). Philosopher, sociologist. Interdependence of the individual & society. Source: Columbia.

1160 FOWLER, HAROLD NORTH (1859-1955), Westfield, Massachusetts, United States. Archeologist. Was one of the first eight students to enroll in the American School of Classical Studies at Athens in 1882. Visited many sites in Greece, the Greek Islands and Asia Minor. Consultant in Classical Literature for the Library of Congress, 1929-1932; Editor-in-Chief of the *American Journal of Archaeology*, 1906-1916. Sources: Biog Index: 4 & 6/Am J Arch 60:285 Jl '56/ Nat Cyc Am Biog 44:341-2 '62.

1161 FOX, CYRIL FRED (1882-1967), England. Archeologist, museum director. Archeology of Great Britain. Director, National Museum of Wales. Sources: Biog Index: 1 7 & 8/Int Dir Anth 1, 2/Antiquity 41:86-8 Je '67/ Britannica Book of the Year 1968:590 '68.

1162 FOX, OSCAR J (1879-), Texas, United States. Song writer, folklorist. Arranged cowboy songs. Sources: Biog Index: 1/Howard, John Tasker. Our American Music. 3rd ed. rev Crowell '46 p 590.

1163 FOX, ROBERT BRADFORD (1917-1985). Archeologist, ethnologist. Archeological fieldwork in Palawan (Philippines); ethnographic fieldwork among the Pinatubo Negritos & the Tagbanua; extensive photographic record of his ethnographic research. Source: Anth News 9/85.

1164 FRANÇOIS, KURT von (1852-1931), Luxemburg. Explorer. Wrote descriptions of German-sponsored travels in Togo in 1888; posted to Southwest Africa (Namibia) in 1895. Published *Die Enforschung des Tschuapa und Lulongo* (1888), *Ohne Schuss durch Dick und Duhn: erste Erforschung des Togohinterlandes* (n.d.). Source: McFarland, Daniel Miles, Historical Dictionary of Upper Volta (1978), p 81.

1165 FRANKE, OTTO (1863-1946), Germode, Harz, Germany. Sinologist. Sources: Biog Index: 2/Monumenta Serica 2:277-96 '47/Isis 41 no 1:56 '60.

1166 FRANKEL, JESSE J (1914-). Cultural anthropologist. Culture & personality in inter-age conflict. Source: Int Dir Anth 5.

1167 FRANKFORT, HENRI (1897-1954), Amsterdam, Netherlands. Archeologist. Archeology & history of the ancient Near East. Sources: Biog Index: 3 & 4/Int Dir Anth 3/Antiquaries Journal 35:285 Jl '55 /Rev Arch series 6 47:211-12 Ap '56/ Warburg & Courtland Institute Journal 17:189 Jl '54.

1168 FRASER, DONALD (1870-1933). Missionary. Wrote extensively on the Tumbuka and Ngoni of Malawi. Source: Crosby, Cynthia A., Historical Dictionary of Malawi (1980), p 54.

1169 FRAZER, JAMES GEORGE (1854-1941), Scotland. Anthropologist, folklorist. Comparative study of primitive religions; author of *The Golden Bough*, 1890. Sources: Biog Index: 1 2 3 5 6 9 10 & 11/Int Dir Anth 2/ Nature 173:191

Ja 30 '54/Dictionary of National Biography 1941-1950:272-8 '59/ Contemporary Review 230:196 Ap '77.

1170 FREEMAN, ETHEL (Cutler) (1886-1972), Morristown, New Jersey, United States. Anthropologist. Expert on the Seminole Indians of the Florida Everglades. Sources: Biog Index: 9/N Y Times p 26 Jl 15 '72.

1171 FREEMAN, JOHN DEREK (1916-), Wellington, New Zealand. Ethnologist. Samoan culture & social organization. Advocate of Boas' anthropological theory correlating human ethnology & ecology. Symbolism & psychoanalytic anthropology. Sources: Int Dir Anth 3, 5.

1172 FREER, ADA GOODRICH (1857-1951). Author, folklorist. Sources: Biog Index: 12/ Hall, Trevor H. Strange Story of Ada Goodrich Freer. Duckworth '80.

1173 FREILE, JUAN RODRÍGUEZ (1566-1640), Bogota, Colombia. Historian. Wrote a history of the Spanish explorations and conquest of Colombia. Source: Davis, Robert H., Historical Dictionary of Colombia (1977), p 114.

1174 FREIRE-MAIA, NEWTON (1918-). Geneticist. Interbreeding levels & effects in Latin America. Source: Int Dir Anth 5.

1175 FRÉMIN, S J, Fr. JACQUES (1628-1691), Rheims, France. Priest. Missionary in New France; wrote on N. American Indians. Source: Jes Rel.

1176 FREUD, SIGMUND (1856-1939), Moravia. Psychiatrist. Major contributions to psychoanalytic theory which he applied to cultural problems. Source: Columbia.

1177 FREYRE, GILBERTO (1900-), Brazil. Anthropologist, ethnologist, social historian. Brazil's foremost ethnologist, whose work has dealt with regionalism and slavery in Brazil. Sources: Biog Index: 1 10 12 & 13/N Y Times Biog Service 11:814 Je '80/ Hispania 64:176 Mr '81/Levine, Robert M., Historical Dictionary of Brazil (1979), p 97-8.

1178 FROBENIUS, LEO VIKTOR (1873-1938), Berlin, Germany. Ethnologist, cultural anthropologist, explorer, historian. Proposed broad classification of world culture-types. Inaugurated ethnographic photography. Studied myths & folklore. Led 12 expeditions to Africa, 1904-1935; created photographic ethnographic collection later to become the Africa Archives; wrote extensively on African peoples. Sources: Biog Index: 10 & 11/Int Dir Anth 1/ International Encyclopedia of the Social Sciences, v. 6/ Negro History Bulletin 41:794-6 Ja '78/Imperato, Pascal J., Historical Dictionary of Mali (1977), p 48/Am Anth 41:173 Ja '39.

1179 FROMM, ERICH (1900-). Psychoanalyst. Argued that man is the product of his culture and that in industrial society man became estranged from himself. Source: Columbia.

1180 FROTHINGHAM, ARTHUR LINCOLN (1859-1923), Boston, Massachusetts, United States. Archeologist. Founded Etruscan archeology as a distinct field; directed excavations of several tombs, 1895-1896. Sources: Biog Index: 11/Archaeology 29:220-8 O '76.

1181 FUCHS, STEPHEN (1908-). Ethnologist. Messianic movements. Untouchability & totemism in religion & magic of the Korkus. Ethnology of Asia & India. Source: Int Dir Anth 5.

1182 FULLER, ANNE HUTCHINSON (1911-1984). Anthropologist, archeologist. Fieldwork in Egypt and Lebanon. Source: Anth News (Sept 1984) p 4.

1183 FULLER, ROBERT G (-1919). Anthropologist. Specialist in archeology of southwestern U.S.; participated in the restoration of Spruce Tree House at Mesa Verde, Colorado. Source: Am Anth 21:113.

1184 FUNKHOUSER, WILLIAM DELBERT (1881-1948), Rockport, Indiana, United States. Entomologist, anthropologist. Archeology of

Kentucky. Sources: Biog Index: 1 & 4/Nat Cyc Am Biog 40:372 '55/N Y Times, Je 10 '48.

1185 FURER-HAIMENDORF, CHRISTOPH von (1909-), Vienna, Austria. Anthropologist, ethnologist. Prominent writer on India; Indian, S.E. Asian, S.W. Pacific & Australian ethnology. Sources: Int Dir Anth 1, 2, 3, 5.

1186 FURER-HAIMENDORF, ELIZABETH von (1902-1987). Anthropologist. Specialized in the cultures of India, particularly the Reddis and Raj Gondes. Compiled lengthy anthropological bibliography of South Asia. Source: Anth News 28;5(1987):4.

1187 FURLONG CARDIFF, GUILLERMO (1889-), Villa Constitucion, Santa Fe, Argentina. Historian. Published accounts of Jesuit mission works in Argentina. Source: Wright & Nelsham, Historical Dictionary of Argentina (1978), p 334-5.

1188 FURTWANGLER, ADOLF (1853-1907). Archeologist. Excavated at Aegina, Olympus & Orchomenus (Greece). Authority on ancient gems, sculpture & vases. Sources: Columbia/Am Anth 9:770-1 O '07.

1189 FUSTEL de COULANGES, NUMA DENIS (1830-1889). Historian. Stressed influence of primitive religion on the development of Greek & Roman institutions. New interpretations of early medieval history. Source: Columbia.

1190 GABELENTZ, HANS CUNON von der (1807-1874). Linguist. Showed relationship among Pacific languages. Source: Columbia.

1191 GADD, CYRIL JOHN (1893-), England. Assyriologist. Scholar of the Babylonians and Sumerians; wrote *Ideas of Divine Rule in the Ancient Near East*. Sources: Biog Index: 1/Int Dir Anth 2/Nature 162:645 O 23 '48.

1192 GAGINI, CARLOS (1865-1925), Costa Rica. Historian. Compiled a dictionary and grammars of Costa Rican colloquial language. Source: Creedman, Theodore, Historical Dictionary of Costa Rica (1977), p 78-9.

1193 GAIDUKEVICH, VIKTOR FRANTSEVICH (1904-1966), St. Petersburg, Russia. Archeologist. Classical archeology north of the Black Sea. Source: Great Soviet Encyclopedia, New York, Macmillan (1975), v. 6, p 37.

1194 GAIGNIÈRES, ROGER de (1642-1715), France. Archeologist, scholar, genealogist, antiquarian. Sources: Dictionary of Universal Biography/Biog Index: 10.

1195 GALAND-PERNET, PAULETTE (1919-). Linguist. Berber dialectology & lexicography. Source: Int Dir Anth 5.

1196 GALE, ALBERT AUGUSTUS (1870-1952). Educator, folklorist. Sources: Biog Index: 3/Hobbies 57:137 F '53.

1197 GALIAY SARAÑANA, JOSÉ (1880-1952). Archeologist. Sources: Biog Index: 3/ Archivo Espanol de Arte y Arqueologia 26 no 1:233 '53.

1198 GALLAGHER, ORVOELL ROGER (1916-1975), Minnesota, United States. Applied anthropologist, ethnologist. Peasant social organization in Central France. Community studies in Northern New York State. Sources: Int Dir Anth 5/Anth News Ja '76.

1199 GALLATIN, ALBERT (1881-1965). Archeologist. Specialist in Greek vases and coinage. Sources: Biog Index: 7/N Y Times p 31 S 2 '65.

1200 GALLIENI, JOSEPH SIMON (1849-1916), France. Civil servant. General & colonial administration in French Sudan, Tonkin & Madagascar. On Madagascar wrote several books on French colonial administration. Source: New Columbia Encyclopedia p 1038.

1201 GALLUS, ALEXANDER (1907-). Archeologist. Theories of archetypes. Paleolithic Australia. Prehistoric times in Slavick countries. Typology & human evolution. Source: Int Dir Anth 5.

1202 GAMA, JOHN. Interpreter. Worked with Theophilus Shepstone to establish early genealogy of the Swazi royal dynasty. Source: Grotpeter, John, Historical Dictionary of Swaziland (1975), p 42.

1203 GAMIO, MANUEL (1883-1960), Mexico City, Mexico. Archeologist, anthropologist, sociologist. Specialized in archeology of Teotihuacan (Mexico). Published widely on archeology (research and conservation); the population of the Teotihuacan valley; migration to the U.S.; Mexican civilization. Sources: Biog Index: 5 & 6/Int Dir Anth 1, 3/ Who's Who in Latin America 3rd ed., Ronald Hilton ed., Stanford Univ. Press (Blaine Ethridge edition, 1971) vol. I, p 43-44/Briggs & Alisky, Historical Dictionary of Mexico (1981), p 89/Am Anth 64:356-66 Ap '62.

1204 GAMS, HELMUT (1893-). Botanist. Conservation. Paleobotany. Climatology. Ecology. Systematic botany & geobotany. Source: Int Dir Anth 5.

1205 GANDAVO, PEDRO de MAGALHÃES de. Historian. Wrote one of the earliest chronicles on the history of Brazilian exploration. Source: Levine, Robert M., Historical Dictionary of Brazil (1979), p 100.

1206 GANN, THOMAS WILLIAM FRANCIS (1867-1938), Westport, County Mayo, Ireland. Archeologist. Middle American archeology. Sources: Biog Index: 2/Int Dir Anth 1/ Dictionary of National Biography 1931-1940:305-6 '49.

1207 GANZO, ROBERT (1898-). Archeologist, poet. Sources: Biog Index: 10/Wakeman, John ed., World Authors, 1950-1970. Wilson '75, p 524-5.

1208 GARCÍA DÍAZ, RICARDO (-1955). Priest, physician, archeologist. Sources: Biog Index: 4/ Archivo Espanol de Arte y Arqueologia 28 no 2:349-50 '55.

1209 GARCÍA PAYÓN, JOSÉ (1893-). Archeologist. Prehispanic religion & archeology in Mexico & Central America. Sources: Int Dir Anth 2, 5.

1210 GARCÍA PELÁEZ, FRANCISCO de PAULO (1785-1867), Guatemala. Clergyman. Wrote a history of Guatemala. Source: Moore, Richard E., Historical Dictionary of Guatemala (1973), p 92.

1211 GARCILASO de la VEGA, (1539-1616), Cuzco, Peru. Historian. Wrote extensive histories on social structure and culture on the pre-Columbian Inca society; bilingual in both Quechua & Spanish, unique source. Sources: Alisky, Historical Dictionary of Peru (1979), p 44/ Heath, Dwight B., Historical Dictionary of Bolivia (1972), p 105.

1212 GARDINER, ALAN HENDERSON (1879-1963), England. Egyptologist. Specialist in ancient Egyptian language; deciphered the inscriptions from the tomb of Tutankhamen in 1920. Sources: Biog Index: 2 6 & 7/ Journal of Egyptian Archaeology 35:1-12 D '49, 50:170-2 D '64/ Illustrated London News 244:27 Ja 4 '64/N Y Times p 26 D 20 '63/ Rev Arch 1:53-5 Ja '64.

1213 GARDNER, ERNEST ARTHUR (1862- 1939), Clapton, England. Archeologist. Classical Greek specialist; excavated at Naucratis, Paphos on Cyprus, and many mainland Greek sites. Sources: Biog Index: 2/ Dictionary of National Biography 1931-1940:307-8 '49.

1214 GARDNER, GUY (1881-1959), England. Archeologist. Prehistory of Africa. Sources: Biog Index: 5/Int Dir Anth 2, 3/Nature 185:655-6 Mr 5 '60.

1215 GARDNER, PERCY (1846-1937), Hackney, England. Archeologist, mathematician. Classical archeologist; specialty in Greek coinage and vase-paintings. Sources: Biog Index: 2/Dictionary of Universal Biography/ Dictionary of National Biography 1931-1940:306-7 '49.

1216 GARDNER, WILLOUGHBY (ca. 1859-1953). Entomologist, archeologist. Organizer of excavations of hill-forts in North Wales; helped organize excavations of Roman sites, such as Segontium

at Caernarvon. Sources: Biog Index: 3/Nature 172:439 S 5 '53.
1217 GARFIELD, VIOLA E (1899-). Social anthropologist. Social organization of N. American Indians. Art & totem poles. Sources: Int Dir Anth 1, 2, 3, 5.
1218 GARIGUE, PHILIPPE (1917-). Sociologist. Sociology of the family. Social change in Canada, Italy & Spain. Source: Int Dir Anth 5.
1219 GARNIER, S J, Fr. CHARLES (1605-1649), Paris, France. Priest. Missionary in New France; wrote on N. American Indians. Source: Jes Rel.
1220 GARNIER, S J, Fr. JULIEN (1643-1730), St. Brieux, France. Priest. Missionary in New France; wrote on N. American Indians. Source: Jes Rel.
1221 GARROD, DOROTHY ANNIE ELIZABETH (1892-1968), London, England. Archeologist. Prehistoric society of Great Britain. Sources: Biog Index: 3 & 8/Int Dir Anth 1, 2/ Britannica Book of the Year 1969:570 '69.
1222 GARSTANG, JOHN (1876-1956), England. Archeologist. Prehistoric archeology of Near East. Sources: Biog Index: 4 & 5/Int Dir Anth 2/Rev Arch 2:102-3 Jl '58.
1223 GARVIN, PAUL L (1919-), Vienna, Austria. Linguist. Linguistic theory & method. Language & culture. Machine translations. Sources: Int Dir Anth 3, 5.
1224 GATSCHET, ALBERT SAMUEL (1832-1907), Switzerland. Ethnologist, linguist. Studied Klamath Indians. Pioneer in scientific study of American Indian languages. Sources: Columbia/Am Anth 9:561-70 Jl '07.
1225 GAUD, FERNAND. Wrote ethnographic works on the Mandjia people of the Central Ubanguian Plateau (Central African Republic). Source: Kalck, Pierre, Historical Dictionary of the Central African Republic (1980), p 56.
1226 GAVAN, JAMES ANDERSON (1916-), Ludington, Michigan, United States. Physical anthropologist. Growth in non-human primates. Sources: Int Dir Anth 3, 5.
1227 GAVAZZI, MILOVAN M (1895-), Gospic, Croatia, Yugoslavia. Ethnologist. Traditional peasant way of life & culture in the Balkans. Sources: Int Dir Anth 1, 2, 3, 5.
1228 GAYA NUÑO, BENITO (1908-1953). Archeologist. Sources: Biog Index: 3/ Archivo Espanol de Arte y Arqueologia 26 no 88:458 '53.
1229 GAYTON, ANNA HADWICK (1899-1977), Santa Cruz, California, United States. Anthropologist. Peruvian archeology. Primitive textiles & historic costume. Studied & catalogued Peruvian textiles & costumes. Curator of textiles at Lowie Museum. Sources: Biog Index: 11/Int Dir Anth 1, 2, 3/Nat Dir Lat Am/ Am Anth 80:653-6 S '78/Anth News D '77.
1230 GEBHARD, PAUL HENRY (1917-), Rocky Ford, Colorado, United States. Ethnologist. Human sexuality, behavior & attitudes. Sources: Int Dir Anth 3, 5.
1231 GEDDES, WILLIAM ROBERT (1916-), New Plymouth, New Zealand. Ethnologist. Dayak social organization & ethnic relations in Australia. Social change in peasant societies of the Southwest Pacific. Sources: Int Dir Anth 3, 5.
1232 GEIST, OTTO WILLIAM (1888-1963), Eiselfing, Bavaria, Germany. Paleontologist, archeologist. Alaskan archeological studies. Sources: Biog Index: 7 & 8/Int Dir Anth 1, 2/ Kein, Charles J. Aghvook, White Eskimo. Otto Geist and Alaskan archeology. Univ. of Alaska Press '69.
1233 GEJVALL, NILS-GUSTAF (1911-), Paryd, Kalmar, Sweden. Anthropologist, osteologist. Human, animal & forensic osteology. Sources: Biog Index: 8/Int Dir Anth 3, 5.
1234 GELL, WILLIAM (1777-1836). Archeologist. Source: Biog Index: 11.
1235 GENET-VARCIN, EMILIENNE (1912-), Paris, France. Paleontologist. Origins of man.

Paleolithic & Mesolithic fossil man. Sources: Int Dir Anth 3, 5.

1236 GENNEP, ARNOLD van (Charles-Arnold Kurr) (1873-1957), Germany. Folklorist. Government worker with cultural organizations. Wrote on rites of passage. Sources: Biog Index: 5 & 11/ International Encyclopedia of the Social Sciences, v. 6.

1237 GÉRARD, JOSEPH-JEAN-CHARLES, Rev (1831-1914), Nancy, France. Missionary. Translated scripture into Sesotho; wrote several volumes on mission life and the Basotho. Source: Haliburton, Gordon, Historical Dictionary of Lesotho (1977).

1238 GERASIMOV, MIKHAIL MIKHAILOVICH (1907-1970), Russia. Anthropologist, archeologist. Pioneer in reconstruction of facial features from skulls. Sources: Biog Index: 9/ Great Soviet Encyclopedia, New York, Macmillan (1975), v. 6, p 309/ N Y Times p 31 Jl 23 '70.

1239 GERBAULT, ALAIN (1893-1941), France. Writer. Collected legends and genealogies of Polynesia, particularly involved with the Marquesas, Tahiti and Bora Bora. Source: Craig & King, Historical Dictionary of Oceania (1981), p 105.

1240 GERBRANDS, ADRIAN ALEXANDER (1917-), Menado, Dutch East Indies, Indonesia. Cultural anthropologist. Visual cultural ethnology. Context of art & artist. Oceania. Sources: Int Dir Anth 3, 5.

1241 GÉRIN-RICARD, HENRY de (1864-1944), Marseilles, France. Archeologist. Prehistory & archeology of Southern France, particularly Provence. Sources: Biog Index: 1/Rev Arch 27:77-80 Ja '47.

1242 GERMAIN, S J, Fr. JOSEPH LOUIS (1633-1722), Clermont, France. Priest. Missionary in New France; wrote on N. American Indians. Source: Jes Rel.

1243 GERMOND, ROBERT CHARLES (1897-1971), Siloe, Lesotho. Physician. Compiled and edited the *Chronicles of Basutoland* (Morija, 1967) based on Paris Evangelical Missionary Society reports, 1830-1902. Source: Haliburton, Gordon, Historical Dictionary of Lesotho (1977), p 51.

1244 GEROW, BERT A (1915-), Lafayette, California, United States. Archeologist. N American folklore & mythology. Sources: Int Dir Anth 3, 5.

1245 GESSAIN, ROBERT (1907-), France. Social anthropologist. Study of small groups, for example, Inuit & isolates of East Senegal. Sources: Int Dir Anth 2, 3, 5.

1246 GHURYE, GOVIND SADASHIV (1893-), Bombay, India. Anthropologist, sociologist. Sources: Biog Index: 10/Int Dir Anth 3.

1247 GIBBONS, MAT. A ST. H. Explorer. Led two expeditions to the Lozi area of western Zambia in 1895-96 and 1898, which resulted in the first accurate maps of the Lozi kingdom and an ethnographic survey of all Lozi territory. Source: Grotpeter, John J., Historical Dictionary of Zambia (1979), p 85.

1248 GIBSON, GORDON D (1915-). Ethnologist. Bantu social organization. Ethnocinematography. African museology. Source: Int Dir Anth 5.

1249 GIBSON, JOHN A (ca. 1849-1912). Seneca chief, ethnologist. Represented Iroquois in dealing with the Canadian government; expert on Iroquois culture. Source: Am Anth 14:692-694 O '12.

1250 GIBSON, SIMEON (1889-1943), Canada. Informant. Dictated legends, translated texts, and interpreted laws, rituals & other data about his people, the Iroquois. Source: Am Anth 46:231-4.

1251 GIDDINGS, JAMES LOUIS (1909-1964), Cladwell, Texas, United States. Anthropologist. Ethnography & folklore of Western Inuit. Sources: Biog Index: 7/Int Dir Anth 3/Am Anth 67:1503-7 D '65/ Am Antiq 31:398-401 Ja '66/N Y Times p 47 D 10 '64.

1252 GIER, GÉRARD de (1858-1943), France. Archeologist. Discovered method of dating "prehistoric time" by the retreat of the ice sheets. Sources: Biog Index: 1/Rev Arch 26:88 Jl '46.

1253 GIFFORD, EDWARD WINSLOW (1887-1959), Oakland, California, United States. Anthropologist, museum curator. Specialized in the surviving California Indian tribes (focusing on kinship terminology & anthropometry), ethnography of Tonga, and archeology of Fiji, Yap, New Caledonia, and Sonora & Nayarit (Mexico). One of the first scholars to publish on acculturation and describe modern lineages. Sources: Biog Index: 5/Int Dir Anth 1, 2, 3/Am Anth 62:327-9 Ap '60/ Am Antiq 25:257-9 O '59/N Y Times p 27 My 18 '59.

1254 GILBERT, WILLIAM HARLEN (1904-), Covington, Kentucky, United States. Socio-cultural anthropologist. Ethnoastronomy. Social organizations. Sources: Int Dir Anth 2, 3, 5.

1255 GILCHRIST, ANNE GEDDES (1864- 1954). Folklorist. Proposed classification scheme for Gaelic and English folkmusic. Sources: Biog Index: 3/Journal of American Folklore 68:87-8 Ja '55.

1256 GILCHRIST, JOHN BORTHWICK (1759-1841), Scotland. Orientalist, physician. Compiled a dictionary and grammar of Hindi. Sources: Biog Index: 5/British Medical Journal no 5144:150-1 Ag 8 '59.

1257 GILES, HERBERT ALLEN (1845-1935), Oxford, England. Sinologist. Pioneer of Chinese studies in Britain, writing everything from dictionaries and textbooks to translations of classical Chinese literature. Sources: Biog Index: 2/Dictionary of National Biography 1931-1940:338-9 '49 /Who Was Who, 1929-1940.

1258 GILES, LIONEL (1875-1958), Sutton, Surrey, England. Sinologist. Wrote extensively on Chinese inscriptions and philosophy; published catalogs of several important collections from the caves of Dunhuang in the British Museum. Sources: Biog Index: 5/Journal of Asian Studies 17:676-7 Ag '58.

1259 GILIJ, FELIPE SALVADOR (1721-1789), Colombia. Missionary. Wrote an account of his 18 years service to the Indians of the Orinoco River area. Source: Davis, Robert H., Historical Dictionary of Colombia (1977), p 116.

1260 GILL, EDMUND DWEN (1908-). Paleoanthropologist. Antiquity & changing environment of Australian aborigines. Source: Int Dir Anth 5.

1261 GILLEN, FRANCIS JAMES (1855-1912), Clare, Australia. Ethnologist. Wrote, with W. Baldwin Spencer, several major works on Aborigines of Central Australia. Sources: Biog Index: 2/Dictionary of Australian Biography 1:346-7 '49/ Am Anth 14:705-6 O '12.

1262 GILLIN, JOHN PHILIP (1907-1973), Waterloo, Iowa, United States. Psychological anthropologist. Culture & psychological theory. Principles of sociocultural integration. Using a psychocultural perspective, studied Latin American social cultural systems & social change. Sources: Int Dir Anth 1, 2, 3, 5/Nat Dir Lat Am/Biog Index: 10 & 12/ Nat Cyc Am Biog 58:429-31 '79/Human Ways (by John P. Gillin)/ N Y Times p 53 Ag 5 '73.

1263 GILLMOR, FRANCES (1903-), Buffalo, New York, United States. Folklorist. Aztec history to 1472. Navajo mythology. Folk drama & dance of Mexican villages. Sources: Int Dir Anth 3, 5/Nat Dir Lat Am.

1264 GIOT, PIERRE-ROLAND (1919-). Geologist, physical anthropologist. Prehistory & protohistory. Quaternary geology & physical anthropology of Brittany. Source: Int Dir Anth 5.

1265 GIRAULT de VILLENUEVE, S J, Fr. ÉTIENNE PIERRE THOMAS (1718-1794), France. Priest. Missionary in New France; wrote on N.

American Indians. Source: Jes Rel.

1266 GJESSING, GUTORM (1906-), Alseuna, Norway. Archeologist. Concept of circumpolar culture. Sources: Int Dir Anth 3, 5.

1267 GLADWIN, HAROLD STERLING (1883-1983). Archeologist. Southwestern U.S. archeology, especially of Pueblo Indians in Arizona; founded Gila Pueblo Archeological Foundation (now Arizona State Museum); published on Gila Pueblo, Mogollon & Hohokam cultures. Source: Anth News 12/85:3.

1268 GLADWIN, THOMAS FAVILL (1917-), New York, New York, United States. Ethnologist. Micronesian specialist and author of *East Is A Big Bird*, on traditional navigation. Source: American Men and Women of Science, ed. by J.C. Press, 12th ed., New York, Bowker, 1973.

1269 GLANVILLE, STEPHEN RANULPH KINGDON (1900-1956), England. Egyptologist. Technological history of ancient Egypt. Sources: Biog Index: 4/Int Dir Anth 2.

1270 GLAPION, S J, Fr. AUGUSTIN LOUIS de (1719-1790), Seez, France. Priest. Missionary in New France; wrote on N. American Indians. Source: Jes Rel.

1271 GLOB, PETER VILHELM (1901-1985), Denmark. Archeologist. Ancient Persia; Vikings in Greenland. Source: Chicago Tribune, July 25, 1985.

1272 GLUCKMAN, HERMAN MAX (1911-1975), Johannesburg, South Africa. Anthropologist, author. Social anthropology. Studied law, ritual & conflict in various groups in Africa. Ethnographic work in Malawi, Zambia, Zimbabwe, & Israel. Sources: Biog Index: 10 & 12/Int Dir Anth 2, 3/ International Encyclopedia of the Social Sciences, v. 18/ Journal of African History 20 no 4:525-41 '79/Anth News Jn '75.

1273 GLUECK, NELSON (1900-1971), Cincinnati, Ohio, United States. Rabbi, biblical scholar, archeologist. Archeology of Israel. Sources: Biog Index: 1 3 6 8 9 11 & 13/Int Dir Anth 2, 3/ Stern, Ellen Norman. Dreamer in the Desert. KTAV Pub House '80.

1274 GODDARD, PLINY EARLE (1869-1928), Lewiston, Maine, United States. Ethnologist, museum curator. Ethnology & language of the Hupa Indians of California; intensive fieldwork & publications on Northwestern U.S. Athapascan groups. Source: Am Anth 31:1-8 Ja '29.

1275 GODFREY, WILLIAM SIMPSON (1916-). Anthropologist, archeologist. Pre-Toltec & Toltec Mexican archeology. Sources: Int Dir Anth 5/Nat Dir Lat Am.

1276 GODLEWSKI, ALEKSANDER L (1905-). Socio- physical anthropologist. Social structure & serological connections. Ethnogenetics & migrations in Oceania. Genealogy in Polynesian clans. Source: Int Dir Anth 5.

1277 GOELL, THERESA M (ca. 1901-1985). Archeologist, architect. Excavated at Nimrud Dagh (Turkey). Source: Anth News 2/86:3.

1278 GOETZE, ALBRECHT (1897-1971), Leipzig, Germany. Assyriologist. Specialist in archeology of Babylon and Assyria; expert on cuneiform writings; founded study of the Hittites as a separate discipline; extensive publications. Sources: Biog Index: 9/American Oriental Society Journal 92:197-203 Ap '72/ N Y Times p 40 Ag 18 '71/Time 98:50-1 Ag 30 '71.

1279 GOFF, CHARLES W (1897-1975), Illinois, United States. Anthropologist. Archeology in Central & South America. Discovered remains of Christopher Columbus. Source: Anth News S '75.

1280 GOGGIN, JOHN MANN (1916-1963), Chicago, Illinois, United States. Anthropologist. Specialist in problems of culture historical; focused on Pueblo & Seminole ethnology, and Florida archeology. Sources: Biog Index: 6 & 7/Int Dir Anth 3/Am Anth 66:385-94 Ap '64.

1281 GOINS, JOHN F (1915-). Anthropologist. Source: Nat Dir Lat Am.

1282 GOLDENWEISER, ALEXANDER ALEXANDROVICH (1880-1940), Kiev, Russia. Anthropologist. An important theorist of post-Boas "American-school;" author of *Early Civilization*. Sources: Biog Index: 4/Int Dir Anth 1, 2/ Dictionary of Australian Biography sup 2:244-5 '58/Am Anth 43:250-5 Ap '41.

1283 GOLDFRANK, ESTHER SCHIFF (1896-), New York, New York, United States. Anthropologist. Sources: Biog Index: 13/Int Dir Anth 3/ Goldfrank, Esther Schiff. Notes on an Undirected Life Queens College Press '78.

1284 GOLDMAN, FRANK PERRY (1912-). Sociologist. Anthropology of learning & educational renewal in Brazil. Source: Int Dir Anth 5.

1285 GOLDMAN, HETTY (1881-1972), New York, New York, United States. Archeologist. Showed early links between Greece and Anatolia. First woman to direct archeological excavations; worked at the American School in Athens and excavated at several locations in Greece and Turkey. Sources: Biog Index: 8 9 11 & 13/Archaeology 20:83 Ap '67/ N Y Times p 38 My 6 '72/Nat Cyc Am Biog 56:509-10 '75/ Notable American Women, the Modern Period. vol. IV, Belknap Press '80, p 280-2.

1286 GOLDMAN, IRVING (1911-), Brooklyn, New York, United States. Ethnologist. Northwest Amazonian ethnology. Polynesian status symbols. Kwakiutl religious thought in British Columbia. Sources: Int Dir Anth 1, 2, 3, 5.

1287 GOLDSCHMIDT, WALTER (1913-), San Antonio, Texas, United States. Ethnologist. Functional, ecological & evolutionary theory. Sources: Int Dir Anth 2, 3, 5.

1288 GOLDSTEIN, MARCUS S (1906-), Philadelphia, Pennsylvania, United States. Physical anthropologist. Dentition & paleopathology. Research on growth of head and face in relation to age & dentition. Sources: Int Dir Anth 1, 2, 3, 5.

1289 GOLDZIHER, IGNÁC (1850-1921). Orientalist. Sources: Biog Index: 1 & 4.

1290 GOLOMSHTOK, EUGENE ALEXANDROVICH (1897-1950), Russia. Anthropologist. Anthropology of Russia. Sources: Biog Index: 2/Int Dir Anth 1 2 3/N Y Times p 25 Je 23 '50/ Science 112:99 Jl 21 '50.

1291 GOLOUBEW, VICTOR (1879-1949), Crimea. Archeologist. Art of Indochina, particularly Angkor. Sources: Biog Index: 2/Isis 42 no 2:146 '51/ Rev Arch series 6 35:102 Ja '50.

1292 GÓMEZ, DIEGO. Explorer. Led expedition to Gambia River in 1457. His reports influenced start of missionary efforts in the valley. Source: Gailey, Harry A., Historical Dictionary of Gambia (1975), p 61.

1293 GÓMEZ, INDALECIO (1850-1920), Molinas, Argentina. Educator. Continued archeological & anthropological studies of Salta province begun by Juan Leguizanon. Source: Wright & Nelsham, Historical Dictionary of Argentina (1978), p 356-7.

1294 GONEIM, MOHAMMED ZAKARIA (1910-1959), Egypt. Archeologist. Discovered the unfinished pyramid at Saqqara (Egypt), and directed excavations at that site. Sources: Biog Index: 5/Illustrated London News 234:107 Ja 17 '59/ N Y Times p 9 Ja 12 '59/Publishers Weekly 175:221 Ja 26 '59/ Time 73:95 Ja 26 '59.

1295 GONIDEC, JEAN FRANCOIS de (1775-1838). Linguist. Pioneer dictionary (1821). of the Celtic language. Source: Columbia.

1296 GONNOR (De Gonnor), S J, Fr. NICHOLAS de (1691-1759), Lucon, France. Priest. Missionary in New France; wrote on N. American Indians. Source: Jes Rel.

1297 GONZÁLEZ, ALBERTO REX (1918-), Argentina. Archeologist. Andean pre-ceramic archeology in Argentina. Source: Int Dir Anth

1298 GONZÁLEZ SUÁREZ, FREDERICO (1844-1917), Quito, Ecuador. Historian, prelate. Specialist in the archeology of southern Ecuador (Canaris); also published an archeological atlas of Ecuador & treatises on the Indians of Imbabura & Carchi; father of Ecuadorean archeology. Source: Am Anth 20:318-321 '18.

1299 GOODE, WILLIAM JOSIAH (1917-). Sociologist. Family & social systems in social theory. Source: Int Dir Anth 5.

1300 GOODENOUGH, WARD HUNT (1919-), Cambridge, Massachusetts, United States. Ethnologist. Social organization, culture & language of Oceania. Formal analysis of culture & culture theory. Sources: Int Dir Anth 3, 5.

1301 GOODMAN, FELICITAS D (1914-). Glosslalia. Mexican linguistic reflections. Source: Int Dir Anth 5.

1302 GOODMAN, JOSEPH THOMPSON (1838-1917), United States. Mayan archeology. Conducted some important deciphering of Maya hieroglyphic writing. Source: Am Anth 21:441-5 O '19.

1303 GOODMAN, MARY ELLEN (1911-1969), Los Angeles, California, United States. Anthropologist. Culture of children; inter-ethnic & urban problems. Sources: Biog Index: 8/Int Dir Anth 3/Am Anth 73:244-7 F '71/ Childhood Education 46:75 N '69.

1304 GOODWIN, ASTLEY JOHN HILARY (1900-1959), Pietermaritzburg, Natal, South Africa. Archeologist. Prehistoric archeology & "primitive" technology in Southern Africa. Sources: Biog Index: 5/Int Dir Anth 1 2 3/Nature 186:761 Je 4 '60.

1305 GOODWIN, GRENVILLE (1907-), New York, New York, United States. Anthropologist. Fieldwork among Western Apache. Sources: Biog Index: 10/Int Dir Anth 2.

1306 GOODWIN, WILLIAM BROWNELL (1866-1950). Archeologist. Conducted excavations in New England, discovering several sites with beehive stone structures which led him to suggest pre-Columbian contact with Ireland via the voyages of St. Brendan. Sources: Biog Index: 2/N Y Times p 28 My 19 '50/ Wasdworth Atheneum Bulletin S 2 no 18:(Insert) O '50.

1307 GOODY, JOHN R (1919-). Ethnologist. Studies in kinship. Source: Int Dir Anth 5.

1308 GORDON, ANTOINETTE K (1892-1975), United States. Anthropologist. Tibetan studies. Interpretation of Tibetan painted religious banners. Founder of the Tibetan Society. Sources: Biog Index: 10/Anth News My '75/N Y Times p 44 Mr 26 '75.

1309 GORDON, CYRUS HERZL (1908-). Orientalist. Source: Biog Index: 6.

1310 GORDON, GEORGE BYRON (1870-1927), Prince Edward Island, Canada. Archeologist, museum curator. Excavated in Central America, Ur (Iraq) & Beisan (Palestine). Director of University of Pennsylvania University Museum. Source: Am Anth 29:366 Jl '27.

1311 GORDON, ROBERT WINSLOW (1888- 1961). Archivist, folklorist. First archivist of Library of Congress Archive of American Folk Song; created collection and preserved much material on cylinders from period, 1922-1929. Sources: Biog Index: 10/Journal of American Folklore 87:12-38 Ja '74.

1312 GORER, GEOFFREY EDGAR (1905-1985), England. Social anthropologist, ethnologist. Ethnological applications of social anthropology. Personality studies of Himalayan cultures, especially Lepcha. Impact of radio and movies (U.S.); national character studies. Sources: Biog Index: 1 & 4/Int Dir Anth 5/ Kunitz, Stanley Jasspon ed., Twentieth Century Authors; 1st sup. Wilson '55 p 375-6/Anth News 9/85.

1313 GORI MOLUBUELA, ENRIQUE (1919-1972). Civil servant. Wrote an ethnographic account of the Bubi people of Equatorial Guinea. Source: Liniger-Gounaz, Max, Historical Dictionary of Equatorial Guinea (1979), p 73-4.

1314 GORMLY, MARY (1919-). Librarian. Indians of Mexico and Northwest Coast, U.S. Source: Int Dir Anth 5.

1315 GORODTSOV, VASILII ALEKSEEVICH (1860-1945), Dubrovichi, Russia. Archeologist. Devised classification of the cultures of the Bronze Age in Russia. Sources: Great Soviet Encyclopedia, New York, Macmillan (1975), v. 7, p 306 /Krainov, D.A. "K stoletiiu so dnia rozhdeniia V.A. Gordtsova" Sovetskaia arkheologiia, 1960, no. 1.

1316 GOSWAMI, M C (1918-). Social anthropologist. Social organization of the Garo, Karbi, Sherdukpen, Bodo Kachari & Lalung of India. Source: Int Dir Anth 5.

1317 GOT'E, IURII VLADIMIROVICH (1873-1943), Moscow, Russia. Historian, archeologist. Undertook the first scientific analysis of the scattered information on the Russians from the Paleolithic to the transformation of the Russian state. Sources: Great Soviet Encyclopedia, New York, Macmillan (1975), v. 7, p 312 /Bogoiavlenskii, S.K. "Akademik Iu. V. Got'e" Izvestiia AN SSR. Seriia istorii i filosofi, 1944, no. 3/ Picheta, V.I. "Akademik Iu. V. Got'e" Istovicheskie zapiski, fasc, 15. Moscow, 1945.

1318 GOTZEN, GUSTOV ADOLF von (1866-). Explorer. Visited Rwanda in 1894; discoverer of Lake Kivu; published account of travels: *Durch Afrika von ust nach west* (1895). Governor of German East Africa until 1906. Source: Weinstein, Warren, Historical Dictionary of Burundi (1976), p 142.

1319 GOUBAUD CARRERA, ANTONIO (1902-1951), Guatemala City, Guatemala. Anthropologist, diplomat. Guatemalan ethnology. Sources: Biog Index: 2/Int Dir Anth 2 3/Am Anth 54:71-3 Ja '52.

1320 GRAEBNER, FRITZ (1877-1934), Germany. Anthropologist, ethnologist, museum curator. Specialist in the cultures of the South Pacific and Australia. Interested in genetic classification of cultures. Curator at Berlin Ethnographic Museum and Cologne Ethnographic Museum. Sources: Biog Index: 11/Anthropos 72 no 1-2:1-55 '77/ Am Anth 320:326 Ap '35.

1321 GRAF, WALTER (1903-). Musicologist. Cross-cultural analysis in musicology. Source: Int Dir Anth 5.

1322 GRAHAM, ROBERT BANTINE CUNNINGHAM (1852-1936), London, England. Writer. Created an excellent historical account of the Jesuit missions to the Guarani Indians. Source: Wright & Nelsham, Historical Dictionary of Argentina (1978), p 368-9.

1323 GRAKOV, BORIS NIKOLAEVICH (1899-1970), Onega, Russia. Anthropologist. Scythian, Sarmatian, and classical Greek anthropology. Sources: Great Soviet Encyclopedia, New York, Macmillan (1975), v. 7, p 331 /"K 70-letiiu Borisa Nikolaevicha Grakova" Sovetskaia arkheologiia, 1969, no. 4.

1324 GRANET, MARCEL (1884-1946), France. Sinologist. Traditional Chinese culture. Published *Festivals and Songs of Ancient China* (1932) and *Chinese Civilization* (1930). Sources: Biog Index: 1/Spectator 176:268-9 Mr 15 '46.

1325 GRANT WATSON, ELLIOT LOVEGOOD (John Lovegood, pseud.) (1885-), England. Scientist, anthropologist. Sources: Biog Index: 1/Grant Watson, Elliot Lovegood. But to what purpose the autobiography of a contemporary. Cresset '46.

1326 GRAVIER, S J, Fr. JACQUES (1651-ca. 1708), Moulins, France. Priest. Missionary in New France; wrote on N. American Indians. Source: Jes Rel.

1327 GRAY, JOHN M, Sir. Judge. Wrote long detailed standard history of the Gambia. Source: Gailey, Harry A., Historical

Dictionary of Gambia (1975), p 63.
1328 GRAY, ROBERT F (1912-). Medical anthropologist, social anthropologist. Social aspects of medicine, magic & religion in African tribes. Source: Int Dir Anth 5.
1329 GRAY, TERENCE (1895-), England. Theatrical producer, Egyptologist. Source: Biog Index: 8.
1330 GRAYSON, GEORGE WASHINGTON (1843-1920), Oklahoma, United States. Businessman, officer of the creek nation. Zealously encouraged the permanent recording of the customs, ceremonies and history of his people, the Creek. Source: Am Anth 23:250-1 Ap '21.
1331 GRAZIOSI, PAOLO (1906-), Florence, Italy. Archeologist. Paleo- & Neolithic art forms. Fossil man in Europe, Asia & Africa. Sources: Int Dir Anth 1, 2, 3, 5.
1332 GREENBERG, JOSEPH HAROLD (1915-), Brooklyn, New York, United States. Anthropological linguist. Regional & general linguistics. Sources: Int Dir Anth 3, 5.
1333 GREENMAN, EMERSON FRANK (1895-1973), Hartwellinkle, Michigan, United States. Anthropologist, archeologist. Archeology & ethnology of North America. Sources: Biog Index: 10/Int Dir Anth 2 3/Am Antiq 39:271-3 Ap '74.
1334 GREENWAY, JOHN (1919-). Ethnomusicologist, folklorist. Worldwide distribution of white & aboriginal folklore. Source: Int Dir Anth 5.
1335 GREER, ISAAC GARFIELD (1881-1967), Zionville, North Carolina, United States. Folk singer, folklorist. Singer of traditional North Carolina folk songs. Sources: Biog Index: 8/Southern Folklore Quarterly 32:265-7 S '68.
1336 GREG, ROBERT HYDE (1876-1953), England. Diplomat, archeologist. Specialist in art of ancient Egypt. Sources: Biog Index: 3/Journal of Egyptian Archaeology 40:1-2 '54.
1337 GREGORY, HERBERT ERNEST (1869-1952), Middleville, Michigan, United States. Scientist, ethnologist. Director of the Bishop Museum in Honolulu; expert on Polynesian culture. Sources: Biog Index: 2 & 3/ Geological Society of America Proceedings 1953:115-23 '54/ Association of American Geographers Annals 42:322-3 D '52/ N Y Times p 25 Ja 29 '52/School & Society 75:93 F 9 '52.
1338 GREGORY, JOHN (1607-1646). Orientalist. Source: Biog Index: 3.
1339 GREMIATSKII, MIKHAIL ANTONOVICH (1887-1963), Russia. Anthropologist, anatomist. Physical anthropology of the Neanderthal stage of human evolution. Sources: Great Soviet Encyclopedia, New York, Macmillan (1975), v. 7, p 415 /Uryson, M. I. "M.A. Gremiatskii" Voprosy antropologii, fasc. 17, Moscow, 1964.
1340 GRENFELL, GEORGE. Explorer, missionary. Explored the Ubangui Basin, Central African Republic. Source: Kalck, Pierre, Historical Dictionary of the Central African Republic (1980), p 62.
1341 GRENIER, ALBERT (1878-1961), Paris, France. Archeologist. Archeology of Gaul (France). Sources: Biog Index: 6 & 7/Rev Arch 2:197-8 O '63.
1342 GRESHOFF, ANTOINE. Trader. First European trader to ascend the Congo River to its falls. Source: Kalck, Pierre, Historical Dictionary of the Central African Republic (1980), p 62.
1343 GREY, GEORGE (1812-1898), Lisbon, Portugal. Civil servant. Collected and published the first compilation of mythology of Polynesia in English and Maori. Source: Craig & King, Historical Dictionary of Oceania (1981), p 110.
1344 GRIAULE, MARCEL HENRI (1898-1956), Aisy-sur-Armancon, Yonne, France. Ethnologist. Ethnography of Africa especially Dogon in French Sudan & several groups in Cameroon. Studied symbolism and ritual of the Dogon and their cosmology; worked in region, 1931-33

& 1946-56. Sources: Biog Index: 4/Int Dir Anth 1 2 3/Imperato, Pascal J., Historical Dictionary of Mali (1977), p 53/Life 41:111-12+ D 3 '56.

1345 GRIERSON, GEORGE ABRAHAM (1851-1941). Philologist. Wrote grammars of many modern Indian vernaculars. Directed the Linguistic Survey of India. Source: Columbia.

1346 GRIEVE, LUCIA CATHERINE GRAEME (1862-1946). Orientalist. Specialist on India; collected an excellent library on that country. Sources: Biog Index: 1/N Y Times p 25 N 27 '46.

1347 GRIFFIN, JAMES BENEDICT (Bennett) (1905-), Atchison, Kansas, United States. Anthropologist, archeologist. Archeology of Eastern United States. Ceramic complexes & prehistoric agricultural societies in North America. Sources: Biog Index: 5/Int Dir Anth 1, 2, 5/Nat Dir Lat Am/ Am Anth 60:760 Ag '58/Am Antiq 23:419 Ag '58.

1348 GRIFFIN, JOHN WALLACE (1919-). Archeologist, cultural ecologist. Archeology of U.S. Source: Int Dir Anth 5.

1349 GRIFFITH, FRANCIS LLEWELLYN (1862-1934), Brighton, England. Egyptologist. Established Archaeological Survey at British Museum; specialist in deciphering hieroglyphic texts, as well as dealing with the languages of Nubia and Meroe and Old Coptic. Sources: Biog Index: 2/Dictionary of National Biography 1931-1940:375-7 '49 /Who Was Who, 1929-1940.

1350 GRIMBLOT, PAUL (1815-1870), France. Orientalist. Source: Biog Index: 3.

1351 GRIMES, WILLIAM FRANCIS (1905-), Pembroke, England. Archeologist. Conducted excavations on prehistoric and Roman sites in Wales. Organized and directed excavations of bombed sites in London (England) during World War II. Sources: Biog Index: 4/Int Dir Anth 3/Nature 177:16 Ja 7 '56.

1352 GRINNELL, GEORGE BIRD (ca. 1849-1938). Published on the Blackfoot & Cheyenne. Source: Am Anth 40:760 O '38.

1353 GROGAN, EWART SCOTT (1874-1964), England. Journalist. Made the journey from the Cape of Good Hope to Cairo in 1898-99 and wrote an account of the trip containing ethnographic data. Source: Ogot, Bethwell A., Historical Dictionary of Kenya (1981), p 67.

1354 GROOTAERS, WILLEM A (1911-). Linguist. Dialectic geography & linguistic atlas of Japan. Source: Int Dir Anth 5.

1355 GROTEFEND, GEORG FRIEDRICH (1775-1853). Archeologist, philologist. Deciphered inscriptions of Persian cuneiform. Wrote on Umbrian & Oscan languages. Source: Columbia.

1356 GROTTANELLI, VINIGI L (1912-), Avigliana, Italy. Ethnologist, archeologist. Religion, magic & morals in Africa. Etruscan archeology. Sources: Int Dir Anth 3, 5.

1357 GUAMÁN POMA de AYALA, FELIPE. Historian. Wrote a detailed chronicle of Peruvian Inca history which is second only to Garcilaso de la Vega's work as a source on early Colonial Peru. Source: Alisky, Historical Dictionary of Peru (1979), p 45.

1358 GUDSCHINSKY, SARAH CAROLINE (1919-), Bay City, Minnesota, United States. Summer Institute of Linguistics. Work in Mexico & Brazil. Wrote: *Protopopotecan* (1959); *How to Learn an Unwritten Language* (1967). Source: Nat Dir Lat Am.

1359 GUERNSEY, SAMUEL JAMES (1868- 1936), Dover, Maine, United States. Archeologist, museum curator. Excavated in New England & at Kayenta (N.E. Arizona); emphasized the development of Pueblo cultures, particularly Basketmaker; focused research on cultural history & lengthened the time perspective for southwest cultures; skilled craftsman in making models for museums. Source: Am Anth

39:135-7 Ja '37.

1360 GUEVARA, DARÍO C (1905-), Pelillo, Ecuador. Folklorist. Collected and studied Ecuadorean folklore and made it a scientific field in that country. Source: Bork & Maier, Historical Dictionary of Ecuador (1973), p 74.

1361 GUHA, BIRAJA SANKAR (1894-1961), Assam, India. Anthropologist. Physical anthropology. Instrumental in laying the foundation of scientific anthropology in India; studied the racial basis of India's caste system; tried to maintain anthropology in India as holistic discipline. Investigated the linguistic affinitive of Central Indian tribes. Worked among tribes of Assam, Bengal, Andaman Islands, Ute & Navajo. Sources: Biog Index: 6/Int Dir Anth 2 3/Am Anth 65:382-7 Ap '63.

1362 GULIAMOV, IA G (1908-), Tashkent, Uzbekistan. Archeologist. Archeology of Uzbekistan. Source: Great Soviet Encyclopedia, New York, Macmillan (1975), v. 7, p 479.

1363 GUMILLA, JOSÉ (1686-1750), Spain. Missionary. Served in Colombia for 23 years; wrote an illustrated account of the Orinoco River area. Source: Davis, Robert H., Historical Dictionary of Colombia (1977), p 121.

1364 GUNDA, BÉLA (1911-), Hungary. Ethnologist. Central & Eastern European ethnology. Origin of plants; cultivation & domestication of animals in the New World. Source: Int Dir Anth 5.

1365 GUNN, BATTISCOMBE GEORGE (1883-1950), England. Egyptologist. Philology and literature of ancient Egypt; assistant to Flinders Petrie who excavated in Upper Egypt in 1913; copied discovered texts and prepared them for publication. Sources: Biog Index: 2 & 5/Journal of Egyptian Archaeology 36:104-5 '50/ Nature 165:549-50 Ap 8 '50/Isis no 3-4:301 '50/ Dictionary of National Biography 1941-1950:334-5 '59.

1366 GUNTHER, ERNA (1896-), Brooklyn, New York, United States. Ethnohistorian. Native art, material culture of the Northwest Coast Indians of North America. Sources: Int Dir Anth 1, 2, 3, 5.

1367 GUPTA, MOTI LAL (1910-), India. Manuscriptologist. Linguistic analyst of Hindi, Sanskrit & Prakrit. Source: Int Dir Anth 5.

1368 GUSINDE, MARTIN (1886-), Breslau, Germany. Anthropologist. Anthropology & ethnology of Americas. Sources: Biog Index: 4/Int Dir Anth 1 3/Time 70:55 Jl 15 '57.

1369 GUTHE, CARL EUGENE (1893-1974), Kearney, Nebraska, United States. Anthropologist, archeologist. Fieldwork & collecting in the Philippines & New Mexico. Studied Pueblo pottery making. Sources: Biog Index: 11/Int Dir Anth 1/Am Antiq 41:168-77 Ap '76/ Anth News F '75.

1370 GUTIERREZ, ALBERTO (1862-1927), Bolivia. Historian. Wrote a social history of Bolivia in the 19th century. Source: Heath, Dwight B., Historical Dictionary of Bolivia (1972), p 113.

1371 GUTIERREZ, JOSÉ ROSENDO (1840-1883), Bolivia. Historian. Source: Heath, Dwight B., Historical Dictionary of Bolivia (1972), p 113.

1372 GUTZLAFF, KARL FRIEDRICH AUGUST (1803-1851), Germany. Sinologist, missionary. Source: Biog Index: 1.

1373 GUY, PHILIP LANGSTAFFE ORD (1885-1952). Archeologist. Director of the Archaeological Survey of Israel; worked at Megiddo, Tell-el Amarna (Egypt), Carchemish (Syria); discovered the stables built by King Solomon at Megiddo. Sources: Biog Index: 3/N Y Times p 41 D 8 '52.

1374 GUZMÁN, AUGUSTO (1903-), Bolivia. Source: Heath, Dwight B., Historical Dictionary of Bolivia (1972), p 113.

1375 GUZMÁN, EULALIA, San Pedro Piedra Gorda, Zacatecas, Mexico. Archeologist. Life and origins of the Indian population of Mexico. Discovered the apparent final resting place of Cuauhtemoc, the last Aztec ruler. Sources: Biog Index: 1 & 2/Americas 2:8-11+ F '50.

1376 HAAS, WILLIAM SAM (1883-1956), Nuremberg, Germany. Orientalist. Specialist in culture and politics of Iran. Sources: Biog Index: 4/N Y Times p 27 Ja 4 '56/ Wilson Library Bulletin 30:500 Mr '56.

1377 HAAVIO, MARTTI HENRIKKI (1899-1973), Temmes, Finland. Folklorist, poet. Folklore of Europe, especially Finland. Sources: Biog Index: 13/Int Dir Anth 2 3/ World Literature Today 54:38-40 Wint '80.

1378 HABERLANDT, MICHAEL (1860-1940), Germany. Ethnologist. Source: Nat Un Cat.

1379 HACHMANN, ROLF GEORG (1917-). Archeologist. Protohistoric Archeology. Protohistory of Germanic peoples. Bronze Age Europe & Iron Age Central Europe. Source: Int Dir Anth 5.

1380 HADDON, ALFRED CORT (1855-1940), London, England. Anthropologist. Led Torres Strait Expedition (1898-1899); wrote a large number of reports on Papua New Guinea and Sarawak; ethnography and material culture. Sources: Biog Index: 2/Int Dir Anth 1 2/ Dictionary of National Biography 1931-40:382-4 '49/ Praeger, Robert Lloyd. Some Irish Naturalists. Tempest '49, p 91-92 il por (80a, 184a).

1381 HADFIELD, PERCIVAL (1903-), Preston, Lancashire, England. Ethnologist. Wrote on primitive society in many geographic areas. Sources: Int Dir Anth 3/Nat Un Cat.

1382 HAEBERLIN, HERMAN KARL (1891- 1918), Akron, Ohio, United States. Ethnologist. Specialized in the tribes of Puget Sound (N. Pacific Coast), Pueblo Indians (Southwest U.S.); studied tribal art, shamanism & Salish languages. Source: Am Anth 22:71-4 Ja '19.

1383 HAEKEL, JOSEF (1907-), Vienna, Austria. Ethnologist. Ethnology of the Bhilala (Rutheva) tribal group in India as well as elsewhere. Sources: Int Dir Anth 3, 5.

1384 HAEUSLER, HEINRICH (1919-). Geologist. Human ecology & geology. Man's role in changing the earth. Source: Int Dir Anth 5.

1385 HAGIWARA, TATSUO (1916-). Ethnologist. Festival structure & history in Japan. Source: Int Dir Anth 5.

1386 HAHN, EDUARD (1856-1928). Geographer. Wrote on animal domestication, on "primitive" agriculture and on ancient economic systems. Source: Am Anth 31:363 Ap '29.

1387 HALBERT, HENRY SALE (1837-1916), Pickens County, Alabama, United States. Archeologist, historian. Colonization agent for removal of Choctaw Indians from Mississippi; historian of Choctaw nation; published on Alabama archeology. Source: Am Anth 18:449-50 Ja '16.

1388 HALE, HORATIO EMMONS (1817-1896). Ethnologist. Member of scientific corps of the Wilkes Exploring Expedition, 1838-1842, which journeyed to the South Pacific; compiled ethnological and philological data, especially linguistic materials, such as a grammar of Fijian which was much in advance of its time; applied the same comparative philological approach in reconstructing the history of the Iroquoian-speaking peoples. Sources: Biog Index: 7/American Philosophical Society Proceedings III no 1:5-37 F 17 '67/Am Anth 10 (old series):25-7 Ja 1897.

1389 HALIBURTON, ROBERT GRANT (1831-1901), Windsor, Nova Scotia, Canada. Attorney. Published on the astronomical elements in tribal myths & ceremonies around the world; collected data on the folklore and mythology of Morocco; "discovered" a population of pygmies in the Atlas Mountains. Source: Am Anth 3:389-90 Ap '01.

1390 HALL, CHARLES FRANCIS (1821-

1871). Explorer. Described Inuit life in 1860s. Source: Columbia.

1391 HALL, EDITH H (1877-1943), Woodstock, Connecticut, United States. Archeologist. Worked at Vrokastro, Crete, 1911-1912; later served as curator of the University Museum (Philadelphia). Sources: Biog Index: 11/Archaeology 31:42 Mr '78.

1392 HALL, EDWARD TWITCHELL (1914-), Webster Grove, Missouri, United States. Applied anthropologist, archeologist. Proxemics & non-verbal communication. Sources: Biog Index: 11 & 12/Int Dir Anth 3, 5/ Psychology Today 13:51 Ag '79, 10:38 Jl '76.

1393 HALL, FITZEDWARD (1825-1901). Orientalist, philologist. Source: Biog Index: 10.

1394 HALL, JAMES NORMAN (1887-1951), Colfax, Iowa, United States. Traveler, writer. Wrote a series of travel articles and novels describing Tahiti in the 1920s, partly in collaboration with Charles Nordhoff. Source: Craig & King, Historical Dictionary of Oceania (1981), p 115.

1395 HALL, RICHARD NICKLIN (1853-1914). Archeologist. Wrote massive works supporting theory of outside origin for Zimbabwean culture; ideas overturned by later works of Randall-MacIver. Source: Rasmussen, R. Kent, Historical Dictionary of Rhodesia/Zimbabwe (1979), p 110-1.

1396 HALLIDAY, WILLIAM REGINALD (1899-1966). Archeologist. Sources: Biog Index: 7/Illustrated London News 249:19 D 3'66.

1397 HALLOWELL, ALFRED IRVING (1892-1974), Philadelphia, Pennsylvania, United States. Theoretical anthropologist. Focused on culture-personality studies; postulated the notion of a culturally constituted behavioral environment to show in part, how human social order is possible. Worked among the Ojibwa. Sources: Biog Index: 3 10 11 & 12/ National Academy of Sciences. Biographical Memoirs v. 51. Columbia Univ. Press, The Academy '80 p 194-213/ Hallowell, Culture & Experience (thru 1954); & Fogelson, Raymond D, Contributions to Anthropology/ International Encyclopedia of the Social Sciences, v. 18/ Am Anth 78:608-11 S '76.

1398 HALPERN, ABRAHAM MEYER (1904- 1985). Folklorist, linguist. Studied Yuman, Pomo & Mayan languages; did thirty years of political analysis on Japan & the Far East. Source: Anth News 1/86:3.

1399 HALPERN, CARL (ca. 1902-1986). Industrialist. Published on the ethnic history of the Bronx (New York, U.S.) and ethnic stratification in industry. Source: Anth News 27:5:4.

1400 HALPERN, KATHERINE SPENCER (1913-). Ethnologist, folklorist. Folklore, psychological & medical anthropology of the U.S. Navajo. Source: Int Dir Anth 5.

1401 HALPERT, HERBERT (1911-). Archivist, folklorist. American & English tales, legends & folk narratives. Source: Int Dir Anth 5.

1402 HALSETH, ODD SIGURD (1893-), Moss, Norway. Archeologist. Southwestern U.S. Indians. Archeology, particularly of Pueblo irrigation works. Sources: Biog Index: 3/Int Dir Anth 1 2 3/Newsweek 42:84-5 Jl 20 '53.

1403 HAMBLY, WILFRID DYSON (1886-), Clayton, Bradford, England. Anthropologist. Africanist. Sources: Nat Un Cat/Int Dir Anth 1 2 3.

1404 HAMDI, OSMAN (1842-1910), Ottoman Empire, Turkey. Statesman, scholar, archeologist. Administrator of archeological excavation in Ottoman Empire for many years. Sources: Biog Index: 4/Rev Arch series 6 46:1-16 Jl '55.

1405 HAMILTON, ALEXANDER (1762-1824). Orientalist. Sources: Biog Index: 8 & 9.

1406 HAMILTON, HENRY WILLIAM (1898-1984). Archeologist. Archeology. Source: Anth News (Oct. 1984) p 3.

1407 HAMILTON, WILLIAM, Sir (1730-1803). Archeologist, diplomat, folklorist. Created a collection of artwork from the classical Greek and Roman periods. Sources: Biog Index: 4 5 6 8 & 11/Horizon 19:66-70 Ja '77.

1408 HAMMOND, DOROTHY (1917-), New Jersey, United States. Ethnologist. Role of women in traditional societies, particularly Africa. Sources: Int Dir Anth 3, 5.

1409 HAMPATÉ BA, AMADOU, see: BA, AMADOU HAMPATE.

1410 HAMPSON, JAMES KELLY (1877-1956), Memphis, Tennessee, United States. Physician, archeologist. Excavated the Mississippian site of Nodena, Arkansas over several decades. Sources: Biog Index: 4/Am Antiq 22:398-400 Ap '57.

1411 HAMPSON, THOMAS (-1888). Anthropologist. Editor of the journal of the Anthropological Society of Washington. Source: Am Anth 1(old series):296 Jl 1888.

1412 HAMY, ERNEST THEODORE (1842-1908), Boulogne-sur-Mer, France. Anthropologist, archeologist. Analyzed Cro-Magnon and other fossil remains. Sources: Dict des A/Am Anth 11:145-7 Ap '09.

1413 HAND, WAYLAND D (1907-), New Zealand. Folklorist. American folk legends & medicines. Sources: Int Dir Anth 3, 5.

1414 HANFMANN, GEORGE M A (ca. 1902-1986), St. Petersburg, Russia. Archeologist. Authority on Classical Greek & Roman art; excavated at Sardis and Tarsus (Turkey); published extensively on the civilizations of Asia Minor. Source: Anth News 27:5:3.

1415 HANKS, JANE RICHARDSON (1908-), Berkeley, California, United States. Ethnologist. U.S. Indian ethnology. Ritual ethnology & birth rituals of the Far East & Southeast Asia. Sources: Int Dir Anth 3, 5.

1416 HANNA, MARCUS ALBERT (1898-). Paleontologist. Source: Biog Index: 6.

1417 HANSEN, ASAEL TANNER (1903-), Collinston, Utah, United States. Ethnologist. Mexican & Central American urbanization. Effects of relocation on Japanese minorities. Cultural change. Sources: Int Dir Anth 2, 3, 5/Nat Dir Lat Am.

1418 HANSEN, HAZEL DOROTHY (1899-1962), San Mateo, California, United States. Archeologist. Led excavations in Aegean, particularly at Skyros (Greece); wrote on Aegean prehistory. Sources: Biog Index: 7/Nat Cyc Am Biog 49:631-2 '66.

1419 HANSON, OLA (1864-1929). Linguist. Wrote on Kachin language of Burma. Source: Nat Un Cat.

1420 HANSSEN, S O BORJE (1917-). Ethnologist. Urban social ecology & social stratification in 19th century Sweden. Sociological history of family & kinship studies. Source: Int Dir Anth 5.

1421 HARCOURT, RAOUL D' (1879-), Oran, Algeria. Wrote on civilization of Central America & Andes. Sources: Int Dir Anth 3/Nat Un Cat.

1422 HARCOURT-SMITH, CECIL, Sir (1859-1944), Staines, Middlesex, England. Archeologist. Began the excavations on the island of Melos (Greece) for British School (1895-1897); first director of Victoria-Albert Museum. Sources: Biog Index: 5/ Dictionary of National Biography 1941-1950:354-5 '59.

1423 HARDEN, DONALD BENJAMINE (1901-). Archeologist. Expert on ancient glass; became the Director of the London Museum in 1956. Sources: Biog Index: 4/Nature 178:240 Ag 4 '56.

1424 HARDING, GERALD WILLIAM LANKESTER (1901-1979), North China. Archeologist. Near Eastern archeology. Sources: Biog Index: 11/Int Dir Anth 2/N Y Times p B-19 F 13 '79.

1425 HARGRAVE, LYNDON LANE (1896-1978), Franklin, Georgia, United States. Archeologist. Using dendrochronology &

ornithological remains, he studied and dated many sites in the Southwest U.S. Sources: Biog Index: 13/Int Dir Anth 1 2/Am Antiq 45:477-82 Jl '80/ Anth News F '79.

1426 HARING, DOUGLAS GILBERT (1894-), Watkins Glen, New York, United States. Ethnologist, sociologist. Interests in Asia especially Japan. Sources: Int Dir Anth 2 3/Nat Un Cat.

1427 HARRINGTON, JOHN PEABODY (1884-1961), Waltham, Massachusetts, United States. Anthropological linguist, ethnologist. Published extensively on American Indians; did field work among the Chumash, Yuma, Mojave, Shoshoni, Tewa; devoted much of his research to searching out the "last survivors" of groups on the verge of extinction; one of early persons to recognize the importance of an interdisciplinary approach to ethnology; his notes are known for their phonetic accuracy. Sources: Biog Index: 6 & 11/Am Anth 65:370-381 Ap '63.

1428 HARRINGTON, MARIE WALSH (ca. 1907-1986). Biographies of Mark Harrington. Specialized in California mission archives and restoration. Source: Anth News 27:7:4.

1429 HARRINGTON, MARK RAYMOND (1882-1971). Museum curator. Collector of specimens. Specialist in American Indian culture. Source: Anth News 4/86:3.

1430 HARRIS, HOWARD L (1917-). Anthropologist. Religion in culture & society. Source: Int Dir Anth 5.

1431 HARRIS, J M (-1909). Businessman. Wrote a brochure calling for changes in British colonial policy in the Sierra Leone area. Source: Foray, Cyril P., Historical Dictionary of Sierra Leone (1977), p 84-5.

1432 HARRIS, ZELLIG SABBETTAI (1909-), Russia. Linguist. Wrote both on structural linguistics and on the grammar of several languages. Source: Int Dir Anth 3.

1433 HARRISON, HERBERT SPENCER (1872-1958), England. Anthropologist. Sources: Biog Index: 5/Int Dir Anth 3/ Illustrated London News 233:353 Ag 30 '58/Museum Journal 58:216 D '58.

1434 HARRISON, JANE ELLEN (1850-1928). Classicist, archeologist. Sources: Biog Index: 5/Stewart, Jessie G. Jane Ellen Harrison: A Portrait from Letters. Merlin '59.

1435 HARRISON, TOM (1911-1976). Anthropologist, archeologist, ethnologist. Stone Age caves. Ethnology & social life of highland people of Borneo (Indonesia). Sources: Biog Index: 11/Int Dir Anth 5/Geography Journal 142:376-7 Jl '76.

1436 HART, CHARLES WILLIAM MERTON (1905-1976), Melbourne, Australia. Social anthropologist. Study of the Tiwi Aborigines of Northern Australia. Also of Natchez social organization; social problems of Natchez Indians in urban & industrial settings. Sources: Biog Index: 11/Int Dir Anth 1 2/Am Anth 79:111-2 Mr '77/ Anth News S '76.

1437 HART, DONN VORHIS (1918-1984). Ethnologist. Peasant culture & folklore of Southeast Asia. Ritual kinship & social organization (compadrazgo) in Latin America & the Philippine Islands. Source: Int Dir Anth 5.

1438 HARTMANN, ROBERT (1832-1893). Wrote about evolution, apes, Africa. Source: Nat Un Cat.

1439 HARTZLER, OMAR LEE (1917-), Elizabethville, Belgian Congo, Zaire. Pastor, ethnologist. Religion & rites of passage in Malanje District (Angola) & Zaire. Sources: Int Dir Anth 3, 5.

1440 HARWOOD, RUTH (1917-). Anthropologist. Community development in El Salvador. Sources: Int Dir Anth 5/Nat Dir Lat Am.

1441 HASKELL, EDWARD (1906-). Ethnologist. Social stratification & culture patterns; advanced classification of cultures. Genetic mental basis of cultural patterns. Source: Int Dir Anth 5.

1442 HASS, MARY R (1910-). Linguist. Grammar of N. American Indian languages. Source: Int Dir Anth 5.

1443 HASSAN, SELIM (1887-1961), Egypt. Egyptologist. Directed excavations at Giza (1928-1936); Assistant Keeper of the Cairo Museum; 45 books published on numerous aspects of Egyptian archeology and history. Sources: Biog Index: 6/Int Dir Anth 1/N Y Times p 86 O 1 '61.

1444 HASSLÖF, OLOF PAUL HERMAN (1901-), Hovenaset, Sweden. Ethnologist. Maritime European social anthropology & ethnology, especially of Sweden. Sources: Int Dir Anth 3, 5.

1445 HASSRICK, ROYAL R (1917-). Ethnologist. Sioux and Dakota Indians, Indian art and history, U.S. & Canada. Source: Int Dir Anth 5.

1446 HASTINGS, JOHN (1875-1976), Cape Province, South Africa. Anthropologist, cartographer. Specialized in anthropological cartography; created numerous climatic-topographic maps. Sources: Biog Index: 10/N Y Times p 34 Ja 27 '76.

1447 HASTINGS, JOHN WALTER (1883-1908). Ethnologist. Collected cultural material in Iceland; did fieldwork in Andean regions of Peru & Bolivia. Source: Am Anth 10:356 Ap '08.

1448 HATTORI, TAKESHI (1909-), Fukuoka, Japan. Ethnologist, linguist. Language & ethnology of Gilyak people of Sakhalin & Amur region (U.S.S.R.). Sources: Int Dir Anth 3, 5.

1449 HAUDRICOURT, ANDRÉ GEORGES (1911-). Linguist. Diachronic phonology. Comparative linguistics. Botanic & ethnobotanic lexicology in Southeast Asia. Source: Int Dir Anth 5.

1450 HAURY, EMIL WALTER (1904-), Newton, Kansas, United States. Anthropologist, archeologist. Preceramic & ceramic archeology in Southwestern U.S. & Mexico. Sources: Biog Index: 8/Int Dir Anth 1, 2, 3, 5/Nat Dir Lat Am/ Men Who Dug Up History. Dodd '68 p 154-66.

1451 HAUSER, WALTER (1893-1959). Museum curator, archeologist. Excavated the Persian site of Ctesiphon, and worked at Nishapur, Iran; was curator of Near Eastern archeology at the Metropolitan Museum of Art in New York. Sources: Biog Index: 5/N Y Times p 29 Jl 15 '59/Am J Arch 64:85 Ja '60.

1452 HAVIGHURST, ROBERT J (1900-). Anthropologist. Cross cultural study of children, adolescents, & retirees in eight cultures. Source: Int Dir Anth 5.

1453 HAWES, HARRIET ANN (Boyd) (1871-1945), Boston, Massachusetts, United States. Archeologist. Discovered and excavated the Cretan site of Gournia in 1901; pioneer archeologist in the field of Minoan culture. Sources: Biog Index: 12/Ms. 8:13-15+ Ja '80.

1454 HAWKES, CHRISTOPHER FRANCIS CHARLES (1905-). Archeologist. Conducted excavations at Colchester, England (Roman Camulodunum); wrote: *The Prehistoric Foundations of Europe*, 1940. Sources: Biog Index: 1/Int Dir Anth 1/Nature 158:300 Ag 31 '46.

1455 HAWKES, JACQUETTA (Hopkins) (1910-). Author, archeologist. Sources: Biog Index: 3 & 4/ Kunitz, Stanley Jasspon ed., Twentieth Century Authors; 1st sup. Wilson '55 p 420-1.

1456 HAWTHORN, HARRY BERTRAM (1910-), Wellington, New Zealand. Wrote about Maori of New Zealand and Indians of British Columbia. Source: American Men and Women of Science, ed. by J.C. Press, 12th ed., New York, Bowker, 1973.

1457 HAY, CLARENCE LEONARD (1884- 1969), Ohio, United States. Archeologist. Mexican & Central American archeology. Sources: Biog Index: 8 & 10/Int Dir Anth 2/Nat Cyc Am Biog 54:554-5 '73/ N Y Times p 39 Je 6 '69.

1458 HAYDU, GEORGE GREGORY (1911-). Psychological

anthropologist. Value genesis, transformation & integration. Similarities & distinctions in enculturation & endoctrination. Source: Int Dir Anth 5.

1459 HAYES, WILLIAM CHRISTOPHER (1903-1963). Egyptologist. Excavated at the sites of Thebes and Lisht for 10 years; curator of Egyptian Antiquities in the Metropolitan Museum. Sources: Biog Index: 6 & 8/N Y Times p 29 Jl 11 '63/ Nature 200:1048-9 D 14 '63/Nat Cyc Am Biog 51:6-7 '69.

1460 HAYNES, HENRY WILLIAMSON (1831-1912), Bangor, Maine, United States. Humanist, teacher. Studied early man in N. America; believed that there had been more than one prehistoric migration of people to the continent and that history of occupation of N. America was longer than was usually supposed; amassed extensive collection of artifacts. Source: Am Anth 15:336-46 Ap '13.

1461 HAZELIUS, ARTUR (1833-1901), Sweden. Wrote about Swedish language, customs. Source: Nat Un Cat.

1462 HEALEY, GILES G (1901-1980), New York, New York, United States. Photographer, archeologist. Discovered the frescoes of Bonampak (Mexico) in 1946; made other discoveries, 1945-1947, and recorded Mayan sites on film. Sources: Biog Index: 12/N Y Times p D-19 Mr 6 '80/ N Y Times Biog Service 11:375 Mr '80.

1463 HEATH, BARBARA HONEYMAN (1910-). Physical anthropologist. Anthropometry & somatypology. Sex studies involving maturation. Source: Int Dir Anth 5.

1464 HEATH, EDWIN. Explorer. Wrote a description of the northern lowland area of Bolivia during the rubber boom. Source: Heath, Dwight B., Historical Dictionary of Bolivia (1972), p 114.

1465 HEBERER, GERHARD (1902-), Halle, Germany. Ethnologist. Wrote on ethnology of Stone Age. Source: Int Dir Anth 2 3.

1466 HEEKEREN, HENDRIK ROBBERT van (1902-1974), Semarang, Java, Indonesia. Archeologist, paleontologist. Paleontology of Indonesia. Sources: Biog Index: 10/Int Dir Anth 3/Mankind 10:48 Je '75.

1467 HEIDEL, ALEXANDER (1907-1955), Argentina. Assyriologist. Specialist on the literature and language of Assyria. Sources: Biog Index: 3/N Y Times p 21 Je 20 '55.

1468 HEILFURTH, GERHARD (1909-). Socio-cultural anthropologist. Cross-cultural mining research. Source: Int Dir Anth 5.

1469 HEILMANN, LUIGI (1911-). Anthropologist, linguist. Historical vs synchronic linguistics in India, Greece & Italy. Source: Int Dir Anth 5.

1470 HEINE-GELDERN, ROBERT von (1885-1968), Grub, Austria. Anthropologist, ethnologist. Investigated trans-Pacific migration theory. Wrote widely on early man. Sources: Biog Index: 8/Int Dir Anth 2 3/N Y Times p 25 My 30 '68/ Oriental Art 15:350 Winter '69.

1471 HEINITZ, WILHELM (1883-). Wrote about traditional non-Western music. Source: Nat Un Cat.

1472 HEINROTH, JOHANN CHRISTIAN AUGUSTUS (1773-1843). Wrote about many subjects including mysticism from cross cultural viewpoint. Source: Nat Un Cat.

1473 HEIZER, ROBERT FLEMING (1915-1979), Colorado, United States. Anthropologist, archeologist. California, Nevada & Alaska archeology. Sources: Biog Index: 12/Int Dir Anth 2 3/Am Anth 82:843-7 D '80/ Anth News S '76, S '79/N Y Times p D-13 Jl 20 '79/ N Y Times Biog Service 10:932 Jl '79.

1474 HELBOK, ADOLF (1883-). Wrote widely on Volksgeschichte, settlements, etc. Source: Nat Un Cat.

1475 HELFRITZ, HANS (1902-). Wrote: *Mexican Cities of the Gods: An Archeological Guide*. New York: Praeger, 1970. Source: Nat Un Cat.

1476 HELLBOM, ANNA-BRITTA (1918-). Ethnologist. Holistic

descriptive models. Cultural participation of women. Acculturation as revealed in Nahuatl language. Mestizo groups in Mexico. Source: Int Dir Anth 5.

1477 HELLMAN, MILO (1872-1947), Jassey, Romania. Dentist, anthropologist. Research on human dentition. Sources: Biog Index: 1/Int Dir Anth 1 2/N Y Times p 21 My 12 '47.

1478 HÉNAULT, MAURICE (1867-1945), France. Archeologist. Sources: Biog Index: 2/Rev Arch series 6 38:53 Jl '51.

1479 HENCKEL CHRISTOPH, CARLOS (1899-). Physical anthropologist. Ontogenesis of the cranium in primates. Ethnic deformations. Source: Int Dir Anth 5.

1480 HENDERSON, NORMAN B (1917-). Ethnologist. Ethnic studies across black & white racial lines. Source: Int Dir Anth 5.

1481 HENDRICK, HAUS (1834-1889), Greenland. Guide, explorer. Guided many exploration parties in the region of the North Pole. Source: Am Anth 3(old series):232 Jl 1890.

1482 HENNEY, JEANETTE HILLMAN (1918-). Ethnologist. Cross-cultural studies of altered state of consciousness. Caribbean religions. Shakers. Source: Int Dir Anth 5.

1483 HENNING, PAUL (-1923). Explorer. Collected anthropological materials; specialized in the manners & customs of Mexican Indian populations. Source: Am Anth 25:586 O '23.

1484 HENNING, WALTER BRUNO (1908-1967), England. Egyptologist. Source: Biog Index: 8.

1485 HENNINGER, JOSEPH ANTON MARTIN (1906-). Ethnologist. Bedouin studies. Religious festivals. Life styles & cattle breeding. Early Semites. Source: Int Dir Anth 5.

1486 HENRIES, RICHARD ABRAM (1908- 1980), Monrovia, Liberia. Lawyer. Wrote a history of the development of Liberia. Source: Dunn & Holsoe, Historical Dictionary of Liberia (1985), p 89-90.

1487 HENRÍQUEZ, DIEGO de (ca. 1900-), Trieste, Italy. Archeologist. Collected ancient & modern weapons; established a military museum. Sources: Biog Index: 5/Time 73:66 Ap 20 '59.

1488 HENRY, JULES (1904-1969), New York, United States. Anthropologist. Psychoanalytic approach to anthropology. U.S. & S. American Indians. Sources: Biog Index: 8 & 9/Int Dir Anth 1 2 3/ Am Anth 73:788-97 Je '71, 74:770 Je '72.

1489 HENRY, MELLINGER EDWARD (1874-1946), Mount Pleasant, Pennsylvania, United States. Folklorist. Specialist in American folksong; edited song collections and compiled song bibliography. Sources: Biog Index: 1/Current Biography 7:31 Mr '46/ Current Biography Yr Bk 1946:252 '47/Journal of American Folklore 59:316 Jl '46/ N Y Times p 24 F 1 '46/School & Society 63:98 F 9 '46/ Southern Folklore Quarterly 10:111-2 Mr '46.

1490 HENRY, TEUIRA (1847-1915), Tahiti. Linguist. Reconstructed J. Orsmond's manuscript and published the works under the title *Ancient Tahiti*; wrote on oral literature and history of Tahiti. Source: Craig & King, Historical Dictionary of Oceania (1981), p 133.

1491 HENSEL, WITOLD (1917-), Poznzn, Poland. Archeologist. Specialized in Slavic archeology. Source: Great Soviet Encyclopedia, New York, Macmillan (1982), v. 28, p 486.

1492 HENSHAW, HENRY WETHERBEE (1850-1930), Cambridgeport, Massachusetts, United States. Ethnologist, ornithologist. Conducted archeological excavations in California; classified & mapped N. American linguistic families; focused on languages of California, Nevada & Washington. Source: Am Anth 33:98-105 Ja '31.

1493 HERBIG, REINHARD (1898-1961). Archeologist. Archeology of classical world, especially Etruria

(Italy). Sources: Biog Index: 6/Am J Arch 67:81 Ja '63.

1494 HERDER, JOHANN GOTTFRIED von (1744-1803), East Prussia, Germany. Philosopher. Wrote on the origin of language. Produced an anthology of folk songs & studies of comparative philology. Worked on comparative religion & mythology. Source: Columbia.

1495 HERNÁNDEZ de ALBA, GREGORIO (1904-), Bogota, Colombia. Ethnologist. Wrote about Colombian ethnology. Sources: Int Dir Anth 3/Nat Un Cat.

1496 HERRERA, PABLO (1820-1896), Pujuli, Ecuador. Folklorist. Source: Bork & Maier, Historical Dictionary of Ecuador (1973), p 75.

1497 HERRERA y TORDESILLAS, ANTONIO (1559-1625), Spain. Historian. Under commission to Philip II, wrote a history of the Spanish conquest of the New World useful as a data source. Source: Davis, Robert H., Historical Dictionary of Colombia (1977), p 123.

1498 HERSENI, TRAIAN (1907-). Anthropologist. Psychological & social studies in cultural & pastoral anthropology of Romania. Source: Int Dir Anth 5.

1499 HERSKOVITS, FRANCES (Shapiro) (1895-1972). Anthropologist. Worked with her husband, Melville Herskovits, on many projects; co-authored several ethnographic works; specialist on culture of Dahomey and Surinam, as well as African art. Sources: Biog Index: 8 & 9/N Y Times p 40 My 8 '72.

1500 HERSKOVITS, MELVILLE JEAN (1895-1963), Bellefontaine, Ohio, United States. Anthropologist. Study of African cultures those of African descent throughout the world. Established one of the first African Studies programs in the U.S. and was the first President of the African Studies Association. Wrote, among other works, *Myth of the Negro Past* (1941) and *Man and His Works* (1948). Sources: Biog Index: 1 4 6 7 9 & 10/Int Dir Anth 1 2 3/ Simpson, George E., Melville Jean Herskovits, New York, Columbia Univ. Press (1973)/Am Anth 66:83-109 F '64.

1501 HERTZBERG, HANS THEODORE EDWARD (1905-), San Antonio, Texas, United States. Physical anthropologist. Anthropometry. Sources: Int Dir Anth 1, 2, 3, 5.

1502 HERZFELD, ERNST EMIL (1880-1948), Celle, Germany. Archeologist. Specialist in archeology of Babylonia and Persia; directed excavations at Persepolis in 1933; did much site survey work throughout the Near East. Sources: Biog Index: 1 2 & 11/Metropolitan Museum Journal 11:119-24 '76/ Art News 46:9 F '48/Museum News 25:3 F 15 '48/N Y Times p 23 Ja 23 '48/ School & Society 67:75 Ja 31 '48/Time 51:68 F 2 '48/Isis 42 no 2:146 '51.

1503 HERZOG, GEORGE (1901-), Budapest, Hungary. Anthropologist. Studied U.S. Indians and other peoples, particularly their music, poetry and folklore. Sources: Int Dir Anth 1 2 3/Nat Un Cat.

1504 HERZOG, ROLF (1919-). Ethnologist. Implications of economics in colonial era. Nomadism and sedentarization in North & Northeastern Africa. Source: Int Dir Anth 5.

1505 HEURTLEY, WALTER ABEL (-1955). Archeologist. Made excavations in Macedonia and on the island of Ithaca (Greece). Sources: Biog Index: 4/Antiquaries Journal 35:285 Jl '55.

1506 HEWES, GORDON WINANT (1917-), San Francisco, California, United States. Anthropologist, archeologist, linguist. Posture & gesture as related to the origin of language. Late Paleolithic to post pharaonic Sudan, archeology. Sources: Int Dir Anth 5/Nat Dir Lat Am/ American Men and Women of Science, ed. by J.C. Press, 12th ed., New York, Bowker, 1973.

1507 HEWETT, EDGAR LEE (1865-

1946), Warren County, Illinois, United States. Archeologist. Numerous excavations in Middle East, Guatemala. Directed the excavation of Quirigua in Guatemala and of cliff dwellings in the Southwest U.S.; also worked in Near East, North Africa and the Mediterranean. Sources: Biog Index: 1/Int Dir Anth 1 2/Am Antiq 13:78-9 Jl '47/ Am Anth 49:260-71 Ap '47/Am J Arch 51:305-6 Jl '47/Museum News 24:3 Ja 15 '47/ N Y Times p 33 Ja 1 '47/School & Society 65:27 Ja 11 '47.

1508 HEWITT, JOHN NAPOLEON BRINTON (1859-1937), England. Anthropologist. Sources: Biog Index: 11/Int Dir Anth 1 2/Am Anth 40:286-90 Ap '38.

1509 HEYERDAHL, THOR (1914-), Norway. Ethnologist, explorer. Specialist in prehistoric navigation and trans-oceanic contacts; excavated on Easter Island; led expeditions in restored ancient craft drifting from Peru to Polynesia, in the Persian Gulf, and elsewhere. Sources: Biog Index: 1 2 3 4 5 6 8 9 10 11 12 & 13/ Heyerdahl, Thor. Tigris Expedition. Doubleday '81/Newsweek 95:16-17 Mr 10 '80/ Makers of Modern Culture. Facts on File '81/Scandinavian Review 68:31-41 Je '80/ Britannica Book of the Year 1970:151 '70/ Current Biography 8:34-5 D '47, 33:30-3 S '72/ Current Biography Yr Bk 1947:300-2 '48, 1972:218-21 '73/ Saturday Review of Literature 41:30-1 O 4 '58/N Y Times Book Review p 8 N 27 '60 /Newsweek 52:99 S 8 '58, 74:69 Jl 28 '69, 73:56+ My 26 '69, 70:11 Ag 7 '67/ Kunitz, Stanley Jasspon ed., Twentieth Century Authors; 1st sup. Wilson '55 p 442-3/Time 110:116 N 28 '77, 98:54 Ag 30 '71/ Commire, Anne. Something about the Author, v 2. Gale '71 p 132-4.

1510 HIBBEN, FRANK CUMMINGS (1910-), United States. Anthropologist, archeologist. Wrote about archeology of Precolumbian North America. Sources: Int Dir Anth 1 2 3/Nat Dir Lat Am/Nat Un Cat.

1511 HIGGS, ERIC (1908-1976). Archeologist, prehistorian. Economic & ecological aspects of plant domestication & subsistence economics. Paleolithic archeology. Sources: Biog Index: 11/Int Dir Anth 5.

1512 HILDER, FRANK FREDERICK (1836-1901), Hastings, England. Military service. Excavated Mississippi Valley mounds; collected ethnological objects in the Philippines. Source: Am Anth 3:205-6 Ja '01.

1513 HILGER, MARY INEZ, OSB Sister (1891-1977), Roscoe, Minnesota, United States. Catholic nun, sociologist, anthropologist, ethnologist. Child life, the family & its cultural setting in N. & S. America. Children's roles in culture. American Indian & Latin American studies. Sources: Biog Index: 11/Int Dir Anth 3, 5/Nat Dir Lat Am/ Am Anth 80:650-3 S '78/Anth News S '77.

1514 HILL, ARCHIBALD A (1902-). Linguist. Phonemic & phonetic changes. Source: Int Dir Anth 5.

1515 HILL, BERT HODGE (1874-1958). Archeologist. Classical archeology; Director of American School in Athens, 1906-1926. Sources: Biog Index: 3 & 5/N Y Times p 37 D 3 '58/Am J Arch 63:193-4.

1516 HILL, GEORGE FRANCIS (1867-1948), England. Art critic, archeologist, numismatist. Sources: Biog Index: 2 & 5/ Dictionary of National Biography 1941-1950:391-2 '59/ Antiquaries Journal 29:246-7 Jl '49.

1517 HILL, IDA CARLETON (Thallon) (1876-1954), Brooklyn, New York, United States. Archeologist. Specialist in Greek archeology. Sources: Biog Index: 3 & 4/Am J Arch 59:241-2 Jl '55/ N Y Times p 83 D 19 '54.

1518 HILL, POLLY (1914-). Anthropologist. Socio-economic life in rural Hausaland (Nigeria). Population density. Rural capitalism, market & house trading. Migrations. Source: Int Dir Anth 5.

1519 HILL, WILLARD WILLIAMS (1902-

1974), San Francisco, California, United States. Anthropologist. Compiled extensive ethnographic data on the Navajo. Sources: Int Dir Anth 1 2/Am Anth 78:87-9 Mr '76.

1520 HILL, WILLIAM CHARLES OSMAN (1901-), Alcester, England. Physical anthropologist. Wrote on early man in Ceylon, India, Middle East. Sources: Int Dir Anth 3/Nat Un Cat.

1521 HILPRECHT, HERMANN VOLLRAT (1859-1925). Assyriologist. Authority on cuneiform writing. Directed expeditions to Nippur (Iraq). Source: Columbia.

1522 HIMMELHEBER, HANS (1908-), Karlsruhe, Germany. Ethnologist. Religion, sculpture & handicrafts in Africa & the Arctic. Sources: Int Dir Anth 3, 5.

1523 HINCKS, EDWARD (1792-1866). Orientalist. Wrote on Egyptians and Assyrians. Source: Nat Un Cat.

1524 HINSDALE, W B (ca. 1851- 1944). University administrator. Specialist in archeology and Indian population of Michigan. Source: Am Anth 47:179 Ja '45.

1525 HINTZE, FRITZ (1915-). Egyptologist, linguist. Phonology, morphology & comparative studies in ancient languages of Egypt and Sweden. Source: Int Dir Anth 5.

1526 HIRSCHBERG, WALTER (1904-). Ethnohistorian. Technology & ergology. African anthropology. Sources: Int Dir Anth 1, 2, 5.

1527 HITCHCOCK, JOHN THAYER (1917-). Cultural ecologist. Systems of generalized exchange & intercaste relations in India. Source: Int Dir Anth 5.

1528 HITTI, PHILIP KHURI (1886-1978), Shimlan, Lebanon. Orientalist. One of the major scholars of his period in Middle East studies. Sources: Biog Index: 1 3 11 & 12.

1529 HO, LIEN K'UEI (1902-), Chekiang Province, China. Wrote on ethnology of China. Sources: Int Dir Anth 3/Nat Un Cat.

1530 HOBHOUSE, LEONARD TRELAWNEY (1864-1929). Philosopher, sociologist. Used evidence from anthropology & comparative psychology to show that the evolution of the human mind was correlated with the development of societies. Source: Columbia.

1531 HOBLEY, CHARLES WILLIAM (1867-), London, England. Civil servant. Wrote two ethnographic accounts of various Kenyan tribal groups and of East African magic in general. Source: Ogot, Bethwell A., Historical Dictionary of Kenya (1981), p 73-4.

1532 HOCART, ARTHUR MAURICE (1884- 1939), Belgium. Anthropologist. Ethnological fieldwork in the Solomon Islands, Fiji, Samoa, Tonga, and elsewhere in Pacific. Focused particularly on religion and symbolism. Source: International Encyclopedia of the Social Sciences, v. 18.

1533 HOCKETT, CHARLES FRANCIS (1916-), Columbus, Ohio, United States. Ethnologist, linguist. N. American Algonkian descriptive & historical linguistics. Sources: Int Dir Anth 3, 5.

1534 HODGE, FREDERICK WEBB (1864-1956), Plymouth, England. Ethnologist, museum administrator, museum curator. Southwestern U.S. anthropology. Headed Smithsonian Institution (1901-1905) and Museum of American Indian (1918-1931). Published first *Handbook of American Indians*; excavated near Zuni (New Mexico). Sources: Biog Index: 4 5 & 6/Int Dir Anth 2 3/Nat Cyc Am Biog 43:28-9 '61/ Am Anth 59:517-20 Ja '57.

1535 HODGKIN, JONATHAN EDWARD (1875-1953). Engineer, archeologist. Sources: Biog Index: 3/Engineer 197:1 Ja 1 '54.

1536 HODGKIN, THOMAS LIONEL (1910-). Wrote about British colonies in Africa, especially the Gold Coast (Ghana). Source: Nat Un Cat.

1537 HODGSON, BRIAN HOUGHTON (1800-1894). Wrote widely on India. Source: Nat Un Cat.

1538 HODGSON, RICHARD (1855-1905), Melbourne, Australia. Published on altered states of consciousness, magic, trances. Source: Am Anth 8:202 Ja '06.

1539 HODSON, THOMAS CALLAN (1871- 1953). Anthropologist. Social anthropology of India. Sources: Biog Index: 3/Int Dir Anth 1 2/ Britannica Book of the Year 1954:529 '54/Nature 171:328-9 F 21 '5.

1540 HOEBEL, EDWARD ADAMSON (1906-), Madison, Wisconsin, United States. Forensic anthropologist, legal anthropologist. Kinship, politics & legal processes of the Shoshone, Cheyenne & Comanche. Also, worked at Keresan Pueblos, & in Pakistan. Developed the ethnography of law. Sources: Int Dir Anth 3, 5/ International Encyclopedia of the Social Sciences, v. 18.

1541 HOERNES, MORITZ (1852-1918), Vienna, Austria. Archeologist. Excavated in Bosnia & Herzegovina. Source: Am Anth 21:113-4 Ja '18.

1542 HOERNLE, AGNES WINIFRED (1885-), South Africa. Wrote about cultural contact and change in Southern Africa, particularly among the Hottentot. Sources: Int Dir Anth 2/Nat Un Cat.

1543 HOFFMAN, WALTER JAMES (1846-1899), Weidasville, Pennsylvania, United States. Diplomat, ethnologist, physician. Ethnology of the Ojibwa & Menomini. Source: Am Anth 2:187-8 Ja '00.

1544 HOFFMANN, MARTA (1913-), Ogna, Norway. Agricultural anthropologist. Textile tools, techniques, crafts, practices & working methods of rural & non-rural Scandinavians. Sources: Int Dir Anth 3, 5.

1545 HOFFMANN, MELVINA (1887-1966), New York, New York, United States. Sculptor. Her 100 bronze portraits of human racial types are in the Field Museum of Natural History (Chicago). Source: Columbia.

1546 HOFSCHLAEGER, REINHARD (1871- 1951), Soldin (Neumark), Germany. Physician, ethnologist. Sources: Biog Index: 3/Isis 43 no 2:118 '52.

1547 HOFSINDE, ROBERT (Gray Wolf) (1902-1973). Folklorist, illustrator. Sources: Biog Index: 5 7 9 & 10/Publishers Weekly 205:62 Ja 14 '74.

1548 HOFSTADTER, RICHARD (1916-1970), Buffalo, New York, United States. Historian. Wrote on social Darwinism. Source: Columbia.

1549 HOGAN, RALPH M (1890-). Ethnologist, linguist. Education & training of professional men & scientists in China. Source: Int Dir Anth 5.

1550 HOGARTH, DAVID GEORGE (1862- 1927), Barton-on-Humber, Linconshire, England. Archeologist. Excavated in Crete, Cyprus, Egypt, Melos, & Syria. Source: Columbia.

1551 HOGBIN, HERBERT IAN (ca. 1905-), England. Social anthropologist. Focused on law & order in fieldwork on Ontong Java. Extensive fieldwork on Guadalcanal, Malaita, & Wogeo, New Guinea, and elsewhere in Oceania. Advised colonial authorities on the British Solomons during World War II. Sources: American Ethnologist 13:4(1986):799-801/Int Dir Anth 1 2 3.

1552 HOHENTHAL, WILLIAM DALTON (1919-), Corning, California, United States. Anthropologist. Culture of Diegueno (Baja California & Mexico). Sources: Int Dir Anth 3/Nat Dir Lat Am.

1553 HOHENWART-GERLACHSTEIN, ANNA (1909-). Egyptologist. Folk culturist of Lower & Upper Egypt. Bedouin & Egyptian Nubians. Source: Int Dir Anth 5.

1554 HOIJER, HARRY (1904-1976), Chicago, Illinois, United States. Anthropologist, linguist. Studied Athapaskan languages, particularly Navajo; U.S. language & culture studies. Researched technical linguistic problems & relations among language, culture & perception. Sources: Biog Index: 10 & 11/Int Dir Anth 1, 2, 3, 5/ International Encyclopedia of the Social

Sciences, v. 18/ International Journal of American Linguistics 43:339-54 O '77/ Am Anth 79:105-10 Mr '77/Anth News My '76/Language 53:169-73 Mr '77/ N Y Times p 28 Mr 6 '76.

1555 HOLAS, BOHUMIL THEOPHILE (1909-), Prague, Czechoslovakia. Cultural ethnologist. Cultural ethnology & sociology of traditional Ivory Coast ethnic groups. Source: Int Dir Anth 5.

1556 HOLE, CHRISTINA (1896-). Editor, folklorist. Editor of the Folklore Society's journal, *Folklore*, 1956-1979; wrote: *Wonder Tales of the British Empire* 1934, and *British Folk Customs*, 1976. Sources: Biog Index: 13/Folklore 90 no 1:4-8 '79, 1:9-10 '79.

1557 HOLE, HUGH MARSHALL (1865-1941). Historian. Wrote a standard history of colonial Rhodesia. Source: Rasmussen, R. Kent, Historical Dictionary of Rhodesia/Zimbabwe (1979), p 116.

1558 HOLINSKI, ALEXANDRE (1816-), France. Traveler. Wrote an account of his trips to South America which treats the abolition of slavery in Ecuador. Source: Bork & Maier, Historical Dictionary of Ecuador (1973), p 76.

1559 HOLLAND, LEICESTER BODINE (1882-1952), Louisville, Kentucky, United States. Architect, archeologist. Studied classical architecture of the Acropolis in Athens in particular the Erechtheum. Sources: Biog Index: 2 3 & 4/Nat Cyc Am Biog 41:270 '56/ N Y Times p 23 F 8 '52.

1560 HOLLAND, WILLIAM JACOB (1848- 1932). Paleontologist. Source: Biog Index: 9.

1561 HOLLIS, ALFRED (1874-), Highgate, London, England. Civil servant. Wrote two volumes on the folklore of the Nandi and Masai of Kenya. Source: Ogot, Bethwell A., Historical Dictionary of Kenya (1981), p 74.

1562 HOLMA, HARRI (1886-1954), Finland. Orientalist, diplomat. Specialist on Assyria and philology of Semitic languages. Sources: Biog Index: 3/N Y Times p 29 Ap 15 '54.

1563 HOLMBERG, ALLAN RICHARD (1909-1966), Renville, Minnesota, United States. Anthropologist. South American ethnology. Sources: Biog Index: 7/Int Dir Anth 3/N Y Times p 40 O 14 '66.

1564 HOLMES, WILLIAM HENRY (1846-1933), Cadiz, Ohio, United States. Anthropologist, artist, scientific illustrator. Surveyed the cliff dwellings & pueblos of the San Juan, Colorado region; first to discredit concept of American Paleolithic; expert in American archeology; also published on the Maya; prominent musicologist. Sources: Biog Index: 3 & 13/ Records of the Columbia Historical Society, v 50 Univ. Press of Virginia. '80 p 252-78/Am Anth 35:752-64 O '33.

1565 HOLTKER, GEORG (1895-1976), Ahaut, Westfalen, Germany. Anthropologist, ethnologist. History & methods in general ethnology. Sources: Biog Index: 11/Int Dir Anth 1, 2, 5/Anthropos 71 no 1-2:1-2 '76.

1566 HOLTOM, DANIEL CLARENCE (1884-1962), Jackson, Mississippi, United States. Anthropologist, ethnologist. Specialist in Shinto, Japanese folk religion. Sources: Biog Index: 6/Am Anth 65:892-3 Ag '63.

1567 HOLUB, EMIL (1847-1902), Bohemia, Czechoslovakia. Surgeon. Traveled widely in Southern & Central Africa, 1883-1887, left a descriptive account of the trip; visited Lozi region and Kafue, Zambia. Source: Grotpeter, John J., Historical Dictionary of Zambia (1979), p 90-1.

1568 HOMET, MARCEL. Trader. Wrote: *Congo, terre de souffrance* (1934) exposing colonial exactions on the Lobaye peoples of what is now the Central African Republic. Source: Kalck, Pierre, Historical Dictionary of the Central African Republic (1980), p 66.

1569 HONEY, DE SYMON. Civil servant. Compiled historical

materials on the Swazi. Source: Historical Dictionary of Swaziland (1975), p 53.

1570 HONIGMANN, JOHN JOSEPH (1914- 1977), Bronx, New York, United States. Anthropologist, ethnologist. Arctic & Subarctic modernization & culture change. Ethnology of the Canadian North. Sources: Biog Index: 11/Int Dir Anth 3, 5/Am Anth 80:630-9 S '78/ Anth News O '77.

1571 HONIGSHEIM, PAUL (1885-1963), Germany. Historian. Formed the link between German sociology & cultural anthropology. Influenced by Max Weber. Source: Am Anth 70:564-9 Je '68.

1572 HOOIJER, DIRK ALBERT (1919-). Paleontologist. Miocene and Pleistocene mammals in South & East Africa. Source: Int Dir Anth 5.

1573 HOOKE, SAMUEL HENRY (1874-), Cirencester, England. Archeologist, linguist. Works on Near East, especially on early Semitic ritual, particularly in Babylon. Sources: Int Dir Anth 1 2 3.

1574 HOOTON, EARNEST ALBERT (1887- 1954), Clemansville, Wisconsin, United States. Physical anthropologist. Relationship of body build to personality. Curator, Peabody Museum. Sources: Biog Index: 3 4 & 13/Int Dir Anth 1 2 3/ Anthropological Quarterly 52:159-64 Jl '79/Am Anth 56:1081-4 D '54.

1575 HORÁK, JIRI (1884-). Folklorist. Slavonic folklore, folksongs & fairy tales. Source: Int Dir Anth 5.

1576 HORI, ICHIRŌ (1910-), Mie prefecture, Japan. Ethnologist, folklorist. Folk religion of Japan and elsewhere in Far East. Sources: Int Dir Anth 3, 5.

1577 HORNELL, JAMES (1865-1949), Manchester, England. Ethnologist. Interest in traditional use of water. Ethnology of fishing and pearl industries; "primitive" water transport. Sources: Int Dir Anth 1 2 3.

1578 HORNER, GEORGE R (1913-). Ethnologist. Folklore & psychological projective systems in Africa. Source: Int Dir Anth 5.

1579 HORSFORD, CORNELIA (1861-1944). Archeologist. Archeology of Norse settlement outside Norway. Source: Siegel, P.A. & K.T. Finley, Women in the Scientific Search, Metuchen, N.J., Scarecrow, 1985.

1580 HORTON, JAMES AFRICANUS BEALE (1835-1883), Freetown, Sierra Leone. Author, social reformer. Wrote several books on political economy of West Africa supporting independence. Sources: Foray, Cyril P., Historical Dictionary of Sierra Leone (1977), p 92-3/Gailey, Harry A., Historical Dictionary of Gambia (1975), p 67.

1581 HOSTOS, ADOLFO de (1887-). Prehistoric archeology and ethnology of the West Indies, Puerto Rico, Santo Domingo, and Cuba. Source: Int Dir Anth 5.

1582 HOUGH, WALTER (1859-1935), Morgantown, West Virginia, United States. Ethnologist, musicologist. Managed collecting of National Museum during period of major acquisitions; did research on ethnobotany; published extensively on fire, and Southwestern U.S. Indians. Source: Am Anth 38:471-81 Jl '36.

1583 HOUSEHOLDER, FRED W (1913-). Classical linguist. Theoretical, historical & comparative linguistics of Greek & Latin. Source: Int Dir Anth 5.

1584 HOVSEPIANTZ, GAREGIN (1866-1952), Armenia. Archeologist. Specialist in Armenian folklore and philology. Sources: Biog Index: 2/Time 60:80 Jl 14 '52/N Y Times p 19 Je 23 '52.

1585 HOW, MARIAN MACGREGOR. Wrote: *The Mountain Bushmen of Basutoland* and other historical materials on Lesotho. Source: Haliburton, Gordon, Historical Dictionary of Lesotho (1977), p 60.

1586 HOWARD, DOROTHY (1902-). Folklorist. Sources: Biog Index:

11/Dorothy's world: childhood in Sabine Bottom, 1902-1910. Prentice-Hall '77.

1587 HOWARD, EDGAR BILLINGS (1887- 1943), New Orleans, Louisiana, United States. Archeologist. Specialist on early man in America and his relationship to man in N.E. Asia. Source: Am Anth 45:452-4 Jl '43.

1588 HOWE, BRUCE (1912-), Washington D.C., United States. Archeologist. Paleo- & Neolithic studies in Morocco, Algeria & African coastal areas. Middle East archeology. Sources: Int Dir Anth 2, 5.

1589 HOWELLS, WILLIAM WHITE (1908-), New York, New York, United States. Physical anthropologist, paleontologist. Craniometric variations of recent man in the Pacific areas. Sources: Int Dir Anth 1, 2, 3, 5/ International Encyclopedia of the Social Sciences, v. 18.

1590 HOWES, FRANK STEWART (1891-), Oxford, England. Folklorist, musician. Principal music critic of the *London Times*, 1943-1960; as editor of the *Folk Song Society Journal* he broadened its content to include folkmusic, dance and folklore of countries other than England. Sources: Biog Index: 10/Folklore 86:48-9 Spr '75.

1591 HOWITT, ALFRED WILLIAM (1830-1908). Ethnologist, explorer. Aboriginal studies in Oceania. Sources: Biog Index: 2 9 & 10/Oceania 46:7-9 S '75/ Dictionary of Australian Biography 1:457-9 '49.

1592 HOYOS SÁINZ, LOUIS de (1861-), Spain. Physical anthropologist. Interested in craniology; broad interests in ethnology, folklore & physical anthropology. Sources: Int Dir Anth 1 2 3.

1593 HOZ, PEDRO SANCHO de la (1547-), Spain. Explorer. Wrote a contemporary account of the conquest of the Inca empire. Source: Bork & Maier, Historical Dictionary of Ecuador (1973), p 76.

1594 HRDLIČKA, ALEŠ (ALEX) (1869-1943), Humpolec, Bohemia, Czechoslovakia. Physical anthropologist. Specialist in anthropometry and human osteology; also published on the physiology of S.W. United States & N. Mexican Indians. Sources: Biog Index: 2 & 3/Int Dir. Anth 1 2/Nat Cyc Am Biog 35:117-18 '49/ Am Anth 54:165-6 Ap '52/Am Anth 46:113-7 Ja '44.

1595 HROZNÝ, BEDŘICH (1879-1952). Assyriologist. Ancient Middle East ethnology, Hittite language. Source: Biog Index: 3.

1596 HSU, FRANCIS LANG KWANG (1911-), China. Psychological anthropologist, ethnologist. Psychological & cultural anthropology in China, India, Japan & U.S. Sources: Biog Index: 10/Int Dir Anth 3, 5/New Yorker 50:34-6 My 13 '74.

1597 HSÜAN, TSANG (ca. 605-664). Buddhist scholar. Translator of Indian Buddhist texts. Source: Columbia.

1598 HUANG, WEN-SHAN (1898-), China. Culturologist. History of Chinese culture. Development of art in China. Taoism & Zen. Acupuncture. Source: Int Dir Anth 5.

1599 HUBER, HUGO (1919-). Ethnologist. Religion, ethnogenesis & social systems in Africa. Source: Int Dir Anth 5.

1600 HUDSON, ALFRED EMMONS (1903-1956), New York, New York, United States. Anthropologist. Central Asian and Hawaiian ethnography. Sources: Biog Index: 4/Int Dir Anth 1 2/N Y Times p 89 My 27 '56.

1601 HUDSON, ARTHUR PALMER (1892- 1978), Attala, Mississippi, United States. Folklorist. Specialized in collecting folklore of the southern United States, with particular emphasis on Mississippian materials. Sources: Biog Index: 4 & 12/Journal of American Folklore 91:968-9 O '78/ Journal of American Folklore 91:968-9 O '78.

1602 HUDSPETH, WILLIAM HARRISON

(1887-). Anthropologist. Southwest China. Anthropology of Far East in general. Sources: Int Dir Anth 3, 5.

1603 HUGEL, ANATOLE, Baron von (1854-1928), England. Ethnologist. Sources: Biog Index: 1/Dublin Review 218:107 Ap '46.

1604 HUGOT, HENRI J (1916-). Paleontologist. Origin of Neolithic cultures in Africa. Source: Int Dir Anth 5.

1605 HULBERT, HOMER BEZALEEL (1863-1949), New Haven, Vermont, United States. Orientalist. Specialist in the history of Korea; wrote several books on this topic, including the first history of Korea in the English language. Sources: Biog Index: 2/N Y Times p 17 Ag 6 '49/Newsweek 34:59 Ag 15 '49/ School & Society 70:111 Ag 13 '49.

1606 HULBERT, KATHARINE W (1909-). Cultural & physical ecologist. Range & adaptation in hominid evolution. Source: Int Dir Anth 5.

1607 HULSE, FREDERICK SEYMOUR (1906-), New York, New York, United States. Physical anthropologist, ethnologist. Body size, social selection, effects of culture on human biology, particularly in Far East. Sources: Int Dir Anth 1, 2, 3, 5.

1608 HUMBOLDT, ALEXANDER von (1769-1859), Germany. Explorer, naturalist, scientist. Wrote widely on his South American explorations, for example to Orinoco and Amazon River Basins and Andes (Venezuela). Sources: Columbia/ Rudolph & Rudolph, Historical Dictionary of Venezuela (1971), p 68.

1609 HUMMEL, SIEGBERT (1908-), Rodewisch, Saxony, Germany. Archeologist, ethnologist. Art, history & religion in Tibet, Himalayas & Central Asia. Sources: Int Dir Anth 3, 5.

1610 HUMPHREY, NORMAN DAYMOND (1911-1955), Detroit, Michigan, United States. Social anthropologist. Specialist in race relations and minority problems; worked with Mexican immigrants in Detroit, Michigan; fieldwork in Tecolotlan, Jalisco, Mexico and with Mexican university students who had studied in the U.S. Source: Am Anth 58:548-50 Je '56.

1611 HUMPHREYS, CLARENCE BLAKE (1873-1949), Dorchester, Massachusetts, United States. Anthropologist, ethnologist. Led an expedition to the New Hebrides (1920s); worked to rebuild South Sea Island section of the Ethnological Museum at Cambridge Univ. Sources: Biog Index: 1/N Y Times p 23 F 11 '49.

1612 HUNG, WILLIAM (1893-), Foochow, China. Sinologist. Member of the faculty and Department of History, Yenching Univ., 1923-1946; editor-in-chief, Harvard-Yenching Institute Sinological Index Series, 1930-1946; research associate of the Harvard-Yenching Institute, 1948-1963. Sources: Biog Index: 6/Harvard Journal of Asiatic Studies 24:7-16 '62-'63.

1613 HUNT, ARTHUR SURRIDGE (1871- 1934), Romford, England. Archeologist. Specialist in papyrology; edited and translated numerous Egyptian texts. Sources: Biog Index: 2/Dictionary of National Biography 1931-1940:455 '49.

1614 HUNT, EDMUND HENDERSON (1874- 1952). Surgeon, anthropologist. Chief medical officer to the Nizam's State Railway, Hyderabad (India); published reports on excavations of the Hyderabad urn-burials and photographs of the rock-cut shrines of Ellora and Buddhist caves of Ajanta; made these sites known throughout the world. Sources: Biog Index: 3/Nature 171:198 Ja 31 '53.

1615 HUNT, GEORGE (1854-1933). Ethnologist. Studied the Kwakiutl. Source: Biog Index: 11.

1616 HUNT, JOHN (1812-1848), England. Missionary. Recorded the customs and conditions of Rotuma and Fiji. Source: Craig & King, Historical Dictionary of Oceania (1981), p 135.

1617 HUNTINGFORD, GEORGE WYNN BRERETON (1901-1978), England. Anthropologist, archeologist. Medieval Ethiopia. Work on culture, language of the Nandi of Kenya. Sources: Biog Index: 11/Int Dir Anth 3, 5/Antiquity 52:92 Jl '78.

1618 HUNTINGTON, ELLSWORTH (1876- 1947), Galesburg, Illinois, United States. Geographer. Focused on anthropogeographic studies of race, human habitats, early human civilizations. Conducted expeditions to Turkistan (Central Asia). Wrote extensively on relationship of nature and culture. Source: Columbia.

1619 HUNTINGTON, ROBERT (1637-1701), England. Orientalist. Sources: Biog Index: 13-1/Journal of Egyptian Archaeology 67:136-42 '81.

1620 HURE, AUGUSTA (1870-1953), Sens, France. Archeologist. Wrote on archeology of Sens region (France). Sources: Biog Index: 4/Rev Arch series 6 47:86 Ja '56.

1621 HURSTON, ZORA NEALE (1901-1960), Eatonville, Florida, United States. Author, folklorist. Specialist in folklore of Black America; wrote widely on the social status of black America in her novels. Sources: Biog Index: 1 2 3 4 5 6 7 8 9 10 11 12 & 13/ Notable American Women, the Modern Period. vol. IV, Belknap Press '80, p 361-3/ Hemenway, Robert E. Zora Neal Hurston, a literary biography. Univ. of Ill. Press '77/Essence 11:100-1+ N '80/ N Y Times Book Review p 8+ D 30 '79/ American Women Writers, v 2. Ungar '80 p 363-6/ 20th Century American Literature. St Martins '80 p 288-90/ Negro History Bulletin 29:149-50 Ap '66.

1622 HURT, WESLEY ROBERT (1917-), New Mexico, United States. Archeologist. Preceramic cultural complexes in Central America. Sources: Int Dir Anth 3, 5/Nat Dir Lat Am.

1623 HUSAYN, TĀHĀ (1889-1976), Egypt. Writer. Composed a study of pre-Islamic Arab poetry. Source: King, Joan W., Historical Dictionary of Egypt (1984), p 332-3.

1624 HUSSEY, MARY INDA (1876-1952). Orientalist. Specialist in Sumerian, Babylonian, and Assyrian; translated and published many cuneiform texts. Sources: Biog Index: 2 & 3/N Y Times p 19 Je 23 '52/ School & Society 75:415 Je 28 '52/Wilson Library Bulletin 27:26 S '52.

1625 HUTTON, JOHN HENRY (1885-1968), England. Anthropologist, ethnologist. Work in India, Indonesia. Sources: Biog Index: 2/Int Dir Anth 3/Nature 165:176 F 4 '50.

1626 IAKIMOV, VSEVOLOD PETROVICH (1912-), Saratov, Russia. Anthropologist. Worked on paleoanthropology and human evolution, with emphasis on Neanderthal man. Source: Great Soviet Encyclopedia, New York, Macmillan (1982), v. 30, p 409.

1627 IARKHO, ARKADII ISAAKOVICH (1903-1935), Moscow, Russia. Anthropologist. Worked on the formation and characteristics of race. Sources: Great Soviet Encyclopedia, New York, Macmillan (1982), v. 30, p 428/"A.I. Iarkho" Antropologicheskii zhurnal, 1935, no. 1.

1628 IBN BATUTA, (1304-1377), Tangier, Morocco. Geographer, traveler. Muslim authority on the cultural & social history of Islam. Described his travels in China, India, Middle East & Africa. His descriptions are the best of the 14th century. Source: Columbia.

1629 IBN KHALDŪN, ABU ZAYD 'ABD AR-RAHMAN (1332-1382), Tunis, Tunisia. Historian, geographer. Compiled an historical work on the world, portions of which describe the Sudan. Wrote a three-volume history of the Islamic Arab stressing social factors as contributing to historical change. Sources: Imperato, Pascal J., Historical Dictionary of Mali (1977), p 55/ King, Joan W., Historical Dictionary of Egypt (1984), p 336-7.

1630 ICAZBALCETA, JOAQUÍN GARCÍA (1825-1894), Mexico City, Mexico. Linguist, historian. Wrote on the early history and languages (Spanish & Native Indian) of Mexico. Source: Am Anth 8(old series):178-9 Ap 1895.

1631 IDRISI, (ca. 1100-ca. 1166), Ceuta, Al-Maghrib, Oman. Geographer. Mapped & described the earth based on his observations & the reports of travelers. *Kitab nuzhat al-mushtaq fi al-ikhtiraq al-afaq*, the most thorough description in existence of the world in the 12th century, particularly important for African studies. Sources: Columbia/Encyclopaedia of Islam, New ed., v. 3, p 1032-5.

1632 IESSEN, ALEKSANDR ALEKSANDROVICH (1896-1964), St. Petersburg, Russia. Archeologist. Bronze Age in the Caucasus and early metallurgy. Sources: Great Soviet Encyclopedia, New York, Macmillan (1976), v. 10, p 124/Krupnov, E.I. and B.B. Piotrovskii. "Pamiati A A Iessena" Sovetskaia arkheologiia, 1965, no. 1.

1633 IKEDA, HIROKO (1914-), Tokyo, Japan. Folklorist. Type & motif analysis of folk literature of Japan. Sources: Int Dir Anth 3, 5.

1634 IMANISHI, KINJI (1902-). Ecologist. Human & non-human primate evolution. Source: Int Dir Anth 5.

1635 IMPERATORI, LEO (1910-). Photographer. Photographic craniometry. Source: Int Dir Anth 5.

1636 INGA, BIRGITTA HULTHEN (1918-). Archeologist. Technological investigation of ceramics. Source: Int Dir Anth 5.

1637 INGHAM, ERNEST GRAHAM, Bermuda. Missionary, historian. Wrote an in-depth history of Sierra Leone. Source: Foray, Cyril P., Historical Dictionary of Sierra Leone (1977), p 94-8.

1638 INVERARITY, ROBERT BRUCE (1909-), Seattle, Washington, United States. Anthropologist, museologist. Microreproductions. Use of computers in Northwest Coast primitive art. Data storage & retrival. "Primitive art.". Sources: Int Dir Anth 3, 5.

1639 IOKHEL'SON, VLADIMIR IL'ICH (1855-1937), Vilnius, Lithuania. Ethnologist, linguist. Specialized in the study of Aleuts, the Yukagir, the Koryak and other peoples of the Arctic. Worked on archeology of Kamchatka Peninsula (Siberia), and Aleut Islands (Alaska). Sources: Great Soviet Encyclopedia, New York, Macmillan (1976), v. 10, p 527/Am Anth 40:345 '38.

1640 IRIBARREN CHARLIN, JORGE (1908-). Archeologist. Prehistoric musical instruments in Chile. Source: Int Dir Anth 5.

1641 IRWIN, ELEANOR CYNTHIA (Evans) (1910-1973), Denver, Colorado, United States. Archeologist, musicologist. Developed new techniques in museum reproduction, particularly epoxy casts of artifacts. Sources: Biog Index: 10/Am Antiq 39:608 O '74.

1642 IRWIN, MARGARET CONSTANCE (1910-), Walla Walla, Washington, United States. Ethnobotanist, ethnologist. Native art of the South Pacific. Sources: Int Dir Anth 3, 5.

1643 ISIDORE, Archbishop of Seville (ca. 560-636), Spain. Churchman. Wrote history of early Spain. Compiled the first encyclopedia (Origins). Source: Columbia.

1644 ITŌ, JINSAI (1627-1705). Sinologist. China as viewed from Tokugawa-period, Japan. Source: Biog Index: 1.

1645 IVANOVSKII, ALEKSEI ARSEN'EVICH (1866-1934), Russia. Anthropologist. Expeditions to the Caucasus, Altai, and Mongolia; editor of *Russkii antropologicheskii zhurnal*, 1900-1914; wrote a major work on the composition of the Russian population. Sources: Great Soviet Encyclopedia, New York, Macmillan (1976), v. 10, p 510/Zalkind, N.G. "A.A. Ivanovskii" Voprosy antropologii, 1966, no. 24/ Nikolaev, L.P. "A.A. Ivanovskii" Antropologicheskii zhurnal, 1934, no. 1-2.

1646 IXTLILXOCHITL, FERNANDO de ALVA (ca. 1568-ca. 1648), Texcoco, Mexico. Historian. Wrote histories of the indigenous peoples of Mexico prior to the Spanish conquest. Source: Juan Lopez de Escalera, Diccionario Biographico y de Historia de Mexico (1964), p. 546.

1647 IZUMI, SEIICHI (1915-1970), Japan. Anthropologist. Asian anthropology. Sources: Biog Index: 9/Int Dir Anth 3/Am Antiq 37:82-5 Ja '72.

1648 AL-JABARTI, ABD AL-RAHMAN (1756-1825), Egypt. Historian. Analyzed the social and economic factors (both rural and urban) causing change in Egyptian society in the 17th & 18th centuries. Source: King, Joan W., Historical Dictionary of Egypt (1984), p 370.

1649 JACKSON, ABRAHAM VALENTINE WILLIAMS (1862-1937). Orientalist. Source: Biog Index: 4.

1650 JACKSON, FREDERICK JOHN (1860-), Oran, Algeria. Civil servant. Author of *Early Days In East Africa*. Source: Ogot, Bethwell A., Historical Dictionary of Kenya (1981), p 87.

1651 JACKSON, GEORGE PULLEN (1874- 1953), Monson, Maine, United States. Folklorist, musicologist. Specialized in the study of shaped-note hymnals of the American South; believed Negro spirituals were derived from traditional white hymn tunes. Sources: Biog Index: 3 5 & 9/Journal of American Folklore 83:446-51 O '70/ Musical America 73:26 Ap 1 '53/N Y Times p 19 Ja 23 '53/ Wilson Library Bulletin 27:478 Mr '53/Nat Cyc Am Biog 42:574-5 '58.

1652 JACOBS, JOSEPH (1854-1916), Sydney, New South Wales, Australia. Folklorist, ethnologist. Wrote much on ethnology and history of Jews, also on fairy tales. Sources: Biog Index: 2 3 & 8/Horn Book 28:385-92 D '52/ Dictionary of Australian Biography 1:470-1 '49/ Doyle, Brian, ed., Who's Who of children's literature. Schacken '68 p 155-6.

1653 JACOBS, MELVILLE (1902-1971), New York, New York, United States. Anthropologist. Recorded oral histories of Indians of Oregon & Washington. Sources: Biog Index: 7 & 11/Int Dir Anth 1 2 3/Am Anth 80:640-9 S '78.

1654 JACOBSTHAL, PAUL FERDINAND (1880-1957), Berlin, Germany. Archeologist. Wrote about Greek vases and pins. Sources: Biog Index: 4 & 5/Int Dir Anth 1 2/Rev Arch 2:103-4 Jl '58.

1655 JACOPI, GIULIO (1898-). Archeologist. Sources: Biog Index: 5/Current Biography 20:21-3 Ja '59/ Current Biography Yr Bk 1959:201-3 '60.

1656 JACOPI, JEAN (1898-). Archeologist. Source: Biog Index: 5.

1657 JACOTTET, ÉDOUARD (1858-1920), Switzerland. Missionary. Compiled grammar of the Sesotho language and a collection of folklore of the Basotho of Lesotho. Source: Haliburton, Gordon, Historical Dictionary of Lesotho (1977), p 60-1.

1658 JAHN, JANHEINZ (1918-). Bibliographer, ethnologist. Literature of sub-Saharan Africa. African religion. Source: Int Dir Anth 5.

1659 JAIMES FREYRE, RICARDO (1868-1933), Bolivia. Historian. Source: Heath, Dwight B., Historical Dictionary of Bolivia (1972), p 130.

1660 JAKOBSON, ROMAN (1896-1982), Moscow, Russia. Linguist. Founded the Prague School of Linguistics. General linguistics, poetics & semiotics of Slavic region. Sources: Int Dir Anth 3, 5/N Y Times, Jl 23, '82.

1661 JALABERT, LOUIS (1877-1943), Lyon, France. Priest, archeologist, epigrapher. Major studies of Greek and Latin inscriptions in Syria. Sources: Biog Index: 2/Rev Arch series 6 34:69 Jl '49.

1662 JALHAY, EUGENIO AUGUSTO (1891-1950), Lisbon, Portugal. Archeologist, priest. European prehistory, especially Portugal, Spain, Belgium. Sources: Biog

Index: 2 & 3/Int Dir Anth 1 2/ Archivo Espanol de Arte y Arqueologia no 23:507 Ja '51/N Y Times p 25 D 1 '50/ Rev Arch series 6 41:196 Ap '53.

1663 JAMES, BENJAMIN VAN RENSSELAER (1814-1869), New York, United States. Printer. First printer in Gabon; issued the first printed works in the Mpongwe language. Source: Gardiner, David E., Historical Dictionary of Gabon (1981), p 119.

1664 JAMES, WILLIS LAURENCE (1900-1979). Folklorist, musicologist. Sources: Biog Index: 12/Negro History Bulletin 43:16-20 Ja '80.

1665 JANKOWSKY, GUSTAV WALTHER (1890-), Wittingen, Germany. Physical anthropologist, geneticist. Pigment & hair color. Sources: Int Dir Anth 1, 2, 5.

1666 JANNORAY, JEAN (1909-1958). Archeologist. Archeology of France, particularly of Enserune. Sources: Biog Index: 5/ Archivo Espanol de Arte y Arqueologia 32 no 1:179-80 '59/ Rev Arch 2:100-2 Jl '59.

1667 JANSEN, WILLIAM HUGH (1914-1979). Archivist, folklorist, linguist. Oral performance, legend, riddles, folktales & epics in U.S., Turkey & Indonesia. Sources: Biog Index: 13/Int Dir Anth 5/ Journal of American Folklore 93:57-9 Ja/Mr '80.

1668 JARAMILLO ALVARADO, PÍO (1889-1922), Loja, Ecuador. Sociologist. Wrote a study of the Indian in Ecuadorean society. Source: Bork & Maier, Historical Dictionary of Ecuador (1973), p 82.

1669 JARVES, JAMES JACKSON (1818-1888), Boston, Massachusetts, United States. Art critic. Art collector. Wrote a history of the Hawaiian Islands. Source: Columbia.

1670 JAW, YORO (1847-1919), Walo, Senegal. Wrote *Cahiers de Yoro Dyao*, most complete early collection of oral tradition on the Wolof of Senegal; collected data on the Wolof of Walo and Kayor; notebooks published in early 20th century. Source: Calvin, Luci Gallistel, Historical Dictionary of Senegal (1981), p 193.

1671 JAYNE, HORACE (1898-1975). Orientalist, art curator. Specialist in Oriental art and participated in expedition to Ur in the 1930s. Sources: Biog Index: 10/N Y Times p 24 Ag 2 '75.

1672 JAZDZEWSKI, KONRAD (1908-1985), Kreuzburg, Silesia, Germany. Prehistorian, museum director. Neolithic Europe. Specialist in N.E. & Central European prehistory from 10,000 B.C. to the Middle Ages; synthesized Polish prehistory; excavated at Brzesc Kujanski. Sources: Int Dir Anth 1, 2, 3, 5/Anth News 2/86:3.

1673 JEANMAIRE, HENRI (1884-1960). Archeologist. Wrote about Greeks from anthropological point of view. Sources: Biog Index: 6/Rev Arch 1:212-13 Ap '61/ Revue des Etudes greques 73, p xxxviii-xxxix.

1674 JEANTON, GABRIEL FRANÇOIS JULES (1881-1943), France. Archeologist. History, archeology and folklore of Macon (France). Sources: Biog Index: 1/Rev Arch 26:89-90 Jl '46.

1675 JEFFREYS, MERVYN DAVID WALDEGRAVE (1890-), Johannesburg, South Africa. Ethnologist. Ceremonial rights of Hottentot & Loboca in South Africa. Primitive religion in general. Sources: Int Dir Anth 2, 3, 5.

1676 JENKS, ALBERT ERNEST (1869-1953), Ionia, Michigan, United States. Anthropologist, ethnologist. Ethnological researches in much of world. Sources: Biog Index: 3/Int Dir Anth 1 2/School & Society 77:399 Je 20 '53/ N Y Times p 27 Je 9 '53.

1677 JENNESS, DIAMOND (1886-1969), Wellington, New Zealand. Anthropologist, ethnologist. Specialist on Inuit of Canada & Alaska (especially Copper Inuit); did additional fieldwork on the Northern D'Entrecasteaux, among Canadian tribes facing extinction, and in

Canadian archeology & ethnology. Sources: Biog Index: 5 6 & 9/Int Dir Anth 2/Am Anth 73:248-54 F '71/ Am Antiq 37:86-8 Ja '72.

1678 JENNINGS, GEORGE JAMES (1914-). Ecologist. Peasant life, religion & personality of U.S. Indians; Middle East studies. Source: Int Dir Anth 5.

1679 JENNINGS, JESSE DAVID (1909-), Oklahoma City, Oklahoma, United States. Anthropologist, archeologist. Supervised archeological work which took place during building of various parkways and monuments. Sources: Biog Index: 5/Int Dir Anth 1 2 3/Am Anth 61:896 O '59.

1680 JENSEN, ADOLF ELLEGARD (1899-), Kiel, Germany. Ethnologist. African art, Indonesian ethnology, especially religion. Sources: Int Dir Anth 1 2 3.

1681 JENSEN, DOROTHY CROSS (1906-1972), New Jersey, United States. Anthropologist, archeologist. Leading authority on Indians of New Jersey. Sources: Biog Index: 10/Am Anth 76:80-2 Mr '74.

1682 JENYNS, ROGER SOAME (1904-1976), England. Sinologist, art historian. Specialist on history of Chinese art, in particular porcelain. Sources: Biog Index: 11/Burlington Magazine 119:119 F '77.

1683 JÉQUIER, GUSTAVE (1868-1946), France. Egyptologist. Wrote in collaboration with Berthelot, Legrain, *Loret et Fouguet*: *Fouilles a Danchour, mars-juin* 1894, 1895. Sources: Biog Index: 1/Chronique d'Egypte 21:207-9 Jl '46.

1684 JEREZ, FRANCISCO de (1497-1563), Seville, Spain. Historian. Wrote an eyewitness account of the conquest of Peru and Ecuador in his capacity as secretary of Francisco Pizarro. Source: Bork & Maier, Historical Dictionary of Ecuador (1973), p 83.

1685 JESUP, MORRIS K (-1908). Businessman. Financed the purchase of anthropological collections and filed research; specialized in early American cultures & their ties to Asia. Source: Am Anth 10:171-2 Ja '08.

1686 JETTMAR, KARL (1917-), Vienna, Austria. Archeologist, ethnologist. Relationship between archeology & ethnology as a theoretical problem. Asian ethnology. Sources: Int Dir Anth 3, 5.

1687 JEWETT, JAMES RICHARD (1862-1943), Westport, Maine, United States. Orientalist. Wrote widely on Arabic language and Arab culture. Sources: Biog Index: 2/Nat Cyc Am Biog 35:126-7 '49.

1688 JIJÓN y CAAMAÑO, JACINTO (1890-1950), Quito, Ecuador. Mayor, historian, archeologist. Archeology and linguistics of Middle and South America, especially Ecuador. Sources: Biog Index: 1/Int Dir Anth 3/Time 49:38 Je 9 '47/Bork & Maier, Historical Dictionary of Ecuador (1973), p 83.

1689 JIMÉNEZ MORENO, WIGBERTO (1910-1985), Mexico City, Mexico. Ethnologist, historian, linguist. Studied colonial history of Spain. Source: Anth News 11/85:3.

1690 JIMERSON, AVERY J (1913-1986). Singer, artist. Iroquois (Seneca) singer and carver of false face masks. Source: Anth News 27:6:4.

1691 JINGOES, STIMELA JASON (1895-), Koeneng, Lesotho. Lesotho leader. Wrote autobiography, *A Chief Is a Chief By the People* (1975). Source: Haliburton, Gordon, Historical Dictionary of Lesotho (1977), p 62.

1692 JOBSON, RICHARD. Explorer, merchant. Led an expedition up the Gambia River in 1621 and 1624; wrote account of these trips. Source: Gailey, Harry A., Historical Dictionary of Gambia (1975), p 74-5.

1693 JOCHELSON, VLADIMIR IL'ICH, see: IOKHEL'SON, VLADIMIR IL'ICH.

1694 JOEL, CLAYTON EDWARD (1906-). Historian. British scholar of general culture history. References to innovation & continuity in history. Source: Int Dir Anth 5.

1695 JOGUES, S J, Fr. ISAAC (1607-1646), Orleans, France. Priest. Missionary in New France; wrote on N. American Indians. Source: Jes Rel.

1696 JOHNSON, FRANKLIN PLOTINUS (1896-1975), Osceola, Missouri, United States. Archeologist. Expert on sculpture and vase painting of ancient Greece; wrote a catalog of sculptures found at Corinth and a basic book on Lysippos. Sources: Biog Index: 11/Am J Arch 80:197 Spr '76.

1697 JOHNSON, FREDERICK (1904-), Everett, Massachusetts, United States. Archeologist, ethnologist. Studied North American Indians. Sources: Int Dir Anth 1 2 3.

1698 JOHNSON, GUY BENTON (1901-), Caddo Mills, Texas, United States. Ethnologist, folklorist. U.S. Negro acculturation, with emphasis on Gullah. Sources: Int Dir Anth 3, 5.

1699 JOHNSON, IRMGARD WEITLANER (1919-). Ethnologist. Meso-America & Peruvian ethnology; primitive spinning, weaving & textile techniques among Mexican Indians. Source: Int Dir Anth 5.

1700 JOHNSON, JOHN (1832-), England. Egyptologist. Source: Biog Index: 1.

1701 JOHNSON, JOTHAM (1905-1967). Archeologist. Founder & editor of *Archeology* magazine; published materials from Dura-Europos (Syria), and Minturno (Italy). Sources: Biog Index: 8/Archaeology 20:82 Ap '67.

1702 JOHNSON, SAMDU JANGABA MOLE (1895-1982), Monrovia, Liberia. Ethnographer. Pioneer Liberian ethnographer and ethnohistorian; wrote extensive literature on the Vai and Kuwaa people, archeological sites, tribal history and cultural associations. Source: Dunn & Holsoe, Historical Dictionary of Liberia (1985), p 96-7.

1703 JOHNSTON, HARRY HAMILTON (1858-1957), London, England. Colonial official. Wrote extensively on Africa as part of the British Empire. Sources: Columbia/Grotpeter, John J., Historical Dictionary of Zambia (1979), p 103.

1704 JOHNSTON, REGINALD FLEMING (1874-1938), Scotland. Sinologist, colonial administrator. Administered Weihriwei (China) and wrote about Chinese civilization. Sources: Biog Index: 2/Who Was Who, 1929-1940.

1705 JOLIS, JOSÉ (1728-1790), Catalonia, Spain. Missionary. Left incomplete natural history of the Chaco region of Argentina containing ethnographic and linguistic detail. Source: Wright & Nelsham, Historical Dictionary of Argentina (1978), p 442.

1706 JONAS, DORIS F (1916-). Medical anthropologist, evolutionist. Studied social malfunctions, stress, caste & psychodynamic formulations. Source: Int Dir Anth 5.

1707 JONES, CHARLES COLCOCK (1831-1893), Savanah, Georgia, United States. Archeologist, historian. Archeology of Georgia (U.S.). Source: Am Anth 6(old series):457-8 O 1893.

1708 JONES, FREDERIC WOOD (1879-1954). Anatomist, anthropologist. Wrote on human and comparative anatomy, anthropology and evolution. Supported Lamarckian conception of evolution; proposed eccentric view of human evolution. Sources: Biog Index: 3 & 4/Royal Society of London. Biographical Memoirs of Fellows of the Royal Society, 1955. The Society of '55 p 119-34/ British Medical Journal no 4892:873-4, no 4894:996 O 9, 23 '54/ Lancet 267:762-3 O 9 '54/Nature 174:772-3 O 23 '54.

1709 JONES, HENRY CLAY (ca. 1844-1912). Indian representative. Gathered and translated material on the Fox; represented his people (Fox) in Washington. Source: Am Anth 14:408-9 Ap '12.

1710 JONES, NEVILLE (1880-1954), Brixton, London, England. Missionary, naturalist, archeologist. Rhodesian prehistory, ethnology;

developed basic sequence of Stone Age cultures of Zimbabwe. Sources: Biog Index: 3/Int Dir Anth 1 2/Rasmussen, R. Kent, Historical Dictionary of Rhodesia/Zimbabwe (1979), p 133/ Nature 174:1037 D 4 '54.

1711 JONES, ROBERT CUBA (1902-). Ethnologist. Studies in Central America, Caribbean, Cuba & some S. American countries, including Venezuela, Ecuador & Chile. Sources: Int Dir Anth 5/Nat Dir Lat Am.

1712 JONES, WILLIAM (1746-1794), Westminster, England. Archeologist, ethnologist, Orientalist. Student of languages, particularly adept at translation; learned Sanskrit in order to know Hindu law with which he was concerned as a judge of the British court in India; while in India, he founded the Asiatick Society (later the Asiatic Society of Bengal), 1784. Sources: Biog Index: 1 3 4 5 7 8 9 11 & 12/Dictionary of National Biography /American Oriental Society Journal 66:230 Jl '46.

1713 JONES, WILLIAM (-1909). Anthropologist, folklorist. Known for his research among Central Algonkian Indians (U.S.), Sauk, Fox, Kickapoo, & Ojibwa; published Fox lore and grammar. His insider status (Fox) enhanced his research. Also did research in Luzon (Philippines). Source: Am Anth 11:137.

1714 JÓNSSON, BRYNJÓLFUR (1838-1914). Folklorist. Sources: Biog Index: 2/ Beck, Richard. History of the Icelandic poets, 1800-1940. Cornell Univ. Press '50 p 75-6.

1715 JORDAN, HARVEY ERNEST (1878-), Coopersburg, Pennsylvania, United States. Anatomist, medical researcher. Source: Int Dir Anth 1 2.

1716 JORDANES, (fl 6th c-), Lower Danube region. Historian. Produced only original source of Ostrogothic history. Source: Columbia.

1717 JOSI, ENRICO (1885-1975), Rome, Italy. Archeologist. Specialist in archeology of the city of Rome; excavated a series of catacombs and early cemeteries; assisted in finding the tomb of St. Peter. Sources: Biog Index: 10/Newsweek 86:49 S 15 '75/N Y Times p 40 S 3 '75/ Time 106:86 S 15 '75.

1718 JOSKE, ADOLPH BREWSTER (1854- 1937). Merchant. Wrote two books describing his 30 years of experiences and contacts with the peoples of Fiji. Source: Craig & King, Historical Dictionary of Oceania (1981), p 139.

1719 JOUBIN, ANDRÉ (1868-1944), France. Archeologist, art historian. Ancient Greek art. Sources: Biog Index: 2/Rev Arch series 6 35:97-101 Ja '50.

1720 JOUSSE, THÉOPHILE (1823-1890). Missionary. Wrote the first work on Paris Evangelical Missionary Society history, much of which relates to Lesotho. Source: Haliburton, Gordon, Historical Dictionary of Lesotho (1977), p 66-7.

1721 JUDD, NEIL MERTON (1887-1976), Cedar Rapids, Nebraska, United States. Archeologist. Excavated in Southwest U.S., especially at Betatakin & Pueblo Bonito in Chaco Canyon (New Mexico). Sources: Biog Index: 1 8 & 11/Int Dir Anth 2 3/ Scientific Monthly 63:iv N '46/Am Anth 80:352-4 Je '78/ Am Antiq 43:399-404 Jl '78/Anth News Mr '77.

1722 JUDD, SYLVESTER (1813-1853). Clergyman, folklorist. Sources: Biog Index: 1 9 & 11/ American renaissance in New England, ed. by Joel Myerson, Gale, 1978.

1723 JULIAN, ANTONIO (1722-), Spain. Missionary. Wrote an account of the natural resources and Indian communities of the province of Santa Marta (Colombia). Source: Davis, Robert H., Historical Dictionary of Colombia (1977), p 133.

1724 JULLIAN, CAMILLE LOUIS (1859-1933). Archeologist. Early history of Bordeaux (France). Sources: Biog Index: 5/Rev Arch 1:103 Ja '60.

1725 JUNGWIRTH, JOHANN (1909-). Physical anthropologist. Dermatoglyphs in Asia Minor. Paleoanthropology & human genetics in Europe. Source: Int Dir Anth 5.

1726 JUNKER, WILHELM JOHANN (1840-1892), Moscow, Russia. Explorer, physician. First European explorer to visit and describe Central Africa and its peoples; wrote *Travels in Africa During the Years 1875-1886* (1890). Source: Kalck, Pierre, Historical Dictionary of the Central African Republic (1980).

1727 JUSSIEU, JOSEPH de (1704-1779). Botanist. Traveled in South America; introduced many plants to Europe. Source: Columbia.

1728 JUYNBOLL, HENDRIK HERMAN (1867-1945), Delft, Netherlands. Ethnologist. Specialist on Old Javanese linguistics and literature; wrote first comprehensive dictionary of Old-Javanese and Dutch. Sources: Biog Index: 1/Far Eastern Quarterly 5:216 F '46.

1729 KAAS, LUDWIG (1881-1952), Germany. Priest, political leader, archeologist. Directed excavations under St. Peter's Basilica in Rome which led to discovery of site of the tomb of St. Peter. Sources: Biog Index: 2/N Y Times p 23 Ap 26 '52/Time 59:92 My 5 '52.

1730 KABERRY, PHYLLIS MARY (1907-1977), England. Anthropologist, economist. Economic & social position of women in the Bamenda Division, British Cameroon. Fieldwork in Cameroon, N.W. Australia, New Guinea. Sources: Biog Index: 11/Int Dir Anth 1 2 3 4/Anth News S '78/ Oceania 48:301-2 Je '78.

1731 AL-KA'BI, HATIM (1917-), Iraq. Sociologist, social-psychologist. National & social movements. Source: Int Dir Anth 5.

1732 KAELAS, LILI S (1919-). Archeologist. Preservation of Neolithic & Megalithic monuments. Source: Int Dir Anth 5.

1733 KAHLER, HANS (1912-). Linguist. Austronesian & Islamic linguistic studies. Sources: Int Dir Anth 4, 4 rev, 5.

1734 KAHN, THEODORE CHARLES (1912-). Psychological anthropologist. Hominology & psychological testing. Human paleontology. Symbols in relation to mental illness. Sources: Int Dir Anth 4, 4 rev, 5.

1735 KALTWASSER PASSIG, JORGE (1917-). Archeologist. Preceramic culture in Argentina, Bolivia, Chile & Peru. Sources: Int Dir Anth 4, 4 rev, 5.

1736 KAMARA, SHAIY MUSA (1863-1943). Historian. Wrote Arabic-language history of Futa Toro (Senegal), one of the two most complete indigenous accounts of the area. Source: Calvin, Luci Gallistel, Historical Dictionary of Senegal (1981), p 205-6.

1737 KANASEKI, TAKEO (1897-), Japan. Folklorist, physical anthropologist. Folktales of Asiatic peoples. Ethnology, physical anthropology, human paleontology and archeology of China, Korea and Japan. Sources: Int Dir Anth 3, 4, 4 rev, 5.

1738 KANE, WILLIAM EDWARD (1866-1945), Baldwinsville, New York, United States. Manufacturer, archeologist. Led expeditions to Latin America and Egypt and wrote on possible connections between ancient peoples of Egypt and Peru. Sources: Biog Index: 2/Nat Cyc Am Biog 34:20-1 '48.

1739 KANG, YOUNGHILL (1903-1972), Korea. Orientalist. Wrote an autobiography useful for its portrayal of traditional Korean culture. Sources: Biog Index: 1 4 & 9/ Kunitz, Stanley Jasspon ed., Twentieth Century Authors, 1st sup. Wilson '55 p 509/N Y Times p 50 D 14 '72.

1740 KAPLAN, BERT (1919-). Ethnologist. Cross-cultural studies of mental illness. Sources: Int Dir Anth 4, 4 rev, 5.

1741 Kappers, see: ARIENS KAPPERS, CORNELIUS UBBOS.

1742 KARGER, MIKHAIL

KONSTANTINOVICH (1903-), Kazan, Russia. Archeologist, art historian. Directed archeological investigations and restoration work in many ancient Russian cities. Sources: Great Soviet Encyclopedia, New York, Macmillan (1976), v. 11, p 449/Vagner, G.K. and A.N. Kirpichnikov. "K 60-letiiu M.K. Kargera" Sovetskaia arkheologiia, 1963, no. 4.

1743 KARLBECK, ORVAR (1879-1967), Sweden. Orientalist. Wrote: *Catalogue of the Collection of Chinese and Korean Bronzes at Nallwyl House*, Stockholm, 1938. Sources: Biog Index: 8/Oriental Art 14:211 Autumn '68.

1744 KARLGREN, KLAS BERNHARD JOHANNES (1889-1978), Sweden. Orientalist. Sources: Biog Index: 12/Int Dir Anth 2.

1745 KARO, GEORG (1872-1963), Venice, Italy. Archeologist. Specialist on Mycenaean and Minoan civilization of Greece. Sources: Biog Index: 7/Am J Arch 70:73 Ja '66.

1746 KAROUZOS, CHRISTOS (1900-1967), Amphissa, Greece. Archeologist. Archeology of classical Greece; director of National Museum. Sources: Biog Index: 8/Rev Arch 1:115-6 '69.

1747 KARPELES, MAUD (1885-1976). Ethnomusicologist, folklorist. Sources: Biog Index: 11/Int Dir Anth 4/Ethnomusicology 21:282-8 My '77.

1748 KASCHNITZ-WEINBERG, GUIDO, von (1890-1958), Austria. Archeologist. Prehistory of southern Europe. Sources: Biog Index: 5/Int Dir Anth 1 2/Am J Arch 63:87 Ja '59.

1749 KASTER, JOSEPH (1912-1968). Egyptologist. Sources: Biog Index: 8/Publishers Weekly 193:48 Je 17 '68.

1750 KATSAROV, GAVRIL ILIEV (1874-1952), Bulgaria. Archeologist. Wrote on ancient Greece, particularly on religion in Thrace. Sources: Biog Index: 3 & 5/Rev Arch 1:94-6 Ja '59.

1751 KAWABATA, TOYOHIKO (1909-), Japan. Folklorist. Folk beliefs, rituals & celebrations of England, Germany & Japan. Sources: Int Dir Anth 4, 4 rev, 5.

1752 KAWAGUCHI, EKAI (1866-1945), Sakai, Japan. Buddhist monk, scholar, explorer. Source: Kodansha Encyclopedia of Japan, v. 4, p 177.

1753 KAYE, HAROLD (1914-). Psychologist. Group dynamics & psychoanalytic theory. Source: Int Dir Anth 5.

1754 KAYOYA, MICHEL (-1972). Priest. Wrote two books on social problems of Burundi: *Sur les Traces de Mon Pere* (1968) and *Entre Deux Mondes* (1970). Source: Weinstein, Warren, Historical Dictionary of Burundi (1976), p 164.

1755 KEAM, THOMAS VARKER (1846-1904), Truro, Cornwall, England. Indian trader. Assembled important collections of S.W. Indian artifacts for three major museums; Hopi expert. Source: Am Anth 7:171-2 Ja '05.

1756 KEANE, AUGUSTUS HENRY (1833- 1912), Ireland. Ethnographer. Studied various ethnic groups from Europe to Central Asia. Source: Am Anth 14:197-8 Ja '12.

1757 KEESING, FELIX MAXWELL (1902-1961). Applied anthropologist. Ethnology of China, Korea, Japan, Indonesia, Micronesia & Polynesia. Applied anthropology of Micronesia and Polynesia. Published on the Maori, Menomini, Samoans and the Philippines; specialist on culture change & the Pacific region. Sources: Biog Index: 5 & 6/Int Dir Anth 1 2 3/Am Anth 64:351-5 Ap '62.

1758 KEILLER, ALEXANDER (1889-1955), Scotland. Archeologist. Amateur archeologist whose excavations, 1925-1929 at Windmill Hill near Avebury revealed the first extensive Neolithic settlement to be explored in Britain. Realized the potentials of air photography for the study of archeological sites. Sources: Biog Index:

4/Int Dir Anth 3/Nature 176:1051-2 D 3 '55.

1759 KEITH, ARTHUR, Sir (1866-1955), Aberdeen, Scotland. Anthropologist. Anatomy and evolution of primates and of man. Sources: Biog Index: 2 3 4 & 9/Int Dir Anth 1/ Kieth, Sir Arthur. Autobiography. Philosophical lib '50/ Illustrated London News 216:488 Ap 1 '50.

1760 KELEMEN, GEORGE (1890-). Physician, anatomist. Aural pathology, comparative anatomy and physiology of vocal organ in the baboon. Sources: Int Dir Anth 4, 4 rev, 5.

1761 KELLER, GORDON N (1919-), United States. Archeologist. Bicultural social work in N. America. Sources: Int Dir Anth 4, 5.

1762 KELLY, CELSUS (1900-1975), Shepparton, Australia. Historian. Collected and published documents relating to the Spanish voyages of Pacific exploration and accounts of Franciscan mission work there. Source: Craig & King, Historical Dictionary of Oceania (1981), p 147.

1763 KELLY, ISABEL TRUESDELL (1906-), Santa Cruz, California, United States. Archeologist, ethnologist. Ethnography of Mexican & other N. American Indians. Wrote: *The Archeology of the Autlan-Tuxcacuesco Area of Jalisco*, 1945-1949. Sources: Int Dir Anth 1, 2, 3, 5.

1764 KELLY, WILLIAM HENDERSON (1902-). Anthropologist. Sources: Int Dir Anth 4, 4 rev/Nat Dir Lat Am.

1765 KELSO, JAMES ANDERSON (1873-1951), Rawalpindi, India. Theologian, archeologist. Excavated at classical Jericho in 1950. Sources: Biog Index: 2 & 3/Archaeology 4:246 Winter '51/Am J Arch 56:182/ N Y Times p 31 N 5 '51.

1766 KELSO, JAMES LEON (1892-1978). Archeologist. Specialist in Biblical archeology of the Middle East; discovered the city of Bethel (Israel) in 1960. Sources: Biog Index: 11/N Y Times p B-2 Je 30 '78.

1767 KENNARD, EDWARD ALLAN (1907-), New York, New York, United States. Ethnologist. Linguistics & ethnography of Hopi Indians. Sources: Int Dir Anth 1, 2, 3, 4, 4 rev, 5.

1768 KENNEDY, RAYMOND (1906-1950), Holyoke, Massachusetts, United States. Ethnologist. Worked in Indonesia. Sources: Int Dir Anth 1 2 3.

1769 KENYATTA, JOMO (1894-1978), Gatndu, Kenya. President of kenya. Held a degree in anthropology from London School of Economics. Leader in self-determination for Africa. Wrote two accounts of Kikuyu culture and social structure. Sources: Ogot, Bethwell A., Historical Dictionary of Kenya (1981), p 98-9/ Anth News F '79.

1770 KENYON, FREDERIC GEORGE (1863-1952). Biblical scholar, archeologist. President of British School of Archeology in Jerusalem (1920-1952); published: *The Bible and Archaeology* (1940). Sources: Biog Index: 3/Antiquaries Journal 32:270-1 Jl '52/ Illustrated London News 221:323 Ag 30 '52/Isis 43 no 4:367 '52/ Journal of Biblical Literature 72:xxiii-xxiv Mr '53/ Library Association Record 54:351-2 383 O-N '52/Library Journal 77:1968 N 15 '52 /Museum Journal 52:254-6 Ja '53/N Y Times p 17 Ag 25 '52/ Nature 170:560-1 O 4 '52/Publishers Weekly 62:918 S 6 '52/ Wilson Library Bulletin 27:123 O '52.

1771 KENYON, KATHLEEN MARY (1906- 1978), London, England. Archeologist, explorer. Archeology of Britain, Near East. Sources: Biog Index: 7 & 11/Int Dir Anth 2, 3/ Rittenhouse, Mignon. Seven Women Explorers. Lippincott '64 p 102-17/ Washington Post p B-6 Ag 25 '78.

1772 KENYON, WALTER A (ca. 1916-1986). Archeologist. Specialized in the Indians of Ontario, Canada, both prehistoric & historic, particularly in fur trade. Source:

1773 KESSLER, EVELYN SEINFELD (1919-1977), New York, United States. Anthropologist, archeologist. Mesoamerican archeology. Cross-cultural studies of women's roles. Classic, post classic, Paleolithic, Mesolithic, Neolithic old world studies of Meso-America. Sources: Int Dir Anth 5/Anth News Ap '77.

1774 KEUR, DOROTHY LOUISE (1904-), New York, United States. Ecologist, ethnologist. Community, comparative & ecological studies in U.S., Mexico & Netherlands. Sources: Int Dir Anth 2, 3, 4, 4 rev, 5.

1775 KEY, HAROLD HAYDEN (1914-). Anthropologist, linguist. Source: Nat Dir Lat Am.

1776 KHAKHETLA, BENNETT MAKALO (1913-). Educator, historian. Wrote an accurate description of the 1970 coup which brought Leabua Jonathan to power in Lesotho. Source: Haliburton, Gordon, Historical Dictionary of Lesotho (1977), p 68-9.

1777 KIDDER, ALFRED VINCENT (1885- 1963), Marquette, Michigan, United States. Archeologist. Used principles of stratigraphic excavation in Southwestern U.S. Wrote classic monograph reconstructing Southwestern prehistory. Advocated multi-disciplinary approach to archeology. Sources: Biog Index: 1 5 6 7 8 & 9/Int Dir Anth 1 2 3/ Woodbury, Richard B., Alfred V. Kidder, New York, Columbia Univ. Press (1973)/ Am Anth 70:320-5 Ap '68.

1778 KIDDER, HOMER HUNTINGTON (1874-1950), Marquette, Michigan, United States. Anthropologist, archeologist. Wrote on Ojibwa. Sources: Biog Index: 2/Int Dir Anth 1 2/N Y Times p 33 D 6 '50.

1779 KIM, CHEWŎN (1909-), Korea. Archeologist, art historian. Art & archeology of Korea & Japan. Sources: Int Dir Anth 4, 4 rev, 5.

1780 KIMBALL, SOLON TOOTHAKER (1909-), Manhattan, Kansas, United States. Applied & urban anthropologist. Culture & community studies. Sources: Int Dir Anth 1, 2, 3, 4, 4 rev, 5.

1781 al-KINDI, ABŪ 'UMAN MUHAMMAD BAN YŪSUP (897-961), Egypt. Historian. Wrote a biographical list of Egypt's governors to 946 and left a record of legal decisions of the period, contributed to the study of Islamic law in action. Source: King, Joan W., Historical Dictionary of Egypt (1984), p 391.

1782 KING, ALFRED RICHARD (1919-). Ethnologist. Culture dynamics, transmission & change; educational processes. Source: Int Dir Anth 5.

1783 KING, ARDEN ROSS (1916-), Francis, Utah, United States. Anthropologist, ethnologist. Worked in Meso-America on persistence of cultural identity & its acquisition. Sources: Int Dir Anth 3, 4, 4 rev, 5/Nat Dir Lat Am.

1784 KING, DALE STUART (1908-), Goodland, Kansas, United States. Anthropologist. Interpretation of technical anthropology to laymen. Sources: Int Dir Anth 1, 2, 3, 4, 4 rev, 5.

1785 KINGSBOROUGH, EDWARD KING, Viscount (1795-1837), Ireland. Archeologist, explorer. Conducted research in the Mayan area; published a 7-volume folio set of his works. Sources: Biog Index: 11/Harper '75 p 204-9/Meyer, Harvey K., Historical Dictionary of Honduras (1976), p 197.

1786 KINGSLEY, MARY HENRIETTA (1862-1900). Ethnologist, traveler. Sources: Biog Index: 2 3 4 6 7 8 9 & 11.

1787 KIRBY, PERCIVAL ROBSON (1887-), Aberdeen, Scotland. Ethnologist. Worked on African ethnological study of music. Sources: Int Dir Anth 1 2 3.

1788 KIRCHER, ATHANASIUS (1602-1680). Scholar, archeologist. Wrote about many subjects, including ancient Egypt. Sources: Biog Index: 4 9 & 12/Godwin, Joscelyn. Athanasius Kirchner; A renaissance

1789 KIRCHOFF, PAUL (1900-), Germany. Anthropologist. Worked on Mexico, Middle America. Studied social organizations. Sources: Int Dir Anth 1, 2, 4, 4 rev.

1790 KIRINO, TADAO (1915-). Anatomist. Tooth form variations in Japanese individuals. Primate dentition. Sources: Int Dir Anth 4, 4 rev, 5.

1791 KIRKLAND, EDWIN CAPERS (1902- 1972). Folklorist. Sources: Biog Index: 10/Southern Folklore Quarterly 37:123-5 Je '73.

1792 KISELEV, SERGEI VLADIMIROVICH (1905-1962), Mytishchi, Russia. Archeologist, historian. Bronze Age through the Middle Ages in Southern Siberia and Mongolia. Sources: Great Soviet Encyclopedia, New York, Macmillan (1976), v. 12, p 521/"S.V. Kiselev" Vestnik drevnei istorii, 1963, no. 1/ Novoe v sovetskoi arkheologii. Moscow, 1965.

1793 KITANO, SEIICHI (1900-), Tanabe, Japan. Sociologist. Japanese kinship systems & socialization process. Sources: Int Dir Anth 3, 4, 4 rev, 5.

1794 KLAATCH, HERMANN (1863-1916), Berlin, Germany. Anatomist, physical anthropologist. Specialized in description & comparative anatomy (especially organography), Paleolithic people, & Australian aborigines; focused on human evolution. Source: Am Anth 18:422-5 Jl '16.

1795 KLEMENTS, DIMITRI ALEKSANDROVICH (1848-1914), Goriainovka, Russia. Ethnologist, archeologist. Archeology of Central Asia and Mongolia. Sources: Great Soviet Encyclopedia, New York, Macmillan (1976), v. 12, p 538/Levin, Sh. M. D.A. Klements. Moscow, 1929/ Tokarev, S.A. "D.A. Klements" Otechestvennye ekonomikogeografy xvii-xx vv. Moscow, 1957/ Devlet, M.A. "D.A. Klements kak arkheolog" Sovetskaia arkheologiia, 1963, no. 4.

1796 KLIMASZEWSKA, JADWIGA (1910-), Poland. Ethnologist, folklorist. Rites, beliefs, magic & cults of Slavic countries. Sources: Int Dir Anth 2, 4, 5.

1797 KLINEBERG, OTTO (1899-), Canada. Anthropologist. Source: Int Dir Anth 1 2.

1798 KLUCKHOHN, CLYDE KAY MABEN (1905-1960), La Mars, Iowa, United States. Cultural anthropologist. Ethnography of the Navajo; theoretician on the concept of culture; popularized anthropology. Sources: Biog Index: 1 2 3 4 5 & 6/Int Dir Anth 1 2 3/ Am Anth 64:140-61 F '62.

1799 KLUCKHOHN, FLORENCE (ROCKWOOD) (ca. 1905-1986). Sociologist. Specialist in variations in values between and within cultures; published on American frontier and women. Source: Anth News 27:5:4.

1800 KNEZ, EUGENE IRVING (1916-). Ethnologist, folklorist. Contemporary village life in Asia & India. Sources: Int Dir Anth 4, 4 rev, 5.

1801 KNIFFEN, FRED BOWERMAN (1900-), Britton, Michigan, United States. Cultural geographer. Settlement patterns. Folk architecture & crafts. U.S. Indians. Sources: Int Dir Anth 1, 2, 3, 4, 5.

1802 KNOBLOCH, JOHANN (1919-). Linguist. Slavic, Caucasian, Oriental & Gypsy languages; cuneiform writing. Sources: Int Dir Anth 4, 4 rev, 5.

1803 KNOTT, SARAH GERTRUDE (ca. 1898-). Folklorist. Sources: Biog Index: 1/Current Biography 8:17-9 Jl '47/ Current Biography Yr Bk revised 1947:357-9 '48/ Independent Woman 26:128-30+ My '47.

1804 KNOWLES, FRANCIS HOWE SEYMOUR (1886-1953). Anthropologist. Practitioner and teacher of physical anthropology; fieldwork on the Iroquois in Ontario led to his appointment as physical anthropologist to the Canadian Government in 1914; studied the techniques used by the Stone Age peoples in the making of tools and weapons. <u>Sources</u>: Biog Index: 3/Int Dir Anth 2 3/Museum Journal 53:88-9 Je '53/ Nature 171:818 My 9 '53.

1805 KOCH, FREDERICK HENRY (1877-1944). Educator, folklorist. <u>Sources</u>: Biog Index: 3 4 & 5/ Juv Lit: Walser, Richard Gaither. Picturebook of Tar Heel Authors. N. C. State Dept of Archives & Hist. '60 p 13.

1806 KOELLE, S W. Linguist, missionary. Wrote a grammar of the Vei (Vy) language and several other works on the languages of Sierra Leone and other parts of Africa. <u>Source</u>: Foray, Cyril P., Historical Dictionary of Sierra Leone (1977), p 110.

1807 KOENIGSWALD, GUSTAV HEINRICH RALPH von (1902-), Berlin, Germany. Paleontologist. Paleontology of mammals including man, especially in Indonesia, China. Worked S.E. & E. Asia. <u>Sources</u>: Int Dir Anth 1, 2, 3, 4, 4 rev, 5.

1808 KOEPP, FRIEDRICH (1860-1944), Biebrich-am-Rhein, Germany. Archeologist. Roman antiquities in Germany. <u>Sources</u>: Biog Index: 2/Rev Arch series 6 35:104 Ja '50.

1809 KOETHE, HARALD LEO BERNHARD (1904-1944), Ludwigsburg, Germany. Archeologist. Roman art and archeology. <u>Sources</u>: Biog Index: 1/Int Dir Anth 1 2/Rev Arch 26:90-1 Jl '46.

1810 KOGANEI, YOSHIKIYO (1859-1944). Physical anthropologist. Wrote on the physical anthropology of the Ainu of Japan. One of founders of physical anthropology in Japan. <u>Source</u>: Kodansha Encyclopedia of Japan (1983), v. 4, p 248.

1811 KONOW, STEN (1867-1948), Norway. Indianist, Orientalist. Student of Indian and Central Asian languages. <u>Sources</u>: Biog Index: 2/Int Dir Anth 2/Isis 41 no 3-4:304 '50/ Journal of the Royal Asiatic Society 99-102 '50.

1812 KONRAD, NIKOLAI IOSIFOVICH (1891-1970), Russia. Orientalist. Specialist on Japanese language and literature. <u>Sources</u>: Biog Index: 9/N Y Times p 40 O 9 '70.

1813 KOOIJMAN, SIMON (1915-), Netherlands. Ethnologist. Material culture & art. Bark cloth (tapa) & iron working in Oceania. <u>Sources</u>: Int Dir Anth 3, 4, 5.

1814 KOPEC, ADA C (1911-). Statistician, geneticist. Distribution of blood groups & other biochemical characteristics. <u>Source</u>: Int Dir Anth 5.

1815 KORNILOV, FEODOR GRIGOR'EVICH (1879-). Folklorist. <u>Sources</u>: Biog Index: 2/ Moisenko, Rena. Realist music. Meridian Bks. '49 p 121-6.

1816 KOROMPAY, BERTALAN (1908-). Cultural anthropologist, ethnologist. Studies of hunting & folklore in Hungary & Finland. Comparative methodology. <u>Sources</u>: Int Dir Anth 4, 4 rev, 5.

1817 KORSON, GEORGE G (1900-1976), Russia. Folklorist. Collected the folklore and folksongs of miners in the coal fields of Pennsylvania, among others. <u>Sources</u>: Biog Index: 7 & 8/Journal of American Folklore 80:343-4 O '67/ N Y Times p 47 My 25 '67.

1818 KORTLANDT, ADRIAAN (1918-). Animal psychologist, ethnologist. Behavior, ecology & evolution of apes, hominids & early man. <u>Sources</u>: Int Dir Anth 4, 4 rev, 5.

1819 KOSKINEN, AARNE A (1917-). Missiologist. Religious views, terminology, missionary influence & thinking in Polynesia. <u>Sources</u>: Int Dir Anth 4, 4 rev, 5.

1820 KOSMOPOULOS, LESLIE (Walker) (1885-1954). Archeologist. Specialist in archeology of Corinth (Greece); worked at American School in Athens. <u>Sources</u>: Biog Index: 3/N Y Times p 27 Je 29 '54.

1821 KOSOK, PAUL (1896-1959). Historian, musician, archeologist. Specialist in Chimu culture of coastal Peru; fieldwork, 1939-1949; authority of native music of Americas. <u>Sources</u>: Biog Index: 5/Musical America 79:33 N 1 '59/N Y Times p 43 O 7 '59 /Wilson

1822 KOSOVA, MARIE (1918-). Folklorist. Historical legends, change of traditional culture, marriage & folk ballads in Europe & the Andes. Source: Int Dir Anth 5.

1823 KOSTRZEWSKI, JÓZEF (1885-1969), Weglewo, Poland. Archeologist. Archeology of Poland. Source: Great Soviet Encyclopedia, New York, Macmillan (1976), v. 13, p 444.

1824 KOTHE, HEINZ E (1914-), Seeberg, Posen, Germany. Ethnohistorian. Ancient European agricultural implements. Sources: Int Dir Anth 3, 4, 4 rev, 5.

1825 KOTZEBUE, OTTO VON (1787-1846), Reval, Estonia. Explorer. Led two voyages which circumnavigated the globe, and left detailed information on the Pacific archipelagos which were published in 1821 and 1830. Source: Craig & King, Historical Dictionary of Oceania (1981), p 150.

1826 KOVALEVSKII, MAKSIM MAKSIMOVICH (1851-1916), Kharkov, Russia. Ethnologist, historian, jurist, sociologist. Peoples of Caucasus. Source: Great Soviet Encyclopedia, New York, Macmillan (1976), v. 12, p 620-1.

1827 KOYAMA, FUJIO (1900-1975). Archeologist, potter. Edited the 16 volume work, *Catalogue of World's Ceramics*, 1955-1958. Sources: Biog Index: 11/Oriental Art 22:108-9 Spr '76.

1828 KRACAW KROEBER-QUINN, THEODORA (1897-1979). Anthropologist. Wrote about her husband, Alfred Kroeber, as well as about California Indians. Source: Anth News 20:7 S '79, p 7.

1829 KRACKE, EDWARD AUGUST, Jr (1908-1976), New York, New York, United States. Sinologist. Studies on Sung China. Sources: Biog Index: 11 & 13-4/Int Dir Anth 4, 4 rev/ American Oriental Society Journal 96:489-91 O '76/Nat Cyc Am Biog 61:147 '82.

1830 KRADER, LAWRENCE (1919-). Ethnologist, anthropologist. Nomadism in Central Asia. Sources: Int Dir Anth 4, 4 rev, 5.

1831 KRAELING, CARL HERMAN (1897-1966), Brooklyn, New York, United States. Archeologist, educator. Specialized in Middle Eastern archeology; directed excavations at Ptolemais, Egypt for Oriental Institute of Chicago. Sources: Biog Index: 7 & 9/N Y Times p 41 N 15 '66/ American School of Oriental Research Bulletin no 198:4-7 Ap '70.

1832 KRAMER, AUGUSTIN FRIEDRICH (1865-1941). Anthropologist. Led several ethnographic expeditions to Samoa, Yap, Palau, the Carolines, and Marshall Islands. Source: Craig & King, Historical Dictionary of Oceania (1981), p 150-1.

1833 KRAMERS, JOHANNES HENDRIK (1891-1951), Rotterdam, Netherlands. Arabist, turcologist, Orientalist. Sources: Biog Index: 3/Isis 43 no 2:118-19 '52/Oriente Moderno 32:56 '52.

1834 KRAPF, JOHANN LUDWIG (1810-1881), Derendingen, Germany. Missionary. Compiled vocabularies of the native languages of Kenya and wrote an account of his 18 years service as a missionary; wrote a grammar of KiSwahili and compiled a KiSwahili dictionary. Sources: Ogot, Bethwell A., Historical Dictionary of Kenya (1981), p 111-3/ Kurtz, Laura S., Historical Dictionary of Tanzania (1978), p 98-9.

1835 KRAPPE, ALEXANDER HAGGERTY (1894-1947). Folklorist. Scholar of Romance-language folklore and literature; nearly 600 publications. Sources: Biog Index: 1/Journal of American Folklore 61:201-2 Ap '48.

1836 KRASHENINNIKOV, STEPAN PETROVICH (1713-1755), Moscow, Russia. Explorer. Wrote accounts of the Kamchatka/Kurile region of Eastern Siberia describing ethnography and geography. Source: Bolshaia Sovetskaia Entsiklopediia, (1972 ed.), vol. 13, p. 358.

1837 KRAUSE, FRITZ (1881-),

Moritsburg bei Dresden, Germany. Anthropologist. Africa, Brazil. Sources: Int Dir Anth 1 2 3.

1838 **KRAUSE, GOTTLOB ADOLF** (1850- 1938), Okrilla, Germany. Explorer. Visited the Sahara, North Africa; first European to reach Ouagadougou area (Burkina Faso). Source: McFarland, Daniel Miles, Historical Dictionary of Upper Volta (1978), p 100-1.

1839 **KREINOVICH, IURII (EURUKHIM) ABRAMOVICH** (1906-1985). Ethnologist. Specialized in the ethnology of the Nivkh (Gilyak) of the Amur region of Siberia & the anthropological linguistics of the Paleosiberians (Ket, Yukagir, Koryak, & Nivkh). Source: Anth News 27:8:4.

1840 **KRESZ, MARIA** (1919-). Ethnologist. Peasant pottery, costumes & folk art in Hungary. Sources: Int Dir Anth 3, 4, 4 rev, 5.

1841 **KRETZOI, MIKLÓS** (1907-). Zoologist. Living & fossil mammalian systematics & phylogeny. Sources: Int Dir Anth 4, 4 rev, 5.

1842 **KRIEGER, ALEX DONY** (1911-), Duluth, Minnesota, United States. Anthropologist, ethnologist. Sources: Int Dir Anth 2, 3, 4, 4 rev/Nat Dir Lat Am.

1843 **KRIGE, EILEEN JENSEN** (1904-), Pretoria, South Africa. Ethnologist. Social structure, kinship, rituals, religion & magic among South African Zulu people. Sources: Int Dir Anth 2, 3, 4, 4 rev, 5.

1844 **KROEBER, ALFRED LOUIS** (1876-1960), Hoboken, New Jersey, United States. Anthropologist. A leading anthropologist of his epoch. Played major role in the development of anthropology in the U.S. as a scientific discipline; focused on ethnography of California & the Great Plains, archeology of Mexico & Peru, linguistics in California, animal communication, and the nature of culture. Sources: Biog Index: 5 6 7 & 9/Int Dir Anth 1 2 3/ Steward, Julian H., Alfred Kroeber, New York, Columbia Univ. Press (1973)/ Current Biography 19:37-8 O '58/ Current Biography Yr Bk 1958:6-8 '58, 1960:226 '61/Am Anth 63:1038-87 O '61/ N Y Times p 41 O '60/Publishers Weekly 178:35 O 31 '61/ Kardiner, Abram, and Preble, Edward. They studied man. World '61 p 187-203/ Am Antiq Soc Proc 71 no 1:10-1 '61/ National Academy of Sciences. Biographical Memoirs v. 36. Columbia Univ. Press. '62 p 192-253/Nat Cyc Am Biog 49:237 '66.

1845 **KROEBER-QUINN, THEODORA** (1897-1979), Colorado, United States. One of the first to develop statistical methods to study cultural relationships, later used by A. Kroeber. Source: Am Anth 82:114-5 Mr '80.

1846 **KROGMAN, WILTON MARION** (1903-), United States. Anthropologist. Physical anthropology. Sources: Biog Index: 3/Int Dir Anth 1, 2, 3, 4, 4 rev/ Saturday Evening Post 227:30+ Ja 15 '55/Readers Digest 66:91-4 Ap '55.

1847 **KROM, NICOLAAS JOHANNES** (1883-1945), Hertogenbosch, Netherlands. Historian, archeologist. Directed Archeological Service of the Netherlands Indies, 1913-1967; extensive excavations and publications on Indonesian archeology, in particular the temple complex of Borobudur. Sources: Biog Index: 1/Far Eastern Quarterly 5:216-7 F '46.

1848 **KROPOTKIN, PETR ALEKSEEVICH** (1842-1921), Moscow, Russia. Geographer. Explored Siberia and Finland. Source: Columbia.

1849 **KRUPNOV, EVGENII IGNATEVICH** (1904-1970), Mozdok, Russia. Historian. Ancient history of the Caucasus. Sources: Great Soviet Encyclopedia, New York, Macmillan (1976), v. 13, p 524/"E.I. Krupnov" Sovetskaia arkheologiia, 1971, no. 1.

1850 **KRUSENSTERN, ADAM JOHANN von** (1770-1846), Estonia. Explorer. Led first Russian circumnavigation-expedition, visiting the Marquesas and Hawaii; left detailed account of trip and sponsored Kotzebue expedition.

1851 **KUBARY, JOHANN STANISLAUS** (1846-1896), Warsaw, Poland. Ethnographer. Pioneer in ethnological studies of Caroline Islands. Wrote 14 major works on Micronesian culture. Source: Craig & King, Historical Dictionary of Oceania (1981), p 151.

1852 **KUBLER, GEORGE** (1912-). Iconographer. Classic Mayan art & architecture. Sources: Int Dir Anth 4, 4 rev, 5.

1853 **KUFTIN, BORIS ALEKSEEVICH** (1892-1953), Samara, Russia. Archeologist, ethnographer. Archeology of Georgia and Transcaucasia. Sources: Great Soviet Encyclopedia, New York, Macmillan (1977), v. 14, p 106/"Pamiati B.A. Kuftina" Vestnik drevnei istorii, 1954, no. 2.

1854 **KUHN, HERBERT** (1895-), Germany. Petroglyphologist. Ice Age rock paintings in France & Spain. Sources: Int Dir Anth 1, 2, 3, 5.

1855 **KUIPER, FRANCISCUS B J** (1907-), The Hague, Netherlands. Linguist. Indo-European linguistics. Vedic mythology & religion in India. Sources: Int Dir Anth 2, 3, 4, 4 rev, 5.

1856 **KUMAR, GURU DAS** (1916-). Anthropologist. Ethnography of peoples of India. Paleoanthropology of ancient peoples of Central & western Asia. Source: Int Dir Anth 5.

1857 **KUMMEL, OTTO** (1874-1952), Germany. Orientalist. Source: Biog Index: 3.

1858 **KUNKEL, PETER H** (1916-). Sociologist. Peasants & political organizations. Black subcultures in United States. Sources: Int Dir Anth 4, 4 rev, 5.

1859 **KUPER, HILDA**, Rhodesia. Africanist, anthropologist. Wrote on the Swazi of Swaziland, and on the Shona & Ndebele of Rhodesia, and on Africa in general. Also wrote a biography of King Sobhuza II of Swaziland. Source: Historical Dictionary of Swaziland (1975), p 67-8.

1860 **KURTH, GOTTFRIED** (1912-). Folklorist. Paleodemography, biology & history of European populations. Sources: Int Dir Anth 4, 5.

1861 **KUTRZEBA-POJNAROWA, ANNA** (1913-), Poland. Ethnologist. Changes of rural areas & theory of culture change in Poland. Sources: Int Dir Anth 4, 4 rev, 5.

1862 **LA BARRE, WESTON** (1911-), Uniontown, Pennsylvania, United States. Anthropologist, ethnologist. Religion of U.S. Indians. Adolescence. Sources: Int Dir Anth 2, 3, 4, 4 rev, 5/Nat Dir Lat Am.

1863 **LACAU, PIERRE LUCIEN** (1873-1963), Brie-Comte-Robert, France. Egyptologist. Eminent Egyptologist; participated in numerous excavations in and wrote widely about ancient Egypt. Sources: Biog Index: 6/Rev Arch 2:55-8 Jl '63.

1864 **La CHASSE, S J, Fr. PIERRE de** (1670-1749), Auxerre, France. Priest. Missionary in New France; wrote on N. American Indians. Source: Jes Rel.

1865 **La COSTE-MESSELIER, PIERRE FROTIER, Marquis de** (1894-1975), Ousches, France. Archeologist. Archeology of Greece, particularly Delphi. Sources: Biog Index: 10/Rev Arch 1:61-2 '75.

1866 **LADENBAUER-OREL, HERTHA** (1912-). Archeologist. European settlement continuity from Roman times through the Middle Ages. Sources: Int Dir Anth 4, 5.

1867 **LADO, ROBERT** (1915-), Tampa, Florida, United States. Linguist. Source: Nat Dir Lat Am.

1868 **La FARGE, OLIVER HAZARD PERRY** (1901-1963). Novelist, anthropologist. Worked in Guatemala. Wrote *The Year Bearer's People*. Pulitzer prize for American Indian novel, *Laughing Boy*. Wrote widely on North American Indians, both as ethnography and fiction, concerned with reservation life and policy. Sources: Biog Index: 2 3 4 5 6 7 8 & 9/Int

Dir Anth 1 2 3/ N Y Times Book Review p 8 Jl 24 '49.

1869 **LAFITAU (La Fitau), S J, Fr. JOSEPH** (1681-1746), Bordeaux, France. Priest. Missionary in New France; wrote on N. American Indians. Source: Jes Rel.

1870 **La FLESCHE, FRANCIS** (1857-1932). Anthropologist, ethnologist, museum curator. Key informant for major ethnography of Omaha; wrote many papers on his culture (Omaha); specialized in rituals of the Osage. Worked in American Indian affairs and as museum curator. Sources: Biog Index: 11/Dockstader, Frederick J. Great North American Indians, Reinhold '77 p 144-5/ Am Anth 34:741, 35:328-31 Ap '33.

1871 **La FLESCHE, SUSAN** (1865-1915). Anthropologist, physician. Omaha Indians. Sources: Biog Index: 11/ Dockstader, Frederick J., Great North American Indians, Von Nostrand Reinhold, p 145.

1872 **LAGARDE, PAUL ANTON de** (1827-1891), Germany. Orientalist. Source: Biog Index: 6.

1873 **LAGDEN, GODFREY** (1851-1934). Civil servant. Wrote on Basotho history. Source: Haliburton, Gordon, Historical Dictionary of Lesotho (1977), p 72-3.

1874 **LAGMAY, ALFREDO V** (1919-). Psychologist. Projective tests, behavioral modification & programmed instruction in the Philippines. Sources: Int Dir Anth 4, 4 rev, 5.

1875 **LAGO, TOMAS** (1903-). Museologist. Popular & native art of South America. Sources: Int Dir Anth 4, 4 rev, 5.

1876 **LAIRD, CAROBETH (Tucker) HARRINGTON** (1895-). Anthropologist. Source: Biog Index: 11.

1877 **LALLEMANT, S J, Fr. CHARLES** (1587-1674), Paris, France. Priest. Missionary in New France; wrote on N. American Indians. Source: Jes Rel.

1878 **LALLEMANT, S J, Fr. JEROME** (1593-1673), Paris, France. Priest. Missionary in New France; wrote on N. American Indians. Source: Jes Rel.

1879 **LAMBERT, ELIE** (1888-1961), Bayonne, France. Archeologist. Wrote about archeology of Europe in Middle Ages. Sources: Biog Index: 6/Rev Arch 1:97-8 Ja '62.

1880 **LAMBERVILLE, S J, Fr. JACQUES de** (1644-1711), Rouen, France. Priest. Missionary in New France; wrote on N. American Indians. Source: Jes Rel.

1881 **LAMBERVILLE, S J, Fr. JEAN de** (1633-1714), Rouen, France. Priest. Missionary in New France; wrote on N. American Indians. Source: Jes Rel.

1882 **LAMBORN, ROBERT HENRY** (1836-1895), Pennsylvania, United States. Engineer, collector, philanthropist. Contributed anthropological artifacts and money to U.S. museums. Source: Am Anth 8(old series):175-6 Ap 1895.

1883 **LAMING-EMPERAIRE, ANNETTE** (1917-). Archeologist. Paleolithic art. Prehistoric sites in S.W. Europe, Brazil, Patagonia (Argentina) & Tierra del Fuego. Sources: Int Dir Anth 3, 4, 4 rev, 5.

1884 **LAMMERHIRT, ANTON** (1911-). Linguist. Semantics, philosophy of language. Culture of Japan. Source: Int Dir Anth 5.

1885 **LAMPRECHT, KARL GOTTAHARD** (1850-1915), at Jessen, Germany. Historian. Advocated a history based on broad social, cultural and psychological trends. Sources: Columbia/New Int Enc, 1914 ed.

1886 **LANDA, DIEGO de** (1524-1579), Spain. Missionary. Wrote a detailed account of Mayan culture and customs. Source: Briggs & Alisky, Historical Dictionary of Mexico (1981), p 63-4.

1887 **LANDES, RUTH** (1908-), New York, New York, United States. Anthropologist, ethnologist. Research among Ojibwa & Potawatomi. Canadian bilingualism & biculturalism. Negro & white relations in U.S. & S. America. Sources: Int Dir Anth 1, 2, 3, 4, 5/Nat Dir Lat Am.

1888 LANDGRAF, JOHN L (1914-), Oregon, United States. Ethnologist, linguist. Fieldwork in Northern Borneo. Sources: Int Dir Anth 3, 4, 4 rev, 5.

1889 LANDIVAR, RAFAEL (1731-1793), Antigua, Guatemala. Priest. Wrote on his service in Guatemala up to 1767. Source: Moore, Richard E., Historical Dictionary of Guatemala (1973), p 118.

1890 LANDTMAN, GUNNAR (1878-1940), Helsingfors, Finland. Ethnologist, sociologist. Interested in primitive folklore. Source: Int Dir Anth 1 3.

1891 LANDY, DAVID (1917-). Ethnologist, anthropologist. Curer's role in cultural & social change. Cross-cultural medical systems. Sources: Int Dir Anth 4, 4 rev, 5/Nat Dir Lat Am.

1892 LANE, EDWARD WILLIAM (1801-1876), England. Orientalist, writer. Wrote an account of the life and culture of Egypt in the early 19th century which was widely read and based on 12 years residence and travel there. Sources: Biog Index: 1 5 11 & 12/King, Joan W., Historical Dictionary of Egypt (1984), p 399.

1893 LANE-POOLE, STANLEY (1854-1931), London, England. Orientalist. Sent by government on archeological missions to Egypt, 1883, & Russia, 1886. Sources: Biog Index: 2/ Dictionary of National Biography 1931-1940:715-16 '49/Who Was Who, 1929-1940.

1894 LANG, ANDREW (1844-1912), Scotland. One of the first to apply anthropological findings to the study of myth and folklore. Sources: Columbia/Am Anth 14:690-1 O '12.

1895 LANGDON, STEPHEN HERBERT (1876-1937), Monroe, Michigan, United States. Assyriologist. Edited & published numerous texts in Sumerian and Babylonian languages; directed field excavations of the city of Kishin (Iraq) 1923, 1925. Sources: Biog Index: 2/Dictionary of National Biography 1931-1940:524 '49/ Who Was Who, 1929-1940.

1896 LANGLOTZ, ERNST (1895-1978). Archeologist. Sources: Biog Index: 11/Int Dir Anth 1 2/Kunstwerk 31:92 Je '78.

1897 LANGSDORF, GEORGE HEINRICH von (1774-1852), Wollstein, Germany. Physician, scientist, explorer, naturalist. Served with Krusenstern expedition, 1802-1806; his account of Hawaii and other groups remains a classic of Polynesian travel literature. Also wrote about Northwest Coast of North America. Sources: Biog Index: 10/Anthropos 70 no 3-4:610-16 '75/Craig & King, Historical Dictionary of Oceania (1981), p 154.

1898 LANTERNARI, VITTORIO (1918-). Cross-cultural ethnologist. Acculturation, primitive religions & syncretism in Sub-Saharan Africa. Sources: Int Dir Anth 4, 4 rev, 5.

1899 LANTIS, MARGARET L (1906-), Dayton, Ohio, United States. Anthropologist. Religion. Arctic ecology. Inuit culture change. Sources: Int Dir Anth 3, 4, 4 rev, 5.

1900 LA PÉROUSE, JEAN-FRANCIS de GALAUP, COMTE de (1741-1788), near Albi, France. Explorer. Led a three-year voyage of exploration and description across the Pacific; his accounts of Hawaii, South Pacific, Central America, China and Philippines contain valuable ethnographic data. Sources: Columbia/New Int Enc, 1914 ed/Craig & King, Historical Dictionary of Oceania (1981), p 154-5.

1901 LA PETIT, S J, Fr. MATHURIN. Priest. Missionary in New France; wrote on N. American Indians. Source: Jes Rel.

1902 Lapouge, Georges Vacher de, see: VACHER de LAPOUGE.

1903 LARCO HOYLE, RAFAEL (1901-1966), Trujillo, Peru. Archeologist. Director of Museo Rafael Larco Herrara. Specialist on pre-Hispanic cultures of north coastal Peru, especially Mochica, Cupisnique and Salinar; created collection of pottery of the region;

explored many coastal valleys for site survey. Sources: Biog Index: 8/ Who's Who in Latin America 3rd ed., Ronald Hilton ed., Stanford Univ. Press (Blaine Ethridge edition, 1971) vol. 2, p 177/ Am Antiq 33:233-6 Ap '68.

1904 LARDE, JORGE (1891-1928), France. Educator. Wrote a volume on the archeology of Cuzcatlan, the ancient Pipil Indian kingdom in central El Salvador. Source: Flemion, Philip F., Historical Dictionary of El Salvador (1972), p 79.

1905 LARREA y RECALDE, JESUS (1878-1955), Spain. Ethnologist. Sources: Biog Index: 4/Int Dir Anth 2/ Archivo Espanol de Arte y Arqueologia 28 no 2:350 '55.

1906 LARSEN, HELGA EYVIN (1905-), Copenhagen, Denmark. Archeologist. Religion. Ecology. Inuit culture change. Sources: Int Dir Anth 1, 2, 3, 4, 4 rev, 5.

1907 LARSSON, KARL ERIK (1918-). Ethnologist. Social structure. Ethnology of the Fiji Islands. Sources: Int Dir Anth 4, 4 rev, 5.

1908 LARTET, EDOUARD (1801-1871), France. Paleontologist. Analyzed fossils, added to study of mammoths and early man. Favored ideas of gradual evolution. Source: Duroux, Paul-Emile, Dictionaire des Anthropologistes, Paris, Editions Universitaires, 1975.

1909 LARTET, LOUIS (1840-1899), France. Discovered first Cro-Magnon skeletons, 1868. Source: Duroux, Paul-Emile, Dictionaire des Anthropologistes, Paris, Editions Universitaires, 1975.

1910 LATCHAM, RICHARD E (1869-1943), Bristol, England. Civil engineer, amateur anthropologist. Specialist on Mapuche (Chile) culture; reorganized Chile's National Museum of Natural History and vastly expanded its collections; published on Araucanian & Diaguita cultures and Chilean prehistory. Source: Am Anth 47:603-8 O '45.

1911 LATCHMAN ALFARO, RICARDO A (1903-1965), Chile. Civil servant, teacher. Wrote a number of works on Chilean history and literature as well as an account of the wars against the Araucanian Indians. Source: Bizzarro, Salvatore, Historical Dictionary of Chile (1972), p 187.

1912 LATHAM, ROBERT GORDON (1812- 1888). Ethnologist, physician, philologist. Sources: Biog Index: 4/Brown, G. H. Comp. Lives of the fellows of the Royal college of physicians of London, 1826-1925. The college '55 p 42.

1913 LATOUR, JACQUES (1918-1956). Archeologist. Archeology of France. Sources: Biog Index: 5/Rev Arch 2:99-101 Jl '58.

1914 LATTIMORE, OWEN (1900-). Sinologist. Specialized in the minority peoples of Western China & Mongolia; extensive publications. Sources: Biog Index: 1 2 3 4 5 6 7 9 & 11/ Saturday Review of Literature 32:10 Ap 9 '49/ N Y Times Book Review p 12 Ag 12 '50/Harper's 201:43-52 Ag, 79-87 S '50/ Newsweek 36:80 Jl 31 '50, 44:28 O 18 '54, 78:55 D 20 '71/America 83:35 Ap 15 '50 /New Republic 131:7-12 D 27 '54/Nation 176:122-14 F 7 '53/ US News 37:16 Jl 16 '54/Kunitz, Stanley Jasspon ed., Twentieth Century Authors; 1st Sup. Wilson '55 p 554-5/Wilson Library Bulletin 37:323 D '62/ Current Biography Yr Bk 1964:246-8 '64.

1915 LAUFER, BERTHOLD (1874-1934), Cologne, Germany. Anthropologist, Orientalist. Conducted fieldwork in China and Tibet; numerous publications on a variety of ethnological topics. Sources: Biog Index: 3/Am Anth 38:101-11, 54:163-4 Ap '52.

1916 LAURE, S J, Fr. PIERRE (1688-1738), Orleans, France. Priest. Missionary in New France; wrote on N. American Indians. Source: Jes Rel.

1917 LAUZON, S J, Fr. PIERRE (1687-1742), Poitiers, France. Priest. Missionary in New France; wrote on N. American Indians. Source: Jes Rel.

1918 LAVACHERY, HENRI ALFRED (1885-), Belgium. Ethnologist. Sources: Biog Index: 3/Int Dir Anth 2, 3, 4, 4 rev/ Brussels, Musees Royaux d'Art et d'Histoire Bulletin S 4 23:106-7 Ja '51.

1919 LAVAL, LOUIS (1808-1880), France. Missionary. Wrote extensively on pre-contact history, religion, culture and language of the Gambier Islands (French Polynesia). Source: Craig & King, Historical Dictionary of Oceania (1981), p 156-7.

1920 LA VALLÉE POUSSIN, LOUIS de (1869-1938), Liege, Belgium. Orientalist. Sanskritist and student of Buddhism. Sources: Biog Index: 2/Isis 41 no 1:56 '50.

1921 LAW, HOWARD WILLIAM (1919-). Descriptive American linguistics. Indian linguistics & culture. Aztec linguistics. Sources: Int Dir Anth 4, 5/Nat Dir Lat Am.

1922 LAWRENCE, THOMAS EDWARD (1888-1935). Archeologist, soldier. Classic literary account of Arab culture during World War I. Sources: Biog Index: 1 2 3 4 5 6 7 8 9 & 13/ International Journal of Middle Eastern Studies 15:154-62 My '79/ Donaldson, Norman & Betty, How did they die? St. Martin's '80 p 218-20/ Makers of Modern Culture. Facts on File '81, p 293/ Lawrence, Arnold Walter, T. E. Lawrence in Arabia & after. Greenwood Press '79/ O'Donnell, Thomas J., Confessions of T. E. Lawrence. Ohio Univ. Press '79/ Robinson, Edward, Lawrence, the story of his life. Folcroft lib. ed. '79/ Tidrick, Kathryn, Heartbeguiling Araby. Cambridge Univ. Press '81 p 163-92.

1923 LAYARD, AUSTEN HENRY L (1817- 1894). Archeologist. Escavated at Nineveh. Sources: Biog Index: 5 6 7 8 9 & 13/ Jameson, Cynthia, Secret of the royal mounds: Henry Leyard & the first cities of Assyria. Coward, McCann & Geoghegan '79.

1924 LAYDEVANT, FRANÇOIS (1878-1954), France. Missionary. Collected and published materials on the ethnology, anthropology, history and geography of Lesotho. Source: Haliburton, Gordon, Historical Dictionary of Lesotho (1977), p 75.

1925 LE BON, GUSTAVE (1841-1931), Nogent-le-Rotron, France. Psychologist. Authored a number of works on social psychology, in which he expounded theories of national traits and racial superiority. Source: Columbia.

1926 LE BRETON, HENRI (1878-1959), Rennes, France. Missionary. Began printing press at Mazenod (Lesotho); wrote and translated a large amount of religious literature in Sesotho. Source: Haliburton, Gordon, Historical Dictionary of Lesotho (1977), p 77.

1927 LE JEUNE, S J, Fr. PAUL (1592-1664), Chalons-sur-Marne, France. Priest. Missionary in New France; wrote on N. American Indians. Source: Jes Rel.

1928 LE MOYNE, S J, Fr. SIMON (1604-1665), Paris, France. Priest. Missionary in New France; wrote on N. American Indians. Source: Jes Rel.

1929 LEACH, EDMUND RONALD (1910-), England. Social anthropologist. Worked in Burma, Ceylon, India & Borneo. Structuralism. Wrote *Political Systems of Highland Burma*; also published on the Kurds and kinship. Sources: Biog Index: 10 & 13/Int Dir Anth 2, 3, 4, 4 rev, 5/ Current Anthropology 27:4 (Aug-Oct 1986) p 375-382/ Makers of Modern Culture. Facts on File '81, p 295.

1930 LEACH, MARIA (1891-1977). Author, folklorist. Edited the *Dictionary of Folklore, Mythology, and Legend* (1944-50); produced several works on folklore related subjects. Sources: Biog Index: 8 & 11/N Y Times p 38 My 24 '77/ School Library Journal 24:16 S '77.

1931 LEAKEY, LOUIS SEYMOUR BAZETT (1903-1972), Kabete, Kenya. Anthropologist, archeologist, paleontologist. Worked with KiSwahili & Kikuyu; excavated

Zinjanthropus & other evidence for evolution at Olduvai Gorge (Tanzania); discovered Homo habilis; wrote extensively on human prehistory. Sources: Biog Index: 6 7 8 9 10 & 11/Int Dir Anth 2, 3, 4, 4 rev/ International Encyclopedia of the Social Sciences, v. 18/Ogot, Bethwell A., Historical Dictionary of Kenya (1981), p 118-9/Kurtz, Laura S., Historical Dictionary of Tanzania (1978), p 105.

1932 LEAKEY, MARY DOUGLAS (Nicol) (1913-). Anthropologist, paleontologist. Studied lower & middle Pleistocene at Olduvai Gorge (Tanzania). Sources: Biog Index: 6 10 & 12/Int Dir Anth 5/ N Y Times Biog Service 11:236-7 F '80.

1933 LEASK, THOMAS SMITH (1839-1912). Merchant. Kept a diary covering history of Mashonaland and Matabeleland (Rhodesia) in the 1860s. Source: Rasmussen, R. Kent, Historical Dictionary of Rhodesia/Zimbabwe (1979), p 148.

1934 LEBEL, PAUL (1901-1965), France. Archeologist. Founded *Revue archeologique de l'Est*; archeology of Burgundy (France). Sources: Biog Index: 8/Rev Arch 2:341 '66.

1935 LEBEUF, JEAN-PAUL (1907-), Paris, France. Archeologist, ethnologist. Worked in Cameroon, Chad & Nigeria on links between African archeology & ethnology. Urbanism and the state in Kotokoland. Sources: Int Dir Anth 3, 4, 4 rev, 5.

1936 LECLERCQ, HENRI (1869-1945), Tournai, Belgium. Priest, archeologist. Archeology of early Christendom. Sources: Biog Index: 2/Rev Arch series 6 37:203-5 Ap '51.

1937 LEE, ALFRED McCLUNG (1906-). Sociologist. Gang & cult formation. Revolts of oppressed. American Blacks, Irish & Sicilians. Sources: Int Dir Anth 4, 4 rev, 5.

1938 LEE, DOROTHY DEMETRACOPOULOU (1905-1975), Constantinople, Turkey. Anthropologist. Existential anthropology. Language & change. Sources: Biog Index: 10/Int Dir Anth 1, 2, 3, 4, 4 rev/ N Y Times p 53 Ap 20 '75/Anth News Jn '75.

1939 LEEDS, EDWARD THURLOW (1877-1955). Archeologist. Keeper of the Ashmolean Museum, Oxford, 1928-1945; major work was in Anglo-Saxon studies. Sources: Biog Index: 4/Int Dir Anth 2/Museum Journal 55:189-90 O '55/ Nature 176:581-2 S 24 '55/ Royal Institute of British Architects Journal S 3 63:215 Mr '56.

1940 LEENHARDT, MAURICE (1878-1954), France. Missionary. Foremost ethnologist for the cultures of New Caledonia, wrote widely on the subject. Sources: Int Dir Anth 2/Craig & King, Historical Dictionary of Oceania (1981), p 157.

1941 LEFEBVRE, GUSTAVE (1879-1959), France. Egyptologist. Wrote on language and literature of ancient Egypt. Sources: Biog Index: 5 & 12/Rev Arch 1:84-6 Ja '58.

1942 LEFEVRE, JOSEPH (1883-1977). Historian, archeologist. Edited: *Documents relatifs a l'admission aux Pays-Bas des nonces et internonces des XVIIe et XVIIe siecles*, 1939; *Correspondance de Philippe II sur les affaires des Pays-Bas*, 2. ptie., 1940-1960. Sources: Biog Index: 13/ Revue Belge d'Archeologie et d'Histoire d'Art 46:166 '77.

1943 LEGGE, JAMES (1815-1897), Scotland. Missionary, sinologist. Source: Biog Index: 1.

1944 LEGRAIN, LEON (1878-1963). Priest, archeologist. Specialist in archeology and languages of Assyria and Sumeria; worked at the sites of Ur (Iraq) and Susa (Iran). Sources: Biog Index: 6 & 7/N Y Times p 25 N 2 '63/ Expedition 6:2 Winter '64.

1945 LEGUIZAMON, JUAN MARTÍN (1833-1881), Cordoba, Argentina. Archeologist. First to study the archeology of the Diaguita peoples of Northwest Argentina. Source: Wright & Nelsham, Historical

1946 LEHMAN, F RUDOLF (1887-), Germany. Ethnologist. Sources: Int Dir Anth 1 2 3.

1947 LEHMANN, DOROTHEA AGNES (1910-). Ethnologist, folklorist, linguist. Bantu languages, dialects. African (Zambian) culture change & folklore. Source: Int Dir Anth 5.

1948 LEHMANN, HENRI (1905-). Archeologist. Central & South American cultures. Religious syncretism among the Maya. Sources: Int Dir Anth 3, 4, 4 rev, 5.

1949 LEHMANN, KARL (1894-1960), Rostock, Germany. Archeologist. Directed the excavations on Samothrace (Greece), which recovered the Winged victory" statue; extensive publications on the island's prehistory. Sources: Biog Index: 5 & 6/Am J Arch 65:307-8 Jl '61/ N Y Times p 27 D 19 '60/Time 77:47 Ja 2 '61/Art Journal 20:174 Winter '60.

1950 LEHMANN, WINFRED PHILIPP (1916-). Linguist. Germanic & classical languages in Indo-European linguistics. Sources: Int Dir Anth 4 rev, 5.

1951 LEHMER, DONALD JAYNE (1918-1975), United States. Anthropologist, archeologist, ethnologist. Village cultures of the N. American Plains Indians. Cultural ecology. Sources: Biog Index: 11/Int Dir Anth 3, 4, 4 rev, 5/ Am Antiq 41:178-80 Ap '76/Anth News S '75.

1952 LEIRIS, MICHEL (1901-), Paris, France. Anthropologist. Ethnology, linguistics and folklore of West Africa. Sources: Biog Index: 10/Int Dir Anth 1 2 3 4/ World Authors, 1950-1970. Wilson '75, Wakeman, John ed., p 854-6.

1953 LEISNER, GEORG KLAUS (1870-1957). Archeologist. Sources: Biog Index: 5/ Archivo Espanol de Arte y Arqueologia 30 no 1:117-18 '57.

1954 LEITE de VASCONCELLOS, JOSE (1858-1943), Ucanha, Portugal. Ethnologist, archeologist. Ethnology and religion of ancient Portugal. Sources: Biog Index: 1/Rev Arch series 6 25:63-4 Ja '46.

1955 LEÓN, NICOLÁS (1859-1929), Michoacan, Mexico. Historian. Wrote widely on Mexican ethnology and anthropology. Source: Briggs & Alisky, Historical Dictionary of Mexico (1981), p 129.

1956 LEONARDI, PIERO (1908-). Paleontologist. Prehistoric art & paleoethnology of Italy. Sources: Int Dir Anth 4, 4 rev, 5.

1957 LEPSIUS, RICHARD (1810-1884), Naumburg, Germany. Archeologist, Egyptologist. Wrote chiefly on paleography, on the Etruscan, Oscan and Umbrian inscriptions. Sources: Columbia/New Int Enc, 1914 ed.

1958 LÉRY, JEAN de (1534-1611), France. Historian. Wrote a chronicle of French involvement in Brazil in the 16th century. Source: Levine, Robert M., Historical Dictionary of Brazil (1979), p 126.

1959 LES TRANGE, GUY (1854-1933), Hunstanton, England. Orientalist. Persian scholar; contributed to historical geography of Middle Eastern culture; translated numerous texts. Sources: Biog Index: 2/Dictionary of National Biography 1931-1940:535 '49.

1960 LESER, PAUL (1899-). Ethnologist. Methods & techniques in source criticism. History of German ethno-historical reconstruction. Tanzania. Sources: Int Dir Anth 4, 4 rev, 5.

1961 LESSA, WILLIAM ARMAND (1908-), Newark, New Jersey, United States. Ethnologist, ethnohistorian. Micronesian folklore. Sources: Int Dir Anth 3, 4, 4 rev, 5.

1962 LESSER, ALEXANDER (1902-1982), New York, New York, United States. Anthropologist. Worked with Plains Indians. Contributed to anthropological theory. Specialized in study of kinship to construct & test social theory; research on Sioux kinship and Pawnee & Kiowa religion; staunch supporter of Native Americans.

Sources: Am Anth 87(1985):637-644/Int Dir Anth 1, 2, 3, 4, 4 rev.

1963 LESSING, FERDINAND DIEDERICH (1882-1961), Essen Altenessen, Germany. Orientalist. Participated in the Scientific Expedition to the North-Western Provinces of China with Sven Hedin, 1930-1932. Sources: Biog Index: 6/Artibus Asiae 25 no 2:193-4 '62.

1964 LESTER, PAUL (1891-), France. Physical anthropologist. Africa. Source: Int Dir Anth 1 2.

1965 LEVEL, ANDRÉS AURELIO, Venezuela. Civil servant. Authored the first census of Venezuela. Source: Rudolph & Rudolph, Historical Dictionary of Venezuela (1971), p 74.

1966 LEVI della VIDA, SAMUELE GIORGIO (1886-1967), Venice, Italy. Orientalist. Specialist on ancient Semitic world and medieval Islam. Sources: Biog Index: 8/N Y Times p 47 N 27 '67.

1967 LÉVI-STRAUSS, CLAUDE (1908-), Brussels, Belgium. Anthropologist. Structuralism. Cognitive & theoretical anthropology. Mythology. Sources: Biog Index: 7 8 9 10 11 & 13-/Int Dir Anth 3, 4, 4 rev, 5/ International Encyclopedia of the Social Sciences, v. 18/ Makers of Modern Culture. Facts on File '81, p 303-6.

1968 LEVIN, MAKSIM GRIGOR'EVICH (1904-1963), Slonim, Belorussia. Anthropologist, ethnographer, archeologist. Specialized in culture of northeastern Asia; also in physical anthropology of Asian peoples and history of physical anthropology in Russia. The peoples of Siberia and Middle Asia. Sources: Biog Index: 7/ Great Soviet Encyclopedia, New York, Macmillan (1977), v. 14, p 451/ "Pamiati M.G. Levina" Sovetskaia etnografiia, 1963, no. 4/ Am Antiq 29:480-3 Ap '64.

1969 LÉVY, ISIDORE (1871-1959), Rixheim, Alsace, France. Archeologist. Wrote on ancient Mediterranean. Sources: Biog Index: 5/Rev Arch 2:98 Jl '59.

1970 LÉVY, PAUL GEORGES VICTOR (1909-). Archeologist. Prehistoric & historic periods in S.E. Asia; ethnology of religions. Sources: Int Dir Anth 2, 3, 4, 4 rev, 5.

1971 LÉVY-BRUHL, LUCIEN (1857-1939), France. Philosopher, psychologist, ethnologist. Known for his research on the mentality of preliterate peoples. Sources: Columbia/ Zusne, L., Biographical Dictionary of Psychology, Westport, Conn., Greenwood, 1984.

1972 LEWIS, ALBERT BUELL (1867-1940), Ohio, United States. Ethnologist. Much fieldwork in Pacific. Sources: Int Dir Anth 1 2/Am Anth 43:256-7 Ap '41.

1973 LEWIS, MARY BUTLER (1903-1970), United States. Archeologist. Contributed to archeology of Mesoamerica & Northeastern U.S. Source: Am Anth 73:255-6 F '71.

1974 LEWIS, OSCAR (1914-1970), New York, New York, United States. Anthropologist, author, ethnologist. Developed the "Culture of Poverty" hypothesis. Did pioneering work in rural-urban studies. Worked in Cuba, Puerto Rico, Mexico & U.S. Sources: Biog Index: 8 9 & 10/Int Dir Anth 3, 4, 4 rev/ International Encyclopedia of the Social Sciences, v. 18/ World Authors, 1950-1970. Wilson '75, Wakeman, John ed., p 866-8/ Am Anth 74:747-57 Je '72.

1975 LEWIS, THOMAS M N (1896-1974), United States. Archeologist. Archeology of Southeast U.S.; founder of Society for American Archeology. Sources: Int Dir Anth 1 2 3/Anth News My '75.

1976 LEYBURN, JAMES GRAHAM (1902-), United States. Anthropologist. Sources: Int Dir Anth 1 2/Nat Dir Lat Am.

1977 LHOTE, HENRI (1903-), Paris, France. Archeologist. Studied rock paintings of the Sahara. Sources: Richard Lawless, Algeria, Clio Press, 1980, p 21/ Who's Who In France, 1983-84 p 895.

1978 LI, FANG KUEI (1902-), China.

Linguist. Historical & modern Chinese grammar & phonology. Sources: Int Dir Anth 2, 3, 5.

1979 LIAVDANSKII, ALEKSANDR NIKOLAEVICH (1893-1942), Iur'evo, Belorussia. Archeologist. Paleolithic, Neolithic and medieval Belorussia. Sources: Great Soviet Encyclopedia, New York, Macmillan (1977), v. 15, p 109/"Pamiati A.N. Liavdanskogo" Sovetskaia arkheologiia 1964, no 1.

1980 LIEBMAN, SEYMOUR BERTRAM (1907-). Cultural anthropologist. Sociocultural & economic status of Jews. Interrelationships of communities. Source: Int Dir Anth 5.

1981 LIESTOL, KNUT (1881-1952), Aseval, Norway. Folklorist. Specialist on folksongs of medieval Norway and their relationship to those of England, Scotland and the family sagas of Iceland; worked to define the folksong tradition of the Northern European area. Sources: Biog Index: 3/Int Dir Anth 3/ Journal of American Folklore 66:332 O '53.

1982 LIEURANCE, THURLOW (1878-1963), Oscaloosa, Iowa, United States. Composer, folklorist. Researched, published and performed U.S. Indian music. Sources: Biog Index: 1 & 8/Nat Cyc Am Biog 51:638 '69/ Howard, John Tasker. Our American music, 3rd ed. rev Crowell '46 p 590-1.

1983 LIKHACHEV, ANDREI FEDOROVICH (1832-1890), Polianki, Russia. Archeologist, numismatist. Bulgarian settlements on the Volga River and Finno-Ugric peoples on the Kama River (Russia). Sources: Great Soviet Encyclopedia, New York, Macmillan (1977), v. 14, p 496/Russkii biograficheskii slovar'. Moscow, 1914, v. 10.

1984 LILLY, ELI (1886-1977). Businessman. Financed much archeological research in Indiana. Source: N Y Times 38:1 Ja '25 '77.

1985 LINDBLOM, KARL GERHARD (1887- 1969), Sweden. Ethnologist. Sources: Biog Index: 9/Int Dir Anth 1, 2, 3, 4, 4 rev.

1986 LINDEGARD, BENGT (1911-). Anthropologist. Somatotyping, cephalometrics & psychometrics in Sweden. Sources: Int Dir Anth 4, 4 rev, 5.

1987 LINDGREN, ETHEL JOHN (1905-), Evanston, Illinois, United States. Anthropologist. Social & economic aspects of reindeer breeding in Scotland. Manchuria. Sources: Int Dir Anth 1, 2, 3, 4, 4 rev, 5.

1988 LINDSKOG, GUSTAV UNO BIRGER (1914-). Sociologist. Secret societies, acculturation, criminology & deviant groups. Forensic anthropology. Sources: Int Dir Anth 4, 4 rev, 5.

1989 LING, SHUN-SHENG (1902-), Chang-Chow, Kiangsu, China. Ethnologist. Trans-Pacific studies. Water transportation in peasant & primitive societies. Sources: Int Dir Anth 1, 2, 3, 4, 4 rev, 5.

1990 LINNE, SIGVALD (1898-), Stockholm, Sweden. Ethnographer. Sources: Int Dir Anth 1 2 3 4.

1991 LINSCOTT, ELOISE HUBBARD (1898-). Folklorist. Collected folkmusic of New England and created superb historical collection of regional primary recordings. Sources: Biog Index: 11/Ms. 6:22 Sept '77.

1992 LINTON, RALPH (1893-1953), Philadelphia, Pennsylvania, United States. Ethnologist. Major figure focused on social structure, cultural process and personality; his *The Study of Man* bridged previously differing theoretical factions of anthropology & provided a common orientation for the discipline. Sources: Biog Index: 3 4 5 & 9/Int Dir Anth 1 2 3/ International Encyclopedia of the Social Sciences, v. 9/Nat Cyc Am Biog/ Who Was Who in America, v. 3/Am Anth 56:274-81 Ap '54/Am Antiq 19:382-3+ Ap '54/ Britannica Book of the Year 1954:531 '54/ Journal of American Folklore 67:309 Jl '54/N Y Times 17:1 D 25 '53/ Wilson Library Bulletin 28:460 F '54/ Kunitz, Stanley Jasspon ed., Twentieth century authors; 1st sup. Wilson '55 p 586-7/Linton, Adelin and Charles Wagely, Ralph Linton,

New York, Columbia Univ. Press (1971).

1993 LIPKIND, WILLIAM (1904-1974), United States. Author, anthropologist, ethnographer. Compiled a dictionary & grammar of Brazilian Indian dialects. Sources: Biog Index: 2 6 7 10 & 13/ Commire, Anne, Something about the Author, v 15. Gale '79 p 178-80/ Anth News D '74.

1994 LIPPOLD, GEORG (1885-1954), Mainz, Germany. Archeologist. Classical archeology. Sources: Biog Index: 3 & 4/Int Dir Anth 1 2/ Rev Arch series 6 47:86-7 Ja '56.

1995 LIPS, EVA (1906-). Economic ethnologist, ethnobotanist. Economics of U.S. & Canadian Indian tribes. Ethnobotany of the sugar maple. Sources: Int Dir Anth 4, 4 rev, 5.

1996 LIPS, JULIUS ERNST (1895-1950), Germany. Anthropologist. Curator of the Ethnological Museum of Cologne, Germany. Sources: Biog Index: 2/Int Dir Anth 1 2 3/Isis 41 no 2:202 '50/ N Y Times p 27 Ja 25 '50/Science 111:213 F 24 '50.

1997 LIPSCHUTZ, ALEXANDER (1883-), Riga, Latvia. Physician, ethnologist. Studies of the last Indian inhabitants of Tierra del Fuego (Chile & Argentina). Sources: Int Dir Anth 3, 4, 4 rev, 5.

1998 LIPTAK, PAL (1914-). Anthropotaxonomist, paleoanthropologist. Studied Huns, Avars & ancient Hungarians. Evolutionary systematics of Hominidae. Sources: Int Dir Anth 4, 4 rev, 5.

1999 LIVI, LIVIO (1891-), Rome, Italy. Physical anthropologist. Source: Int Dir Anth 1 2.

2000 LIVINGSTONE, DAVID (1813-1873), Blanktyre in Lanarkshire, Scotland. Missionary, explorer. Wrote large number of diaries, letters and researches useful for documenting history of Zimbabwe, 1840s and 1850s; explored large areas of central Botswana, Lake Ngami, Victoria Falls. Sources: Columbia/New Int Enc, 1914 ed/Rasmussen, R. Kent, Historical Dictionary of Rhodesia/Zimbabwe (1979), p 154/ Stevens, Richard P., Historical Dictionary of the Republic of Botswana (1975), p 91.

2001 LLOYD, SETON (1902-), England. Archeologist. Fieldwork on excavation sites in Egypt, Iraq; worked on the Sumerian temples of Tell Asmar and Tell Ajrab; became director of the British Institute of Archeology in Ankara (Turkey) in 1948. Sources: Biog Index: 1/Int Dir Anth 3/Nature 162:327 Ag 28 '48.

2002 LOCKARD, DERWOOD W (1907-1977), Chicago, Illinois, United States. Anthropologist. Established center for the study of cultures of the Middle East at Harvard University. Sources: Int Dir Anth 1 2/Anth News 18:7 S '77, p 3.

2003 LOCKERBIE, LESLIE (1911-). Archeologist. New Zealand C-14 dating. Sources: Int Dir Anth 4, 4 rev, 5.

2004 LOCKERBY, WILLIAM (1782-1853), Ashbridge, Scotland. Merchant. Wrote memoir of his stay on Fiji, 1808-1809, which is useful as an ethnographic source. Source: Craig & King, Historical Dictionary of Oceania (1981), p 160-1.

2005 LOCKETT, CLAIBORNE (1907-1984). Ethnologist. Specialist on the art of the Indians of Arizona. Source: Anth News (Sept 1984) p 4.

2006 LOE, ALFRED, Baron de (1858-1947), Valenciennes, France. Archeologist, museum curator. Studied prehistoric sites in Belgium; curator of the Musees Royaux d'Art et d'Histoire, Brussels. Sources: Biog Index: 1/ Brussels, Musees Royaux d'Art et d'Histoire Bulletin S 4 19:101-3 Jl '47.

2007 LOEB, EDWIN MEYER (1894-1966), New York, United States. Anthropologist. Worked in Indonesia, Southwestern U.S. & Polynesia. Studied the diffusion of trait complexes. Precise field monographs remain invaluable. Sources: Biog Index: 7 & 8/Int Dir Anth 1 2 3/Am Anth 69:200-3 Ap '67.

2008 LOEFLING, PETTER (-1756), Sweden. Naturalist. Studied the natural environment of the Cumana region of Venezuela. Source: Rudolph & Rudolph, Historical Dictionary of Venezuela (1971), p 77.

2009 LOEHR, MAX (1903-). Sinologist. Sources: Biog Index: 10/Int Dir Anth 4.

2010 LOESCHCKE, SIEGFRIED (1883-1956), Dorpat, Estonia. Archeologist. Director of Roman Department of the Rheinische Landesmuseum in Trier; most important excavation was made in the Altbach river valley (Germany), 1924-1945. Sources: Biog Index: 4/Am J Arch 62:105 Ja '58.

2011 LOMAX, ALAN (1915-). Folklorist. Sources: Biog Index: 2 4 & 5/Int Dir Anth 4, 4 rev/Reporter 24:48+ F 2 '61.

2012 LOMAX, JOHN AVERY (1867-1948), Goodman, Mississippi, United States. Folklorist. Collected and published American folksongs. Sources: Biog Index: 1 2 3 4 & 5/N Y Times, Ja 27 '48/ Saturday Review of Literature 41:37+ Ag 30 '58.

2013 LOMBARD, LAMBERT (1506-1566). Archeologist, architect, painter. Source: Biog Index: 10.

2014 LOMBARDI-SATRIANI, RAFFAELE (1873-1966), Italy. Folklorist. Expert on folklore of Calabrian region of Italy. Sources: Biog Index: 8/Int Dir Anth 2/ Journal of American Folklore 81:66-7 Ja '68.

2015 LOMMEL, ANDREAS (1912-), Munich, Germany. Archeologist. Rock-painting. Australian acculturation & aboriginal art. Prehistoric & contemporary primitive art in the S. Pacific. Sources: Int Dir Anth 3, 4, 4 rev, 5.

2016 LONGYEAR, JOHN MUNRO (1914-), Houghton, Michigan, United States. Anthropologist, archeologist. Meso-America work includes Mayan & El Salvador sites. Sources: Int Dir Anth 3, 4, 4 rev, 5/Nat Dir Lat Am.

2017 LONNROT, ELIAS (1802-1884). Philologist, folklorist. Sources: Biog Index: 5 & 7.

2018 LOOMIS, CHARLES GRANT (1901-1963), Worcester, Massachusetts, United States. Folklorist. Wrote on folklore, particularly German folklore. Sources: Biog Index: 3 6 7 & 8/Nat Cyc Am Biog 50:356-7 '68.

2019 LOOMIS, CHARLES P (1905-). Rural sociologist. Social change in Costa Rica, Peru, Bolivia, western S. America. Source: Int Dir Anth 5.

2020 LOPEZ, CECILIO (1898-1979), Markins, Rizal, Philippines. Linguist, grammarian. Studies of Philippine languages. Sources: Int Dir Anth 3, 4, 4 rev, 5/Am Anth 82:555-6 S '80/ Anth News N '79.

2021 LOPEZ, JULIUS (1918-1961). Archeologist. Specialist in urban archeology of New York State; authority on pottery from coastal regions of the state. Sources: Biog Index: 4 & 6/Am Antiq 28:82 Jl '62.

2022 LÓPEZ CUEVILLAS, FLORENTINO (1886-1958). Archeologist. Sources: Biog Index: 6/ Archivo Espanol de Arte y Arqueologia 34 no 103:222 '61.

2023 LORENZ, KONRAD ZACHARIAS (1903-), Austria. Ethnologist, naturalist, zoologist. Postulated domestication as a potential cause for man's destruction of successive cultures. Sources: Biog Index: 13/ International Encyclopedia of the Social Sciences, v. 18/ Makers of Modern Culture. Facts on File '81, p 312-13.

2024 LORET, VICTOR (1859-1946), France. Egyptologist. Source: Biog Index: 2.

2025 LOTH, EDWARD (1885-1944), Poland. Anthropologist. Physical anthropology. Source: Int Dir Anth 1 2.

2026 LOTHROP, SAMUEL KIRKLAND (1892-1965), United States. Anthropologist, archeologist.

Expert on the regional ceramics of Costa Rica and Nicaragua; excavated areas in Guatemala. Sources: Biog Index: 1 6 7 & 11/Meyer, Harvey K., Historical Dictionary of Nicaragua (1972), p 241/ Samuel Kirkland Lothrop (In National academy of sciences, Biographical memoirs (v 48) The academy '76 p 253-72).

2027 LOTI, PIERRE (1850-1923), France. Writer. His novel *Le Mariage de Loti*, is useful for its accurate depiction of Tahitian customs and court life in the 1870s. Source: Craig & King, Historical Dictionary of Oceania (1981), p 163.

2028 LOUBAT, JOSEPH FLORIMOND (1831-1927), New York, New York, United States. Financed archeology including prizes for manuscripts and three endowed professorships in archeology. Source: Am Anth 29:340.

2029 LOUD, LLEWELLYN LEMONT (1879- 1946), Woodland, Aroostook County, Maine, United States. Archeologist. Worked at Lovelock Cave, Nevada; surveyed pre-contact Wiyot Indian site in California; excavated four mounds in the San Francisco area. Sources: Biog Index: 1/Am Antiq 12:180 Ja '47.

2030 LOUIS, ANDRÉ (1912-). Ethnosociologist. Rural social change & ecology of Berber-speaking populations. Source: Int Dir Anth 5.

2031 LOUKATOS, DEMÉTRIOS (1908-). Ethnologist. Popular Greek culture. Proverbs & superstitions in Epirus & the Ionian Islands. Source: Int Dir Anth 5.

2032 LOUNSBURY, FLOYD GLENN (1914-), Stevens Point, Wisconsin, United States. Anthropologist, linguist. Sources: Int Dir Anth 3, 4, 4 rev/Nat Dir Lat Am.

2033 LOW, IMMANUEL (1854-1944). Orientalist. Source: Biog Index: 2.

2034 LOWE, CLARENCE van RIET (1894-1956). Archeologist, engineer. Excavations of Stone Age sites in South Africa; co-authored with A.J.H. Goodwin, *The Stone Age Cultures of South Africa*, in 1929; was the first director of the Archaeological Survey of the Union of South Africa in 1935. Sources: Biog Index: 4/Int Dir Anth 1 2/Nature 178:179 Jl 28 '56.

2035 LOWIE, ROBERT HARRY (1883-1957), Vienna, Austria. Anthropologist, ethnologist, musicologist. Distinguished American ethnologist & theorist. Specialist in Crow culture; fieldwork among the Shoshone, Ute, Chippewa, Hidatsa, Mandan, Arikara, Hopi & Washo cultures. Sources: Biog Index: 4 5 6 9 & 11/Int Dir Anth 1 2 3/ Robert Harry Lowie (In National academy of sciences, Biographical memoirs v 44) The academy '74, p 175-212/Am Anth 60:358-75 Ap '58.

2036 LOYARD, S J, Fr. JEAN-BAPTISTE (1674-1731), Pau, France. Priest. Missionary in New France; wrote on N. American Indians. Source: Jes Rel.

2037 LOZANO, PEDRO (1647-1752), Madrid, Spain. Historian. Wrote two books on the geography of the Chaco and the conquest of Paraguay & Argentina. Source: Wright & Nelsham, Historical Dictionary of Argentina (1978), p 513.

2038 LUCAS, ALFRED (1867-1945). Egyptologist, archeologist. Contributed knowledge of chemistry to excavation work in Egypt, for example, in analysis of tomb of Tutankhamen. Sources: Biog Index: 1/Chemical Society Journal p 558 Je '46/ Chronique d'Egypte 21:205-6, 22:301-4 Jl '46, Jl '47/ Nature 157:98-9 Ja 25 '46, 157:433 Ap 6 '46.

2039 LUCAS-SHADWELL, WILLIAM NOEL (1882-1943), England. Archeologist. Archeology of Correze (France). Sources: Biog Index: 1/Rev Arch series 6 25:63 Ja '46.

2040 LUGLI, GIUSEPPE (1890-1967). Archaeologist. Specialist on archeology of the City of Rome and the surrounding region. Sources: Biog Index: 9/Paladio ns 19:184 Ja-D '69.

2041 LUGO, BERNARDO de (1675-), Bogota, Colombia. Grammarian.

Documented language of the Chibcha Indians of Colombia. Source: Davis, Robert H., Historical Dictionary of Colombia (1977), p 140.

2042 LUKAS, JOHANNES (1901-), Karlsbad, Germany. Ethnologist, linguist. African language studies. Sources: Int Dir Anth 2, 3, 4, 4 rev, 5.

2043 LUMLEY, MARIE-ANTOINETTE de. Archeologist, human paleontologist. Human paleontology. Sources: Biog Index: 10/Time 103:100 Ap 29 '74/ Mary, Leakey, Disclosing the Past, an Autobiography, Leakey, Mary D., McGraw-Hill, 1986, p 174.

2044 LUND, PETER WILHELM (1801-1880), Denmark. Wrote about paleontology of Brazil. Source: Nat Un Cat.

2045 LUNET de LAJONQUIERE, ETIENNE EDMOND (1861-). Wrote about archeology of China. Source: Nat Un Cat.

2046 LUNSFORD, BASCOM LAMAR (1882- 1973), North Carolina, United States. Folk musician, folklorist. Collected and recorded folklore of the North Carolina mountains. Sources: Biog Index: 1 & 10/Journal of American Folklore 87:155 Ap '74/ Newsweek 82:78-9 Ag 20 '73.

2047 LUOMALA, ELLEN KATHARINE (1907-), Cloquet, Minnesota, United States. Ethnologist. Oral art & its cultural context in Polynesia. Sources: Int Dir Anth 1, 2, 3, 4, 4 rev, 5.

2048 LUZBETAK, LOUIS JOSEPH (1918-), Joliet, Illinois, United States. Anthropologist. Cross-cultural communication. Applied anthropology for Catholic missionaries. Sources: Int Dir Anth 5/ American Men and Women of Science, ed. by J.C. Press, 12th ed., New York, Bowker, 1973.

2049 LUZEL, FRANÇOIS MARIE (1821-1895). Folklorist. Collected legends and tales of the Breton people. Sources: Biog Index: 5/ Modern Language Association, Publications, 73 pt 1:545-8 D '58.

2050 LYND, ROBERT STAUGHTON (1892- 1970), New Albany, Indiana, United States. Sociologist. With his wife he made a study of Muncie, Indiana published as *Middletown: A Study in Contemporary American Culture*. Source: Columbia.

2051 LYON, DAVID GORDON (1852-1935). Orientalist. Source: Biog Index: 3.

2052 LYONNE, S J, Fr. MARTIN (1614-1661), Paris, France. Priest. Missionary in New France; wrote on N. American Indians. Source: Jes Rel.

2053 MACALISTER, ROBERT ALEXANDER STEWART (1870-1950), England. Archeologist. Sources: Biog Index: 2 & 3/Antiquaries Journal Jl '50/ Rev Arch series 6 43:67 Ja '54.

2054 McALLESTER, DAVID PARK (1916-), Everett, Massachusetts, United States. Ethno-musicologist. Ceremonial use of music and poetry by N. American Indians. Sources: Int Dir Anth 3, 5.

2055 McALLISTER, J GILBERT (1904-), San Antonio, Texas, United States. Ethnologist, archeologist. N. American Indian social organization & archeology; Hawaiian archeology. Sources: Int Dir Anth 1, 2, 3, 5.

2056 McARTHUR, MARGARET (1919-). Social anthropologist. Social aspects of nutrition & public health in Malaya & West Coast of New Guinea. Source: Int Dir Anth 5.

2057 MACAULAY, THOMAS BABINGTON (1800-1859), Rothley Temple, Leicestershire, England. Historian. Wrote major history of England. Early in career, reformed educational system and legal code of India. Sources: New Int Enc, 1914 ed/Columbia.

2058 McBURNEY, CHARLES BRIAN MONTAGU (1914-), Stockbridge, Massachusetts, United States. Archeologist. Upper, middle & lower Paleolithic chronology & statistical analysis. Sources: Int Dir Anth 3, 5.

2059 McCALL, DANIEL FRANCIS

(1918-). Ethnologist. African arts, aesthetics, urbanization, religion & reconstruction of W. African culture history. Source: Int Dir Anth 5.

2060 McCARTHY, FREDERICK DAVID (1905-), Sydney, New South Wales, Australia. Archeologist, ethnologist. Australian aboriginal rock art. Sources: Int Dir Anth 2, 3, 5.

2061 McCLINTOCK, WALTER (1870-1949), Pittsburgh, Pennsylvania, United States. Ethnologist. Studied Blackfoot of Indiana & Montana. Sources: Biog Index: 1/Int Dir Anth 1 2/N Y Times p 76 Mr 27 '49.

2062 McCONE, R CLYDE (1915-). Archeologist, ethnologist. Fertile Crescent. Origins of civilization. Mesopotamia & Egypt. Study of N. American cultures. Source: Int Dir Anth 5.

2063 McCORKLE, (Homer) THOMAS (1914-). Anthropologist, ethnologist. Health & medical behavior in urban Mexico, Latin America & U.S. Sources: Int Dir Anth 5/Nat Dir Lat Am.

2064 McCOWN, THEODORE DONEY (1908- 1969). Anthropologist. Sources: Biog Index: 8 & 9/Britannica Book of the Year 1970:585 '70.

2065 MacCURDY, GEORGE GRANT (1863- 1947), Warrensburg, Missouri, United States. Paleo-anthropologist, museologist. Published on prehistoric archeology; specialized in European prehistory; stimulated research on prehistory. Sources: Biog Index: 1 & 2/Am Anth 50:516-524 Jl '48, 52:513-15 O '50/ Rev Arch series 6 38:56 Jl '51.

2066 McDAVID, RAVEN I (1911-1984). Linguist. Editor of Linguistic Atlas Project. Source: Anth News 10/85.

2067 MACDONALD, ARTHUR (1856-1936). Anthropologist. Sources: Biog Index: 11/History of Education Quarterly 17:169-95 Sum '77.

2068 MACDONALD, C K (1820-1871). Egyptologist. First to excavate at Serabit el-Khadim, Sinai, site of temple of Hathor (1849). Sources: Biog Index: 10/Journal of Egyptian Archaeology 58:280 Ag '72.

2069 MACDONALD, GEORGE (1862-1940), Elgin, Scotland. Classical archeologist, numismatist. Archeology focusing on Roman Britain; excavated at several sites along the Antonine wall. Sources: Biog Index: 2/Int Dir Anth 2/ Dictionary of National Biography 1931-1940:560-1 '49.

2070 MACDONALD, NORMAN (1911-). Physician. Aetiology of war. Source: Int Dir Anth 5.

2071 McEWAN, CALVIN WELLS (1906-1950), Pittsburgh, Pennsylvania, United States. Archeologist. Specialist in Near Eastern archeology; conducted excavations in Syria for Oriental Institute of Chicago in 1930s. Sources: Biog Index: 2/Int Dir Anth 2/Am J Arch 55:101-2 Ja '50, Ja '51/ Museum News 27:3 F 1 '50/N Y Times p 85 Ja 15 '50/Science 111:159 F 10 '50.

2072 McFEAT, TOM (1919-). Ethnologist. Small-group culture studies. Proxemics. N. American settlement patterns. Communication networks. Change & community integration. Source: Int Dir Anth 5.

2073 McFEE, MALCOM (1917-). Ethnologist. Blackfoot Indian culture change. Oceania. Source: Int Dir Anth 5.

2074 McGEE, WILLIAM JOHN (1853-1912), Iowa, United States. Anthropologist, ethnologist. Studied the American Indians of Iowa, the Mississippi Valley, and California; was the first president of the American Anthropological Association. Source: Am Anth 14:683-7 O '12.

2075 McGILL, JOSEPHINE (1877- 1919). Song writer, folklorist. Sources: Biog Index: 1/Howard, John Tasker. Our American Music. 3rd ed. rev Crowell '46 p 589.

2076 MACGREGOR, FRANCES C (1906-). Anthropologist, sociologist. Medical areas including motor behavior of children in Bali (Indonesia), facial deformities & plastic surgery. Source: Int Dir Anth 5.

2077 MACGREGOR, GORDON (1902-1984). Anthropologist. Early advocate of applied anthropology among Indians of the U.S. Source: Anth News (May 1984) p 3.

2078 MACGREGOR, JAMES J (1861-1935). Translated Ellenberger's *History of the Basuto* into English. Wrote a volume on traditions of Lesotho. Source: Haliburton, Gordon, Historical Dictionary of Lesotho (1977), p 97.

2079 McGREGOR, JOHN C (1905-), Pontiac, Illinois, United States. Archeologist. Prehistoric human ecology. Reconstruction of tissues. Sources: Int Dir Anth 1, 2, 3, 5.

2080 McGUIRE, JOSEPH DEAKINS (1842-1916), Washington D.C., United States. Attorney. Assembled large collection of stone tools from Indian cultures of Maryland area; published on drillings, pipes & smoking customs of American Indians. Source: Am Anth 18:450-1 Ja '16.

2081 McILWRAITH, THOMAS FORSYTH (1899-1964), Hamilton, Ontario, Canada. Anthropologist. Studied social and religious life of primitive peoples. Sources: Biog Index: 1 & 6/Int Dir Anth 1 2 3/N Y Times p 39 Ap 1 '64.

2082 MacINTOSH, NEIL WILLIAM GEORGE (1906-1977). Anthropologist, anatomist. Sources: Biog Index: 13/ American Journal of Physical Anthropology 50:151-52 F '79/ Archaeology & Physical Anthropology, Oceania 14:78-80 Ap '79.

2083 MACKAY, ERNEST JOHN HENRY (1880-1943). Archeologist. Sources: Biog Index: 1/Nature 157:220 F 23 '46/ Chronique d'Egypte 21:206 Jl '46.

2084 McKENNAN, ROBERT ADDISON (1903-), Helena, Montana, United States. Ethnologist. Arctic, Alaskan & Northwest Coast prehistory. Athapaskan demography, somatology & blood types. Sources: Int Dir Anth 1, 2, 3, 5.

2085 MACKENZIE, JOHN C (1835-1899), Scotland. Missionary. Wrote account of his contacts with and visits to the Ndebele of Rhodesia in 1800s. Explored central Botswana; contributed to spread of British influence in the region. Sources: Rasmussen, R. Kent, Historical Dictionary of Rhodesia/Zimbabwe (1979), p 163/ Stevens, Richard P., Historical Dictionary of the Republic of Botswana" (1975), p 94.

2086 McKERN, WILL C (1892-), Medical Lake, Wisconsin, United States. Archeologist, ethnologist. Tonga & Mississippi Valley. Hopewell culture. Sources: Int Dir Anth 1, 2, 3, 5.

2087 MACKEY, JAMES LOVE (1820-1867). Missionary. Wrote the first scientific study of the Benga people of Equatorial Guinea. Source: Liniger-Gounaz, Max, Historical Dictionary of Equatorial Guinea (1979), p 95.

2088 MacMICHAEL, HAROLD ALFRED (1883-1969), England. Civil servant. Wrote on the ethnographic composition of the Sudan prior to Islam as well as on its subsequent history, including much on Sudanese manuscript records invaluable to the ethnographer. Source: Voll, John Obert, Historical Dictionary of the Sudan (1978), p 63.

2089 MacMILLAN, WILLIAM MILLER (1885-1974). Historian. Founded social and economic historical writing in South Africa; favored liberal approach to social issues. Source: Saunders, Christopher, Historical Dictionary of South Africa (1983), p 102.

2090 MacNEISH, RICHARD STOCKTON (1918-). Anthropologist, archeologist. Sources: Biog Index: 9/Nat Dir Lat Am/Am Antiq 37:393 Jl '72.

2091 McNICKLE, d'ARCY (1904-1977), Flathead Reservation, Montana, United States. Anthropologist, writer, historian, government official. Worked with Bureau of Indian Affairs & Agency for Indian Development. Presented authentic & responsible Indian viewpoints on the encounter between Indians & whites in the Western Hemisphere; maintained that an essential core of Indian cultural integrity was being preserved; published on N. American Indians. Sources: Biog Index: 9 & 13/Am Anth 81:632-36 S '79.

2092 McPHEE, COLIN (1901-1964), Montreal, Quebec, Canada. Ethnomusicologist. Music in Bali (Indonesia). Source: The New Grove Dictionary of Music and Musicians, vol 11, 1980, p. 449.

2093 McQUOWN, NORMAN ANTHONY (1914-), Peoria, Illinois, United States. Anthropologist, linguist. Mayan language studies. Micro-analysis of sound in modern Mexican speech patterns. Use of filmed interviews. Sources: Int Dir Anth 2, 3, 5/Nat Dir Lat Am.

2094 MADAY, BELA CHARLES (1912-). Anthropologist, ethnologist. Mental health in acculturation of immigrants. U.S. & Hungary. Source: Int Dir Anth 5.

2095 MADEIRA, PERCY CHILDS, Jr (1889-1967), Philadelphia, Pennsylvania, United States. Anthropologist, archeologist, lawyer. Conducted aerial survey of Mayan sites in Yucatan (Mexico) and Northern Guatemala. Sources: Biog Index: 8 & 9/Nat Cyc Am Biog 53:326 '71.

2096 MADIGAN, FRANCIS C (1917-). Anthropologist. Philippine medical anthropology. Folk religion, rituals for agriculture health. Dual system analysis of fertility, mortality & migration. Source: Int Dir Anth 5.

2097 MAENCHEN, OTTO JOHN (1894-1969). Sinologist. Sources: Biog Index: 9 & 10/Oriental Art 17:183 Summer '71.

2098 MAGALHAES, COUTO de, Brazil. Folklorist. Collected a volume of legends of the Tupi Indians of Brazil in the late 19th century. Source: Levine, Robert M., Historical Dictionary of Brazil (1979), p 133.

2099 MAGET, MARCEL JEAN (1909-), Vincennes, France. Ethnologist. Problems in European ethnography & technology, especially in France. Sources: Int Dir Anth 3, 5.

2100 MAGLIONI, RAPHAEL (1890-1953), Florence, Italy. Priest, archeologist. Specialist in archeology of South China; collected in the Hoifung district. Sources: Biog Index: 3/N Y Times p 25 My 29 '53.

2101 MAGNUSSON, FINNUR (1781-1947). Archeologist. Sources: Biog Index: 3/ Journal of English & German Philology 52:71-5 Ja '53.

2102 MAHLER, EDUARD (1857-1945), Ciffer, Pozsony County, Hungary. Orientalist. Oriental astronomy and chronology. Sources: Biog Index: 1/Isis 38:108 '47 pts. 1-2, nos. 112-112.

2103 MAIR, LUCY PHILIP (1901- 1986), England. Social anthropologist, applied anthropologist. Specialized in British colonial administration, social anthropology, marriage, witchcraft, social change & development; did fieldwork in Uganda. Sources: Int Dir Anth 3, 5/Anth News 27:8:4.

2104 MAIURI, AMEDEO (1886-1963). Archeologist. Director of excavations at Herculaneum and Pompeii for several decades; also worked on Crete, Rhodes; Director of National Museum in Naples. Sources: Biog Index: 6 & 7/Bollettino d'Arte 48 287-8 Jl '63/ Rev Arch 1:104-6 Ja '65/N Y Times p 47 Ap 8 '63/Time 81:98 Ap 19 '63.

2105 MAJUMDAR, DHIRENDRA NATH (1903-1960). Anthropologist. Pioneer in anthropology in India; published on race in Bengal, the city of Kampur, several rural villages, and Khasa polyandry; conducted extensive anthropometric & sociological studies on tribes and castes in five Indian states; first acculturation research done in India. Sources: Biog Index: 6/Int Dir Anth 3/Am Anth 63:369-74 Ap '61.

2106 **MAKARIUS, RAOUL** (1916-). Ethnologist, anthropologist. Ethnology and structuralism. Kinship, social organization & totemism in Egypt, Syria & Lebanon. Source: Int Dir Anth 5.

2107 **MAKINO, TATSUMI** (1905-), Tokyo, Japan. Ethnologist. Chinese family & kinship system. Comparative studies of East Asian peoples. Sources: Int Dir Anth 3, 5.

2108 **MALASPINA, ALESSANDRO** (1754-1809), Italy. Explorer. Led an expedition to the Pacific, 1789-1794, which yielded valuable ethnographic data on Hawaii, Tonga and other areas. Source: Craig & King, Historical Dictionary of Oceania (1981), p 168.

2109 **MALEFIJT, ANNEMARIE de WAAL** (1914-). Cultural anthropologist, mythologist. Cultural & religious anthropology. House types & social organization in Java. Source: Int Dir Anth 5.

2110 **MALINOWSKI, BRONISLAW KASPAR** (1884-1942), Krakow, Poland. Anthropologist. A major theorist in social anthropology. Associated with functionalism. Did research in Pacific, especially in Trobriand Islands, as well as in Africa, Mexico, Australia and elsewhere. Sources: Biog Index: 6 7 9 11 & 13/Int Dir Anth 1 2/ Makers of Modern Culture. Facts on File '81, p 332-33/ Zusne, L., Biographical Dictionary of Psychology, Westport, Conn., Greenwood, 1984/Am Anth 45:441-51 Jl '43.

2111 **MALKIEL, YAKOV** (1914-), Kiev, Russia. Linguist. Wrote: *Reconstruction of Hispanic-Latin Word Families* (1954); *Essays on Linguistic Themes* (1967). Source: Nat Dir Lat Am.

2112 **MALLERY, GARRICK** (1832-1894), Pennsylvania, United States. Soldier, anthropologist. Conducted field studies and wrote descriptions of the sign language and pictographs of North American Indian tribes. Source: Am Anth 8(old series):79-80 Ja 1895.

2113 **MALLOWAN, MAX EDGAR LUCIEN** (1904-1978), England. Archeologist. Excavation at Nimrud (Iraq), the ancient Assyrian capital. Sources: Biog Index: 7 8 & 11/Int Dir Anth 2/Anth News N '78/ Publishers Weekly 214:94 S 18 '78/Washington Post p C-10 Ag 22 '78.

2114 **MALO, DAVID** (1793-1853), Keaufou, Hawaii, United States. Folklorist, writer. Collected and published a basic compendium of the legends and traditions of pre-contact Hawaii. Source: Craig & King, Historical Dictionary of Oceania (1981), p 169.

2115 **MALOUF, CARLING ISAAC** (1916-), Filmore, Utah, United States. Ethnohistorian. Social change among intermountain & plains N. American Indians. Sources: Int Dir Anth 3, 5.

2116 **MALTHUS, THOMAS ROBERT** (1766- 1834), England. Economist, sociologist. Pioneer in modern population studies. Source: Columbia.

2117 **MAMMERI, MOULOUD** (1917-). Ethnolinguist. Berber grammar & oral literature. Source: Int Dir Anth 5.

2118 **MANA de ANGULO, JOSE M** (1912- 1964). Archeologist. Sources: Biog Index: 7/ Archivo Espanol de Arte y Arqueologia 37 no 109:205-6 '64.

2119 **MANDEL, WILLIAM MARX** (1917-). Ethnologist, ethnolinguist. Marxist analysis. Social organization. Women in Soviet society. Minorities, social, economic & political change. Source: Int Dir Anth 5.

2120 **MANDELBAUM, DAVID GOODMAN** (1911-), Chicago, Illinois, United States. Anthropologist. Transcendence & pragmatic aspects of religion. Priests & shamans. Comparative life histories. Sources: Int Dir Anth 1, 2, 3, 5.

2121 **MANNERS, ROBERT ALAN** (1913-). Anthropologist, ethnologist. Culture theory. N. American Indians. Puerto Rico. The Kipsigis of Kenya. Editor-in-chief of *American Anthropologist*, 1974-1976. Sources: Int Dir Anth

5/Nat Dir Lat Am.

2122 MANNING, THOMAS (1772-1840), England. Sinologist. Sources: Biog Index: 5 & 12.

2123 MANOUVRIER, LÉONCE PIERRE (1850-1927), France. Anthropologist. Worked on physical anthropology, human evolution, and contemporary human variation. Source: Am Anth 29:340-1 Ap '27.

2124 MANSOUR UDDIN, M (1904-). Folklorist. Bengali folksongs & folk tales. Language, literature & poetry. Source: Int Dir Anth 5.

2125 MANUEL, E ARSENIO (1909-). Anthropologist. Morphemes & morphology of Philippine languages. Philippine folk epics. Manuvu epic songs & traditional law. Source: Int Dir Anth 5.

2126 AL-MAQRIZI, AHMAD IBN 'ALI AHMAD (1364-1442), Egypt. Historian. Wrote a detailed history of the Islamization of Egypt, giving due attention to factors such as position of nearby religions and the immigration of Arab tribes into Egypt. Source: King, Joan W., Historical Dictionary of Egypt (1984), p 422.

2127 MAQUET, JACQUES JEROME (1919-), Brussels, Belgium. Anthropologist. Aesthetic & symbolic components in Black African political systems. Fieldwork in Rwanda. Sources: Int Dir Anth 3, 5.

2128 MARCHAND, ÉTIENNE (1755-1793), France. Explorer. Visited the Marquesas in 1791 and left an unpublished manuscript journal which has useful information on the area. Source: Craig & King, Historical Dictionary of Oceania (1981), p 171.

2129 MARCOZZI, VITTORIO (1908-), Chioggia, Italy. Paleontologist. Evolution of man. Australopithecine & palaeoveneti. Italy, Kenya & Tanzania, Africa. Sources: Int Dir Anth 3, 5.

2130 MARDRUS, JOSEPH CHARLES VICTOR (1868-1949), France. Orientalist. Translated the *Book of 1001 Nights* from Arabic to French. Sources: Biog Index: 1 & 2/France Illustration 5:VI Ap 9 '49.

2131 MAREK, KURT W (Pseud: C W Ceram) (1915-1972). Archeologist. Popular historian of archeology. Sources: Biog Index: 3 4 9 & 10/World Authors, 1950-1970, Wilson '75, Wakeman, John ed., p 946-7.

2132 MAREST, S J, Fr. PIERRE GABRIEL (1662-1727), Laval, Mayenne, France. Priest. Missionary in New France; wrote on N. American Indians. Source: Jes Rel.

2133 MARETT, ROBERT RANULPH (1866- 1943), Jersey, Channel Islands, New Zealand. Anthropologist, philosopher. Studied comparative religion. Sources: Biog Index: 5/Int Dir Anth 1 2/ Dictionary of National Biography 1941-1950:572-4 '59.

2134 MARGARY, IVAN DONALD (1898-1976). Archeologist. Surveyed and excavated the Roman palace at Fishbourne, England; specialist on Roman Britain. Sources: Biog Index: 11/Geography Journal 142:377 Jl '76.

2135 MARGOLIOUTH, DAVID SAMUEL (1858-1940), London, England. Orientalist. Sources: Biog Index: 2/Who Was Who, 1929-1940.

2136 MARIETTE, AUGUSTE EDOUARD (1821-1881), France. Egyptologist. Combined excavation with museum curatorship, monuments conservation and diplomacy. Sources: Biog Index: 9 10 11 & 12/Antiquity 51:55 Mr '77.

2137 MARINATOS, SPYRIDON (1901-1974), Greece. Archeologist. Discovered and excavated the ruined cities on the island of Thera (Greece), 1967; director of Museum at Heraklion, 1919-1939. Sources: Biog Index: 10/Archaeology 28-59 Ja '75/N Y Times p 46 03 '74/ Time 104:86 O 14 '74.

2138 MARINER, WILLIAM (1791-1853), England. Sailor. Lived, 1806-1810, on Tonga and learned about Tongan society; wrote the first grammar and vocabulary of the Tongan language. With John Martin recorded memoirs on Tongan society. Source: Craig & King, Historical Dictionary of Oceania (1981), p 172.

2139 MARINGER, JOHANNES (1902-). Archeologist, prehistoric ethnologist. Paleolithic & Neolithic art & religion. Sources: Biog Index: 11-/Int Dir Anth 5/Anthropos no 5-6:699-82 '72.

2140 MARINOV, VASSIL (1907-). Ethnologist. Geographical settlement research in ethnography & prehistory of Bulgaria. Source: Int Dir Anth 5.

2141 MARKMAN, SIDNEY DAVID (1911-). Art historian. Colonial architecture of Central America, especially Guatemala. Source: Int Dir Anth 5.

2142 MARQUAND, ALLAN (1853-1924). Archeologist. Sources: Biog Index: 1 3 & 11.

2143 MARR, NIKOLAI IAKOVLEVICH (1864-1934), Kutasi, Russia. Orientalist, linguist. Basic work on Caucasian languages. Source: Great Soviet Encyclopedia, New York, Macmillan (1977), v. 15, p 492.

2144 MARR, WILHELM (1819-1904), Magdeburg, Germany. Journalist. Left a description of Costa Rican life in the 1860s. Source: Creedman, Theodore, Historical Dictionary of Costa Rica (1977), p 122.

2145 MARRIOTT, ALICE LEE (1910-). Ethnologist. Sources: Biog Index: 2 7 & 8.

2146 MARROQUIN ZAVALETA, ALEJANDRO DAGOBERTO (1911-). Ethnologist. Mexican & Central American socio-economics; markets of Meso-American natives. Source: Int Dir Anth 5.

2147 MARSHACK, ALEXANDER (1918-). Anthropologist, archeologist. Paleo- & Mesolithic engraving. Cognitive symbol systems. Sources: Biog Index: 9/Int Dir Anth 5/Newsweek 80:70 D 18 '72.

2148 MARSHALL, DONALD STANLEY (1919-). Linguist. Dictionary of Tuamotuan dialects of the Polynesian languages. Human sexual behavior. Source: Int Dir Anth 5.

2149 MARSHALL, JOHN HUBERT (1876-1958). Archeologist, anthropologist. Sources: Biog Index: 5 6 & 12/ Daugherty, Charles Michael. Great Archaeologists. Crowell '62 p 87-93/ Am Anth 61:1071-4 D '59.

2150 MARSTON, CHARLES (1867-1946), England. Archeologist. Studied Biblical & Roman archeology. Sources: Biog Index: 1/Int Dir Anth 2/N Y Times p 21 My 23 '46/ Nature 157:867 Je 29 '46.

2151 MARSTRANDER, SVERRE (1910-), Oslo, Norway. Archeologist. Rock carvings & prehistoric boats. Sources: Int Dir Anth 3, 5.

2152 MARTIN, MUNGO (ca. 1879-1962), Fort Rupert, British Columbia, Canada. Kwakiutl chief. Carved, restored & copied totem poles; collected, recorded & preserved songs, stories, names, & ceremonial heirlooms of his people. Source: Am Anth 65:894-6 Ag '63.

2153 MARTIN, PAUL SIDNEY (1899-1974), Chicago, Illinois, United States. Archeologist. Research in New Mexico & Arizona, especially on Mogollon culture. Sources: Int Dir Anth 1 2 3/Am Anth 78:90-2 Mr '76.

2154 MARTIN, RUDOLF (1864-1925), Zurich, Switzerland. Anthropologist. Wrote on methodology in physical anthropology. Source: Am Anth 28:414-7 Mr '76.

2155 MARTÍNEZ del RÍO, PABLO (1892-1963), Mexico City, Mexico. Anthropologist, archeologist. Specialist on prehistory of Tlatelolco and much of ancient Mexico. Sources: Biog Index: 6/Int Dir Anth 2 3/Am Antiq 29:221-7 O '63/ Americas 19:424-5 Ap '63.

2156 MARTÍNEZ HERNÁNDEZ, JUAN (1866-1959), Merida, Yucatan, Mexico. Archeologist. Made extensive translations of Mayan sacred books (codices); wrote Maya-Spanish half of Motul dictionary, 1929. Sources: Biog Index: 5/Int Dir Anth 1/Am Antiq 25:397-9 Ja '60.

2157 MARTÍNEZ SANTA-OLALLA, JULIO (1905-), Burgos, Spain. Archeologist. Archeology of Spain's quaternary period. Neolithic & Bronze Age Mediterranean sites. Sources: Int Dir Anth 1, 2, 3, 5.

2158 MARTÍNEZ TORNER, EDUARDO (1888-1955). Folklorist. Sources: Biog Index: 4/Revista Interamericana de Bibliografia 6:95 Ja '56.

2159 MARWICK, BRIAN ALLEN, England. Civil servant. Published an ethnographic study of the Swazi. Source: Historical Dictionary of Swaziland (1975), p 91.

2160 MARYON, HERBERT (1874-1966), England. Archeologist. Specialized in ancient metallurgy of Middle East, Egypt, Greece, Rome, China and Japan. Sources: Biog Index: 7/Am J Arch 70:287 Jl '66.

2161 MASON, GREGORY (1889-1968), New York, New York, United States. Anthropologist, journalist. Engaged in both scholarly and popular writing on South America, particularly Mexico, from anthropological point-of-view. Sources: Biog Index: 3 8 & 10/Nat Cyc Am Biog 54:263-4 '73.

2162 MASON, JOHN ALDEN (1885-1967), Philadelphia, Pennsylvania, United States. Anthropologist, archeologist. Excavated in Latin America, especially Colombia & Peru. Interested in linguistics, classified Indian languages. Sources: Biog Index: 8/Int Dir Anth 1 2 3/Am Anth 71:871-9 O '69/ Expedition 10:2 Winter '68/Journal of American Folklore 82:266-7 Jl '69/ N Y Times p 47 N 9 '67.

2163 MASON, LEONARD E (1913-), Seattle, Washington. Ethnologist. Contemporary change, displaced communities & cultural ecology in Micronesian atolls. Primitive art. Sources: Int Dir Anth 2, 3, 5.

2164 MASON, OTIS TUFTON (1838-1908), United States. Ethnologist. Studied the cultures of various North American Indian groups. Source: Am Anth 10:660-7 O '08.

2165 MASPERO, GASTON CAMILLE CHARLES (1846-1916), Paris, France. Egyptologist. Followed Mariette as the director of the Boolag Museum and related excavations in Cairo in 1881; this directorship saw the beginning of the excavations of the Egypt Exploration Fund. Excavated at Karnak and Luxor. Sources: Biog Index: 1/Journal of Egyptian Archaeology 3:227-234 '16/ Columbia/New Int Enc, 1914 ed.

2166 MASPERO, HENRI (1883-1945), France. Sinologist. Source: Biog Index: 1.

2167 MASSÉ, S J, Fr. ENNEMOND (1575-1646), Lyons, France. Priest. Missionary in New France; wrote on N. American Indians. Source: Jes Rel.

2168 MASSEY, WILLIAM CLIFFORD (1917-), California, United States. Anthropologist. Ethnology of California. Sources: Int Dir Anth 3/Nat Dir Lat Am.

2169 MASSICOTTE, EDOUARD ZOTIQUE (1867-1947), Canada. Historian, folklorist. Sources: Biog Index: 1/Royal Society of Canada, Proceedings. Transactions, S 3 42:103-5 '48.

2170 MATEESCO, CORNELIUS (1911-). Archeologist. Vadastra cultural studies. Archeology of Romania. Source: Int Dir Anth 5.

2171 MATHEW, JOHN (1849-1929). Clergyman, ethnologist. Aboriginal studies. Sources: Biog Index: 2 & 10/Dictionary of Australian Biography 2:122-3 '49/ Oceania 46:15-20 S '75.

2172 MATHEWS, ROBERT HAMILTON (1841-1918). Anthropologist. Oceanic aboriginal studies. Sources: Biog Index: 10/Oceania 46:1-24 S '75.

2173 MATIEGKA, JINDRICH (1862-1941), Benesov, Czechoslovakia. Anthropologist. Worked on the physical anthropology of Czechoslovakia. Source: Great Soviet Encyclopedia, New York, Macmillan (1977), v. 15, p 587.

2174 MATLUCK, JOSEPH H (1917-), Brooklyn, New York, United States. Linguist. Wrote: *La Pronunciacion en el Espanol del Valle de Mexico*, 1951. Source: Nat Dir Lat Am.

2175 MATSON, DANIEL SHAW (1908-).

Anthropologist, linguist. Source: Nat Dir Lat Am.

2176 MATTESON, ESTHER L M (1912-), Willits, California, United States. Linguist. Source: Nat Dir Lat Am.

2177 MATTHEWS, JOHN. Merchant. Wrote account of the Sierra Leone peoples during 1785, 1787 and 1788. Source: Foray, Cyril P., Historical Dictionary of Sierra Leone (1977), p 137.

2178 MATTHEWS, WASHINGTON (1843-1905), Killiney, Dublin, Ireland. Military surgeon. Specialist in Hidatsa and other Plains cultures & Navajo; studied myths, ritual, craniology & anthropometry. Source: Am Anth 7:514-23 Ap '05.

2179 MATTHEWS, ZACHARIAH KEODIRELANG (1902-1968), Kimberley, South Africa. Anthropologist. Specialist in anthropology and native law of South African black nations. Sources: Biog Index: 2 & 8/Int Dir Anth 3/Commentary in Time, Je 30 '52/ N Y Times p 84 My 12 '68.

2180 MAUCH, KARL (1837-1875), Germany. Explorer. Wrote first descriptions and created first maps of the ruins at Great Zimbabwe. Source: Rasmussen, R. Kent, Historical Dictionary of Rhodesia/Zimbabwe (1979), p 178.

2181 MAUDSLAY, ALFRED PERCIVAL (1850-1931), England. Archeologist, explorer. Specialist in Maya archeology; first to make an extensive study of the ruins of Copan (Honduras), 1881-1894; published a 5-volume work on the study (1889). Sources: Biog Index: 6 & 10/Meyer, Harvey K., Historical Dictionary of Honduras (1976), p 222-3/History Today 25:680-8 O '75/ Am Anth 33:403-12 Ap '31.

2182 MAURICE, JAN-BAPTISTE (1707-1746), Rouen, France. Wrote on N. American Indians. Source: Jes Rel.

2183 MAUS, HEINZ (1911-). Sociologist. History of sociology. Source: Int Dir Anth 5.

2184 MAUSS, MARCEL (1872-1950), Epinal, France. Ethnologist. Source: La Grande Encyclopedie, Larousse, 1975.

2185 MAXIA, CARLO LUIGI GIUSSEPPE (1907-), Rome, Italy. Physical anthropologist. Human anatomy, ethnology & history of science. Sources: Int Dir Anth 2, 3, 5.

2186 MAYER, LEON ARY (1895-1959). Archeologist. Sources: Biog Index: 5 & 6/Ars Orientalis 4:454-62 '61.

2187 MAYER, PHILIP (1910-), Benin. Anthropologist. Cross-cultural urban studies. Socialization of youths. Social structure, law & ritual. Theory of witchcraft in Africa. Sources: Int Dir Anth 3, 5.

2188 MAYR, THOMAS E (ca. 1912-1986). Avocational archeologist. Specialized in Maryland archeology, particularly Middle Patuxent Valley prehistory; recognized Middle Woodland Selby Bay complex. Source: Anth News 27:7:4.

2189 MBA, LEON (1902-1967), Libreville, Gabon. Civil servant. Specialist in customary law of the Fang people of Gabon; wrote a study of Fang customs in the 1940s. First president of Gabon. Source: Gardiner, David E., Historical Dictionary of Gabon (1981), p 132-7.

2190 MEAD, MARGARET (1900-1978), Philadelphia, Pennsylvania, United States. Anthropologist, cross-cultural ethnologist, museologist. Extensive Oceanic & American fieldwork over fifty years, 1925-1975. Cross-cultural studies in culture, personality change & education. Created & fostered an understanding of & interest in anthropology among the public. Wrote, researched widely on Samoa, Bali, New Guinea and the Admiralty Islands. Sources: Biog Index: 2 3 4 5 6 7 8 9 10 11 12 & 13/Int Dir Anth 1, 2, 3, 5/ International Encyclopedia of the Social Sciences, v. 18/ Reviews in Anthropology 12:1 (1985):15-20/Craig & King, Historical Dictionary of Oceania (1981), p 175-6/ Am Anth 82:262-9,

82:270-7, 354-61 Je '80/Anth News Ja '79/ American Journal Orthopsychiatry 49:2 Ja '79/ Current Biography Yr Bk 1979:468 '80/Natural History 88:84+ N '79/ Science 208:41-2 Ap 4 '80/Newsweek 94:165 N 19 '79/ Film News 35:10 N '78, 35:41 N '78/UNESCO Courier 32:39-40 Je '79/ Howard, J. Margaret Mead: a Life. Simon & Schuster '84/ Bateson, Mary Catherine, With a Daughter's Eye. Morrow '84/ Commire, Anne. Something about the Author, v 20. Gale '80 p 123-4/ Kuper, Adam. Makers of Modern Culture. Facts on File '81 p 350/ Mead, Margaret. Margaret Mead, Some Personal Views, Walker '79.

2191 MEADER, ROBERT ELI (1912-), Rochester, New Hampshire, United States. Missionary, linguist. Summer Institute of Linguistics. Brazil. Source: Nat Dir Lat Am.

2192 MEANS, PHILIP AINSWORTH (1892-1944), Boston, Massachusetts, United States. Ethnologist, historian, archeologist. Studied relations of native cultures to white invaders in Hispanic America. Specialist in Peruvian archeology, particularly art, art styles & textile weavings. Sources: Biog Index: 1/Int Dir Anth 1 2/Commentary in Time, Je 30 '52/ Am Anth 48:234-7 Ap '46.

2193 MEDHURST, WALTER HENRY (1796- 1857), England. Sinologist, missionary. Source: Biog Index: 1.

2194 MEDINA, JOSÉ TORIBIO (1852-1930). Anthropologist. Sources: Biog Index: 3 5 & 7.

2195 MEDINA ROJAS, ALBERTO (1916-), Chile. Ethnohistorian, archeologist. Central & Southern Chile. Ethnohistories of Patagonian Araucanian & natives of Tierra del Fuego. Source: Int Dir Anth 5.

2196 MEEK, CHARLES KINGSLEY (1885-), Larne, Ireland. Cultural anthropologist. Government anthropologist in Nigeria. Source: Int Dir Anth 2 3.

2197 MEERTENS, PIETER JACOBUS (1899-). Cultural anthropologist, folklorist, bibliographer. Onomastics & dialectology of the Netherlands. Source: Int Dir Anth 5.

2198 MEEUSSEN, ACHIEL EMEIL IEPERSTR (1912-), Jette, Belgium. Linguist. African & Amerindian languages. Sources: Int Dir Anth 3, 5.

2199 MEJÍA, JOSÉ VICTOR (1877-1945), Guatemala. Army officer. Wrote a history & geography of the Peten region of Guatemala. Source: Moore, Richard E., Historical Dictionary of Guatemala (1973), p 132.

2200 MEKEEL, HAVILAND SCUDDER (1902-1947), St. Louis, Missouri, United States. Psychological anthropologist. Socio-economic study of a Pueblo group. Focused on social action & social improvement by getting at the root of fundamental contemporary social problems; studied child development, Sioux acculturation, and social prejudices. Sources: Biog Index: 1/Int Dir Anth 1 2/Am Anth 50:95-100 Ja '48/ N Y Times p 17 Jl '25 '47/School & Society 66:88 Ag 2 '47.

2201 MELO de MORAES de FILHO, ALEXANDRE JOSE de, Brazil. Folklorist. Wrote several works on Brazilian customs and folklore in the early part of the 20th century. Source: Levine, Robert M., Historical Dictionary of Brazil (1979), p 141.

2202 MELVILLE, ELISABETH HELEN CALLANTER. Author. Wrote a voluminous journal on life, customs and history of Sierra Leone; extracts from it were later published in book form. Source: Foray, Cyril P., Historical Dictionary of Sierra Leone (1977), p 139-40.

2203 MÉNARD, S J, Fr. RENÉ (1604-1661), Paris, France. Priest. Missionary in New France; wrote on N. American Indians. Source: Jes Rel.

2204 MENCUS FRANCO, AGUSTIN (1862- 1902), Guatemala. Historian. Compiled a history of colonial Guatemalan literature and a history of city of Antigua. Source: Moore, Richard E., Historical Dictionary of Guatemala (1973), p 132.

2205 MENDAÑA DE NEIRA, ALVARO de (1542-1595), Galicia, Spain. Explorer. First to locate and describe the Marquesas Islands in 1595; his journal is valuable for descriptions of the area at that time. Source: Craig & King, Historical Dictionary of Oceania (1981), p 180.

2206 Mendes Corrêa, Antonio see: CORRÊA, ANTONIO AUGUSTO MENDES.

2207 MENDIETA, Fr. JERANIMO de (1525-1604), Vitaria, Spain. Missionary. Wrote an account of the conversion of Mexico's Indians in the 16th century. Source: Briggs & Alisky, Historical Dictionary of Mexico (1981), p 143.

2208 MENDOZA, VICENTE T (1894-1964), Cholula, Puebla, Mexico. Folklorist. Specialist in Mexican music, pre-Conquest and corrida music, also the decima; made many sketches of folk arts and crafts. Sources: Biog Index: 7/Journal of American Folklore 78:154-5 Ap '65.

2209 MENDOZA DE BARATTA, MARIA (1894-), El Salvador. Musician. Noted for her interest in preserving the native music of El Salvador. Source: Flemion, Philip F., Historical Dictionary of El Salvador (1972), p 87-8.

2210 MENZIES, JAMES MELLON (1885-1957), Clinton, Ontario, Canada. Missionary, archeologist. Expert on the Shang period of Chinese history; translated many oracle bone inscriptions; first to identify the site of An-yang as the Shang capital. Sources: Biog Index: 4/Journal of Asian Studies 16:672-3 Ag '57.

2211 MERA, HARRY PERCIVAL (1875-1951), Pottsville, Pennsylvania, United States. Physician, archeologist. Studied Indian art. Sources: Biog Index: 2/Int Dir Anth 1 2/Am Antiq 17:47-8 Jl '51.

2212 MERA MARTÍNEZ, JUAN LEÓN (1832-1891), Atocha, Ecuador. Historian. One of early collectors of Ecuadorean folklore. Source: Bork & Maier, Historical Dictionary of Ecuador (1973), p 94.

2213 MERCER, HENRY CHAPMAN (1856- 1930). Archeologist. Sources: Biog Index: 10 & 11/Archaeology 31:41-51 Jl '78/ Popular Science 210:158-60 Ap '77.

2214 MERCER, SAMUEL ALFRED BROWNE (1880-), Bristol, England. Clergyman, Egyptologist. Translated the Pyramid Texts from Saqqara (Egypt); compiled grammars of Assyrian and Ethiopic languages; wrote 18 books on Egyptology. Sources: Biog Index: 3/Current Biography 14:34 F '53.

2215 MERCKLIN, EUGEN VIKTOR (1884-). Archeologist. Sources: Biog Index: 9/ Jahrbuch der Hamburger Kunstsammlungen 14-15:297-302 '70.

2216 MERIAT, PIERRE (1911-1959), France. Archeologist. Archeology of Syria, Anatolia (Turkey), and Armorica (Northwestern France). Sources: Biog Index: 6/Rev Arch 1:49-50 Ja '61/ Annales de Bretagne, 67, 1960, fasc. 1, 1-32.

2217 MERITT, LUCY (Shoe) (1906-). Archeologist. Expert on Classical Greek architecture; studied moldings used in Greece and regional architectural variants in Asia Minor, Etruria, Republican Rome and western Greece. Sources: Biog Index: 11/Archaeology 30:74-5 Mr '77.

2218 MERMET, S J, Fr. JEAN (1664-1716), Grenoble, Isere, France. Priest. Missionary in New France; wrote on N. American Indians. Source: Jes Rel.

2219 MERRITT, ROBERT L (1919-). Archeologist. Astronomical & metrological significance of Megalithic monuments in England, Scotland, Brittany & France. Source: Int Dir Anth 5.

2220 MERTON, ROBERT KING (1910-), Philadelphia, Pennsylvania, United States. Sociologist. Social structure, sociology of science, bureaucracy & mass communication.

Source: Columbia.

2221 MESHCHIANINOV, IVAN IVANOVICH (1883-1967), Ufa, Russia. Linguist, archeologist. Specialist in the dead languages of the Caucasus and Asia Minor. Sources: Great Soviet Encyclopedia, New York, Macmillan (1977), v. 16, p 145/Zhirmunskii, V.M. "Pamiati akademika I.I. Meshchianinova" Voprosy iazykoznaniia, 1967, no. 3/ Panfilov, V.Z. "Ivan Ivanovich Meshchianinov" Izvestiia A N SSSR ser. literatury i iazyka, 1967, no. 4.

2222 MESSINA, GIUSEPPE (1893-1951), San Cataldo (Caltanisetta), Italy. Priest, Orientalist. Student of Iranian religion and influences. Sources: Biog Index: 3/Isis 43 no 2:119 '52/Oriente Moderno 31:216 '51.

2223 MESTORF, JOHANNA (1829-1909), Bramstedt, Holstein, Switzerland. Anthropologist. Translated Scandinavian archeological material into German; specialist in the archeology of Schleswig-Holstein & the Danish Islands; also published articles on ethnology and folklore; the leading female archeologist of her generation. Source: Am Anth 11:536-7 Jl '09.

2224 METCALF, GEORGE S (1900-1975), United States. Archeologist. U.S. Plains archeology. Source: Anth News Ap '76.

2225 MÉTRAUX, ALFRED (1902-1963), Lausanne, Switzerland. Ethnographer. Worked on prehistory of Easter Island, emphasizing possible outside contacts. Foremost authority on South American Indians; focused on synthesis & historical research, particularly on the Tupinamba of Brazil & tribes of Argentina, Paraguay, and Bolivia. Sources: Biog Index: 7/Int Dir Anth 2/Craig & King, Historical Dictionary of Oceania (1981), p 180-1/Am Anth 66:603-13 Je '64.

2226 MÉTRAUX, RHODA (1914-), Brooklyn, New York, United States. Anthropologist. Current issues in culture & applied anthropology. Anthropological methods in personality, mental health studies. Attitudes & change in complex societies, especially toward science, scientists & education. Sources: Int Dir Anth 3, 5/Nat Dir Lat Am.

2227 MEURIN, S J, Fr. SEBASTIEN LOUIS (1707-1777), Charleville, France. Priest. Missionary in New France; wrote on N. American Indians. Source: Jes Rel.

2228 MEYER, ROBERT EUGENE (1911-). Folklorist. Compiled directories to local, regional, state and national festivals in both Europe and the United States. Sources: Biog Index: 2/N Y Times Book Review p 8 Ap 8 '51.

2229 MICHAEL, HENRY N (1913-). Archeologist, ethnologist, economic geographer. Economic geography. Carbon-14 dating techniques for archeology. Source: Int Dir Anth 5.

2230 MICHAELIS, JOHANN DIVID (1717-1791), Germany. Orientalist. Source: Biog Index: 2.

2231 MICHALOWSKI, KAZMIERZ (1901-1980), Tarnopol, Poland. Egyptologist, archeologist. Specialized in Egyptian art & architecture; wrote extensively about Egypt and several major sites. Led archeological teams to Egypt, Nubia, Syria, and the Crimea. Sources: Biog Index: 12/Int Dir Anth 1 2/Time 117:86 Ja 19 '81/ Great Soviet Encyclopedia, New York, Macmillan (1977), v. 16, p 246.

2232 MICHÉA, JEAN (1919-). Ethnologist. Human ecology. Prehistoric Arctic & palaeoethnography of S.W. Alaska. Source: Int Dir Anth 5.

2233 MICHELIS, PANAYOTIS A (1903-). Archeologist, author, poet. Sources: Biog Index: 9/ Journal of Aesthetics and Art Criticism 28:569-70 Summer '70.

2234 MICHELSON, TRUMAN (1879-1938). Ethnologist. Specialist in Algonkian linguistics & social organization. Source: Am Anth 41:281-5 Ap '39, 41:173.

2235 MIDELFORT, CHRISTIAN FREDRIK (1906-). Anthropologist. Psychiatric treatment in the context of the Church. Religious denomination, change in occupation & residence. Ethnicity. Source: Int Dir Anth 5.

2236 MIDVALE, FRANK J (1903-1971), Cedar Rapids, Iowa, United States. Archeologist. Expert on prehistoric canal systems on the Gila and Salt Rivers of Arizona; preserved site of Mesa Grande, Arizona; produced several useful maps of these systems and sites. Sources: Biog Index: 10/Am Antiq 39:452-3 Jl '74.

2237 MIECZYSŁAW, GLADYSZ (1903-). Folklorist. Cultural processes in western Slavic regions. Contemporary changes in folk culture in Polish Carpathians. Source: Int Dir Anth 5.

2238 MIGEOD, FREDERICK WILLIAM HUGH (1872-1952), Chislehurst, Kent, England. Anthropologist, linguist, colonial civil servant. Wrote extensive linguistic works on the Mende language of Sierra Leone. Spent most of his service in West Africa and as a result was able to write five volumes on languages and four travel books; acted as general overseer of the British Museum East Africa Expedition starting in 1925. Sources: Biog Index: 3/Foray, Cyril P., Historical Dictionary of Sierra Leone (1977), p 143/Nature 170:184 Ag 2 '52.

2239 MIGOT, ANDRÉ (1892-). Archeologist, physician, traveler. Source: Biog Index: 9.

2240 MIKAMI, TSUGIO (1907-). Archeologist, ethnologist. Stone Age, Bronze Age megalithic cultures. Japanese & Korean ceramics. Source: Int Dir Anth 5.

2241 MIKLUKHO-MAKLAI, NIKOLAI NIKOLAEVICH (1864-1888), Rozhdestvenskoe, Russia. Anthropologist, ethnologist. Studied the Papuans (New Guinea) and other peoples of Oceania. Sources: Great Soviet Encyclopedia, New York, Macmillan (1977), v. 16, p 299/Tumarkin, D.D., "Velikii russkii uchenyi-gumanist" Sovetskaia etnografiia (1963), no. 6.

2242 MILCU, STEPHAN (1903-). Physical anthropologist. Anthropological atlas of Oltentia (Romania). Source: Int Dir Anth 5.

2243 MILES, GEORGE CARPENTER (1904-1975). Archeologist. Specialist in Islamic coinage; participated in excavations at Heraklion (Greece); published extensively on Islamic coins and inscriptions. Sources: Biog Index: 1 10 & 11/Am J Arch 81:113 Win '77/ International Journal of Middle East Studies 7:290-1 Ap '76.

2244 MILET (Millet), S J, Fr. PIERRE (1635-1709), Bourges, France. Priest. Missionary in New France; wrote on N. American Indians. Source: Jes Rel.

2245 MILL, JOHN STUART (1806-1873), England. Economist, philosopher. Developed the social philosophy of Utilitarianism. Source: New Columbia Encyclopedia p 1778.

2246 MILLER, PAUL AUSBORN (1917-). Anthropologist. Source: Biog Index: 8.

2247 MILLER, VSEVOLOD FEDOROVICH (1848-1913), Moscow, Russia. Linguist, folklorist, ethnographer. Collected much material on the Russian byliny (epic folktales) and other aspects of folklore. Sources: Great Soviet Encyclopedia, New York, Macmillan (1977), v. 16, p 317/Ol'denburg, S. "V.F. Miller" Russkaia mysl', 1913 book 12/ Speranskii, M. V.F. Miller. Moscow, 1914/ Azadovskii, M.K. Istoriia russkoi fol'kloristiki, Moscow, 1963, v. 2, p 296-306.

2248 MILLET, GABRIEL (1867-1953). Archeologist. Wrote on Byzantine art. Sources: Biog Index: 3/Rev Arch series 6 43:214-7 Ap '54.

2249 MILLS, JAMES, PHILIP (1890-1960), Cheshire, England. Ethnologist. Anthropology of Assam (India). Sources: Biog Index: 5/Int Dir Anth 1 2 3/Geography Journal 126:380-1 S '60 /Nature 186:1015 Je 25 '60.

2250 MILUTINOVIC, VERA (1913-). Ethnologist. Serbian wedding songs, customs & baked goods. Source: Int Dir Anth 5.

2251 MINA, TOGO (1906-1949), Asyut, Egypt. Museum director, Egyptologist. Egyptian coptic scholar; discoverer of papyri from library of Chenoboskion (Egypt); Director of Coptic Museum in Cairo. Sources: Biog Index: 2/Isis 42 no 2:146 '51.

2252 MINER, HORACE MITCHELL (1912-), St. Paul, Minnesota, United States. Ethnologist. African culture of Algerian oases; Timbuctoo (Mali); Hausa ecology. Sources: Int Dir Anth 2, 3, 5.

2253 MINNS, ELLIS HOVELL (1874-1953), England. Archeologist. Wrote about Scythians and Greeks. Sources: Biog Index: 3/Int Dir Anth 2/Archaeology 6:244 D '53/ Artibus Asiae 17 no 2:168-73 '54.

2254 MINTO, ANTONIO (1880-1954), Pieve di Sacco, Italy. Archeologist. Expert on Etruscans. Sources: Biog Index: 3 & 4/Rev Arch series 6 47:88-9 Ja '56/ Am J Arch 59:241.

2255 MIRSKY, ALFRED E (1901-1974), United States. Biochemist. Social implications of biology. Source: Anth News N '74.

2256 MISHKIN, BERNARD (1913-1954), Theodhosia, Crimea, Ukraine. Anthropologist. Specialist in rank & warfare among the Kiowa Plains Indians; also did field research in Wapi area (New Guinea) and Kauri (Peru). Sources: Biog Index: 4/Am Anth 57:1033-5 O '55.

2257 MITCHELL, JAMES CLYDE (1918-), Rhodesia. Anthropologist, sociologist. Sociology of the Bantu-speaking peoples; demography and social change in Africa. Urban networks in Zambia. Source: Social Scientists Specializing in African Studies, Unesco, 1963.

2258 MITCHELL, JAMES LESLIE (1901-1935). Archeologist. Source: Biog Index: 10.

2259 MIYAMOTO, NOBUTO (1901-), Tokyo, Japan. Archeologist, ethnologist. Material culture of Southwest Asia, Formosa, & Oceania. Sources: Int Dir Anth 3, 5.

2260 MIZUNO, SELICHI (1905-1971). Sinologist, Orientalist, archeologist. Sources: Biog Index: 10/Artibus Asiae 35 no 1-2:163-4 '73.

2261 MNYANDA, BRADFIELD JACOB MABHASO (1906-1970), Cape Province, South Africa. Clergyman. Wrote the first book by an African describing life of the black community of Zimbabwe. Source: Rasmussen, R. Kent, Historical Dictionary of Rhodesia/Zimbabwe (1979), p 193.

2262 MOBERG, CARL-AXEL AXELSSON (1915-). Prehistorian. General prehistory, especially of Europe. Source: Int Dir Anth 5.

2263 MODDERMAN, PIETER JAN REMEES (1919-), Tanah Radja, Dutch East Indies, Indonesia. Prehistorian. Middle Neolithic cultures, especially prehistoric barrows of the Netherlands. Sources: Int Dir Anth 3, 5.

2264 MODRIJAN, WALTER (1911-). Archeologist. Megalithic edifices in France. Ice Age man in Europe. Source: Int Dir Anth 5.

2265 MOE, JORGEN ENGEBRETSEN (1813-1882), Norway. Folklorist, bishop. Sources: Biog Index: 1 7 & 8/Who's Who in Children's Literature.

2266 MOERENHOUT, JACQUES-ANTOINE (1796-1879), Belgium. Diplomat. Wrote an account of traditional Tahitian culture and political development up to 1837. Source: Craig & King, Historical Dictionary of Oceania (1981), p 193.

2267 MOGAMI, TAKAYOSHI (1898-), Kanazawa City, Japan. Ethnologist. Primitive Japanese fishing & funeral rites. Sources: Int Dir Anth 3, 5.

2268 MOHAPELOA, JOSIAS MAKIBINYANE (1914-), Molumong, Lesotho. Educator, historian. Wrote a study of the absentee rule of Lesotho by the British, 1871-1881. Source: Haliburton, Gordon, Historical Dictionary of Lesotho (1977), p 117-8.

2269 MOLEMA, MODIRI SILAS (1892-

1965), Mafeking, Botswana, Bechuanaland. Historian, journalist. Wrote history of the Bantu (1920), and biographies of two leading Tswana chiefs. Source: Stevens, Richard P., Historical Dictionary of the Republic of Botswana (1975), p 103.

2270 MOLET, LOUIS (1915-). Ethnologist, linguist. Central African & French Polynesian studies. Source: Int Dir Anth 5.

2271 MOLYNEUX, GEORGE EDUARD STANHOPE (1866-1923), England. Egyptologist. Discovered (with Howard Carter) the tomb of King Tutankhamen. Sources: Biog Index: 3 9 11 & 12/Columbia.

2272 MONBODDO, JAMES BURNETT, Lord (1714-1790), Scotland. Linguist, physical anthropologist, judge. Sources: Biog Index: 5 9 & 11.

2273 MOND, ROBERT LUDWIG (1867-1938), Farmworth, Lancashire, England. Chemist, archeologist. Financed many Egyptian expeditions and worked at several sites; supported British School in Palestine; also paid for numerous publications on Libyan materials. Sources: Biog Index: 2 & 3/Dictionary of National Biography, '49/ Metallurgia 48:92 Ag '53/Chemical Age 69:119 Jl 18 '53.

2274 MONGE MEDRANO, CARLOS (1884-), Lima, Peru. Physician, surgeon. Specialized in human adaptation to living at high elevations; Andean populations. Source: Who's Who in Latin America 3rd ed., Ronald Hilton ed., Stanford Univ. Press (Blaine Ethridge edition, 1971) 184-185.

2275 MONIER-WILLIAMS, MONIER (1819-1899), Bombay, India. Linguist. Expert in Sanskrit and religions of India, especially Hindu. Source: Am Anth 1:794 O 1899.

2276 MONNERET de VILLARD, UGO (1881-1954), France. Orientalist, archeologist. Archeology of Nubia, Ethiopia and Italy, particularly Christian antiquities. Wrote: *Aksum, ricerche di topografia generale*, 1938; *Mission archeologique de Nubie*, 1924-1934, 1935; *Storia della Nubia cristiana*, 1938. Sources: Biog Index: 5 & 12/Rev Arch series 6 49:78 Ja '57/ Revista degli studi orientali, 30, I-II:72-188, 1955/Ars Orientalis 2:627 '57.

2277 MONOD, THÉODORE (1902-), Rouen, France. Naturalist, anthropologist. French West Africa & Sahara. Source: Int Dir Anth 3.

2278 MONTAGU, ASHLEY (1905-). Anthropologist. Popular writer on comparative bio-anthropology, race, sex roles, aggression & cooperation. Sources: Biog Index: 3 4 7 8 & 11/Int Dir Anth 5/ International Encyclopedia of the Social Sciences, v. 18/ Psychology Today 11:50 Ag '77.

2279 MONTEIL, PARFAIT LOUIS (1855-1925). Explorer. Extensive exploration of Senegal area, 1885; crossed the Sahara from the south via Lake Chad, 1890-1892; wrote description of this *De St. Louis a Tripoli par le lac Chad*, 1895. First European to cross Upper Volta from west to east. Source: McFarland, Daniel Miles, Historical Dictionary of Upper Volta (1978), p 110-1.

2280 MONTELIUS, OSCAR (1843-1921), Sweden. Archeologist. Established the chronology for the Bronze Age in Europe and the Mediterranean. Source: Am Anth 23:531 O '21.

2281 MONTENEGRO, PEDRO (1663-1728), Galicia, Spain. Physician. Collected and described native medicines of Guarani Indians. Source: Wright & Nelsham, Historical Dictionary of Argentina (1978), p 586.

2282 MONTS de SAVASSE, FELICIEN de (1700-1760). Archeologist. Source: Biog Index: 7.

2283 MOOK, MAURICE ALLISON (1904-1973), Saegertown, Pennsylvania, United States. Anthropologist, sociologist. American Indian, Amish & Quaker social history & Pennsylvania folklore. Sectarian societies in the U.S. Sources: Biog Index: 12-/Int Dir Anth 1, 2,

5/Nat Cyc Am Biog 58:342-3 '79/ Anth News Mr '75.

2284 MOONEY, JAMES (1861-1921). Ethnologist. Member of first generation of U.S. government ethnologists who studied Native American cultures, especially Cherokee and Kiowa; studied the Ghost Dance & Indian-white relations. Sources: Biog Index: 2/Moses, L.G., The Indian Man, A Biography of James Mooney (1984)/ Banta, Richard Elwell, comp. Indiana authors & their books, 1816-1916. Wabash College '49 p 227-8/Am Anth 23:530 '21/ Am Anth 24:209-14 Ap '22.

2285 MOORE, FRANCES. Merchant. Wrote detailed description of Gambian social, economic and political institutions during a five year residency (1735). Source: Gailey, Harry A., Historical Dictionary of Gambia (1975), p 94.

2286 MOORE, HARVEY CLEAVER (1918-). Ethnologist, psychological anthropologist. Community organizations & psychological anthropology of Navajo Indians. Source: Int Dir Anth 5.

2287 MOORE, JOSEPH GRAESSLE (1904-), Dubuque, Iowa, United States. Anthropologist, ethnologist, linguist, musicologist. Contemporary Cumana music & dance in Jamaican revival. Sources: Int Dir Anth 3, 5/Nat Dir Lat Am.

2288 MOORE, RILEY D (1883-1949). Osteopath, anthropologist. Sources: Biog Index: 2/Numismatist 62:362 Je '49.

2289 MOOREHEAD, ALAN (1910-). Writer. Wrote *The White Nile*, New York, Harper & Row, 1960 and *The Blue Nile*, New York, 1962, popular histories of the Sudan. Source: Nat Un Cat.

2290 MOOREHEAD, WARREN KING (1866- 1939), Sienia, Italy. Archeologist. Wrote widely on N. American Indian archeology; led numerous excavations in U.S; specialist in Illinois & Ohio archeology, particulary Hopewell and Fort Ancient, contemporary Sioux religion and "uprising," southwestern U.S. archeology (San Juan River Valley, Chaco Canyon, LaPlata Valley); championed fair play for Indians, especially Ojibwa; focused on archeological surveys of new & little known regions. Sources: Biog Index: 2/Int Dir Anth 1/Am Anth 41:286-94 Ap '39/ Nat Cyc Am Biog 36:70-1 '50.

2291 MOPELI-PAULUS, ATWELL SIDWELL (1913-), Witzie's Hock, Orange Free State, South Africa. Novelist. Wrote poetry and novels discussing ritual murder in Lesotho and the conflict of traditional & changing value systems. Source: Haliburton, Gordon, Historical Dictionary of Lesotho (1977), p 124-5.

2292 MORAIN, S J, Fr. JEAN (1630-1688), Coustances, Manche, France. Priest. Missionary in New France; wrote on N. American Indians. Source: Jes Rel.

2293 MORALES-PATINO, OSWALDO IGNACIO (1899-1978), Cuba. Anthropologist. West Indian archeology. Source: Anth News 20:2 F '79, p 3.

2294 MORAN, PEDRO. Priest. Compiled several dictionaries of the Pokomam dialect of Maya. Source: Moore, Richard E., Historical Dictionary of Guatemala (1973), p 139.

2295 MORAN BARDON, CÉSAR (1882-1952). Priest, archeologist. Sources: Biog Index: 3/ Archivo Espanol de Arte y Arqueologia 25 no 1:210 '52.

2296 MORDINI, ANTONIO (1904-). Archeologist, ethnologist. Archeology of Brazil & Middle East. Religious rites & monastaries of Ethiopia. Sources: Int Dir Anth 2, 5.

2297 MORENO, FRANCISCO PASCACIO (1852-1919), Buenos Aires, Argentina. Explorer, naturalist. Conducted anthropological & archeological research in southern Argentina. Source: Wright & Nelsham, Historical Dictionary of Argentina (1978), p 591.

2298 MORGAN, LEWIS HENRY (1818-1881), Aurora, New York, United States. Anthropologist, lawyer, ethnologist. Pioneer theorist. Proposed system accoridng to which world cultures are said to have evolved. Described culture of Iroquois and other U.S. Indians in great detail. Sources: Biog Index: 1 2 3 5 7 & 11/Columbia/ International Encyclopedia of the Social Sciences, vol. 10, p 496-498/ Science & Society 42:344-6 Fall '78.

2299 MORGAN, RICHARD G (1903-1968), Middletown, Ohio, United States. Archeologist. Specialist in archeology of Ohio; worked on Fort Ancient culture; focused on lithic materials. Sources: Biog Index: 8/Int Dir Anth 1 2 3/Am Antiq 34:467-70 O '69.

2300 MORICE, ADRIEN GABRIEL (ca. 1859-1938). Reverend. Published on Northwest Athapascan groups, especially the Dene. Source: Am Anth 40:760 O '38.

2301 MORLAND, JOHN KENNETH (1916-). Ethnologist. Comparison of racial attitudes in Thailand, Hong Kong, Philippines & U.S. Source: Int Dir Anth 5.

2302 MORLEY, SYLVANUS GRISWOLD (1883-1948), Chester, Pennsylvania, United States. Anthropologist, archeologist. Directed research and excavation on Mayan archeological and ethnology for 40 years; wrote a basic work on Mayan culture. Leading figure in Maya archeology of his generation; specialized in Maya hieroglyphic writing. Sources: Biog Index: 1 2 3 5 7 & 9/Meyer, Harvey K., Historical Dictionary of Honduras (1976), p 234-44/Am Anth 51:293-7 Ap '49.

2303 MORRIS, ANN AXTELL (1900-1945). Archeologist, artist. Specialist in the archeology of the Maya & the southwestern U.S.; copied wall paintings at Chichen-Itza (Mexico), recorded pictographs & cave paintings. Source: Am Anth 47:645 O '45.

2304 MORRIS, EARL HALSTEAD (1889-1956), Chama, New Mexico, United States. Archeologist. Excavated in S.W. Colorado, Guatemala, N.W. New Mexico, Chichen Itza (Mexico), and Arizona. Sources: Biog Index: 3 4 & 8/Am Anth 59:521-3 Je '57.

2305 MORRIS, HAROLD STEPHEN (1913-), Weymouth, England. Ethnologist. Rank & kinship in S.E. Asia & Africa. Sources: Int Dir Anth 3, 5.

2306 MORSE, DAN (1906-1985). Physical anthropologist, physician. Specialized in tuberculosis; published on paleopathology of the Midwest U.S. and forensic anthropology. Source: Anth News 12/85:3.

2307 MORTILLET, LOUIS LAURENT GABRIEL de (1820-1899), Meilan, Isere, France. Archeologist, geologist, zoologist. Specialist in the development of the early history of humanity; explored the remains of the Gallic peoples. Source: Am Anth 1:199-200 Ja 1899.

2308 MOSHOESHOE, NEHEMIAH (1824-1906), Thaba Basiu, Lesotho. Historian. Son of Moshoeshoe I, was first Basotho historian; wrote a pamphlet on the Basotho. Source: Haliburton, Gordon, Historical Dictionary of Lesotho (1977), p 136.

2309 MOSS, FREDERICK JOSEPH (1829-1904), New Zealand. Civil servant, writer. Wrote several books describing Fiji, the Cook Islands and Maori culture. Source: Craig & King, Historical Dictionary of Oceania (1981), p 198.

2310 MOSTNY-GLASER, GRETA (1914-), Linz, Austria. Museologist. Prehistory of Chile. Museology & personnel selection for museums. Sources: Int Dir Anth 3, 5.

2311 MOTOLINIA, F TORIBIO de BENAVENTE, O.F.M. (1490-1568), Spain. Missionary. Wrote *Historia de los Indios de la Nueva Espana*. Wrote several histories of the conquest of Mexico; sought better treatment for the Indians. Sources: Briggs & Alisky, Historical Dictionary of Mexico (1981), p 22-3/ Diccionario de Historia

Ecclesiastica de Espana, 1972-75, p 1746.

2312 MOUNTFORD, CHARLES PEARCY (1890-), Hallett, South Australia, Australia. Ethnologist. Ethnology of Aborigines. Traditional Australian art. Ethnophotography. Sources: Biog Index: 10-/Int Dir Anth 3, 5.

2313 MOURANT, ARTHUR ERNEST (1904-). Population geneticist. Population distributions of blood groups & genetic polymorphisms, especially among Jews, Arabs & Basques. Source: Int Dir Anth 5.

2314 MOUTERDE, RENÉ (1880-1962), Lyon, France. Priest, archeologist. Wrote on archeology of Lebanon and Syria. Sources: Biog Index: 6/Rev Arch 1:240-1 Ap '62.

2315 MOVIUS, HALLAM L, Jr (1907-), Newtown, Massachusetts, United States. Archeologist. Studied Ireland, particularly Irish Stone Age. Sources: Int Dir Anth 1 2 3.

2316 MUBĀRAK, ALI (1823-1893), Egypt. Civil servant. Authored a 20-volume work covering all aspects of life and society in 19th-century Egypt. Source: King, Joan W., Historical Dictionary of Egypt (1984), p 442.

2317 MUCKERMANN, HERMANN (1877-). Priest, anthropologist. Sources: Biog Index: 3/Hoehn, Matthew, ed. Catholic Authors; v 2, St. Mary's Abbey '52 p 371-4.

2318 MUELLE-ROJAS, JORGE C (1903-1974), Lima, Peru. Archeologist. Peruvian primitive art & archeology in the Andes. Sources: Int Dir Anth 2, 5/Anth News D '74.

2319 MUENSTERBERGER, WERNER (1913-), Hoerde, Germany. Anthropologist. Psychoanalytic differentiation of ethnic defenses & reaction patterns. Sources: Int Dir Anth 3, 5.

2320 MUHLMANN, WILHELM EMIL (1904-), Dusseldorf, Germany. Sociologist. Sociology of religion & politics in the Mediterranean region. Sources: Int Dir Anth 1, 2, 3, 5.

2321 MUIR, JOHN (1810-1882), Scotland. Orientalist. Source: Biog Index: 4.

2322 MUKHERJEE, RAMKRISHNA (1919-). Sociologist. Social science research methodology. Social change. Source: Int Dir Anth 5.

2323 MULLER, FREDERICK MAX (1823-1900), Dessau, Germany. Anthropologist, philologist. Specialist in Indian languages (particularly Sanskrit) and religion (particularly Buddhism). Source: Am Anth 2:776-7 O '00.

2324 MULLER, HERMAN JOSEPH (1890-1967), New York, New York, United States. Specialist in field of mutation: discovered a method of inducing mutation via X-rays; background for human evolution studies. Source: New Columbia Encyclopedia, p 1856.

2325 MULLER, KARL OTFRIED (1797-1840), Brieg, Silesia, Germany. Archeologist. Sources: Columbia/ New Int Enc, 1914 ed.

2326 MULLER, KURT RICHARD VALENTIN (1889-1945), Berlin, Germany. Archeologist. Classical archeology; special interest in the interrelations between the Oriental and Mediterranean cultures. Sources: Biog Index: 1/Am J Arch 50:172-3 Ja '46.

2327 MULLER, ROLF (1898-). Archeologist, archeological astronomer. Astronomy of Inca, and Maya and in the Old Testament. Source: Int Dir Anth 5.

2328 MULLOY, WILLIAM THOMAS (1917- 1978), Salt Lake City, Utah, United States. Anthropologist, archeologist. Archeology of N. American Plains Indians and Easter Island. Sources: Biog Index: 13/Int Dir Anth 2, 3, 5/Anth News Jn '78/ Oceania 49:226-29 Mr '79.

2329 MUMFORD, WILLIAM BREGANT (1900-1951). Educator. Attempted to create culturally adapted system of education for Africa. Source: Kurtz, Laura S., Historical Dictionary of Tanzania (1978), p 138.

2330 MUNCH, PETER A (1909-1984), Norway. Sociologist,

anthropologist. Culture of the people of Tristan da Cunha; Norwegian immigration to the United States. Source: Anth News (May 1984) p 3.

2331 MUNIZAGA AGUIRRE, CARLOS (1917-). Anthropologist. Incorporation of indigenous Araucanians (Mapuche) to urban environment in Chile. Source: Int Dir Anth 5.

2332 MUNRO, ROBERT (1835-1920). Archeologist. Specialized in the investigation of European lake dwellings. Source: Am Anth 22:308 Jl '20.

2333 MUNTSCH, ALBERT (1873-), St. Louis, Missouri, United States. Priest, anthropologist. Acculturation processes among Germanic, Slavic, and Romance nations. Sources: Biog Index: 3/Int Dir Anth 1 2 3/ Hoehn, Matthew, ed. Catholic Authors; v 2, St. Mary's Abbey '52 p 374-5.

2334 MUNZINGER, WERNER (1832-1875). Merchant. Studied language and culture of the Belen (or Bogos) people of northern Ethiopia's Tigre province. Source: Prouty & Rosenfeld, Historical Dictionary of Ethiopia (1981), p 137.

2335 MURAMATZU, YUJI (1911-1974), Hachioji, Japan. Sinologist. Wrote two important historical studies of Chinese economic organizations, focusing in particular on the tenant-landlord relationship. Sources: Biog Index: 10/Journal of Asian Studies 33:651 Ag '74.

2336 MURDOCK, GEORGE PETER (1897- 1985), Meriden, Colorado, United States. Applied anthropologist, comparative ethnologist. A founder of ethnology. Developed the *Outline to Cultural Materials* (1938), 5th edition (1975). Worked for creation (1949) of the Human Relations Area Files (1937) at Yale Univ. Fieldwork in the Northwest Coast of U.S., Asia, Europe, Hawaii, Micronesia, among the Jaida and Tenino, and in Truk; systematic cross-cultural & comparative study; extensive publications on social structure. Sources: Biog Index: 4/Int Dir Anth 1, 2, 3, 5/ International Encyclopedia of the Social Sciences, v. 18/ Current Biography 18:30-2 Mr '57/Current Biography Yr Bk 1957:390-2 '58/ Anth News 9/85.

2337 MURDOCK, JOHN PETER (-1926). Anthropologist. Wrote on ethnology of Inuit. Sources: Biog Index: 4/Am Anth 28:580-1 Jl '26.

2338 MURRA, JOHN VICTOR (1916-), Odessa, Ukraine. Anthropologist, ethnologist. Andean ethnohistory & Inca economic organization. Sources: Int Dir Anth 3, 5/Nat Dir Lat Am.

2339 MURRAY, ALEXANDER STUART (1841-1904), Arbroath, Scotland. Archeologist. Keeper of Greek & Roman antiquities at the British Museum. Excavations in Cyprus. Source: Columbia.

2340 MUS, PAUL (1902-1969), Bourges, France. Educator, Orientalist. Specialist on Vietnamese culture; worked & lived in Hanoi, 1927-1940; one of few U.S. scholars on Vietnam at the beginning of U.S. involvement. Sources: Biog Index: 8/N Y Times p 27 Ag 16 '69.

2341 MUSIL, ALOIS (1868-1944). Orientalist. Source: Biog Index: 1.

2342 MYER, WILLIAM E (-1923), Tennessee, United States. Businessman. Specialist in Tennessee archeology; compiled complete map of Indian trails in Tennessee & Southwest U.S. Source: Am Anth 25:585 O '23.

2343 MYRES, JOHN LINTON (1869-1954). Anthropologist, archeologist. Sources: Biog Index: 3 & 4/Brit Sch Athens Ann bibliog no 49:311-14 '54.

2344 NADEL, SIEGFRIED FREDERICK STEPHEN (1903-1956), Vienna, Austria. Social anthropologist, colonial administrator. Wrote on several African cultures, especially Nupe & Tiv of Nigeria and Nubia of Sudan. Analyzed political and religious structures of primitive man. Sources: Biog Index: 4/Int Dir Anth 3/Am Anth 59:117-24 F '57.

2345 NAHMAN, MAURICE (-ca. 1945), France. Egyptologist. Sources: Biog Index: 1/Chronique d'Egypte 22:300-1 Jl '47.

2346 NAKAZAWA, KEN (1883-1953), Fukashima Province, Japan. Orientalist. Specialist on Oriental art, literature and languages. Sources: Biog Index: 3/N Y Times p 31 S 30 '53.

2347 NAMBA, MONKICHI (1898-), Japan. Cultural anthropologist, social anthropologist. Japanese cultural change. Source: Int Dir Anth 5.

2348 NAPIER, JOHN RUSSEL (1917-). Primatologist. Ecology & behavior of non-human primates. Source: Int Dir Anth 5.

2349 NASH, CHARLES H (1908-1968), Illinois, United States. Archeologist. Geology and ceramics. Analyzed archeological materials from Gilbertsville Basin, Tennessee. Sources: Biog Index: 8/Int Dir Anth 2/Am Antiq 34:172-4 Ap '69.

2350 NASH, PHILLEO (1909-), Wisconsin Rapids, Wisconsin, United States. Cross-cultural urban ethnologist. Indian religion. Indian & non-Indian relations in N. America. Sources: Int Dir Anth 1, 2, 3, 5.

2351 NASH-WILLIAMS, VICTOR ERLE (1897-1955), Cardiff, Wales. Archeologist. Early Christian inscriptions in Wales, archeology and linguistics of Europe. Sources: Biog Index: 4/Int Dir Anth 2 3/ Illustrated London News 227:1088 D 24 '55/Museum Journal 55:289-90 F '56/ Nature 177:163-4 Ja 28 '56.

2352 NASSAU, ROBERT HAMELL (1835-1921), Lawrenceville, New Jersey, United States. Linguist, missionary, physician. Wrote extensively on history and culture of the Benga, Fang, Galoa and Bakelle peoples of Gabon. Source: Gardiner, David E., Historical Dictionary of Gabon (1981), p 144-5.

2353 NASSAU, ROBERT HAMILTON (1835-1921). Folklorist, missionary. Translated the Bible into the Benga language of Equatorial Guinea and Gabon; wrote widely on West Africa. Source: Liniger-Gounaz, Max, Historical Dictionary of Equatorial Guinea (1979), p 111.

2354 NATHAN, HILEL (1917-). Medical anthropologist, physical anthropologist. Medical & physical anthropology of ancient & living Jewish populations in Israel. Source: Int Dir Anth 5.

2355 NAU, S J, Fr. LUC FRANÇOIS (1703-1753), Noirmoutiers, France. Priest. Missionary in New France; wrote on N. American Indians. Source: Jes Rel.

2356 NEEDHAM, JOSEPH (1900-), England. Orientalist, biochemist. Wrote the series of volumes entitled *Science and Civilization in China*, a standard overview of the growth and history of science throughout Chinese history. Sources: Biog Index: 9 10 11 & 12/N Y Times Book Review p 2 Je 20 '71.

2357 NEKRASOV, OLGA (1910-), Romania. Bio-anthropologist, primate osteologist. Ancient populations of Europe especially Romania. Source: Int Dir Anth 5.

2358 NELSON, HAROLD HAYDEN (1915-). Egyptologist, ethnologist. Fossil man. Armenian acculturation in the U.S. Sources: Biog Index: 3/Int Dir Anth 5.

2359 NELSON, NELS CHRISTIAN (1875-1964), Denmark. Archeologist. Prehistoric archeology of Mongolia and New Mexico. Sources: Biog Index: 6 & 7/Int Dir Anth 1 2/Am Antiq 31:393-7 Ja '66.

2360 NELSON, OLAF FREDERICK (1883- 1944), Savai'i, Samoa. Educator, politician. Recorded and published a volume on Samoan myths and legends. Source: Craig & King, Historical Dictionary of Oceania (1981), p 204-5.

2361 NELSON, WILLIAM (1847-1915), Newark, New Jersey, United States. Lawyer, historian. Published on the Indians of New Jersey. Source: Am Anth 17:217 Ja '15.

2362 NEMESKÉRI, JÁNOS (1914-), Budapest, Hungary. Paleodemographer.

Population genetics of small populations & isolates. Interested in physical and family anthropology and human paleontology. Sources: Int Dir Anth 3, 5.

2363 NESBITT, PAUL H (1904-), Savanna, Illinois, United States. Anthropologist, archeologist, ethnologist, museologist. Mogollon prehistory & archeology of U.S.; techniques in exhibition of museum collection. Sources: Int Dir Anth 1, 2, 3, 5/Nat Dir Lat Am.

2364 NESHEIM, ASBJORN (1906-), Trondheim, Norway. Lapp linguist. Cultural & linguistic contacts of the Lapps. Comparative research in Lapp fishing and fishing terminology. Sources: Int Dir Anth 3, 5.

2365 NESTOR, JON J (1905-), Focsani, Romania. Historian. Prehistory, protohistory of Central & Eastern Europe. Sources: Int Dir Anth 1, 2, 5.

2366 NESTURKH, MIKHAIL FEDOROVICH (1895-), Pskov, Russia. Anthropologist, primatologist. Research on the origins of man and the ecology, taxonomy, and paleontology of primates. Source: Great Soviet Encyclopedia, New York, Macmillan (1978), v. 17, p 477.

2367 NETTLESHIP, ANDERSON (1910-). Bio-anthropologist, medical anthropologist. Symbolism in primitive medicine. Bio-anthropology of war. Source: Int Dir Anth 5.

2368 NEUGEBAUER, KARL ANTON (1886- 1945). Archeologist, curator. Curator of the Antiquarium in the Berlin Museum. Main interest was in Greek bronzes. Sources: Biog Index: 1/Am J Arch 50:406-7 Jl '46.

2369 NEUSTUPNÝ, JIŘÍ (1905-), Pilsen, Czechoslovakia. Prehistorian, museologist, archeologist. Ethnic classification of prehistoric societies of Europe. Paleolithic art in Bohemia. Stone Age in Czechoslovakia. Sources: Int Dir Anth 3, 5/ Great Soviet Encyclopedia, New York, Macmillan (1978), v. 17, p 518.

2370 NEUVILLE, RENÉ (1899-1952), Gibraltar. Archeologist, diplomat. Correlations between quaternary geology and prehistory in North Africa and Middle East. Sources: Biog Index: 1 2 & 3/Int Dir Anth 1 2 3/ Rev Arch series 6 44:79-80 Jl '54/N Y Times, Je 24 '52.

2371 NEWALL, ROBERT STIRLING (1884-1978), England. Archeologist. Prehistoric archeology of Wiltshire (England). Sources: Biog Index: 11/Int Dir Anth 2/Antiquity 52:91 Jl '78.

2372 NEWBERRY, PERCY EDWARD (1869- 1949), England. Egyptologist. Surveyed the Necropolis at Thebes (Egypt), 1895-1901; was present at opening of Tutankhamen's tomb; wrote widely on Egyptology, Thebes. Sources: Biog Index: 2 5 & 12/Int Dir Anth 3/N Y Times p 15 Ag 8 '49.

2373 NEWBOLD, DOUGLAS (1894-1945), Tunbridge Wells, England. Colonial administrator, archeologist. Civil servant in Anglo-Egyptian Sudan; explored Libyan desert; attempted to structure transitional institutions for independence; classical scholar. Sources: Biog Index: 3 & 5/ Dictionary of National Biography 1941-50:623-4 '59.

2374 NEWCOMBE, CHARLES F (1852-1924), Newcastle-upon-Tyne, England. Physician. Authority on early voyages to the Pacific coast; studied Haida; assembled ethnological collections of the material culture of the Indians of British Columbia for major museums. Source: Am Anth 27:352-3 Ap '25.

2375 NEWELL, WILLIAM WELLS (1839-1907), Cambridge, Massachusetts, United States. Folklorist. Studied games & songs of American children, voodoo, Negro folklore, English folktales in America; emphasized the importance of collecting folklore of changing cultures (American Indians, Cajuns in Louisiana, Spanish Americans). Source: Am Anth 9:366-76 Ap '07.

2376 NEWMAN, STANLEY STEWART

(1905-1984), Chicago, Illinois, United States. Linguist. Studies include Bella Coola, Zuni, Yokut & Nahuatl languages. Aztec (Milpa Alta dialect) and comparative study of Otomi language. Language and cultural relationships. Sources: Int Dir Anth 1, 2, 3, 5/Am Anth 86:151-153.

2377 NEWTON, HENRY (1866-1947), Victoria, Australia. Clergyman. Wrote accounts of the peoples of Papua New Guinea and the Anglican mission work there. Source: Craig & King, Historical Dictionary of Oceania (1981), p 206-7.

2378 NIANE, DJIBRIL TANSIL. Historian. Wrote account of oral traditions relating to Mali Empire *Soundjata ou l'epopee Mandingue* (1960). Source: O'Toole, Thomas E., Historical Dictionary of Guinea (1978), p 52.

2379 NICHOLSON, REYNOLD ALLEYNE (1868-1945), Keignley, Yorkshire, England. Orientalist. Specialist in literature of Sufism; made many translations and contributions to Near Eastern scholarship on mysticism. Sources: Biog Index: 1 & 5/ Dictionary of National Biography 1941-1950:628 '59.

2380 NICOLAS, S J, Fr. LOUIS (1634-), Aubenas, France. Priest. Missionary in New France; wrote on N. American Indians. Source: Jes Rel.

2381 NIDA, EUGENE ALBERT (1914-), Oklahoma City, Oklahoma, United States. Anthropologist, linguist. Techniques for syntactic and morphological analysis. Interested in general ethnology, linguistics and applied anthropology. Sources: Int Dir Anth 3/Nat Dir Lat Am.

2382 NIEDERLE, LUBOR (1865-1944), Czechoslovakia. Archeologist, historian. Slavic prehistory. Archeology of Greece and Rome. Sources: Biog Index: 2/ Great Soviet Encyclopedia, New York, Macmillan (1978), v. 17, p 556/ Rev Arch series 6 34:73 Jl '49.

2383 NIGGEMEYER, HERMANN (1908-), Arnsberg, Westfalen, Germany. Ethnologist. Technology & ornaments of Indonesian textiles. Linguistics of Indonesia. Sources: Int Dir Anth 2, 3, 5.

2384 NIKOLAEV, LEV PETROVICH (1898-1954), Taganrog, Russia. Anthropologist, anatomist. Physical anthropology in the Ukraine. Source: Great Soviet Encyclopedia, New York, Macmillan (1978), v. 18, p 208.

2385 NILES, JOHN JACOB (1892-1980), Louisville, Kentucky, United States. Song writer, folklorist. Collected and recorded songs of the southern Appalachians. Sources: Biog Index: 1 2 5 8 12 & 13/Museum Journal 38:12-14+ Ja/F '80/ Current Biography 41:46 Ap '80/Current Biography Yr Bk 1980:461 '80/ N Y Times p D-11 Mr 3 '80/N Y Times Biog Service 11:422 Mr '80.

2386 NILLES, JOHN (1905-). Missionary, ethnologist. Society, religion & languages in Papua New Guinea, especially Chimbu District. Source: Int Dir Anth 5.

2387 NILSSON, NILS MARTIN PERSSON (1874-1967), Sweden. Archeologist. Interested in Greek archeology and religious history as well as in Swedish folklore. Sources: Biog Index: 8/Int Dir Anth 1 2/Archaeology 20:299 O '67.

2388 NIMUENDAJU, CURT (1883-1945), Jena, Germany. Ethnologist. Archeology and ethnology of Brazil. Authority on the Indians of Brazil: Tukuna, Apapocuva-Guarani, Kaingang, Apinaye, and Canela. Sources: Biog Index: 1/Int Dir Anth 1 2/Am Anth 48:238-43 Ap '46.

2389 NISHIMURA, ASAHITARO (1909-). Ethnologist. Traditional Indochinese. Indonesian & Malaysian fishing cultures. Source: Int Dir Anth 5.

2390 NISHIMURA, MASAE (1915-), Japan. Ceramicist. Chronological development of Jomon culture (Japan). Source: Int Dir Anth 5.

2391 NIZA, MARCOS de (ca. 1500- after 1543), Nice, France. Explorer, priest. Wrote two historical works on the pre-conquest Inca/Scyri wars and subsequent history of the Peru/Ecuador region. Source: Bork & Maier, Historical Dictionary of Ecuador (1973), p 104-5.

2392 NOBACK, CHARLES ROBERT (1916-). Anatomist. Structure & function of primitive nervous systems. Source: Int Dir Anth 5.

2393 NOBLE, HAROLD JOYCE (1903-1953), Pyongyang, Korea. Diplomat, Orientalist. Specialist on Far East language & culture; acted as advisor during occupation and Korean war. Sources: Biog Index: 3 & 10/N Y Times p 15 D 24 '53.

2394 NOGARA, BARTOLOMEO (1868-1954), Bellano, Italy. Archeologist. Director of Pontifical Galleries and Monuments at the Vatican; expert on Etruscans. Sources: Biog Index: 3 & 4/Am J Arch 59:241/ Rev Arch series 6 47:87-8 Ja '56.

2395 NOGUERA, EDUARDO (1896-1977), Mexico City, Mexico. Archeologist. Archeology of the Americas, pottery of Mexican archeological sites. Sources: Biog Index: 12/Int Dir Anth 1 2 3/Am Antiq 43:618-21 O '78.

2396 NOLDEKE, THEODOR (1836-1930), Germany. Orientalist. Source: Biog Index: 11.

2397 NOONE, HERBERT DEANE (1907-), Madras, British India. Anthropologist. Interested in ethnology of S.E. Asia and Archipelago, and in social anthropology, acculturation and prehistoric archeology of the Malay Peninsula; studied Shamanism in its relation to integration among Malayan aborigines. Sources: Biog Index: 5/Int Dir Anth 2/ Holman, Dennis. Noone of the Ulu. Heinemann. '58.

2398 NORBECK, EDWARD (1915-), Canada. Ethnologist. Human play. Japanese culture, kinship & society. Sources: Int Dir Anth 3, 5.

2399 NORDENSKIOLD, NILS ERLAND HERBERT (1877-1932), Stockholm, Sweden. Ethnographer. Wrote extensively on archeology, history, and ethnography of the provinces of Bolivia. Pioneered the field of ethnology in Argentina; specialist in Paraguay, Argentine Chaco, South American Indians in general. Sources: Heath, Dwight B., Historical Dictionary of Bolivia (1972), p 165/ Wright & Nelsham, Historical Dictionary of Argentina (1978), p 623/ Am Anth 35:158-61 Ja '33.

2400 NORLUND, POUL (1888-1951), Denmark. Archeologist. Archeology of Europe, especially in the Viking and Middle Ages. Sources:' Biog Index: 1 2 & 3/Int Dir Anth 1 2 3/ Antiquaries Journal 32:268 Jl '52/N Y Times, Je 1 '51.

2401 NORTHROP, GORDON DOUGLAS (1919-). Anthropologist, ethnologist. Pan-Indianism among urban American Indians. Source: Int Dir Anth 5.

2402 NORTON, CHARLES ELIOT (1827-1908), Cambridge, Massachusetts, United States. Classicist. Founder of Archeological Institute of America; specialist in the archeology of Asia Minor (Assos, Turkey); argued that the only culture worthy of serious study are those with great art traditions. Source: Am Anth 10:704-5 O '08.

2403 NORTON, IRENE MILLS (1903-1985). Social worker. Cultural backgrounds of children. Source: Anth News 10/85.

2404 NORTON, RICHARD (1872-1918). Archeologist. Sources: Biog Index: 3/Russel, Foster William. Mount Auburn biographies. Mount Auburn Cemetery '53 p 121.

2405 NOTT, HENRY (1774-1844), England. Missionary. Produced Tahiti's first law code, translated and published the Bible in Tahitian. Source: Craig & King, Historical Dictionary of Oceania (1981), p 209.

2406 NOUVEL, S J, Fr. HENRI (1621-1702), Pezenas, France. Priest. Missionary in New France; wrote on N. American Indians. Source: Jes Rel.

2407 NOVAKOVA, MARIE (1914-). Physical anthropologist. Growth & development among Czechoslovakian children. Source: Int Dir Anth 5.

2408 NOYES, GEORGE RAPALL (1798-1868). Orientalist. Sources: Biog Index: 3 & 6.

2409 NUMAZAWA, KIICHI (1907-), Japan. Ethnologist. Mythology in Japanese Shintoism. Source: Int Dir Anth 5.

2410 NUNES CABRAL de CARVALHO, JOSE (1913-). Anatomist, histologist. Micropaleontology & comparative anatomy. Source: Int Dir Anth 5.

2411 NUÑEZ CHINCHILLA, JESÚS (1915-), Ocotepeque, Honduras. Archeologist. Archeology of Meso-America, especially Honduras. Sources: Int Dir Anth 3, 5.

2412 NUSBAUM, JESSE LOGAN (1887-1975), Colorado, United States. Museum director, archeologist. Preservation work on Southwest U.S. Indian ruins. Sources: Biog Index: 13/Int Dir Anth 1 2/ Nusbaum, Rosemary, Tierra Dulce: reminiscences from the Jesse Nusbaum Papers. Sun Stone Press '80/Anth News My '76.

2413 NUSSBAUM, WILLIAM (1896-), Frankfurt Ammain, Germany. Physician. Physical features of Sephardic & Ashkenasim Jews. Identical and non-identical twins. Sources: Int Dir Anth 3, 5.

2414 NUTTALL, ZELIA MARIA MAGDALENA (1857-1933), San Francisco, California, United States. Archeologist. A founder of the American Anthropological Association. Specialized in Mexican archeology & was last of great pioneers in the field; located lost and forgotten manuscripts on early Mexican culture; first to recognize the Archaic culture. Sources: Notable American Women, 1607-1950, vol. II, Belknap Press '71, p 640-2/Am Anth 33:475-82 Jl '33.

2415 OBERG, KALERVO (1901-1973), Nanaimo, British Columbia, Canada. Applied anthropologist. Background studies for planning projects in agriculture in Surinam, Brazil. Coined the term "culture shock.". Sources: Biog Index: 10 & 12/Int Dir Anth 2 3/Nat Cyc Am Biog 58:464-5 '79/ Nat Dir Lat Am/Am Anth 76:357-60 Je '74.

2416 OBERMAIER, HUGO (1877-1946), Regensburg, Bavaria, Germany. Paleontologist, physician. Interested in Quaternary man. Sources: Biog Index: 1 & 2.

2417 OBOOKIAH, HENRY (1792-1818), Hawaii, United States. Missionary. Hawaiian native who began translation of the Bible into Hawaiian; left memoirs valuable for account of Hawaii in the early 19th century. Source: Craig & King, Historical Dictionary of Oceania (1981), p 211.

2418 OBREGON LIZANO, MIGUEL (1861-1935), Costa Rica. Geographer. Compiled several volumes on the natural history and geography of Costa Rica. Source: Creedman, Theodore, Historical Dictionary of Costa Rica (1977), p 137.

2419 O'CALLAGHAN, ROGER TIMOTHY (1912-1954), New York, New York, United States. Orientalist, priest. Taught Biblical history, archeology, Ugaritic, and Akkadian languages and comparative semiotics at Pontifico Istituto Biblico in Rome; was involved in archeological work in the Near East at Karatepe and Babylos. Sources: Biog Index: 3/ American School of Oriental Research Bulletin no 134:3 Ap '54.

2420 OCKLEY, SIMON (1628-1720), England. Orientalist. Sources: Biog Index: 5 & 12.

2421 ODUM, HOWARD WASHINGTON (1884-). Sociologist, folklorist. Sources: Biog Index: 3 4 6 7 & 10/ American Journal of Sociology 79:278-95 S '73.

2422 OETTEKING, BRUNO (1871-1960), Hamburg, Germany. Physical anthropologist. Interested in general physical & applied anthropology and human paleontology. Expert morphologist; his materials on human craniology used widely in chiropractic. Sources: Biog Index: 5/Int Dir Anth 1 2 3/Am Anth 62:675-80 Ag '60/ N Y Times p 27 Ja 18 '60.

2423 OGATA, TAMOTSU (1916-).

Anatomist. Relationship of environment to man's physical characteristics in Japan and Peru. Source: Int Dir Anth 5.

2424 OIKONOMOS, GEORGIOS P (1883-1951), Athens, Greece. Archeologist. Wrote on archeology of classical Greece. Sources: Biog Index: 3/Rev Arch series 6 44:81-3 Jl '54.

2425 OINAS, FELIX J (1911-). Linguist, mythologist. Heroic epic, ballads & legends of Russia, Finland & Estonia. Source: Int Dir Anth 5.

2426 OJEDA, ALONSO de (-1516), Spain. Sailor. First European to explore Caribbean coast of Venezuela. Source: Rudolph & Rudolph, Historical Dictionary of Venezuela (1971), p 88.

2427 OKA, MASAO (1898-), Matsumoto City, Nagano Prefecture, Japan. Ethnologist. Source: Japan Biographical Encyclopedia and Who's Who (3rd ed., 1964/65) p 1143.

2428 OLAON, RONALD LEROY (1895-1980). Anthropologist. Source: Am Anth S '81.

2429 OLIVEIRA LIMA, MANUEL de (1867-1928), Brazil. Historian. Most thorough historian of Brazilian society in the 19th century. Source: Levine, Robert M., Historical Dictionary of Brazil (1979), p 152.

2430 OLIVER, DOUGLAS LLEWELLYN (1913-), United States. Ethnologist. Ethnography of Melanesia, Micronesia and Polynesia. Sources: Int Dir Anth 3, 5.

2431 OLIVER, NICOLAAS JOHANNES JACOBUS (1919-), Pearston, South Africa. Legal anthropologist. African forensic anthropology. Bantu & comparative South African law. Phonetics and morphology of Xhosa language. Sources: Int Dir Anth 3, 5.

2432 OLIVIER, GEORGES (1912-). Physical anthropologist, primatologist. Application of biometrics to anthropological osteology. Hominization. Sources: Int Dir Anth 5/ Duroux, Paul-Emile, Dictionnaire des Anthropologistes, Paris, Editions Universitaires (1975).

2433 OLSEN, STANLEY JOHN (1919-). Zooarcheologist. Faunal analysis of archeological materials, especially in Southwest U.S. Source: Int Dir Anth 5.

2434 OLSON, RONALD LEROY (1895-1979), Mankato, Minnesota, United States. Anthropologist, ethnologist, ethnographer. Ethnography of the Northwest Coast peoples (U.S.). Specialist in Quinault ethnography, the origins of social structure among N. American Indians, and "salvage ethnography" on various northern Kwakiutl groups. Sources: Int Dir Anth 1, 2, 3, 5/Am Anth 83:605-7 S '81.

2435 O'NEALE, LILA MORRIS (1886-1948), North Dakota, United States. Anthropologist. Specialist on Peruvian textile weaving. Source: Am Anth 50:1948 p 657.

2436 O'NEIL, BRYAN HUGH St. JOHN (1905-1954), England. Archeologist. Archeology in Britain, especially Wales and particularly of the early Iron Age and medieval period. Sources: Biog Index: 3 & 4/Int Dir Anth 2/ Antiquaries Journal 35:285-6 Jl '55.

2437 ONESIMOS, NESIB (1856-1931). Clergyman. Produced a reader/speller in the Oromo language of Ethiopia; translated Bible into Oromo. Source: Prouty & Rosenfeld, Historical Dictionary of Ethiopia (1981), p 141-2.

2438 OPIE, PETER (1918-). Folklorist, author. Source: Biog Index: 9.

2439 OPLER, MARVIN KAUFMANN (1914- 1981), Buffalo, New York, United States. Anthropologist, social psychiatrist. Applied anthropology; analyzed cultural and economic factors leading to & consequences of war relocation of Japanese in the U.S.; psychopathology & ethno-social psychiatry. Sources: Int Dir Anth 2, 3, 5/Am Anth 83:617-21 S '81.

2440 OPLER, MORRIS EDWARD (1907-), Buffalo, New York, United States. Ethnologist. History & culture of Chiricahua & Mescaler

Apache Indians. Sources: Int Dir Anth 1, 2, 3, 5.

2441 OPPENHEIM, ADOLF LEO (1904-1974). Assyriologist, paleontologist. Directed the Assyrian Dictionary project; wrote widely on the civilizations of Assyria and Babylon. Sources: Biog Index: 10 & 11/N Y Times p 44 Jl 24 '74.

2442 OPPENHEIMER, ARMAND M (1906-). Physical anthropologist. Hominid evolution. Dental & facial anatomy. Source: Int Dir Anth 5.

2443 ORACIÓN, TIMOTEO S (1911-). Cultural anthropologist. Folk medicine among the Magahat people of the Philippines. Total culture. Source: Int Dir Anth 5.

2444 ORBIGNY, ALCIDES DESSALINES d' (1802-1857), France. Naturalist. Wrote on the ethnology and history of the Oriente region of Bolivia. Source: Heath, Dwight B., Historical Dictionary of Bolivia (1972), p 168.

2445 ORELLANA POZO, J. GONZALO (1904-), Cuenca, Ecuador. Historian. Created a history of Ecuador. Source: Bork & Maier, Historical Dictionary of Ecuador (1973), p 107.

2446 O'RIORDAIN, SEAN PADRAIG (1904-1957), Cork Co., Ireland. Archeologist. Interested in archeology of Europe, especially of Ireland. Sources: Biog Index: 4/Int Dir Anth 1 2 3/ Illustrated London News 230:695 Ap 27 '57/Nature 179:1053 My '57.

2447 OROZCO y BERRA, MANUEL (1816- 1881), Mexico. Archeologist, historian. Left a four-volume history of the conquest of Mexico. Source: Briggs & Alisky, Historical Dictionary of Mexico (1981), p 166-7.

2448 ORR, KENNETH GORDON (1916-), Long Island City, New York, United States. Applied cultural anthropologist, archeologist. Applications of cultural anthropology to problems of socio-economic change. Archeology of U.S. Plains and lower Mississippi regions. Sources: Int Dir Anth 2, 3, 5.

2449 ORR, PHIL C (1903-), Dillon, Montana, United States. Archeologist. Pleistocene man & mammals in N. America. Source: Int Dir Anth 5.

2450 ORREGO, ANTENOR (1892-1960), Peru. Philosopher. Promulgated the philosophy of "indigenismo" in the 1920s, stressing the cultural heritage of the Indians of Peru as a vital force in Peruvian society. Source: Alisky, Historical Dictionary of Peru (1979), p 69.

2451 ORSMOND, JOHN (1788-1856), England. Missionary. Compiled a dictionary of the Tahitian language and recorded volumes of genealogical and cultural data on Tahiti; later published by his granddaughter, the linguist Teuira Henry. Source: Craig & King, Historical Dictionary of Oceania (1981), p 216-7.

2452 ORTIZ, FERNANDO (1881-1969), Havana, Cuba. Anthropologist, ethnologist. Professor of Law. Leader in Afro-Cuban studies and pioneer in Afro-American studies; identified the Yoruba (Nigeria) as the major influence on Afro-Cuban religion; published on the Indian & African influences on Cuban culture. Sources: Biog Index: 8/Am Anth 72:816-819 Ag '70/N Y Times p 35 Ap 12 '69.

2453 ORTIZ CORTES, SERGIO ELIAS (1894-), Pasto, Narino, Colombia. Linguist. Native languages & dialects in Colombia. Sources: Int Dir Anth 3, 5.

2454 ORTUTAY, GYULA (1909-1978). Ethnologist, folklorist, government official. Folklore of Europe, especially of Hungary. Sources: Biog Index: 11-/Int Dir Anth 5/N Y Times p A-25 Mr 24 '78.

2455 OSBORNE, DOUGLAS (1912-), Helena, Montana, United States. Archeologist. Pacific, Micronesian & Southwest U.S. archeology; studied possible prehistoric migration route through Northern Canada and Alaska. Sources: Int Dir Anth 2, 3, 5.

2456 OSBORNE, LILLY DE JONGH (1884-1975), Costa Rica. Authority on crafts & textiles of

Guatemala & El Salvador. Source: Anth News My '75.

2457 OSHANIN, LEV VASIL'EVICH (1884-1962), Tashkent, Uzbekistan. Anthropologist. Investigated the ethnic background of the peoples of Middle Asia and the Transcaspian region. Sources: Great Soviet Encyclopedia, New York, Macmillan (1978), v. 19, p 121/Miklashevskaia, N.N. "Pamiati L.V. Oshanin" Voprosy antropologii, 1962, no. 12.

2458 OSTRIC, ANTHONY (1913-). Cultural anthropologist, social anthropologist. Man's origin and biological & cultural development. Source: Int Dir Anth 5.

2459 OSWALD, FELIX (1866-1958), England. Geologist, archeologist. Interested in Roman archeology, specializing in Roman Terra Siggillata pottery. Sources: Biog Index: 5/Int Dir Anth 2/Am J Arch 63:194 Ap '59/ Nature 182:1549 D 6 '58.

2460 OTIENDE, JOSEPH DANIEL (1917-), Maragoli, Kenya. Teacher. Wrote an ethnography of the Abaluhya of Kenya. Source: Ogot, Bethwell A., Historical Dictionary of Kenya (1981), p 177.

2461 OTTEN, CHARLOTTE M (1915-). Cross-cultural ethnologist, bio-anthropologist. Bio-social interaction. Primitive art. Cross-cultural aesthetics. Source: Int Dir Anth 5.

2462 OUDNEY, WALTER (1801-1824). Explorer. Traveled to Hausa states in northern Nigeria in the early 1820s; left a journal account of his trip. Source: Levine & Nye, Historical Dictionary of Cameroon, (1974), p 27.

2463 OUTES, FÉLIX (1878-1939), Buenos Aires, Argentina. Anthropologist. Founded anthropology as a discipline in Argentina; fieldwork done in Pampas region and in Patagonia. Source: Wright & Nelsham, Historical Dictionary of Argentina (1978), p 659.

2464 OVIEDO y BANOS, JOSÉ de. Historian. Wrote a history (incomplete) of the Spanish conquest of Venezuela. Source: Rudolph & Rudolph, Historical Dictionary of Venezuela (1971), p 89.

2465 OVIEDO y VALDEZ, FRANCISCO GONZALO FERNANDEZ (1478-1557), Madrid, Spain. Historian. Wrote a history of Spanish exploration detailing early penetrations of Costa Rica. Wrote an account of the conquest of Nicaragua in his general history of the Americas. Sources: Bork & Maier, Historical Dictionary of Ecuador (1973), p 61-2/ Meyer, Harvey K., Historical Dictionary of Nicaragua (1972), p 315.

2466 OWEN, WALTER EDWIN (1878-1945), Northern Ireland. Missionary. Amateur archeologist active in Kenya in the 1930s & 1940s. Source: Ogot, Bethwell A., Historical Dictionary of Kenya (1981), p 178.

2467 OXE, AUGUST (1863-1944), Germany. Archeologist. Studied Roman-German archeology, particularly interested in Roman Terra Siggillata pottery, both Italian and provincial. Sources: Biog Index: 1/Am J Arch 51:219 Ap '47.

2468 PACE, BIAGIO (1889-1955), Italy. Archeologist, historian. Wrote about ancient world in general, particularly about Sicily (Italy). Sources: Biog Index: 5/Rev Arch 2:101-2 Jl '58/ Rivista di Antropologia 42:483ff 1955.

2469 PADDOCK, JOHN G (1918-). Archeologist, ethnologist. Demography, social psychiatry & ethnohistory of the Mexican Mixtec Indians. Source: Int Dir Anth 5.

2470 PAINTER, MURIEL THAYER (1892- 1975), United States. Anthropologist. Yaqui Indians of Mexico, especially their Easter ceremony. Source: Anth News Jn '75.

2471 PALACIOS, ENRIQUE JUAN (1891-1953), Mexico. Archeologist. Mexican & Mayan archeology; art and philosophy of the Orient. Panoramic view of prehistory and history of Mexico. Sources: Biog Index: 3/Int Dir Anth 1 2/Am Antiq 19:152 O '53.

2472 **PALERM VICH, ANGEL** (1917-1980), Ibiza, Spain. Anthropologist, ethnologist. Irrigation & its relevance to Mesoamerican culture; Mexican peasant economic systems. Influenced the direction of anthropology in Mexico. Specialist in the Tajin Totonac, & the implications of irrigation systems for Mesoamerican cultural development; used his leadership post in the Organization of American States to solve major problems (land reform, development & planning). <u>Sources</u>: Am Anth 83:612-615, 911 S '81/Int Dir Anth 5.

2473 **PALMER, EDWARD** (-1911). Ethnological collector. Carefully put together early collection of artifacts from St. George (Utah), and the Verde River area (Arizona), as well as of the Apache. <u>Source</u>: Am Anth 13:173 Ja '11.

2474 **PALMER, EDWARD HENRY** (1840-1882), England. Orientalist. <u>Sources</u>: Biog Index: 5 & 12.

2475 **PANCHANADIKAR, KRISHNA CHINTAMANI** (1919-). Ethnologist. Social structure & change in rural Indian communities. <u>Source</u>: Int Dir Anth 5.

2476 **PANE, IGNACIO ALBERTO** (1880-1920), Paraguay. Sociologist. Specialist on Paraguayan family and social characteristics. <u>Source</u>: Kolinski, Charles J., Historical Dictionary of Paraguay (1973), p 177.

2477 **PANEK, STANISŁAW** (1916-), Poland. Ethnologist. Ontogenetic development of young people in Poland & Egypt. <u>Source</u>: Int Dir Anth 5.

2478 **PANETTA, ESTER** (1895-), Reggio, Italy. Ethnologist, folklorist. Ethnology of N.E. Africa, especially, Somalia and Ethiopia. Songs & folktales of N.E. Africa. Libyan Arabic. <u>Sources</u>: Int Dir Anth 3, 5.

2479 **PAPADIMITRIOU, JOHN** (1904-1963), Skyros, Greece. Archeologist. Excavated and wrote on ancient Greece; director of Greek archeology services. <u>Sources</u>: Biog Index: 6 & 7/Rev Arch 2:206-7 O '63.

2480 **PAPE, MAX A** (1914-). Anthropologist, sociologist. Physical & cultural anthropology of Mexico & the Philippines. <u>Source</u>: Int Dir Anth 5.

2481 **PARAIN, CHARLES** (1893-), France. Anthropologist, ethnologist. History of ancient agrarian techniques & structure of rural communities. <u>Sources</u>: Int Dir Anth 3, 5.

2482 **PARANAVITANA, SENARAT** (1896-), Metaramba, Galle, Ceylon. Archeologist, epigraphist, philologist. Participated in the excavations at Mohenjodaro (Pakistan); Archaeological Commissioner, Ceylon Department of Archeology, 1940-1956. Epigraphy of Ceylon. <u>Sources</u>: Biog Index: 10/Artibus Asiae 35 no 3:273-7 '73.

2483 **PARATORE, ANGELA** (1912-), Madison, Wisconsin, United States. Fieldwork, Mexico. <u>Source</u>: Nat Dir Lat Am.

2484 **PAREDES, AMÉRICO** (1915-). Folklorist. <u>Source</u>: Nat Dir Lat Am.

2485 **PAREDES, MANUEL RIGOBERTO** (1870-1950), Bolivia. Geographer, historian. Compiled detailed information on small regions of the Bolivian altiplano. <u>Source</u>: Heath, Dwight B., Historical Dictionary of Bolivia (1972), p 178.

2486 **PARENTI, RAFFAELLO** (1907-), Florence, Italy. Osteometrist, paleontologist. Elementary application of biometrics to anthropology. Neolithic and Mesolithic man in Italy. <u>Sources</u>: Int Dir Anth 3, 5.

2487 **PARIBENI, ROBERT** (1876-1956). Archeologist. Specialist in archeology of Greece, Crete and Albania. <u>Sources</u>: Biog Index: 4/N Y Times p 61 Jl 15 '56.

2488 **PARK, MUNGO** (1771-1806), Selkirk, Scotland. Explorer. One of first explorers to follow Niger River in Mali; left account of travels. <u>Sources</u>: Columbia/Imperato, Pascal J., Historical Dictionary of Mali (1977), p 82.

2489 PARK, WILLARD Z (1906-1965), Silt, Colorado, United States. Ethnologist. Conducted research among the Paviotso (Nevada), especially on their social organization & religion, and in Andean Colombia. Source: Am Anth 68:135-6 F '66.

2490 PARKER, ARTHUR CASWELL (1881-1955), New York, United States. Archeologist. Comparison of Indian populations of Middle Atlantic States and evidences of migration. Sources: Biog Index: 3 4 11 & 12/Int Dir Anth 1 2/ American Philosophical Society Proceedings 123 no 1:47-72 F 20 '79.

2491 PARKER, WILLIAM NELSON (1919-). Anthropologist. Techniques & market organization in U.S. agriculture. Source: Int Dir Anth 5.

2492 PARKES, JAMES CHRISTOPHER ERNEST (1861-1899). Civil servant. Wrote an extensive survey of the various peoples and regions of Sierra Leone for the Colonial Office. Source: Foray, Cyril P., Historical Dictionary of Sierra Leone (1977), p 170-1.

2493 PARRIS, WAYNE LAVERN (1918-). Ethnologist. Religious acculturation among the Bura & Hausa of Nigeria. Source: Int Dir Anth 5.

2494 PARROT, ANDRÉ (1901-1980). Museum director, archeologist. Excavated the Iraqi site of Mari in 1933; expert on ancient Mesopotamia. Sources: Biog Index: 13/N Y Times p B-5 Ag 27 '80.

2495 PARSONS, ELSIE CLEWS (1875-1941), New York, New York, United States. Anthropologist, ethnologist. Fieldwork among Zapotec in Mexico, among Zuni and N. American Plains Indians, and in the Ecuadorean Andes. Negro folklore. Sources: Biog Index: 2/Int Dir Anth 1 2/ Notable American Women, 1607-1950, vol. III, Belknap Press '71, p 20-2/ Am Anth 45:244-55 Ap '43/ American Philosophical Society Proceedings 94 no 3:308-9 '50.

2496 PARSONS, TALCOTT (1902-1979), Colorado Springs, Colorado, United States. Sociologist, evolutionist. Major social theorist. "Structural-functional theory.". Source: International Encyclopedia of the Social Sciences, v. 18.

2497 PASHA, EMIN (1840-1892), Oppelu, Prussia. Civil servant. Wrote account of his experiences as Governor of Southern Sudan during Ottoman rule. Source: Kurtz, Laura S., Historical Dictionary of Tanzania (1978), p 54.

2498 PASSEK, TAT'IANA SERGEEVNA (1903-1968), St. Petersburg, Russia. Archeologist. Neolithic to Bronze Age in European Russia. Sources: Great Soviet Encyclopedia, New York, Macmillan (1978), v. 19, p 322/"Pamiati T.S. Passek" Sovetskaia arkheologiia, 1969, no. 2.

2499 PATAI, RAPHAEL (1910-), Budapest, Hungary. Mythologist. Near Eastern religion & mythology of Biblical Jews to 1000 A.D. Sources: Int Dir Anth 3, 5.

2500 PATON, ALAN (1903-), Pietermaritzburg, Natal, South Africa. Author. Wrote influential novels calling for removal of apartheid and vividly depicting social conditions in South Africa. Source: Saunders, Christopher, Historical Dictionary of South Africa (1983), p 134.

2501 PATON, LEWIS BAYLES (1864-1932). Archeologist. Source: Biog Index: 7.

2502 PATSCH, GERTRUD (1910-). Ethnologist, linguist. History of Georgian language. Ethnography of Georgia, U.S.S.R. Source: Int Dir Anth 5.

2503 PAUL, BENJAMIN D (1911-), New York, New York, United States. Anthropologist. Community study of highland Indians, ethnology and applied anthropology of Middle America. Sources: Int Dir Anth 3/Nat Dir Lat Am.

2504 PAUL, IRVEN (1894-). Cultural anthropologist, museologist. Latin American culture, history & literature. Source: Int Dir Anth 5.

2505 PAUL, LOIS (1915-1975), United States. Anthropologist. Medical anthropology. Studied marriage patterns & life cycles in Guatemala; child development & the role of women. Source: Anth News F '76.

2506 PAULSEN, ALLISON C (1918-). Archeologist. Andean ceramics. Source: Int Dir Anth 5.

2507 PAVELČIK, JAN (1906-). Physical anthropologist. Analysis of 8th-10th century Moravian (Czechoslovakia). Ethnography of S.E. Moravia. Source: Int Dir Anth 5.

2508 PAYNE, HUMFRY GILBERT GARTH (1902-1936), Wendover, England. Archeologist. Excavated the site of Perachora near Corinth; specialist in archaic Greek art; director, British School at Athens, 1924-1936. Sources: Biog Index: 2/ Dictionary of National Biography 1931-1940:680-1 '49.

2509 PAZDUR, JAN (1909-), Poland. Historian. History of material culture of Poland, 7th-20th centuries. Source: Int Dir Anth 5.

2510 PAZOS KANKY, VICENTE (1779-1853). Historian. Indigenista. Source: Heath, Dwight B., Historical Dictionary of Bolivia (1972), p 185.

2511 PEABODY, ROBERT SINGLETON (1837-1904), Muskingum Co., Ohio, United States. Philanthropist. Put together a systematic collection of more than 30,000 archeological artifacts from the Ohio Valley, the South Atlantic and Gulf states, and the Plains. Source: Am Anth 6:745-6 O '04.

2512 PEAKE, HAROLD JOHN EDWARD (1867-1946), Ellesmere, Shropshire, England. Anthropologist. Most interested in environment and archeological sites; always related prehistoric remains to the place, time and peoples in an effort to humanize the subject. Sources: Biog Index: 1 2 & 5/ Dictionary of National Biography 1941-1950:663 '59.

2513 PEARCE, JAMES EDWIN (1868-1938). Archeologist. Specialist in the archeology of Texas. Source: Am Anth 41:173 Ja '39.

2514 PEDERSEN, ASBJORN (1903-). Petroglyphologist. Prehistoric S. American metallurgy. Rock paintings & engravings. Source: Int Dir Anth 5.

2515 PEDRO, ARMILLAS (1915-1984), Spain. Archeologist. Archeology and pre-Columbian art in Mexico. Source: Anth News (Sept 1984) p 3.

2516 PEET, THOMAS ERIC (1882-1934), Liverpool, England. Egyptologist. Conducted excavations in Egypt for Egypt Exploration Fund, after 1909. Sources: Biog Index: 2/Who Was Who, 1929-1940.

2517 PEIRCE, HAYFORD (1883-1946), Bangor, Maine, United States. Businessman. Specialist in Byzantine art; collaborated with Royall Tyler on *Byzantine Art*, 1926. Sources: Biog Index: 1 & 2/Am J Arch 50:293 Ap-Je '46/ Nat Cyc Am Biog 34:531 '48.

2518 PELLIOT, PAUL (1878-1945), France. Sinologist. Sources: Biog Index: 1 & 2/Int Dir Anth 2.

2519 PEÑA y MONTENEGRO, ALONSO de (-1688), Villa del Padron, Galicia, Spain. Wrote works on missionary methods which contain much information of interest to anthropologists. Source: Bork & Maier, Historical Dictionary of Ecuador (1973), p 113.

2520 PENARD, ARTHUR PHILIP (1880-1932), Paramaraibo, Surinam, Dahomey. Ethnologist, ornithologist. Collected facts about the language and habits of the Carib Indians; with his brother, Frederick Paul Penard, in 1907-1908 published in three volumes, *De Menschetende Aanbidders der Zonneslang* (The man-eating adorers of the Snake of the Sun) which was an account of the psychology, folklore and customs of the Carib. Sources: Biog Index: 2/ Auk, a Quarterly Journal of Ornithology 66:56-60 Ja '49.

2521 PENAVIN, OLGA (1916-). Folklorist, linguist. Hungarian folk languages, ballads & tales. Source: Int Dir Anth 5.

2522 PENCK, ALBRECHT (1858-1945),

Leipzig, Germany. Geographer, geologist. Concerned with and wrote on the morphology of the earth's surface. Researched Ice Age in the Alps and early man in Europe. **Sources**: Int Dir Anth 1 2/Columbia/New Int Enc, 1914 ed.

2523 PENDLEBURY, JOHN DEVITT STRINGFELLOW (1904-1941), England. Archeologist. Archeology of Crete and prehistoric archeology of Greece; relations between Egypt and the Aegean. **Sources**: Biog Index: 1/Int Dir Anth 2/Rev Arch 26:153-4 O '46.

2524 PENOYRE, JOHN (1870-1954). Archeologist. **Sources**: Biog Index: 3/Journal of Hellenic Studies 74:183-4 '54.

2525 PENZER, NORMAN MOSLEY (1892-1960). Historian. History of exploration. **Sources**: Biog Index: 6/Geographical Journal 127:142 Mr '61.

2526 PEPPER, GEORGE HUBBARD (1873- 1924), Tottenville, Staten Island, New York, United States. Museum curator. Excavated at Pueblo Bonito (New Mexico), in Michoacan (Mexico), Manabi (Ecuador), New Jersey & Georgia (U.S.); conducted ethnological survey of all occupied Pueblos of Southwest U.S.; specialist in Navajo weaving. **Source**: Am Anth 26:566-7 O '24.

2527 PERALIA y ALFARO, MANUEL MARÍA (1840-1937), Costa Rica. Historian. Wrote a history of Costa Rica, Nicaragua and Panama in the 16th century. **Source**: Creedman, Theodore, Historical Dictionary of Costa Rica (1977), p 156.

2528 PÉRATÉ, ANDRÉ (1862-1947), France. Archeologist, art historian, translator. Christian archeology. **Source**: Rev Arch series 6 39:94-5 Ja '52.

2529 PEREIRA da COSTA, FRANCISCO AUGUSTO (1851-1923), Brazil. Writer. Collected a volume of legends, tales and poems from the state of Pernambuco (Brazil). **Source**: Levine, Robert M., Historical Dictionary of Brazil (1979), p 165.

2530 PEREIRA de QUEIROZ, MARÍA ISAURA (1918-). Sociologist. Rural environment of Brazil. Sociology of Messianism in Brazil. **Source**: Int Dir Anth 5.

2531 PERICOT GARCÍA, LUIS (1899-), Gerona, Spain. Cultural anthropologist, petroglyphologist. Prehistoric Iberia. Balearic Islands. Early man. **Sources**: Int Dir Anth 1, 2, 3, 5.

2532 PERROT, GEORGES (1832-1914), Villeneuve-Saint-Georges, France. Archeologist. While a member of an archeological expedition to Asia Minor, he reconstructed the text of a bilingual record of the reign of Augustus on the walls of a temple of Ankana (Turkey). **Sources**: Columbia/New Int Enc, 1914 ed.

2533 PERRY, WILLIAM JAMES (1889-1940). Anthropologist, ethnologist. Sought to demonstrate the diffusion of archaic cults throughout Southern Asia, the Pacific and N. America. **Sources**: Biog Index: 2/Int Dir Anth 2/Nature 163:865-6 Je 4 '49.

2534 PERSSON, AXEL WALDEMAR (1888- 1951), Sweden. Archeologist. Led several excavations in Greece and S.W. Asia Minor. **Sources**: Biog Index: 2 & 3/Int Dir Anth 2/Am J Arch, Ja '52/ Rev Arch series 6 43:217-20 Ap '54.

2535 PETER, Prince of Greece & Denmark (1908-1980). Anthropologist, ethnologist. Polyandry in Central Asia and among various peoples of Himalayas & South India. Nomadism of Central Asia. **Sources**: Biog Index: 1 & 13/Int Dir Anth 5/New Yorker, Ap 17 '48/ Am Anth 83:616-7 S '81/N Y Times p D-19 O 17 '80/ Far Eastern Economic Review il 110:74 N 21-27 '80.

2536 PETERS, EMRYS LLOYD (1916-), Merthyr Tydfil, Wales. Social anthropologist. Traditional society of Cyrenaica (Libya) and of Shi'-ites of South Lebanon. **Sources**: Int Dir Anth 3, 5.

2537 PETERSON, MENDEL L (1918-). Archeologist, museum curator. **Source**: Biog Index: 8.

2538 PETRIE, HILDA (Urlin) (1871-1956), England. Egyptologist. Worked with her husband Flinders Petrie on drawings of finds from excavations; led two excavations of her own: the opening of Osireion (Abydos) and the clearing of tomb-chapels at Saqqara (Egypt). Sources: Biog Index: 4/Nature 179:71 Ja 12 '57.

2539 PETRIE, WILLIAM MATTHEW FLINDERS, Sir (1853-1942). Egyptologist. Sources: Biog Index: 5 6 7 & 9.

2540 PETRYSHYN, JAROSLAW THEODORE (1917-). Ethnologist. Mythology of the Lacondon Maya, of Mexico. Source: Int Dir Anth 5.

2541 PFEIFFER, JOHN E (1914-). Cultural ethnologist, primatologist, petroglyphologist. Origins of agriculture. Prehistoric art & archeology. Source: Int Dir Anth 5.

2542 PFEIFFER, ROBERT HENRY (1892-1958), Bologna, Italy. Biblical scholar, Orientalist. Wrote on era when Biblical events occurred. Sources: Biog Index: 3 4 5 & 6/Nat Cyc Am Biog 43:511 '61.

2543 PHILIP, JOHN (1777-1851). Missionary. Advocated full legal rights for the Khoisan peoples of Cape Province; tried to work for equality of races. Source: Saunders, Christopher, Historical Dictionary of South Africa (1983), p 136.

2544 PHILIPPE, JOSEPH (Abbe) (1876-1950), Plasnes, France. Priest, archeologist. Archeology of Normandy (France). Sources: Int Dir Anth 1/Rev Arch series 6 40:72-4 Jl '52.

2545 PHILLIPS, PHILIP (1900-), Buffalo, New York, United States. Archeologist. Archeology of S.E. United States, especially Lower Mississippi Valley. Sources: Int Dir Anth 1, 2, 3, 5.

2546 PICARD, CHARLES (1883-1965). Archeologist. Sources: Biog Index: 7 & 8/Monuments Piot 55:1-6 '67.

2547 PICKETT, VELMA BERNICE (1912-), Dunning, Nebraska, United States. Linguist. Summer Institute of Linguistics. Mexico. Wrote: *The Grammatical Hierarchy of Isthmus Zapotec* (1960). Source: Nat Dir Lat Am.

2548 PICKTHALL, MARMADUKE (1875-1936), England. Orientalist. Source: Biog Index: 4.

2549 PICON SALAS, MARIANO (1901-), Venezuela. Diplomat, historian. Wrote several historical works useful to the ethnographer. Source: Rudolph & Rudolph, Historical Dictionary of Venezuela (1971), p 95.

2550 PIERRON, S J, Fr. JEAN (1631-1700), Dan-sur-Meuse, France. Priest. Missionary in New France; wrote on N. American Indians. Source: Jes Rel.

2551 PIERSON, DONALD (1900-), Indianapolis, Indiana, United States. Anthropologist, sociologist. Race in Brazil. Interested in social anthropology of S. America. Sources: Int Dir Anth 3, 5/Nat Dir Lat Am.

2552 PIERSON, S J, Fr. PHILIPPE (1642-1688), Ath, Hainaut, Belgium. Priest. Missionary in New France; wrote on N. American Indians. Source: Jes Rel.

2553 PIGAFETTA, ANTONIO (1491-1534), Italy. Wrote account of Magellan's circumnavigation of the earth. Sources: Webster's Biographical Dictionary/ Chamber's Biographical Dictionary, p 1011.

2554 PIGAFETTA, FILIPPO (ca. 1533-ca. 1604). Traveler. Described kingdom of Kongo (Angola), India, and other lands. Source: Nat Un Cat.

2555 PIGGOTT, STUART (1910-), Petersfield Hants., England. Archeologist. Survey of Neolithic cultures in Britain; Indian prehistory. Sources: Biog Index: 1/Int Dir Anth 2 3/Nature 158:91 Jl 20 '46.

2556 PIKE, EUNICE VICTORIA (1913-), Woodstock, Connecticut, United States. Missionary, linguist. Summer Institute of Linguistics. Mexico. Source: Nat Dir Lat Am.

2557 PIKE, KENNETH LEE (1912-),

Woodstock, Connecticut, United States. Linguist. Methodology of linguistic analysis; phonetics of various American Indian languages. Sources: Int Dir Anth 3, 5/Nat Dir Lat Am.

2558 PILLET, MAURICE (1881-1964), Mantes-sur-Seine, France. Egyptologist. Led and wrote about the results of numerous excavations to Middle East. Sources: Biog Index: 7/Rev Arch 1:179-184 Ap '64.

2559 PILLING, JAMES CONSTANTINE (1846-1895). Linguist, administrator, bibliographer. Wrote about the languages of North American Indians. Source: Am Anth 8(old series):407-9 O 1895.

2560 PINKLEY, JEAN McWHIRT (1910-1969), Miami, Arizona, United States. Archeologist. Specialist in the sites of Mesa Verde, California and Pecos Mission, New Mexico. Sources: Biog Index: 8/Am Antiq 34:471-3 O '69.

2561 PINO, JOSÉ, see: Son of Many Beads.

2562 PIOTROVSKII, BORIS BORISOVICH (1908-), St. Petersburg, Russia. Archeologist, Orientalist. Archeology of the Caucasus, Armenia, and Egypt. Specialist on archeology of Urartu. Source: Great Soviet Encyclopedia, New York, Macmillan (1978), v. 19, p 551.

2563 PISCHEL, ANNA BARBARA (1912-). Anthropologist. Applied & urban anthropology. Folk art, handicrafts, ceramics, tools & wovenware. Source: Int Dir Anth 5.

2564 PITT-RIVERS, AUGUSTUS HENRY LANE FOX (1827-1900). Archeologist. Developed a systematic scientific approach to the preservation and analysis of archeological remains. Sources: Biog Index: 4 6 & 11.

2565 PITT-RIVERS, JULIAN (1919-). Ethnologist. Cross-cultural ethnology of Spanish-speaking communities. Source: Int Dir Anth 5.

2566 PITTARD, EUGENE AMI (1867-1963), Geneva, Switzerland. Anthropologist. Racial incidence of disease; serology; physical anthropology of Bushmen, Hottentot and Griqua of Southern Africa; prehistory of Dordogne, France. Sources: Biog Index: 6/Int Dir Anth 1 2 3/Nature 200:120 O 12 '63.

2567 PITTIONI, RICHARD (1906-1985), Vienna, Austria. Prehistorian, archeologist. Prehistoric & early history of European copper mining. Specialist in European prehistory, particularly Austria; identified prehistoric copper mines and ores in the Alps & assigned specific artifacts to them. Sources: Int Dir Anth 1, 2, 3, 5/Anth News 27:6:4.

2568 PLAATJE, SOLOMON T (1876-1932). Writer. Wrote a diary of the siege of Mafeking (South Africa); active in founding forerunner of African National Congress; protested Native Land Act of 1900s. Source: Saunders, Christopher, Historical Dictionary of South Africa (1983), p 137.

2569 PLANCQUAERT, MICHEL (1897-). Missionary, cultural anthropologist. Prehistoric archeology of the Yuka of the Kwango River area (Zaire). Source: Int Dir Anth 5.

2570 PLUMER, JAMES MARSHALL (1899- 1960), Newton Center, Massachusetts, United States. Sinologist, art historian. Wrote at length on Far Eastern, particularly Chinese, art. Sources: Biog Index: 7/Nat Cyc Am Biog 49:82 '66.

2571 POCH, RUDOLF (-1921). Anthropologist. Source: Am Anth 23:389 Jl '21.

2572 POCOCKE, EDWARD (1604-1691), England. Orientalist. Sources: Biog Index: 1 & 4.

2573 POEBEL, ARNO (1881-1958), Germany. Orientalist. Expert in the Sumerian language and culture. Sources: Biog Index: 4/N Y Times p 29 Mr 4 '58.

2574 POIGNANT, AXEL (ca. 1907-1986). Photographer. Documented the native peoples of Australia, particularly in Arnhem Land. Source: Anth News 27:7:4.

2575 POISSON, GEORGES (1861-1943),

France. Anthropologist. Prehistory especially protohistory; ethnology of the ancient peoples of Europe, the Aryan question. Sources: Biog Index: 2/Int Dir Anth 1 2/Rev Arch series 6 34:69 Jl '49.

2576 POLANYI, KARL (1886-1964), Hungary. Economist. Economic anthropology. Wrote on the economic systems of ancient and non-Western societies. Described economic histories of Kingdom of Dahomey. Source: Am Anth 67:1508-11 D '65.

2577 POLEMAN, HORACE IRVIN (1905-1965), Philadelphia, Pennsylvania, United States. Librarian, Orientalist. Developed South Asia collection at Library of Congress and was instrumental in setting up PL480 program; contributed bibliographies of materials on India and Tibet. Sources: Biog Index: 7 & 9/Nat Cyc Am Biog 53:202 '71.

2578 POLI, ODDONE C (1907-). Sociologist. Sociology of the U.S. Source: Int Dir Anth 5.

2579 POLIKARPOVICH, KONSTANTIN MIKHAILOVICH (1889-1963), Belaia Dubrovska, Belorussia. Archeologist. Archeology of Belorussia. Source: Great Soviet Encyclopedia, New York, Macmillan (1979), v. 20, p 327.

2580 POLLOCK, HARRY EVELYN DORR (1900-), Utah, United States. Anthropologist. Interested in archeology of Middle America; survey of Maya architecture. Sources: Int Dir Anth 1 2 3/Nat Dir Lat Am.

2581 POLO, MARCO (ca. 1254-1324), Venice, Italy. Traveler, merchant. Described 13th century China and much of rest of Asia. Source: Columbia.

2582 POMPONAZZI, PIETRO (1462-1525), Mantua, Italy. Philosopher. Wrote: *De Incantationibus*, in which he stressed the evolution of man and nature. Sources: Columbia/New Int Enc, 1914 ed.

2583 POND, ALONZO WILLIAM (1894-), Janesville, Wisconsin, United States. Author, archeologist. Ethnology and archeology of desert areas. Sources: Biog Index: 10/Int Dir Anth 1 2 3.

2584 PONS, JOSÉ (1918-). Biostatistician, physical anthropologist. Dermatoglyphs, craniology & blood groups in Spain. Source: Int Dir Anth 5.

2585 POP, MIHAI (1907-). Ethno-sociologist. Romanian ethno-sociology. European ethnology & mythology. Source: Int Dir Anth 5.

2586 POPE, ARTHUR UPHAM (1881-1969), Phoenix, Rhode Island, United States. Orientalist. Specialist on art & culture of Persian empire; created a comprehensive survey of Persian art. Sources: Biog Index: 1 & 8/N Y Times p 47 S 4 '69.

2587 POPE, GUSTAVUS D (1911-), Detroit, Michigan, United States. Archeologist. Archeology of the New England area. Sources: Int Dir Anth 3, 5.

2588 POPE, J KEITH (1919-). Archeologist. Sources: Biog Index: 12/ Pope, J. Keith. Decade of adventure. Rose Print, Co. '79.

2589 POPE, SAXTON TEMPLE (1875-1926), Texas, United States. Surgeon, archer. Published on the medical history of the Ishi the last Yahi Indian, and bow & arrow technology. Source: Am Anth 29:341-342 '27.

2590 POPESCU, DORIN (1904-), Faget, Severin, Romania. Archeologist. Bronze Age cultures of Romania. Sources: Int Dir Anth 1, 2, 5.

2591 PORADA, EDITH (1912-). Art historian, archeologist. Specialist in Near Eastern & Greek seals and their cultural significance; established this field as a part of Near East archeology. Sources: Biog Index: 11/Am J Arch 82:248 Spr '78.

2592 PORRAS GARCES, PEDRO IGNACIO (1915-). Archeologist. Petroglyphs of the upper Napo Valley in Ecuador. Source: Int Dir Anth 5.

2593 PORTER, LUCIUS CHAPIN (1880-1958), Tientsin, China. Sinologist, missionary. Wrote about Chinese history and philosophy. Sources: Biog Index: 1 5 & 7/Nat

Cyc Am Biog 47:162 '65.

2594 POSNANSKY, ARTURO (1878-1946), Poland. Archeologist, soldier. Amateur archeologist who excavated at Tiahuanaco (Bolivia). Sources: Biog Index: 1/Int Dir Anth 1/Heath, Dwight B., Historical Dictionary of Bolivia (1972), p 143/N Y Times p 21 Jl 30 '46.

2595 POSSELT, FRIEDRICH WILHELM (-1950). Ethnographer. Wrote a large number of books and articles on the Ndebele and Shona of Rhodesia. Source: Rasmussen, R. Kent, Historical Dictionary of Rhodesia/Zimbabwe (1979), p 253.

2596 POTEKHIN, IVAN IZOSIMOVICH (1903-1974), Krivosheino, Krasnoiarsk Krai, Russia. Anthropologist. One of founders of Soviet African studies; works focused on modern history, economics and ethnography. Source: Great Soviet Encyclopedia, New York, Macmillan (1979), v. 20, p 473.

2597 POTIER, S J, Fr. NICOLAS (Jean) (1642-1689), Chauny, Ausne, France. Priest. Missionary in New France; wrote on N. American Indians. Source: Jes Rel.

2598 POTIER, S J, Fr. PIERRE (1708-1781), Blandain, France. Priest. Missionary in New France; wrote on N. American Indians. Source: Jes Rel.

2599 POTOCKI, JAN HRABIA (1761-1815). Historian, archeologist. Source: Biog Index: 7.

2600 POTTIER, EDMOND (1855-1934). Archeologist. Editor of *Revue Archeologique*. Sources: Biog Index: 6/Rev Arch II:v-xvii 1934.

2601 POUGET, JEAN FRANÇOIS ALBERT du (Maruis de Nadaillac) (ca. 1818-1904). Public servant. Published widely on the prehistoric Americas, archeology of Africa and Europe, and ethnology. Source: Am Anth 7:169-170.

2602 POULÍK, JOSEF (1910-), Czechoslovakia. Archeologist. Slavic culture of Moravia (Czechoslovakia). Source: Great Soviet Encyclopedia, New York, Macmillan (1979), v. 20, p 484.

2603 POULSEN, FREDERIK (1876-1951), Jutland, Denmark. Archeologist. Wrote widely on Classical Greek & Roman culture. Sources: Am J Arch 56:182-3 Jl '52/Rev Arch series 6 41:197-9 '53.

2604 POUNAH, PAUL-VINCENT (1914-), Lambarene, Gabon. Author. Specialist on the folklore and history of the Galoa people and the Moyen-Ogooue province of Gabon. Source: Gardiner, David E., Historical Dictionary of Gabon (1981), p 165.

2605 POUND, ALONZO W (1894-1986). Archeologist. Led expeditions to the Sahara, North Africa. Specialist in deserts & lithic studies. Source: Anth News 28:3:4.

2606 POUND, LESLIE (1872-1958). Philologist, folklorist. Sources: Biog Index: 3 4 5 6 & 13.

2607 POUND, LOUISE (1872-1958). Philologist, folklorist. Sources: Biog Index: 3 4 5 6 & 13/ Notable American Women, the Modern Period. vol. IV, Belknap Press '80, p 557-9.

2608 POURCHET, MARIA JULIA (1906-), Rio de Janeiro, Brazil. Bio-anthropologist, anthropometrist. Human biology & bio-social interrelations among indigenous groups in Brazil. Sources: Int Dir Anth 3, 5.

2609 POWDERMAKER, HORTENSE (1903- 1970), Philadelphia, Pennsylvania, United States. Anthropologist. Fieldwork and writing on New Ireland, Mississippi, and Zambia. Interested in race relations & labor issues. Her study of Indianola, Mississippi is one of the first anthropological studies of a modern U.S. community. Sources: Biog Index: 1 5 6 7 8 9 10 & 13/ Notable American Women, the Modern Period. vol. IV, Belknap Press '80, p 559-61/ Am Anth 73:783-7 Je '71.

2610 POWELL, JOHN WESLEY (1834-1902), Mt. Morris, New York, United States. Ethnologist, geologist, soldier, public servant. Led explorations of the Southwest U.S. for the Bureau of American Ethnology. Sources: Columbia/Am Anth

4:564-5 Jl '02.

2611 POWELL, THOMAS GEORGE EYRE (1913-1975). Art historian, archeologist. Studied megaliths of Wales, Ireland, Brittany and England; Celtic art and archeology. Sources: Biog Index: 11/Antiquity 49:247-8 D '75.

2612 PRADEL, LOUIS (1906-). Archeologist. Mousterian & Upper Paleolithic archeology in France. Source: Int Dir Anth 5.

2613 PRADERE, BERTRAND (1861-1949). Archeologist. Conservator of Musee Alaoui in Tunis (Tunisia), which he helped transform into a major museum for North American Antiquities. Sources: Biog Index: 3/Rev Arch series 6 40:68-9 Jl '52.

2614 PRASCHNIKER, CAMILLO (1884-1949). Archeologist. Director of the Austrian Archeological Institute; an authority on classical Greek sculpture who made investigations of the work of Phidias and his pupil Alkamenes. Sources: Biog Index: 2/Am J Arch 54:253 Jl '50.

2615 PRESTON, IRA (1818-1886), Danvers, Massachusetts, United States. Missionary. Languages of Gabon. First to reduce Bakele language (Dikele) to writing and did pioneering linguistic work on the Fang language; translated scriptures into Dikele. Source: Gardiner, David E., Historical Dictionary of Gabon (1981), p 165-6.

2616 PREUSS, KONRAD THEODOR (ca. 1857-1938). Anthropologist. Director of the Museum fur Volkerkunde, Berlin. Wrote on anthropology of Middle America. Source: Am Anth 41:173 Jl '39.

2617 PRICE, MAURICE THOMAS (1888-1964), United States. Anthropologist. Contributed to the understanding of the necessity for recognizing Indian social & cultural institutions. Worked with the Bureau of Indian Affairs. Sources: Biog Index: 6 & 7/American Sociological Review 29:581 Ag '64/ Am Anth 70:943 O '68.

2618 PRIETO, JUSTO (1897-), Paraguay. Sociologist. Authored a sociological study of Paraguay. Source: Kolinski, Charles J., Historical Dictionary of Paraguay (1973), p 197.

2619 PRIMOVSKI, ANASTAS (1911-), Bulgaria. Ethnologist, folklorist. Bulgarian ethnography & folklore. Source: Int Dir Anth 5.

2620 PROPP, VLADIMIR JAKOVLEVIC (1895-1970), Russia. Folklorist. Specialized in the analysis of plot and structure in folktales, using 1500 Russian specimens as a basis. Sources: Biog Index: 9 & 11/Film Quarterly 30:19-28 Spr '77.

2621 PROSKOURIAKOFF, TATIANA (1909-1985), Siberia. Anthropologist, archeologist. Mayan art & epigraphy, history of the lowland Maya based on inscriptions. Sources: Int Dir Anth 2, 5/Nat Dir Lat Am/Am Anth 11/85:3.

2622 PROVINSE, JOHN HENRY (1897-1965), Carbon County, Montana, United States. Anthropologist, soil conservationist. Ethnology and applied anthropology of N. America; applied social science especially in its relationship to government. Focused on bringing anthropology to bear on practical human problems such as Indian affairs in the U.S. & community development in Egypt & the Philippines; studied acculturation in Borneo & social control in Plains Indian (U.S.) cultures. Sources: Biog Index: 7/Int Dir Anth 1 2 3/Am Anth 68:990-4 Ag '66.

2623 PRUDDEN, THEOPHIL MITCHELL. Scientific research administrator. Mapped, surveyed, photographed & described archeological sites of the Southwestern U.S. during late 19th century, particularly pueblos and cliff dwellings; first to describe early Basket Maker culture & identify the old "unit-type" of pueblo structure; founded archeological expeditions; focused on San Juan watershed (Colorado, Utah, Arizona). Source: Am Anth 27:149-50 Ja '25.

2624 PRZEWORSKA (Rosen-Przeworska), JANINA (1906-). Archeologist. History of primitive dress. Celtic archeology. Source: Nat Un Cat.
2625 PRZYLUSKI, JEAN (1885-1944). Orientalist. Annamite & Buddhist studies. Sources: Biog Index: 2/Rev Arch series 6 35:101-2 Ja '50.
2626 PUGIN, AUGUSTUS CHARLES (1762-1838). Archeologist, architect. Sources: Biog Index: 9 & 11/Connoisseur 198:118-23 Je '78.
2627 PUIG y CADAFALCH, JOSÉ (1867-1956), Mataro, Catalonia, Spain. Architect, archeologist. Specialist on Roman Spain; wrote widely on Greek and Roman archeological remains in all of Spain with emphasis on Catalonia. Sources: Biog Index: 4 & 5/Speculum 34:535-6 Jl '59.
2628 PUSINERI SCALA, CARLOS ALBERTO (1919-), Paraguay. Numismatist. Author of several works on Paraguayan archeology. Source: Kolinski, Charles J., Historical Dictionary of Paraguay (1973), p 200.
2629 PUTNAM, FREDERIC WARD (1839-1915), Salem, Massachusetts, United States. Anthropologist, naturalist, museum curator. Conducted archeological excavations in numerous states of the U.S. Curator of the Peabody Museum of American Archeology and Ethnology at Harvard; assembled first major collection of ethnographic materials from around the world for the World's Columbian Exposition, Chicago, 1893; became known as the "Father of American Archeology" and is credited with introducing and popularizing anthropology to the American public. Sources: Biog Index: 3 & 7/American Scientist 54:315 Aut '66/ Am Anth 17:712-8 O '15.
2630 PUTNAM, PATRICK TRACEY LOWELL (1904-1953), New York, United States. Anthropologist. Studied introduction of iron working and South American food plants into Africa; frontier between Bantu and non-Bantu languages in the Belgian Congo and links to pygmy languages. Sources: Biog Index: 3/Int Dir Anth 1 2/N Y Times p 23 D 29 '53.
2631 QUAIN, BUELL (-1939). Ethnologist. Published on Fijian poetry; worked in Brazil. Source: Am Anth 42:180 Ja '40.
2632 QUASTEN, JOHANNES (1900-). Priest, archeologist, educator. Sources: Biog Index: 1/Hoehn, Matthew, ed. Catholic Authors. St. Mary's Abbey '48 p 633.
2633 QUEN, S J, Fr. JEAN de (1603-1659), Amien, France. Priest. Missionary in New France; wrote on N. American Indians. Source: Jes Rel.
2634 QUENUM, MAXIMILIEN POSSEY BERRY (1911-). Wrote *Au Pays du Fon*: *Usages et Coutumes de Dahomey* (1938). Source: DeCalo, Samuel, Historical Dictionary of Dahomey (1976), p 107.
2635 QUIMBY, GEORGE IRVING (1913-), Grand Rapids, Michigan, United States. Museologist. Hawaiians in American fur trade. American museums. Sources: Int Dir Anth 3, 5.
2636 QUIQUANDON, F. Explorer, administrator. Left detailed descriptions of the Sikasso area of Mali in late 19th century. Source: Imperato, Pascal J., Historical Dictionary of Mali (1977), p 85.
2637 QUIROGA, ADAN (1863-1904), San Juan, Argentina. Archeologist, folklorist. Did archeological work in the province of Catamarca and Tucuanan (Argentina); collected & preserved folklore literature of the Argentine northwest. Source: Wright & Nelsham, Historical Dictionary of Argentina (1978), p 745.
2638 QUIRÓS, PEDRO FERNANDEZ de (ca. 1565-1615), Evora, Portugal. Explorer. Led an expedition to the Tuamotu Archipelago and New Hebrides in 1605-1606. Source: Craig & King, Historical Dictionary of Oceania (1981), p 248-9.
2639 RABEL-HEYMANN, LILI (1913-).

Linguist. Description of Khasi language of Assam, India. Methodology of foreign language teaching. Source: Int Dir Anth 5.

2640 RABIN, EMILY (1917-). Ethnohistorian. Zapotec writing & Mixtec codices. Ethnohistory of Mexico. Source: Int Dir Anth 5.

2641 RACHLIN, CAROL K (1919-). Ethnologist. Prehistoric & historic U.S. Indian weaving. Source: Int Dir Anth 5.

2642 RADCLIFFE-BROWN, ALFRED REGINALD (1881-1955), Warwickshire, England. Anthropologist, ethnologist. A major figure in social anthropology. Did fieldwork in Australia, Andaman Islands, and Africa, among American Indians. Believed in scientific study of societies. Sources: Biog Index: 1 4 & 13/Int Dir Anth 1 2 3/ Makers of Modern Culture. Facts on File '81, p 431/Am Anth 58:544-7 Je '56.

2643 RADET, GEORGES ALBERT (1859-1941), France. Archeologist. Archeology of Hellenic Anatolia (Turkey). Sources: Biog Index: 2/Rev Arch series 6 34:66-7 Jl '49.

2644 RADIN, PAUL (1883-1959), Lodz, Poland. Anthropologist, ethnologist. Expert on ethnography of Indians of North and South America; 17 books. Specialized in religion and mythology, particularly among the Winnebago; emphasized an empirical approach & depended largely upon native documents, texts secured from informants. Sources: Biog Index: 5/Int Dir Anth 1 2/Am Anth 61:839-43 O '59/ Journal of American Folklore 74:65-7 Ja '61/N Y Times p 88 F 22 '59/ Wilson Library Bulletin 33:560 Ap '59.

2645 RADLOFF, FRIEDRICH WILHELM (1837-ca. 1920), Berlin, Germany. Museum director. Specialist in Turkic culture, the Altaian & Kirghiz tribes & West Siberian shamanism. Source: Am Anth 22:308 Jl '20.

2646 RADLOV, VASILII VASIL'EVICH (1837-1918), Berlin, Germany. Archeologist, ethnologist. Gathered information on all aspects of the Turkic peoples, with special emphasis on their language. Sources: Great Soviet Encyclopedia, New York, Macmillan (1978), v. 21, p 461/Biobibliograficheskii slovar' otechestvennykh tiurkologov, Moscow, 1974.

2647 RAFFEIX, S J, Fr. PIERRE (1635-1724), Clermont, France. Priest. Missionary in New France; wrote on N. American Indians. Source: Jes Rel.

2648 RAGLAN, FITZ ROY RICHARD SOMERSET (1885-1964), London, England. Anthropologist. Social anthropology, military & political employment in Middle East; general ethnology, archeology, linguistics and folklore. Sources: Biog Index: 4 & 7/Int Dir Anth 2 3/ Illustrated London News 254:475 526 '64/N Y Times p 37 S 15 '64/ Newsweek 64:67 S 28 '64/Publishers Weekly 186:49 O 5 '64/Time 84:97 S 25 '64.

2649 RAGUENEAU, S J, Fr. PAUL (1608-1680), Paris, France. Priest. Missionary in New France; wrote on N. American Indians. Source: Jes Rel.

2650 RAHDER, JOHANNES (1898-), Loeboeg, Begalung, Netherlands. Linguist. Comparative linguistics & religion. Philosophy, literature and history of the Japanese Middle Ages. Sources: Int Dir Anth 1, 2, 5.

2651 RAHMANN, RUDOLF (1902-), Germany. Historian, folklorist. Philippine folklore, religion & shamanism. India. Ethnology of South & East Asia. Sources: Int Dir Anth 2, 5.

2652 RAINEY, FROELICH GLADSTONE (1907-). Anthropologist. Archeological research in Arctic and West Indies, ethnological research in the Arctic & North America. Sources: Biog Index: 1 7 8 & 11/Int Dir Anth 1 2 3/Expedition 18:2 Sum '76.

2653 RAJEWSKI, ZDZISŁAW ADAM (1907-), Dubin, Poland. Anthropologist, museologist. Central

European settlements & culture of the Hallstatt period. Slavic history, anthropology, ethnology, Polish literature and economics. Studied treatment of bone and horn in protohistory. Sources: Int Dir Anth 1, 2, 3, 5.

2654 RALE (Rasles, Racles), S J, Fr. SEBASTIEN (1657-1724), Pontarlier, France. Priest. Missionary in New France; wrote on N. American Indians. Source: Jes Rel.

2655 RAMNEANTZU, PETER (1902-), Timisoara, Romania. Ethnologist, physician, anthropologist. Aging, constitution & diseases in Romanian ethnic groups. Sources: Int Dir Anth 3, 5.

2656 RAMÓN y RIVERA, LUÍS FELIPE (1913-), San Cristobal, Venezuela. Folklorist, museum director. Director, Venezuelan National Institute of Folklore. Worked with wife, Isabel Ortez, in researching and recording as much folkmusic as possible. Sources: Biog Index: 4/Americas 8:15-20 S '56.

2657 RAMOS, JOSÉ LUÍS (1790-1849), Venezuela. Educator. Authored several grammars & dictionaries of Venezuelan Spanish. Source: Nat Un Cat.

2658 RAMSAY, WILLIAM MITCHELL (1851-1939), Glasgow, Scotland. Classical archeologist. Specialized in Asia Minor; contributed to the historical geography of this region. Sources: Biog Index: 2 & 7/Dictionary of National Biography, '49.

2659 RAMSKOU, THORKILD LOUISON (1915-). Historian. Viking Period (700/1100 AD) of Northern Europe. Source: Int Dir Anth 5.

2660 RAMSTEDT, GUSTAF JOHN (1873-1950), Tammisaari, Finland. Orientalist. Founder of Mongolian dialectology and Altaic linguistics; wrote on the phonology of the Khalkha-Mongolian language; published a Kalmuck dictionary, the first scientific dictionary of that language; also studied the language of the Mongols of Afghanistan. Sources: Biog Index: 2/Harvard Journal of Asiatic Studies 14:315-22 Je '51.

2661 RANDALL, FRANCIS EUGENE (1914-1949), New Philadelphia, Ohio, United States. Applied physical anthropologist. Specialist in the practical applications of anthropometric data in the military; developed a data bank in anthropometry from survey of 109,000 people, which was used to address military clothing and equipment problems. Sources: Biog Index: 2/Science 110:578 N 25 '49/Am Anth 52:243-4 Ap '50.

2662 RANDALL-MACIVER, DAVID (1873- 1945), England. Archeologist, librarian. Classical archeology and prehistoric anthropology. First trained archeologist to work in Zimbabwe, his work demonstrated African origins of Great Zimbabwe. Sources: Biog Index: 1 2 & 5/Int Dir Anth 2/ Dictionary of National Biography 1941-1950:709-10 '59/Rasmussen, R. Kent, Historical Dictionary of Rhodesia/Zimbabwe (1979), p 259-60/ Chronique d'Egypte, Ja '46.

2663 RANDLE, MARTHA CHAMPION (1910-1965), Los Angeles, California, United States. Anthropologist, musicologist. One of the first investigators of Peyote music; focused on N. American Indians, particularly the Iroquois. Sources: Biog Index: 7/Am Anth 68:995-6 Ag '66.

2664 RANDOLPH, VANCE (1892-). Folklorist. Sources: Biog Index: 3 & 4/ Kunitz, Stanley Jasspon ed., Twentieth Century Authors; 1st sup. Wilson '55 p 813-4.

2665 RANK, GUSTAV (1902-), Estonia. Ethnologist. Agricultural tools, plow. Popular architecture & lifestyles. Ethnology of N. America, Europe, N. & N.E. Asia. Sources: Int Dir Anth 3, 5.

2666 RANKE, HERMANN (1878-1953), Germany. Egyptologist, museum curator. Curator of the Egyptian Section of the University Museum, Univ. of Pennsylvania; in 1911, translated James H. Breasted's *History of Egypt* into German;

prepared a new edition of Adolf Erman's *Aegypten und Aegyptisches Leben in Altertum* in 1885 with an English edition in 1894 entitled *Life in Ancient Egypt*. Sources: Biog Index: 3/ Pennsylvania University Museum Bullletin 17:57 Dec '53.

2667 RAPONDA-WALKER, ANDRÉ (1871- 1968). Priest. Leading native Gabonese scholar; extensive publications on peoples, languages and botany; notable for anthropologists is the *Rites et Croyances des Peuples du Gabon* (1962). Source: Gardiner, David E., Historical Dictionary of Gabon (1981), p 194.

2668 RASMUSSEN, HOLGER (1915-), Reero, Denmark. Ethnologist, museologist. Fishing & peasant culture in Denmark. Ethnology, archeology and folklore of Europe. Sources: Int Dir Anth 3, 5.

2669 RASMUSSEN, KNUD JOHAN VICTOR (1879-1933), Jakobshaun, Greenland. Ethnologist, explorer. Expert on the group with which he identified, namely, the Inuit; sought origins of Inuit peoples; collected folklore, described religion, recorded biographies in several Inuit groups. Sources: Biog Index: 5 & 11/ Rasky, Frank. North Pole or bust. McGraw '77 p 358-83/Am Anth 36:585-94 O '34.

2670 RASPE, RUDOLF ERICH (1737-1794). Archeologist. Sources: Biog Index: 2 3 4 5 & 8.

2671 RATTRAY, ROBERT SUTHERLAND (1881-1938). British colonial officer, anthropologist. Wrote important ethnographies of Hausa (of Nigeria) and of Ashanti (of Ghana). Sources: Who Was Who, 1929-1940/Am Anth 41:130-1 Ap '39.

2672 RAULIN, HENRI (1918-). Ethnologist. Evolution of traditional African agricultural organization. Source: Int Dir Anth 5.

2673 RAVDONIKAS, VLADISLAV IOSIFOVICH (1894-1976), Tikhvn, Russia. Archeologist, historian. Archeology of northwestern Russia. Source: Great Soviet Encyclopedia, New York, Macmillan (1978), v. 21, p 509.

2674 RAWLINSON, HENRY CRESWICKE (1810-1895), England. Government official, Orientalist. Sources: Biog Index: 7 & 8.

2675 RAY, GAUTAM, SANKAR (1919-). Archeologist. Prehistoric & contemporary pottery in India. Source: Int Dir Anth 5.

2676 RAYFIELD, JOAN RACHEL (1919-). Anthropologist. Structure of oral narrative. Rural & urban migration. Source: Int Dir Anth 5.

2677 READE, WILLIAM WINWOOD (1838-1873). Explorer. Wrote three travel accounts of West Africa, describing among other places, Sierra Leone. Source: Foray, Cyril P., Historical Dictionary of Sierra Leone (1977), p 182-3.

2678 REAGAN, ALBERT B (1871-1936). Civil servant. Specialist in ethnology & archeology of American Indian peoples. Source: Am Anth 39:187 Ja '37.

2679 REAL y RAMOS, CARLOS ALONSO DEL (1914-). Prehistoric sociology, prehistoric religion & Paleolithic art of Europe, Siberia, Africa and Asia. Source: Int Dir Anth 5.

2680 RECINOS, ADRIAN (1886-1962), Guatemala. Historian. Wrote a treatment of the Popol Vuh and a history of the Huehuetenango area of Guatemala. Source: Moore, Richard E., Historical Dictionary of Guatemala (1973), p 171.

2681 REDFIELD, MARGARET PARK (1899-1977). Anthropologist. Specialist in folklore of the Yucatan peninsula; did work on the American family and China. Sources: Biog Index: 11/N Y Times p 34 F 8 '77.

2682 REDFIELD, ROBERT (1897-1958), Chicago, Illinois, United States. Anthropologist, sociologist. Ethnology of Middle America, especially Mexico and Guatemala. Social anthropology of "Folk" peoples. Comparative study of civilizations. Sources: Int Dir Anth 1 2 3/Biog Index: 3 4 5 & 6/

Nat Cyc Am Biog 44:76-7 '62/Columbia/Am Anth 61:652-62 Ag '59.

2683 REDHOUSE, JAMES WILLIAM (1811-1892), Suffolk, England. Orientalist. Turkish lexicography. Major work, *Turkish and English Lexicon*, published in 1890. Sources: Biog Index: 2 & 12/American Oriental Society Journal 99:573 O '79.

2684 REDINHA, JOSÉ PEDRO DOMINGUES (1905-). Sociologist. Ethno-sociology of Angola. Source: Int Dir Anth 5.

2685 REED, ALMA M (-1966). Archeologist. Excavated in Yucatan in the 1920s; author of several books in Mexico. Sources: Biog Index: 7/N Y Times p 45 N 21 '66.

2686 REED, CHARLES A (1912-). Bibliographer, anthropologist, primatologist. Primate evolution; early animal domestication. Agricultural origins. Source: Int Dir Anth 5.

2687 REED, ERIK KELLERMAN (1914-), Quincy, Massachusetts, United States. Archeologist. Archeology & prehistoric Southwest U.S. Sources: Int Dir Anth 1, 2, 3, 5/Nat Dir Lat Am.

2688 REED, FREDERICK RICHARD COWPER (1869-1946), England. Paleontologist, geologist. Geological Survey of India. Sources: Biog Index: 1/Nature 157:400 Mr 30 '46/es; worked for the.

2689 REEVE, HENRY. General work on the Gambian region in the early 20th century. Source: Gailey, Harry A., Historical Dictionary of Gambia" (1975), p 106.

2690 REGNAUT (Renant, Renaut), S J, Br. CHRISTOPHE (1613-1697), Paris, France. Priest. Missionary in New France; wrote on N. American Indians. Source: Jes Rel.

2691 REICHARD, GLADYS AMANDA (1893-1955), Bangor, Pennsylvania, United States. Anthropologist, folklorist, linguist. Primitive arts, languages, religion, especially of Navajo Indians. Also studied Melanesian design, Coeur d'Alene mythology, and Salish linguistics. Sources: Biog Index: 4 & 13/Int Dir Anth 1 2 3/ Notable American Women, the Modern Period. vol. IV, Belknap Press '80, p 573-4/ Am Anth 58:913-6 O '56/Journal of American Folklore 69:53-4 Ja '56/ N Y Times p 25 Jl 26 '55/Plateau 28:48 O '55.

2692 REICHEL-DOLMATOFF, GERARDO (1912-). Archeologist. Colombian archeology, chronology & early ceramics. Source: Int Dir Anth 5.

2693 REINING, CONRAD C (1918-). Anthropologist. Tropical agricultural E. African development. Source: Int Dir Anth 5.

2694 REISNER, GEORGE ANDREW (1867- 1942). Egyptologist. Sources: Biog Index: 2 & 9.

2695 REITER, PAUL DAVID (1909-1953), Pittsburgh, Pennsylvania, United States. Anthropologist, archeologist. Interested in archeology of S.W. United States. Researched Pueblo population of Chaco Canyon, physical anthropology of children of Rh-crossed parents. Escavated near Lincoln, New Mexico, and researched Jemez Cave, New Mexico. Primarily an archeologist, he utilized the perspectives of physical anthropology & ethnology. Maintained that pit houses and great Kivas were derived from the Old World. Sources: Biog Index: 3/Int Dir Anth 1 2 3/Am Anth 56:1085-7 D '54/ Am Antiq 19:67-8 Jl '53.

2696 RELLINI, UGO (1870-1943), Florence, Italy. Archeologist. Prehistoric anthropology, researched Paleolithic, Mesolithic, & Neolithic and civilizations of the Bronze Ages. Sources: Biog Index: 2/Int Dir Anth 1 2/Rev Arch series 6 34:71 Jl '49.

2697 REMESAL, ANTONIO de (1570-1627). Priest. Wrote a history of Guatemala which was very critical of the settlers' treatment of the Amerindians. Source: Moore, Richard E., Historical Dictionary of Guatemala" (1973), p 172.

2698 RENAUD, ÉTIENNE BERNARDEAU (1880-1973), Billancourt, France. Philologist, archeologist.

Archeology of Western Plains and Southwest U.S. in Paleolithic Old World and physical and racial anthropology. Studied religion of prehistoric Indians of Mexico. Source: Biog Index: 10/Int Dir Anth 1 2 3/French Review 47:613-4 F '74.

2699 RENÉ-MORENO, GABRIEL (1836-1908), Bolivia. Historian. Compiled a large collection of historical materials on Bolivia. Source: Heath, Dwight B., Historical Dictionary of Bolivia (1972), p 203.

2700 RENOUF, PETER Le PAGE (1822-1897), England. Egyptologist. Source: Biog Index: 4.

2701 REOHRIG, FREDERIC LOUIS OTTO (1819-1908), Prussia. Orientalist, philologist. Published on the Dakota Indians; specialist in Sanskrit. Source: Am Anth 10:502-503.

2702 REQUENA, RAFAEL (1876-1946), Carupano, Venezuela. Anthropologist, archeologist, physician. Excavated tombs in the Lake Valencia region of Venezuela in 1932, said Atlantis was founder of that culture. Sources: Biog Index: 1/N Y Times p 46 Ap 21 '46.

2703 RETZIUS, ANDERS (-1860). Anatomist. Founder of modern craniometry; classified human races on the cephalic-gnatic index basis; the first to recognize the mixed character of Europe's population and challenged the validity of the Aryan hypothesis. Source: Am Anth 22:173-177 '20.

2704 RETZIUS, GUSTAF (1842-1919), Stockholm, Sweden. Anatomist, physical anthropologist. Pioneer physical anthropologist; specialized in craniology (particularly Finnish & Swedish skulls); described Finnish culture and Lapp distribution; prepared study of physical characteristics of 45,000 Swedes. Sources: Biog Index: 9/Am Anth 21:345, 22:173-7 Ap '20.

2705 REY, LÉON (1887-1954), Faremoutiers, France. Archeologist. Led excavations in Greece and Albania. Sources: Biog Index: 4/Rev Arch series 6 47:202-4 Ap '56.

2706 REYNOLDS, HARRIET ROBERTSON (1910-). Missionary, ethnologist. Philippine kinship & social structure. Source: Int Dir Anth 5.

2707 REYNOLDS, I HUBERT (1914-). Missionary, ethnologist. Acculturation in Philippine minority groups. Source: Int Dir Anth 5.

2708 RIBAS, OSCAR BENTE (1909-), Luanda, Angola. Writer. Published collections of Angolan folktales. Source: Martin, Phyllis M., Historical Dictionary of Angola (1980), p 77-8.

2709 RIBEIRO, RENE (1914-), Recife, Brazil. Ethnologist. Afro-Brazilian cult groups & messianic movements. Influence of African family patterns on the Recife Negro family. Sources: Int Dir Anth 3, 5.

2710 RIBERO, JUAN de (1681-1736), Spain. Missionary. Left an account of the Jesuit missions at the Orinoco and Meta Rivers and in the plains of Casanare (Colombia). Source: Davis, Robert H., Historical Dictionary of Colombia (1977), p 192.

2711 RICCI, S J, Fr. MATTEO (1552-1610), Italy. Missionary to China. Brought many facets of Western culture to China and reported on Chinese culture to West. Source: Columbia.

2712 RICE, DAVID TALBOT (1903-1972). Archeologist, art historian. Sources: Biog Index: 9 & 10/Britannica Book of the Year 1973:516 '73.

2713 RICHARDS, AUDREY ISABEL (1899-1984), London, England. Sociologist. Fieldwork among the Bemba of Zambia and Ganda of Uganda. Director and founder of the Institute of Social Research in East Africa. Comparison of Zambians with other Bantu. Subsistence, nutrition, and socialization of women. Sources: Int Dir Anth 1 2 3/ International Encyclopedia of the Social Sciences, v. 18/ American Ethnologist 13:2(1986):338-362.

2714 RICHMOND, IAN ARCHIBALD (1902-1965), Rochdale, Lancashire, England. Archeologist. Specialized on archeology of Roman Britain and in particular military sites; extensive publications. Sources: Biog Index: 4 & 7/Int Dir Anth 2/Am J Arch 70:179 Ap '66/ Journal of Roman Studies 55:xiii-xiv '65/Nature 208:831 N 27 '65.

2715 RICKETSON, EDITH HILL BAYLES (1899-1976). Archeologist. Interested in Mayan ceramics and in Guatemalan textiles. Sources: Biog Index: 12/Int Dir Anth 1 2/Am Antiq 43:615-17 O '79.

2716 RICKETSON, OLIVER GARRISON (1894-1952), Pennsylvania, United States. Archeologist. Middle American archeology and geography, researched pre-Columbian geography of Middle America. Sources: Biog Index: 3/Int Dir Anth 1 2/N Y Times p 87 O 19 '52/ Am Antiq 19:69-72 Jl '53.

2717 RIEFSTAHL, ELIZABETH (1889-1986). Egyptologist, museum curator. Specialized in ancient art, especially that of Egypt of 13th century, B.C. Source: Anth News 27:8:4.

2718 RIESENBERG, SAUL H (1911-), Newark, New Jersey, United States. Ethnohistorian. Aboriginal ethnohistory & political structure in Micronesia. Sources: Int Dir Anth 3, 5.

2719 RIIS, POUL JORGEN (1910-), Denmark. Archeologist. Classical art & archeology of Greece, Italy & Syria. Sources: Int Dir Anth 2, 3, 5.

2720 RINCHEN, YONGSIYEBU (1905-). Linguist. Grammar of written & spoken Mongolian. Mongolian shamanism. Source: Int Dir Anth 5.

2721 RIPAULT, LOUIS MADELEINE (1775-1823), France. Orientalist. Went with Napoleon to Egypt. Sources: Biog Index: 10/Wilson Library Bulletin 49:229 N '74.

2722 RITCHIE, WILLIAM AUGUSTUS (1903-), Rochester, New York, United States. Archeologist. Prehistoric archeology & physical anthropology of Northeast U.S.; interested in general European archeology. Did extensive excavations in New York & Pennsylvania. Researched cultural manifestations and chronology of N.E. North American Indians; paleopathology of New York Indians. Sources: Biog Index: 1/Int Dir Anth 1, 2, 3, 5/Hobbies 53:157 N '48.

2723 RITTER, DALE WILLIAM (1919-). Archeologist, ethnologist. Petroglyphs, pictographs & prehistoric medicine. Source: Int Dir Anth 5.

2724 RITTER, KARL (1779-1859), Quedlinburg, Prussia. Geographer. A founder of modern human geography. He emphasized the influence of natural environment on the development and activities of man. Sources: Columbia/New Int Enc, 1914 ed.

2725 RITZENTHALER, ROBERT EUGENE (1911-1980), Milwaukee, Wisconsin, United States. Archeologist, medical anthropologist. Worked with Ojibwa studying effects of change & urbanism. First ethnographic study of Kickapoo of Mexico. Primitive art & medicine of N. American Indians. Polynesian ethnology; Chippewa health, Palau native wealth. Sources: Int Dir Anth 2, 3, 5/Am Anth 83:607-11 S '81.

2726 RIVAS, PEDRO (1889-1955). Anthropologist. Sources: Biog Index: 4/Revista Interamericana de Bibliografia 5:137 Ja '55.

2727 RIVERS, WILLIAM HALSE R (1864-1922), Luton, Kent, England. Anthropologist, physician. Medical anthropology. Sources: Biog Index: 11 & 13/Slobodin, Richard, W.H.R. Rivers, New York, Columbia Univ. Press (1978)/Makers of Modern Culture. Facts on File '81, p 445/ Zusne, L., Biographical Dictionary of Psychology, Westport, Conn., Greenwood, 1984/Am Anth 24:117 Ja '22.

2728 RIVET, PAUL (1876-1958), France. Anthropologist, physician, ethnographer. American ethnology and linguistics. Published on the archeology & ethnology of Ecuador, several languages of South American Indians, and metallurgy in pre-Columbian America. Founded Societe des Americanistes and other anthropological study centers and international institutions. Sources: Biog Index: 4 & 5/Int Dir Anth 1 2/Am Anth 60:1180-1 D '58.

2729 RIVIÈRE, GEORGES HENRI (1897-1985). Musicologist. Brought together folklore and anthropology in France. Source: Anth News 10/85.

2730 ROBERTS, FRANK HAROLD HANNA, Jr (1897-1966), Centerburg, Ohio, United States. Archeologist, ethnologist, civil servant. American archeology and ethnology. Specialized in Southwestern U.S. cultures; authority on early humans in North America; last director of Bureau of American Ethnology. Produced archeological survey of U.S. river basins which would be flooded by dam construction. Excavated at Pueblo Bonito (New Mexico) & Lindenmeier site (Colorado). Sources: Biog Index: 7/Int Dir Anth 1 2 3/Am Anth 68:1226-32 O '66.

2731 ROBERTS, HENRY BUCHTEL (1903- 1960). Archeologist. Conducted excavations in Mexico & Central America in 1930s; discovered Cocle gold-working culture of Panama. Sources: Biog Index: 5 & 13/Int Dir Anth 1 2/N Y Times p 37 Ap 5 '60.

2732 ROBERTS, JOHN MILTON (1916-), Omaha, Nebraska, United States. Anthropologist, linguist. Legal & psychological aspects of U.S. games & folktales. Sources: Int Dir Anth 3, 5.

2733 ROBERTS, ORLANDO W. Trader. Wrote an account of his experiences trading from Panama to Honduras which contains much ethnographic information. Source: Meyer, Harvey K., Historical Dictionary of Honduras (1976), p 305.

2734 ROBERTS, ROBERT E T (1915-). Ethnologist, anthropologist. Comparative analysis of inter-caste & inter-racial marriage. Source: Int Dir Anth 5.

2735 ROBESON, ESLANDA CARDOZA (Goode) (1896-1965). Anthropologist. Sources: Biog Index: 1 7 & 13/ Notable American Women, the Modern Period. vol. IV, Belknap Press '80, p 583-4.

2736 ROBINSON, DAVID MOORE (1880-1958). Archeologist. Sources: Biog Index: 4 & 5/College Art Journal 18:76 Fall '58.

2737 ROCHE, JEAN (1913-). Paleontologist. Mesolithic shell hoards in Mediterranean & Portuguese areas. Sources: Int Dir Anth 2, 5.

2738 ROCK, MILES (1840-1901), Ephrata, Pennsylvania, United States. Civil engineer. Studied Indian pictographs in New Mexico. Source: Am Anth 3:208 Ja '01.

2739 RODAS CORZO, OVIDIO (1906-1955), Chichicastenango, Guatemala. Journalist. Wrote several volumes dealing with arts and legends of Guatemalan Indians. Source: Moore, Richard E., Historical Dictionary of Guatemala (1973), p 176.

2740 RODAS NORIEGA, FLAVIO (1882-), Chichicastenango, Guatemala. Ethnologist. Collaborated with Rodas Corzo on a book on Quiche Maya symbolism and did one of the earliest translations. Source: Moore, Richard E., Historical Dictionary of Guatemala (1973), p 176.

2741 RODENWALDT, GERHARD (1866-1945), Germany. Archeologist. Greek and Roman art, studied ancient sarcophagus reliefs. Sources: Biog Index: 1/Int Dir Anth 1 2/Am J Arch 50:405-6 Jl '46.

2742 RODINSON, MAXIME (1915-), Paris, France. Ethnologist, anthropologist. Ethno-alimentation. Demoniac possession. Magical medicine of Middle East. Islam. Ethiopia. Sources: Int Dir Anth 3, 5.

2743 RODNICK, DAVID (1909-), New Haven, Connecticut, United States. Anthropologist. Contemporary U.S. industrial civilization.

Researched acculturation among the Assiniboines of Fort Belknap Reservation, Montana. Sources: Int Dir Anth 1, 2, 3, 5.

2744 RODRÍGUES, JOSÉ BONIFACIO MARTINS (1915-). Anthropologist. Brazilian Indians. Urban anthropology of Brazil. Slum areas. Source: Int Dir Anth 5.

2745 RODRÍGUES, LUCIO (1915-). Folklorist. Christian folklore & folk music. English Literature. Source: Int Dir Anth 5.

2746 ROEHRIG, FREDERIC LOUIS OTTO (1819-1908), Halle, Prussia. Orientalist, philologist. Studied Dakota Indian language; published on the languages of California Indians. Source: Am Anth 10:502-3.

2747 ROERICH, NIKOLAI KONSTANTIN (1874-1947), St. Petersburg, Russia. Archeologist. Specialist on India, Tibet and Central Asia; expedition on a search for drought-resistant plants (1934-35); excavated at Pondicherry, India. Sources: Biog Index: 1 & 10/American Artist 38:32-6 D '74/ N Y Times p 33 D 16 '47.

2748 ROGACHEV, ALEKSANDR NIKOLAEVICH (1912-1984), Russia. Archeologist. Theoretical and methodological writings on archeology. Source: Anth News (Oct. 1984) p 3.

2749 ROGERS, DAVID BANKS (1868-1954), Paw Paw, Illinois, United States. Anthropologist. Wrote on Indians of Western U.S. Sources: Biog Index: 6/Int Dir Anth 1/Nat Cyc Am Biog 44:284-5 '62.

2750 ROGERS, MALCOLM JENNINGS (1890-1960), Fulton, New York, United States. Archeologist. Anthropology of S.W. United States, researched Yuman pottery. Sources: Int Dir Anth 1 2/Biog Index: 6/Am Anth 63:1323-4 D '61/ Am Antiq 26:532-4 Ap '61.

2751 ROGERS, SPENCER LEE (1905-), Topeka, Kansas, United States. Anthropologist. Craniometry. Osteometry. Aboriginal medicine. Southwestern agricultural folklore. Sources: Int Dir Anth 1, 2, 3, 5.

2752 ROGGEVEEN, JACOB (1659-1729), Middelburg, Zeeland, Netherlands. Explorer. Led a search for the mythical southern continent and visited Easter Island and the Tuamotu area. Source: Craig & King, Historical Dictionary of Oceania (1981), p 252.

2753 ROGINSKII, IAKOV IAKOVLEVICH (1895-), Mogilev, Russia. Anthropologist, biologist. Origin, classification, and variation in human morphology. Sources: Great Soviet Encyclopedia, New York, Macmillan (1979), v. 22, p 224/Zalkind, N.G. "75 let so dnia rozhdeniia Ia. Ia/ Roginskogo", Voprosi antropologii, 1970.

2754 ROHEIM, GEZA (1891-1953), Budapest, Hungary. Psychoanalyst, anthropologist. Psychology of primates, religion, myth and ritual of Australia and Melanesia. Conducted fieldwork in Papua New Guinea; regarded as founder of psychological anthropology. Sources: Biog Index: 2 3 & 7/Int Dir Anth 2 3/Craig & King, Historical Dictionary of Oceania (1981), p 252-3/Am Anth 55:420 Ag '53.

2755 ROHRLICH-LEAVITT, RUBY (1913-). Ethnologist. Cultural change in Puerto Rico. Women's cross-cultural roles & status. Source: Int Dir Anth 5.

2756 ROJAS, ARISTIDES (1826-1894), Venezuela. Writer. Wrote compilations of historical legends of Venezuela. Source: Rudolph & Rudolph, Historical Dictionary of Venazuela (1971), p 102.

2757 ROLAND, AUGUSTIN (1868-1943), France. Archeologist. Archeology of the Marne. Sources: Biog Index: 1/Rev Arch series 6 25-63 Ja '46.

2758 ROLLAND, HENRI (1887-1970), Nice, France. Archeologist. Excavated Glanum (France), a Roman town. Sources: Biog Index: 10/Rev Arch 2:299-302 '73.

2759 ROLLAND, PAUL (1896-1949), Tournai, Belgium. Archeologist, art historian. Specialist in presentation of historic sites and in Belgian archeology. Sources: Biog Index: 2/College Art Journal 10:60 Fall '50.

2760 ROMAIN, JEAN-BAPTISTE (1916-). Ethnologist. Physical anthropology. Haitian pre-Columbian ethnology. Primitive religion. Source: Int Dir Anth 5.

2761 ROMER, BELA J (1912-). Ethnologist. Geography. Food & primitive food technology. Source: Int Dir Anth 5.

2762 ROMERO, PABLO BUSH (1905-). Archeologist, diver. Source: Biog Index: 9.

2763 RONEY, JAMES G (1918-). Museologist, paleontologist. Folk medicine. Culture change in health care. Medical anthropology. Source: Int Dir Anth 5.

2764 ROONEY, MARIE (Collins) (ca. 1870-1949), Minnesota, United States. Folklorist. Specialist in American Indian folklore; collected tales and legends of the Sioux. Sources: Biog Index: 2/N Y Times p 21 D 23 '49.

2765 ROOT, WILLIAM CAMPBELL (1904- 1969). Archeologist. Specialist on pre-Columbian metallurgy; worked on materials from the Sacred Well at Chichen Itza (Mexico). Peru and Southwest U.S. Sources: Biog Index: 9/Am Antiq 35:363-4 Jl '70.

2766 ROPEID, ANDREAS (1916-). Folklorist, museologist. Cattle breeding & food economy in Norway. Source: Int Dir Anth 5.

2767 ROPITEAU, ANDRE (1904-1940), Bourguignon, France. Compiled a collection of books & documents relating to Tahiti which later was codified into a massive bibliography. Source: Craig & King, Historical Dictionary of Oceania (1981), p 253.

2768 ROSEN-PRZEWORSKA, JANINA (1906-). Archeologist. Source: Int Dir Anth 5.

2769 ROSS, EDWARD DENISON (1871-1940), London, England. Orientalist, linguist. Translated many historical works from Persian and Gujarati; numerous publications useful as background sources to fieldwork. Sources: Biog Index: 2/ Dictionary of National Biography 1931-1940:750-1 '49.

2770 ROSTOVTZEFF, MICHAEL IVANOVICH (1870-1952), Kiev, Russia. Historian, archeologist. Wrote widely on many subjects in Old World history and archeology. Sources: Biog Index: 3 & 4/Nat Cyc Am Biog 39:558-9 '54.

2771 ROTH, GEORGE KINGSLEY (1903-1960). Anthropologist, ethnologist, colonial administrator. Leading authority on Fiji. Sources: Biog Index: 6/Am Anth 64:822-825 Ag '62.

2772 ROTH, HENRY LING (1855-1925), London, England. Ethnologist. Wrote standard works of day on Tasmanian aborigines and natives of Sarawak and Borneo; also wrote on Benin. Sources: Biog Index: 2/Dictionary of Australian Biography 2:289-90 '49.

2773 ROTH, WALTER EDMUND (1861-1933), London, England. Ethnologist, civil servant. Aboriginal studies. Expert on the cultures of the natives of Western Australia, his work led to reform of the penal system there; expert on the Guyana Indians for whom he authored the Aboriginal Protection Acts; translated ethnographies about early British Guyana. Sources: Biog Index: 2 & 10/Oceania 46:20-21 S '75/ Am Anth 36:266-70 Ap '34.

2774 ROUCH, JEAN (1917-), Paris, France. Anthropologist, ethnologist, documentary filmmaker. Researched religion and magic of the Songhay and ethnography of other peoples of Mali and Niger. Made ethnographic films on Africans. Sources: Biog Index: 9 11 12 & 13-/Int Dir Anth 3, 5/DeCalo, Samuel, Historical Dictionary of Niger, p 196/Film Library Quarterly 11 no 4:21-23 '79/ Cinema, v. 2. Viking Press '80 p 901-9.

2775 ROUILLARD, GERMAINE (-1946), France. Egyptologist. Wrote: *L'administration civile de l'Egypte byzantine*, 1923; *Les papyrus grecs de Vienne*, 1923. Sources:

Biog Index: 1/Chronique d'Egypte 22:174-6 Ja '47.

2776 ROUSE, IRVING (1913-), Rochester, New York, United States. Anthropologist, archeologist, ethnohistorian. Ethnohistory & Caribbean prehistory. Sources: Biog Index: 5/Int Dir Anth 1, 2, 3, 5/Nat Dir Lat Am/ Am Antiq 25:289 Ap '60.

2777 ROUTLEDGE, KATHARINE (1866-1935), Darlington, Australia. Anthropologist. Led the first archeological expedition to Easter Island and collected island traditions; her work was valuable for the examination of the petroglyphs, scripts and statues of Easter Island. Source: Craig & King, Historical Dictionary of Oceania (1981), p 254.

2778 ROWE, CHANDLER W (1917-), Torrington, Connecticut, United States. Archeologist. Archeology of Wisconsin, Tennessee & Hawaii, U.S. Sources: Int Dir Anth 3, 5.

2779 ROWE, JOHN HOWLAND (1918-), Sorrento, Maine, United States. Anthropologist, archeologist, ethnologist. Peruvian Inca history & culture. Andean archeology. Sources: Int Dir Anth 3, 5/Nat Dir Lat Am.

2780 ROY, CARMEN (1919-), Bonaventure, Gaspe, Canada. Folklorist. Oral literature, tales & culinary anthropology of Canada and Saint-Pierre of Miquelon. Sources: Int Dir Anth 3, 5.

2781 ROY, WILLIAM (1726-1790), Miltonhead, Lanarkshire, Scotland. Archeologist, engineer, general. Specialized on the Roman antiquities in Scotland. Sources: Biog Index: 11/Geography Journal 143:439-50 N' 77.

2782 ROYS, LAWRENCE (1884-1977), Saginaw, Michigan, United States. Engineer. Mayan astronomy, mathematics & engineering. Sources: Int Dir Anth 1 2 3/Anth News F '78.

2783 ROYS, RALPH LOVELAND (1879-1965), Greenville, Michigan, United States. Anthropologist. Ethnology, linguistics and native history of Middle America; researched pre- & post-Spanish Yucatan peninsula (Mexico). Sources: Biog Index: 7/Int Dir Anth 1 2 3/Am Antiq 32:95-9 Ja '67.

2784 RUBIN, VERA D (1911-), Moscow, Russia. Anthropologist. Medical Anthropology. Population studies. Cannabis & culture in Jamaica. Cultural and applied anthropology in the Caribbean and United States. Sources: Int Dir Anth 5/Nat Dir Lat Am/ American Men and Women of Science, ed. by J.C. Press, 12th ed., New York, Bowker, 1973.

2785 RUBIN de la BORBOLLA, DANIEL FERNANDO (1907-), Puebla, Mexico. Anthropologist. Physical anthropology, especially of Middle & South America; archeology, especially of Middle America; musicology. Researched food habits of pre-Columbian Indians, architectural reconstruction of Tzintzuntzan (Mexico). Sources: Biog Index: 5/Int Dir Anth 3/Current Biography 21:34-5 F '60/ Current Biography Yr Bk 1960:349-50 '61.

2786 RUBIO ORBE, GONZALO (1909-), Otavalo, Ecuador. Anthropologist. Indigenismo in Meso-American & South American educational & applied anthropology. Specialized on rural Ecuadorean life and the Indian population. Sources: Int Dir Anth 5/Bork & Maier, Historical Dictionary of Ecuador (1973), p 130.

2787 RUCK, ERNESTO O, Germany. Archivist. First archivist of Bolivia. Source: Heath, Dwight B., Historical Dictionary of Bolivia (1972), p 209.

2788 RUCKERT, FRIEDRICH (1788-1866). Orientalist. Source: Biog Index: 7.

2789 RUDENKO, SERGEI IVANOVICH (1885-1969), Kharkov, Russia. Archeologist, anthropologist, ethnologist. Worked at site of Pazynzk. Sources: Great Soviet Encyclopedia, New York, Macmillan (1979), v. 22, p 326/Masson, V. "K 80-letiiu S. I. Rudenko" Sovetskaia arkheologiia, 1965, no. 4.

2790 RUDNER, JOHAN JALMAR (1917-). Archeologist. Non-Bantu S. African ethnology, pottery & rock art. Source: Int Dir Anth 5.

2791 RUDNYEKYJ, J B (1910-). Folklorist. Slavic folklore, language & onomastics. Ukrainian. Manitoba place names. Source: Int Dir Anth 5.

2792 RUEY, YIH-FU (1898-), Liyang, Kiangsu, China. Ethnologist. Kinship patterns & family systems in Central China. Ceremonial customs of the Miao tribe. Sources: Int Dir Anth 3, 5.

2793 RUGE, GEORG HERMANN (ca. 1852-1919). Anatomist. Specialist in the growth of human lower jaw. Source: Am Anth 21:113.

2794 RUHLMANN, ARMAND (1896-1948), Mulhouse, France. Archeologist. Prehistory of Morocco. Source: Rev Arch series 6 40:69-71 Jl '52.

2795 RUIZ de MONTOYA, ANTONIO (1585-1652), Lima, Peru. Missionary. One of the first to study language of the Guarani Indians of Paraguay and Argentina; wrote on the vocabulary and art of the language. Source: Wright & Nelsham, Historical Dictionary of Argentina (1978), p 820-1.

2796 RUPPERT, KARL (1895-1960), Phoenix, Arizona, United States. Archeologist. Mayan archeology, especially Southern Campeche (Mexico) as related to the Maya area. Sources: Biog Index: 6/Int Dir Anth 1 2 3/Am Antiq 27:101-3 Jl '61.

2797 RUSSEL, JAMES TOWNSEND (1902- 1962). Archeologist. Worked for Smithsonian Institution in Mexico and on Paleolithic sites in the Pyrenees. Sources: Biog Index: 6/Int Dir Anth 1/N Y Times p 23 Je 23 '62.

2798 RUSSELL, FRANK (1868-1903), Iowa, United States. Arctic explorer, ethnologist. Specialized in the peoples of Northern Canada and in those of Arizona (Pima & Papago). Source: Am Anth 5:737-8 O '05.

2799 RUST, ALFRED (1901-1984), Germany. Anthropologist. Specialist in the Paleolithic and Mesolithic. Source: Anth News (Oct. 1984) p 3.

2800 RUST, HORATIO NELSON (1828-1906), Amherst, Massachusetts, United States. Businessman. Assembled important collections of Southern California artifacts; active in improving situation of Mission Indians. Source: Am Anth 8:737-8 O '06.

2801 RUZ LHUILLIER, ALBERTO (1906-). Archeologist. Classic & postclassic Mayan ceramics. Ceremonial architecture. Source: Int Dir Anth 5.

2802 RYBAKOV, BORIS ALEKSANDROVICH (1908-), Moscow, Russia. Archeologist, historian. Archeology and socioeconomic development of early Russian cities. Sources: Great Soviet Encyclopedia, New York, Macmillan (1979), v. 22, p 519/B.A. Rybakov. Moscow, 1968 (AN SSSR: Materialy k bibliografi ycheni'kh SSSR, Seriia istorii, no. 9).

2803 RYERSON, EGERTON (1876-1960), Canada. Orientalist. Wrote: *The Netsuke of Japan*, illustrating legends, history, folklore & customs, 1958; wrote with Alexander Newman, *Japanese Art: a collector's guide*, 1966. Sources: Biog Index: 6/Oriental Art 6:168 Winter '60.

2804 RYKOV, PAVEL SERGEOVICH (1884-1942), Russia. Archeologist. Archeology of the Lower Volga River region. Sources: Great Soviet Encyclopedia, New York, Macmillan (1979), v. 22, p 523/Sinitsin, I.V. and P.D. Stepanov. "Pamiati P.S. Rykova" Sovetskaia arkheologiia, 1964, no. 1.

2805 RYMER, THOMAS (1641-1713). Archeologist, critic. Sources: Biog Index: 3 & 10/Philological Quarterly 54:152-77 Win '75.

2806 SAAKE, WILHELM (1910-). Ethnologist. Acculturation problems among Indians of Brazil. Source: Int Dir Anth 5.

2807 SAAVEDRA CERON, ALVARO de

(-1529), Spain. Explorer. First European to cross the Pacific; journal valuable source of information on Guam, Marshalls, Carolines and New Guinea. Source: Nat Un Cat.

2808 EL-SA'DI, 'ABD AL-RAHMAN IBN 'ABD ALLAH (1596-ca. 1656). Historian. Created the historical work, *Tarikh es-Sudan*, a major source of Malian history prior to the 17th century. Source: Imperato, Pascal J., Historical Dictionary of Mali (1977), p 47.

2809 SAENZ de SANTA MARIA, CARMELO (1913-). Linguist, historian. Mayan languages in Guatemala & Mexico. Written testimonies. Paganism in contemporary Christianity. Source: Int Dir Anth 5.

2810 SAEZ MARTIN, BERNARDO (1913-). Archeologist. Excavations of quaternary terraces. Neolithic & Visigothic archeology. Source: Int Dir Anth 5.

2811 SAFFORD, WILLIAM EDWIN (1859-1926). Botanist, ethnologist, ethnobotanist. Specialized in Guam, Peru & Bolivia; assembled valuable collection of Peruvian & Bolivian Indian material culture; saw close relationship between man & plants. Sources: Biog Index: 3 & 6/ Humphrey, Harry Baker. Makers of North American botany. Ronald '61 p 213-15/ Am Anth 28:453 Ap '26.

2812 SAHAGUN, BERNARDINO de (1500- 1590), Leon, Spain. Priest. Wrote a detailed history of New Spain and described many pre-conquest Aztec institutions. Source: Briggs & Alisky, Historical Dictionary of Mexico (1981), p 198.

2813 SAINT-PÉRIER, RENÉ de POILLOUE (1877-1950), Huisseau sur Cosson, France. Archeologist. Classical and prehistoric archeology, natural and regional history; excavated caves of Lower Pyrenees. Sources: Biog Index: 3/Int Dir Anth 1 2 3/Rev Arch series 6 41:87-9 Ja '53.

2814 SAINTE FARÉ GARNOT, JEAN (1908-1963), Paris, France. Archeologist. Wrote widely on ancient Egypt. Sources: Biog Index: 7/Rev Arch 2:198-204 O '63.

2815 SAKAI, TAKURO (1917-). Physical anthropologist. Dentition of Japan, Polynesia & Afghanistan. Comparative odontology of small mammals. Source: Int Dir Anth 5.

2816 SALCEDO, FRANCISCO (ca. 1540-1600), Guatemala. Priest. Compiled a dictionary of the Mexican language. Source: Moore, Richard E., Historical Dictionary of Guatemala (1973), p 182.

2817 SALT, HENRY (1780-1827). Egyptologist. Sources: Biog Index: 10 11 & 12.

2818 SALVADOR, VINCENTE de. Priest. Author of the first history of Brazil (1627). Source: Levine, Robert M., Historical Dictionary of Brazil (1979), p 191.

2819 SALZ, BEATE R (1913-). Ethnologist. Sociocultural change. Andean & Meso-American economic development. Sources: Int Dir Anth 5/Nat Dir Lat Am.

2820 SAMAYOA CHINCHILLA, CARLOS (1898-), Guatemala. Diplomat, folklorist. Sources: Biog Index: 1/Onis, Harriet de, ed. Golden Land. Knopf '48 p 310.

2821 SAMOKVASOV, DMITRII IAKOVLEVICH (1843-1911), Estate of Molotech', Russia. Archeologist, historian. Excavated many sites in Russia and donated his collection of artifacts to the Historical Museum in Moscow. Source: Great Soviet Encyclopedia, New York, Macmillan (1979), v. 22, p 583.

2822 SANABRIA FERNANDEZ, HERNANDO (1913-), Bolivia. Folklorist, historian. Specialized in history and folklore of the Oriente region of Bolivia. Source: Heath, Dwight B., Historical Dictionary of Bolivia (1972), p 210.

2823 SANBORN, CYRUS ASHTON ROLLINS (1882-1970), New Hampshire, United States. Archeologist. Long association with the Boston Museum of Fine Arts in many capacities; assistant in charge of the Egyptian Department; member of the

Harvard University Museum of Fine Arts Expedition in Egypt after WWI; became Librarian of the Museum from 1923-1952; was also secretary of the Museum and editor of Museum publications. Sources: Biog Index: 10/Boston Museum Bulletin 68 no 353:215-7 '70.

2824 SÁNCHEZ BUSTAMENTE, DANIEL (1870-1933), Bolivia. Historian. Source: Heath, Dwight B., Historical Dictionary of Bolivia (1972), p 210.

2825 SÁNCHEZ LABRADOR, JOSÉ (1717- 1798), La Guardia, Spain. Missionary. Left some 20 works dealing with the history, environment and ethnology of the Rio de La Plata area (Argentina). Source: Wright & Nelsham, Historical Dictionary of Argentina (1978), p 863.

2826 SANDOVAL, LISANDRO (1862-1946), San Francisco, California, United States. Philologist. Wrote several works on the languages of Guatemala. Source: Moore, Richard E., Historical Dictionary of Guatemala (1973), p 200.

2827 SANFORD, MARGARET SELLARD (1912-). Ethnologist. Ethnology of kinship, marriage, families & fosterage among the Kiowa, Apache, Creole & Caribs. Source: Int Dir Anth 5.

2828 SANGMEISTER, EDWARD (1916-). Archeologist. Early Neolithic band & cord ceremonies of central Europe. Source: Int Dir Anth 5.

2829 SANKALIA, HASMUKH DHIRAJLAL (1908-), Bombay, India. Archeologist, prehistorian. Paleolithic & Neolithic cultures of India. History, geography and ethnology of Gujarat, Deccan and Bellary. Sources: Biog Index: 11/Int Dir Anth 3, 5.

2830 SANTILLAN, FERNANDO de (-1575), Spain. Civil servant. Wrote an early history of the Incas. Source: Bork & Maier, Historical Dictionary of Ecuador (1973), p 136.

2831 SAPIR, EDWARD (1884-1939), Lauenburg, Germany. Anthropological linguist. Worked in linguistics, American Indian ethnology, cultural theory. Focused on N. American Indian languages (Takelma, Yana, Southern Paiute, Nootka), Indo-Germanic and Semitic languages. Specialized in linguistic change and the relationship between language & culture. Sources: Biog Index: 1 2 4 7 & 13/Int Dir Anth 1/ Makers of Modern Culture. Facts on File '81, p 461-2/ Zusne, L., Biographical Dictionary of Psychology, Westport, Conn., Greenwood, 1984/Am Anth 41:465-77 Jl '39.

2832 SARBEH, JOHN MENSAH (1864-1910), Cape Coast, Ghana. Lawyer, politician. Wrote *Fanti Customary Laws* (1897) and *Fanti National Constitution* (1906). Source: Dictionary of African Biography: vol. 1, Ethiopia-Ghana. New York: Reference Publication, Inc., 1977, p 313-4.

2833 SARRE, FRIEDRICH (1865-1945), Germany. Archeologist. Sources: Biog Index: 1/Burlington Magazine, 88 F '46/ Ars Islamica 11-12:210-12 '46/College Art Journal 5:359-60 My '46.

2834 SARTIAUX, FÉLIX (1876-1944), France. Archeologist. Archeology of Greek civilization. Source: Rev Arch series 6 39:98-100 Ja '52.

2835 SARZEC, ERNEST de (1836-1901). Archeologist, diplomat. Led archeological excavations in Iraq. Sources: Biog Index: 4/Rev Arch series 6 46:1-16 Jl '55.

2836 SATRIANI, RAFFAELE LOMBARDI (1873-1966), Italy. Folklorist. Specialist in folklore of Calabria (Italy), especially songs, popular beliefs, folktales, proverbs, riddles, tongue twisters, festivities, and customs. Aimed at reconstructing the nature of gentry-peasantry relation. Source: Am Anth 70:571-2 Je '68.

2837 SATTERTHWAITE, LINTON (1897-1978), Trenton, New Jersey, United States. Archeologist. Mesoamerican archeology & ethnology. Research on ruins of Piedras Negras (Mexico), calendar, math &

astronomy of ancient Maya; correlation of ancient Maya and Christian chronologies. Sources: Int Dir Anth 1 2 3/Anth News S '78.

2838 SAUER, JONATHAN D (1918-). Geographer, ethnobotanist. Ethnobotany of amaranthus & canavalia and interactions between man & vegetation. Source: Int Dir Anth 5.

2839 SAUTER, MARC-RANDOLPHE (1914- 1983), Geneva, Switzerland. Paleontologist, archeologist. Human paleontology & archeology of Paleolithic Western Europe and the Mediterranean. Researched historical anthropology of Switzerland. Published on Switzerland prior to the Roman Conquest, races of Europe, and the Mediterranean Paleolithic-Mesolithic. Sources: Anth News 28:5(1987):4/Int Dir Anth 2, 3, 5.

2840 SAVEL'EV, PAVEL STEPANOVICH (1814-1859), St. Petersburg, Russia. Conducted excavations to trace the origins of the Russian people. Used written Arabic manuscripts and archeological materials to trace early contacts between Arabs and Slavs. Sources: Great Soviet Encyclopedia, New York, Macmillan (1979), v. 22, p 655/Grigor'ev, V.V. Zhizn' i trudy P.S. Savel'eva. St. Petersburg, 1861.

2841 SAWYER, ALAN REED (1919-). Anthropologist. Source: Nat Dir Lat Am.

2842 SAYCE, ARCHIBALD HENRY (1845- 1938), Shirehampton, England. Archeologist, linguist. Ancient Near East. Sources: Who Was Who, 1929-1940/Nat Un Cat.

2843 SAZ, ANTONIO de. Linguist. Wrote two books on Guatemalan languages. Source: Moore, Richard E., Historical Dictionary of Guatemala (1973), p 208.

2844 SBATH, PAUL (-1945). Orientalist, priest. Published religious, philosophical, medical texts in Arabic. Sources: Biog Index: 1/Isis 36 no 3-4: 250 '46.

2845 SCANDURA, ANTONIO (1904-). Sociologist, ethnologist. History & ethnography of Islamic cultures. Source: Int Dir Anth 5.

2846 SCARPA, ANTONIO (1903-). Medical anthropologist. Bio-medical interpretation & criteria. Source: Int Dir Anth 5.

2847 SCHADEN, EGON (1913-), Sao Bonifacio, Brazil. Ethnologist. Indian acculturation & messianic movements in Brazil. Sources: Int Dir Anth 3, 5.

2848 SCHAEFFER, CLAUDE EVERETT (1901-1969), Dayton, Ohio, United States. Anthropologist, ethnologist. Cultural anthropology, ethnology & ecology, especially of Northern Plains Indians. Began *Studies in Plains Anthropology & History* series. Sources: Biog Index: 9/Int Dir Anth 1 2 3/Am Anth 72:1409-11 D '70.

2849 SCHAPERA, ISAAC (1905-), Garies, Little Namaqualand, Cape Province, South Africa. Social anthropologist, ethno-linguist. Social anthropology and sociology. Research on the Tswana, for example, on Tswana customary law. Wrote on effects of contact with Europeans on South African Bantu. Also wrote ethnographic works on various peoples of Southern Africa, including the Khoisan. Sources: Biog Index: 2/Int Dir Anth 1 2 3/ International Encyclopedia of the Social Sciences, v. 18/ Nature 165:793-4 My 20 '50/Saunders, Christopher, Historical Dictionary of South Africa (1983).

2850 SCHEBESTA, PAUL JOACHIM (1887-1967), Gross-Peterwitz, Silesia. Missionary. Extensive fieldwork among and writing on the Mbuti pygmies of Zaire & Negritos of the Philippines and Malaya. Sources: Int Dir Anth 2 3/Am Anth 70:537-45 Je '68.

2851 SCHEFFER, JOHANNES (1621-1679). Classicist, archeologist. Sources: Biog Index: 4/ Warburg & Courtland Institute Journal 20:59-74 Ja '57.

2852 SCHENCK, WILLIAM EGBERT (1884-1956), Memphis, Tennessee, United States. Anthropologist, businessman. Published on the Indians and archeology of California. Sources: Biog Index: 4/Int Dir Anth 1 2/Am Anth 59:326-7 Ap '57.

2853 SCHLEICHER, CHARLES (1871-1943), Paris, France. Publisher, archeologist. Prehistory. Sources: Biog Index: 1/Int Dir Anth 1 2/Rev Arch series 6 25:204-5 Ap '46.

2854 SCHLENTHER, URSULA (1919-). Ethnologist. Inca & Aztec socioeconomics. Source: Int Dir Anth 5.

2855 SCHLIEMANN, HEINRICH (1822-1890), Neubukow, Germany. Archeologist. Discovered site of Troy. Excavated there and at several other ancient sites. Sources: Biog Index: 1 2 4 6 7 8 9 10 11 & 12/ Education Digest 45:52-4 D '79/Modern Language Journal 63:273-6 D '79/ Classical Journal 74:348-55 Ap '79.

2856 SCHLUMBERGER, DANIEL (1904-1972). Archeologist. Sources: Biog Index: 8 9 & 10/Britannica Book of the Year 1973:516 '73.

2857 SCHMELTZ, J D E (1839- ca. 1909), Hamburg, Germany. Ethnographer. Developed collections in State Museum of Ethnography, Leiden, Holland. Source: Am Anth 11:324-5 Ap '09.

2858 SCHMERLER, HENRIETTA (-1931). Anthropology student. Her death while conducting field research sparked an extensive debate about the preparation of students for their field experiences. Source: Anth News 28:1:3-4.

2859 SCHMID, ELIZABETH (1912-), Freiburg, Germany. Osteologist. Osteology of central European mammals. Researched sedimentary deposits in excavation as aids in dating; prehistoric pottery. Sources: Int Dir Anth 3, 5.

2860 SCHMIDT, EMIL (1837-1906), Obereichstadt, Germany. Physician. Published on prehistoric North America, craniology of Italy (Pompeii) & Egypt. Ethnology of South India. Source: Am Anth 9:236-7 Mr '07.

2861 SCHMIDT, ERICH FRIEDRICH (1897-1964), Baden-Baden, Germany. Archeologist. Interested in archeology of the Near East & Iran; aerial survey of Iran. Sources: Biog Index: 7 & 8/Int Dir Anth 1 2/ Journal of Near Eastern Studies 24:145-8 Jl '65/Am Antiq 3 0 '65.

2862 SCHMIDT, NATHANIEL (1862-1939). Orientalist, paleontologist. Sources: Biog Index: 2 & 4/ Dictionary of Australian Biography sup 2:596-7 '58.

2863 SCHMIDT, P WILHELM (1868-1954), Horde-Dortmund, Germany. Priest, ethnologist. Ethnology of Northern South America, East & South Africa, China, Korea & Japan, N & N.E. Asia; folklore of Europe. Sources: Biog Index: 1 3 4 7 & 13/Int Dir Anth 1/ Anthropos 74 no 5-6:908-9 '79/Am Anth 56:868-70 O '54.

2864 SCHMIDT, ULRICH, Germany. Explorer. Wrote an account of his participation in the 1535 expedition of Pedro Mendoza to the Paraguayan region. Source: Kolinski, Charles J., Historical Dictionary of Paraguay (1973), p 228.

2865 SCHMITT, KARL (1915-1952), Albany, New York, United States. Anthropologist, ethnologist. Ethnology and archeology of North America; studied culture change of the Wichita and Caddo Indians of Oklahoma. Sources: Biog Index: 3/Int Dir Anth 3/Am Anth 55:237-9 Ap '53/ Am Antiq 18:259-60 Ja '53.

2866 SCHNEIDER, DAVID M (1918-), New York, United States. Ethnologist. American culture, family & kinship. Ethnology of Oceania. Folklore of Micronesia. Sources: Int Dir Anth 3, 5.

2867 SCHOOLCRAFT, HENRY ROWE (1793-1864). Ethnologist, explorer. Sources: Biog Index: 1 3 4 8 & 9.

2868 SCHOUTEN, WILLIAM CARNELISEN (1567-1625), Hoarn, Netherlands. Explorer. Led a voyage which visited Tonga, New Guinea and several other islands. Source: Craig & King, Historical

Dictionary of Oceania (1981), p 261.

2869 SCHRADER, HANS (1869-1948), Germany. Archeologist. Classical archeology. Sources: Biog Index: 2/Int Dir Anth 2/Am J Arch 53:58-9 Ja '49.

2870 SCHRANIL, JOSEF (1893-1949). Archeologist. Czechoslovakian archeology. Ancestors of the Bohemians & Moravians. Sources: Biog Index: 2/Int Dir Anth 2/Rev Arch series 6 34:67 Jl '49.

2871 SCHREINER, OLIVE (1855-1920). Writer, social reformer. Wrote novels depicting South African life; feminist and opponent of Second Boer War. Source: Saunders, Christopher, Historical Dictionary of South Africa (1983), p 153.

2872 SCHROEDER, ALBERT HENRY (1914-), Brooklyn, New York, United States. Anthropologist, archeologist. S.W. United States archeology, dendrochronology and laboratory methods. Sources: Int Dir Anth 2 3/Nat Dir Lat Am.

2873 SCHRUMPF, CHRISTIAN (1818-1884). Missionary. Wrote pamphlets on Basotho customs and language. Source: Haliburton, Gordon, Historical Dictionary of Lesotho (1977), p 157.

2874 SCHUCHERT, CHARLES (1858-1942). Paleontologist. Sources: Biog Index: 3/ National Academy of Sciences. Biographical Memoirs v. 27. Columbia Univ. Press, The Academy '52 p 363-89.

2875 SCHULTEN, ADOLF (1870-1960), Elberfeld, Germany. Archeologist. Archeology of Spain. Sources: Biog Index: 5 & 6/ Archivo Espanol de Arte y Arqueologia 33 no 101-102:222-8 '60/ Rev Arch 2:223-4 O '62.

2876 SCHULTZ, ADOLPH H (1891-1976), Stuttgart, Germany. Anthropologist, primatologist. Human evolution. Primate biology. Sources: Biog Index: 11-/Int Dir Anth 1, 2, 3, 5/ American Journal of Physical Anthropology 46:191-2 Mr '77.

2877 SCHULTZ, HARALD (1909-1966), Porto Alegre, Brazil. Anthropologist, author. Wrote about ethnology of Indians in Brazil. Sources: Biog Index: 7/Am Anth 68:1233-5 O '66/ Publishers Weekly 189:278 Ja 24 '66.

2878 SCHURTZ, HEINRICH (1863-1903). Ethnographer. Built up ethnographic section of Bremen Museum. Wrote on folklore. Source: Am Anth 5:583 '03.

2879 SCHWAB, WILLIAM B (1917-). Anthropologist. African urban field methods. Social change in Nigeria. Source: Int Dir Anth 5.

2880 SCHWABEDISSEN, HERMANN (1911-). Archeologist. Paleo- & Mesolithic Europe. Source: Int Dir Anth 5.

2881 SCHWEINFUIRTH, GEORG AUGUST (1836-1925), Germany. Studied the Stone Age in Tunisia, Egypt and Palestine. Source: Am Anth 29:342 Ap '27.

2882 SCHWIDETZKY, ILSE (1907-), Lissa, Germany. Physical anthropologist. Biology of skeletal populations of Europe. Sources: Int Dir Anth 1, 3, 5.

2883 SCOTT, DAVID CLEMENT RUFFELLE (1853-1907). Missionary. Wrote a survey of his mission work in Malawi and compiled a dictionary of Nyanja, language of Malawi. Source: Crosby, Cynthia A., Historical Dictionary of Malawi (1980), p 103.

2884 SCOTT, HUGH LENOX (-1934). Specialized in the ethnology of N. American Plains Indians, particularly Arapaho and Kiowa. Source: Am Anth 36:490 Jl '34.

2885 SCOTT, JOHN PAUL (1909-). Behavioral geneticist. Social behavior of non-human animals. Behavioral development. Source: Int Dir Anth 5.

2886 SCOTT, W LINDSAY (1892-1952), England. Archeologist. Neolithic and early Bronze Age culture of Atlantic coast of Europe. Study of prehistoric Scotland. Sources: Biog Index: 2 & 3/Int Dir Anth 2/Isis 43 no 4:367 '52/ Nature 170:184 Ag 2 '52/N Y Times, Je 20 '52.

2887 **SCOTTI, PIETRO** (1899-). Ethnologist, medical anthropologist. Ethnology of Congo & Paraguay. Source: Int Dir Anth 5.

2888 **SCOVILLE, ANNIE BEECHER** (1865-1953), Norwich, New York, United States. Educator, folklorist. Specialist in folklore of American Indians; first women to supervise Omaha and Winnebago reservations. Sources: Biog Index: 3/N Y Times p 92 Mr 15 '53.

2889 **SECHEFO, JUSTINUS** (1870-1938). Wrote two studies of Basotho traditional customs and clothing. Source: Haliburton, Gordon, Historical Dictionary of Lesotho (1977), p 158.

2890 **SEELE, KEITH CEDRIC** (1898-1971), Warsaw, Indiana, United States. Egyptologist. Worked at Saqqara and Luxor (Egypt) as an epigrapher; made drawings also of Medinet Habu and Karnak; prepared the New Kingdom collections from Nubia for publication. Sources: Biog Index: 9 & 10/Journal of Near Eastern Studies 32:1-3 Ja '73.

2891 **SEELY, FRANKLIN AUSTIN** (1834-1895), Pennsylvania, United States. Administrator, anthropologist. Wrote about the development of technological innovations. Source: Am Anth 8(old series):177-8 Ap 1895.

2892 **SEEWALD, OTTO** (1898-), Vienna, Austria. Prehistorian. Prehistory and prehistorical musical instruments and art. Sources: Int Dir Anth 1 2 3.

2893 **SEKELJ, TIBOR** (1912-). Art historian. Aboriginal art. Comparative study of masks & their uses. Source: Int Dir Anth 5.

2894 **SEKESE, AZARIELE M** (1849-1930). Historian. Wrote a series of articles on Basotho folklore later collected and published as *Mekhoa ea Basotho*. Source: Haliburton, Gordon, Historical Dictionary of Lesotho (1977), p 160.

2895 **SELIGMAN, BRENDA ZARA** (1883-1965), London, England. Anthropologist. Fieldwork in Ceylon and the Sudan, interested in social anthropology, especially kinship & religion. Sources: Biog Index: 7/Int Dir Anth 1 2 3/Oriental Art 11:189 Autumn '65.

2896 **SELIGMAN, CHARLES GABRIEL** (1873-1940), London, England. Physician, ethnologist, ethnographer. Studied in the Torres Straits, New Guinea, the Sudan. Oceanic anthropology. Interested in Chinese art and in psychology in relation to anthropology. Conducted fieldwork in New Guinea, Sarawak, Ceylon & the Sudan; published on racial differences & material culture. Sources: Biog Index: 2 4 & 10/Int Dir Anth 1 2/Oceania 45:472-82 Je '75/ Am Anth 43:437-9 Jl '41.

2897 **SELLING, DAGMAR K M** (1912-). Archeologist. Prehistoric & medieval pottery of northern Europe. Source: Int Dir Anth 5.

2898 **SELOUS, FREDERICK COURTENEY** (1851-1917). Hunter, author. Wrote descriptions of wildlife of Rhodesia in numerous articles and three books, covering the Shona Revolt and his travels over South Africa as well. Source: Rasmussen, R. Kent, Historical Dictionary of Rhodesia/Zimbabwe (1979), p 290-1.

2899 **SEMPER, CARL GOTTFRIED** (1832-1893), Altona, Germany. Ethnographer. Researched & published widely on Palau and the Philippines. Source: Craig & King, Historical Dictionary of Oceania (1981), p 263.

2900 **SEMPLE, ELLEN CHURCHILL** (1863-1932), Louisville, Kentucky, United States. Geographer. Wrote on effect of environment on human development. Sources: Biog Index: 2/Nat Cyc Am Biog 35:139 '49.

2901 **SENSENIG, E CARL** (1910-1974), Gloucester, Massachusetts, United States. Anatomist, anthropologist. Chairman of the Department of Anatomy, Univ. of Alabama; helped to develop that university's programs in physical anthropology and marine sciences; began the first graduate program in physical anthropology in a medical school in the southern U.S. Sources: Biog Index: 10/ American Journal of

Physical Anthropology 42:347 My '75.
2902 SEQUOYAH (ca. 1766-1843), Loudon Co., Tennessee, United States. Compiled Cherokee language syllabary. Source: Columbia.
2903 SERVICE, ELMAN ROGERS (1915-), Tecumseh, Michigan, United States. Social anthropologist. Mexican & Paraguayan ethnology. Primitive social organization. Researched acculturation of the Guarani Indians during the colonial period in Paraguay. Sources: Int Dir Anth 3, 5/Nat Dir Lat Am.
2904 SETA, ALESSANDRO della (1879-1944), Italy. Archeologist. Archeology of Greece and ancient Italy; director of Italian School in Athens. Sources: Biog Index: 2/Rev Arch series 6 34:71-2 Jl '49.
2905 SETZLER, FRANK MARYL (1902-1975), Fremont, Ohio, United States. Anthropologist, archeologist, curator. Head Curator, Dept. of Anthropology, U.S. Nat. Museum, Smithsonian Institute. Archeology and material culture of U.S. & Australia. Sources: Biog Index: 12/Int Dir Anth 1, 2, 3, 5/Nat Cyc Am Biog 58:68-9 '79 /Anth News Ap '75.
2906 SEURE, GEORGES (1873-1944), France. Archeologist. Archeology of Thrace. Source: Rev Arch series 6 36:106-8 Jl '50.
2907 SEVERUS (-980), Egypt. Clergyman. Coptic bishop who wrote a history of that church detailing its rise and spread into Nubia and Ethiopia. Source: King, Joan W., Historical Dictionary of Egypt (1984), p 559-60.
2908 SEYRIG, HENRI (1895-1973). Archeologist. Director of the French Institute of Archaeology in Beirut, 1945-1966; excavated chiefly in Syria, Lebanon. Sources: Biog Index: 9/N Y Times p 42 Ja 25 '73.
2909 SHAE, JOHN GILMARY (1824-1892), New York, United States. Historian, linguist. Wrote on the early exploration of the Mississippi Valley and on the languages of North American Indians. Source: Am Anth 5(old series):104 Ap 1892.
2910 SHAKESPEAR, WILLIAM HENRY I (1878-1915), England. Orientalist. Made six exploratory journeys through Arabia (- 1914); notebooks contain valuable regional information. Sources: Biog Index: 11 & 12/Geography Journal 142:512 N '76.
2911 SHAPIRO, HARRY LIONEL (1902-), Boston, Massachusetts, United States. Bio-anthropologist, curator. Physical anthropology, studied race mixtures in Hawaii and South Pacific. Sources: Biog Index: 3 5 & 12/Int Dir Anth 2, 3, 5/ Natural History 89:96-7+ F '80.
2912 SHARP, CECIL JAMES (1859-1924), London, England. Musician, folklorist. Collected folksongs in England and in Appalachian Mountains. Sources: Biog Index: 2 4 5 8 & 12/ Dictionary of Australian Biography 2:316-318 '49/Fox-Strangways, Arthur Henry & Karpeks, Maud. Cecil Sharp. DaCopa Press '80.
2913 SHAW, CHARLES THURSTON (1914-), Plymouth, England. Archeologist. Igbo-Ukwu culture of Nigeria. Archeology of Europe. Sources: Int Dir Anth 3, 5.
2914 SHEAR, THEODORE LESLIE (1880- 1945), New London, New Hampshire, United States. Archeologist. Several field trips to Greece; professor of classical archeology. Sources: Biog Index: 5/Int Dir Anth 1 2/Nat Cyc Am Biog 42:208-9 '58.
2915 SHEDDICK, VERNON G J (1915-), England. Ecologist, social anthropologist. Human ecology. Social organization of N.W. European local populations. Ethnology of E. & S. Africa; studied land tenure practice of Basutoland (Lesotho). Sources: Int Dir Anth 3, 5.
2916 SHELLABEAR, WILLIAM GIRDLESTONE (1862-1947). Orientalist. Sources: Biog Index: 1/Moslem World 167-8 Ap '47, 37:177-84 Jl '47/ School & Society 65:59 Ja 25 '47.

2917 SHEPARD, ANNA OSLER (1903-1973), Merchantville, New Jersey, United States. Anthropologist, archeologist. Scientific analysis of pottery from Pecos (Texas) and Chichen Itza (Mexico); technical aspects of primitive pottery. Sources: Biog Index: 10/Int Dir Anth 1 2 3/Am Antiq 39:448-51 Jl '74.

2918 SHEPARDSON, MARY T (1906-). Social anthropologist. Legal, political & social anthropology of U.S. Apache & Navajo Indians. Source: Int Dir Anth 5.

2919 SHETELIG, HAAKON (1877-1955), Oslo, Norway. Archeologist. Prehistoric and protohistoric archeology of Scandinavia. Prehistoric art of Northern Europe. Sources: Biog Index: 4/Int Dir Anth 2 3/Nature 176:582 S 24 '55.

2920 SHETRONE, HENRY CLYDE (1876-1954), Millersport, Ohio, United States. Archeologist. Archeology of the Mound area. Museum administration. Sources: Biog Index: 4/Int Dir Anth 1 2/Am Antiq 21:296-9 Ja '56.

2921 SHIBATA, MINORU (1906-), Japan. Historian. Japanese folk belief & ancestor worship. Source: Int Dir Anth 5.

2922 SHIBUSAWA, KELZO (1896-1963), Tokyo, Japan. Folklorist. Ethnology and linguistics of China, Korea and Japan. Studied history, techniques and folklore of Japanese fishing. Sources: Biog Index: 6/Int Dir Anth 3/N Y Times p 27 O 26 '63.

2923 SHINER, JOEL L (1919-). Archeologist, prehistorian. Archeology of Africa, particularly Sudan. Source: Int Dir Anth 5.

2924 SHINNIE, PETER LEWIS (1915-). Archeologist, linguist. Ancient cultures of the Nile Valley, particularly Meroe. Source: Int Dir Anth 5.

2925 SHIPEK, FLORENCE CONNOLLY (1918-), Massachusetts, United States. Applied anthropologist, ethnologist. Comparative land use from demographic & ecological perspective. General human paleontology and museum techniques. Sources: Int Dir Anth 3, 5.

2926 SHISHKIN, VASILII AFANAS'EVICH (1893-1966), Shopsino, Russia. Archeologist. Conducted excavations in Central Asia. Sources: Great Soviet Encyclopedia, New York, Macmillan (1982), v. 29, p 605/V.A. Shishkin kak uchenyi-arkheolog i obshchestvennyi diatel' Istoriia material'noi Kul'tury Uzbekistana, fasc. 6, Tashkent, 1965.

2927 SHOOK, EDWIN MARTIN (1911-), Newton, North Carolina, United States. Anthropologist, archeologist. Archeology of Middle America, highlands and Pacific coast of Guatemala. Sources: Int Dir Anth 3/Nat Dir Lat Am.

2928 SHUQAYR, NA'UM BEY (1863-1922). Civil servant. Compiled the *Tarikh al-Sudan*, a source of Sudanese history. Source: Voll, John Obert, Historical Dictionary of the Sudan (1978), p 86.

2929 SIBATA, TAKESI (1918-). Idiolects & linguistic lexicography. Source: Int Dir Anth 5.

2930 SIBTHORPE, A B C (ca. 1829-1916). Geographer, historian. First native of Sierra Leone to write a history of the country. Source: Foray, Cyril P., Historical Dictionary of Sierra Leone (1977), p 194.

2931 SIEGEL, BERNARD JOSEPH (1917-), Superior, Wisconsin, United States. Social anthropologist. N.E. Brazil. Conflict in anthropology. Personality stereotypes by status roles on regional basis in the U.S. Sources: Int Dir Anth 3, 5/Nat Dir Lat Am.

2932 SIEGEL, MORRIS (1906-1961), New York, New York, United States. Anthropologist, sociologist. Published on the ethnology of Guatemala & several African colonies. Sources: Biog Index: 7/Int Dir Anth 3/Am Anth 66:395-6 Ap '64.

2933 SIERKSMA, FOKKE (1917-1977). Anthropologist. Cross-cultural theological anthropology. Acculturation, Messianism & comparative religion. Tibet. Source: Int Dir Anth 5.

2934 SIEROSZEWSKI, WACŁAW (1858-1946). Author, ethnologist. Sources: Biog Index: 13/Ethnohistory 24:103-15 Spr '77.

2935 SIGAL, LOUIS (1877-1945), France. Priest, archeologist. Archeology of Narbonne (France). Sources: Biog Index: 2/Rev Arch series 6 37:199-203 Ap '51.

2936 SIIGER, HALFDAN (1911-). Anthropologist. Culture & religion of India & Pakistan. Source: Int Dir Anth 5.

2937 SILLERY, ANTHONY (1903-). Historian. Wrote extensively on history and culture of Botswana. Source: Stevens, Richard P., Historical Dictionary of the Republic of Botswana (1975), p 133.

2938 SILVERMAN, FREDERIC N (1914-). Radiologist. Diagnostic radiology & skeletal dysplasias. Source: Int Dir Anth 5.

2939 SILVY, S J, Fr. ANTOINE (1638-1711), Aix, Provence, France. Priest. Missionary in New France; wrote on N. American Indians. Source: Jes Rel.

2940 SIMMONS, OZZIE GORDON (1919-). Anthropologist. Source: Nat Dir Lat Am.

2941 SIMOES, MARIO FERREIRA (1915-1985). Archeologist, ethnologist, musicologist. Archeology of Brazil & the Amazon basin. Archeological fieldwork on Marajo Island and coastal Brazil. Sources: Int Dir Anth 5/Anth News 9/85.

2942 SIMON, PEDRO (1581-), Spain. Missionary. Wrote an account of the Spanish conquests on the South American continent. Source: Davis, Robert H., Historical Dictionary of Colombia (1977), p 206.

2943 SIMON, S J, Fr. CHARLES (1620-1697), Bourges, France. Priest. Missionary in New France; wrote on N. American Indians. Source: Jes Rel.

2944 SIMPSON, GEORGE EATON (1904-), Knoxville, Iowa, United States. Medical anthropologist. Medical & religious cults of the Caribbean. Haitian ethnology. Sources: Int Dir Anth 2, 3, 5/Nat Dir Lat Am.

2945 SIMPSON, GEORGE GAYLORD (1902-). Bio-anthropologist, physical anthropologist. Evolution, structure & affinities of primates. Sources: Biog Index: 1 3 4 7 & 11/Int Dir Anth 5/ Chronicle of Higher Education 16:14 My '78/ Simpson, George G. Concession to the Improbable, Yale Press 78.

2946 SIMPSON, RUTH de ETTE (1918-). Archeologist. Lithic typology. Archeology of California, Nevada. Source: Int Dir Anth 5.

2947 SINEL'NIKOV, NIKOLAI ALEKSANDROVICH (1885-1941), Moscow, Russia. Anthropologist. Specialized in physical anthropology and the primate-human evolutionary development. Source: Great Soviet Encyclopedia, New York, Macmillan (1979), v. 23, p 475.

2948 SINGER, MILTON B (1912-). Ethnologist. Cultural traditions & social change in India and elsewhere. Source: Int Dir Anth 5.

2949 SIO, ARNOLD A (1917-). Ethnologist, historian. Comparative race relations in U.S., West Indies & Brazil. Ethnology of the West Indies. Source: Int Dir Anth 5.

2950 AL-SIYUTI, JALAL AD-DIN (1445-1505). Author. Compiled a voluminous encyclopedia on Egypt and is credited with some 560 books on many societies. Source: King, Joan W., Historical Dictionary of Egypt (1984), p 581-2.

2951 SIZOV, VLADIMIR IL'ICH (1840-1904), Moscow, Russia. Archeologist. Archeology of the Russian people. Sources: Great Soviet Encyclopedia, New York, Macmillan (1979), v. 23, p 496/Anuchin, D.N. "Pamiati V.I. Sizova" Drevnosti: Tr. Moskovskogo arkheologicheskogo obshchestva, vol. 21, no. 1, Moscow, 1906.

2952 SJOVOLD, THORLIEF (1914-), Tonsberg, Norway. Historian. Iron Age settlement history of northern Norway. Sources: Int Dir Anth 3, 5.

2953 SKARLAND, IVAR (1899-1965), Hoylandet, Namdel, Norway. Anthropologist. Physical anthropology. Studied anthropometric data of Alaskan Indians. Specialist in the archeology and cultures of the natives of Alaska. Sources: Biog Index: 7/Int Dir Anth 2 3/Am Anth 68:132-3 F '66.

2954 SKEAT, WALTER WILLIAM (1866-1912), London, England. Malay ethnology, especially magic and folklore. Sources: Columbia/Int Dir Anth 2.

2955 SKINNER, ALANSON BUCK (1885-1925), Buffalo, New York, United States. Ethnologist, museum curator. Specialist in the archeology of New York State and the ethnology of the Menomini and other Plains Indians. Source: Am Anth 28:275-80 Ja '26.

2956 SKY, HOWARD (1900-1971). Cayuga faith keeper. Working with anthropologists, he was a valued informant & interpreter of Iroquois life. Source: Am Anth 74:758-63 Je '72.

2957 SLAVEYKOV, PETKO RACHEV (1827-1895). Folklorist, poet. Source: Biog Index: 7.

2958 SLEIGHT, FREDERICK WINFIELD (1918-), Corning, New York, United States. Anthropologist. Archeology of Florida & Virgin Islands. Source: Nat Dir Lat Am.

2959 SLOBODIN, RICHARD (1915-), New York, New York, United States. Ethnologist. Northern Canadian Athapaskan community organization & religion. Sources: Int Dir Anth 3, 5.

2960 SLOLEY, ROBERT WALTER (1879-1958), England. Engineer, Egyptologist. Expert on Egyptian mathematics and science, particularly Egyptian astronomy and methods of measuring time. Sources: Biog Index: 5 & 12/Nature 182:1128 O 25 '58.

2961 SLOTKIN, JAMES SYDNEY (1913-1958), New York, New York, United States. Anthropologist, social scientist. General social anthropology; studied social and cultural factors in personality development, methodology of the social sciences. Specialized in historical documentary research, Menomini culture, Peyote religion, the adaptation of native peoples to industrial labor, and psychological anthropology. Sources: Biog Index: 5/Int Dir Anth 3/Am Anth 61:844-7 O '59.

2962 SMIRNOV, ALEKSEI PETROVICH (1899-1974), Moscow, Russia. Archeologist. Archeology of the Volga and Kama regions, Russia. Source: Great Soviet Encyclopedia, New York, Macmillan (1979), v. 23, p 561.

2963 SMITH, ALLAN HATHORN (1913-), Norwood, Pennsylvania, United States. Cultural anthropologist, ethnohistorian. Cultural ethnohistory of American Indians. Sources: Int Dir Anth 3, 5.

2964 SMITH, ANDREW (1797-1872). Physician. Led the first scientific expedition to visit Lesotho; wrote a study of the San (Bushmen) of the valley of the Orange River (South Africa); left a diary of an 1834-35 expedition containing ethnographic records. Source: Haliburton, Gordon, Historical Dictionary of Lesotho (1977), p 163.

2965 SMITH, ANNE MILLSPAUGH (Cooke) (1900-1981), New York, New York, United States. Anthropologist. Worked with Indians of Great Basin & Southwest U.S.; leader in applied anthropology. Source: Am Anth 84:395-6 Je '82.

2966 SMITH, ARTHUR HAMILTON (1860- 1941), London, England. Archeologist. Produced several catalogs of the holdings in the classical section of the British Museum; Keeper of Greek-Roman Antiquities, British Museum. Sources: Biog Index: 5/ Dictionary of National Biography 1941-1950:791-2 '59.

2967 SMITH, AUGUSTUS LEDYARD (ca. 1901-1985). Archeologist. Archeology of the Maya. Source: Anth News 3/86.

2968 SMITH, BENJAMIN MOSBY (1811-1893). Orientalist, theologian. Sources: Biog Index: 2/ Flourney,

Francis Rosebro. Benjamin Mosby Smith, 1811-1893. Richmond Press '47.

2969 SMITH, CARLYLE STANLEY (1915-), Great Neck, New York, United States. Archeologist. Evolution of firearms in historical archeology of W. Europe & N. America; archeology of coastal New York, lower Republican River and Kanopolis River, Kansas. Sources: Int Dir Anth 3, 5.

2970 SMITH, EARL BALDWIN (1888-1956), Topsham, Maine, United States. Archeologist, architectural historian. Wrote extensively on architecture in ancient world. Sources: Biog Index: 4 & 7/Nat Cyc Am Biog 48:46 '65.

2971 SMITH, ELMER RICHARD (1909-1960), St. Anthony, Idaho, United States. Anthropologist. Cultural anthropology, historical sociology and social psychology; studied ecological factors, cave cultures, early Indian in Utah. Specialist in the cave cultures of Utah and applied anthropology (race relations & minority problems). Sources: Biog Index: 5 & 6/Int Dir Anth 2 3/Am Anth 62:1047-9 D '60/ Am Antiq 26:535-6 Ap '61.

2972 SMITH, ERMINNIE ADELE PLATT (1836-1886), Marcellus, New York, United States. Ethnologist, geologist. Iroquois language and myths. Sources: Notable American Women, 1607-1950, vol. III, Belknap Press '71, p 312-3/ Siegel, P.A. & K.T. Finley, Women in the Scientific Search, Metuchen, N.J., Scarecrow, 1985.

2973 SMITH, GEORGE (1840-1876), Chelsea, England. Orientalist. Wrote about Assyria and Babylonia. Sources: New Int Enc, 1914 ed/Columbia.

2974 SMITH, GRAFTON ELLIOT (1871-1937). Anatomist, anthropologist. Aboriginal studies. Sources: Biog Index: 2 4 & 10/Dictionary of National Biography, '49/ Oceania 3:169-73 O '74.

2975 SMITH, HALE GILLIAM (1918-1977), Jacksonville, Illinois, United States. Archeologist. Prehistoric & Spanish colonial archeology. Historical archeology of Florida, especially of Spanish colonial period. Sources: Int Dir Anth 3, 5/Nat Dir Lat Am/Anth News O '77.

2976 SMITH, HENRY LEE (1913-). Linguist. Historical & contemporary dialects of English. Source: Int Dir Anth 5.

2977 SMITH, HERSCHEL C (1907-1966), Salt Lake City, Utah, United States. Archeologist. Worked at Tule Springs Project (1962-1963) near Las Vegas, and at Pintwater Cave, Nevada. Sources: Biog Index: 8/Am Antiq 32:389-90 Jl '67.

2978 SMITH, JOSEPH LINDON (1863-1950). Painter, archeologist. Sources: Biog Index: 2 4 & 6/ Smith, Corinna Haven (Putman). Interesting people; 80 years with the great & near-great. Univ. of Oklahoma Press '62/ Am J Arch, Jl '51.

2979 SMITH, M BREWSTER (1919-). Psychologist. Culture, personality & social psychology. Source: Int Dir Anth 5.

2980 SMITH, MARIAN WESLEY (1907-1961), New York, United States. Anthropologist. Ethnology of Americas and Asia, archeology and folklore of North America, Europe, Near and Middle East and India. Fieldwork on the Indians of Washington State and British Columbia. Publications on the Puyallup and Nisqualli (1940) and the archeology of the Columbia-Fraser River (1950); honorary secretary of the Royal Anthropological Institute in 1956. Sources: Biog Index: 5 & 6/Int Dir Anth 2/Am Antiq 27:567 Ap '62/ Nature 192:917 D 9 '61.

2981 SMITH, MAURICE G (-1930). Social anthropologist. Specialized in the Indians of Oklahoma and the Peyote cult. Source: Am Anth 33:230 Ap '31.

2982 SMITH, MILES (1554-1624). Orientalist, bishop. Sources: Biog Index: 3/ Fuller, Thomas. Worthies of England. Abr ed. Allen '52.

2983 SMITH, MYRON BEMENT (1897-

1970), Newark Valley, New York, United States. Archeologist. Archeology of North America, Near and Middle East and India; researched Islamic architecture of Persia; Islamic archives. Expert on Islamic and Iranian architecture; created a photographic archive on Islamic construction. Sources: Biog Index: 9 & 10/Int Dir Anth 3/Nat Cyc Am Biog 55:539-40 '74/ Archaeology 23:251 Je '70.

2984 SMITH, ROBERT ELLIOT (1899-), Arachon, France. Anthropologist, archeologist, ceramicist. Meso-American ceramics. Mayan archeology. Sources: Int Dir Anth 1, 2, 3, 5/Nat Dir Lat Am.

2985 SMITH, SIDNEY (1889-), England. Assyriologist. One of the first to make a correlation between the complicated stratigraphic and epigraphic data yielded from excavations in Syria and Hatay (Turkey); Keeper of the Department of Egyptian and Assyrian Antiquities at the British Museum, 1930-1948. Sources: Biog Index: 1/Int Dir Anth 2/Nature 162:645 O 23 '48.

2986 SMITH, STANLEY (1883-1955), Middlesborough, England. Paleontologist. Leading authority on Paleozoic corals; knowledgeable in Greek and Roman antiquities; worked with D.E. Eicholz on reinterpreting the geological references in the treatise of Theophrastus. Sources: Biog Index: 4/Nature 176:377 Ag 27 '55.

2987 SMITH, WILLIAM RAMSAY (1859-1937), King Edward, Scotland. Ethnologist. Wrote extensively on Australian aborigines. Sources: Biog Index: 2/Dictionary of Australian Biography 2:338-9 '49.

2988 SMITH, WILLIAM STEVENSON (1907-1969). Archeologist, Egyptologist. Excavated principally at Giza and Saqqara, 1930-1939; specialized in Egyptian art and architecture; directed later work at Giza for Harvard. Sources: Biog Index: 8/N Y Times p 53 Ja 14 '69.

2989 SMOLLA, GUNTER (1919-). Archeologist. History & theory of prehistoric research. Source: Int Dir Anth 5.

2990 SMYTH, ROBERT BROUGH (1830-1889), Carville, England. Geologist, ethnologist. Wrote on Australian aborigines. Sources: Biog Index: 2/Dictionary of Australian Biography 2:340 '49.

2991 SNELL, WAYNE WALTER (1918-), Jewell, Iowa, United States. Summer Institute of Linguistics. Staff member, Peru. Bilingual education & community development. Source: Nat Dir Lat Am.

2992 SNODGRASSE, RICHARD M (1903-). Physical anthropologist. Human morphology & growth appraisal by anthropometry & roentgenography. Sources: Int Dir Anth 1, 2, 5.

2993 SNYDERMAN, GEORGE S (1908-), Philadelphia, Pennsylvania, United States. Ethnohistorian. Primitive medicine & folklore in U.S. ethnohistory. Ethnology of Africa, N. America, folklore of N. & Middle America, primitive psychology and ethnohistory of N. America; studied wampum among Iroquois, Jamaican folklore, and Seneca education and surgery. Sources: Int Dir Anth 3, 5.

2994 SOBRINO, JOSEPHINE (1915-), San Antonio, Texas, United States. Folklorist. Mexican folklore. Source: Nat Dir Lat Am.

2995 SODERBERG, BERTIL K J (1912-). Ethnologist. Musical instruments & folklore of the Lower Congo. Source: Int Dir Anth 5.

2996 ŠOLC, VÁCLAV (1919-). Ethnologist. Material culture of Aymara Indians of Chile & Bolivia. Source: Int Dir Anth 5.

2997 SOLECKI, RALPH STEFAN (1917-), Long Island, New York, United States. Archeologist, prehistorian. Prehistory, photo-interpretation & aerial photography in Northeastern U.S. Researched Arctic Alaskan and pre-Inuit archeology. Sources: Int Dir Anth 3, 5.

2998 SOLEY GUELL, TOMAS (1875-1943), Costa Rica. Economist.

Wrote an economic history of Costa Rican development. Source: Creedman, Theodore, Historical Dictionary of Costa Rica (1977), p 188.

2999 SON of MANY BEADS, THE (BIDAGA or JOSÉ PINO) (1866-1954), New Mexico, United States. Key Navajo informant. Source: Am Anth 57:1036-7 O '55.

3000 SOON-CHANG, HONG (1917-), Korea. Ethnologist. Ethnography & national consciousness in Korea. Source: Int Dir Anth 5.

3001 SOROKIN, PITIRIM (1889-), Russia. Sociologist. Contributed to sociocultural systems studies. Source: International Encyclopedia of the Social Sciences, v. 15.

3002 SOUTHORN, BELLA. Writer. Wrote an essay on Gambian politics, history and society. Source: Gailey, Harry A., Historical Dictionary of Gambia (1975), p 120.

3003 SPAULDING, ALBERT C (1914-), Choteau, Montana, United States. Archeologist. Quantitative methods in theoretical archeology of Eastern U.S. Sources: Int Dir Anth 2, 3, 5.

3004 SPECK, FRANK GOULDSMITH (1881-1950), Brooklyn, New York, United States. Anthropologist, folklorist, ethno-musicologist. Worked with Native N. Americans, especially N.E & S.E. American Indians. Researched ceremonialism, linguistic texts, art and social organizations of Algonkian, Iroquoias and Sioux. Specialized in American Indians & folk science, Algonkian & other U.S. Indian languages, material culture, songs & ceremonies. Sources: Biog Index: 2/Int Dir Anth 1 2 3/ Journal of American Folklore 64:415-18 O '51/Am Anth 53:67-87 Ja '51/ Pennsylvania University Museum Bulletin 15:3-5 Jl '50/ Archaeology 8:58 Spring '50/N Y Times p 27 F 8 '50/ School & Society 71:109 F 18 '50/Science 111:213 F 24 '50/ Wilson Library Bulletin 24:554 Ap 50.

3005 SPECTOR, JOHANNA (1915-). Ethnomusicologist. Ethnomusicology of Jews in Europe. Source: Int Dir Anth 5.

3006 SPEISER, EPHRAIM AVIGDOR (1902-1965), Galicia, Pennsylvania, United States. Orientalist. Prehistoric and Oriental archeology, ancient Oriental history and comparative linguistics. Sources: Biog Index: 7/Int Dir Anth 2/ American School of Oriental Research Bulletin (cover) no 179:2-6 O '65/ N Y Times p 33 Je 17 '65/Publishers Weekly 188:49 Jl 5 '65.

3007 SPEISER, FELIX (1880-1949), Basel, Switzerland. Ethnologist. Ethnology and physical anthropology of Melanesia. Sources: Biog Index: 2/Int Dir Anth 1 2 3/Phoebus 2 no 4:191 '49.

3008 SPEKE, JOHN HANNING (1827-1864), Somersetshire, England. Explorer. Explored much of Tanzania and Uganda; credited with discovery of the source of the Nile; wrote descriptive account of the region. Source: Kurtz, Laura S., Historical Dictionary of Tanzania (1978), p 199.

3009 SPELEERS, LOUIS (1882-), Anvers, Belgium. Egyptologist. Conservator, Oriental section Musees Royaux d'Art et d'Historire, Brussels. Sources: Biog Index: 2/ Brussels, Musees Royaux d'Art et d'Histoire Bulletin S 4 20:108-10 '48.

3010 SPENCE, LEWIS (1874-1955), Broughty Terry, Scotland. Poet, folklorist. Ethnology and folklore of Middle America and Europe, archeology of the Americas and Europe; studied mythology of pre-Columbian Mexico, Celtic divine forms. Sources: Biog Index: 3 & 4/Int Dir Anth 3/ Kunitz, Stanley Jasspon ed., Twentieth Century Authors; 1st sup. Wilson '55 p 939-40.

3011 SPENCER, J E (1907-). Geographer. Agricultural & sedentary gardening systems of S.E. Asia. Source: Int Dir Anth 5.

3012 SPENCER, KATHERINE (1913-). Anthropologist. Sources: Biog Index: 2/Survey 87:84 F '51.

3013 SPENCER, WALTER BALDWIN (1860-1929). Ethnologist. Aboriginal studies. Sources: Biog Index: 2 & 10/Oceania 46:21-4 S '75.

3014 SPENCER, WILLIAM KINGDON (1878-1955), England. Paleontologist. Sources: Biog Index: 4/ Royal Society of London. Biographical memoirs of fellows of the Royal Society, 1956. The Society of '56 p 291-8.

3015 SPENGLER, OSWALD (1880-1936), Germany. Historian, philosopher. Formulated a cyclical theory of development and decline operative in all cultures. Sources: International Encyclopedia of the Social Sciences, vol. 15/ Columbia.

3016 SPICER, EDWARD HOLLAND (1906-), Chettenham, Pennsylvania, United States. Anthropologist, ethnologist. Mexican & U.S. ethnology. Yaqui & Sonora culture change and religion. Sources: Int Dir Anth 1, 2, 3, 5/Nat Dir Lat Am.

3017 SPIEGAL, HEDWIG (1903-). Art critic. Chalk figures & art of Oceania. Source: Int Dir Anth 5.

3018 SPIER, LESLIE (1893-1961), New York, New York, United States. Ethnologist, anthropologist. Antiquity of man in America, ethnology of western Indians. Specialized in the archeology of New Jersey, Delaware & New York, and American Indian ethnology (particularly the Havasupai & Klamath); focused on the distribution of cultural phenomena, culture processes & culture growth, and kinship. Sources: Biog Index: 6/Int Dir Anth 1 2 3/ International Encyclopedia of the Social Sciences, v. 15/ Am Anth 63:835-7 Ag '61, 67:1258-77 O '65/Am Antiq 28:379-81 Ja '63.

3019 SPINDEN, HERBERT JOSEPH (1879-1967), Huron, South Dakota, United States. Anthropologist, archeologist. Ancient art and American history, explored Central America. In 1919 solved the chronology of Mayan inscriptions and estimated Toltec eras. Studied sequence and meaning in art, development of group mind through cultural leadership. Worked at Copan (Honduras) in 1913; produced a possible correlation scheme for the Mayan calendar. Sources: Biog Index: 2 & 8/Int Dir Anth 1 2 3/Museum News, Ja 15 '51/ Meyer, Harvey K., Historical Dictionary of Honduras (1976), p 333/ N Y Times p 44 O 24 '67.

3020 SPINDLER, LOUISE SCHAUBEL (1917-). Anthropologist. N. American Indian psycho-cultural anthropology. Adaptation & culture change among the Menomini Indians. Source: Int Dir Anth 5.

3021 SPITSYN, ALEKSANDR ANDREEVICH (1858-1931), Iaransk, Russia. Archeologist. Classified many of the existing archeological artifacts of the Russian Bronze Age, Scythian-Sarmatian, Volga-Kama, and other Slavic areas. Sources: Great Soviet Encyclopedia, New York, Macmillan (1980), v. 24, p 428/Passek, T.S. and B.A. Latynin. "K stoletiiu dnia rozhdeniia A.A. Spitsyna" Sovetskaia arkheologiia, 1958, no. 3.

3022 SPOEHR, ALEXANDER (1913-), Tuscon, Arizona, United States. Archeologist, ethnologist. Archeology & ethnic group relations of the Philippines & S. Pacific. Sources: Int Dir Anth 3, 5.

3023 SPOTT, ROBERT (1888-1953), Requa, California, United States. Important mediator in Yurok-white relations in California; key Yurok informant & interpreter. Source: Am Anth 56:282 Ap '54.

3024 SPUHLER, JAMES NORMAN (1917-), Tucumcari, New Mexico, United States. Physical anthropologist. Inbreeding in human populations in Japan. Human biology and public health of the Navajo. Sources: Int Dir Anth 3, 5.

3025 SPYRIDAKIS, GEŌRGIOS (1909-). Ethnologist, folklorist. Greek folklore & history of Greek ethnology. Source: Int Dir Anth 5.

3026 SQUIER, EPHRAIM GEORGE (1821- 1888), Bethlehem, New York, United States. Archeologist, ethnologist. Specialized in the ethnology, archeology and linguistics of American Indians; wrote several books describing Honduras and Nicaragua as they were in 1852; also wrote on prehistory of Mississippi Valley and New York. Sources: Biog Index: 4 5 & 13/American History Illustrated 15:30-5 Jl '80/ Meyer, Harvey K., Historical Dictionary of Honduras (1976), p 333-4/ Meyer, Harvey K., Historical Dictionary of Nicaragua (1972), p 427.

3027 SRINIVAS, MYSORE NARASIMHACHAR (1916-). Anthropologist, sociologist. Rural studies, social structure & analysis of disputes in India. Sources: Biog Index: 10-/Int Dir Anth 5/ International Social Sciences Journal 25 no 1/2:129-48 '73.

3028 SRODON, ANDRZEJ (1908-). Paleobotanist. Vegetation of the Quaternary period. Source: Int Dir Anth 5.

3029 STAHELIN, FELIX (1873-1952), Basel, Switzerland. Archeologist. Wrote on Roman antiquities. Sources: Biog Index: 3/Rev Arch series 6 44:81 Jl '54.

3030 STANISCHEV, DIMITR (1906-). Anatomist, physical anthropologist. Growth rhythms. Proportions of growing bodies of boys & girls in Bulgaria. Source: Int Dir Anth 5.

3031 STANLEY, HENRY MORTON (1841- 1904). Explorer. Visited Uganda, Tanzania; circumnavigated Lake Victoria; led an expedition across Africa, 1887-1889; left detailed journals of these travels. Source: Kurtz, Laura S., Historical Dictionary of Tanzania (1978), p 200.

3032 STARK, DONALD STEWART (1915-), Wilkes-Barre, Pennsylvania, United States. Linguist. Translated Bible into Mixtec language of Mexico. Source: Nat Dir Lat Am.

3033 STARR, BETTY WARREN (1906-1964), Chicago, Illinois, United States. Anthropologist, secretary. Studied levels of communal relations in Veracruz (Mexico), and early British travelers to Eastern Europe. Sources: Biog Index: 7/Am Anth 68:128-131 F '66.

3034 STARR, FREDERICK (1859-1933). Ethnologist. Did field research among various Indian tribes (U.S. & Mexico), in Japan, the Philippines & Africa; also published on Buddhism in Korea; identified himself closely with the native population; stimulated wide interest in anthropology. Source: Am Anth 36:271 Ap '34.

3035 STEED, GITEL POZNANSKI (1914-1977), United States. Social anthropologist. Ethnological work in India. Power politics, women, religion & ritual in rural India. Sources: Biog Index: 11 & 13-/Int Dir Anth 5/Am Anth 81:88-91 Mr '79/ Anth News D '77.

3036 STEENSBERG, AXEL (1906-), Sinding, Denmark. Anthropologist. Agricultural practices of Asia, Europe & Indonesia. Sources: Int Dir Anth 3, 5.

3037 STEENSBY, H P (-1920). Geographer. Specialist in Inuit culture; maintained that the center of Inuit culture was the Coronation Gulf region. Source: Am Anth 23:115 Ja '21.

3038 STEERE, BISHOP. Missionary. Compiled a handbook of KiSwahili in 1865 and wrote widely on the language. Source: Kurtz, Laura S., Historical Dictionary of Tanzania (1978), p 201.

3039 STEFANISZYN, BRONISŁAW (1906-). Social anthropologist. Medicine & lyrics of Ambo of Zaire. Source: Int Dir Anth 5.

3040 STEFFENSEN, JON (1905-), Reykjavik, Iceland. Physical anthropologist. Origin & development of Icelanders. Sources: Int Dir Anth 3, 5.

3041 STEGGERDA, MORRIS (1900-1950), Holland, Michigan, United States. Anthropologist. Maya Indians. Growth of Maya, Navajo, Negro and Dutch children. Development of anthropometric instruments. Sources: Biog Index: 3/Int Dir Anth 1 2 3/Nat Cyc Am Biog 38:345 '53.

3042 STEIN, MARC AUREL (1862-

1943), Budapest, Hungary. Archeologist, antiquarian. Antiquarian and geographical research in India, Central Asia and Iran. Sources: Biog Index: 4 5 6 8 & 11/Int Dir Anth 1 2/Apollo 107:80-5/ Smithsonian 8:95-6 My '77/ Mirsky, Jeannette. Sir Arthur Stein, archeological explorer. Univ. of Chicago Press '77.

3043 STEINDORFF, GEORG (1861-1951), Germany. Egyptologist. Sources: Biog Index: 1 2 & 3/Isis 43 no 1:56 '52.

3044 STEINER, ROLAND B (ca. 1840-1906). Planter. Collected archeological artifacts; published on folklore of the "Southern Negro". Source: Am Anth 8:204.

3045 STEKELIS, MOSHE (1898-1967), Russia. Archeologist. Prehistoric archeology and physical anthropology. Sources: Biog Index: 7/Int Dir Anth 2/N Y Times p 47 Mr 16 '67.

3046 STEPHENS, FERRIS J (1893-1969), Fayette County, Indiana, United States. Assyriologist. Numerous studies of Assyrian documents; assembled major American collection of Babylonian artifacts at Yale Univ. Sources: Biog Index: 9 & 11/Nat Cyc Am Biog 57:487-8 '77.

3047 STEPHENS, JOHN LLOYD (1805-1852), Shrewsbury, New Jersey, United States. Writer, diplomat. Wrote accounts of his travels in Middle East, Europe, and Central America, in each case detailing the prehistory of the region. With Frederick Catherwood produced two volumes depicting many ancient sites in Central America, in particular Copan (Honduras). Sources: Columbia/Creedman, Theodore, Historical Dictionary of Costa Rica (1977), p 190/Meyer, Harvey K., Historical Dictionary of Honduras (1976), p 335-6.

3048 STEPHENSON, ROBERT LLOYD (1919-), Portland, Oregon, United States. Archeologist. Preceramic & ceramic archeology of U.S.; excavated at Accokeek (Maryland). Archeological surveys of reservoir areas in Texas to be inundated by dams. Sources: Int Dir Anth 3, 5.

3049 STERN, THEODORE (1917-). Ethnologist. Published on religion among Karen of Thailand and linguistics, ethnology of Klamath Indians. Source: Int Dir Anth 5.

3050 STERNBERG, LEO (1861-1927), Russia. Ethnologist. Ethnology of the peoples of Eastern Siberia, especially the Gilyak, Orochi, Goldi, and Ainu. Comparative ethnographic research. Source: Am Anth 31:568-71 Jl '29.

3051 STEVENS, GORHAM PHILLIPS (1876-1963), Staten Island, New York, United States. Archeologist. Wrote widely on classical Greek architecture. Sources: Biog Index: 7 & 9/Nat Cyc Am Biog 52:71-2 '70.

3052 STEVENSON, JAMES (1840-1888), Maysville, Kentucky, United States. Explorer, surveyor. Specialized in the archeology & ethnology of Arizona & New Mexico, particularly the Navajo, Zuni, and Hopi. Source: Am Anth 18:557-8 O '16.

3053 STEVENSON, MATILDA COXE (EVANS) (1850-1915), San Augustine, Texas, United States. Ethnologist, ethnographer. Authority on Zuni and other Pueblo Indians, especially San Ildefonso Pueblos, of the Southwest United States. Focused on role of women, child life & religion. Sources: Notable American Women, 1607-1950, vol. III, Belknap Press '71, p 33-4/ Siegel, P.A. & K.T. Finley, Women in the Scientific Search, Metuchen, N.J., Scarecrow, 1985/Am Anth 18:552-9 O '16/Anth News 3/86.

3054 STEVENSON, PAUL HUSTON (1892- 1971), Monmouth, Illinois, United States. Physician, anthropologist. Physical anthropology and human anatomy, anthropomorphic and constitutional problems of Chinese. Sources: Biog Index: 11/Int Dir Anth 1 2/Nat Cyc Am Biog 56:37-8 '75.

3055 STEVENSON, SARA (Yorke)

(1847-1921), Paris, France. Archeologist. Sources: Biog Index: 12/Meyerson, Martin & Winegrad, Dilys P. Gladly learn & gladly teach. Univ. of Pennsylvania Press '78 p 116-29.

3056 STEWARD, JULIAN HAYNES (1902- 1972), Washington D.C., United States. Anthropologist, cultural ethnologist. Archeology of western U.S., ecology of primitive cultures. Cultural ecology; area studies; peasant populations. Advanced the notion of "cultural evolution". Founded Smithsonian Institution's Institute of Social Anthropology. Sources: Biog Index: 9 & 10/Int Dir Anth 1 2 3/ International Encyclopedia of the Social Sciences, v. 18/Nat Dir Lat Am/ Am Anth 75:886-903 Je '73.

3057 STEWART, JAMES RIVERS BARRINGTON (1913-1962), Australia. Archeologist. Near Eastern archeology, especially of early Bronze Age. Sources: Biog Index: 6/Int Dir Anth 2/Am J Arch 66:411-12 O '62/ Illustrated London News 240:423 Mr 17 '62.

3058 STEWART, KENNETH MALCOLM (1916-), Tecumseh, Nebraska, United States. Ethnohistorian. Chemehuevi, Mohave, Papago, Yuman & Pima ethnography. N. American shamanism, primitive warfare and Pima acculturation. Sources: Int Dir Anth 3, 5.

3059 STEWART, KILTON RIGGS (1902-1965), Salt Lake City, Utah, United States. Anthropologist, physiologist. Ethnology and folklore of S.E. Asia, China, Korea, Japan and Indonesia. Application of therapeutic methods of trance dream reconstruction practiced among Negritoes of Luzon (Philippines) and of dream interpretations of Senoi Shamans (of Malaya). Sources: Biog Index: 7/Int Dir Anth 3/N Y Times p 47 My 19 '65.

3060 STEWART, OMER CALL (1908-), Provo, Utah, United States. Ethnologist. Ute acculturation in Mexico & U.S. Great Basin Indians. General and S.W. United States ethno-geography. Indian burning and landscape, analysis of Mormon villages; intergroup relations in Colorado. Sources: Int Dir Anth 1, 2, 3, 5.

3061 STEWART, THOMAS DALE (1901-), Delta, Pennsylvania, United States. Anthropologist, ethnologist, paleopathologist. Identification of human skeletons for forensic anthropology. Anthropometry of American Indians & Inuit. Comparative primate anatomy, musculature and hair directions, craniometry of various Inuit and Indian groups. Sources: Biog Index: 2/Int Dir Anth 1, 2, 3, 5/Nat Dir Lat Am/ Popular Mechanics 93:122-5+ F '50.

3062 STIEDA, LUDWIG (1837-1918), Riga, Russia. Anatomist. Surveyed Russian anthropological literature. Source: Am Anth 21:344 Jl '19.

3063 STIMSON, JOHN FRANCIS (1883-1958), New Jersey, United States. Ethnologist. Editor of *Webster's Dictionary* for Polynesia, Melanesia & Micronesia. Interested in linguistics, ethnology and anthropology. Worked on dictionary of the Tuamotuan dialect of the Polynesian language. Sources: Biog Index: 5/Int Dir Anth 1 2/N Y Times p 19 N 1 '58.

3064 STIRLING, EDWARD CHARLES (1848-1919), Strathalbyn, South Australia, Australia. Physiologist, ethnologist. Wrote widely on many subjects including Australian aborigines. Sources: Biog Index: 2/Dictionary of Australian Biography 2;365-6 '49.

3065 STIRLING, GENE McNAUGHTON (1905-1977), California, United States. Expert on Seminole Indians. Source: Anth News Mr '77.

3066 STIRLING, MATTHEW WILLIAMS (1896-1975), Salinas, California, United States. Anthropologist, archeologist, ethnologist, museum curator. Worked in Mexican archeology. Presented first solid evidence that the Olmec was the oldest civilization in Mesoamerica. Worked on New Guinean,

African, & Seminole Indian ethnology. Stimulated anthropology as director of Bureau of American Ethnology for 30 years. Sources: Biog Index: 10 11 & 12/Int Dir Anth 1 2 3/Nat Dir Lat Am/ Nat Cyc Am Biog 58:307-8 '79/Am Antiq 41:63-67 '76/Am Anth 78:886-8 D '76/ Anth News Ap '75.

3067 STIRLING, PAUL (1912-). Rural social structure of Turkey; general ethnology of the Middle East, especially Turkey. Source: Int Dir Anth 5.

3068 STJERNQUIST, BERTA (1918-). Archeologist, prehistorian. Bronze & Iron Age cultural connections in Scandinavia. Source: Int Dir Anth 5.

3069 STOKOE, WILLIAM C (1919-). Linguist. Sign languages. Semiotics, American sign language. Source: Int Dir Anth 5.

3070 STOŁYHWO, KAZIMIERZ (1880-), Brailov, Poland. Anthropologist. The origin and culture of the Slavs. Source: Great Soviet Encyclopedia, New York, Macmillan (1980), v. 24, p 565.

3071 STONE, DORIS ZEMURRAY (1909-), New Orleans, Louisiana, United States. Anthropologist, archeologist. Central America archeology & ethnology. Delimitation of pre-Columbian cultures of Honduras. Talamanca. Metallurgy. Research Associate, Peabody Museum. Wrote: *Archeology of the North Coast of Honduras* (1941); *Archeology of Southern & Central Honduras* (1957); *The Talamancan Tribes of Costa Rica* (1961). Sources: Biog Index: 3/Int Dir Anth 1, 2, 3, 5/Nat Dir Lat Am/ Americas 5:9-11+ Ja '53.

3072 STONE, JOHN FREDERIC SMERDON (1899-1957), Bath, England. Archeologist. European prehistory, especially Neolithic and Bronze Ages; excavated Late Bronze Age sites in southern England. Petrological identification of stone axes and other tools, distribution of faience beads derived from E. Mediterranean. Sources: Biog Index: 4/Int Dir Anth 2 3/Nature 179:1165 Je 8 '57.

3073 STONEHILL, BEN (1906-1965). Folklorist. Hebrew folklore. Sources: Biog Index: 7/N Y Times p 25 D 28 '65.

3074 STONER, VICTOR ROSE (1893-1957), Victoria, Texas, United States. Priest, archeologist. Authority on the old Spanish colonial missions of the Pimeria Alta; co-founder of archeological journal, *The Kiva*. Sources: Biog Index: 5/Am Antiq 23:420 Ap '58.

3075 STOPA, ROMAN (1895-), Wola Batorska, Poland. Linguist, social anthropologist. S. & W. African clicks & clicking languages. Relation between language, psychology and culture. Sources: Int Dir Anth 3, 5.

3076 STOUCH, GEORGE W H (1842-1906), Gettysburg, Pennsylvania, United States. Military officer. Fighter against and later agent for U.S. Indians, particularly Northern Cheyennes and Crows, Southern Cheyennes and Arapaho. Source: Am Anth 8:738-9 O '06.

3077 STOUT, DAVID BOND (1913-1968), Stoughton, Wisconsin, United States. Anthropologist. Principal ethnologist & one of the founders of the Department of Anthropology at State Univ. of New York at Buffalo. American archeology and ethnology, especially South American; studied design areas, games, toys, etc., in South America. Sources: Int Dir Anth 2 3/Am Anth Mr '74 Mr '74.

3078 STREHLOW, THEODOR GEORGE HEINRICH (1908-), Hermannsburg, Northern Territories, Australia. Folklorist, linguist. Folklore. Songs & traditions of the Aranda. Aboriginal myths & songs of Australia. Analysis of the rhythms, structure, diction, poetic devices and themes of Central Australian aboriginal chants. Sources: Int Dir Anth 2, 3, 5.

3079 STRESSER-PEAN, GUY (1913-), Paris, France. Ethnologist, archeologist. Mexican ethnobotany & ethnozoology. Researched rite of the "Volador" in Mexico and

Central America. Sources: Int Dir Anth 3, 5.

3080 STROMBACK, DAG ALVAR (1900-1978), Jarbo, Sweden. Folklorist, philologist. Ethnology, linguistics and folklore of Europe. Researched Swedish tradition and dialects; medieval folklore in Scandinavia. Sources: Biog Index: 13/Int Dir Anth 3/Folklore 90:98-104 '79.

3081 STROMSVIK, GUSTAV (1901-). Archeologist. Directed excavations at Copan (Honduras), 1935-1942, and did stela restorations at Quirigua (Guatemala). Source: Meyer, Harvey K., Historical Dictionary of Honduras (1976), p 336.

3082 STRONG, EUGENIE (Sellers) (1860-1943), England. Archeologist. Art & sculpture of Ancient Rome. Sources: Biog Index: 2 & 5/ Dictionary of National Biography 1941-1950:848-9 '59/Rev Arch, Ja '50.

3083 STRONG, WILLIAM DUNCAN (1899- 1962), Portland, Oregon, United States. Anthropologist, archeologist. Archeology and ethnography of the Americas, including especially coastal Peru, Central America, Nebraska, Southwestern U.S. Known for putting cultural phenomena into historical context. Sources: Biog Index: 6 & 7/Int Dir Anth 1 2 3/Nat Cyc Am Biog 49:385-6 '66/ Am Anth 65:1102-11 O '63.

3084 STUBBS, STANLEY ALGER (1906-1959), Albuquerque, New Mexico, United States. Archeologist, museum curator. Archeology of N. America, material culture of S.W. Indians; surveyed Pueblo Villages. Southwestern (U.S.) archeology, particularly Pueblo cultures; stimulated interest in Southwestern culture. Sources: Biog Index: 5/Int Dir Anth 1 2 3/Am Anth 62:1045-6 O '60/ Am Antiq 25:587-8 Ap '60.

3085 STUMPF, FRIEDRICH CARL (1848- 1936), Wiesentheid, Lower Franconia, Germany. Psychologist, philosopher, ethno-musicologist. Published in German. Often considered founder of ethnomusicology. Source: International Encyclopedia of the Social Sciences, v. 15.

3086 STUTTERHEIM, WILLEM FREDERIK (1892-1942), Rotterdam, Netherlands. Archeologist, museum conservator. Worked in Indonesia & Bali. Prehistory & art history. Sources: Biog Index: 1/Int Dir Anth 1/Far Eastern Quarterly 5:217-8 F '46.

3087 SULLIVAN, HARRY STACK (1892-1949), Norwich, New York, United States. Psychiatrist. Wrote on theoretical psychiatry. Dealt with relation between culture and personality. Source: International Encyclopedia of the Social Sciences, v. 15.

3088 SULLIVAN, LOUIS ROBERT (1892- 1925), Houlton, Maine, United States. Physical anthropologist. Specialist in Polynesian anthropometry. Source: Am Anth 27:357-8 Ap '25, 38:313 Ja '26.

3089 SUMI, TOKAN (1914-). Linguist. Sanskrit lore & Turkish languages. Source: Int Dir Anth 5.

3090 SUMMERS, ROGER F H (1907-). Archeologist. Wrote extensively on Iron Age of Rhodesia and the Ndebele state. Source: Rasmussen, R. Kent, Historical Dictionary of Rhodesia/Zimbabwe (1979), p 315.

3091 SUMNER, WILLIAM GRAHAM (1840- 1910), Paterson, New Jersey, United States. Stressed evolutionary social science studies. Folkways. Social Darwinism. Social classes. Sources: International Encyclopedia of the Social Sciences, v. 15/ Am Anth 12:118-9 Ja '10.

3092 SUSTO, JUAN ANTONIO (1896-), Panama City, Panama. Historian. Wrote an account of early Panamanian history citing many primary Spanish documentary sources. Source: Hedrick & Hedrick, Historical Dictionary of Panama (1970), p 92-3.

3093 SUTTLES, WAYNE PRESCOTT (1918-). Ethnologist. Economic anthropology. Salish language & ethnology. Okinawan peasant culture. Source: Int Dir Anth 5.

3094 SUZUKI, HISASHI (1912-). Physical anthropologist. Microevolution of the Japanese. Twin studies. Source: Int Dir Anth 5.

3095 SUZUKI, JIRO (1916-). Social anthropologist. Racial problems. Unemancipated minorities in Japan. Source: Int Dir Anth 5.

3096 SUZUKI, MAKOTO (1914-), Japan. Anatomist, physician. Craniotomy of Hawaiians, Japanese and Maori. Archeological studies on prehistoric age in Chugoku and Shikoku (Japan). Sources: Int Dir Anth 3, 5.

3097 SVOB, TVRTKO (1917-). Bio-museologist. Growth & development in Yugoslavia. Source: Int Dir Anth 5.

3098 SWADESH, FRANCES LEON (1917-). Linguist, social anthropologist. Ethnohistory of Mexican & U.S. Hispanics. Value orientations. Source: Int Dir Anth 5.

3099 SWADESH, MORRIS (1909-1967), Holyoke, Massachusetts, United States. Linguist, anthropologist. Tarascan language & cultural relationships. Nootka language & economy. Linguistic work led him to develop a method for measuring the separation in time of any two languages (lexico-statistical method for dating linguistic separation). Sources: Int Dir Anth 1 2 3/American Indigena 27:240-246/ Am Anth 70:755-6 Ag '68.

3100 SWAN, CHARLES L (1909-). Social anthropologist. Madiga untouchables of India. Source: Int Dir Anth 5.

3101 SWANTON, JOHN REED (1873-1958), Gardiner, Maine, United States. Anthropologist, ethnologist, ethnohistorian. Historical ethnology of North American Indians & their geographical distribution. Definitive works on the Haida. Also wrote about Southwestern U.S. & Mexican Indians (Tunica, Chitimacha, & Atakapa) Indians and ethnography of Northwest Coast and Southeast. Developed & refined the methods used in ethnohistory; discovered, identified, traced the movements of, and wrote the histories of ethnic entities; disproved the evolutionary contentions about the social organization of American Indian tribes. Sources: Biog Index: 5/Int Dir Anth 1 2/ International Encyclopedia of the Social Sciences, v. 15/ Steward, Julian H., John Reed Swanton. New York, Columbia Univ. Press (1960), p 329-49/Am Anth 61:633-8 Ag '59.

3102 SWAUGER, JAMES L (1913-). Petroglyphologist, archeologist. Petroglyphs of the Ohio Valley. Historic archeology of Ft. Pitt (Pittsburg, Pennsylvania). Jordan. Source: Int Dir Anth 5.

3103 SWEET, LOUISE ELIZABETH (1916-). Ethnologist, ethnoecologist. Ethnology. Peasant & nomadic pastoralists of the the Near & Middle East. Source: Int Dir Anth 5.

3104 SWIFT, EMERSON HOWLAND (1889- 1975), West Orange, New Jersey, United States. Archeologist. Specialist on ancient Corinth (Greece) with emphasis on sculpture; contributed to various volumes on materials from this site. Sources: Biog Index: 11/Am J Arch 80:197 Spr '76.

3105 SWINDLER, MARY HAMILTON (1884-1967). Archeologist. Ancient art. Pre-Christian painting. Sources: Biog Index: 2 7 8 10 & 13/Am J Arch, O '67/ Notable American Women, the Modern Period. vol. IV, Belknap Press '80, p 667-69.

3106 SWINGLE, WALTER TENNYSON (1871-1952), Canaan, Pennsylvania, United States. Sinologist, botanist. Wrote on traditional Chinese agriculture. Sources: Biog Index: 6 & 10/Nat Cyc Am Biog 54:13-4 '73.

3107 SWINTON, GEORGE (1917-). Anthropologist. Inuit sculpture. Prehistoric & contemporary Inuit art. Source: Int Dir Anth 5.

3108 SYMMONS-SYMONOLEWICZ, KONSTANTIN (1909-). Sociologist. Social movements, political sociology & nationalism. Source: Int Dir Anth 5.

3109 TACITUS, CORNELIUS (A.D. 55-A.D. 117), Italy. His *Germania* is the earliest ethnology of Germany. Source: Columbia.

3110 TAIT, CHARLES (1768-1835). Paleontologist, jurist, planter. Sources: Biog Index: 1/Journal of Southern History 14:206-33 My '48.

3111 TAIT, DAVID (1912-1956). Anthropologist, ethnographer. Ghana & Konkomba. Studied the Konkomba and Dagomba (Ghana) in which he examined particularly their social structure and religion & relations with surrounding peoples. Sources: Biog Index: 4/Am Anth 59:325 Ap '57.

3112 TAKAHASHI, RYO (1911-). Physician. Human, mammalian nasal cartilage & nasal system deviations. Source: Int Dir Anth 5.

3113 TAKAHITO, MIKASA, Prince of Japan (1915-). Orientalist. Sources: Biog Index: 4/Time 66:48+ Jl 11 '55/Life 39:72 O 17 '55.

3114 TAKÁTS, ZOLTÁN FELVINCZI (1880-1964), Hungary. Orientalist, museum curator. Sources: Biog Index: 7/Oriental Art 11:125 Summer '65.

3115 TAKEDA, SHOSHU (1916-). Folklorist, historian. Folk Buddhism & history of folk temples in Japan. Source: Int Dir Anth 5.

3116 TALCOTT, LUCY (1899-1970), New Britain, Connecticut, United States. Archeologist. Devised improved system of record-keeping for archeological expeditions; wrote about Greek vases. Sources: Biog Index: 8 9 & 10/Nat Cyc Am Biog 54:627-8 '73.

3117 TALLGREN, AARNE MICHAEL (1885-1950), Finland. Archeologist. Prehistory, especially early history of Asia and Bronze Age of Eastern Europe. Sources: Biog Index: 2/Int Dir Anth 1 2/Rev Arch series 6 37:207 Ap '51.

3118 TANAKA, SUMIKO (1909-), Japan. Matriculturist. Status & history of women in Japan. Source: Int Dir Anth 5.

3119 TANNENBAUM, JANE BELO (1904-1968), Texas, United States. Anthropologist, artist. Studied ceremonial life, trance, religion & children's art of Balinese society (Indonesia). Sources: Biog Index: 8/Am Anth 70:1168-9 D '68.

3120 TANNER, CLARA LEE (1906-), Biscoe, North Carolina, United States. Folk artist. Southwest U.S. Indian paintings, arts & crafts. Ethnology of N. America, archeology of N. America, Europe, Near & Middle East. Sources: Int Dir Anth 3, 5.

3121 TANTAQUIDGEON, GLADYS (1889-). Anthropologist. Sources: Biog Index: 9/Int Dir Anth 2.

3122 TANZER, HELEN HENRIETTA (1876-1961). Archeologist. Classical archeology in Rome. Sources: Biog Index: 1 & 6/Nat Cyc Am Biog, '46/N Y Times p 36 D 24 '61.

3123 TAPLIN, GEORGE (1831-1879). Missionary, folklorist. Aboriginal studies. Sources: Biog Index: 10/Oceania 46:9-12 S '75.

3124 TARDE, JEAN GABRIEL de (1843-1904), Sarlat, France. Sociologist. Wrote on criminology, communication, cultural diffusion. Source: International Encyclopedia of the Social Sciences, v. 15.

3125 TASMAN, ABEL JANSZOAN (1603-1659), Lutjegasti, Netherlands. Explorer. Led a voyage of discovery, 1642-1643, which located New Zealand and Tasmania; journal of this trip is richly illustrated as well as being ethnographically valuable. Source: Craig & King, Historical Dictionary of Oceania (1981), p 283.

3126 TAULI, VALTER EVALD (1907-). Linguist. Estonian grammar. Theory of language planning. Comparative Uralic morphology. Source: Int Dir Anth 5.

3127 TAX, SOL (1907-), Chicago, Illinois, United States. Ethnologist, social anthropologist. Founder of "action anthropology"; founder of L.A.R.G.; founder & first editor (1958-1974) of *Current Anthropology*. President of many organizations including American

Anthropological Association & IX *International Congress of Anthropological & Ethnological Sciences* (1973). Editor, *World Anthropology*. Specialist on N. American Indian problems. Primitive social organization and kinship, Maya Indians, acculturation, culture change and race relations; fieldwork in Guatemala. Sources: Int Dir Anth 1, 2, 3, 5/ International Encyclopedia of the Social Sciences, v. 18/Nat Dir Lat Am.

3128 TAYLOR, ARCHER (1890-1973), Philadelphia, Pennsylvania, United States. Folklorist. Specialist in folk speech, riddles, proverbs, folktales, folksongs & ballads, especially of Europe; created many bibliographies on these topics. Sources: Biog Index: 10/Journal of American Folklore 87:2-9 Ja '74.

3129 TAYLOR, DONALD LAVOR (1916-), Ephriam, Utah, United States. Human sexuality, marriage and family relations in Germany. Source: American Men and Women of Science, ed. by J.C. Press, 12th ed., New York, Bowker, 1973.

3130 TAYLOR, DOUGLAS MACRAE (1907-), Bately, Yorkshire, England. Cultural anthropologist, linguist. Island Carib culture & language. West Indian Creole languages. Sources: Int Dir Anth 3, 5.

3131 TAYLOR, RICHARD MORRIS STOVIN (1903-). Physical anthropologist. Dental science & surgery. Source: Int Dir Anth 5.

3132 TAYLOR, WALTER WILLARD (1913-), Chicago, Illinois, United States. Archeologist. Mexican, U.S. & European Neolithic & Paleolithic archeology. Pueblo ethnography. Theory in archeology. Archeology of Southeast and Southwest Americas, especially Northern Mexico; researched cave cultures of Coahuila (Mexico), "Great Drought" in Southwestern U.S. Sources: Int Dir Anth 2, 3, 5/Nat Dir Lat Am.

3133 TAYLOR, WILLIAM BOWER (1821-1895), Pennsylvania, United States. Physicist, administrator, anthropologist. Wrote on technological innovation. Source: Am Anth 8(old series):184 Ap 1895.

3134 TAYLOR, WILLIAM ROBERT (1882- 1951), Canada. Orientalist, theologian. Sources: Biog Index: 2/Journal of Biblical Literature 71:xx-xi Mr '52/ Royal Society of Canada, Proceedings and Transactions, '53.

3135 TECHNAU, WERNER (1902-1941), Germany. Archeologist. Archeology of Classical Greece. Sources: Biog Index: 1/Rev Arch series 6 25:64 Ja '46.

3136 TEGGART, FREDERICK JOHN (1870-1946), Belfast, Ireland. Historian. Contributed to theory of history, comparative history, ethnic history. Source: International Encyclopedia of the Social Sciences, v. 15.

3137 TEILHARD de CHARDIN, S J, Fr. PIERRE (1881-1955), Clermont-Ferrand, France. Priest, anthropologist. Human paleontology and Cenozoic stratigraphy in Asia and India; development of science of anthropogenesis. Sources: Biog Index: 3 4 5 6 7 8 9 10 11 12 & 13/Int Dir Anth 1 2 3/ Lucas, Mary & Ellen, Teilhard. McGraw-Hill '81/ UNESCO Courier 34:24-29, 30-2 N '81/ America 142:384 My 3 '80, 144:418-20, 422-24, 424-27 My 23 '81/ N Scientist 90:280-2 Ap 30, 540 My 14, 647-8 Je 4, 710-11 Je 11 '81/ Natural History 89:8+ Ag '80/ Makers of Modern Culture. Facts on File '81, p 515-16/ Teilhard de Chardin, Pierre. Letters from my friend Teilhard de Chardin. Paulist Press/ Am Anth 58:147-50 F '56.

3138 TEIT, JAMES A (-1922), Shetland Islands, Zetland Islands, Scotland. Ethnographer, ethno-geographer. Specialist on the Thompson, Shuswap, Lillooet & Salish Indians and other native groups of interior British Columbia; specialist on Salish basketry. Source: Am Anth 24:490-2 O '22.

3139 TELETOR, CELSO NARCISO (1891-). Priest. Compiled

dictionaries of several Maya dialects spoken in Guatemala. Source: Moore, Richard E., Historical Dictionary of Guatemala (1973), p 220.

3140 TELLO, JULIO CÉSAR (1880-1947), Peru. Archeologist, physician. Founder of archeology in Peru and most prominent Peruvian archeologist of his time. Director of several museums and head of several expeditions. Published on syphilis, trepanning, Nazca cemeteries, mummified heads, and other features of pre-Hispanic Peru; origin and also on development of Andean civilizations. Sources: Biog Index: 1/Int Dir Anth 1/ Alisky, Historical Dictionary of Peru (1979), p 102/ Who's Who in Latin America 3rd ed., Ronald Hilton ed., Stanford Univ. Press (Blaine Ethridge edition, 1971) 201/ Niles, Blair (Rice), ed. Journeys in Time. Coward McCann '46 p351-64/ Am Antiq 14:50-6/Am J Arch 51:433-4 O '47/N Y Times p 26 Je 5 '47.

3141 TEMPLE, RICHARD CARNAC (1850- 1931), Allahabad, India. Army officer, Orientalist. Studied and collected Indian folklore and wrote on ethnography of India's peoples; edited explorers' accounts. Sources: Biog Index: 2/ Dictionary of National Biography 1931-1940:850-1 '49.

3142 TEN KATE, HERMAN FREDERIK CAREL (1858-1931), Amsterdam, Netherlands. Anthropologist. Published on the ethnography & physical anthropology of 20 southwestern (U.S.) Indian tribes; studied Indians & Bush Negroes of Dutch Guyana; traveled around the world and assembled collections for major European museums. Source: Am Anth 33:415-18 Jl '31.

3143 TEPLOUKHOV, SERGEI ALEKSANDROVICH (1888-1932), Il'inskoe, Russia. Archeologist. Archeology of southern Siberia, Kirghizia and Mongolia. Source: Great Soviet Encyclopedia, New York, Macmillan (1980), v. 25, p 516.

3144 TEPPER, JOHANNES (1907-). Prehistorian. Finno-Ugaritic prehistory in Eastern Europe. Source: Int Dir Anth 5.

3145 TERESHCHENKO, ALEKSANDR VLAS'EVICH (1806-1865), Zen'kovo, Russia. Ethnographer, archeologist. Studied the cultural and physical characteristics of the Russian people and their links with other Slavic peoples. Source: Great Soviet Encyclopedia, New York, Macmillan (1980), v. 25, p 522.

3146 THAKKAR, AMRITLAL VITHALDUS (1869-1951). Anthropologist. Specialist on tribal peoples of India, in particular those of Assam, Orissa, and Khandesh. Strove with Mohatmas Ghandi to eliminate stigma of "untouchability.". Sources: Biog Index: 2 & 11/N Y Times, Ja 20 '51.

3147 THAUNG, MAUNG PE (1919-). Cultural geographer. Cultural geography of S.E. Asia. Indigenous races of Burma. Source: Int Dir Anth 5.

3148 THAUSING, GERTRUD (1915-). Linguist, Egyptologist. African languages. Problems of religion & philosophy. Source: Int Dir Anth 5.

3149 THEAL, GEORGE McCALL (1837-1919). Archivist, historian. Wrote thorough history of South Africa (11 volumes); prepared colonial records for publication; helped create mythology to support apartheid. Source: Saunders, Christopher, Historical Dictionary of South Africa (1983), p 169.

3150 THEIL, BERNHARD AUGUST (1850- 1901), Elberfeld, Prussia. Priest. Published on the languages of the native peoples of Costa Rica. Source: Am Anth 4:358-9 Ap '02.

3151 THOMAS, CYRUS (1825-1910), Kingsport, Tennessee, United States. Lutheran minister, lawyer, ethnologist. Extensive work in anthropology & entomology. Ohio Mounds, anthropology & ethnology. Sources: Biog Index: 1 & 9/Columbia/Am Anth 12:337-43 Ap '10.

3152 THOMAS, FREDERICK WILLIAM (1867-1956), England. Orientalist. Boden Professor of Sanskrit at Oxford, 1927-1937. Sources: Biog Index: 4/Illustrated London News 228: 565 My 19 '56.

3153 THOMAS, THOMAS MORGAN (1828- 1884). Missionary. Wrote account of Ndebele life in mid-19th century Rhodesia. Source: Rasmussen, R. Kent, Historical Dictionary of Rhodesia/ Zimbabwe (1979), p 320-1.

3154 THOMAS, WILLIAM ISAAC (1863-1947), Virginia, United States. Cultural evolutionist. Source: International Encyclopedia of the Social Sciences, v. 15.

3155 THOMPSON, EDWARD HERBERT (1856-1935). Archeologist. Owned Chichen Itza (Mexico); specialist in Maya archeology & folklore; assembled collections of artifacts for major U.S. museums. Sources: Biog Index: 4 6 & 8/Am Anth 37:711-12 O '35.

3156 THOMPSON, HAROLD WILLIAM (1891-1964), Buffalo, New York, United States. Folklorist, philologist. Established folklore study as part of American academic life; specialized in folklore of New York state. Sources: Biog Index: 7/Journal of American Folklore 77:346-7 O '64.

3157 THOMPSON, HERBERT (1859-1944), London, England. Egyptologist. Specialist in Demotic and Coptic forms of Egyptian language; translated texts and papyri. Sources: Biog Index: 1 & 5/ Dictionary of National Biography 1941-1950:880-1 '59.

3158 THOMPSON, HOMER ARMSTRONG (1906-). Archeologist. Specialized in topography & monuments of Athens (Greece); directed excavation of the Agora, 1947-1967; pioneered study of Attic pottery. Sources: Biog Index: 1 & 10/Archaeology 26:84 Ap '73/C B, Ap '48.

3159 THOMPSON, JOHN ERIC (1898-1975), London, England. Anthropologist, archeologist. Scholar of Mayan writing, history & religion. Latin American archeology and ethnology. Directed excavations at several sites in the Mayan area over a period of 25 years and wrote extensively on Mayan archeology. Sources: Biog Index: 10 & 11/Int Dir Anth 1 2 3/Nat Dir Lat Am/ Meyer, Harvey K., Historical Dictionary of Honduras (1976), p 348/ Am Anth 78:317-20 Je '76/Am Antiq 42:180-90 Ap '77/Antiquity 49:245-6 D '75.

3160 THOMPSON, LAURA (1905-), Honolulu, Hawaii, United States. Anthropologist. Ecology & culture change. U.S. Indians, Iceland & Fiji Islands. Ethnology of N. America & Oceania, pottery and acculturation studies of Lau and Fiji Islands; culture theory; Indian personality research, theory and method of cooperative, integral social action research. Sources: Int Dir Anth 1, 3, 5.

3161 THOMPSON, LEONARD M (1916-). Historian. Compiled extensive written historical literature on South Africa; wrote biography of Moshoeshoe I of Lesotho. Source: Saunders, Christopher, Historical Dictionary of South Africa (1983), p 169.

3162 THOMPSON, REGINALD CAMPBELL (1876-1941), England. Assyriologist, archeologist. Assyriology, cuneiform, excavated in Near East; researched a dictionary of Assyrian botany. Sources: Biog Index: 1 & 5/Int Dir Anth 2/ Dictionary of National Biography 1941-1950:881-2 '59/ Driver, Godfrey Rolles. Reginald Campbell Thompson, 1876-1941. (Brit Acad, proceedings, v 30) Oxford '46.

3163 THOMPSON, STITH (1885-1976), Bloomfield, Kentucky, United States. Folklorist. International & comparative folklore. Studied motif-index of folk literature and motif and type analysis of oral tales of India. Sources: Biog Index: 10 & 11-/Int Dir Anth 3, 5.

3164 THOMPSON, WILLIAM ISAAC (1775-1833), Cork, Ireland. American ethnology, Polish peasant, sex. Promoted womens' rights.

Source: International Encyclopedia of the Social Sciences, v. 15.

3165 THOMSEN, CHRISTIAN JURGENSEN (1788-1865), Denmark. Archeologist. Sources: Biog Index: 4 & 6/ Daugherty, Charles Michael. Great Archaeologists. Grigson, Geoffrey & Gibbs-Smith, C. H. eds. Crowell '62 p 23-8.

3166 THOMSON, BASIL HOME (1861-1939), England. Civil servant. Wrote accounts of the society of Tonga and Fiji as they were ca. 1900. Source: Craig & King, Historical Dictionary of Oceania (1981), p 286-7.

3167 THOMSON, JOSEPH (1858-1895), Scotland. Explorer. Explored much of area between Tanzanian coast and Lake Victoria, particularly in the Masai area. Led two expeditions to the lake areas of East Africa, 1878-1880 and 1882-1884, the account of which contain data on the Masai. Sources: Ogot, Bethwell A., Historical Dictionary of Kenya (1981)/ Kurtz, Laura S., Historical Dictionary of Tanzania (1978), p 221.

3168 THOMSON, ROBERT (1816-1851), England. Missionary. Wrote five journals of his work on Marquesan and Tahitian history. Source: Craig & King, Historical Dictionary of Oceania (1981), p 281.

3169 THORNDIKE, EDWARD LEE (1874-1949), Williamsburg, Massachusetts, United States. Psychologist. Contributed to many fields of psychology, especially learning theory. Favored hereditarian theories of human behavior. Source: International Encyclopedia of the Social Sciences, v. 16.

3170 THORNER, DANIEL (1915-). Historian. Economic history. Problems of economic development. Source: Int Dir Anth 5.

3171 THUREAU-DANGIN, FRANÇOIS (1872-1944), Paris, France. Orientalist. One of the editors and contributors to *Revue d'Assyriologie* for 34 years. Sources: Biog Index: 1/Isis 36 no 3-4: 250 '46/ Revue d'Assyriologie 39:1-3 '42-44.

3172 THURNWALD, RICHARD (1869-1954), Vienna, Austria. Sociologist, anthropologist. Did extensive studies in Germany, Yugoslavia, Micronesia, New Guinea, East Africa. As a functionalist, he looked for the ways in which diverse aspects of culture were interwoven; provided the first systematic up-to-date account of primitive economies. Sources: Biog Index: 3/Int Dir Anth 1 3/ International Encyclopedia of the Social Sciences, v. 16/Am Anth 56:863-7 O '54.

3173 TIEDKE, KENNETH E. R (1911-), Neshkoro, Wisconsin, United States. Archeologist, ethnologist. Midwestern U.S. cross-cultural archeology & ethnology. Researched Rosebud Sioux acculturation. Sources: Int Dir Anth 3, 5.

3174 TINBERGEN, NIKOLAAS (1907-), The Hague, Netherlands. Ethologist. Introduced controlled experiments in the field. Made discoveries among wasps, butterflies, gulls. Brought ethology to the status of a unique science. Explored significance of findings of ethology to human society. Sources: Biog Index: 10 & 13/ International Encyclopedia of the Social Sciences, v. 18/ Makers of Modern Culture. Facts on File '81, p 519-20/ Current Biography 36:39-42 N '75/Current Biography Yr Bk 1975:4:14-6 '76/ Time 102:62 O 22 '73.

3175 TINDALE, NORMAN BARNETT (1900-). Ethnologist. Australian archeology & ethnology. Stone tool hafting. Source: Int Dir Anth 5.

3176 TISCHENDORF, LOBEGOTT FREIDER (1815-1874), Germany. Orientalist, bibliographer. Source: Biog Index: 10.

3177 TISSERANT, CHARLES. Botanist, missionary. First to study history and customs of the Banda people of the Central African Republic; studied traditional practices of agriculture among these people. Source: Kalck, Pierre, Historical Dictionary of the Central African Republic (1980), p

3178 **TITIEV, MISCHA** (1901-1978), Krementchug, Russia. Anthropologist. His ethnographic research on Hopi became a model for studies of western Pueblos. Sources: Int Dir Anth 1 2 3/Nat Dir Lat Am/Am Anth 81:342-44 Je '79/ Anth News Mr '79.

3179 **TODD, THOMAS WINGATE** (1885-1938), England. Physician. Contributed to physical anthropology, especially to the study of the development and variations in the human skeleton. Source: Am Anth 41:458-61 Jl '39.

3180 **TOKAREV, SERGEI ALEXANDROVICH** (1899-). Religious ethnologist. Religious beliefs & ethnogenesis of the Siberian & Slavic peoples. History of Russian ethnography. Source: Int Dir Anth 5.

3181 **TOKUDOME, MITOSHI** (1919-), Japan. Physical anthropologist. Studies of the origin of the Japanese people. Source: Int Dir Anth 5.

3182 **TOLEDO, FRANCISCO de**, Spain. Civil servant. Collected and sent to Spain much information on pre-Columbian Peru via interviews with surviving Inca nobles on their families, thus creating an excellent source of data useful to ethnographers. Source: Alisky, Historical Dictionary of Peru (1979), p 103.

3183 **TOLSTOV, SERGEI PAVLOVICH** (1907-1976), St. Petersburg, Russia. Ethnographer, archeologist, historian. Specialized on Central Asia and directed the Khorezm Archeological and Ethnographic Expedition, 1937-69. Sources: Great Soviet Encyclopedia, New York, Macmillan (1981), v. 26, p 215/Zhdanko, T.A. "S.P. Tolstov (k 60-letiiu so dnia rozhdeniia)" Sovetskaja etnografiia, 1967, no. 1.

3184 **TOMAŠIĆ, DINKO ANTUN** (1902-). Sociologist. Russia. Eastern Europe. Personality, culture & politics of Eastern & Western Europe. Source: Int Dir Anth 5.

3185 **TONNIES, FERDINAND** (1855-1936), Schleswig-Holstein, Germany. Sociologist. Major social theorist. Source: International Encyclopedia of the Social Sciences, v. 16.

3186 **TOOKER, WILLIAM WALLACE** (1848-1917). Authority on Indian nomenclature & archeology. Source: Am Anth 19:458 Jl '17.

3187 **TOOR, FRANCES** (1890-1956). Folklorist. Mexican popular arts. Sources: Biog Index: 4/N Y Times p 25/Publishers Weekly 169:2766 Je 25 '56/ Wilson Library Bulletin 31:36 S '56.

3188 **TOPINARD, PAUL** (1830-1911), France. Physician, anthropologist. Contributed to the development of physical anthropology. Source: Am Anth 14:196-7 Ja '12.

3189 **TORGERSEN, JOHAN** (1906-), Oslo, Norway. Physical anthropologist. Neolithic & historic comparative anatomy. Scandinavian pathology & craniometry. Application of x-rays in physical anthropology. Sources: Int Dir Anth 3, 5.

3190 **TORII, RYUZO** (1870-1953). Archeologist. Specialist on Japanese prehistory; studied ethnography of Manchuria. Sources: Biog Index: 3/Int Dir Anth 3/N Y Times p 27 Ja 15 '53.

3191 **TORRES, LUIS VAEZ de**, Portugal. Explorer. Led two ships of Quiros expedition through the New Guinea area in 1605-1606 and wrote an account of this effort. Source: Craig & King, Historical Dictionary of Oceania (1981), p 295-6.

3192 **TOULOUSE, JOSEPH HARRISON** (1916-1977), Albuquerque, New Mexico, United States. Archeologist. Excavated Pueblo Pardo site (New Mexico). Discovered San Jose preceramic culture. Mission archeology, world prehistory, especially lithic industries; cremation cult, bibliography of early man in the New World. Sources: Int Dir Anth 2 3/Anth News F '78.

3193 **TOURVILLE, HENRI de** (1842-1903), France. Contributed nomenclature for cross-cultural analysis. Source: International Encyclopedia of the Social Sciences, v. 15.

3194 TOUTAIN, JULES (1865-1961), Vincennes, France. Archeologist. Wrote about religion in Roman Empire and in Carthage. Sources: Biog Index: 6/Rev Arch 1:95-7 Ja '62.

3195 TOWNSEND, ELAINE MIELKE (1915-), Chicago, Illinois, United States. Summer Institute of Linguistics, Mexico & Peru, consultant. Source: Nat Dir Lat Am.

3196 TOYNBEE, ARNOLD JOSEPH (1889- 1975), London, England. His *A Study of History* proposed broad patterns underlying history of all civilizations. Source: International Encyclopedia of the Social Sciences, v. 18.

3197 TOZZER, ALFRED MARSTON (1877- 1954), Lynn, Massachusetts, United States. Anthropologist, archeologist, ethnologist. Maya specialist; worked on ethnology & archeology of Lacandon Indians. Contributed to anthropological conception of culture. Sources: Biog Index: 3 & 4/Int Dir Anth 1 2 3/ International Encyclopedia of the Social Sciences, v. 16/ Am Anth 57:614-18 Je '55/Am Antiq 21:72-80 Jl '55/ National Academy of Sciences. Biographical Memoirs. Columbia Univ. Press '57 p 383-97.

3198 TRAGER, GEORGE L (1906-), Newark, New Jersey, United States. Linguist. Taos Pueblo language & ethnography. Sources: Int Dir Anth 3, 5.

3199 TRAORE, DOMINIQUE AMADOU (1890-1972), Nigeria. Ethnographer. Expert on West African herbal medicines. Source: Imperato, Pascal J., Historical Dictionary of Mali (1977), p 101.

3200 TREGANZA, ADAM EDUARDO (1916- 1968), Salt Lake City, Utah, United States. Anthropologist. Specialized in archeology of Baja California (Mexico), and the Topanga culture of Southern California; worked extensively in California salvage archeology. Sources: Biog Index: 8/Int Dir Anth 3/Am Antiq 34:462-6 O '69.

3201 TREITSCHKE, HEINRICH von (1834-1896), Dresden, Germany. Historian. Defended authoritarianism in extinct cultures. Sources: New Int Enc, 1914 ed/Columbia/ International Encyclopedia of the Social Sciences, v. 16.

3202 TRET'IAKOV, PETR NIKOLAEVICH (1909-1976), Kostroma, Russia. Archeologist, historian. Expert on ancient history & archeology of the Slavic peoples; directed excavations on the Volga in the 1930s. Traced the development of the Russian people. Sources: Biog Index: 10/ Great Soviet Encyclopedia, New York, Macmillan (1981), v. 26, p 329/ N Y Times p 42 Je 16 '76.

3203 TREVOR, JACK CARRICK (1908-1967), Bath, England. Anthropologist. Ethnology and physical anthropology, studied ethnology of Virgin Islands, race crossings, craniology of medieval England & Negroes. Somatometry of Sandawe (Tanganyika). Sources: Biog Index: 8/Int Dir Anth 2 3/Nature 216:523 N 4 '67.

3204 TRIK, AUBREY S (1910-1968), Jacksonville, Florida, United States. Archeologist. Archeology of Middle America, restoration and excavation of ruins of Zaculeu (Guatemala). Sources: Biog Index: 8/Int Dir Anth 3/Expedition 10:15 Spring '68.

3205 TRILLES, HENRI (1866-1949), Clermont-Ferrand, France. Priest. Wrote about the Fang and the Pygmies of northeastern Gabon. Source: Gardiner, David E., Historical Dictionary of Gabon (1981), p 188.

3206 TRITTON, A S (1881-1973), England. Orientalist. Wrote on Muslim theology and education. Sources: Biog Index: 10/Asian Affairs 61:117 F '74.

3207 TROLL, CARL TH (1899-). Geographer, anthropologist. Indian culture & agriculture in the Andes of Bolivia & Peru. Source: Int Dir Anth 5.

3208 TROTTER, MILDRED (1899-), Monaca, Pennsylvania, United States. Anatomist. Interested in hair, vertebral column & vascular system. Sources: Int Dir Anth 1, 2, 3, 5.

3209 TROXELL, WILLIAM S (1893-1957). Columnist, folklorist. Collected and published folklore of the Pennsylvania Dutch. Sources: Biog Index: 4/N Y Times p 81 Ag 11 '57.

3210 TSCHOPIK, HARRY SCHLESSINGER (1915-1959), New Orleans, Louisiana, United States. Ethnologist. Southwestern U.S. & S. American ethnology and archeology. Role of magic in Aymara culture, Peru. Sources: Biog Index: 4 & 6/Int Dir Anth 2 3/Nat Cyc Am Biog 45:264-5 '62/ Am Anth 60:132-40 F '58.

3211 TSUKISHIMA, KENZO (1911-). Cultural psychologist. Ethno-psychology of language in Japan. Source: Int Dir Anth 5.

3212 TU, ER-WEI (1913-). Mythologist. Interrelations of Chinese & American Indian mythologies. Source: Int Dir Anth 5.

3213 TUBAKI, KOZI (1907-). Physical anthropologist. Physical anthropology of Asian peoples. Craniometry & physiognomy. Source: Int Dir Anth 5.

3214 TUGGLE, WILLIAM ORRIE (1841-1885). Folklorist. Sources: Biog Index: 6 & 10.

3215 AL-TUNISI, ZAYN AL-ABIDIN (19th century-), Tunisia. Explorer. Wrote account of journey through Wadai and Darfur (now in Chad and Sudan respectively) in the first years of the 19th century; described metallurgy of the Banda peoples. Source: Kalck, Pierre, Historical Dictionary of the Central African Republic (1980), p 3.

3216 TURGOT, ANNE ROBERT JACQUES (1727-1781), Paris, France. Sociologist. Worked in sociocultural studies. Source: International Encyclopedia of the Social Sciences, v. 15.

3217 TURNER, GEOFFREY E S (ca. 1910-1984). Museum curator. Specialist in N. American ethnology; published on hair embroidery in Siberia & N. America. Source: Anth News 3/86.

3218 TWEDDELL, COLIN ELLIDGE (1899-). Ethnologist, linguist. Ethnology & language of Tuli in China. Source: Int Dir Anth 5.

3219 TWIESSELMANN, FRANCOIS (1910-), Bouillon, Belgium. Physical anthropologist. Compared growth in Belgian & other populations. Sources: Int Dir Anth 3, 5.

3220 TYLDEN, GEOFFREY (-1970). Merchant, military officer. Wrote an historical account of the Basotho, plus articles and pamphlets. Source: Haliburton, Gordon, Historical Dictionary of Lesotho (1977), p 175.

3221 TYLOR, EDWARD BURNETT (1832- 1917), London, England. Anthropologist. Exposed ethnocentrism. Often considered the inventor of the anthropological concept of "culture.". Sources: Biog Index: 4 & 6/Am Anth 65:783-99 Ag '63/ International Encyclopedia of the Social Sciences, v. 15/ Kardiner, Abram, & Preble, Edward. They Studied Man. World '61 p 56-7/ Zusne, L., Biographical Dictionary of Psychology, Westport, Conn., Greenwood, 1984.

3222 TYTUS, ROBB de PEYSTER (1876- 1913), Ashville, North Carolina, United States. Archeologist. Excavated tomb of Amenhotep III near Thebes (Egypt). Sources: Biog Index: 7/Nat Cyc Am Biog 47:541 '65.

3223 U, DAW KHIN KHIN (1918-). Ethnologist. Marriage customs of Burmese Moslems. Burmese ethnology. Source: Int Dir Anth 5.

3224 UHLE, MAX (1856-1944), Dresden, Germany. Archeologist. Considered father of Peruvian and Ecuadorean archeology. Much writing on anthropology and sociology of Americas, both North & South. Sources: Biog Index: 3/Int Dir Anth 1 2/Bork & Maier, Historical

Dictionary of Ecuador (1973), p 146/ Rowe, John Howland. Max Uhle, 1856-1944 a memoir of the father of Peruvian archaeology. Univ. of California Press '54.

3225 UHLENBECK, EUGENIUS MARIUS (1913-), The Hague, Netherlands. Linguist. Javanese language & literature, S.E. Asian languages in general. Sources: Int Dir Anth 3, 5.

3226 UNDERHILL, RUTH MURRAY (1884- 1984), Ossining, New York, United States. Social anthropologist. Southwest U.S. Indian social conditions, including problem of alcoholism; Papago culture. Sources: Biog Index: 3 & 7-/Int Dir Anth 1, 2, 3, 5/ Anth News (Sept. 1984) p 3.

3227 UNDERWOOD, FRANCES WENRICH (1917-), Philadelphia, Pennsylvania, United States. Cultural anthropologist. Peasantry of Haiti, Bangladesh Buddhists. Sources: Int Dir Anth 3, 5/Nat Dir Lat Am.

3228 UNDERWOOD, PAUL A (1902-1968), Puerto Rico. Archeologist, architect. Directed the restoration of the Church of Kariye Djami in Istanbul (Turkey) in the 1950s; specialist on Byzantine architecture and archeology. Sources: Biog Index: 8/N Y Times p 47 S 27 '68.

3229 UNWIN, GEORGE (1870-1925), Stockport, England. Economic historian. Wrote about English economic history, defending economy free of state interference. Source: International Encyclopedia of the Social Sciences, v. 16.

3230 URDANETA, ANDRÉS de (1508-1568), Guipuzcoa, Spain. Geographer. Participated in several trans-Pacific voyages in the 16th century; journals of these trips are useful for ethnographic data on Cebu, Philippines. Source: Craig & King, Historical Dictionary of Oceania (1981), p 313.

3231 URI, JOHN (1724-1796), Nagykoros, Hungary. Calvinist theologian, Orientalist. Scholar of Semitic languages; compiler of the catalogue of the Oriental manuscripts of the Bodleian Library of Oxford Univ. Sources: Biog Index: 1/Isis 39, pts. 1-2, nos. 115 and 116:61-3 '48.

3232 URICOECHEA, EZEQUIEL (1834-1880), Colombia. Linguist. Wrote several works on the Indian languages of Colombia. Source: Davis, Robert H., Historical Dictionary of Colombia (1977), p 222.

3233 USEEM, JOHN (1911-), Erie Co., New York, United States. Sociologist. Comparative study of Asian societies. Scientific communities, culture contact & change. Sources: Int Dir Anth 3, 5.

3234 USENER, HERMANN (1834-1905). Folklorist. Source: International Encyclopedia of the Social Sciences, v. 15.

3235 UTLEY, FRANCIS LEE (1907-1974). Folklorist. International folktales. History of cultural contrast. Sources: Biog Index: 10 & 12-/Int Dir Anth 5/Nat Cyc Am Biog 58:47 '79.

3236 UVAROV, ALEKSEI SERGEEVICH (1825-1884), Russia. Archeologist. Major figure in the early years of Russian archeology. Established the Russian Archeological Society. Source: Great Soviet Encyclopedia, New York, Macmillan (1981), v. 26, p 648.

3237 VACAS GALINDO, PEDRO ENRIQUE (1865-1938), Cotacachi, Ecuador. Historian, writer. Wrote a novel depicting the customs and mores of the Jivaro Indians of Ecuador. Source: Bork & Maier, Historical Dictionary of Ecuador (1973), p 149.

3238 VACHER de LAPOUGE, GEORGES (1854-1936), France. Scientist. Published on social selection, the social role of the Aryan "race", and race in its social milieu; research on human skeletal material, physical types derived from photography and national expansion. Sources: Biog Index: 2/Am Anth 52:287-91 Ap '50.

3239 VAILLANT, GEORGE CLAPP (1901- 1945), Boston, Massachusetts, United States. Anthropologist, archeologist, ethnographer, museologist. Archeologist of Aztec, Maya, & other Mexican Indian civilizations. Sources: Biog Index: 2/Int Dir Anth 1 2/ International Encyclopedia of the Social Sciences, v. 16/ Nat Cyc Am Biog 34:194-5 '48/Am Anth 47:589-602 O '45.

3240 VAILLANT de GUESLIS (Guelis), S J, Fr. FRANCOIS (1646-1677). Priest. Missionary in New France; wrote on N. American Indians. Source: Jes Rel.

3241 VAKARELSKI, CRISTO (1896-), Plovdiv, Bulgaria. Ethnologist. Comparative ethnology of Balkan & Slavic peoples, particularly Bulgarian mythology & folklore. Sources: Int Dir Anth 2, 3, 5.

3242 VALCÁRCEL, LUIS EDUARDO (1891-), Ilo, Moquegua, Peru. Archeologist, ethnologist, historian. Peruvian archeology, especially of Inca of Cuzco region; Peruvian ancient art; Peruvian history. Gave important direction to Peruvian museums of archeology & anthropology. Sources: Biog Index: 2/Int Dir Anth 1 2 3/Americas 1:46 O '49/ Who's Who in Latin America 3rd ed., Ronald Hilton ed., Stanford Univ. Press (Blaine Ethridge edition, 1971) 205-206.

3243 VALDIVIA, LUIS de (1560- 1642), Spain. Priest. Compiled a grammar of the language spoken in the Spanish colonies which is useful for linguistic research. Source: Bizzarro, Salvatore, Historical Dictionary of Chile (1972), p 285.

3244 VALENTINE, EDWARD PLEASANTS (1864-1907), Virginia, United States. Museum curator. Virginia archeology. Source: Am Anth 10:501-2 Jl '08.

3245 VALENTINI, PHILIPP JOHANN JOSEPH (1824-1899), Berlin, Germany. Published on the archeology of the Maya & Toltec cultures as well as artifacts from Mexico & Guatemala; studied early Costa Rican history & migration of early Mexican peoples. Source: Am Anth 1:391-4 Ap 1899.

3246 VALLE, MANUEL M (1905-), Peru. Anthropologist, ethnologist. Biocultural adapability & racial classifications. Andes. Inca. Sources: Int Dir Anth 2, 3, 5.

3247 VALLOIS, HENRI VICTOR (1889-). Human paleontologist, primatologist, physical anthropologist, archeologist. Comparative anatomy of primates. Human paleontology. Sources: Biog Index: 5 & 6-/Int Dir Anth 3, 5/Am Anth 61:896 O '59.

3248 VALLOIS, RENÉ (1882-1962), Brienne-le-Chateau, France. Archeologist. Wrote on architecture in ancient Greece, particularly that of Delos. Sources: Biog Index: 6/Rev Arch 1:225-33 Ap '62.

3249 VALONEN, NIILO EEMIL TAPIO (1913-), Uriala, Finland. Ethnologist. Primitive technology in European, Finnish & Swedish farm buildings. Ethnology of Europe and North Asia. Sources: Int Dir Anth 3, 5.

3250 VALSIK, J A (1903-), Prague, Bohemia, Czechoslovakia. Physical anthropologist. Anthropology of Gypsies. Sources: Int Dir Anth 2, 3, 5.

3251 VÁMBÉRY, ARMIN (1832-1913), Szerdahely, Hungary. Orientalist. Wrote on his travels in Persia and Armenia. Sources: Biog Index: 12/Columbia/New Int Enc, 1914 ed.

3252 Van BUREN, ELIZABETH (Douglas) (-1961). Archeologist. A pioneer in ancient Near Eastern iconography beginning in 1930; her collections of types of objects, such as animal representations of ancient Mesopotamia, became the standard for scholarly work in the Near East. Sources: Biog Index: 6/Am J Arch 67:83 Ja '63.

3253 VANCOUVER, GEORGE (1757-1798), Kings Lynn, England. Explorer, naval officer. Contributed to the exploration of the northern Pacific and led an expedition, 1790-95, whose accounts give data on Hawaii, during the reign of Kamehameha I, and Tahiti. Source: Craig & King, Historical Dictionary of Oceania (1981), p 315.

3254 Van DEMAN, ESTHER BOISE (1862-1937). Archeologist. Sources: Biog Index: 4/Dictionary of Australian Biography sup 2:676-7 '58.

3255 Van den STEENHOVEN, GEERT (1919-). Adat Law, Indonesia. Source: Int Dir Anth 5.

3256 VANDENBERG, STEVEN G (1915-). Psychologist, physical anthropologist. Genetics. Source: Int Dir Anth 5.

3257 VANDENHOUTE, JAN L (1913-). Ethnologist, museologist. Popular art, especially African. European ethnology & museology. Sources: Int Dir Anth 3, 5.

3258 Van der MERWE, P J (1912-1979). Historian. Works on the history of the Voortrekkers and Boer migration. Source: Saunders, Christopher, Historical Dictionary of South Africa (1983), p 80.

3259 VANDIER, JACQUES (1905-1973). Egyptologist. Curator of Department of Egyptian Antiquities, the Louvre (1940-1973); wrote widely on Egyptian archeology; edited several manuscripts. Sources: Biog Index: 10/Journal of Egyptian Archaeology 60:4 '74.

3260 Van HEEKEREN, HENDRIK ROBBERT (1902-). Prehistory of Southeast Asia. Source: Int Dir Anth 5.

3261 VANNICELLI, PRIMO LUIGI (1907-). Ethnologist. History of religions, especially in Asia. Source: Int Dir Anth 5.

3262 Van VALKENBURGH, RICHARD FOWLER (1904-1957), Newark, California, United States. Anthropologist. American Indian anthropology. Sources: Biog Index: 5/Int Dir Anth 1 2/Am Antiq 23:421 Ap '58.

3263 Van ZINDEREN BAKKER, EDUARD M (1907-). Quaternary paleoenvironment of East and South Africa. Source: Int Dir Anth 5.

3264 VARAGNAC, ANDRÉ (1894-), Paris, France. Archeologist, folklorist. European prehistory. Influence of energy sources on spiritual orientation of European cultures. Sources: Int Dir Anth 3, 5.

3265 VARGAS, JOSÉ MARÍA (1902-), Chardeleg, Ecuador. Art historian, folklorist. Specialized in history of Ecuadorean art and folklore of the colonial period. Source: Bork & Maier, Historical Dictionary of Ecuador (1973), p 150-1.

3266 VARGAS-BARON, EMILY (1904-), Seattle, Washington, United States. Anthropologist. Education in Mexico & Central America. Source: Nat Dir Lat Am.

3267 VARGYAS, LAJOS (1914-), Budapest, Hungary. Folklorist. Folk music & theatre of Hungary. Sources: Int Dir Anth 3, 5.

3268 VARILLE, ALEXANDRE (1909-1951), France. Egyptologist. Archeology of Egypt; worked particularly at Karnak. Sources: Biog Index: 2 & 3/Rev Arch series 6 41:194-6 Ap '53.

3269 VASIĆ, MILOJE M (1869-1956). Archeologist. Archeology of Yugoslavia. Sources: Biog Index: 5/Int Dir Anth 2/Rev Arch 1:87-8 Ja '58.

3270 VAUGHAN, ORVAL DOUGLAS (1900-), Canada. Archeologist. Sources: Biog Index: 1/Royal Canadian Institute, Toronto. Centennial volume, 1849-1949. The Institute '49, p 228.

3271 VAUX, ROLAND de (1903-1971). Priest, archeologist. Directed the excavations at Qumran; headed the team that restored the Dead Sea Scrolls; excavated also at Tell Kisan near Haifa. Sources: Biog Index: 9/ American School of Oriental Research Bulletin no 207:3-5 O '72/ Gazette des Beaux Arts 78:40 N '71/N Y Times p 40 S 13 '71/Time 98:84 S 27 '71.

3272 VÁZQUEZ, JUAN ADOLFO (1917-). Linguist. Symbolism in pre-Columbian Inca & Mapuche oral literature. Source: Int Dir Anth 5.

3273 VEGA, GARCILASO de LA.

3274 VELASCO, JUAN (1727-1792), Riobamba, Ecuador. Historian. Wrote a history of the lands of the Inca Empire from mythological times to the 18th century, which included much primary source material and documentation. Source: Alisky, Historical Dictionary of Peru (1979), p 109-10.

3275 VELEVA, MARIA (1914-). Folk culturist. Bulgarian folk art, folk culture & textile technology. Source: Int Dir Anth 5.

3276 VELKOV, IVAN (1891-1958), Bulgaria. Archeologist. Archeology of Bulgaria. Sources: Biog Index: 5/Rev Arch 1:208-9 Ap '59.

3277 VERDELIS, NICOLAS (1908-1966), Nisyros, Greece. Archeologist. Archeology of classical Greece; led excavations at several sites. Sources: Biog Index: 8/Rev Arch 1:100 '66.

3278 VERHOEVEN, THEODORUS L (1907-). Anthropologist. Prehistoric Southwest Indonesia. Source: Int Dir Anth 5.

3279 VERWEY, ANTONY H N (1918-). Ethnologist. Buddhist art of 8th-12th centuries in India. Source: Int Dir Anth 5.

3280 VESELOVSKII, NIKOLAI IVANOVICH (1848-1918), Moscow, Russia. Archeologist. Archeology of the city of Afrasiab (Uzbekistan) in Middle Asia and burial mounds in southern Russia. Source: Great Soviet Encyclopedia, New York, Macmillan (1974), v. 4, p 624.

3281 VIATKIN, VASILII LAVRENT'EVICH (1869-1932), Semirechenskaia Oblast', Russia. Archeologist. Excavations at Afrasiab (Uzbekistan). Source: Great Soviet Encyclopedia, New York, Macmillan (1974), v. 5, p 413.

3282 VICO, GIOVANNI BATTISTA (Giambiattista) (1668-1744), Naples, Italy. Philosopher, historian, linguist. Formulated theory of history focussing on idea of societal development. Sources: Encyclopedia of the Social Sciences, v. 15/Columbia.

3283 VICUNA MACKENNA, BENJAMIN (1831-1886), Chile. Lawyer. Wrote over 100 historical works dealing with Chilean affairs. Source: Bizzarro, Salvatore, Historical Dictionary of Chile (1972), p 290-1.

3284 VIDAL de la BLACHE, PAUL (1845-1918), France. Geographer. French pioneer in modern human geography. Believed "possibilism," as opposed to determinism, characterized man-environment relationship. Source: International Encyclopedia of the Social Sciences, v. 16.

3285 VILETTE, JEANNE (1897-). Archeologist. Source: Biog Index: 5.

3286 VILLACORTA CALDERÓN, JOSÉ ANTONIO (1879-), Guatemala. Anthropologist, historian. Wrote on archeology and ethnology of Guatemala; edited several of the Maya sacred books. Source: Moore, Richard E., Historical Dictionary of Guatemala (1973), p 235.

3287 VILLAMIL de RADA, EMETÉRIO (1804-1880), Bolivia. Philologist. Wrote on the theory that Tiahuanaco (Bolivia) was the site of the tower of Babel. Source: Heath, Dwight B., Historical Dictionary of Bolivia (1972), p 246.

3288 VILLAVICENCIO, MANUEL (1822-1871), Quito, Ecuador. Geographer. Wrote the first comprehensive geography of Ecuador. Source: Bork & Maier, Historical Dictionary of Peru (1973), p 155.

3289 VIMONT, S J, Fr. BARTHELEMY (1594-1667), Lisieux, France. Priest. Missionary in New France; wrote on N. American Indians. Source: Jes Rel.

3290 VIRCHOW, RUDOLPH LUDWIG KARL (1821-1902), Germany. Physical anthropologist, archeologist. The founder of cellular pathology. Introduced measuring bones in physical anthropology. Studied skull pathology, distribution of physical characteristics in Germany, and early history of human races in Europe; debunked notion that human physical types coincide with languages & cultures. Source: Am Anth 4:568-71 Jl '02, 4:796-7 O '02.

3291 VIRÉ, ARMAND (1869-1951), France. Archeologist, biologist. Research on cave fauna, including prehistoric era. Sources: Biog Index: 3/Int Dir Anth 2/Rev Arch series 6 44:79 Jl '54.

3292 VIVIAN, RICHARD GORDON (1908- 1966), Michigan, United States. Archeologist. Research in Chaco Canyon (New Mexico). Sources: Biog Index: 7/Int Dir Anth 2/Am Antiq 32:100-3 Ja '67.

3293 VIVIER, S J, Fr. LOUIS (1714-1756), Issodun, France. Priest. Missionary in New France; wrote on N. American Indians. Source: Jes Rel.

3294 VOEGELIN, CHARLES FREDERICK (1906-1986), New York, New York, United States. Linguistic anthropologist. Classification of languages of the world. Work on N. American Indian languages. Most prominent American anthropological linguist. Sources: Int Dir Anth 1, 2, 3, 5/Anth News 27:6:4.

3295 VOGT, EVON ZARTMAN (1918-). Social anthropologist. Contemporary social organization of Mexican Maya. Sources: Int Dir Anth 5/Nat Dir Lat Am.

3296 VOGT, FRANCIS-XAVIER (1870-1943), Marlenheim, France. Missionary. Wrote an Ewondo-French syllabus. Source: Levine & Nye, Historical Dictionary of Cameroon (1974), p 125-6.

3297 VOGT, HANS KAMSTRUP (1903-), Fredrikstad, Norway. Linguist. Grammar of old & modern Georgian. Sources: Int Dir Anth 3, 5.

3298 VOLK, ERNEST (1845-1919), Waldkirch, Germany. Archeologist. Specialist in the archeology of the Delaware Valley (New Jersey). Source: Am Anth 22:97 Ja '20.

3299 VOLKOV, FEDOR KONDRAT'EVICH (1847-1918), Kriachkova, Ukraine. Ethnographer, anthropologist, archeologist. Ethnography in the Ukraine. Source: Great Soviet Encyclopedia, New York, Macmillan (1974), v. 5, p 574.

3300 VOLLAMAERE, ANTON LEON, Belgium. Linguist, epigrapher. Deciphered several of the Mayan hieroglyphs and offered a key to reading the inscriptions with verb conjugations. Source: Meyer, Harvey K., Historical Dictionary of Honduras (1976), p 371-2.

3301 VORREN, FRUNLV (1916-), Harstad, Norway. Ethnologist, museologist. Lapp reindeer nomadism in the Arctic. Ethnography of N. Scandinavia. Sources: Int Dir Anth 3, 5.

3302 VOUGA, PAUL (1880-1940), Switzerland. Archeologist. Worked in Lake Village sites, Switzerland; interest in "protohistory.". Sources: Biog Index: 1/Int Dir Anth 1 2/Rev Arch 28:62 Jl '47.

3303 VULCANESCU, ROMULUS (1912-), Romania. Ethnologist. Funeral rites & Romanian mythology. Source: Int Dir Anth 5.

3304 VULIĆ, NIKOLA (1872-1945), Yugoslavia. Archeologist. Prehistory of Yugoslavia. Sources: Biog Index: 2/Int Dir Anth 2/Rev Arch series 6 37:207 Ap '51.

3305 WACE, ALAN JOHN BAYARD (1879- 1957), England. Archeologist, classicist. Fieldwork in Greece. Sources: Biog Index: 2 4 & 5/Int Dir Anth 2/Rev Arch 1:91-94 Ja '59.

3306 WADDELL, LAWRENCE AUSTINE (1854-1938), Cumbernauld, Dumbartonshire, Scotland. Orientalist. Specialist in Buddhist culture, with emphasis on Lamaism; Tibetan and Indian culture, history. Sources: Biog Index: 2/ Dictionary of National Biography 1931-1940: 882-3 '49.

3307 WAGLEY, CHARLES W (1913-). Ethnologist. Studies in Brazil, Hispanic South & Central America. Sources: Int Dir Anth 5/Nat Dir Lat Am.

3308 WAGNER, EMILIO RODGER (1868-1949). Archeologist. Researched the pre-Columbian culture of the northern region of Argentina. Sources: Biog Index: 2/N Y Times p 13 S 24 '49.

3309 WAINRIGHT, GERALD AVERY (1879-1964), Clifton, England. Archeologist. Specialized in hieroglyphics; was involved with studies of the Sea People and technical and religious studies of ancient Egypt. Sources: Biog

Index: 7/Journal of Egyptian Archaeology 50:173-6 D '64.

3310 WAITZ, FRANZ THEODOR (1821-1864). Pioneered in psychological anthropology. Source: Encyclopedia of the Social Sciences, v. 15.

3311 WAKAMORI, TARO (1915-), Chosi, Japan. Educator. Mountain worship & folk beliefs in Japan. Sources: Int Dir Anth 3, 5.

3312 WAKE, CHARLES STANILAND (1835-1910), Kingston-on-Hull, England. Anthropologist. Specialist in early human social structure & primitive beliefs; published on evolution and morality, serpent worship, & the development of marriage & kinship. Source: Am Anth 12:343-4 Ap '10.

3313 WALCOTT, CHARLES DOOLITTLE (1850-1927). Geologist. Sources: Biog Index: 1 & 8/ National Academy of Sciences. Biographical Memoirs v. 39. Columbia Univ. Press, '67 p 471-540.

3314 WALDECK, JEAN FREDERIC MAXIMILIEN (1766-1875), France. Archeologist, explorer. Gave early descriptions of Maya sites, including Palenque. Sources: Biog Index: 1/Natural History 55:450-6 D '46.

3315 WALEY, ARTHUR (1899-1966). Sinologist. Wrote elegant translations of Chinese and Japanese classics; wrote on traditional Far Eastern culture. Sources: Biog Index: 4 7 8 9 12 & 13-4/ N Y Times Book Review p 10t Ap 24 '83/ Waley, Alison. Half of Two Lives. McGraw-Hill '83 p 326.

3316 WALIGÓRSKI, ANDRZEJ (1908-). Ethnologist. Peasant communities of Europe, especially Poland. Source: Int Dir Anth 5.

3317 WALKER, ERIC ANDERSON (1886-1976). Historian. Wrote a basic history of South Africa in 1920s; defined the "frontier" tradition in South African culture. Source: Nat Un Cat.

3318 WALKER, WILLIAM (1808-1896), Vershire, Vermont, United States. Missionary. Translated large portions of Bible into Mpongwe; left diaries which are an important source of Gabonese history for the period 1842-1882. Source: Gardiner, David E., Historical Dictionary of Gabon (1981), p 194-5.

3319 WALLACE, ALFRED RUSSEL (1823- 1913), England. Naturalist. Proposed the theory of evolution from evidence in biogeography. Sources: Encyclopedia of the Social Sciences, v. 15/Columbia.

3320 WALLACE, RUTH SAWTELL (1895-1978), Massachusetts, United States. Cultural anthropologist. Canadian Santee beliefs & tales. Excavated first Azilian skeletons in France. Anthropometric study of children. Sources: Biog Index: 6 11 & 13/Int Dir Anth 3, 5/Am Anth 81:85-7 Mr '79/ Anth News Mr '78.

3321 WALLIN, GEORGE AUGUST (1811-1852). Orientalist. Sources: Biog Index: 3/ Studia orientalia, v 18 no 1. Societas orientalis Fennica '52.

3322 WALLIS, WILSON DALLAM (1886-1970), Maryland, United States. Anthropologist. Interested in archeology & linguistics. Stressed behavioral aspect of culture. Wrote extensively in physical anthropology. Following Edward B. Tylor, he favored diffusion. Cross-cultural approaches. New emphasis on messianic movements in primitive religions. Sources: Biog Index: 6 & 8/Int Dir Anth 1 2 3/ International Encyclopedia of the Social Sciences, v. 16/ N Y Times p 43 Mr 17 '70/Am Anth 73:257-66 F '71.

3323 WALSH, RAYMOND COLLINGE (1910-). Archeologist. Fluctuations of sea levels & dating of raised beaches by archeological methods. Source: Int Dir Anth 5.

3324 WALTER, MICHAEL ALI HAROLD BURGOYNE (1913-). Sociologist. Marital instability & rural economic development in Malaysia. Source: Int Dir Anth 5.

3325 WALTON, JAMES (1911-), England. Historian. Wrote about rock paintings and vernacular architecture of Lesotho and prepared maps of Lesotho & Botswana. Source:

Haliburton, Gordon, Historical Dictionary of Lesotho (1977), p 178.

3326 WARD, LAURISTAN (1882-1960), Andover, Massachusetts, United States. Archeologist. Research on archeology & prehistory of Eastern Hemisphere, especially Asia, Africa, also America. Sources: Biog Index: 5 & 7/Int Dir Anth 1 2 3/Nat Cyc Am Biog 48:664-5 '65.

3327 WARD, WILLIAM (1917-). Demographer. U.S. Urban social planning & urban-ethnic settlement patterns. Source: Int Dir Anth 5.

3328 WARDLE, HARRIET NEWELL (1875- 1964), Philadelphia, Pennsylvania, United States. Anthropologist, archeologist, museum curator. American archeology & ethnology. Primarily interested in material culture and technology and American Indian cultures. Source: Expedition 6:40 Summer '64.

3329 WARING, ANTONIO JOHNSTON (1915-1964), Savannah, Georgia, United States. Archeologist. Worked to establish pottery horizons of Georgia coast; contributed basic work on Southern Archaic culture and the Southern Cult. Sources: Biog Index: 7/Am Antiq 31:552-4 Ap '66.

3330 WARNER, FRANK (1903-1978), Selma, Alabama, United States. Folklorist. Collected traditional songs of rural eastern seaboard states, U.S. Sources: Biog Index: 11/Anth News Ap '78/N Y Times p B-2 Mr 1 '78/ N Y Times Biog Service 9:406-7 Mr '78.

3331 WARNER, WILLIAM LLOYD (1898-), Redlands, California, United States. Anthropologist. Social anthropology of several contemporary U.S., Irish, and Australian towns, including "Yankee city.". Sources: Biog Index: 5 8 & 9/Int Dir Anth 1 2 3/ International Encyclopedia of the Social Sciences, vol. 18/ American Journal of Sociology 76:561 Ja '71/Current Biography 31:47 Jl '70/ Current Biography Yr Bk 1970:422 '71.

3332 WARREN, HENRY CLARKE (1854-1899). Orientalist. Sources: Biog Index: 3/Russel, Foster William. Mount Auburn biographies. Mount Auburn Cemetary '53 p 173.

3333 WARSHER, TATIANA (1880-1960), Moscow, Russia. Archeologist. Compiler of thirty-seven manuscript volumes of the *Codex Topographicus Pompeianus*, a record of all that had been cleared of the site of Pompeii (Italy); became the assistant to Rostovtzeff in 1923 and became devoted to the detailed description of the site. Sources: Biog Index: 6/Am J Arch 66:95-6 Ja '62.

3334 WASHBURN, SHERWOOD LARNED (1911-), Cambridge, Massachusetts, United States. Physical anthropologist. Studies of skeleton; of sex differences among Bantu and Bushmen; and of the social behavior of baboons. Sources: Biog Index: 6/Int Dir Anth 3/Am Anth 63:835-7 Ag '61.

3335 WASLEY, WILLIAM WARWICK (1919-1970), El Tigre, Sonora, Mexico. Archeologist. Southwestern U.S. specialist; worked on Hohokam, site of Snaketown (Arizona); focused on relationship of prehistoric Southwest with Mexico; also did extensive salvage work. Sources: Biog Index: 9/Am Antiq 37:89-92 Ja '72.

3336 WASSEN, SVEN HENRY (1908-), Goteberg, Sweden. Ethnologist, medical anthropologist, archeologist. Medical anthropology. Drugs among Indians of Central & South America. South American ethnology, archeology. Sources: Int Dir Anth 1, 2, 3, 5.

3337 WASSON, ROBERT GORDON (1898- 1986). Banker, folklorist, ethnopharmacologist. Pioneer in ethnomycology specializing in usage of hallucinogenic drugs in ancient religions. Published on the mind-altering fungi in Old & New World Cultures, particularly mushrooms in Russia & Mesoamerica. Sources: Biog Index: 13/Anth News 28:3:4/Science News 118:Ag 2 '80.

3338 WATANABE, HITOSHI (1919-), Hisni-cho, Japan. Archeologist. Behavioral ecology of northern hunters & gatherers of Eurasia. Prehistoric man in Eastern Hemisphere. Sources: Int Dir Anth 3, 5.

3339 WATANABE, NAOTSUNE (1919-), Tokyo, Japan. Physical anthropologist, archeologist. Natural scientific researches in prehistory of Japan. Natural selection. Sources: Int Dir Anth 3, 5.

3340 WATERMAN, LEROY (1875-1972), Pierpoint, Ohio, United States. Archeologist, biblical scholar. Excavated Seleucia (Iraq) and other Middle Eastern cities. Sources: Biog Index: 12/Nat Cyc Am Biog 58:511-512 '79.

3341 WATERMAN, RICHARD ALAN (1914- 1971), California, United States. Anthropologist, ethnomusicologist. Researched the influence of African music on the Americas. Sources: Biog Index: 10 & 11/Ethnomusicology 27:89-94 '73/ Nat Cyc Am Biog 57:207-8 '77/Am Anth 76:76-7 Mr '74.

3342 WATERMAN, THOMAS TALBOT (1885-1936), Missouri, United States. Ethnologist. Worked with several American Indian groups. Source: Am Anth 39:527-9 Jl '37.

3343 WATKINS, ALFRED E (1855-). Archeologist, photographer. Source: Biog Index: 10.

3344 WATKINS, LEE HENDERSON (1908- 1972), California, United States. Entomologist, anthropologist. Gathered ethnographic data on beekeepers in particular & agriculture in general. Sources: Biog Index: 10/Bibliography on file at Univ. of California, Davis/ Am Anth 76:355-6 Je '74.

3345 WATKINS, MARK HANNA (1903-1976), Huntsville, Texas, United States. Anthropologist, educator. Introduced anthropology to black students. Research on American blacks and Africans. Sources: Biog Index: 11/Int Dir Anth 1 2 3/Am Anth 78:889-90 D '76/ Anth News My '76.

3346 WATRIN, S J, Fr. PHILIBERT (Philippe) (1697-1764), Metz, France. Priest. Missionary in New France; wrote on N. American Indians. Source: Jes Rel.

3347 WATROUS, BLANCHE GREENE. (1909-), Cleveland, Tennessee, United States. Ethnologist, folklorist. Childhood in contemporary African & N. American cultures. Sources: Int Dir Anth 3, 5.

3348 WATSON, JAMES BENNET (1918-), Chicago, Illinois, United States. Social anthropologist, ethnologist. Social organization & acculturation of Cayua of Brazil and Tairora of New Guinea. Sources: Int Dir Anth 3, 5/Nat Dir Lat Am.

3349 WATSON, LINVILL (1918-). Ethnologist. Ethnicity & inter-ethnic relations in Nigeria & Canada. African & N. American ethnology. Source: Int Dir Anth 5.

3350 WATSON, VIRGINIA DREW (1918-), Tomah, Wisconsin, United States. Archeologist, ethnologist. Worked in Meso-America; studied sex roles & sociocultural change among the Agarabe and Tairora of New Guinea. Sources: Int Dir Anth 3, 5/Nat Dir Lat Am.

3351 WATZINGER, CARL (1877-1948), Darmstadt, Germany. Archeologist. Hellenistic prehistory. Sources: Biog Index: 2/Int Dir Anth 1 2/Am J Arch 54:133-4 Ap '50.

3352 WAUCHOPE, ROBERT (1909-1979), Columbia, South Carolina, United States. Anthropologist, archeologist. Archeological survey of Northeastern Georgia. Research in Mexico, Guatemala. Sources: Int Dir Anth 1 2 3/Nat Dir Lat Am/Anth News Mr '79.

3353 WAUTERS, ALPHONSE. Geographer. Published articles in 1885 supporting King Leopold's claim to the Ubangui basin of Central Africa. Source: Kalck, Pierre, Historical Dictionary of the Central African Republic (1980), p 132-3.

3354 WAX, ROSALIE H (1911-). Ethnologist. World view & ethos of old Scandinavians of Iceland & Norway. American Indian ethnology. Source: Int Dir Anth 5.

3355 WEAKLAND, JOHN H (1919-). Psychiatrist. Communication & behavior in family & other systems. Source: Int Dir Anth 5.

3356 WEBER, MAX (1864-1920). Sociologist. Analyzed the nature of social science; introduced the concept "ideal type;" believed in a comparative approach. Sources: Encyclopedia of the Social Sciences, v. 16/Columbia.

3357 WECKLER, JOSEPH EDWIN, Jr (1906-1963), Mapleton, Iowa, United States. Social anthropologist. Conducted twenty year study of Cundiyo (New Mexico), a Spanish-American village as well as ethnological research on Mokil (Micronesia); specialized in reducing tensions among different racial, religious & ethnic groups, and in improving intergroup relations. Sources: Biog Index: 7/Int Dir Anth 3/Am Anth 66:1348-50 D '64.

3358 WEDEL, WALDO RUDOLPH (1908-), Newton, Kansas, United States. Archeologist. Human ecology & U.S. archeology. Sources: Int Dir Anth 2, 3, 5.

3359 WEDGWOOD, CAMILLA HILDEGARDE (1901-1955), Newcastle-upon-Tyne, England. Social anthropologist, applied anthropologist, academic administrator. Social anthropology of Western Pacific. Fieldwork on Nauru, New Guinea, Manam I: kinship & the activities of women & children on Manam (Melanesia); colonialism and native education on Nauru (Micronesia). Sources: Biog Index: 4/Int Dir Anth 1 2 3/ American Ethnologist 13:4(1986):776-798/Nature 176:144-5 Jl 23 '55.

3360 WEIANT, CLARENCE WOLSEY (ca. 1898-1986), Peekskill, New York, United States. Anthropologist, archeologist, linguist, chiropractor. Focused on the Tarascan Indians (Mexico), prehistoric Mexican archeology, and parapsychology. Ceramics of Valley of Mexico & Gulf Coast. Sources: Int Dir Anth 2, 3, 5/Anth News 28:2:4/Nat Dir Lat Am.

3361 WEIDENREICH, H FRANZ (1873-1948), Edenkoben, Germany. Anthropologist, anatomist, paleontologist. Peking Man & human evolution. Published on the origin of humanity and the significance of anatomical features for speech and gait; published on human fossil remains. Sources: Biog Index: 1 & 2/Int Dir Anth 1/Columbia/ International Encyclopedia of the Social Sciences, v. 16/Am Anth 51:85-90 Ja '49 /Far Eastern Quarterly 8:95 N '48/Isis 42 no 2:147 '51.

3362 WEILL, RAYMAND (1874-1950), Elbeuf, France. Archeologist, Egyptologist. Managed several excavations in Egypt and wrote widely on Middle Eastern archeology. Source: Rev Arch series 6 42:93-6 Jl '53.

3363 WEINBERG, SAUL S (1911-). Archeologist, prehistorian. Neolithic & Early Bronze Age classical prehistoric archeology of Greece & the Aegean. Source: Int Dir Anth 5.

3364 WEINER, JOSEPH SIDNEY (1915-), Transvaal, South Africa. Biologist, physical anthropologist, paleontologist. Physiological responses to climate. Sources: Int Dir Anth 3, 5.

3365 WEISMANN, AUGUST (1834-1914), Germany. Zoologist. Applied theoretical analysis of data to question of evolution in physical anthropology. Source: Encyclopedia of the Social Sciences, v. 15.

3366 WEITLANER, ROBERT J (1883-1968), Steyr, Austria. Archeologist, linguist. Work in Mexico, reconstructed the language of the Otomi. Ethnographic work on the Chinantec. Sources: Biog Index: 9/Int Dir Anth 1 2/Am Anth 72:343-8 Ap '70.

3367 WELLING, JAMES CLARKE (-1894), New Jersey, United States. Historian, linguist. Wrote on early cultural developments of Europe and United States. Source: Am Anth 7(old series):418 O 1894.

3368 WELLS, CALVIN PERCIVAL BAMPFYLDE (1907-1978), England.

Medical anthropologist, paleopathologist. Medical history. Medical anthropology. Founder of the International Paleopathology Association. Sources: Int Dir Anth 5/Anth News N '78.

3369 WELLS, LAWRENCE HERBERT (1908-), Handsworth, England. Anatomist, physical anthropologist. Physical anthropology of Southern African Bantu and primates. Sources: Biog Index: 4/Int Dir Anth 1 2 3/Nature 177:873 My 12 '56.

3370 WELTE, CECIL RICE (1915-). Ethnohistorian. Settlement patterns & ethnohistory of Oaxaca Valley (Mexico). Source: Int Dir Anth 5.

3371 WELTER, GABRIEL (1890-1954), ALsace-Lorraine, Germany. Archeologist. Wrote on archeology of classical Greece. Sources: Biog Index: 4/Rev Arch series 6 48:70-1 Jl '56.

3372 WELTFISH, GENE (1902-1980), New York, New York, United States. Anthropologist. N. American Indian art and its relation to art of other cultures. Sources: Biog Index: 3 & 13/Int Dir Anth 1 2/N Y Times p B-10 Ag 5 '80/ N Y Times Biog Service 11:1211 Ag '80.

3373 WENINGER, MARGARETE (1896-), Vienna, Austria. Bio-anthropologist, physical anthropologist, geneticist. Dermatoglyphic research. Sources: Int Dir Anth 3, 5.

3374 WENTWORTH, WILLIAM CHARLES (1896-). Ethnologist. Ethnology of Australian Aborigines. Source: Int Dir Anth 5.

3375 WERTHEIMER, MAX (1880-1943), Prague, Czechoslovakia. Analyzed numbers as they are used in some primitive societies. Source: International Encyclopedia of the Social Sciences, v. 16.

3376 WESSEL, BESSIE BLOOM (1889-1969), Ukraine. Anthropologist, sociologist. Methodology for study of urban areas. Ethnic study of Woonsocket, Rhode Island. Sources: Biog Index: 9/Int Dir Anth 3/Am Anth 72:555-7 Je '70.

3377 WEST, ROBERT COOPER (1913-), Enid, Oklahoma, United States. Geographer. Historical geography of Latin America. Source: Nat Dir Lat Am.

3378 WESTERMANN, WILLIAM LINN (1873-1954), Illinois, United States. Historian, Orientalist. Specialized in the social and economic history of the classical world, with emphasis on slavery. Sources: Biog Index: 3 & 4/Political Science Quarterly 70:481-2 S '55.

3379 WESTERMARCK, EDWARD ALEXANDER (1862-1939), Helsingfors (Helsinki), Finland. Ethnologist. Started cross-cultural research through questionnaires to missionaries & others living with primitive peoples. Research over broad area. Sources: Int Dir Anth 1/ International Encyclopedia of the Social Sciences, v. 16.

3380 WESTPHAL, ERNST O J (1907-). Comparative African linguistics. Classification of dialects & Bantu languages. Source: Int Dir Anth 5.

3381 WESTPHAL-HELLBUSCH, SIGRID (1916-1984), Germany. Anthropologist. Field studies of Arabs of southern Iraq. Source: Anth News (Sept 1984) p 4.

3382 WETHERILL, LOUISA (Wade) (-1945). Anthropologist. With John Wetherill collected Navajo artifacts. Sources: Biog Index: 12/Comfort, Mary Apolline. Rainbow to yesterday: the John & Louisa Wetherill story. Vantage Press. '80.

3383 WETHERILL, RICHARD (1858-1910). Archeologist. Sources: Biog Index: 4/McNitt, Frank. Richard Wetherill: Anasazi. Univ. of New Mexico Press '57.

3384 WEYER, EDWARD MOFFAT (1904-), Pennsylvania, United States. Archeologist, ethnologist. Inuit & Aleut archeology & ethnology from Alaska to Greenland. Sources: Int Dir Anth 2, 3, 5.

3385 WHEAT, JOE BEN (1916-), Van Horn, Texas, United States. Archeologist. Pueblo archeology & textile of Southwest U.S.

Sources: Int Dir Anth 5/ American Men and Women of Science, ed. by J.C. Press, 12th ed., New York, Bowker, 1973.

3386 WHEELER, ROBERT ERIC MORTIMER (1890-1976), Scotland. Archeologist. Archeology in India and Pakistan. Sources: Biog Index: 1 3 4 5 6 8 9 & 11/Am Anth 79:894-5 D '77/ Antiquity 50:180 S '76/Current Biography 37:45 S '76/ Current Biography Yr Bk 1976:478 '77/Gazette des Beaux Arts 88:supp 33 N '76/ N Y Times p D-12 Jl 23 '76/Time 108:63 Ag 2 '76.

3387 WHEELOCKE, ABRAHAM (1593-1653), England. Orientalist. Sources: Biog Index: 3/ Fuller, Thomas. Worthies of England. Abr ed. Allen '53 p 484-5.

3388 WHITAKER, JOSEPH PEPPINO (1850-). Wine merchant, archeologist. Source: Biog Index: 9.

3389 WHITE, LESLIE ALVIN (1900-1975), California, United States. Anthropologist. Invented "culturology", a theory of cultural evolution. Made major theoretical contributions to cultural anthropology via application of Socratic logic. Wrote on Pueblo and Seneca Indians. Sources: Biog Index: 5 10 & 11/Int Dir Anth 1, 2, 3, 5/ International Encyclopedia of the Social Sciences, v. 18/Am Anth 78:612-17 S '76 /Anth News My '75/N Y Times p 36 Ap 4 '75.

3390 WHITE, RALPH GARDNER (1918-). Linguist. Polynesian languages, especially Tahitian. Source: Int Dir Anth 5.

3391 WHITE, ROBERT MANSON (1916-). Anthropometrist. Human factors in applied anthropometry. Source: Int Dir Anth 5.

3392 WHITEFORD, ANDREW HUNTER (1913-), Winnepeg, Manitoba, Canada. Anthropologist, archeologist. Social stratification & urban change in Latin America. Sources: Int Dir Anth 2, 3, 5/Nat Dir Lat Am.

3393 WHITING, ALFRED FRANK (1912-1978), Burlington, Vermont, United States. Anthropologist, ethnobotanist. Study of the Hopi. Material culture & ethnobotany of the Hopi Indians. Sources: Int Dir Anth 1, 2, 3, 5/Anth News 0 '78.

3394 WHITING, JOHN W M (1908-), Chilmark, Martha's Vineyard, Massachusetts, United States. Psychoanthropologist, ethnologist. Worked especially with developmental problems of children. Fieldwork in New Guinea. Family life in E African tribes of Kenya. Sources: Int Dir Anth 2, 3, 5/ International Encyclopedia of the Social Sciences, v. 18.

3395 WHITMAN, WILLIAM (-1940). Ethnologist. Known for his extensive fieldwork among the Rio Grande Pueblo Indians and with the southern Sioux tribes of the Great Plains. Source: Am Anth 42:180 Ja '40.

3396 WHITNEY, WILLIAM DWIGHT (1827-1894), Northampton, Massachusetts, United States. Orientalist, comparative philologist. Wrote: *Language and the Study of Language*, 1885; *The Life and Growth of Language: an outline of linguistic science*, 1876. Sources: Biog Index: 7 & 12.

3397 WHITTEMORE, THOMAS (1871-1950). Archeologist. Expert on Byzantine archeology; worked on the mosaics of Hagia Sophia in Istanbul (Turkey) in the 1930s. Sources: Biog Index: 1 & 2/Archaeology S 6 36:117-8 Jl '50/ College Art Journal 9:420 Summer '50/Isis 41 no 3-4:303 '50/ N Y Times p 23 Je 9 '50/Revue Historique 205:365 Ap '51/ School & Society 71:388 Je 17 '50/Time 55:83 J3 19 '50.

3398 WHITTEN, NORMAN EARL, Sr (1912-1986). Ethnologist. Specialist in African ethnology & popular culture studies. Source: Anth News 27:6:4.

3399 WHORF, BENJAMIN LEE (1897-1941), Winthrop, Massachusetts, United States. Linguist. Consolidated the concrete phrase "language & culture" to synthesise the mutual impact of these two entities. Wrote widely in linguistics and on relation of language to culture, did much work with American Indian languages. Sources: Biog Index: 3 7 & 13/Int Dir Anth 1 2/ International Encyclopedia of the Social Sciences, v. 16/ Makers of Modern Culture. Facts on File '81, p 569.

3400 WHYMPER, EDWARD (1840-1911), London, England. Explorer. Wrote a travel account containing a valuable chapter on the archeology of Ecuador. Source: Bork & Maier, Historical Dictionary of Ecuador (1973), p 155-6.

3401 WHYTE, ROBERT ORR (1903-). Nutritionist. Practices & standards of nutrition among rural peoples of monsoonal & equatorial Asia. Source: Int Dir Anth 5.

3402 WIDDICOMBE, JOHN (-1928). Missionary. Wrote two accounts of his forty years of mission work in Lesotho during the 19th century. Source: Haliburton, Gordon, Historical Dictionary of Lesotho (1977), p 181-2.

3403 WIENER, CHARLES (1851-1913), Austria-Hungary. Anthropologist. Led an expedition from Guayaquil (Ecuador) to the Atlantic in 1876-1877, studying linguistics and archeological remains en route; published a detailed account of the journey. Source: Bork & Maier, Historical Dictionary of Ecuador (1973), p 156.

3404 WIK, REYNOLD MILLARD (1910-). Anthropologist. American agricultural technology & social change. Steam power on U.S. farms. Source: Int Dir Anth 5.

3405 WIKANDER, OSCAR STIG (1908-). Linguist. Sanskrit epics. Zoroastrian fire cult of Iran & Asia Minor. Indo-European linguistics. Source: Int Dir Anth 5.

3406 WIKMAN, KARL ROBERT VILLEHAD (1886-), Wasa, Finland. Social anthropologist. Studies on Northern European social anthropology and folklore. Sources: Int Dir Anth 1, 2, 3, 5.

3407 WILDER, RAYMOND LOUIS (1896-). Cultural anthropologist. Applications of cultural anthropology to mathematics & science. Source: Int Dir Anth 5.

3408 WILDHABER, ROBERT (1902-). Bibliographer, cultural anthropologist, folklorist. Religious iconography & European legends. Source: Int Dir Anth 5.

3409 WILHELM, ADOLF (1864-1950), Tetschen-Liebwerd, Bohemia, Czechoslovakia. Hellenist, archeologist. Wrote widely on Greek texts. Sources: Biog Index: 4/Rev Arch series 6 45:47-8 Ja '55.

3410 WILHELM, OTTMAR E (1898-). Ethno-zoologist, genealogist, anthropologist. Sero-anthropology & genealogy of Easter Islanders. Source: Int Dir Anth 5.

3411 WILKES, CHARLES (1798-1877), New York, New York, United States. Naval officer. Led the U.S. Exploring Expedition, 1838-1842; journal of the trip valuable for ethnographic data on Hawaii and other groups of Pacific islands. Source: Craig & King, Historical Dictionary of Oceania (1981), p 337.

3412 WILKINSON, DAVID (1831-1910), England. Linguist. Supported the rights of Fijian people to separate cultural identity in the 19th century. Source: Craig & King, Historical Dictionary of Oceania (1981), p 337-8.

3413 WILKINSON, JAMES VERE STEWART (1885-1957), England. Orientalist. Joined the Indian Civil Service in 1911 and with knowledge acquired there became a member of the staff of the Department of Oriental Manuscripts in the British Museum in 1924; interested in Persian and Mogul painting. Sources: Biog Index: 5 & 12/Ars Orientalis 3:259-62 '59.

3414 WILLARD, SIDNEY (1780-1856). Orientalist. Sources: Biog Index: 3/Russel, Foster William. Mount Auburn biographies. Mount Auburn Cemetary '53 p 180.

3415 WILLEMS, EMILIO (1905-), Brazil. Anthropologist. Worked in Brazil, Chile, & Columbia. Sources: Int Dir Anth 3/Nat Dir Lat Am.

3416 WILLEY, GORDON RANDOLPH (1913-), Chariton, Iowa, United States. Anthropologist, archeologist. Mayan & Peruvian archeology of Central & South America. Southwest U.S. archeology. Sources: Biog Index: 3 & 8/Int Dir Anth 2, 3, 5/Nat Dir Lat Am/ Men Who Dug Up History, Dodd '68.

3417 WILLIAMS, BARNETT OSBORNE (1897-1969), Easley, South Carolina, United States. Anthropologist, sociologist. Focused research on the changing rural southern U.S. Sources: Biog Index: 9/Rural Sociology 35:321-2 Je '70.

3418 WILLIAMS, JOHN (1796-1839), England. Missionary. Wrote a description of mission efforts in Polynesia useful as a summary of early 19th century efforts. Source: Craig & King, Historical Dictionary of Oceania (1981), p 338.

3419 WILLIAMS, JOHN BROWN (1810-1860), Salem, Massachusetts, United States. Civil servant, ethnographer. Wrote in detail on customs, culture and politics of Fijian and New Zealand peoples. Source: Craig & King, Historical Dictionary of Oceania (1981), p 338-9.

3420 WILLIAMS, JOSEPH JOHN (1875-1940), Boston, Massachusetts, United States. Ethnologist, priest. Study of Negro in W. Africa and West Indies. Sources: Biog Index: 1/Int Dir Anth 1 2/ Hoehn, Matthew, ed. Catholic Authors. St. Mary's Abbey '48 p 785-6.

3421 WILLIAMS, MARY (1882-1977). Philologist, philosopher, folklorist. An Arthurian scholar concentrating on the relationship of French Arthurian romance to Welsh literature and tradition. Sources: Biog Index: 12/Folklore 89:104-5 Spr '78.

3422 WILLIAMS, SAMUEL WELLS (1812-1884). Sinologist, missionary. Sources: Biog Index: 1/ Mueller, John Theodore. Great Missionaries to China. Zondervan '47 p56-8.

3423 WILLIAMS-FREEMAN, JOHN PEERE (1858-1943), Southhampton, England. Archeologist. Investigated prehistoric earthworks of England; his 1915 book on field archeology was the first to attempt to set prehistoric man in his natural environment. Sources: Biog Index: 5/ Dictionary of National Biography 1941-1950:960-1 '59.

3424 WILLIAMS-HUNT, PETER DARRELL RIDER (1919-1953), Caversham, England. Archeologist, ethnologist. Neolithic Period and Bronze Age in S.E. Europe. Sources: Biog Index: 3/Int Dir Anth 3/Museum Journal 53:138 Ag '53.

3425 WILLSON, ROBERT W (-1922). Anthropologist. Specialist in the astronomical features of the Maya codices, especially the Dresden Codex. Source: Am Anth 24:492 O '22.

3426 WILSDORF, HELMUT M (1912-). Ethnologist. Theory of metallurgy in Classical & Near Eastern ethnology. Mining lore. Source: Int Dir Anth 5.

3427 WILSON, JOHN ALBERT (1899-1976). Egyptologist, Orientalist, missionary. Director of Oriental Institute, Univ. of Chicago. Sources: Biog Index: 3 11 & 12/ David, M. D. John Wilson and his institution. John Wilson Educ. Soc. '76.

3428 WILSON, MONICA HUNTER (1908-), Lovedale, South Africa. Social anthropologist. Growth & decline of peasant communities in Tanganyika. Sources: Int Dir Anth 3, 5.

3429 WILSON, THOMAS (1832-1902), United States. Specialist on European prehistory. Source: Am Anth 4:286-91 Ap '02.

3430 WINCKELMANN, JOHANN JOACHIM (1717-1768), Steldal, Prussia, Germany. Art critic, archeologist. Called the father of modern history of art; wrote: *History of Ancient Art*, 1753, which laid down the principles for the scientific study of a nation's art, principles still adhered to today. Sources: Biog Index: 1 2

6 7 9 & 10/ Metropolitan Museum of Art, Bulletin, Ap '49.

3431 WINCKLER, HUGO (1863-1913), Grafenhainichen, Germany. Orientalist. Excavations at Sidon (Lebanon) and Bogazkoy (Turkey). Source: Columbia.

3432 WINLOCK, HERBERT EUSTIS (1884-1950). Archeologist, Egyptologist. Directed excavations at Deir-el-Bahri, 1911-1931; wrote widely on ancient Egyptian civilization. Sources: Biog Index: 2 & 3/Nat Cyc Am Biog 37:217-18 '51/ Archaeology, Spring '50.

3433 WINNING, HASSO LEOPOLD von (1914-), Heidelberg, Germany. Anthropologist. Meso-American archeology, pre-Columbian art of Mexico & Central America. Source: Nat Dir Lat Am.

3434 WINTEMBERG, WILLIAM JOHN (1876-1941), New Dundee, Ontario, Canada. Archeologist, folklorist. Studies on Canadian archeology and folklore. Sources: Biog Index: 5/Int Dir Anth 1/ Swayze, Nansi. Man Hunters. Clarke '60 p 143-78.

3435 WIRTH, LOUIS (1897-1952), Germany. Sociologist. Analysis of urban life. Source: International Encyclopedia of the Social Sciences, v. 16.

3436 WIRZ, PAUL (1892-1955), Moscow, Russia. Ethnologist. Ethnology of S.E. Asia, S. Asia, Ivory Coast. Sources: Biog Index: 4/Int Dir Anth 1 2 3/ Brussels, Musees Royaux d'Art et d'Histoire Bulletin S 4 27:111-2 '55.

3437 WISSLER, CLARK (1870-1947), Wayne Co., Indiana, United States. Anthropologist, ethnologist, museum curator. Curator of Anthropology, American Museum of Natural History. N. American Indian studies. Published on the Blackfoot & Sioux. Relation of nature and culture; developed the culture-area and age-area concept. Sources: Biog Index: 1 2 & 3/Int Dir Anth 1/ International Encyclopedia of the Social Sciences, vol. 16/ Am Anth 54:164 Ap '52, 50:292-304 Ap '48.

3438 WITHERS, ARNOLD M (1916-), Pueblo, Colorado, United States. Archeologist. Archeology of the Plains, Southwest U.S. & Northern Mexico. Sources: Int Dir Anth 3, 5.

3439 WITHERS, CARL A (James West) (1900-1970), Sheldon, Missouri, United States. Anthropologist, author, folklorist. Investigated American rural life, especially the reaction of rural farmers to urban influences; wrote on "Plainville," Missouri; also specialized on children's folklore. Sources: Biog Index: 13/Int Dir Anth 3/ Commire, Anne. Something about the Author, v 14. Gale '78 p 261-2/ Am Anth 74:764-9 Je '72.

3440 WOKROJ, FRANCISZEK (1906-), Twow, Poland. Geneticist, anthropologist. Polish ontogenetics. Paleo-Slavic ethnogenetics. Sources: Int Dir Anth 3, 5.

3441 WOLF, SIEGFRIED (1907-). Museologist. Benin bronze & copper casting technology. Metallurgy & history of metals. Source: Int Dir Anth 5.

3442 WONO, NDOLE. Writer. Worked to preserve the cultural heritage of the Vai people of Liberia and participated in the development of a distinctive script for the Vai language. Source: Dunn & Holsoe, Historical Dictionary of Liberia (1985), p 189.

3443 WOOD, JOSEPH GARBETT (1833-1894). Merchant. Wrote account of negotiations and land disputes between concessionaires and the Ndebele king, Lobengula. Source: Rasmussen, R. Kent, Historical Dictionary of Rhodesia/Zimbabwe (1979), p 350.

3444 WOODBURY, NATHALIE FERRIS SAMPSON (1918-). Bibliographer, ethnologist. Prehistory, history & ethnology of Zuni & Papago Indians. Sources: Int Dir Anth 5/Nat Dir Lat Am.

3445 WOODBURY, RICHARD BENJAMIN (1917-), Indiana, United States. Anthropologist. Mexican & Southwest U.S. arid land agricultural anthropology. Preindustrial technology. Sources: Int Dir Anth 3,

5/Nat Dir Lat Am.

3446 WOODWARD, ARTHUR (ca. 1898-1986). Museum curator. Specialist in the archeology & ethnology of the Southwest U.S.; also did field research in French Oceania. Source: Anth News 4/86:3.

3447 WOODWARD, ARTHUR SMITH (1864- 1944), Macclesfield, England. Paleontologist. Reconstructed "Piltdown man", claiming it was real. Sources: Biog Index: 5 11 & 12/Int Dir Anth 1 2/Time 112:82 N 13 '78.

3448 WOOLLEY, CHARLES LEONARD (1880-1960). Archeologist, historian. Principal excavator of Ur and the Sumerian civilization; wrote: *Ur of the Chalders*, *A record of Seven years of excavation*, 1920; edited *Ur Excavations*, the report of the Joint Expedition of the British Museum and of the Museum of the Univ. of Pennsylvania to Mesopotamia, 1927. Sources: Biog Index: 3 5 6 & 11/Expedition 20:3-4 Fall '77.

3449 WORMINGTON, HANNAH MARIE (1914-), Denver, Colorado, United States. Archeologist. Early man in N. America. Sources: Int Dir Anth 2, 3, 5.

3450 WORRELL, WILLIAM HOYT (1879-1952). Orientalist. Specialized in Arabic and Coptic languages. Sources: Biog Index: 3/N Y Times p 21 Ja 5 '53/ School & Society 77:14 Ja 3 '51/Wilson Library Bulletin 27:408 F '53.

3451 WRIGHT, GEORGE ERNEST (1909-1974), Zanesville, Ohio, United States. Biblical archeologist. Near East archeology, especially of Old Testament period. Sources: Biog Index: 1 6 & 10/Int Dir Anth 2 3/Archaeology 28:59 Ja '75.

3452 WRIGHT, GEORGE FREDERICK (1838-1921). Geologist. Concerned with the antiquity of man. Source: Am Anth 23:392.

3453 WRIGHT, JOHN HENRY (1852-1908), Urmia, Persia, Iran. Classicist. Specialist in Greek archeology & philology. Source: Am Anth 10:706 O '08.

3454 WURZBACHER, GERHARD (1912-). Linguist, social anthropologist. Studies in African & Indian socialization & innovation. Source: Int Dir Anth 5.

3455 WYLIE, LAURENCE WILLIAM (1909-). Cultural anthropologist. Comparison of U.S. & French cultures. Source: Int Dir Anth 5.

3456 WYMAN, LELAND CLIFTON (1897-), Livermore Falls, Maine, United States. Physical anthropologist. Navajo Indian ethno-biology and ethnology. Interested in art and physical anthropology. Sources: Int Dir Anth 1, 2, 3, 5.

3457 WYSS, JOHANN RUDOLF (1781-1830). Anthropologist, folklorist, philosopher. Sources: Biog Index: 5 & 8/Who's Who in Children's Literature.

3458 XENOPHON, (428-354 BC), Athens, Greece. Author. History & ethnography of the Persians. Source: Columbia.

3459 XIMENEZ, FRANCISCO (1666-1729), Guatemala. Priest. Discovered the manuscript of the Popol Vuh and translated it into Latin; wrote on Cakchiquel, Quiche and Tzutuhil and conducted archeological excavations. Source: Moore, Richard E., Historical Dictionary of Guatemala (1973), p 237.

3460 YADIN, YIGAEL (1917-1984). Archeologist. Directed excavations at Hazor, Megiddo, and Masada (Israel); worked on translation of Dead Sea Scrolls. Sources: Biog Index: 6 7 8 9 10 & 11/Anth News (Oct 1984) p 3/ New Republic 176:6+ F 26 '77/Time 109:57-8 Ja 24 '77.

3461 YAMADA, KAZUMARO (1903-), Japan. Physical anthropologist, geneticist. Anthropometry & human genetics in Japan. Source: Int Dir Anth 5.

3462 YAMAMOTO, MIKIO (1913-), Japan. Computerized ecological studies for Japanese community health planning. Health indices. Source: Int Dir Anth 5.

3463 YAMANE, TSUNEO (1917-), Japan. Sociologist. The family in Japanese sociological analysis. Source: Int Dir Anth 5.

3464 YANG, HSI-MEI (1916-). Physical anthropologist. Bibliographer of Ancient Chinese. Source: Int Dir Anth 5.

3465 YASA, IBRAHIM (1915-). Sociologist, anthropologist. Turkish rural sociology. Urban anthropology. Occupational patterns. Source: Int Dir Anth 5.

3466 YELMA, DERESSA (1907-1974). Economist, historian. Wrote a book on the history of the Galla (Oromo) people of Ethiopia (1967). Source: Prouty & Rosenfeld, Historical Dictionary of Ethiopia (1981), p 186.

3467 YETTS, WALTER PERCEVAL (1878- 1957), England. Orientalist, physician, art historian. Sources: Biog Index: 4 5 & 12/Ars Orientalis 3:262-3 '59/ Artibus Asiae 20 no 2-3:184-5 '57.

3468 YINGER, J MILTON (1916-). Sociologist. Ethnic & racial relations. Theory of religion & religious movements. Theory of personality & U.S. culture. Source: Int Dir Anth 5.

3469 YOUNG, CHUNG-CHIEN (1897-), China. Vertebrate paleontologist. Fossil man, human evolution & Chinese paleo-vertebrates. Source: Int Dir Anth 5.

3470 YOUNG, JOHN HOWARD (1913-1978). Archeologist. Worked at Curium (Cyprus); directed excavations at Nimrud Dagh (Turkey); specialist in Greek & Turkish archeology. Sources: Biog Index: 11/Am J Arch 82:427 Sum '78.

3471 YOUNG, ROBERT (1822-1888), England. Theologian, Orientalist. Sources: Biog Index: 3/Journal of Religion 32:258-60 O '52.

3472 YOUNG, RODNEY STUART (1907-1974), Bernardsville, New Jersey, United States. Archeologist. Directed excavations at the city of Gordion in Turkey, 1950-1974. Sources: Biog Index: 10/Am J Arch 79:112 Ap '75/Archaeology 28:129 Ap '75/ N Y Times p 65 O 27 '74.

3473 YOUNG, THEODORE CUYLER (1900- 1976). Orientalist, missionary. Expert on Iran. Sources: Biog Index: 11/ International Journal of Middle East Studies 8:267-9 Ap '77/ Middle East Journal 30:517-8 Aut '76.

3474 YU, CHIN CHUAN (1914-). Anatomist. Anthropometry & dermatoglyphics of Formosan aborigines on Taiwan. Source: Int Dir Anth 5.

3475 ZABELIN, IVAN EGOROVICH (1820-1908), Tver, Russia. Historian, archeologist. Ethnography and customs of the Russian people. Sources: Great Soviet Encyclopedia, New York, Macmillan (1975), v. 9, p 544 /Artsikhovskii, A.V. "Zabelin-arkheolog." Istoriko-arkheologicheskii sbornik. Moscow, 1948.

3476 ZAEHNER, ROBERT CHARLES (1913-1974), England. Orientalist. Source: Biog Index: 11.

3477 ZAKAR, ANDRÁS (1912-), Hungary. Linguist. Sumerian roots of modern languages. Source: Int Dir Anth 5.

3478 ŽAMCARANO, CYBEN ŽAMCARANOVIČ (1880-1940), Aginsk area of Transbaikalia, Mongolia. Folklorist. Collected and recorded epics, songs and stories of the Mongolian peoples; also made available information on native law of the Khalkha and Buryat of Mongolia. Sources: Biog Index: 4/Harvard Journal of Asiatic Studies 19:126-45 Je '56.

3479 ZAMIATNIN, SERGEI NIKOLAEVICH (1899-1958), Pavlovsk, Russia. Archeologist. The Paleolithic era in the U.S.S.R. Sources: Great Soviet Encyclopedia, New York, Macmillan (1975), v. 9, p 578 /"S.N. Zamiatnin" Sovetskaia arkheologiia, 1959, no. 2.

3480 ZEČEVIĆ, SLOBODAN (1918-). Folklorist, musicologist, mythologist. Dances, folk festivals, funeral rites, music & mythology of Serbs. Source: Int Dir Anth 5.

3481 ZENEB, ALEQA. Historian. Wrote a chronicle covering the life of Emperor Tewodros II, 1825-1857. Source: Prouty & Rosenfeld, Historical Dictionary of Ethiopia (1981), p 190.

3482 ZERRIES, OTTO HEINRICH JOSEPH (1914-), Pforzheim, Germany.

Ethnologist, art critic. Ethnology & art of Yanoama Indians of Brazil and Venezuela. Religion, material culture & social organization in the Amazon region. Sources: Int Dir Anth 3, 5.

3483 ZEUNER, FREDERICK EVERARD (1905-1963), Berlin, Germany. Physical anthropologist, archeologist. Early man in Europe. Sources: Illustrated London News 243:825 N 16 '83/N Y Times p 37 N 7 '63/ Nature 200:1263 D 28 '63.

3484 ZIMMER, HEINRICH ROBERT (1890-1943), Germany. Orientalist. Specialist on cultures, philosophy and symbols of Indian mythology. Sources: Biog Index: 3/Partisan Review 20:444-51 Jl '53.

3485 ŽLÁBEK, KAREL (1902-). Comparative anatomy of vertebrate renal vessels, kidney & masticatory apparatus. Variability of muscles & evolution of the chin. Source: Int Dir Anth 5.

3486 ZNAMIEROWSKA-PRUFFEROWA, MARIA (1898-), Lithuania. Ethnologist, museologist. Traditional fishing in Poland. Material culture & folklore. Education, documentation & open air museums. Sources: Int Dir Anth 2, 5.

3487 ZOJZI, RROK (1908-). Cultural anthropologist. Customary law, popular customs, primitive socioeconomic structures. Swing plow. Source: Int Dir Anth 5.

3488 ŻUROWSKI, KAZIMIERZ JOSEF (1909-), Poland. Archeologist. Polish archeology. European metallurgy in the Bronze Age. Art in primitive European communities. Sources: Int Dir Anth 2, 5.

-A-

Abaluhya 2460
aboriginal 0215 0281 0819 1025 1126
    1334 1591 2015 2060 2171 2172 2718
    2751 2773 2893 2974 3013 3078 3123
Abydos 0561 2538
Acahualinca 1132
accadian 2419
Accokeek 3048
acculturation 0121 0137 1055 1253
    1476 1698 1898 1988 2015 2094 2105
    2200 2333 2358 2397 2493 2622 2707
    2743 2806 2847 2903 2933 3058 3060
    3127 3160 3173 3348
Acolhua 0633
Acropolis 0302 1559
acupuncture 1598
Adat Law 3255
Aden 2068
administrator 0440 0469 0797 1404
Admiralty Islands 2190
adolescence 0656 1452 1862
adzes 0975
Aegean 1418 2523 3363
Aegina 1188
aesthetics 0802 0845 0936 0952 2059
    2127 2461
Afghanistan 0178 0207 2660 2815
Afrasiab 3280 3281
Africa 0001 0049 0082 0085 0091 0104
    0105 0128 0132 0168 0206 0214 0218
    0238 0244 0286 0355 0363 0434 0453
    0499 0607 0621 0631 0672 0695 0742
    0754 0755 0766 0808 0843 0844 0845
    0846 0855 0927 0930 0961 1008 1023
    1069 1070 1089 1137 1150 1178 1214
    1248 1272 1318 1328 1331 1344 1356
    1403 1408 1438 1499 1500 1522 1526
    1536 1578 1588 1599 1604 1628 1631
    1658 1680 1703 1726 1769 1787 1806
    1837 1859 1935 1947 1964 2042 2059
    2110 2127 2129 2187 2198 2252 2257
    2261 2305 2329 2344 2431 2452 2596
    2601 2630 2642 2662 2672 2679 2709
    2774 2879 2923 2932 2993 3031 3034
    3066 3148 3257 3326 3341 3345 3347
    3349 3380 3398 3454
Africa, Central 0249 0374 0436 0672
    0695 0710 0787 0809 0877 1225 1340
    1567 1568 1726 2270 3177 3353
Africa, East 0177 0277 0394 0531
    1318 1531 1572 1650 2238 2693 2713
    3167 3172 3394
Africa, North 0124 0453 0756 0999
    1504 1507 1838 2370 2478 2605
Africa, South 0109 0178 0341 0443
    0465 0488 0560 0572 0769 0773 0826
    0844 0860 0885 0905 1304 1542 1675
    1843 2034 2089 2179 2431 2500 2543
    2566 2568 2790 2849 2863 2871 2898
    2915 2964 3149 3161 3263 3317 3369
Africa, Southwest 1164
Africa, West 0019 0206 0279 0320
    0362 0470 0555 0607 0693 0826 0844
    0887 1069 1072 1580 1952 2059 2238
    2277 2353 2677 3075 3199 3420
Afrikaans 0969
Agarabe 3350
aggression 0316 2278
aging 0412 0447 0863 2655
Agora 3158
agriculture 0169 0243 0274 0350 0433
    0455 0610 0694 1042 1090 1347 1364
    1386 1402 1511 1824 2096 2415 2472
    2481 2491 2541 2665 2672 2686 2693
    2713 2751 3011 3036 3106 3177 3207
    3249 3344 3404 3439 3445 3487
Ainu 0088 0681 1810 3050
Ajanta 1614
Akan 0842
Aksum 2276
Alabama 0884 1387 2901
Alaska 0006 0422 0889 1232 1473
    1639 1677 1850 2084 2232 2455 2953
    2997 3384
Albania 2487 2705
alcoholism 3226
Aleut 1639 3384
Alexandria 0439
Algeria 1588 2252
Algonkian 0817 1533 1713 2234 3004
almanac 0993
Alps 2522 2567
Altai 0285 1645 2645
Altaic 2660
Altbach 2010
Altiplano 2485
Amahuaca 0941
amaranthus 2838
Amarna 1373
Amazon Basin 0020 0242 0624 1286
    1608 2941 3482
Ambo 3039
Amenhotep III 3222
America 0036 0073 0100 0243 0301
    0318 0400 0428 0615 0659 0699 0705
    0740 0760 0786 0856 0952 0955 0964
    1282 1368 1401 1413 1489 1564 1587
    1621 1685 1799 1821 1921 1962 2012
    2190 2198 2284 2375 2395 2402 2465
    2472 2601 2629 2635 2681 2697 2728

              2730 2866 2980 3004 3010 3018 3019
              3046 3069 3077 3083 3132 3156 3164
              3224 3294 3326 3328 3341 3345 3404
              3439
America, Central   0103 0191 0271
              0314 0349 0370 0415 0417 0580 0629
              0661 0740 0781 0988 0996 1147 1206
              1209 1310 1417 1421 1457 1622 1711
              1789 1900 2141 2146 2503 2580 2616
              2682 2716 2731 2783 2785 2927 2993
              3010 3019 3047 3071 3079 3083 3204
              3266 3307 3433
America, Hispanic   0035 1154 2192
              2375 3357
America, Latin   0235 0254 0930 1032
              1090 1154 1174 1262 1437 1513 1738
              2063 2162 2504 3159 3377 3392
America, Meso-   0023 0254 0276 0430
              0802 0878 1699 1773 1783 1973 2016
              2146 2411 2472 2786 2819 2837 2984
              3066 3337 3350 3433
America, North   (227 individual references, too many to list)
America, South   0009 0059 0089 0093
              0170 0267 0326 0368 0692 0730 1279
              1488 1513 1558 1563 1608 1651 1688
              1711 1727 1875 1887 1948 2019 2161
              2225 2399 2514 2551 2630 2644 2728
              2785 2786 2863 2942 3077 3210 3336
              3416
American Anthropological Association   0481 0666 1129 2074 2414
              3127
Amish   2283
Ammon's Law   0064
amulet   1059
Amur   1448 1839
Anasazi   0514
Anatolia   1285 2216 2643
anatomy   0080 0164 0541 0578 0841
              0965 0973 1708 1759 1760 1794 2185
              2410 2442 2901 3054 3061 3189 3247
              3361 3485
ancestors   0930 0932 1253 2870 2921
Andaman Islands   1361 2642
Andes   0430 0608 0613 0730 0804 1297
              1421 1447 1608 1822 2274 2318 2338
              2489 2495 2506 2779 2819 3140 3207
              3246
Angkor   1291
Anglo-Saxon   0569 1939 2377
Angola   0050 0109 0183 0224 0762
              0918 1439 2554 2684 2708
animals   0846 0978 1034 1112 1137
              1233 1364 1386 1438 1818 1844 2686
              2885 3174 3252

Ankana   2532
Ankara   2001
Anthropological Institute   0538
Anthropological Society   1411
anthropometry   0050 0090 0226 0290
              0329 0447 0476 0507 0690 1110 1130
              1253 1463 1501 1594 2105 2178 2661
              2953 2992 3041 3054 3061 3088 3320
              3391 3461 3474
Antigua   2204
Antilles   0505
Antioch   1021
Antonine   2069
Anuak   1062
Apache   0216 0431 1305 2440 2473
              2827 2918
apartheid   2500 3149
apinaye   2388
Appalachia   0741 2385 2912
Arabia   0068 0178 0284 0303 0531
              0756 1127 1623 1629 1687 1736 1922
              2126 2130 2313 2478 2840 2844 2910
              3381 3450
Aramaic   0785
Aranda   3078
Arapaho   0948 1014 2884 3076
Araucanian   1910 1911 2195 2331
Arawakan   0604
archaic, southern   3329
Archeological Institute   0947 2402
              2614
Archeological Survey   0813 1349 1373
              2034
archetypes   1201
archipelago   0405 1825 2397 2638
architecture   0167 0184 0268 0418
              0571 0705 0768 0913 0947 0951 1039
              1559 1679 1743 1801 1852 2141 2217
              2231 2264 2580 2665 2785 2801 2970
              2983 2988 3051 3228 3248 3249 3325
archivist   1311 2787
Arctic   1481 1522 1570 1639 1899 2084
              2232 2652 3301
Argentina   0024 0035 0057 0058 0059
              0078 0098 0252 0383 0448 0550 0565
              0582 0594 0770 0920 0956 1078 1187
              1297 1705 1735 1883 1945 1997 2037
              2225 2297 2399 2463 2637 2795 2825
              3308
Arikara   2035
Arizona   0173 0428 0739 1144 1267
              1359 2005 2153 2236 2304 2473 2623
              2798 3052 3335
Arizona State Museum   1267
Arkansas   1410
Armenia   0099 1584 2358 2562 3251

Armorica   2216
Arnhem   2574
art   0013 0017 0033 0053 0108 0141
     0184 0214 0268 0272 0307 0313 0361
     0378 0418 0443 0473 0502 0509 0550
     0587 0599 0604 0657 0674 0733 0759
     0781 0802 0845 0863 0902 0904 0918
     0927 0936 0937 0952 0968 1006 1058
     1063 1070 1158 1217 1240 1291 1331
     1336 1366 1382 1407 1414 1445 1451
     1499 1598 1609 1638 1642 1669 1671
     1680 1682 1719 1779 1809 1813 1840
     1852 1875 1883 1956 2005 2006 2015
     2047 2059 2060 2139 2163 2192 2208
     2211 2231 2248 2312 2318 2346 2369
     2394 2402 2461 2471 2508 2515 2517
     2541 2563 2570 2586 2611 2621 2679
     2691 2717 2719 2725 2739 2741 2790
     2795 2823 2892 2893 2896 2919 2988
     3004 3009 3017 3019 3082 3086 3105
     3107 3119 3120 3187 3242 3257 3259
     3265 3275 3279 3372 3430 3433 3456
     3482 3488
art, ancient   3430
artist   1240
Aryan   2575 2703 3238
Ashanti   2671
Ashmolean Museum   1939
Asia   0099 0108 0261 0262 0264 0265
     0363 0543 0806 0844 1020 1089 1181
     1331 1426 1647 1685 1686 1800 1856
     1968 2336 2581 2679 2980 3036 3117
     3137 3213 3233 3261 3326 3401
Asia Minor   0045 0269 1023 1160 1414
     1725 2217 2221 2402 2532 2534 2658
     3405
Asia, Central   0088 0285 0590 0644
     0825 1600 1609 1618 1756 1795 1811
     1830 1968 2457 2535 2747 2926 3042
     3183 3280
Asia, Southwest   1110 2259
Asiatic Society   0325 0812 1712
Assam   .361 2249 2639 3146
Assiniboine 2743
Assos   0144 2402
Assyria   0747 1278 1467 1523 1562
     1624 1944 2113 2214 2441 2973 2985
     3046 3162 3171
astronomy   1004 1389 2102 2219 2327
     2782 2837 2960 3425
Aswan   1043
Atacama Desert   0383
Atahualpa   0559
Atakapa   3101
Athapaskan   1274 1554 2084 2300 2959
Athens   0397 0947 0982 1160 1285
     1515 1559 1820 2508 2904 3158
Atlantic   1093 2511 2886 3403
Atlantis   2702
atolls   2163
Australia   0182 0200 0215 0244 0281
     0282 0327 0588 0616 0673 0735 0819
     0856 0893 0932 0979 1025 1046 1057
     1077 1185 1201 1231 1260 1261 1320
     1436 1794 2015 2060 2110 2312 2397
     2574 2642 2754 2772 2905 2987 2990
     3064 3078 3175 3331 3374 3474
Australia, Central   1261 3078
Australia, North   1436
Australia, Northwest   1730
Australia, Western   2773
Australopithecus   0465 0572 0846 2129
Austria   2567
Austronesia   1733
Autlan   1763
Avars   1998
Avebury   1758
Awe Cave   0070 0514
axes   3072
Aymara   2996 3210
Azande   1062
Azerbaijan   0084
Azilian   3320
Aztec   0666 1046 1263 1375 1921 2376
     2812 2854 3239

-B-

Babel   3287
baboon   1760 3334
Babylon   0747 1191 1278 1502 1573
     1624 1895 2441 2973 3046
Babylos   2419
Bagendon   0707
Bahamas   0391
Bahrein Islands   0269
Baja California   1552 3200
Bakele   2352 2615
Balearic Islands   2531
Bali   2076 2092 2190 3086 3119
Balkans   0586 0756 0862 1116 1227
     3241
ballads   0243 1822 2425 2521 3128
Baltic 0371
Baluchistan 0178
Bamenda   1730
Banda   3177 3215
Bangladesh   3227
Bantu   0940 1248 1947 2257 2269 2431
     2630 2713 2849 3334 3369 3380
baptist   0597

Baromo	0320					
Barrows	0707 2263					
basins	2730 2941 3353					
Basketmakers	2623					
basketry	0514 1359 3138					
Basotho	0094 0485 0614 0836 0928 1026 1106 1237 1657 1873 2308 2873 2889 2894 3220					
Basques	1093 2313					
Bedouin	1485 1553					
beehive	1306					
beekeepers	3344					
Beirut	1064 2908					
Beisan	1310					
Belen	2334					
Belgium	0332 0886 1662 2006 2759 3219					
Bella Coola River	2376					
Bellary	2829					
Belorussia	1979 2579					
Bemba	0441 2713					
Benga	2087 2352 2353					
Bengal	0597 0834 1361 1712 2105 2124					
Benghazi	0901					
Benin	0017 0985 2772 3441					
Berber	1195 2030 2117					
Berlin	2616					
Berlin Museum	2368					
Bertillon system	0290					
Betatakin	1721					
Bethel	1766					
Bhilala	1383					
Bible	0034 0527 0597 1766 1770 2150 2353 2405 2417 2419 2437 2499 2542 3032 3318					
bibliography	0170 0276 0689 0735 1186 1489 2577 2767 3128 3192					
biculturalism	0042 1761 1887					
Bijugo	0050					
bilingualism	0429 1211 1887 2532 2991					
biochemistry	1814					
biology	0044 0080 0447 0607 1607 1860 2255 2278 2367 2458 2461 2608 2846 2876 2882 3024 3290 3456					
biometrics	0356 0880 2432 2486					
birds	0975 3174					
Bishop Museum	1337					
Black Sea	0288 0340 1080 1193					
Blackfoot	1063 1352 2061 2073 3437					
Blacks, American	0121 0137 0218 0822 1621 1937 3345					
blood	0419 0491 1814 2084 2313 2584 2695					
Blue Mountains	0851					
Boas, Franz	1171 1282					
boats	0567 2151 3191 3485					
Bobo	0791					
Bodleian Library	3231					
Boer	3258					
Boer War	2871					
Bogazkoy	3431					
Bohemia	1109 2369 2870					
Bolivia	0111 0267 0383 0772 0793 0795 0922 1370 1447 1464 1735 2019 2225 2399 2444 2485 2594 2699 2787 2811 2822 2996 3207 3287					
Bombay	0325 1049					
Bonampak	1462					
bones	0456 0752 0768 1112 2210 2653 2793 3112 3290					
Boolag Museum	2165					
Bora Bora	1239					
Bordeaux	1724					
Borneo	0899 1435 1888 1929 2622 2772					
Borobudur	1847					
Bororo	0725					
Bosnia	1541					
Boston	0972					
Boston Museum	2823					
botany	0019 0032 0455 1204 1449 2667 3162 3208 3337					
Botswana	2000 2085 2937 3325					
bow	2589					
boys	3030					
brain	0746 0846 0971					
Brandberg	0443					
Brazil	0002 0074 0107 0120 0137 0170 0203 0218 0224 0384 0567 0725 0929 0941 1177 1205 1284 1358 1837 1883 1958 1993 2044 2098 2191 2201 2225 2296 2388 2415 2429 2529 2530 2551 2608 2631 2744 2806 2818 2847 2877 2931 2941 2949 3307 3348 3415 3482					
Brazzaville	0132					
breeding	1485 1987 2766					
Bremen Museum	2878					
British Columbia	0193 0356 0869 1286 1456 2374 2376 2980 3138					
British Empire	0595 1556 1703					
British Guyana	2773					
British Honduras	0070					
British Institute	2001					
British Museum	0190 0194 0257 0260 0455 0484 0835 0901 1258 1349 2339 2966 2985 3413 3448					
British Ordinance Survey	0789					
Brittany	1264 2049 2219 2611					
Bronx	1399					
bronze	0112 0886 1061 1545 1743					

```
                 2368 3068 3441                    0757 0779 0792 0829 0833 0868 0869
Bronze Age            0149 0457 0460 1131          0908 0917 0960 0966 0967 1048 1175
   1315 1379 1632 1792 2157 2240 2280              1218 1219 1220 1242 1249 1265 1270
   2498 2590 2696 2886 3021 3057 3072              1296 1326 1445 1570 1677 1695 1772
   3117 3363 3424 3488                             1804 1864 1869 1877 1878 1880 1881
Brussels         0587 2006 3009                    1887 1901 1916 1917 1927 1928 1962
Bubi       1313                                    1995 2036 2052 2132 2167 2203 2218
Buddhism         0325 0898 0939 1022 1597          2227 2244 2292 2355 2376 2380 2406
   1614 1920 2323 2625 3034 3115 3227              2455 2550 2552 2597 2598 2633 2647
   3279 3306                                       2649 2654 2690 2780 2798 2939 2943
buffalo          3077                              2959 3240 3289 3293 3346 3349 3434
Bulgaria         1983 2140 2619 3030 3241       Canaris          1298
   3275 3276                                    Canary Islands        0677
bullfights       2208                           Canavalia        2838
Bura       2493                                 Canela           2388
Burgundy         1934                           cannabis         2784
burials          0371 0939 1614 3280            cannibalism      0931
Buriat     3478                                 Cape of Good Hope      1353
Burkina Faso     1838                           capitalism       1518
Burma      1419 1929 3147 3223                  Caracol          0070
Burundi          0680 1754                      Carbon-14        1092 2229
Bushmen          0846 1027 1585 2566 2964       Carchemish       1373
   3142 3334                                    Carchi           1298
butterflies      3174                           Caribbean        0214 0314 0472 0916 1163
Byblos           1064                              1482 1711 2426 2452 2520 2776 2784
Byci Skala       0008                              2850 2944 3059
byliny     2247                                 Caribs           2520 2827
Byzantine        0926 2248 2517 2775 3228       Caroline Islands      1832 1851 2807
   3397                                         Carthage         0302 3194
                                                cartography           0433 0565 1446
                                                carvings         1107 1690 2151
                   -C-                          Casacare         2710
                                                caste      1361 1706 2105 2734 3100
Caddoan          0862 2865                      catacombs        1717
Cadiueios        0368                           Catamarea        2637
Caernarvon       1216                           catechism        0379
Cairo      1353 2165 2251                       Catholic         0934 2048 2394
Cairo Museum          1443                      cattle     1485 2766
Cajuns           2375                           Caucasus         0112 0263 0507 1118 1632
Cakchiquel       3459                              1645 1802 1826 1849 2143 2221 2562
Calchaqui        0058                           caves      0443 0550 1258 1435 1614 2303
calendar         0666 0992 2837 3019               2813 2971 3132 3291
California       0589 0821 0932 0964 1253       Cayua      3348
   1274 1428 1473 1492 1552 1828 1844           Cebu       3230
   2029 2074 2168 2560 2746 2800 2852           Celts      0015 0553 0732 0883 1059 1115
   2946 3023 3200                                  1295 2611 2624 3010
calligraphy      0676                           cemeteries       0901 0939 1717 3140
Cambodia         1158                           cenozoic         3137
Cambridge University       0699 1611            Central African Republic    0249 0374
Cameroon         0206 0686 0693 0787 0899          0710 0787 0877 1225 1340 1568 3177
   1344 1730 1935                               cephalic         2703
Camulodunum, Roman         1454                 cephalometry     ·1986
Canada           0029 0047 0075 0122 0127       ceramics         0005 0023 0184 1044 1054
   0131 0160 0240 0293 0308 0317 0319              1109 1297 1347 1450 1636 1682 1827
   0387 0389 0403 0414 0423 0438 0486              2026 2240 2349 2506 2563 2692 2715
   0539 0598 0618 0659 0664 0665 0683              2801 2984 3048 3192 3360
```

ceremonial	1675	2054	2152	2792	2801	Chogha	0895				
3004 3119						Chou Dynasty	0689				
ceremonies	1330	1389	2470	2828	3004	Christianity		0041	0296	0557	0642
Ceylon	0906	1520	1929	2482	2895	1936 2276 2351 2528 2745 2809 2837					
2896						3105					
Chaco	0252	0368	0795	1705	2037 2399	Chugoku	3096				
Chaco Canyon		1721	2290	2695	3292	Chukchee	0372				
Chad	0899	1935	2279	3215		Chumash	1427				
Chad, Lake		0693	0899	2279		Cibao	0472				
Champlain Valley			0158			circumnavigation		1825	1850	2553	3031
chants	0278	3078				circumpolar	1266				
charaxes	0340					Civil War	1130				
Chari River		0899				classes	0464	0742	0893	1399	1420
Chavin	0608					1441 2836 3182 3392					
Chemehuevi		3058				clicking languages		3075			
chemistry	0752	2038				climate		1446	3364		
Cherokee	2284	2902				climatology	1204				
Cheyenne	0073	0914	0995	1014	1352	Coahuila	3132				
1540 3076						coal	1817				
Chiapas	0350					Cocle	2731				
Chibcha	0992	2041				Codex, Dresden		1147	3425		
Chicago	0426	0895	1545	1831	2071	codices		2156	2640	3425	
2629 3427						coinage		1199	1215	2243	
Chichen Itza		0629	2303	2304	2765	coins	0184	0288	0442	0732	1061 2243
2917 3155						Colchester	1454				
chiefs	0657	1691	2269			Cologne	1996				
childhood	0852	1513	2200	2505	3053	Cologne Ethnographic Museum					1320
3347						Colombia		0010	0022	0069	0407 0620
childrearing		0915				0804 0805 0992 0993 1091 1102 1104					
children	0189	0300	1303	1452	1513	1133 1173 1363 1495 1723 2041 2162					
2076 2187 2375 2403 2407 2695 3030						2453 2489 2692 2710 3232					
3041 3119 3320 3359 3394 3439						colonies		0005	0011	0024	0030 0111
Chile	0066	0179	0202	0383	0448 0660	0199 0203 0595 0606 0645 0831 1046					
1640 1711 1735 1910 1911 1997 2195						1073 1076 1099 1200 1431 1504 1536					
2310 2331 2996 3283 3415						1551 1557 1568 1689 2103 2141 2204					
Chile's National Museum				1910		2903 2932 2975 3074 3149 3243 3265					
Chimbu District		2386				3359					
Chimu	1821					colonization		0010	1090	1387	
China	0001	0061	0097	0108	0141 0151	Colorado		1183	1564	2304	2623 2730
0330 0456 0599 0651 0652 0674 0675						3060					
0689 0780 0807 0843 0997 1004 1006						Columbia		0093	2980	3415	
1052 1145 1257 1258 1324 1529 1549						Columbia University			1082		
1596 1598 1602 1628 1644 1682 1704						Comanche		0599	0613	1540	
1737 1743 1757 1807 1829 1900 1914						Compadrazgo			1437		
1915 1963 1978 2045 2100 2107 2160						Congo River		0754	1342		
2210 2335 2356 2570 2581 2593 2681						conquests		0098	0920	0921	1104 1173
2711 2792 2863 2896 2922 3054 3059						1497 1593 1646 1684 2037 2208 2311					
3106 3212 3218 3315 3464 3469						2391 2447 2464 2465 2812 2942					
Chinantec	3366					conservation		1109	1203	1204	2136
Chinook	1010					Cook Islands		2309			
Chippewa	0196	0995	2035	2725		Cook, Captain James			0182	0233	1148
Chiricahua	2440					1149					
chiropractic		2422				Copan	0629	2181	3019	3047	3081
Chisona	1030					Copenhagen			0344		
Chitimacha	3101					copper		2567	3441		
Choctaw	0875	1014	1387			Coptic	0542	0801	1349	2251	2907 3157

                              3450
Coptic Museum   2251
corals   2986
Corinth   0463 1696 1820 2508 3104
Coronation Gulf   3037
Correze   0187 2039
corrida   2208
Costa Rica   0023 0040 0315 0643 1101
   1105 1192 2019 2026 2144 2418 2465
   2527 2998 3071 3150 3245
costumes   0981 1229 1840
cowboy   1162
cranial   0777 1592 2178 2422 2584
   2704 2860 3203
craniometry   0392 1589 1635 2703
   2751 3061 3189 3213
craniotomy   3096
cranium   1479
crats   1423
Cree   0469 0995
Creek   1073 1330
cremation   3192
Creole   0286 2827
Crete   0397 0524 0528 1391 1453 1550
   2104 2487 2523
crime   0645 2291 2773
Crimea   0310 2231
criminology   0080 1130 1233 1988 2306
   2431 3061 3124
Cro-Magnon   0850 1412 1909
Crow   2035 3076
Ctesiphon   1451
Cuauhtemoc   1375
Cuba   0214 0391 1581 1711 1974 2452
cults   0101 1021 1796 1937 2533 2709
   2944 2981 3192 3405
culture   (273 individual references, too many to list)
Cunana   2008 2287
Cundiyo   3357
cuneiform   0523 1278 1355 1521 1624
   1802 3162
Cupisnique   1903
curator   0174 0229 1229 1320 1391
   1451 1459 1574 1870 1996 2006 2136
   2368 2629 2666 2905 3259 3437
Cuzcatlan   1904
Cuzco   3242
Cyprus   0840 1213 1550 2339 3470
Cyrenaica   0706 2536
Czechoslovakia   0008 0373 1660 2173
   2369 2407 2507 2602 2870

                   -D-

Dagomba   3111
Dahomey   0289 0531 1499 2576 2634
Dahshur   0986
Dakota   0894 1143 1445 2701 2746
dams   2730 3048
dance   0266 0509 0806 0948 1263 1590
   2287
Danchour   1683
Danish National Museum   0344
Darfur   3215
Darwinism   0020 0848 1548
Dayak   1231
Dead Sea Scrolls   0527 3271 3460
death   0324 0494 0939 2221 2858
Deccan   2829
decima   2208
Deir el Bahri   0637 3432
Delaware   3018
Delaware Valley   0003 3298
Delhi   0273
Delos   0498 3248
Delphi   0749 1865
demography   0014 0080 0605 0672
   0739 0752 0863 0877 0935 0978 1042
   1051 1116 1203 1375 1389 1483 1518
   1524 1645 1860 2030 2084 2096 2116
   2257 2274 2313 2354 2357 2362 2469
   2490 2695 2703 2784 2786 2882 2915
   2925 3024 3034 3056 3219
demotic   1050 2742 3157
dendrochronology   0258 1425 2872
Dene   2300
Denmark   0360 2668
dentition   0200 0541 0841 1046 1288
   1477 1790 2442 2815 3131
dermatoglyphics   0491 0811 1130 1725
   2584 3373 3474
desert   1039 2373 2583 2605
Detroit   1610
Dhlo-Dhlo   0631
Diaguita   1910 1945
dialects   0652 0741 0763 0783 1127
   1152 1195 1354 1947 1993 2148 2197
   2294 2376 2453 2660 2976 3063 3080
   3139 3380
Dick   1164
dictionaries   0035 0060 0068 0298 0321
   0324 0368 0452 0461 0686 0762 0763
   0791 0801 1030 1085 1192 1256 1257
   1295 1728 1834 1930 1993 2148 2156
   2294 2441 2451 2657 2660 2816 2883
   3063 3139 3162
Diegueno   1552
Dikele   2615
Dionysius   0033
diplomacy   2136

diplomat 0493
disease 0777 2306 2566 2655 3140
Diyala 0895
Dnestr River 0310
Dobu 0461
Dogon 0927 1344
domestication 0881 1034 1364 1386 1511 2023 2686
Dominican Republic 0472
Dordogne 0684 2566
Douala 0686
dreams 1012 3059
drought 2747 3132
drugs 2784 3336 3337
Dunhuang 1258
Dura Europos 1701
Dutch 1728 3041
dwellings 1507 1564 2332 2623
dynasties 0456 0689 1202
dysplasias 2938
Dzibilchaltun 0076

-E-

Easter 2470
Easter Island 1047 1509 2225 2328 2752 2777 3410
eastern hemisphere 3326 3338
ecology 0080 0265 0386 0412 0878 0978 1042 1171 1204 1287 1384 1420 1511 1774 1818 1899 1906 1951 2030 2079 2163 2232 2252 2348 2366 2848 2915 2925 2971 3056 3160 3338 3358 3462
economy 0081 0294 0354 0507 0679 0715 0737 0766 0809 0830 1075 1386 1504 1511 1518 1580 1648 1730 1769 1882 1974 1980 1987 1995 2089 2119 2146 2200 2229 2285 2335 2338 2439 2448 2472 2576 2596 2653 2725 2766 2819 2998 3093 3099 3170 3172 3229 3324 3378 3487
Ecuador 0030 0036 0258 0537 0563 0613 0639 0667 0712 0763 1056 1298 1360 1558 1668 1684 1688 1711 2212 2391 2445 2526 2592 2728 2786 3224 3237 3265 3288 3400 3403
Edfu 0046
education 0159 0359 0397 0469 0720 0982 1160 1284 1285 1422 1515 1549 1660 1769 1770 1782 1820 2057 2190 2226 2273 2329 2508 2786 2904 2991 2993 3206 3266 3359 3486
Egypt 0046 0060 0102 0133 0227 0231 0260 0280 0284 0336 0419 0426 0439 0482 0484 0494 0561 0611 0629 0631 0637 0649 0801 0859 0871 0907 0962 0974 0986 1001 1009 1039 1043 1050 1074 1085 1125 1157 1182 1212 1269 1294 1336 1365 1373 1443 1459 1523 1525 1550 1553 1613 1648 1738 1781 1788 1831 1863 1892 1893 1941 2001 2038 2062 2106 2126 2160 2214 2231 2251 2271 2273 2316 2372 2373 2477 2516 2523 2538 2562 2622 2666 2717 2721 2775 2814 2823 2860 2881 2890 2950 2960 2985 2988 3157 3222 3259 3268 3309 3362 3432
Egyptology 0494 0649 0871 1009 1043 1506 1863 2165 2214 2372 2516 2666 2823
El Salvador 0199 0549 0641 1111 1440 1904 2016 2209 2456
Ellora 1614
encomienda 0615
enculturation 0081 1458
England 0005 0455 0503 0520 0534 0701 0707 0976 1022 1076 1095 1255 1343 1351 1401 1454 1590 1605 1751 1758 1981 2057 2078 2134 2219 2371 2375 2611 2666 2912 2976 3072 3203 3229 3423
engravings 1084 1137 2147 2514
entomology 3151
Entrecasteaux 1677
environment 0059 0866 1260 1397 2008 2331 2423 2512 2530 2724 2825 2898 2900 3284 3423
epics 0353 1667 2125 2247 2425 3405 3478
epigraphy 0324 0494 0496 0523 0561 0649 0732 0859 1074 1093 1147 1212 1258 1302 1349 1355 1661 1957 2210 2243 2302 2351 2482 2621 2890 2985 3019 3300 3309
Epirus 2031
Equador 1298
Equatorial Guinea 0435 1313 2087 2353
ergology 1526
Estonia 0126 2425 3126
ethics 0405 1356 3237 3312
Ethiopia 0178 0269 0363 0394 0443 0477 0634 0638 0748 1617 2214 2276 2296 2334 2437 2478 2742 2907 3466
ethnicity 1099 2235 3349
ethnoarcheology 0230
ethnoastronomy 1254
ethnobiology 0430
ethnobotany 1449 1582 1995 2838 3079 3393

ethnocentrism 0262 3221
ethnocinematography 1248
ethnoesthetics 0105
ethnogenetics 1276 1599 3180 3440
ethnographer 0088 0844 0869 1702
 2088 2549 3182
ethnography 0026 0032 0035 0054
 0139 0206 0213 0216 0315 0320 0368
 0405 0453 0521 0546 0575 0586 0589
 0595 0728 0735 0751 0791 0797 0830
 0889 0948 0952 0980 0996 1000 1020
 1049 1078 1092 1099 1148 1149 1163
 1178 1225 1247 1251 1253 1272 1313
 1320 1344 1353 1380 1499 1519 1531
 1540 1600 1705 1763 1767 1798 1832
 1836 1844 1856 1868 1870 1900 2004
 2088 2099 2108 2140 2159 2399 2430
 2434 2460 2502 2507 2596 2619 2629
 2644 2671 2725 2733 2773 2774 2845
 2849 2857 2878 2964 3000 3050 3058
 3083 3101 3125 3132 3141 3142 3178
 3180 3183 3190 3198 3230 3299 3301
 3344 3366 3411 3458 3475
ethnohistory 0071 0093 0121 0152
 0873 0875 0930 0937 1062 1096 1702
 2195 2338 2469 2640 2718 2776 2963
 2993 3098 3101 3370
ethnolinguistics 0613
Ethnological Survey 0869
ethnomedicine 1130 3337
ethnomusicology 3005 3085
ethnophotography 2312
ethnopsychology 0703
ethnozoology 3079
ethology 3174 3354
Etruria 0033 0208 0583 0974 1180
 1356 1957 2254 2394
Eurasia 0042 1084 3338
Europe 0049 0091 0097 0108 0147
 0169 0247 0248 0251 0262 0263 0264
 0274 0281 0320 0339 0363 0374 0393
 0433 0443 0460 0497 0555 0599 0649
 0693 0709 0769 0835 0897 0972 0977
 0999 1023 1046 1051 1109 1118 1146
 1331 1342 1377 1379 1444 1454 1662
 1672 1725 1726 1727 1748 1756 1822
 1824 1838 1855 1860 1866 1879 1950
 2065 2099 2228 2262 2264 2279 2280
 2332 2336 2351 2357 2369 2400 2426
 2446 2454 2522 2567 2575 2585 2601
 2665 2668 2679 2703 2722 2807 2828
 2839 2849 2859 2863 2880 2882 2886
 2897 2913 2980 3005 3010 3036 3047
 3072 3080 3120 3128 3132 3142 3249
 3257 3264 3290 3316 3367 3405 3408
 3429 3483 3488
Europe, Central 0119 0275 0507 1115
 1379 1672 2653
Europe, Eastern 0209 0378 0981 1124
 1364 2365 3033 3117 3144 3184
Europe, Northern 1981 2659 2919
 3406
Europe, Northwestern 0696 2915
Europe, Southeastern 3424
Europe, Southwestern 1883
Europe, Western 0453 0460 0883 1140
 2839 2969 3184
evolution 0103 0221 0222 0327 0386
 0635 0695 0745 0766 0776 0846 0847
 0870 0935 0941 0965 0971 1201 1339
 1438 1530 1606 1626 1634 1708 1759
 1794 1818 1908 1931 2123 2129 2324
 2442 2582 2672 2686 2876 2945 2969
 3056 3312 3319 3361 3365 3389 3469
 3485
Ewondo 3296
expeditions 0020 0032 0182 0341 0417
 0432 0484 0568 0572 0628 0634 0661
 0710 0787 0910 0972 1091 1178 1247
 1292 1380 1388 1509 1521 1611 1618
 1645 1671 1692 1738 1832 1850 1897
 1963 2108 2238 2273 2532 2605 2623
 2638 2747 2777 2823 2864 2964 3031
 3116 3140 3167 3183 3191 3253 3403
 3411 3448
explorations 0045 0069 0094 0165
 0182 0233 0271 0320 0405 0430 0546
 0594 0692 0693 0706 0751 0782 0795
 0958 1039 1072 1099 1173 1205 1340
 1481 1608 1758 1762 1900 1903 2000
 2085 2279 2307 2373 2426 2465 2488
 2525 2610 2909 2910 3008 3019 3141
 3167 3174 3253
explorer 1023 1726
extermination 1027
extinct 1112 1427 1677 3201

-F-

families 0685 1133 1218 1299 1420
 1492 1513 1981 2107 2111 2362 2476
 2681 2709 2792 2827 2866 3129 3182
 3355 3394 3463
Fang 1055 2189 2352 2615 3205
Fanti 1099 2832
Far East 0141 1398 1415 1576 1602
 1607 2393 2570 3315
fauna 0182 1018 2433 2838 3028 3291
Fayum, Lake 0631
female 1044 2223
feminist 2871

Fergana	0285					
Feronia	0208					
Fertile Crescent	2062					
fertility	2096					
festivals	0041	0360	1324	1385	1485 1751 2228 2836 3480	
Field Museum	1545					
Fiji	0562 0751 0932 1053 1253 1388 1532 1616 1718 1907 2004 2309 2631 2771 3160 3166 3412 3419					
films	1312 1462 2093 2774					
Finland	1022 1377 1816 1848 2425 2704 3249					
Finno-Ugric	0627 1983 2419 3144					
fire	1582 3405					
fishing	0567 1577 2267 2364 2389 2668 2922 3486					
Fitzwilliam Museum	0699					
floods	2730 3401					
flora	0019 0597 3337					
Florida	1170 1280 2958 2975					
Fly River	0032					
folklore	(206 individual references, too many to list)					
Folklore Society	0455 0520 1556					
folkmusic	0743 1255 1590 1651 1991 2656					
folksongs	0209 0551 1041 1162 1311 1324 1335 1489 1494 1575 1817 1981 2012 2124 2125 2152 2250 2375 2385 2478 2836 2912 3004 3078 3128 3330 3478					
folktales	0452 0551 0765 0891 1667 1737 2247 2375 2478 2620 2708 2732 2836 3128 3235					
Folsom	1112 2953					
Fon	0985 2634					
food	2520 2780					
Formosa	2259 3474					
Fort Ancient	0072 2290 2299					
Fort Belknap Reservation	2743					
fossils	0059 0190 0465 0755 0777 1034 1235 1331 1412 1841 1908 2358 3361 3469					
Fox	1709 1713					
France	0052 0095 0124 0187 0253 0358 0377 0381 0404 0410 0432 0436 0453 0554 0670 0684 0685 0688 0764 0780 0839 0876 0891 0898 0928 0945 0963 0977 1072 1088 1198 1200 1241 1341 1620 1666 1674 1677 1724 1854 1913 1934 1958 2039 2099 2130 2216 2219 2264 2270 2544 2566 2612 2729 2757 2758 2775 2935 3284 3320 3455					
Franciscan	1762					
Fraser River	2980					
Frejus region	0945					
French Institute	2908					
frescoes	1462					
Fuegians	0448 0449 1883 1997 2195					
Fulani	0139 0206 0791					
functionalism	2110 3172					
funeral	0260 0611 0839 0859 0939 1180 1212 1614 1717 1729 2038 2267 2271 2372 2538 2702 3222 3303 3480					
fungi	3337					
Futa Toro	1736					

-G-

Gabon	0295 0535 0787 0972 1663 2189 2352 2353 2604 2615 2667 3205 3318					
Gaelic	1255					
Galla	3466					
Gallic	2307					
Gallo-Roman	0888					
Galoa	2352 2604					
Gambia	1327 2285 2689 3002					
Gambia River	1292 1692					
games	0807 2375 2732 3077					
Ganbier Islands	1919					
Ganda	2713					
Garo	1316					
genealogy	1202 1239 1276 2451 3410					
genetics	0096 0195 0316 0327 0420 0479 0849 0853 0932 0935 0965 0998 1174 1320 1441 1725 1925 2007 2313 2324 2362 2413 3024 3094 3256 3461					
Geneva	0904					
gentry	2836					
geobotany	1204					
geography	0035 0136 0140 0265 0606 0634 0751 0857 0980 1099 1102 1354 1381 1836 1924 1959 2037 2140 2199 2229 2418 2658 2716 2724 2761 2829 3042 3060 3101 3147 3284 3288 3377					
Geological Survey	2688					
geology	0190 0310 0393 0404 0410 0489 0631 0674 0753 1061 1084 1107 1137 1264 1306 1384 1614 1854 1977 2015 2060 2080 2151 2349 2370 2514 2790 2859 2986 3072 3175 3325 3441					
Georgia	1109 1707 1853 2502 2526 3329 3352					
Georgian	2502 3297					
Germany	0140 0275 0287 0352 0474 0502 0553 0709 0783 1138 1164 1379 1571 1751 1808 1950 1960 1996 2010 2018 2223 2333 2467 2666 2831 3085 3109 3129 3172 3290					
geysers	0182					

Ghana	0320	0595	0842	1099	1536	2671						
3111												
Gandhi, Mahatma			3146									
Ghost Dance		2284										
Gila Pueblo	1267	2236										
Gilbert Island			0321	0546								
Gilbertsville Basin			2349									
Gilyak	1448	1839	3050									
girls	3030											
Giza	0986	1443	2988									
Glanum	2758											
glossolalia	1301											
Gloucester	0707											
gods	1475											
Gold Coast	0320	0595	0842	1099	1536							
2671	3111											
Gordion	3472											
gorillas	1040											
Gournia	1453											
grammar	0295	0421	0461	0686	0762							
0791	0940	0969	0998	1000	1022	1152						
1192	1256	1345	1388	1432	1442	1657						
1713	1806	1834	1978	1993	2117	2138						
2214	2547	2657	2720	3126	3243	3297						
Grand Bassam			0320									
Great Basin		2965										
Great Britain		0206	0397	0452	0518							
0732	0773	0839	0867	0885	0982	1061						
1099	1161	1221	1257	1264	1422	1431						
1536	1556	1694	1712	1758	1770	1771						
2069	2085	2103	2134	2219	2238	2268						
2273	2436	2508	2555	2611	2714	3033						
Great Plains			1129	1361	1951	2256						
2328	2495	2622	2848	2884								
Greece		0033	0080	0241	0272	0302						
0313	0342	0361	0397	0408	0460	0462						
0463	0498	0502	0554	0591	0606	0622						
0657	0904	0946	0947	0982	1060	1080						
1160	1188	1189	1199	1213	1215	1285						
1323	1407	1414	1418	1422	1469	1505						
1517	1583	1654	1661	1673	1696	1719						
1745	1746	1750	1820	1865	1949	2031						
2137	2160	2217	2243	2253	2339	2368						
2382	2387	2424	2479	2487	2508	2523						
2534	2591	2603	2614	2627	2705	2719						
2741	2834	2904	2906	2914	2966	2986						
3025	3051	3104	3116	3135	3158	3248						
3277	3305	3363	3371	3409	3453	3470						
Greenland		0329	0889	1271	3384							
Gribingui	0249											
Griqua	2566											
Guadalcanal			1551									
Guam	2807	2811										
Guarani		0292	0379	0547	0552	1079						
1322	2281	2388	2795	2903								
Guatemala		0110	0298	0517	0544	0623						
	0626	0744	1210	1319	1507	1868	1889
2026	2095	2141	2199	2204	2304	2456
2505	2680	2682	2697	2715	2739	2809
2826	2843	2927	2932	3081	3127	3139
3204	3245	3286	3352			
Guayabo	0023						
Guayaquil		0036	0667	3403			
Guaycurue	0368						
Guinea	0120						
Gujarati	2769	2829					
Gulf Coast	3360						
Gullah	0214	1698					
gulls	3174						
Guyana Indians		2773					
gypsies		0765	1136	1802	3250		

-H-

habitats	0981	1618				
Hadhramaut		0269	0631			
Hagia Sophia		3397				
Haida	0869	2374	3101			
Haifa	3271					
Haiti	0742	2375	2760	2944	3227	
Hallstatt	0008	2653				
hallucinogens		3337				
Hanoi	2340					
Harvard	2002	2629	2988			
Harvard University Museum					2823	
Harvard Yenching Institute				1612		
Harvey Rockshelter			0471			
Hatay	2985					
Hausa	0206	0693	1518	2252	2462	2493
2671						
Havasupai	3018					
Hawaii	0246	0322	0525	0574	0751	1031
1036	1337	1600	1669	1850	1897	1900
2055	2108	2114	2336	2417	2635	2778
2911	3096	3253	3411			
Hazor	3460					
headwaters	0165					
health	0080	0469	1044	1119	1123	2056
2063	2094	2096	2226	2725	2763	3024
3462						
Hebrew	0870	3073				
Hebrides	0182					
Hehe	0469					
Hellenistic	3351					
Herakleion	2137	2243				
herbs	0728	3199				
Herculaneum		2104				
heredity	0228	3169				
Herzegovina		1541				
Hidatsa	2035	2178				
hierarchies	0979	2547				

hieroglyphics   0649 2214
Himalayas   0343 1312 1609 2535
Hindi   1022 1049 1256 1367 1712 2275
Hinduism   0557
Hispanic   0071 0481 0573 0802 1903
    2111 3098 3140 3307
history   (261 individual references, too many to list)
Hittites   0524 1278 1595
Hohokam   1267 3335
Hoifung   2100
holistic   1361 1476
Holland   2857
holocene   1042
hominids   0465 0467 0695 0776 0850
    0965 1412 1606 1818 1909 1931 1998
    2442
hominology   1734
Homo Habilis   1931
Homo Sapiens   0776
Honduras   2181 2411 2733 3019 3026
    3047 3071 3081
Hong Kong   2301
Hopewell   1142 2086 2290
Hopi   0045 0234 0914 0915 1012 1014
    1755 1767 2035 3052 3178 3393
Hottentot   0844 0846 1542 1675 2566
Huascal   0559
Huehuetenango   2680
Human Relations Area Files   1141
    2336
Hungary   0167 0209 0944 1816 1840
    1998 2094 2454 2521 3267
Huns   1998
hunters   0975 3338
hunting   1816
Hupa   1274
Huron   0438
Hut Tax War   0043
Hyderabad   1614
hymnals   1651

                    -I-

Iberia   2531
Ice Age   1854 2264 2522
Iceland   0106 0182 1447 1981 3040
    3160 3354
iconography   3252 3408
idiolects   2929
Ifugao   0212
Igbo   0138 2913
Ikhtiraq   1631
Illinois   0158 0230 0426 0471 2290
Imbabura   1298

immigration   0137 0723 1610 2094 2126
    2330
Inca   0559 0608 0713 0816 1211 1357
    1593 2327 2338 2391 2779 2830 2854
    3182 3183 3242 3246 3272 3274
India   0026 0097 0161 0163 0196 0247
    0261 0273 0284 0325 0353 0354 0431
    0440 0473 0513 0521 0531 0557 0575
    0590 0597 0615 0663 0697 0719 0797
    0813 0979 0990 1015 1029 1098 1158
    1181 1185 1186 1316 1345 1346 1361
    1383 1469 1520 1527 1537 1539 1596
    1614 1625 1628 1712 1800 1855 1856
    1929 2057 2105 2249 2275 2535 2554
    2577 2639 2651 2675 2688 2747 2829
    2860 2936 2948 2980 2983 3027 3035
    3042 3100 3137 3141 3146 3163 3279
    3386
Indian Civil Service   0440 0797 3413
Indiana   0334 1984 2050 2061
Indiana University Folklore Institute   0950
Indianola   2609
Indians, Southwestern U.S.   1402
    1582 1755
indigenismo   2450 2786
Indochina   0280 0388 0724 1158 1291
    2389
Indonesia   0244 0291 0719 0788 1435
    1466 1625 1667 1680 1757 1768 1807
    1847 2007 2076 2092 2383 2389 3036
    3059 3086 3119 3255 3278
Indus Valley   0524
industries   0085 0357 1179 1399 1436
    1577 2743 2961 3192
informant   0943 1870 2644 2956 2999
    3023
Ingrians   0126
institutes   0025 0426 0441 0538 0895
    0947 0950 1144 1358 1534 1612 1831
    2001 2071 2191 2402 2547 2556 2614
    2656 2713 2797 2905 2908 2980 2991
    3056 3195 3427
instruments   0067 0082 0626 0918
    1640 2892 2995 3041
International Congress   3127
International Paleopathology Association   3368
Inuit   0329 0356 0431 0733 0881 0889
    0917 0989 1245 1251 1390 1677 1899
    1906 2337 2669 2997 3037 3061 3107
    3384
inventor   3221
Ionian Islands   2031
Iowa   0158 2074
Iran   0108 0570 0895 1376 1451 1944

```
                2222 2861 2983 3042 3405 3473      Jivaro    3237
Iraq            1310 1521 1895 1944 2001 2113      joking    0949
                2494 2835 3340 3381                Jomon     2390
Ireland              0821 1306 1937 2315 2446      Jordan         3102
                2611 3331
Irene Mound          1109
iron       1813 2630                                              -K-
Iron Age        0112 0245 0460 0503 0860
      0862 0886 1131 1379 2436 2952 3068           Kachari   1316
      3090                                         Kachin    1419
Iroquois        0438 0750 0817 0821 1096           Kafue     1567
      1249 1250 1388 1690 1804 2298 2663           Kaimiloa       0331
      2956 2972 2993 3004                          Kaingang       2388
Ishi       2589                                    Kalinga        0212
Isis       0041                                    Kalmuck        2660
Islam           0108 0231 1058 1623 1628 1629      Kama      1983 2962 3021
      1733 1781 1966 2088 2126 2243 2742           Kamchatka      1639 1836
      2845 2983                                    Kamehameha I        0574 3253
Israel          0025 0034 0706 1272 1273 1310      Kampur         2105
      1373 1766 2273 2354 2881 3460                Kaniye Djami        3228
Istanbul        3228 3397                          Kanopolis River     2969
Isthmia         0463                               Kansas         0466 2969
Italy           0137 0198 0208 0307 0347 0460      Karaja    0929
      0510 0589 0634 0771 0901 1218 1469           Karatepe       2419
      1493 1701 1956 2014 2129 2217 2276           Karbi     1316
      2467 2468 2486 2719 2836 2860 2904           Karnak         2165 2890 3268
      3333                                         Kassena        0791
Ithaca     1505                                    Kauri     2256
Ivory Coast          0320 1555 3436                Kawaiisu       0589
                                                   Kayenta        1359
                                                   Kayor     1670
                     -J-                           Kazakhstan     0285
                                                   Kentucky       1184
Jaida      2336                                    Kenya     1531 1561 1617 1834 2121 2129
Jainism         0325                                     2460 2466 3394
Jalisco         1610 1763                          Keresan Pueblo      1540
Jamaica         0266 0286 0391 2287 2784           Ket       1839
      2993                                         Ketou     0985
Japan           0012 0088 0090 0097 0141 0151      Khadim         2068
      0237 0694 0939 1024 1036 1354 1385           Khalkha        2660 3478
      1398 1417 1426 1566 1576 1596 1633           Khandesh       3146
      1644 1737 1751 1757 1779 1790 1793           Kharge         0631
      1810 1812 1884 2160 2240 2267 2347           Khasi     2105 2639
      2390 2398 2409 2423 2439 2650 2803           Khazars        0112
      2815 2863 2921 2922 3024 3034 3059           Khmer     0759
      3094 3095 3096 3115 3118 3181 3190           Khoisan        2543 2849
      3211 3311 3315 3339 3461 3462 3463           Kickapoo       1713 2725
Java            0283 0916 1158 1551 1728 2109      Kikuyu         1769 1931
      3225                                         Kimbundu       0762
jaw        2793                                    Kincaid Mounds      0471
Jemez Cave      2695                               kinesics       0328
Jericho         1765                               kinship        0006 0192 0214 0242 0651
Jerusalem       0345 1770                                0929 0941 0943 0979 1077 1083 1150
Jesuit     0061 0620 1187 1322 2710                      1253 1307 1420 1437 1540 1793 1843
Judaism              0785 1124 1652 1980 2313            1929 1962 2106 2107 2305 2398 2413
      2354 2413 2499 3005                                2706 2792 2827 2866 2895 3018 3094
```

```
                3127 3312 3359
Kiowa      0214 1962 2256 2284 2827 2884
Kipsigis        2121
Kirghizia       0285 2645 3143
Kish       1110
Kishin     1895
Kiswahili       1834 1931 3038
Kitab      1631
Kivas      2695 3074
Kivu, Lake      1318
Klamath         1224 3018 3049
Knossos         1060
Kongo      0224 0320 0844 2554
Konkomba        3111
Kordofan        0374
Korea      0097 1605 1737 1739 1743 1757
      1779 2240 2393 2863 2922 3000 3034
      3059
Korhus          1181
Koryak          1639 1839
Kota       0440
Kotokoland      1935
Kotzebue        1850
Kromdraai       0465
Krusenstern          1897
Ksar Akil       1064
Kuikuru         0941
Kuka       0899
Kukukuku        0337
Kurds      1929
Kuril      1836
Kuwaa      1702
Kwakiutl        0715 0869 1286 1615 2434
Kwango River         2569


                     -L-


La Plata Valley      0057 2290 2825
Lacandon        0350 2540 3197
Lacondon        0350 2540 3197
Lalung          1316
Lamaism         0343 3306
Lamarckian theory    1708
languages       (261 individual references, too many to list)
Lapps      2364 2704 3301
Las Vegas       2977
Latin      1583 1661 3459
Latvia     0126 0176
law, Roman      0493
laws       0064 0166 0493 0924 1250 1272
      1540 1551 1712 1781 2057 2125 2179
      2187 2189 2405 2431 2452 2543 2634
      2732 2773 2832 2849 2918 3255 3478
      3487
```

```
Lebanon         0045 0072 1064 1182 2106
      2314 2536 2908 3431
Leiden          2857
Lepchas         1312
Leptis Magna         0208
Lesotho         0094 0485 0836 0851 1027
      1243 1585 1657 1720 1776 1924 1926
      2078 2268 2291 2915 2964 3161 3325
      3402
lexicography         0027 1195 2683 2929
Lexicon         2683 3099
lexicostatistics     0998
Liberia         0117 0305 0490 0621 0723
      1071 1486 1702 3442
librarian       2823
library         0116 1160 1311 1346 2251
      2577 3231
Library Anthropology Research
      Group      3127
Libya      0102 0208 0307 0901 2273 2373
      2478 2536
Lilooet         3138
Lima       0608
Limpopo Basin        0905
Lindenmeier          2730
Lindos          0344
Linear B        0342 1060
Linguistic Atlas Project     2066
Linguistic Survey         1345
linguistics          0027 0054 0074 0097 0140
      0267 0320 0356 0421 0515 0521 0565
      0588 0613 0691 0716 0719 0721 0783
      0791 0826 0894 0940 0983 0998 1008
      1010 1047 1099 1156 1223 1301 1332
      1354 1358 1361 1367 1388 1432 1449
      1469 1492 1533 1554 1583 1660 1688
      1705 1728 1733 1767 1839 1844 1855
      1921 1950 1952 2111 2125 2162 2191
      2234 2238 2351 2364 2381 2383 2547
      2556 2557 2615 2648 2650 2660 2691
      2728 2783 2831 2922 2929 2991 3004
      3006 3026 3049 3063 3080 3099 3195
      3243 3300 3322 3325 3380 3396 3399
      3403 3405
literature      0064 0074 0104 0264 0303
      0482 1052 1106 1152 1160 1257 1365
      1467 1490 1633 1658 1702 1728 1812
      1835 1897 1911 1926 1941 2117 2124
      2204 2346 2379 2504 2637 2650 2653
      2745 2780 3062 3161 3163 3225 3272
      3421
lithics         1044 2299 2605 2946 3192
Lobaye          1568
Loboca          1675
London          0493 1351 1769
London Museum        1423
```

London Times	1590				
Loti	2027				
Louisiana	1151 2375				
Louvre	0657 0902 3259				
Lovelock Cave	2029				
Lowie Museum	1229				
Lozi	0171 1247 1567				
Luando	0183				
Lulongo	1164				
Lusaka	0441				
Luxor	0611 2165 2890				
Luzon	1713 3059				
Lydian	0493				
Lysippos	1696				

-M-

Macaque	0605				
Macedonia	1505				
Machu Picchu	0323				
Macon	1674				
Madagascar	1075 1084 1200				
Madiga	3100				
Mafeking	2568				
Magahat	2443				
Magellan	2553				
magic	1181 1328 1356 1531 1538 1796 1843 2742 2774 2954 3210				
Magyars	0821				
Malaita	1551				
Malanje District	1439				
Malawi	0004 1168 1272 2883				
Malaya	0338 0788 2056 2397 2850 3059				
Malaysia	0727 2389 2397 2954 3324				
Mali	0139 0206 0320 0555 0910 0927 1072 2252 2378 2488 2636 2774 2808				
mamalik	0168				
mammals	0059 0541 0755 0965 1572 1807 1841 2449 2815 2859 3112				
mammoth	1112 1908				
Manabi	2526				
Manam	3359				
Manchu	0061				
Manchuria	1987 3190				
Mandan	2035				
Mandingue	2378				
Mandjia	1225				
Manitoba	2791				
Manuvu	2125				
Maori	0297 0492 0975 1343 1456 1757 2309 3096				
maps	1099 1247 1446 1492 1631 2180 2236 2342 2623 3325				
Mapuche	1910 2331 3272				
Marajo	2941				
Mari	2494				
Mariana Islands	0837				
markets	0235 0619 1518 2146 2491				
Marksville	1142				
Marne	2757				
Maronites	1064				
Marquesas Islands	1239 1850 2128 2205 3168				
Marri Baluchis	0478				
marriage	0790 0893 1822 2103 2505 2734 2827 3129 3223 3312 3324				
Mars	1683				
Marshall Islands	1832 2807				
marsupial	0182				
Martin Wagner Museum	0502				
Martinique	0391				
martyr	0438				
Maryland	2080 2188 3048				
Masada	0025 3460				
Masai	1561 3167				
masks	1690 2893				
Massawa	0634				
masticatory	3485				
Matengo	0216				
Mato Grosso	0725				
Maund Ruin	0631				
Maya	0076 0349 0350 0428 0623 0629 0661 0744 0753 0924 1046 1147 1302 1398 1462 1564 1785 1852 1886 1948 2016 2093 2095 2156 2181 2294 2302 2303 2327 2471 2540 2580 2621 2715 2740 2782 2796 2801 2809 2837 2967 2984 3019 3041 3127 3139 3155 3159 3197 3239 3245 3286 3295 3300 3314 3416 3425 3459				
Mazenod	1926				
Mbomou River	0374				
Mbuti	2850				
measurement	1082 2219				
medicine	0009 0050 0226 0318 0325 0533 0728 0765 0871 0892 1001 1046 1143 1328 1400 1413 1614 1891 2063 2076 2096 2281 2354 2367 2443 2505 2589 2723 2725 2727 2742 2751 2763 2844 2846 2901 2944 2993 3039 3199 3336 3368				
Medina	0637				
Mediterranean	0080 0177 0590 0606 0974 1507 1969 2157 2280 2320 2326 2737 2839 3072				
megalithic	0839 0883 1732 2219 2240 2264 2611				
Megiddo	1373 3460				
Melanesia	0221 0337 0716 0915 1153 2430 2691 2754 3007 3063 3359				

Melos   0397 1422 1550
Melungeons 0522
Menard   1142
Mende   0728 2238
Menominee   1543 1757 2955 2961 3020
Meroe   0986 1349 2924
Mesa Grande   2236
Mesa Verde 1183 2560
Mesolithic 1235 1773 2147 2486 2696
    2737 2799 2839 2880
Mesopotamia   0895 1110 2062 2494
    3252 3448
Messianism 1181 2530 2709 2847 2933
    3322
mestizo   1476
Meta River 2710
metallurgy 0023 1632 2160 2514 2728
    2765 3071 3215 3426 3441 3488
metrological   2219
Mexican-American   0189 0571
Mexico   0071 0076 0103 0150 0191
    0276 0349 0350 0356 0369 0399 0417
    0418 0432 0481 0518 0544 0566 0617
    0619 0623 0629 0666 0687 0704 0740
    0744 0781 0828 0830 0843 0845 0921
    0949 0996 1046 1067 1092 1156 1203
    1209 1253 1263 1275 1301 1314 1358
    1375 1417 1450 1457 1462 1475 1476
    1483 1552 1594 1610 1630 1646 1699
    1763 1774 1789 1844 1955 1974 2063
    2093 2095 2110 2146 2155 2161 2174
    2207 2208 2303 2304 2311 2395 2414
    2447 2469 2470 2471 2472 2480 2483
    2495 2515 2526 2540 2547 2556 2640
    2682 2685 2698 2725 2731 2765 2783
    2785 2796 2797 2809 2816 2837 2903
    2917 2994 3010 3016 3032 3033 3034
    3060 3066 3079 3098 3101 3132 3155
    3187 3195 3200 3239 3245 3266 3295
    3335 3352 3360 3366 3370 3433 3445
Mexico City   0912
Miao   2792
Michigan   1524 1610
Michoacan   2526
microevolution 0080 0923 3094
Micronesia 0090 0193 0278 1268 1757
    1851 1961 2163 2336 2430 2455 2718
    2866 3063 3172 3357 3359
micropaleontology 1120 2410
microreproductions 1638
Middle Ages   1672 1792 1866 1879
    2400
Middle Atlantic States   2490
Middle East 0091 0097 0408 0453 0570
    0663 0748 0789 0913 0999 1507 1520
    1528 1588 1595 1628 1678 1766 1831
    1959 2002 2160 2296 2370 2558 2648
    2742 2980 2983 3047 3067 3103 3120
    3340 3362
Middletown 2050
Midwest   0239 0758 0914 2306 3173
migration   0371 0492 0932 1107 1203
    1276 1460 1470 1518 2096 2455 2490
    2676 3245 3258
Military   1130 1487 2648 2661 2714
Milpa Alta 2376
Mindanao   0727 1064
minerals   0310 3441
mining   0203 1468 1817 2567 3426
Minnesota   0466 0471
Minoans   1060 1453 1745
minorities 0042 0954 1118 1417 1610
    1914 2119 2707 2971 3095
Minturno   1701
Miocene   1572
Miquelon   2780
missionaries   0029 0047 0061 0075
    0122 0127 0131 0160 0240 0293 0308
    0317 0319 0387 0389 0403 0414 0438
    0486 0515 0539 0597 0598 0618 0659
    0664 0665 0683 0779 0792 0829 0833
    0934 0960 0966 0967 1048 1175 1219
    1220 1242 1265 1270 1292 1296 1326
    1695 1819 1834 1864 1869 1877 1878
    1880 1881 1901 1916 1917 1927 1928
    2036 2048 2052 2132 2167 2203 2218
    2227 2244 2292 2355 2380 2406 2519
    2550 2552 2597 2598 2633 2647 2649
    2654 2690 2711 2939 2943 3240 3289
    3293 3346 3379
Mississippi   0705 1142 1387 2448 2609
Mississippi Valley   0258 0727 1512
    2074 2086 2909 3026
Mississippian Culture   1410 1601
Missouri   0653 1044 3439
Mixezoque   1156
Mixtecs   0617 0830 0845 2469 2640
    3032
Moa   0975
Moabite Stone   0706
Mocabi   0582
Mochica   1903
Modoc   0821
Mogollon   1267 2153 2363
Mogul   3413
Mohenjodaro   2482
Mojave   0915 1083 1427 3058
Mokil   3357
mollusk   1120
monasteries   2296
Mongolia   1645 1792 1795 1914 2359
    2660 2720 3143 3478

Mongols	0821	2660				
Montana	2061	2743				
Monte Alban		0617	0740			
monuments	0239	0260	0376	0396	0534	
1679	1732	2136	2219	2394	3158	
Moravia	2507	2602	2870			
Mormon	3060					
Morocco	1389	1588	2794			
morphology	0507	0746	0841	0973	0978	
1525	2125	2381	2422	2431	2522	2753
2992	3126					
Morija	0485	1243				
Moscow		0113	0371	2821		
Moscow University			0088	0366		
Moshoeshoe I		0094	0614	2308	3161	
Motilone	0391					
Motul	2156					
Mound builders		0072	0371	0471	0705	
1109	1129	1140	1512	2029	2920	3151
3280						
Mousterian	2612					
Moyen Ogooue		2604				
Moza	0183					
Mozambique	0183	0918				
Mpongwe	0295	0535	1663	3318		
mummies	0419	3140				
Muncie	2050					
murder	2291					
musculature		3061	3485			
Musee Alaoui		2613				
museology	1248	2310	3257			
museums		0088	0174	0190	0194	0257
0260	0344	0370	0439	0440	0455	0459
0484	0502	0608	0617	0699	0717	0818
0835	0901	0932	0936	0948	0952	0972
1109	1129	1161	1229	1258	1267	1310
1320	1337	1349	1359	1391	1422	1423
1425	1443	1451	1459	1487	1534	1545
1574	1582	1611	1641	1746	1755	1870
1882	1910	1939	1996	2010	2104	2136
2137	2165	2251	2310	2339	2363	2368
2374	2613	2616	2629	2635	2666	2821
2823	2857	2878	2905	2920	2925	2966
2985	3071	3140	3142	3155	3242	3413
3437	3448	3486				
mushrooms	3337					
music	0067	0074	0082	0116	0125	0163
0209	0551	0607	0626	0741	0822	0918
1129	1162	1311	1324	1335	1471	1489
1494	1503	1590	1640	1651	1690	1787
1821	1982	2054	2092	2125	2152	2208
2209	2250	2287	2375	2385	2478	2663
2745	2836	2892	2995	3004	3030	3078
3264	3267	3330	3341	3478	3480	
musicology		0163	1321	1564	2785	
Muslim		0168	1628	3206		

Mycenaean		0167	0188	0342	0441	0512
0613	0874	0887	1071	1231	1303	1399
1479	1480	1555	1745	1756	2319	2369
2457	2655	3022	3101	3136	3327	3349
3357	3376	3468				
mysticism		1472	2379			
myth	0577	0750	0830	0927	1130	1178
1389	1500	1894	2178	2360	2752	2754
2972	3078					
mythology		0039	0138	0278	0318	0368
0750	0821	0932	0977	1025	1047	1239
1244	1250	1263	1343	1389	1401	1413
1494	1667	1822	1855	1930	1967	2049
2098	2114	2360	2409	2425	2499	2529
2540	2585	2644	2691	2739	2756	2764
2803	3010	3149	3212	3241	3274	3303
3408	3480	3484				

-N-

Nachez	1318	1436				
Nallwyl		1183	1743	2695		
Namibia	1164					
Nandi	1561	1617				
Naples	2104					
Napo Valley		2592				
Narbonne	2935					
Natal	0341					
nationalism		0429	3108			
Native Land Act			2568			
natives		0559	0740	0920	0955	1366
1642	1821	1834	1875	2146	2179	2192
2195	2209	2281	2417	2453	2574	2644
2667	2725	2772	2773	2783	2930	2953
2961	3034	3138	3150	3359	3478	
Naucratis	1213					
Nauhautl	1476	2376				
Nauru	3359					
Navaho		0613	1000	1263	1361	1400
1519	1554	1798	2178	2286	2526	2691
2918	2999	3024	3041	3052	3382	3456
navigation		1268	1509			
Nayarit	1253					
Nazca	3140					
Ndebele		0506	1030	1859	2085	2595
3090	3153	3443				
Neanderthal			0385	0393	0756	1018
1339	1626					
Near East		0099	0184	0378	0426	0570
0596	0629	0669	0835	1125	1167	1191
1222	1424	1451	1502	1507	1573	1771
2071	2379	2419	2499	2591	2842	2861
3057	3162	3252	3426	3451		
Nebraska	3083					
necropolis	2372					

Negro   0093 0846 1500 1651 1698 1887
  2375 2495 2709 3041 3044 3142 3203
  3420
Neolithic   0245 0310 0457 0460 0586
  0862 0863 0906 0975 1109 1131 1331
  1588 1604 1672 1732 1758 1773 1979
  2139 2157 2263 2486 2498 2555 2696
  2810 2828 2829 2886 3072 3132 3189
  3363 3424
Netherlands   1774 2197 2263 2857
Netsuke   2803
Nevada   1473 1492 2029 2489 2946
  2977
New Caledonia   1053 1253 1940
New England   1306 1359 1991 2587
New Guinea   0032 0125 0221 0337
  0461 0532 0680 1153 1380 1551 1730
  2056 2190 2241 2256 2377 2386 2754
  2807 2868 2896 3066 3172 3191 3348
  3350 3359 3394
New Hebrides   0716 0931 1053 1611
  2638
New Ireland   2609
New Jersey   0003 1681 2361 2526 3018
  3298
New Mexico   1144 1369 1534 1721 2153
  2304 2359 2526 2560 2695 2730 2738
  3052 3192 3292 3357
New Spain   2311 2812
New Testament   0800
New World   0399 0958 1020 1364 1497
  3192 3337
New York   0158 0438 0717 0750 1096
  1198 1399 1451 1475 2021 2289 2722
  2955 2969 3018 3026 3077 3156
New Zealand   0232 0297 0492 0932
  1120 1456 2003 3125 3419
Ngami, Lake   2000
Ngoni   1168
Nias   0841
Nicaragua   0415 1132 2026 2465 2527
  3026
Niger   0899 2774
Niger River   2488
Nigeria   0138 0206 0693 0800 0899
  1070 1144 1518 1935 2196 2344 2452
  2462 2493 2671 2879 2913 3349
Nile   0165 1009 2289 2924 3008
Nilgiri Hills   0440
Nimrud 2113
Nimrud Dagh   1277 3470
Nineveh   1923
Nippur   1521
Nishapur   1451
Nisqualli   2980
Nivkh   1839

Nodena   1410
nomadism   0285 1504 1830 2535 3103
  3301
Nootka   2831 3099
Normandy   0778 2544
North Carolina   0718 1335 2046
North Pole   1481
north woods   0243
Norway   0053 0881 1107 1579 1981
  2330 2766 2952 3354
nose   3112
Novgorod   0113
Nubia   0223 0907 1349 2231 2276 2344
  2890 2907
Nubian   1553
Nuer   1062
Nupe   2344
nursery   0300
nutrition   0476 0809 1046 1082 2056
  2713 3401
Nyamwezi   0602
Nyanja   2883

-O-

Oaxaca   0617 0619 0830 3370
obstetrics   0578
Oceania   0588 0845 1240 1276 1300
  1551 1591 1813 2073 2241 2259 2866
  3017 3160 3446
Oglala   0894
Ohio   0072 0172 1129 1140 2290 2299
Ohio Mounds   3151
Ohio Valley   2511 3102
oil   0357
Ojibwa   1397 1543 1713 1778 1887
  2290 2725
Okinawa   3093
Oklahoma   2865 2981
Old Testament   2327 3451
Old World   1017 1034 2695 2698 2770
Olduvai Gorge   1931 1932
Olmec   3066
Oltenia   2242
Olympus   1188
Omaha   1129 1870 1871 2888
Ona   0448
Oneida   0216
onomastics   0828 2197 2791
Ontario   0423 1037 1772 1804
ontogenesis   1479 2477 3440
oracles   0456 2210
Orange River   0094 2964
Orchomenus   1188
Oregon   0821 1010 1653

organography 1794
Orient 0642 1089 1671 1802 2102 2326 2346 2444 2471 2822 3006 3009 3231
Oriental Institute 0426 0895 1831 2071 3427
Orinoco 0620 0644 1259 1363 1608 2710
Orissa 3146
ornaments 0981 2383
ornithology 1425
Oroche 3050
Oromo 2437 3466
Osireion Abydos 2538
Ossage 0653 1870
osteology 1233 1594 2432 2859
osteometry 2751
Ostia 0564
ostrogothic 1716
Otomi 2376 3366
Ottoman 2497
Ottoman empire 1404
Ouagadougou 0320 1838
Ouidah 0021
Ouro Preto 0203
Oxford 0174 1939 3152
Oxford University 3231

-P-

Pacific 0069 0125 0233 0372 0492 0574 0616 0692 0751 0837 0857 0866 0980 1148 1185 1190 1231 1320 1382 1388 1470 1532 1589 1642 1757 1762 1825 1900 1972 1989 2015 2108 2110 2374 2455 2533 2807 2896 2911 2927 3022 3230 3253 3359 3411
paganism 0338 2809
paintings 0053 0859 0974 1084 1215 1696 1854 1977 2015 2303 2514 3105 3120 3325 3413
Paiute 2831
Pakistan 0478 1540 2482 2936 3386
palace 2134
Palau 0193 1832 2725 2899
Palawan 1163
Palenque 0623 0629 0666 3314
paleoanthropology 1201 1626 1725 1856 3440
paleobotany 0724 0870 1204
paleodemography 0080 1860
paleoecology 0152
paleoenvironment 3263
paleoethnography 2232
paleoethnology 0709 1956
paleography 1957

paleolimnology 0878
Paleolithic 0149 0275 0310 0385 0393 0396 0443 0512 0544 0684 0862 0906 1011 1018 1201 1235 1317 1506 1511 1564 1773 1794 1839 1883 1979 2058 2139 2369 2612 2679 2696 2698 2797 2799 2829 2839 3132 3440 3479
paleontology 0091 0147 0465 0724 0896 0906 1331 1466 1588 1734 1737 1807 1839 2043 2044 2129 2147 2362 2366 2422 2839 2880 2925 3137 3247 3469
paleopathology 0080 1288 2306 2722 3368
Paleozoic 2986
Palermo 0901
Pamir 0285
Pamiro Alai 0285
pampas 0059 2463
Pan Indianism 2401
Panama 0315 0625 2527 2731 2733 3092
Papago 0943 2798 3058 3226 3444
Paphos 1213
Papua New Guinea 0032 0532 0680 1380 2241 2377 2386 2754
papyrology 0197 0257 0785 1613 2251 2775 3157
Paracas Peninsula 0608
Paraguay 0057 0136 0153 0292 0314 0368 0547 0552 0594 0635 0920 0934 1079 2037 2225 2399 2476 2618 2628 2795 2864 2887 2903
paralanguage 0328
parapsychology 3360
Paris 0421
Paris Evangelical Missionary Society 1027 1243 1720
pastoralists 0087 1498 3103
Patagonia 1078 1883 2195 2463
pathology 0009 0850 1760 3189 3290
Patuxent Valley 2188
Paviotso 2489
Pawnee 0983 1129 1962
Pazynzk 2789
Peabody Museum 0932 1574 2629 3071
peasantry 0065 0235 0336 0529 0589 0599 1032 1154 1198 1227 1231 1437 1678 1840 1858 1989 2472 2668 2836 3056 3093 3103 3164 3227 3316 3428
Pecos 2917
Peking 0333
Peking Man 3361
pelvis 0768
Pembrokshire 1095
Pennsylvania 0003 0474 1817 2283

	2666 2722 3102 3448
Pennsylvania-Germans	1138 3209
Pennsylvania University Museum	1310
Penobscot	1007
Perachora	0982 2508
Pernambuco	2529
Persepolis	0523 1502
Persia	0523 1158 1271 1355 1451 1502 1959 2586 2769 2983 3251 3413 3458
Persian Gulf	1509
Peru	0011 0213 0323 0422 0537 0556 0608 0692 0941 1042 1054 1229 1357 1447 1509 1684 1699 1735 1738 1821 1844 1903 2019 2162 2192 2256 2318 2391 2423 2435 2450 2765 2779 2811 2991 3083 3140 3182 3195 3207 3210 3224 3242 3416
Peten	2199
petroglyphs	0550 2592 2723 2777 3072 3102
peyote	2663 2961 2981
pharaonic	0649 1506
pharmacopias	0927
Philadelphia	0972 1391
Philip II	1497
Philippines	0212 0236 0304 0727 1013 1064 1139 1163 1369 1437 1512 1713 1757 1874 1900 2020 2096 2125 2301 2443 2480 2622 2651 2706 2707 2850 2899 3022 3034 3059 3230
philology	0068 0074 0341 0361 0421 0496 0702 1050 1127 1158 1365 1388 1494 1562 1584 3453
philosophy	0312 0473 1258 1884 2245 2450 2471 2593 2650 2844 3148 3484
phonetics	0027 1127 1427 1514 2431 2557
phonemic	1514
phonology	0015 1449 1525 1978 2660
photography	0273 0337 0561 0661 0687 1163 1178 1614 1635 1758 2623 2983 2997 3238
phylogeny	0965 0971 1841
physiognomy	3213
physiology	0892 1594 1760 3364
pictographs	2112 2303 2723 2738
Piedras Negras	2837
Piltdown Man	0190 3447
Pima	2798 3058
Pimeria Alta	3074
Pintwater Cave	2977
Pipil indian	1904
Pitt Rivers Museum	0174
Pittsburg	3102
Pizarro	0030 1684
plants	1034 1364 1511 1727 2630 2747 2811
play	2290 2398 3077
Pleistocene	0404 0755 1572 1932 2449
plowing	0169 0433 2665 3487
poetry	0300 0549 0836 0944 1503 1623 1660 2054 2124 2291 2529 2631 3039 3078
Pokomam	2294
Poland	0087 0529 1217 1672 1823 1861 2152 2237 2477 2509 2653 3164 3316 3440 3486 3488
politics	0171 0238 0488 0614 0715 0766 0842 1072 1099 1150 1375 1376 1398 1540 1580 1776 1858 1929 2119 2127 2266 2285 2320 2344 2648 2718 2918 3002 3035 3108 3184 3404 3419
polyandry	2105 2535
polymorphism	0853 2313
Polynesia	0246 0492 0515 0525 0691 0937 0975 1031 1239 1276 1286 1337 1343 1509 1757 1819 1897 1919 2007 2047 2148 2270 2430 2725 2815 3063 3088 3390 3418
Polynesian Society	0297
Pomo	0589 1398
Pompeii	0771 2104 2860 3333
Ponape	0214 0278
Pondicherry	2747
Popol Vuh	2680 3459
populations	0080 0605 0672 0739 0752 0863 0877 0935 1051 1116 1203 1375 1389 1483 1518 1524 1645 1860 2030 2116 2274 2313 2354 2357 2362 2490 2695 2703 2784 2786 2882 2915 3024 3034 3056 3219
porcelain	1682
Poro	0728
Portugal	0007 0762 0767 1662 1954 2737
Poseidon	0463
positivism	0745
postnatal	0824
Potawatomi	0821 0983 1887
Potosi	0078 0111
pottery	0241 0502 0534 1188 1199 1215 1369 1654 1696 1840 1903 2021 2395 2459 2467 2675 2750 2790 2859 2897 2917 3116 3158 3160 3329
Prague	1660
Prakrit	1367
praxiteles	0033
prehistory	(174 individual references, too many to list)
prejudice	0384 0720 2200
preservation	0190 1009 1129 1311

pretoltec--Rhode Island

	1732	2091	2152	2209	2236	2412 2564
	2637	3442				

pretoltec 1275
primates 0195 0386 0541 0695 0846
 1226 1438 1479 1634 1759 1790 1818
 2348 2366 2686 2754 2876 2945 2947
 3061 3247 3369
primatology 0973
privateering 0837
propylaea 0302
protoculture 0846
protohistory 0085 0087 0881 1088
 1264 1379 2365 2575 2653 2919 3302
Provence 1241
provincial 2467
proxemics 1392 2072
psychiatry 0532 2235 2439 2469 3087
psychoanalytic 1171 1176 1488 1753
 2319
psychodynamics 1706
psycholinguistics 0613
psychology 0009 0065 0221 0232 0351
 0364 0589 0843 1045 1262 1400 1498
 1530 1578 1596 1734 1885 1925 2286
 2520 2732 2754 2896 2961 2971 2979
 2993 3020 3075 3169 3211 3310
psychometrics 1986
psychopathology 0656 2439
psychotherapy 0863 1119
Ptolemaic 1074 1831
Pueblo 0005 0045 0173 0508 0823
 0955 1108 1267 1280 1359 1369 1382
 1402 1540 1564 2200 2526 2623 2695
 3053 3084 3132 3178 3198 3385 3389
 3395
Pueblo Bonito 0349 1721 2526 2730
Pueblo Pardo 3192
Puerto Rico 0038 0391 0551 0605
 1581 1974 2121 2755
Puget Sound 1382
Pukapuka 0234
Puyallup 2980
Pygmies 1389 2630 2850 3205
Pylos 0342
pyramids 1294

-Q-

Quakers 2283
Quaternary 1264 2157 2370 2416 2810
 3028 3263
Quechua 0763 1211
Queensland 0735
Quiche 2740 3459
Quinault 2434
Quirigua 0629 1507 3081
Quiros 3191
Quito 0030
Qumran 3271

-R-

race 0137 0218 0262 0338 0384 0469
 0507 0532 0740 0756 0776 0811 0819
 0874 0932 0942 1046 1361 1480 1545
 1610 1618 1627 1925 2105 2278 2301
 2543 2551 2566 2609 2698 2703 2734
 2839 2896 2911 2931 2949 2971 3095
 3127 3147 3203 3238 3246 3290 3357
 3468
radio 1312
radiocarbon 0862
radiology 2938
Recife 2709
Red Sea 0628
Reddis 1186
reforestation 0350
regionalism 1177
reindeer 1987 3301
religion 0023 0093 0214 0218 0277
 0376 0379 0408 0413 0442 0518 0561
 0577 0682 0830 0843 0927 0931 0939
 1021 1022 1052 1122 1157 1158 1169
 1181 1189 1209 1236 1286 1308 1328
 1356 1382 1430 1439 1482 1485 1494
 1522 1532 1566 1576 1599 1609 1614
 1658 1675 1678 1680 1750 1796 1819
 1843 1847 1855 1862 1898 1899 1906
 1919 1926 1948 1954 1962 1970 2001
 2059 2068 2081 2096 2109 2120 2126
 2133 2139 2156 2222 2235 2267 2275
 2290 2296 2320 2323 2344 2350 2386
 2387 2397 2452 2489 2493 2499 2532
 2644 2645 2650 2651 2667 2669 2679
 2691 2698 2720 2754 2760 2774 2844
 2895 2921 2933 2936 2944 2959 2961
 3016 3035 3049 3053 3058 3059 3079
 3111 3115 3119 3148 3159 3180 3194
 3206 3261 3286 3303 3309 3311 3312
 3322 3337 3357 3408 3468 3480 3482
Republican River 2969
reservations 0995 1143 1868 2743
 2888
restoration 0076 0190 0203 0527 1183
 1428 1509 1742 2152 3081 3204 3228
 3271
retirees 1452
revolts 0030 0037 0148 0153 0836
 1937 2290 2898
Rhode Island 2695 3376

Rhodes Livingstone Institute						0441
Richborough		0534				
riddles		2836				
Rig Veda		0353				
rites	0260	0611	0839	0859	1180	1212
	1717	1729	2038	2250	2271	2372	2538
	2702	3222				
ritual	0039	0238	0379	0927	0939	1236
	1250	1272	1344	1415	1437	1439	1538
	1573	1751	1796	1843	1870	2096	2178
	2187	2267	2291	2296	2667	2754	3035
	3059	3079	3119	3303	3480		
rockshelters			0471			
roentgenography				2992		
Roman Empire			0033	0063	0079	0124
	0287	0313	0397	0534	0583	0657	0701
	0707	0888	1189	1216	1351	1407	1414
	1808	1809	1866	2010	2134	2150	2339
	2459	2467	2585	2603	2627	2655	2741
	2758	2781	2839	2966	2986	3029	3194
	3303					
Romance		0512	1835	2333	3421	
Rosetta Stone			0649			
Rotuma		1616				
Royal Anthropological Institute						2980
Royal Scottish Museum					0818	
rubber		1464				
Rumania		0079	0743	0765	1498	2170
	2242	2357	2590			
rural	0253	0589	1518	1544	1648	1861
	1974	2030	2105	2475	2481	2530	2676
	2786	3027	3035	3067	3324	3330	3401
	3417	3439	3465			
Russia		0018	0088	0108	0112	0113
	0149	0204	0366	0371	0373	0385	0396
	0421	0457	0507	0671	0821	0874	1011
	1290	1315	1317	1323	1448	1645	1742
	1850	1853	1893	1968	1983	2119	2247
	2253	2425	2457	2498	2502	2620	2673
	2802	2821	2840	2951	2962	3021	3062
	3145	3180	3184	3202	3236	3280	3337
	3475	3479				
Russian Archeological Society						3236
Rwanda		0680	0715	1318	2127	

-S-

Sacred Well		2765				
Sahara		1658	1838	1898	1977	2277
	2279	2605				
Sakaptin		0909				
Sakhalin		1448				
Sakkara		0986	1294	2214	2538	2890
	2988					
Salinar		1903				
Salish	0193	1033	1382	2691	3093	3138
Salt River		2236				
Salta		1293				
Samoa	0469	1053	1171	1532	1757	1832
	2190	2360				
Samothrace		1949				
San		2964				
San Cristobal			0350			
San Francisco			2029			
San Ildefonso Pueblo					3053	
San Jose		3192				
San Juan		1564	2623			
San Juan River			2290			
Sanai	0176					
Sandawe		3203				
Sangha		0710				
Sanskrit		0264	0473	0496	0697	1367
	1712	1920	2275	2323	2701	3089	3152
	3405					
Santa Fe		0582				
Santa Marta			1723			
Santee		3320				
Santiago Island			0605			
Santo Domingo			0391	1581		
Sarawak		0877	1380	2772	2896	
sarcophagus			2741			
Sardis	0493	1414				
Sarmatians		1323	3021			
Sauk	0821	1713				
Scandinavia			0245	0274	0459	1271
	1544	2223	2400	2919	3068	3080	3189
	3301	3354				
Scotland		0247	0818	1981	1987	2219
	2781	2886				
scriptures		0535	0642	0870	1237	2615
sculpture		0033	0591	0676	1188	1522
	1696	1949	2614	2777	3081	3082	3104
	3107					
Scyri	2391					
Scythians		0112	0373	1323	2253	3021
sea	0288	0340	0628	1080	1193	3323
sedentarization			1504	2859	3011	
Segontium		1216				
Seleucia		3340				
semantics		1156	1884			
Seminole		1073	1170	1280	3065	3066
semiotics		0253	1127	1660	2419	3069
Semirech'e		0285				
Semites		0303	0827	1485	1562	1573
	1966	2831	3231			
Seneca		1690	2993	3389		
Senegal		1245	1670	1736	2279	
Senoi	3059					
Sens	1620					
Sephardic		2413				
Serabit		2068				

Serampore	0597
Serbia	2250 3480
serology	1276 2566 3410
Serpent Mound	1129 3312
Sesebi	0335
Sesotho	0928 1026 1237 1657 1926
Seti I	0260 0561
sexuality	0405 0915 1230 1463 2148 2278 3129 3164 3334 3350
Shakers	1482
Shamanism	0023 0413 1382 2120 2397 2645 2651 2720 3058 3059
Shang	0456 2210
Shawnee	0821
Shi'ites	2536
Shikoku	3096
Shintoism	1566 2409
Shona	0007 0037 0148 0506 0722 1152 1859 2595 2898
Shoshoni	1427 1540 2035
Shropshire	0520
Shuswap	0869 3138
Siam	0280
Siberia	0108 0372 0682 0825 1639 1792 1836 1839 1848 1968 2645 2679 3050 3143 3180 3217
Sicily	2468
Sidon	3431
Sierra Leone	0043 0055 0700 0728 1076 1431 1637 1806 2177 2202 2238 2492 2677 2930
Sierra Nevada	0964
sigillata	2459 2467
Sikasso	2636
silting	0753
Sinai	2068
Sind	0196
Sindebele	1030
Sinology	0898 1612
Sioux	0894 1129 1445 1962 2200 2290 2764 3004 3173 3395 3437
Six Nations	0750 2993
skeletons	0290 0504 0572 0768 1909 2882 2938 3061 3179 3238 3320 3334
skull	1238 2704 3290
Skyros	1418
slavery	0615 0877 1177 1558 3095 3378
Slavonic	1575
Slavs	0087 0112 0821 0826 1019 1491 1660 1796 1802 2237 2333 2382 2602 2653 2791 2840 3021 3070 3145 3180 3202 3241 3440
Slovakia	1019
slums	2744
Smithsonian Institution	1534 2797
	2905 3056
smoking	2080
Smyrna	0901
snake	2520
Snaketown	3335
Sobhuza II	1859
socioeconomics	2802 2854
sociology	0052 0222 0294 0364 0446 0679 0721 0830 0868 0977 1084 1218 1420 1518 1555 1571 2105 2146 2183 2200 2220 2257 2320 2448 2530 2578 2585 2618 2679 2684 2713 2849 2971 3108 3224 3463 3465 3487
sociopathology	0656
Socratic	3389
Solomon Islands	0716 1122 1532 1551
Somali	2478
somatology	2084
somatometry	3203
somatotyping	1128 1463 1986
Songhay	2774
Sonora	1253 3016
South Asia	0473 1186 1737
Southern Cult	3329
Soviet Union	2119 2596
Spain	0011 0418 0573 0606 0615 0684 0692 0805 1055 1104 1131 1133 1173 1211 1218 1497 1630 1643 1646 1662 1689 1762 1854 2157 2174 2464 2465 2565 2584 2627 2797 2810 2813 2875 2942 2975 3074 3092 3182 3243
Sparta	0397
speech	2093 3128 3361
spirituals	0125 1651 3264
sports	0768 0790
St. Brendan	1306
St. Peter	1717 1729
stables	1373
statistics	0356 0671 0690 0783 0880 0993 1845 2058 3099
stereotypes	2931
Sterkfontein	0465 0572
Stockholm	1743
Stone Age	0085 0251 0337 0754 1435 1465 1710 1804 2034 2240 2315 2369 2881
stratigraphy	0356 1134 1777 2985 3137
stress	1706
structuralism	1929 1967 2106
subarctic	1570
subcultures	1858
Sudan	0102 0165 0280 0335 0477 0494 0789 0809 0986 1062 1200 1344 1506 1629 2088 2289 2344 2373 2497 2808 2895 2896 2923 2928 3215

Sufism	2379					
Sumeria	1191	1624	1895	1944	2001	
2573	3448	3477				
sun	2520					
surgery	2076	2993	3131			
Surinam	0916	1499	2415	3142		
Susa	1944					
Swaziland	0488	1202	1569	1859	2159	
Sweden	0051	0108	0126	1420	1444	
1461	1525	1986	2387	2704	3080	3249
Switzerland	0296	0512	0904	1089	2839	
3302						
syllabary	2902					
symbols	0577	0652	0684	1098	1122	
1171	1286	1344	1532	1734	2127	2147
2367	2740	3272	3484			
syncretism	1898	1948				
syntax	0027	2381				
syphilis	3140					
Syria	0284	0345	0669	0706	0907	1373
1550	1661	1701	2071	2106	2216	2231
2314	2719	2908	2985			

-T-

Tagbanuwa	1163					
Tahiti	0016	0100	0405	0406	1239	1394
1490	2027	2266	2405	2451	2767	3168
3253	3390					
Tairora	3348	3350				
Taiwan	2259	3474				
Takelma	2831					
Talamanca	3071					
Tanganyika	0680	0777	3203	3428		
Tanzania	0216	0469	0602	0680	0777	
0808	0809	1931	1932	1960	2129	3008
3031	3167	3203	3428			
Taoism	1598					
Taos Pueblo		3198				
tapa	1813					
Tarascan	1156	3099	3360			
Tarsus	1414					
Tasmania	0932	2772	3125			
Taung Baby		0846				
taxonomy	0005	2366				
technology	0174	0393	0404	0444	0802	
0845	0866	0897	1112	1269	1304	1526
1544	1636	1804	2080	2099	2383	2563
2589	2665	2761	2891	3072	3133	3175
3249	3275	3328	3404	3441	3445	
Tecolotlan	1610					
Tel Aviv	0025					
Tell Kisan	3271					
temples		0561	1847	2001	2068	2532
3115						

Tenayuca	0633					
Tenino	2336					
Tennessee	0230	2342	2349	2778		
Teopanzolco		0633				
Teotihuacan		0633	1203			
Tepexpan Man		0912				
Tepoztlan	0633					
teratology	0973					
Tewa	1427					
Tewodros II		3481				
Texas	0121	0357	1046	1065	2513	2917
3048						
textiles	0687	1042	1229	1544	1699	
1813	2192	2383	2435	2456	2526	2563
2641	2661	2715	2889	3217	3275	3385
Thailand	0280	0364	1036	2301	3049	
theater	0086	0502	0944	3267		
Thebes	0859	1459	2372	3222		
theorist	0994	1282	1798	2035	2110	
2298	2496	3185				
Thera	2137					
therapeutic	3059					
Thrace	1750	2906				
Tiahuanaco	0267	2594	3287			
Tibet	0145	1308	1609	1915	2577	2747
2933	3306					
Tibetan Society		1308				
Tigre River		2334				
Tikal	0623					
Tikopia	1122					
Timbuctoo	0555	2252				
Timor	0050					
Tinguian	0727					
Tiv	2344					
Tiwi	1436					
Tlatelolco	2155					
Toda	0440					
Togo	0289	0766	1164			
Toltecs	1275	3019	3245			
tombstones	0939					
Tomi	0249					
Tonga	0166	1053	1253	1532	2086	2108
2138	2868	3166				
tools	0393	0404	1112	1544	1804	2080
2563	2665	3072	3175			
Topanga	3200					
Torres Strait		1380				
Torres Straits		2896				
totemism	1181	1217	2106	2152		
Totonac	2472					
trading	0451	1098	1342	1518	1772	
2635	2733					
transcendence		2120				
trepanning	3140					
Trinidad	0391					
tripartite	0977					

Tripoli	2279					
Tripolitania	0706					
Tristan	2330					
Tristan da Cunha		2330				
Trobriand Islands		2110				
Troy	0342	2855				
Truk	2336					
Tschuapa	1164					
Tswana	2269	2849				
Tuamotu Islands		0234	0405	0546	0751	
2148	2638	2752	3063			
Tuhoe	0297					
Tukuna	2388					
Tulum	0629	3218				
Tumacacori	0239					
Tumbuka	1168					
Tunica	3101					
Tunis	2613					
Tunisia	2613	2881				
Tupi	2098					
Tupinamba	2225					
Turkey		0001	0080	0144	0493	0702
0825	0840	0901	1021	1277	1285	1414
1667	2001	2216	2402	2532	2643	2645
2646	2683	2985	3067	3089	3228	3397
3431	3465	3470	3472			
Turkistan	1618					
Turrialba	0023					
Tusculum	0583					
Tutankhamen		0611	1212	2038	2271	
2372						
Tuxcacuesco		1763				
Twana	1010					
typology		0914	0975	1201	2946	
Tyre	0045					
Tzeltzal		0744				
Tzintzuntzan		2785				
Tzutuhil		3459				

-U-

Ubangui		0831	1225	1340	3353	
Udmurts		0126				
Uganda		1008	2103	2713	3008	3031
Ukraine		0112	2384	2791	3299	
Umbrian		1355	1957			
U.S.S.R		0385	0396	0507	0874	1316
1448	2502	3479				
United States			0052	0072	0080	0152
0239	0255	0369	0378	0466	0469	0536
0599	0606	0613	0653	0656	0718	0720
0782	0786	0862	0875	0914	0915	0930
0951	0952	1033	1041	1073	1098	1109
1183	1203	1312	1314	1347	1348	1399
1415	1445	1488	1500	1503	1554	1596
1601	1610	1667	1678	1707	1713	1774
1801	1844	1858	1862	1882	1887	1974
1982	1995	2063	2077	2094	2228	2283
2284	2290	2298	2301	2303	2306	2330
2336	2340	2358	2363	2434	2439	2490
2491	2526	2578	2609	2622	2641	2730
2732	2743	2778	2784	2901	2905	2931
2949	2993	3003	3004	3016	3034	3048
3056	3060	3076	3084	3098	3132	3142
3155	3160	3173	3330	3331	3358	3367
3404	3417	3455	3468			
United States, National Park Service					0239	
United States, Northeastern						1973
2722	2997					
United States, Southeastern						0039
0505	1975	2545				
United States, Southwestern						0028
0121	0422	0444	0514	0810	1081	1267
1382	1425	1450	1507	1534	1594	1721
1777	2007	2342	2412	2433	2455	2526
2610	2623	2687	2695	2698	2730	2750
2765	2872	2965	3053	3060	3083	3101
3120	3132	3210	3226	3335	3385	3416
3438	3445	3446				
United States, Western					0006	0048
0180	0181	0572	0782	0858	2749	
untouchability		1181	3146			
Upper Chari		0645				
Upper Volta		0791	2279			
Ur	1310	1671	1944	3448		
Uralic	3126					
Urals	0310					
Urartu	2562					
urbanism		0097	1303	1420	1436	1648
1935	1974	2021	2063	2187	2257	2331
2401	2563	2676	2725	2744	2879	3327
3376	3392	3435	3439	3465		
urbanization		0742	1417	2059		
urn	1614					
Utah	2473	2623	2971			
Ute	0045	1361	2035	3060		
utilitarianism		2245				
Uxmal	0629					
Uzbekistan		1362	1631	3280	3281	

-V-

Vai	1702	3442			
Valencia, Lake		2702			
Vanuatu		0931			
Vatican		2394			
Vedic	1855				
Vei	1806				
Venezuela		0054	0096	0391	0644	0802

```
                0923 0991 1608 1711 1965 2008 2426    Wiyot      2029
                2464 2657 2702 2756 3482              Wogeo      1551
Veracruz        3033                                  Wolof      1670
Verde River          2473                             women      0512 0863 1032 1123 1408 1476
Vermont         0158                                             1730 1773 1799 2119 2505 2713 2755
vernacular      3325                                             2888 3035 3053 3118 3164 3359
vertebrates     0467 0881 0971 3208 3469              Woonsocket      3376
                3485                                  World War I          1922 2823
Victoria Albert Museum          1422 1425             World War II         1036 1351 1551
Victoria Falls       2000                             writing      0524 2591 2777 3442
Vienne          2775                                  Wroxeter     0534
Vietnam         0915 1200 2340 2625                   Wurzberg     0502
Viking Ship Museum        0459
Vikings         2659
Virgin Islands       2958 3203                                   -X-
Virginia        0236 3244
vocabularies         0800 1834 2138 2795              Xhosa      2431
Volga      1983 2804 2962 3021 3202                   Xuantunica      0070
Voltaic         1099
voodoo          2375
voortrekkers         3258                                        -Y-
Vrokastro       1391
Vulci      0208                                       Yahgan          0449
                                                      Yaki       2589
                                                      Yakima Band          0909
                 -W-                                  Yale University      0229 2336 3046
                                                      Yana       2831
Wadaii     3215                                       Yang       2210
Wales      0397 1093 1095 1161 1216 1351              Yanoama         3482
           2351 2436 2611 3421                        Yao        0004
Wallis Island        0219                             Yap        1253 1832
Walo       1670                                       Yaqui      1092 2470 3016
wampum          2993                                  Yemen      0269 0631
Wapi       2256                                       Yokut      2376
war        0043 0202 0469 0559 0877 1036              Yoro Dyao       1670
           1053 1107 1130 1351 1487 1551 1804         Yoruba          0800 2452
           1911 1922 2070 2192 2256 2367 2391         Yucatan         0076 2095 2681 2685 2783
           2393 2439 2823 2871 3058                   Yuchi      0821
warriors        0977                                  Yugoslavia      0188 0209 0500 0862 1541
Washington State          1411 1492 1653                   3097 3172 3269 3304
           1709 2980                                  Yuka       2569
Washo      2035                                       Yukagir         1639 1839
wasps      3174                                       Yukon Valley         0869
weapons         1107 1487 1804 2969                   Yuma       1112 1427
Weihriwei       1704                                  Yupas      0923
Wenner Gren Foundation          1092                  Yurok      3023
West Indies     0120 0391 0505 1108 1581
           2652 2949 3130 3420
Wichita         2865                                             -Z-
wildlife        2898
Wiltshire       2371                                  Zaculu          3204
Windmill Hill        1758                             Zaire      0109 0332 0470 0499 0607 0645
Winnebago       1129 2644 2888                             0826 1439 1568 2569 2630 2850 2887
Wisconsin       2778                                       2995 3039
Wishram         1000                                  Zambezi         0905
witchcraft      2103 2187                             Zambia          0109 0171 0441 0695 0737
```

	1247	1272	1567	1947	2257	2609	2713
Zapotec			0617	2495	2547	2640	
Zen	1598						
Zimbabwe		0007	0037	0148	0269	0506	
	0601	0631	0722	0736	1030	1152	1272
	1395	1557	1710	1859	1933	2000	2085
	2180	2261	2595	2662	2898	3090	3153
Zinjanthropus		1931					
Zomba	0214						
zoology		0602	1149				
Zoroastrianism		3405					
Zulu	0488	0560	1843				
Zuni	0508	0823	1108	1534	2376	2495	
	3052	3053	3444